Financial Accounting and Reporting

A Contemporary Emphasis

JOHN DEARDEN and JOHN SHANK

Harvard Business School

PRENTICE-HALL, INC., Englewood Cliffs, N.J.

Library of Congress Cataloging in Publication Data

Dearden, John.
  Financial accounting and reporting.

  Includes index.
  1. Financial statements. 2. Accounting. I. Shank,
John K., joint author. II. Title.
HF5681.B2D43   657'.3   75-2005
ISBN 0-13-314757-6

Printed in the United States of America.

10 9 8 7 6 5 4 3 2 1

Prentice-Hall International, Inc., *London*
Prentice-Hall of Australia, Pty. Ltd., *Sydney*
Prentice-Hall of Canada, Ltd., *Toronto*
Prentice-Hall of India Private Limited, *New Delhi*
Prentice-Hall of Japan, Inc., *Tokyo*

The task which Financial Accounting has faced has been to move in the direction of certainty and simplicity in an economy which was moving rapidly in the direction of complexity and uncertainty, if not confusion. The task may be likened to that of the billiard sharper in *The Mikado*—to control, as it were, the cue ball (of accounting classification) to bring together in proper relation the two object balls (of revenue and cost) on a cloth untrue (of contractual relations indefinite or deceptive in expression) with the twisted cue (of ambiguous terminology and conventions) and the elliptical billiard balls (of an unstable monetary symbol). And this has to be done for an audience wholly unaware of the defects of the equipment provided, which has been led to believe that the task is easy.

George O. May

Contents

Case Listing

Chapter 6

Chapter 7

Chapter 8

Chapter 9

Chapter 10

Chapter 11

Chapter 12

Chapter 13

Chapter 14

Acknowledgements

Most of this book was written while we were teaching at the Graduate School of Business, Harvard University. We wish, therefore, to express our thanks to Dean Lawrence E. Fouraker for providing us with the opportunity to write this book and, also, for allowing us to use 42 cases that hold Harvard University copyrights.

The book contains cases written by several other professors. We wish to express our great appreciation to the following scholars for allowing us to use their material in this book: Professor Robert N. Anthony, Harvard University; Associate Professor M. Edgar Barrett, Harvard University; Emeritus Professor Walter F. Frese, Harvard University; Professor David Hawkins, Harvard University; Professor Henry Key, Texas Christian University; Dr. Robert T. Sprouse, Financial Accounting Standards Board; and Professor Richard F. Vancil, Harvard University.

Several people read all or part of this book in manuscript form. We wish to express our great appreciation to the following scholars for their many helpful suggestions: Professor William H. Beaver, Stanford University; Professor N. H. Hakansson, University of California at Berkeley; Professor Henry B. Reiling, Columbia University; Professor Lawrence Revsine, Northwestern University; Mr. Frank T. Weston, Arthur Young and Company; and Professor Jerry J. Weygandt, University of Wisconsin.

Finally, we would like to express our appreciation to Mrs. Jane Barrett who typed the manuscript.

John Dearden
John Shank

Preface

Most people's problem with accounting is that they don't realize that there is less there than meets the eye.

Charles J. Christenson

If we wished to describe as succinctly as possible what the accountant does, we would say that he/she *measures* and *communicates*. The accountant measures the economic status of an organization and the changes in that status between two points in time. Then the accountant communicates the results of these measurements to those who are interested in knowing them.

It is common to divide accounting into financial accounting and management accounting. Financial accounting is concerned with providing information to people outside the firm: creditors, suppliers, stockholders, potential stockholders, the government, and so forth. Management accounting is concerned with providing information to people inside the firm. (Strictly speaking, of course, all accounting is management accounting, since financial accounting information is also used by management.) This book is concerned with financial accounting. The authors believe, however, that as a general rule financial accounting should always reflect the way managers look at the business in evaluating it themselves.

One characteristic that distinguishes financial accounting is that the users of financial accounting information really have little power to specify what information they will receive and little or no power over the preparation of this information. Furthermore, the accountant who prepares financial accounting information often is preparing it for a wide audience with varying degrees of interest, knowledge, and expertise. Consequently, if the financial accountant is to be able to communicate with the people interested in the financial affairs of a company, he/she must use a terminology that is understood by most readers. To facilitate this communication, it is important that companies use a reasonably consistent vocabulary in financial reports. One purpose of this book is to acquaint you with that vocabulary.

A common misconception is that accounting is exact or precise. Accounting measures can be subject to a great deal of judgment. To minimize bias in the financial reports, therefore, the accountant preparing these reports must consistently follow an agreed-upon set of principles and procedures. Furthermore, the accountant's work must be reviewed by an independent expert to be sure that the ground rules have been followed and that the accounting estimates are not biased. In the United States these ground rules are called generally accepted accounting principles (GAAP) and the independent party is called a certified public accountant (CPA). Another purpose of this book is to acquaint you with GAAP and with the functions of the CPA. Even within GAAP, however, there is considerable opportunity for differences. It is important to keep in mind that accounting is more of an "art" than a "science."

One dichotomy into which organizations may be divided is "profit" and "non-profit." Accounting systems are used in both types of organizations, of course. Financial accounting systems, however, are primarily concerned with providing relevant information on economic changes, particularly with respect to profitability, to the investor or potential investor. Since non-profit institutions do not have investors in the traditional sense, financial accounting is primarily concerned with profit-making institutions. Consequently, this book is principally concerned with profit-making organizations. The major form of organization for profit-making concerns in the U.S. is the corporation.

To summarize, this book deals with the art/science of financial accounting. Within the framework of financial accounting the book is concerned primarily with public reporting by American corporations.

PLAN OF THE BOOK

The book is divided into two parts. The first seven chapters are concerned with basic financial statements and how they are prepared. In these chapters, our approach is from the viewpoint of the insider who is preparing these financial reports. We believe that a basic knowledge of how financial reports are prepared is very useful to the reader of such statements. The last seven chapters are concerned with published financial reports. In these chapters, our approach is from the point of view of the outsider who must read and understand published financial statements. The overall emphasis of the book is on interpreting financial statements rather than preparing them. Those things that are of primary interest to the *preparer* of financial statements have been either omitted or presented in a summary fashion.

Definitions of Accounting

Before you begin your study of financial accounting, we think it is useful for you to consider the following definitions of accounting. As you will see in reading them, they differ dramatically in their conception of accounting. After finishing this book you should re-read them to see which, if any, you have come to accept.

Accounting is:

The art of recording, classifying, and summarizing in a significant manner and in terms of money, transactions and events which are, in part at least, of a financial character, and interpreting the results thereof.

The American Institute of Certified
Public Accountants

Identifying, measuring and communicating economic information to permit users to form judgments and make decisions.

American Accounting Association

A method of retrospective and contemporary monetary calculation designed to provide a continuous source of financial information as a guide to future actions in markets.

Raymond J. Chambers

The quantitative description and projection of income flows and wealth aggregates based on (certain) basic assumptions.

Richard Mattessich

The Balance Sheet

A balance sheet is a statement of the financial condition of the enterprise. *

A balance sheet does not purport to reflect and could not usefully reflect the value of the enterprise. **

These are old fond paradoxes to make fools laugh i' the alehouse. ***

  *AICPA, CPA Handbook
 **AICPA, Committee on Terminology
***William Shakespeare

Howard Ross

1

The purpose of a balance sheet is to show the financial position of a business on a given date. It shows the financial resource a business owns, the debts that the business owes, and the residual interest of the business, which is the difference between what it owns and what it owes. The things that a business owns are called *assets*. The debts that a business owes are called *liabilities*. The difference between assets and liabilities is called *owners' equity*.

A balance sheet, then, is a statement of financial condition. In its traditional format a balance sheet shows assets on the left-hand side of the page and liabilities and owners' equity on the right-hand side. When the liabilities and owners' equity are added together, they will be equal to the assets. Therefore, the statement is said to "balance" because the left-hand column is equal to (i.e., balances with) the right-hand column. Notice that this balance must be true *by definition*. If owners' equity is defined as the difference between assets and liabilities, then assets *must equal* liabilities plus owner's equity. This can be proved algebraically:
If:

Assets − Liabilities = Owners' Equity
Then, changing Liabilities to the other side of the equation:
Assets = Liabilities + Owners' Equity

The balance sheet is important to the extent that it provides a comprehensive overview of the financial position of a business. Things that happen in a business that affect its financial status in any way will ultimately be reflected in the balance sheet. This attempt at comprehensiveness, however, also accounts for its principal limitation. It is simply impossible to express on one sheet of paper the complete financial status of a business.

BALANCE SHEET FORMAT

Following is an example of a typical balance sheet. The purpose of this section of the chapter is to explain its format and terminology.

Assets, in general, are the things that are owned by the business. Assets consist principally of goods held for sale, items which will be converted into goods for sale, expenses applicable to future periods, and claims to value, such as cash or notes or accounts receivable. The following points are important to remember about assets.

1. It is ownership, not physical possession, that determines whether a particular item is an asset or not. For example, a rented building is an asset to the business that has legal title to it, not the business that is in physical possession of it.
2. A business is a separate entity and the assets of the owners of the business should not be confused with the assets of the business.
3. What is considered to be an asset and how it is valued are determined by accounting principles. These principles are arbitrary in many instances. For example, physical equipment is included on the balance sheet at "cost," rather than at replacement value or potential sales value.

Traditionally, assets are listed on the balance sheet in the general order of their liquidity (potential conversion into cash).

Current Assets are those assets that are in the form of cash or are expected to be turned into cash in the short run, usually within 1 year. Following is a brief description of the principal types of current assets.

THE ABC COMPANY
Balance Sheet
As of December 31, 1974 ($000)

Assets			Liabilities and Owners' Equity		
Current Assets			**Current Liabilities**		
Cash		$ 346	Accounts Payable		$ 568
Marketable Securities		1,928	Notes Payable		2,000
Accounts Receivable		894	Taxes Payable		385
Notes Receivable		200	Prepaid Income		53
Inventories		1,893	Total		$3,006
Prepaid Expenses		56			
Total Current Assets		$5,317			
Investments		*1,000*			
Property Assets			*Long-term Liabilities*		
Land	$2,669		Mortgage Payable		$1,000
Buildings	2,346		Bonds Payable		4,000
Machinery	4,291		Total		5,000
Other Property			Total Liabilities		$8,006
Assets	163	9,469			
Less Accumulated					
Depreciation		2,100			
Net Property Assets		$7,369			

Intangible Assets			*Owners' Equity*	
Goodwill	$ 991		Capital Stock	$4,500
Patents	385	1,376	Retained Earnings	1,846
Less Accumulated				6,346
Amortization		710		
Net Intangible Assets		666		
			Total Liabilities and	
Total Assets		$14,352	Owner's Equity	$14,352

Cash includes cash in bank accounts, as well as any currency that the business may have. For any item to be considered "cash," there should be no restrictions on its availability. For example, a deposit in a bank that requires a waiting period for withdrawal is not considered "cash" on a balance sheet.

Marketable Securities are securities, such as government bonds, that are being held instead of cash. If a business has more cash on hand than it needs in the immediate future, it often invests in marketable securities so that it can earn a return on its idle money. The fact that marketable securities are listed under current assets means that the business intends to liquidate these investments when it needs the cash.

Accounts Receivable represent money owed to a business by its customers on "open account." Open account simply means that customers are allowed a certain amount of time to pay for the goods that they have purchased. The amount of money that the customers owe between the time of sales and the time of payment is shown as accounts receivable.

Notes Receivable are the amounts that are owed to the business for which a legal document, called a "note," has been given. A note is a piece of paper that states that a given amount will be paid at a given date, usually at a specified interest rate. Notes receivable differ from accounts receivable in several ways. First, a note represents a "secured" claim, whereas, an open account is "unsecured." Second, a note usually bears interest. Third, it is not necessarily owed by a customer. For example, a note could represent a loan to an officer or employee.

Inventories are the goods that a business holds for sale to its customers. The classification of goods as inventory is determined by what the business intends to do with them. The same product could be classified as inventory in one company and as a fixed asset in another. For instance, an automobile could be an item of inventory to an automobile dealer and a fixed asset to a company that sells vacuum cleaners. Inventories not only consist of goods held by immediate sale to customers, but also include items in the process of being made into finished products.

Prepaid Expenses result from paying an item of expense in advance. For example, assume that an insurance premium of $1,000 is paid to cover the year beginning July 1, 1974. If a balance sheet were prepared on December 31, 1974, $500 of that premium would be an asset (prepaid expense) because it covers the first half of 1975. This is an asset in the sense that it represents an expenditure that will benefit the business in the future.

Noncurrent assets are those assets that are not expected to be turned into cash in the short run. Following are brief descriptions of the principal types of non-current assets.

Investments are notes or securities held by a business for investment purposes. That is to say, the intention is to hold those securities for the long run, at least longer than a year. They are classified separately from short-term marketable securities (which are current assets) because the intent of management regarding the holding period is different.

Property Assets are those physical assets that are to be used in the conduct of the business. The expectation is that they will be used, rather than sold. Property assets are usually divided into several categories such as land, buildings, machinery and equipment, delivery equipment, and so forth.

Nearly all property assets, except land, are subject to reductions in value over time. The process of accounting for this reduction in value is called "depreiation" and an asset is said to depreciate if its value is reduced over time. The total amoung of this depreciation is called "accumulated depreciation." Property assets, therefore, are shown at cost less accumulated depreciation. Depreciation is a process of spreading the depreciable value (cost less estimated future salvage value) over the estimated useful life of an asset in the rational and consistent way. Cost less accumulated depreciation at any intermediate time thus may bear little relationship to the asset's sales value at that point. For example, assume that a business purchased a delivery truck for $4,000 and estimated that it would last for 5 years and then be sold for $1,000. The value of the truck would decline from $4,000 to $1,000 (or $3,000) over the next 5 years. This means it would lose value at an average rate of $600 a year.[1] At the end of 2 years, the truck would be valued on the balance sheet at $2,800 ($4,000 - [2 X $600]), regardless of what it could be sold for at that time. The cost of a fixed asset is frequently called its "gross book value." The cost minus accumulated depreciation is called "net book value" or just "book value."

Intangible Assets include non-physical assets having a longer time span than 1 year. Intangible assets include such things as good will, patents, copyrights, and franchises. These assets must be included at the purchase price, less the estimated reduction in value since the date of purchase. There is considerable flexibility with respect to writing off[2] these assets over a period of time. The process of writing off intangible assets (called "amortization") is exactly the same as the process of depreciating fixed assets. For example, suppose that you purchased a patent for $10,000 and this patent has 10 years left to run; you would reduce your patent value, for example, by $1,000 a year. Some intangibles, however, have no definite life and can be written off pretty much as the accountant or manager wishes. For example, companies sometimes write off goodwill as quickly as possible, even though the goodwill might still exist. It is important to remember that intangible assets show on a balance sheet only if they have been purchased. The value of the Coca-Cola trademark, for example, does not appear on the balance sheet of the

---

[1] This is called the straight-line method of depreciation, because the same amount of depreciation is taken each year. Other methods of depreciation are discussed in Chapter 6.

[2] The process of reducing the value of an asset or eliminating it entirely is called "writing off" the asset.

Coca-Cola Company because it has been developed gradually over the years; it was not purchased.

Many people believe that the intangible asset values shown on a balance sheet are not particularly useful in helping to assess the condition of the business. Consequently, many firms do not show intangible assets on their balance sheet even though they exist. Profitable firms are likely to write off intangible assets that really exist, whereas marginal firms may list intangible assets of questionable value. In evaluating a firm's financial condition, it is important to find out as much as possible about those intangible assets shown on the balance sheet and those not shown.

Liabilities are claims against the business—i.e., they represent amounts owed to people or firms outside the business. As we will show later, the liability figures are no more precise or "correct" than the asset values. There is just as much reliance on accounting conventions, many of them arbitrary, in determining the amounts shown for liabilities as there is for the amounts shown as assets. For the most part, liabilities represent an estimate of amounts the business will have to pay.

1. *Current Liabilities* are debts that must be paid off within the short run, usually 1 year. Following is a description of the principal types of current liabilities.

(a) *Accounts Payable* are debts owed to suppliers on open account (the counterpart of accounts receivable).

(b) *Notes Payable* are debts for which the business has given a legal document (called a note) as evidence of liability. These notes are usually given to a bank but may also be given to a supplier. The date when the note must be paid determines whether it is a current liability or a long-term liability. If it is due within a year, it is a current liability. Sometimes a note does not designate any specific due date. In this case, the classification is determined by the intent of the parties. If the intention is to pay the note in less than a year, it is classified as a current liability. Otherwise, it is considered long term. As with notes receivable, a note payable will usually require that interest be paid on the face amount for the period that it is outstanding.

(c) *Taxes Payable*, as the name indicates, are amounts owed to federal, state, or local governments for taxes. Usually, the largest proportion of this item is for federal income taxes, although state income taxes and federal social security and unemployment taxes can be substantial. In some instances, federal income taxes are shown separately because they are such a significant item.

(d) *Prepaid Income* is income received in advance. For example, suppose that a business rents part of its office space to a tenant who has paid $500 covering the months of December 1974 and January 1975. The balance sheet as of December 31, 1974, would show prepaid income of $250 as a current liability. The business owes the tenant the *use* of the office space for a month.

2. *Long-term Liabilities* are those debts that are not due for at least a year. Long-term liabilities usually consist of long-term notes, mortgages and bonds.

A mortgage payable is a debt for which some or all of the business property has been placed as security or "collateral" for the debt. This means that the mortgage holder has a prior claim on those assets of the business if the business defaults on the debt. This could be an important consideration in deciding whether to lend money to a business.

A business often borrows money, through the capital markets, using an instrument called a bond. A bond is a promise by a business to pay a given amount (usually $1,000) at some time in the future and to pay a specified interest rate until that time. The company sells as many bonds as necessary to raise the amount of money needed. Bonds are covered in more detail in Chapter 7. For the moment, consider them as any other long-term liability.

Owner's Equity is the difference between the assets and the liabilities of a business. In this book we are concerned nearly exclusively with those businesses called corporations. A corporation is a legal entity, apart from any of its owners. The owners of a corporation are called stockholders. A stockholder owns a number of shares of stock in a corporation. The proportion of a stockholder's ownership is determined by the number of shares he holds divided by the total number of shares outstanding. For example, a woman holds 100 shares of stock in Corporation A, which has a total of 500 shares outstanding. She has a one-fifth (100/500) interest in the company. The owners' equity of a corporation is divided into two parts. The first is the "capital stock," which is the amount invested in the company by stockholders. The second part is called "retained earnings," which represent the cumulative earnings of the company less any distribution of these earnings (called dividends). Chapter 7 considers capital stock in more detail. For the next six chapters, it is sufficient for you to understand that the owners' equity part of the balance sheet consists of (1) the stockholder investment, and (2) the cumulative earnings less dividends. It is also important to emphasize that there is no necessary relationship between the amount of retained earnings and the amount of cash in a business.

Not all businesses are corporations. There are unincorporated businesses called individual proprietorships (if owned by a single person) and partnerships (if owned by more than one person). Unincorporated businesses are those started by individuals who do not go through the legal process of setting up a separate legal entity. Individual proprietorships and partnerships are given different legal and tax treatment from corporations. These differences need not be considered here. From a balance sheet point of view, the only difference is that, instead of capital stock and retained earnings, the owners' equity of a company is designated as "John Jones, Capital," if a single proprietorship, or as John Jones, Capital, Fred Smith, Capital, and so forth, if it is a partnership. The amount shown after each of the partners' names represents that person's share of the owners' equity of the partnership.

BALANCE SHEET CHANGES

As we indicated earlier, anything that directly affects the financial resources of business will be reflected in the balance sheet. The purpose of this part of the chapter is to show how the balance sheet is affected by events that occur in a typical business day.

The ABC Corporation starts business on January 1, 1974. It has capital of

$100,000 that was raised through the sale of stock. The balance sheet as of January 1 is:

Assets		*Owners' Equity*	
Cash	$100,000	Capital Stock	$100,000

On January 3, the manager of the company:

1. purchased $25,000 worth of inventory on open account;
2. leased a building, paying 1 year's rent of $12,000 in advance in cash;
3. purchased $30,000 worth of equipment for cash.

At the end of the day, the balance sheet is as follows:

THE ABC CORPORATION
Balance Sheet
As of January 3, 1974

Assets		*Liabilities and Owners' Equity*	
Cash	$ 58,000	Accounts Payable	$ 25,000
Inventory	25,000	Capital Stock	100,000
Prepaid Rent	12,000		
Equipment	30,000		
	$125,000		125,000

During the remainder of January, the following activities occurred:

1. Sales were as follows:
   (a) Inventory that cost $5,000 was sold for $7,500 on open account.
   (b) Inventory that cost $3,000 was sold for $4,000 in cash.
2. $10,000 was borrowed on a 60-day noninterest-bearing note.
3. The manager paid himself a salary of $1,000 for the month of January.
4. The life of the equipment is estimated to be 10 years. One month's depreciation, therefore, is $250 (30,000 ÷ 120).

The balance sheet as of January 31 is as follows:

THE ABC CORPORATION
Balance Sheet
As of January 31, 1974

Assets		*Liabilities and Owners' Equity*	
Cash	$ 71,000[a]	Accounts Payable	$ 25,000
Accounts Receivable	7,500	Notes Payable	10,000
Inventory	17,000[b]	Capital Stock	100,000
Prepaid Rent	11,000[c]	Retained Earnings	1,250[e]
Equipment*	29,750[d]		
	$136,250		$136,250

*For the purpose of these examples, we are deducting depreciation directly from the asset, rather than showing a separate accumulated depreciation amount.

[a]58,000 + 4,000 (1b) + 10,000 (2) − 1,000 (3) = 71,000
[b]25,000 − 5,000 (1a) − 3,000 (1b) = 17,000
[c]One month's rent (12,000 ÷ 12) has expired
[d]Original cost of the equipment ($30,000) less 1 month's depreciation ($250)
[e]The earnings of the business during January (ignoring income taxes) can be calculated as follows:

Sales (1a + 1b)	$11,500
Cost of Goods Sold (1a + 1b)	8,000
Depreciation	250
Rent	1,000
Manager's Salary	1,000
Total Expenses	$10,250
Earnings	$ 1,250

During the month of February, the following activities occurred:

1. $15,000 worth of inventory was purchased on account.
2. $20,000 was paid to suppliers.
3. Sales were as follows:
   (a) Inventory costing $10,000 was sold on open account for $15,000.
   (b) Inventory costing $5,000 was sold for $8,000 in cash.
4. $5,000 was collected from customers.
5. $1,000 was paid to the manager as a salary for February.
6. A dividend of $500 was paid to the stockholders.

The balance sheet as of February 28, 1974 is as follows:

THE ABC CORPORATION
Balance Sheet
As of February 28, 1974

Assets		*Liabilities and Owners' Equity*	
Cash	$ 62,500[a]	Accounts Payable	$ 20,000[e]
Accounts Receivable	17,500[b]	Notes Payable	10,000
Inventory	17,000[c]	Capital Stock	100,000
Prepaid Rent	10,000[d]	Retained Earnings	6,500[f]
Equipment	29,500[d]		
	$136,500		$136,500

[a]71,000 − 20,000 (2) + 8,000 (3b) + 5,000 (4) − 1,000 (5) − 500 (6) = 62,500
[b]7,500 + 15,000 (3a) − 5,000 (4) = 17,500 .
[c]17,000 + 15,000 (1) − 10,000 (3a) − 5,000 (3b) = 17,000
[d]These are the January 31 balances less 1 additional month's rent and one additional month's depreciation
[e]25,000 + 15,000 (1) − 20,000 (2) = 20,000
[f]Retained earnings January 31, $1,250 + profits of $5,750 less dividend of 500 = 6,500

Earnings for February
(Again ignoring taxes)

Sales	$23,000
Cost of Goods Sold	15,000
Manager's Salary	1,000
Rent	1,000
Depreciation	250
Total Expenses	$17,250
Earnings Before Taxes	$ 5,750

BOOKKEEPING

The examples that we have just presented represent one way of keeping track of the impact of financial activities on the balance sheet of the business (financial activities are called "transactions"). In the typical business, however, there could well be hundreds of transactions daily. Obviously, a systematic efficient method for recording transactions is required. The technique for recording and classifying transactions is called "bookkeeping." There are two interesting things about the simple bookkeeping we have been doing in this part of the chapter.

First, every transaction affected two items on the balance sheet. For instance, cash received from customers affected cash and accounts receivable. Furthermore, the amount by which one of the affected items changed was always equal to the amount by which the other item changed. The method of bookkeeping that records this dual aspect of every transaction is called "double entry bookkeeping." Occasionally, more than two items are affected by a single transaction. When this occurs, it is always possible to group the items so that the total changes in one sub-group will equal the total changes in the other sub-group. This is called the "duality" principle.

The second point to emphasize is that the balance sheet always stayed in balance. Even though we calculated the balance of each item separately, the assets still equaled liabilities plus owners' equity. The preservation of this fundamental accounting equation is also a result of the method of bookkeeping. Not only will each transaction affect two items by an equal amount, but it also will affect these items in such a way that the fundamental accounting equations always remain in balance. For example, the cash received from customers increased cash and decreased accounts receivable by the same amount, thus keeping total assets the same. Cash paid to suppliers reduced cash and reduced accounts payable; thus both assets and liabilities were reduced, maintaining the balance. Cash sales increased assets and increased owners' equity, again preserving the balance. In short, the fundamental accounting equation (Assets = Liabilities + Owners' Equity) is always preserved.

In Chapter 4 we will describe the bookkeeping process in more detail.

THREE BALANCE SHEET LIMITATIONS

When using a balance sheet to assess the financial status of a business, there are three important limitations to the data that must be kept constantly in mind. These are:

1. The balance sheet reflects only those activities that can readily be reduced to monetary terms;
2. The amounts shown are calculated in accordance with accounting conventions and they are only useful to the extent those conventions are useful;
3. Many things that a layman would consider as assets or liabilities are not shown at all on the balance sheet.

Each of these limitations is discussed in this part of the chapter.

EVERYTHING IN MONETARY TERMS

Accounting deals only in activities that can be expressed in monetary units. It is true that, in the long run, all activities of a business will have a financial impact on it. The problem is that, at any given time, their effects may not have been reflected in the monetary flow. For example, an efficient executive organization is of utmost importance to the success of any business. Suppose that near the end of the year, a successful company lost its entire top management team. The balance sheet would be exactly the same as if the management team had remained intact, yet the company's status might have changed considerably. On the other hand, a company could have achieved a major research breakthrough, yet not had time to exploit its advantage when the balance sheet was prepared. The balance sheet of this company would be exactly the same as if the research had been a complete failure. Although these are exaggerated examples, they demonstrate this basic limitation of the balance sheet.

ITEMS VALUED BY APPLYING CONVENTIONS

One of the most basic and more arbitrary accounting principles is that assets are shown on the balance sheet at their cost. If the asset is one that loses its value over time (e.g., wears out), it is carried at the original cost of the asset less the estimated proportion of this cost that has expired. This principle causes many problems for the user of the balance sheet. With changing price levels, the cost of an asset purchased several years ago may have no relationship to its current replacement cost or its current selling value.

Assets have traditionally been shown at cost because alternative means of valuing them have been viewed to cause even greater problems. Resale value, for example, can be very misleading because special-purpose equipment may have no value for anyone except the business for which it was designed. Furthermore, many people question the relevance of resale value for assets that are intended to be *used* rather than *sold*. Replacement cost creates two problems. First, if you were to replace an asset today, you would probably buy something different and presumably better adapted to your business. Replacement cost would, therefore, have to be adjusted for improvements in technology and engineering adaptations. A second problem with replacement cost is that its determination is subject to a considerable degree of uncertainty, so that balance sheet amounts would be less objective. In spite of its limitations, modern accounting statements are required to follow the principle that assets be reflected on the balance sheet at their cost. If you buy something, you can indicate it on your balance sheet as an asset for the amount that you paid for it. Otherwise, you cannot include it as an asset and you cannot enter it at any amount higher than the amount that you paid for it.

MANY ITEMS NOT SHOWN

There are certain types of assets that are not shown on the balance sheet at all. As mentioned earlier, for example, some intangible assets are not reflected on the balance sheet. Building a dealer organization may require a considerable investment and there is no question that a good dealer organization can be of great value to a company. Yet because of the intangible nature of this asset, it is practically never shown on the balance sheet. Other intangible assets include research findings, organizational and personnel development, and customer goodwill from advertising. The rule with such intangible assets is that if you buy it from someone else, you may carry it as an asset. If you develop it yourself, you may not. Following are two examples that demonstrate this rule.

Example 1–goodwill. If you buy a business for more than the value of the physical assets, you can consider the excess payment to be goodwill and include it as an asset on your balance sheet. If you develop this goodwill through advertising, quality control, service, and so forth, you cannot include it on your balance sheet as an asset.

Example 2–patents. If you buy a patent from someone outside your business, you can enter it on your balance sheet at the price that you paid for it. If you develop your own patent, you can value it only at the cost of obtaining the patient.

Similarly, some items that involve obligations by the corporation to make future payments are not shown as liabilities. Specifically, lease payments, pension liabilities, and the debt of unconsolidated affiliated companies are often not fully reflected in financial statements. We will discuss these areas in later chapters.

BALANCE SHEET ANALYSIS

A single balance sheet contains only a limited amount of information about a company. You need to analyze a company over a period of time and also analyze the balance sheet in conjunction with the income statement (to be described in

Chapter 2) and the funds flow statement (to be described in Chapter 3). As we pointed out earlier in the chapter, accounting deals only with the flow of values that can be expressed in monetary terms. Thus, even with all of these statements, the outsider can gain only a limited knowledge of a company. Nevertheless, there is some important information that you can obtain from the balance sheet alone and this part of the chapter describes this information. In the next chapter we will describe how other balance sheet data can be meaningful when used in conjunction with the income statement.

LIQUIDITY

Perhaps the most important information that the balance sheet provides concerns the liquidity of the business. Liquidity relates directly to "solvency," which is the ability of a business to meet its financial obligations as they come due. The more cash and cash equivalent assets that a company has, compared to its obligations, the more liquid (and, thus, the more solvent) it is said to be. Liquidity is, of course, of vital importance because a business can be forced into bankruptcy if it cannot pay its debts.[3]

Working Capital

The most common measure of liquidity is *working capital*, which is current assets minus the current liabilities. For the ABC company shown previously, working capital is $5,317 − $3,006, or $2,311. Working capital can be thought of as revolving funds. Goods are purchased, creating a current liability and increasing the inventory; the inventory is sold increasing accounts receivable and decreasing the inventory; the accounts receivable are collected, increasing cash and decreasing amounts of accounts receivable; the accounts payable are paid, decreasing cash and decreasing accounts payable; and so the cycle continues. In a going business, these items are continually revolving, and although the balances may remain fairly constant, the composition of these items will be constantly changing. For example, although the level of inventory may remain constant, the actual physical inventory changes, at least partially, every day.

The amount of working capital indicates the protection that a company has against adverse conditions. For example, what happens when a company is closed down by a strike? Presumably, the business would have to pay its current liabilities and this could be done by liquidating the current assets. If the current assets were exactly equal to the current liabilities, the business would quickly be in financial difficulties. In another instance, a recession could cause operating losses. If a company had little or no liquidity to cushion its losses, it would quickly be facing serious financial problems.

The Current Ratio

Relative liquidity is expressed by the *current ratio*, which is the amount of current assets divided by the amount of current liabilities. For the ABC Company, the

---

[3] Bankruptcy involves the forced sale of assets to pay the debts of a business.

current ratio is $5,317 ÷ $3,006, or 1.77. One common rule of thumb is that the current ratio should be at least 2. In other words, a company should have twice as much current assets as it has current liabilities. Like all rules of thumb, this generalization is of limited usefulness. The important consideration is the amount and type of current assets and the impact of likely misfortunes. A ratio cannot be used without a knowledge of the business.

Notice that borrowing money from a bank on a short-term loan will not change the working capital, but it will reduce the current ratio. The loan will increase the amount of cash but it will also increase the current liabilities. If a business is deficient in working capital, it can correct the deficiency by long-term borrowing, added investments by stockholders, or retaining profits in the business (assuming, of course, the business is earning profits).

Some Comments On Liquidity

In general, the balance sheet gives an accurate indication of the liquidity of a company. Cash, receivables, and payables should be almost exactly as indicated on the balance sheet. (We are assuming, of course, that the balance sheet has been properly prepared.) It is really only the inventory that might be misleading. In general, inventory values tend to be understated for two reasons: (1) Inventories are valued at cost, which usually is less than the amount for which they can be sold. (If they cannot be sold for more than cost, how can the business earn a profit?) (2) In an inflationary economy, acquisition cost will continually lag replacement cost. To the extent that selling prices rise because of inflation, valuation of inventories at acquisition cost thus further understates current values. (This condition is examined in Chapter 5. For the present, it is sufficient that you understand that, in a going business, inventories tend to be valued at considerably less than the amount for which they could be sold.)

Although inventory values tend to be understated, their liquidity can often be overstated. Many items of inventory could not be liquidated within a year and, in fact, might take several years. For example, service parts inventories might take years to liquidate.

Another factor that should be considered is that there could be a wide difference between the price received from selling an inventory item in the regular process of business and the price one could get in case of a forced liquidation of all inventories. In other words, although inventories tend to be undervalued in a going concern, they *could be overvalued*, particularly if a company might be going out of business.

In summary, then, the key to the usefulness of the working capital figure is the inventory figure. If inventory values can affect a decision (e.g., if you were considering lending the company money), you should find out what comprises the inventory and how it has been valued. Although the inventory values are usually understated in profitable businesses, their liquidity can be seriously overstated in some instances.

DEBT-EQUITY RATIO

A balance sheet can provide important information about how a business has been financed—that is, information about who has provided the money to buy the property assets and to finance the working capital. This money comes from two sources: creditors who lend the company money and owners who invest in the business. The relative amounts provided by these two sources can be an important consideration in making certain types of decisions about a business.

The relationship between creditor and owner financing is shown by the "debt-equity ratio." This is the amount of long-term debt divided by the sum of long-term debt plus owners' equity. (We consider only long-term liabilities because short-term loans are a means of obtaining cash when working capital is tied up in other current assets. Short-term loans, therefore, are not a part of the permanent financing of a business.) For the ABC Company the debt-equity ratio is $5,000 ÷ (5,000 + $6,346) = 44 per cent.

As a rule of thumb, many lenders feel the debt-equity ratio should be no higher than 40 per cent to 50 per cent. That is, the stockholders should put up at least half of the money to finance a business. This rule of thumb, of course, is subject to the same type of limitations as the current ratio. Some businesses with a very high debt-equity ratio are safe investments; others with a low debt-equity ratio can be very risky investments.

The debt-equity ratio can be very important when a company is looking for additional long-term financing. Since the liabilities will be paid off first in case of liquidation, the fewer long-term liabilities a company has in relation to its owners' equity, the safer it is to lend the business additional funds (other things being equal, of course).

If the values of any assets are overstated or understated, it will affect the amount of owners' equity, but not the long-term liabilities. (Since owners' equity is assets minus liabilities, the equity would be reduced if the asset values were reduced.) This means that the debt-equity ratio is only as accurate as the values of the assets and, as we have already pointed out, the balance sheet values of assets can be quite arbitrary. The debt-equity ratio must be considered with this fact in mind.

SUMMARY

The right-hand side of the balance sheet shows where the resources of the company have come from. The left-hand side of the balance sheet shows where these resources have been invested. Although the balance sheet appears to be precise, it is not necessarily so. First, the balance sheet is prepared in accordance with accounting conventions and, thus, the figures are only as precise as these conventions allow. Second, there are many areas where in subjective judgment is required and, thus, the figures are only as precise as the judgment involved. Throughout the book, we will show how accounting conventions and subjective judgments can affect accounting results. At this point, it is sufficient to be generally aware of these limitations of the balance sheet.

QUESTIONS

1. Explain why a balance sheet balances. Can you see any benefits from this type of presentation? Can you think of any better way to do it?

2. What is the benefit of separating current assets from other assets and current liabilities from other liabilities?

3. What is a prepaid expense? Give some examples of prepaid expenses. Why are they an asset? Give some examples of prepaid income. Why are they liabilities?

4. Give some examples of products that might be inventory to one type of company and a property asset to another type of company. What, if any, are the advantages of treating the same product differently in different companies?

5. Explain the meaning of the term "goodwill." How does a company acquire goodwill to include on its balance sheet? How would you go about deciding how to write it off?

6. What is the rationale for including assets at cost and only cost? What alternatives are there? Which would you recommend? Why?

7. Describe some events (other than those listed in the text) that could have an important impact on a company's future profitability, but which would not affect the balance sheet at the time that the event occurred.

8. Why do you think it is important to have a set of accounting principles that everyone must follow? Why not let each business prepare a balance sheet in any way that seems reasonable to the management of the business?

9. Explain the current ratio? How is it important in balance sheet analysis? Can you think of a circumstance in which a low current ratio (e.g., less than 1) might not be unfavorable? Can you think of a circumstance in which a high current ratio (e.g., greater than 3) might not necessarily indicate adequate liquidity?

10. Explain the debt-equity ratio. How is it important in analyzing the balance sheet? Can you think of a circumstances where in a company with a low debt-equity ratio (e.g., .2) might not be a good risk for a loan? Can you think of a circumstance where in a company with a high debt-equity ratio (e.g., .8) might be a good risk for a loan?

Problem 1-1

Identify how each of the following items would be classified on the balance sheet (current asset, property asset, current liability, etc.)

1. A note payable, due in 10 years; as security for this note, a mortgage has been placed on the office building.

2. The office building mentioned in 1, above.

3. Deposits of Swiss francs in a Geneva bank account that is being used by the Swiss branch of the company.

4. Debts owed to suppliers.

5. Amounts owed by customers.

6. Short-term government bonds.

7. Land on which the factory is located.

8. Patents.

9. Prepaid insurance.

10. Capital stock.

11. Taxes currently owed to the federal government.

12. Goods held for resale.

13. Investments in subsidiary companies.

14. Wages due employees.

15. A 3-month loan made to an officer of this company.

Problem 1-2

Prepare a balance sheet from the information provided below. Calculate the current ratio and the debt-equity ratio. On the basis of this balance sheet, would you lend this company $25,000 on a 1-year, unsecured loan? Why or why not?

THE XYZ COMPANY
(Account balances on December 31, 1974)

Mortgage Payable	$40,000
Property Assets	52,691
Cash	10,460
Accounts Payable	31,569
Notes Receivable	1,000
Inventories	23,481
Notes Payable (short-term)	20,000
Accounts Receivable	20,390
Capital Stock	20,000
Retained Earnings	?

Problem 1-3

Prepare a balance sheet from the information provided below. Assume that you are a loan officer in a bank, and the UVW Company requests a loan of $100,000 on a 5-year note. What balance sheet information would be useful in making this decision? What other information would you need?

THE UVW COMPANY
(Account balances on December 31, 1974)

Investments: Cost = $164,000; market value =	$298,426
Cash	25,692
Accounts Payable	43,689
Notes Receivable	20,000
Property Assets	489,463
Capital Stock	500,000
Inventories	48,005
Federal Income Taxes Payable	10,984
Prepaid Expenses	4,296
Accounts Receivable	46,981
Retained Earnings	?

Problem 1-4

Prepare a balance sheet from the information provided below. If you were a loan officer in a bank, would you lend this company $50,000 on a 90-day note? There are 10,000 shares of stock outstanding. What is the maximum amount you would pay for a share?

THE RST COMPANY
(Account balances as of December 31, 1974)

Accounts Payable	$ 75,432
Cash	6,398
Property Assets	25,746
Bonds Payable	200,000
Goodwill	100,000
Notes Payable	30,000
Inventories	98,698
Taxes Payable	6,483
Patents	146,291
Accounts Receivable	25,432
Capital Stock	150,000
Prepaid Expense	583
Retained Earnings	?

Problem 1-5

The January 1975 transactions for the NOQ Company are as follows. Prepare a balance sheet as of January 31.

1. The NOQ Corporation was formed by selling 1,000 shares of capital stock for $200,000 cash.

2. On January 2, a 10-year lease on a building was signed. The first year's rent of $6,000 was paid.

3. A total of $120,000 worth of equipment was purchased on January 15. Of the purchase price, $50,000 was paid in cash; the NOQ Corporation gave a 90-day noninterest-bearing note for the remaining $70,000. The equipment is expected to last for 10 years.

4. Inventory costing $60,000 was bought on open account.

5. Goods costing $30,000 were sold for $45,000 on open account.

6. The following salaries were paid in cash:

President	$1,000
Bookkeeper	400

Problem 1-6

The February 1975 transactions for the NOQ Company are as follows. Prepare a balance sheet as of February 28.

1. Payments of $20,000 were received from customers.

2. Payments of $50,000 were made to suppliers.

3. Inventory costing $40,000 was purchased on open account.

4. Goods costing $40,000 were sold for $60,000 on open account.

5. The following salaries were paid in cash:

President	1,000
Bookkeeper	400
Salesman	600

Problem 1-7

The balance sheet of the KLM Corporation as of December 31, 1974, is as follows:

Assets		*Equities*	
Cash	$ 16,936	Accounts Payable	$ 41,983
Accounts Receivable	22,498	Notes Payable	20,000
Inventories	34,852	Mortgage Payable	50,000
Supplies	3,980	Capital Stock	100,000
Land	6,734	Retained Earnings	10,017
Buildings	75,000		
Equipment	50,000		
Goodwill	12,000		
Total Assets	$222,000	Total Equities	$222,000

Balance Sheet Notes:

1. Five years ago the building had cost $100,000. It has an estimated life of 20 years. Consequently, its net book value is equal to $100,000–$25,000 (5 years' depreciation), or $75,000.

2. Five years ago the equipment was purchased for $100,000. This equipment has an estimated life of 10 years.

3. The goodwill resulted from purchasing a company several years ago and paying $12,000 more than the fair value of the assets acquired.

4. The note payable is a 3-month's note dated December 31, 1974, bearing interest at 6 percent per annum. The interest is payable with the principal on April 1, 1975.

5. The mortgage bears interest at 4 per cent per year, payable June 30 and December 31 of each year.

The following transactions took place during January:

1. Inventory was purchased for $8,925 on open account.

2. Goods costing $25,420 were sold for $43,982 on open account. Commissions on these sales were $2,469 and were paid in cash to the salesmen.

3. Customers paid $20,396 on their accounts.

4. Suppliers were paid $10,498.

5. It was decided to amortize goodwill over 10 years, beginning January 1, 1975.

6. Supplies worth $1,482 were purchased for cash. Supplies worth $3,840 were used during the month.

7. The following salary payments were made:

Administrative Staff	$2,680
Sales Salaries	4,180
Total	$6,860

Prepare a balance sheet as of January 31, 1975.

Problem 1-8

The following transactions took place in the KLM Corporation during the month of February 1975:

1. Inventory was purchased for $19,827 on open account.

2. Goods costing $29,830 were sold for $47,230 on open account. Sales commission on these sales of $2,980 was paid in cash.

3. Customers paid $24,960 on their accounts.

4. Suppliers were paid $11,260.

5. Supplies worth $4,830 were purchased for cash during the month. On February 28, on inventory of supplies revealed that $2,692 worth were still on hand at that date.

6. The following salary payments were made:

Administrative Staff	$2,700
Sales Salaries	5,190
Total	$7,890

Required:

1. Prepare a balance sheet as of February 28, 1975.

2. Prepare an analysis of the change in retained earnings during the month. (This analysis can be in any format that you wish.)

Problem 1-9

Explain how each of the following transactions would affect the balance sheet. Name the items on the balance sheet that would be changed, the amounts of the change, and whether the changes are an increase or a decrease in the items affected. Assume that each event is independent.

1. A total of $1,000 is borrowed on January 15 from a bank on a 30-day, 6 per cent note. What is the effect of this transaction on:

   (a) January 15, when the money is borrowed.
   (b) January 31, when the balance sheet is to be prepared.
   (c) February 14, when the note is paid.

2. Assume the same facts as in 1, above, except that it is a noninterest-bearing note and the bank "discounted" the note at 6 per cent annual rate—that is, the bank reduced the cash given to the company by the amount of interest. (In other words, the bank took out its interest first.) When the note comes due in 30 days, only $1,000 will be paid because the note does not bear interest.

3. A company lends an employee $5,000 on January 15. The employee gives the company a 60-day note for $5,000. The note bears interest at the rate of 9 per cent a year. What is the effect of this transaction on:

   (a) January 15.
   (b) January 31.
   (c) February 28.
   (d) March 17.

4. On March 15 a company buys a 3-year fire insurance policy for $3,600. What is the effect of this transaction on:

   (a) March 15.
   (b) December 31, when the year-end balance sheet is prepared. (Assume that no interim balance sheets have been prepared.)

5. A company has the following property assets as of the beginning of the year:

Type of Asset	Original Cost	Estimated Life
Land	$ 1,496,500	
Buildings	33,568,940	30 years
Machinery	150,268,830	10 years
Delivery Equipment	5,733,480	5 years

On July 1 the company purchased $250,000 worth of machinery for cash. On October 1 the company purchased $50,000 worth of delivery equipment for cash. No property assets were retired or sold during the year. What changes will be made in the balance sheet on:

   (a) July 1.
   (b) October 1.
   (c) On December 31 in connection with the preparation of the year-end balance sheet. (Assume that no interim balance sheets have been prepared.)

Problem 1-10

Prepare a balance sheet as of June 30, 1975, for the R.D. Morison Company, using the following data:

Retained Earnings	$438,000
Inventories	420,000
Investment in the Peerless Company	250,000
Accounts Payable	200,000
Accounts Receivable	385,000
Accumulated Depreciation on Buildings	420,000
Capital Stock	750,000
Equipment (at cost)	570,000
Notes Payable	100,000
Estimated Tax Liability	100,000
Marketable Securities	150,000
Accrued Expenses Payable	89,000
Land (at cost)	175,000
Accumulated Depreciation on Equipment	300,000
Bonds Payable	400,000
Buildings (at cost)	800,000
Cash	47,000

The Income Statement

The typical accountant?
*A man past middle age, spare, wrinkled, intelligent,
cold, passive, noncommittal, with eyes like a codfish,
polite in contact, but at the same time unresponsive, calm
and damnably composed as a concrete post or a plaster-
of-Paris cast; a human petrification with a heart of feldspar
and without charm of the friendly germ, minus bowels,
passion or a sense of humor. Happily, they never reproduce
and all of them finally go to Hell.*

Elbert Hubbard

2

The most important change in a balance sheet between two periods of time is the change in owners' equity. It is important that the potential creditor or investor know not only the amount of this change, but also the principal factors that have contributed to it. One such factor is the operating results of the business. Consequently, in addition to a balance sheet, the publicly held corporation must also publish an income statement. The income statement provides the details of the changes in owners' equity between two periods that have resulted from the operations of the business.

The principal objective of most private businesses is to earn profits.[1] The purpose of the income statement is to indicate how successful the business has been in meeting this objective. Profits are of primary importance to the board of directors in evaluating the management of a company, to stockholders or potential stockholders in making investment decisions, and to banks and other creditors in deciding on action to be taken with respect to loans. Other things being equal, a profitable company is a good company to invest in, lend money to, work for, and deal with in general. An unprofitable company, on the other hand, presents problems on all of these counts, because if the profit situation is not changed, it must eventually go out of business. When this happens, most of the persons or companies dealing with it are likely to be affected adversely. As a result, the income statements of a business are carefully scrutinized by all interested parties.

MATCHING COSTS AGAINST REVENUES

Income can be defined as the excess of revenues over expenses in a given period of time. In accounting, we measure income by attempting to match the costs against the revenue that they generate. In general, the process, first, is to measure all revenue earned over a period of time, and then to measure all expenses related to

[1] In this book, we will use the terms "income," "profit," and "earnings" interchangeably.

that same period. If an expense can be directly associated with an item of revenue (such as the inventory cost of an item sold), we charge it off in the same period that the revenue is recognized. If an expense cannot be associated directly with an item of revenue (such as the president's salary), we write it off in the period when it is incurred. One can thus think of an income statement in the following way:

Revenues earned from sales during the period
— Expenses directly relatable to the items sold
— Expenses relatable to the period
— Income for the period

The purpose of this part of the chapter is to describe the accounting process of income measurement.

Revenue

In business, revenue is counted in the earliest period in which it is considered earned. The earning of revenue does not necessarily mean the receipt of cash. The receipt of cash represents the culmination of a series of events that begins when raw materials are purchased. The following diagram shows these various events for a typical business.

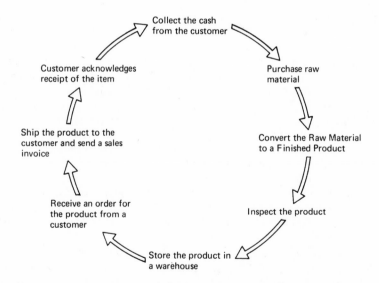

Each step in this process contributes to the creation of value, which is ultimately reflected in the amount of cash received. In effect, the sales revenue is "earned" a little bit at a time as each of the steps is completed. The accountant's problem is to decide when to count the sales revenue.

A criterion of timeliness—accounting for something as soon as possible—suggests using as early a point in the process as is feasible for determining that sales revenue has been earned. On the other hand, there are two criteria that tend to suggest using a later point in the process. These are "uncertainty resolution" and "performance." "Uncertainty resolution" means that the accountant wants to wait until the uncertainty about the actual amount of cash to be received has been largely resolved—that is, until the uncertainty has been reduced to a low level. Accepted accounting practice requires that we do not recognize revenue before we are reasonably sure of the actual amount to be received. What constitutes reasonable certainty, however, will differ in different industries and also can differ according to the judgment of the parties involved—primarily management and the accountant.

The "performance" criterion means that the accountant does not want to count sales revenue until the critical tasks involved in earning that revenue have been performed. Revenue should not be recognized until the important functions to be performed in generating that revenue have been completed. Thus, a manufacturing company does not count a firm, fixed price order it has received as a sale until the product has been produced and, in most cases, shipped to the customer. Accepted accounting practice requires that we do not count revenue before all the critical tasks have been performed.

In the great majority of cases, however, the recognition of revenue presents no serious problem. Revenue is usually recognized: (1) when the title to goods has passed, or (2) when a service has been rendered.

Costs, Expenditures, and Expenses

The *cost* of any item is the *value* given up in order to obtain it. An *expenditure* is a payment. An *expense* is a cost that has been "used up," presumably in obtaining revenue. A *loss* is a cost that has been used up but which has resulted in no benefit to the business—for example, the destruction of inventory in a fire. These distinctions are not always made in actual business practice. It is quite common to use costs and expenses interchangeably, and often no distinction is made between an expense and a loss. For the purpose of understanding the accounting theory of income measurement, it may be well to keep the definitions of these terms in mind, at least for this chapter.

In measuring income or earnings, we try to calculate those *costs* that have become expenses in generating sales revenues. Notice also that in calculating the amount of *expense*, the period in which the *expenditure* was made is not the determining factor.

The first and most obvious expense is for the inventory sold. This is usually called the "cost of goods sold." Any other costs directly incurred in making the sales (such as sales commissions) also become expenses. In addition, any other costs that have expired during the period in question become expenses. The principle is to reflect as expenses only the cost of these items that benefited the firm during the period. Any costs that would benefit the firm in future periods should be charged against those future periods.

The following generalizations concern expenses:

1. Many *costs* are automatically treated as *expenses* in the period in which

they are incurred (but not necessarily paid) because they can not readily be related to the items the firm sells. Examples include administrative salaries, rent of the office building, office supplies used, and so forth. Some *costs* may benefit the firm in the future but are treated as *expenses* immediately because of the difficulty in determining what, if any, this future benefit is worth. Advertising, sales promotion, and research are included in this category.

2. Some assets, either partially or totally, become expenses in any accounting period. Inventory items that have been sold are one example already mentioned. In addition, a portion of the property assets may have been used up and the amount of this used-up portion is an expense (depreciation). Also, prepaid expenses may be partially or wholly used up.

3. There may be expenses related to the current period that will not be paid until some future period. Interest, property taxes, and rent may fall in this category. For example, on July 1, 1975, a business borrows $10,000 on a 1-year note that bears interest at the rate of 6 per cent. By December 31, the business has incurred an expense of $300, even though it may not have to pay it until the note matures in 6 months. The interest expense for 1975 would be $300 and the balance sheet would show a liability of $300. We call this liability "accrued interest payable" to indicate that payment is not yet due.

4. There may be costs incurred during the period that are really assets. For example, if insurance or rent is paid in advance, the proportion applying to a future period is an asset on the balance sheet date. The expense of the current period, therefore, is equal to the total cost reduced by the amount applicable to the future period.

Capitalization vs. Expensing

When a cost is incurred, the accountant must treat it as either an asset or an expense. If he treats it as an asset, he is said to "capitalize" it. If he treats it as an expense, he is said to "expense" it. In most instances, there is no problem deciding what to do. An item that has permanent value (e.g., an investment) or long-term value (e.g., a property asset) is always capitalized, whereas items that have already been or clearly will be used up during the period are always expensed. There are some optional cases, however. In particular, items like prepaid insurance or prepaid rent can be treated as either an asset or an expense at the time they are paid. At the end of the period, however, it is necessary to adjust these items so that only the expired part is included in expenses and only the unexpired part is included among the assets.

The Accrual Concept

The concept of recognizing revenues when they are earned, rather than when they are realized (converted to cash), and of recognizing costs when the benefits have expired, rather than when the cash is paid out, is called the "accrual concept." An income statement for a corporation should always be prepared using the accrual concept. In Chapter 3, we will describe an accounting statement that shows the flow of cash into and out of the business. For now, it is sufficient to understand that the income statement is not intended to measure the movement of cash.

SUMMARY

During the accounting period, the accountant records as revenues all sales of goods and services billed to customers; he records as expenses the cost of the inventory sold and the costs directly applicable to the sale or service rendered. As he pays bills, he records all items as either assets (e.g., inventories, property assets, prepayments, etc.) or expenses (salaries, wages, telephone and telegraph, etc.). At the end of the period, before preparing financial statements, the accountant makes the following adjustments in his data:

1. He records as an asset and as an item of income any product sales or service revenues that have been earned but not yet billed.
2. He records as a liability and reduces income for any product sales or service revenues that the business has billed but which are not yet earned at the date on which the financial statements are prepared—for example, advance magazine subscriptions for a magazine company.
3. He reduces his assets for the amounts that have expired during the period and treats these amounts as expenses—for example, depreciation.
4. He reduces expenses for the value applicable to future periods. This amount is an asset—a prepaid expense—on the balance sheet.
5. He treats as an expense any service or product that has been received by the business but not paid for. The amount of such items is set up as a liability.

These five items are called "adjusting" entries and are treated in more detail in Chapter 4.

INCOME STATEMENT FORMAT

The income statement is traditionally divided into at least two sections. One is the income from operations; the other is the non-operating income and expense section. Often a section is included for extraordinary items. The following is an example of a typical income statement.

THE ABC CORPORATION
Income Statement
For Year Ending December 31, 1974 ($000)

Sales (net)	$30,486
Cost of Goods Sold	17,391
Gross Margin	$13,095

Other Operating Expenses		
Selling Expenses		$6,431
Administrative Expenses		2,982
Research and Development		1,489
Total		$10,902
Operating Profit		$ 2,193
Other Income and Expenses		
Interest Expense	$420	
Interest Income	(12)	
		408
Net Income before Taxes		$ 1,785
Income Taxes		805
Net Income		$ 980

Developing an Income Statement

The balance sheet of the DEF Corporation on December 31, 1974, is as follows:

Assets		Liabilities and Owners' Equity	
Cash	$ 25,492	Accounts Payable	$ 20,460
Accounts Receivable	30,640	Notes Payable[b]	20,000
Inventories	60,920	Capital Stock	200,000
Property Assets (net)[a]	150,130	Retained Earnings	26,722
	$267,182		$267,182

[a]Property assets consisted of land, $35,000; building cost, $60,000; accumulated depreciation, $20,000; life, 20 years; equipment cost, $120,000; accumulated depreciation, $44,870; life, 10 years.

[b]This is a 5-year note issued on January 1, 1974, bearing interest at 6 per cent. Interest is due June 30 and December 31 of each year.

The following activities took place during the month of January 1975:

1. Merchandise costing $40,000 was sold for $65,000 on open account. (This transaction will increase accounts receivable by $65,000, increase sales by $65,000, decrease inventory by $40,000, and increase cost of sales by $40,000. Notice that the impact on owners' equity is an increase of $25,000 [$65,000 − $40,000], the gross margin on the sale. It is necessary, however, to keep track of both sales and cost of sales so that an income statement can be developed.)
2. Inventory costing $35,000 was purchased on open account.
3. A total of $29,000 was collected in cash from customers.
4. Suppliers were paid $19,000.
5. A premium of $3,600 was paid for fire insurance. The policy was issued on January 15, and the premium covered 3 years from the date of issue. (This increases prepaid expenses and reduces cash by $3,600.)

6. The following expenses were paid during the month in cash:

Sales Salaries	$6,800
Sales Commissions	1,300
Administrative Salaries	5,000
Telephone and Telegraph	400
Electricity	385

7. On January 15, an officer of the company was loaned $2,000. He gave the company a promissory note, due in 90 days, with interest at an annual rate of 6 per cent.

At the end of January, but before adjustments, the income statement and balance sheet figures will be as follows:

Income Statement

Sales		$65,000
Cost of Goods Sold		40,000
Gross margin		$25,000
Selling expenses		
Sales Salaries	6,800	
Sales Commission	1,300	8,100
Administrative Expenses		
Administrative Salaries	5,000	
Telephone and Telegraph	400	
Electricity	385	5,785
Net profit before Taxes		$11,115

Balance Sheet

Assets		Liabilities and Owners' Equity	
Cash	$ 16,007[a]	Accounts Payable	$ 36,460[d]
Accounts Receivable	66,640[b]	Notes Payable	20,000
Notes Receivable	2,000		
Inventories	55,920[c]	Capital Stock	200,000
Prepaid Expenses	3,600	Retained Earnings	37,837[e]
Property Assets (net)	150,130		
	$294,297		$294,297

[a]25,492 + 29,000 (3) − 19,000 (14) − 3,600 (5) − 13,885 (6) − 2,000 (7) = 16,007
[b]30,640 + 65,000 (1) − 29,000 (3) = 66,640
[c]60,920 + 35,000 (2) − 40,000 (1) = 55,920
[d]20,460 + 35,000 (2) − 19,000 (4) = 36,460
[e]26,722 + 11,115 (income statement) = 37,837

The income statement and the balance sheet shown above are not correct because the only activities taken into account have been the discrete, day-to-day financial transactions. Other changes in values have been occurring continuously over the period. We take these into account just before preparing the financial statements. (There would be no point, for example, in taking depreciation into account daily if financial statements are prepared only monthly.) These are called adjustments and are calculated, in this example, as follows:

1. Some more of the property assets have been used up during January. The amount is calculated as follows:

   Land does not depreciate because it is not subject to wear.

   Building: $60,000 ÷ 20-year life = $3,000 depreciation per year; 3,000 ÷ 12 = $250 depreciation per month.

   Equipment: $120,000 ÷ 10-year life = $12,000 depreciation per year; $12,000 ÷ 12 = $1,000 depreciation per month.

   Total depreciation equals $1,250; this is subtracted from the amount of property assets and included in the income statement as an expense.

2. One-half month's worth of fire insurance has been used up. $3,600 ÷ 36 months = $100 insurance expense per month. One-half a month's expense, therfore, is $50. This is subtracted from the asset, prepaid expense, and included as an expense on the income statement.

3. We have a note receivable for $2,000. This note earns 6 per cent, or $120 per year. One-half month's interest, therefore, is $5. We have earned $5 interest income over this period, even though it has not yet been paid. We set up an asset called "accrued interest receivable" and an income item called "interest income" for this amount.

4. The company has a note payable outstanding of $20,000 on which it has agreed to pay 6 per cent a year, or $1,200. For January, therefore, the company has incurred a liability of $100. We set up a liability called "accrued interest payable" and an expense called "interest expense."

5. Assume in this example that the business must pay income taxes of 50 per cent of its profit before taxes. This adjustment cannot be made until the income statement has been prepared. When we calculate the amount of tax, we set up a liability, "taxes payable," and an item of expense, "income taxes."

We are now ready to prepare an adjusted income statement and balance sheet.

THE DEF COMPANY
Income Statement
For the Month of January 1975

Sales		$65,000
Cost of Goods Sold		40,000
Gross Margin		$25,000
Selling Expenses		
Sales Salaries	$6,800	
Sales Commissions	1,300	8,100
Administrative Expenses		
Administrative Salaries	5,000	
Telephone and Telegraph	400	
Electricity	385	
Depreciation Expense	1,250	
Insurance Expense	50	7,085
Operating Profit		$9,815

Other Income and Expense		
Interest Expense	$100	
Interest Income	(5)	95
Income before Taxes		$ 9,720
Income Taxes	4,860	
Net Income	$ 4,860	

THE DEF COMPANY
Balance Sheet
As of January 31, 1975

Assets		*Liabilities and Owners' Equity*	
Cash	$ 16,007	Accounts Payable	$ 36,460
Accounts Receivable	66,640	Accrued Interest Payable	100
Notes Receivable	2,000	Taxes Payable	4,860
Accrued Interest		Notes Payable	20,000
Receivable	5		
Inventories	55,920	Capital Stock	200,000
Prepaid Expenses	3,550	Retained Earnings	31,582[a]
Property Assets	148,880		
	$293,002		$293,002

[a]26,722 + 4,860 = 31,582

INCOME STATEMENT AND RETAINED EARNINGS

Notice on the above balance sheet that the net income is added to the retained earnings. In this example the difference between the beginning and ending owners' equity is the income for the period. This means that items of income are really increases in owners' equity and items of expenses are decreases in owners' equity. They are segregated into income and expense categories so that it is possible to show the *details* of the changes.

There are other changes in retained earnings that may not be reflected in the income statement. For practical purposes, those can be divided into three types:

1. Dividends paid to stockholders.
2. Corrections to past years' statements. For example, a company may discover an accounting error that has resulted in expenses being understated for the past few years. The correction for this error would be made directly to retained earnings, without showing the item on the income statement. Such items are rare in modern accounting.
3. Amounts transferred to capital stock in connection with stock dividends. This is described in Chapter 7.

INCOME STATEMENT ANALYSIS

This part of the chapter describes the principal financial statement ratios used by financial analysts. All ratios involving income statement items are for a period of 1 year. If the income statement covers less than a year, it can be "annualized" by multiplying each item by a factor that converts it to 12-month period.

Return on Investment

A most important financial statement ratio is the return on investment. This is a measure of the success of the company in achieving its financial objectives during the period under analysis.

There are two usual ways of calculating return on investment: (1) after-tax earnings before interest expense divided by owners' equity + long-term debt, and (2) after-tax earnings divided by owners' equity. Each of these calculations is explained in this part of the chapter.

After-tax earnings before interest expense divided by owners' equity plus long-term debt. The purpose of this ratio is to evaluate the earnings performance of a business without regard to the way in which it has been financed. The investment in a business is the working capital plus non-current assets, which is equivalent to long-term debt plus owners' equity. This can be shown mathematically as follows:

$$CA + NCA = CL + NCL + OE$$

Then, $CA - CL + NCA = NCL + OE$; but $(CA - CL)$
= Working Capital = WC

Therefore,

$$WC + NCA = NCL + OE$$

CA = current assets
NCA = non-current assets
CL = current liabilities
NCL = non-current liabilities
OE = owners' equity

The interest on long-term debt is added back to the income because the long-term debt has been included in the investment base. (In other words, we are eliminating the entire effects of long-term debt and assuming that the business is entirely financed by the stockholders.)

The ratio tells you what percentage a business has earned on its overall investment. In short, it is designed to tell you how well the business has utilized the assets that it controls.

Sometimes, this ratio is subdivided into two parts: the return on sales (earnings ÷ sales) and the investment turnover (sales ÷ investment). For example, a business shows the following:

Sales	$20,000,000
Net Earnings	$ 2,000,000
Investment	$10,000,000

The return on investment is $\dfrac{\$\ 2,000,000}{\$10,000,000}$ or 20%. This can be divided into:

Return on Sales = $\dfrac{\$\ 2,000,000}{\$20,000,000}$ = 10%

Investment Turnover = $\dfrac{\$20,000,000}{\$10,000,000}$ = 2

Return on Sales X Investment Turnover = Return on Investment
10% X 2 = 20%

Businesses vary widely in both return on sales and investment turnover, so these ratios mean little in themselves. When analyzing profits over a period of time for the same company, however, dividing the return on investment into these two ratios can provide some insight into the reasons for changes. Also, when analyzing the results of comparable companies, comparing these two ratios might make it possible to ascertain some of the reasons for differences in the return on investment.

After-tax earnings divided by owners' equity. Net earnings after taxes divided by owners' equity shows how well the management of the company is doing with the money invested by stockholders. This rate of return will be higher than the one described in the preceding section if the company has been able to earn more on its borrowed money than it is paying for it. This, of course, is to be expected. Lending money to a business tends to be less risky than investing in it because creditors have prior claim on the funds of a business if it gets into financial trouble. Also, the interest payments are a contractual obligation of the business, whereas dividends depend on earnings.

This ratio is of special interest to the investor or potential investor in a company because it gives him an idea of how much he will earn on his investment.

Turnover Ratios

There are several ratios involving the turnover of balance sheet items that are used in analyzing a company's financial statements. Two of these are described in this part of the chapter.

Sales/Receivables. This ratio is used to calculate the number of days' sales that are uncollected. For example, if annual sales were $500,000 and receivables $100,000, we would have a turnover of five. This means that receivables equal to 1/5 of a year's sales were outstanding. Expressed in terms of number of days, this is 1/5 X 360 = 72 days.

We can say, therefore, that receivables are equal to 72 days' sales. This is useful principally when compared with the company's credit policy. If the credit policy is 1 month, this would indicate that the company is having problems collecting its receivables.

Cost of goods sold/inventory. This ratio provides inventory turnover and the number of days inventory on hand. For example, suppose that the annual cost of goods sold was $2,000,000 and the inventory was $500,000. The inventory turnover would be 2,000,000/500,000, or 4 times a year. To express this turnover in days: 1/4 X 360 days = 90 days. The inventory, therefore, is equal to 3 months' sales.

Limitation of Turnover Ratios. Although turnover ratios can be useful in analyzing financial statements, they have at least three limitations that should be kept in mind.

First, the absolute ratios are not particularly useful because satisfactory ratios can vary considerably among different businesses. It is necessary, therefore, to have some standard of evaluation for the particular businesses that you are analyzing.

Second, turnover ratios can be misleading if the sales volume is seasonal. Consider, for example, a company with annual sales of $6,000,000 and year-end accounts receivable of $500,000. As we calculated it earlier, this is a turnover of twelve times. Receivable seem to be equal to 30 days' sales, a very reasonable level. If, however, sales are highly seasonal such that sales in the last 2 months of the year were only $500,000, the year-end receivables actually represent 60 days' sales, at current levels, not 30.

Third, the method of valuing inventories can be important in measuring inventory turnover. These methods are described in Chapter 5.

LIMITATIONS OF THE INCOME STATEMENT

It is important in evaluating a business to realize that the income statement has certain inherent limitations. The first of these results from the inability of the accounting system to recognize and measure all changes in values that have occurred during the year. The second limitation results from the unwillingness of almost all companies to provide more information than is required by law or regulation. Each of these is discussed in this part of the chapter.

Recognition and Measurement

For a going concern, complete accuracy would require that we measure all the changes in values that have occurred during the period for which the income statement has been prepared. Clearly, this is not practical because we are limited in accounting practice to those changes that can be measured in financial terms. Furthermore, we are restricted by accounting practice to recognizing only those changes that can be measured with a resonable degree of objectivity. The conditions that limit the accuracy of the balance sheet also affect the income statement, but in a somewhat different way. The purpose of this part of the chapter is to explain the impact of these limitations on the income statement. Notice that these limitations are the result of our attempts to measure "interim" earnings. If we waited until a business was liquidated, we could measure income precisely; it is the difference between the cash invested and the cash taken out. Since the total income must be the same under any system of measurement, the effect of imperfect measurement is to reflect the *timing* of income incorrectly. Consequently, understatement of profit in one period will result in overstatement of profit in some subsequent period, and vice versa. In the phrase "periodic earnings measurement" you should remember that it is the measurement that is periodic, not the earnings.

1. *Assets Shown at Cost*   It is a well-established principle in economics that an on-going business has not earned a trading or operating profit until it has covered, out of sales revenues, the cost of replacing the items used up in generating the sale. The annual depreciation expense is based on the original cost of the property assets. Thus, if the cost of an asset is significantly less than its replacement value, the operating income will be overstated. What has happened, in effect, is that the company has non-operating income resulting from the increased values of the property

assets. This would be offset by the increased depreciation cost of using the higher-valued assets. The problem is that the increase in the value of property assets will probably be different from the increase in depreciation during a given time period. Furthermore, the depreciation is an operating expense, whereas the change in value is non-operating income.

2. *Non-Recognition of Certain Types of Assets* According to the accounting principle called "conservatism," if there is any doubt about how an item should be treated, the alternative that reflects the lower profit should be chosen. Expressed in different terms: "anticipate all losses; never anticipate a profit." The principle of conservatism goes back many years, when accounting statements were used principally for information for potential lenders; therefore, the accountant who understated values was rarely subject to criticsm. Now, however, with financial statements being used by potential investors, the understatement of profits can have serious effects. For instance, it could result in stock prices being undervalued. Anyone realizing that profits were understated could take advantage of this situation to the detriment of other people who accepted the financial statements as a fair reflection of earnings. As a result, the idea of conservatism is not now followed so blindly as it was in past years. Nevertheless, it is an accepted accounting convention and it can distort the profit picture from period to period. The major effect of conservatism on the income statement is that certain costs are expensed in the period in which they occurred, even though they may benefit a firm in the future. Advertising, training, and research and development are typical examples.

In summary, then, two factors that limit the accuracy of income statements are (1) using original cost as a basis for depreciation, and (2) writing off certain types of costs in the period in which they were incurred rather than in the future period in which their benefit is realized. Notice that although these factors are both based on conservatism, they can cause *the profit to be overstated* in a given year. For example, if certain costs whose benefits are realized in 1974 and 1975 are written off in 1974, the 1974 profits will be understated but the 1975 profits will be *overstated*. Consequently, before you draw any conclusion with respect to an increasing *trend* in profits, be sure that the trend is not caused by understating profits at the beginning of the trend and overstating them in subsequent years.

Limitations in the Amount of Profit Information

An income statement provides only a fraction of the accounting information available in the typical company. Almost without exception, the income statement shows earnings for the total company only. Product-line profitability or profitability by organizational unit are usually omitted. Furthermore, the revenue and expense items are shown in a condensed form. For example, typically only net sales dollars are shown. Manufacturing costs are shown as one figure in "cost of goods sold." Consequently, it is difficult to draw anything but broad conclusions about why profits have changed from year to year. Sometimes the annual report gives a general explanation of changes but these explanations are also very broad. Whatever the reason, most companies provide only the information that they are required to provide and this practice, in the authors' opinion, is very likely to continue.

QUESTIONS

1. Why is it important to know the reasons for the change in owners' equity? What could be some of the causes of change? What action could you take if you knew the reasons for change?

2. How would you explain the concept of matching costs against revenues to a person generally unacquainted with business (e.g., a doctor)?

3. Give some examples wherein revenue would not be recognized because of the uncertainty of the amount of cash that was to be received.

4. Give some examples of different critical tasks that determine when revenue is to be recognized.

5. Why is it important to distinguish between an expense and a loss?

6. Give examples of costs that will nearly always be capitalized. Give some examples of costs that will nearly always be expensed.

7. Explain the relationship between the income statement items and the retained earnings. Why is it necessary to record the effect of financial transactions in terms of the items appearing on the income statement?

8. How would you go about deciding if a particular company was earning a satisfactory return on its investment?

9. Explain why turnover ratios are useful only when compared to a standard or norm. Give examples of how two different companies could have significantly different receivable and inventory turnover and yet both be performing in a satisfactory manner.

10. What would you recommend that the accounting profession do to increase the usefulness of the income statement to stockholders and potential stockholders?

Problem 2-1

Prepare an income statement for the KLM Company for January 1975. (See Problem 1-7.)

Problem 2-2

Prepare an income statement for the KLM Company for February 1975. (See Problem 1-8.)

Problem 2-3

The Cennet Corporation has the following balance sheet and income statement amounts as of December 31, 1974. These amounts are before any adjustments have been made for 1974.

	Amount
Cash	$ 10,887
Accounts Receivable	30,468
Notes Receivable	20,000

Inventories	$86,439
Prepaid Expenses	200
Property Assets (net of accumulated depreciation)	148,932
Accounts Payable	29,832
Notes Payable	15,000
Capital Stock	200,000
Retained Earnings (as of January 1, 1974)	37,223
Sales	85,963
Cost of Goods Sold	52,435
Selling Expense	12,132
Administrative Expense	4,825
Interest Expense	900
Interest Income	1,200
Dividends Paid	2,000

Notes:

1. Property assets include:
   (a) A building, costing $50,000, with a life of 20 years.
   (b) Equipment, costing $100,000, with a life of 10 years. No property assets were bought or sold during the year.
2. The prepaid expense is an insurance premium covering 4 years, beginning January 1, 1974.
3. The note receivable is a 1-year note dated October 1, 1974, bearing 6 percent interest. At the time the note was received, an interest payment of $1,200 was made and recorded as interest income.
4. The note payable is a 1-year note, dated July 1, 1974, bearing interest at 6 per cent. Interest of $900 was paid in advance when the note was given and was recorded as interest expense.
5. The corporation pays income taxes of 50 percent of income before taxes.

Required:

1. Prepare an income statement for the year 1974 and a balance sheet as of December 31, 1974.

2. Calculate the following ratios:
   (a) Current
   (b) Debt-equity
   (c) Return on investment
   (d) Inventory turnover
   (e) The number of days outstanding for accounts receivable

Problem 2-4

The Dennett Company has the following balance sheet and income statement amounts as of December 31, 1974. These amounts are before any adjustments have been made in 1974.

Item	Amount
Cash	$ 40,730
Accounts Receivable	65,924
Inventories	206,483
Prepaid Expenses	700
Property Assets (net of accumulated depreciation)	209,836
Goodwill	10,000
Accounts Payable	102,674
Notes Payable	30,000
Mortgage Payable	100,000
Capital Stock	200,000
Retained Earnings (as of January 1, 1974)	85,187
Sales	235,698
Cost of Goods Sold	170,439
Selling Expenses	35,965
Administrative Expenses	10,482
Interest Expense	3,000

Notes:

1. The corporation has the following depreciable assets:
   (a) A building costing $100,000, that has a life of 25 years;
   (b) Machinery, costing $50,000, that has a life of 10 years;
   (c) Delivery equipment, costing $10,000 that has a life of 5 years.
2. Prepaid expenses consist of the following items:
   (a.) Prepaid insurance, costing $100. The policy extends from July 1, 1974 to July 1, 1975.
   (b.) The note payable is a 90-day note, dated December 1, 1974 and bearing interest at the rate of 6 per cent per year. The interest of $450 was paid in advance.
   (c.) Supplies costing $150 have been included in prepaid expenses. It is estimated that $50 worth of supplies are still on hand on December 31, 1974.
3. The mortgage payable bears interest at the rate of 6 percent per year, payable July 1 and January 1 of each year.
4. The management of the company has decided to write-off the good-will before publishing the balance sheet.
5. Assume that the corporation paid no income tax in 1974.

Required:

1. Prepare an income statement for the year 1974 and a balance sheet as of December 31, 1974.
2. Calculate the ratios indicated in Problem 2-3.

Problem 2-5

The balance sheet of the Ennett Company as of December 31, 1974, is as follows:

THE ENNETT COMPANY
Balance Sheet as of December 31, 1974
($000)

Cash	$ 1,439	Accounts Payable	$ 1,362
Accounts Receivable	2,260	Taxes Payable	489
Inventories	5,490	Capital Stock	8,000
Property Assets	3,438[a]	Retained Earnings	2,776
Total Assets	$12,627	Total Liability and Net Worth	$12,627

[a]Fixed assets are as follows: land, $1,200; building: cost, $1,000; estimated life, 25 years; accumulated depreciation, $400; equipment: cost, $3,200; estimated life, 10 years; accumulated depreciation, $1,562.

The following transactions occurred during 1975:

1. Goods costing $4,632 were sold on open account for $6,398.
2. Inventory costing $5,190 was purchased during the year on open account.
3. Cash of $6,920 was received in payment of accounts receivable.
4. Accounts payable of $4,980 were paid in cash.
5. On July 1, $1,000 worth of machinery was purchased for cash. It is estimated that this machinery will have a 10-year life.
6. The company borrowed $1,000 on a 5-year note to pay for the machinery. The note was dated July 2 and bears interest at the rate of 6 per cent annually, payable on January 1 and July 1 of each year.
7. The following expenses were paid:

Sales Salaries	$450
Administrative Salaries	320
Telephone and Telegraph	10
Utilities	5
Advertising	40
Insurance*	10

8. Office space was leased out to an outside business for an annual rental of $120. This amount was paid on July 1, 1975, to cover the year ending July 1, 1976.
9. A dividend of $500 was paid.
10. The $489 owed for taxes was paid.
11. On December 31, 1975, the company owed the following salaries:

Sales Salaries	$5
Administrative Salaries	4

12. The company pays income taxes equal to 50 per cent of the income before taxes. This had not been paid as of December 31, 1975.

Required:

Prepare an income statement for 1975 and a balance sheet as of December 31, 1975.

*Payment for a 2-year fire insurance policy, effective January 1, 1975.

EXHIBIT 1
CENTRAL LAUNDRY
Record of Cash Receipts and Disbursements

Cash Receipts		Cash Disbursements	
Cash Sales	$ 76,100	Wages and Salaries	$ 58,300
Collection of Accounts		Repairs	6,200
Receivable Arising from		Property and Misc. Taxes	1,900
the Sale of Laundry			
Services	38,600	Heat, Light, and Power	5,500
		Additional Laundry Supplies	8,800
		Selling and Administration	13,100
		Interest[a]	720
		Insurance[b]	3,400
		Partial Payment of Bank Loan	
		on December 31, 1975	6,000
		Payment of Accounts Payable	1,185
	$114,700		$105,105

Unpaid bills from suppliers (representing purchases of laundry supplies)	$ 2,900
Unpaid customer accounts (representing laundry services to them)	$ 4,400

[a]Interest at 6 per cent on the bank loan was payable June 30 and December 31. Interest payments for 1975 were made when due.

[b]Of the total insurance premiums of $3,400 paid in 1975, $1,200 constituted the full premium on a 2-year policy due to expire on December 31, 1976.

EXHIBIT 2
CENTRAL LAUNDRY
Other Information Relative to Operations

1. Wages and salaries were paid monthly on the second of each month for the preceding month. Wages and salaries earned during December but not yet paid totaled $3,000.
2. The yearly depreciation expense on the buildings and equipment was figured at $7,500 and on the trucks at $1,400.
3. Interest on the mortgage at 4 per cent was payable annually on January 1. No such interest had yet been paid.
4. An inventory taken of the laundry supplies at the end of the year revealed a supply on hand costing $1,000.
5. Federal income taxes for 1975 would have to be based on current tax rates:

> 22 per cent for taxable income up to and including $25,000
> 48 per cent for taxable income in excess of $25,000

Required:

Prepare a balance sheet as of December 31, 1975, and an income statement for the year ending December 31, 1975.

Problem 2-10

For each of the following situations, indicate the balance sheet and income statement amounts as of December 31, for the items described. (Assume that each situation is independent.)

1. Before adjustment, the interest expense account shows a balance of $5,000 and accrued interest payable shows a zero balance. A 1-year note payable with a face value of $10,000 bearing interest at the rate of 8 per cent, was given to the bank on October 1. No interest has been recorded for this note.

2. Assume the same facts as in 1, above, except that the bank discounted the note. (Discounting means that the bank took its interest in advance.) The interest of $800 was recorded as an asset called prepaid interest.

3. One year's rent of $2,000 on part of the office building was received on July 1. This was recorded as prepaid rent.

4. On January 1, the inventories were $426,000. During the year, $1,962,000 was purchased. A physical inventory on December 31 showed that the inventory on hand had cost $397,000.

5. On January 1, accrued wages payable showed a balance $4,692. During the year, $198,620 was paid in cash for wages. On December 31, wages earned but not paid amounted to $5,678.

6. On January 1, accounts receivable showed a balance of $82,690. During the year, $3,496,720 was collected from customers. On December 31, accounts receivable amounted to $98,639. What is the amount of the sales?

7. In a retail store, the merchandise inventory account showed a balance of $10,672 on January 1 and $12,943 on December 31. Accounts payable showed a balance of $4,982 on January 1 and $3,673 on December 31. During the year the store paid $40,920 to its suppliers for merchandise purchased from them. What is the cost of sales?

The Statement of Changes in Financial Position

If you must make mistakes, it will be more to your credit to make a new one each time.

3

The third major financial statement is the statement of changes in financial position (also called a statement of sources and uses of funds). This statement shows the flow of funds into, through, and out of a business. Until September 30, 1971, the statement of changes in financial position was not required in annual reports, although it was often provided. Minimal requirements included only a balance sheet and an income statement. In March 1971, however, the Accounting Principles Board issued Opinion Number 19, "Reporting Changes in Financial Position." The Board concluded that information concerning the *financing and investing activities* of a business enterprise, and the resulting *changes in financial position* during the accounting period, is essential to financial statement users in making economic decisions.[1]

What is a statement of changes in financial position? Let us begin by reviewing briefly the nature of the balance sheet and the income statement. The balance sheet is a summary of the financial position of a firm as of a given point in time. Essentially, it provides answers to questions such as, What are the total financial resources of the firm at that point in time? From what sources were they obtained? In what categories of assets are they invested? The income statement is a summary of the financial effects of operations over a specified accounting period, focussing on the extent to which the *business operations* of the period have increased or decreased the owners' equity in the firm. Notice, however, that "business operations" are usually only a part of the firm's financial activities. The income statement deals only with those items that affect the retained earnings account of the firm. During the accounting period, however, the firm may have been involved in other financial transactions that provided resources or called for the use of resources to either increase various categories of assets or to reimburse some previous source of funds (resources). These other transactions may well have had little or no effect on the retained earnings account.

---

[1] The origins, composition, functions, and demise of the Accounting Principles Board are discussed in Chapter 8.

Although the income statement shows changes only in retained earnings, the statement of changes in financial position[2] shows how the other balance sheet items have also been changed during the period. Basically, the funds flow statement provides the same information provided by the balance sheet and income statement, but with a different emphasis. In fact, given a beginning and ending balance sheet and an income statement for a period, a funds flow statement can generally be prepared.

ELEMENTS OF A STATEMENT OF CHANGES IN FINANCIAL POSITION

A statement of changes in financial position consists of two elements: (1) the source of funds and (2) the use of funds. Each element is described in this part of the chapter.

What Are Funds?

Funds refer to the liquid financial resources of a business—cash and items nearly equivalent to cash. In common practice, however, this definition is broadened to include all current assets less current liabilities, or what we have called working capital. We define funds as working capital (rather than cash) because items of working capital will soon be turned into cash or will consume cash and can be considered, therefore, equivalent to cash. For example, it makes very little difference, financially, whether you sell for cash or on open account. You make the same profit and receive the same amount of cash eventually. By the same token, it makes little difference, financially, whether you purchase for cash or on open account. If you purchase on open account, you keep the cash, but you are committed to pay off the accounts payable in a short time. You can, therefore, think of all changes in financial position as being measured by the receipt and expenditure of cash or of items that will be turned into cash (current assets) or paid with cash (current liabilities) in the normal course of operating the business. The change in the balance of cash is, of course, important to the person responsible for seeing that the company has enough money in the bank to meet its commitments. The cash balance alone, however, is not normally regarded as the most useful way of measuring the funds position of a firm.

Changes in Funds Available

The change in funds is simply the working capital at the beginning of a period subtracted from the working capital at the end of the period. A negative number means, of course, that funds have decreased. A positive number means that funds have increased. For example:

---

[2] In this book, we will use the terms "statement of changes in financial position" and "funds flow statement" interchangeably.

Figure 3-1
THE ATAX COMPANY
Comparative Balance Sheet
($000)

	December 31, 1973	December 31, 1974
Assets		
Current Assets		
Cash	$ 6,491	$ 3,678
Accounts Receivable	10,387	12,947
Inventories	25,346	26,385
	42,224	43,010
Property Assets	35,925	40,185
	$78,149	$83,195
Liabilities and Owners' Equity		
Current Liabilities		
Accounts Payable	$10,865	$12,647
Notes Payable	5,000	2,000
Taxes Payable	4,289	3,847
	20,154	18,494
Bonds Payable	10,000	10,000
Capital Stock	30,000	30,000
Retained Earnings	17,995	24,701
	$78,149	$83,195

The change in the working capital is:
Working capital on December 31, 1974 ($ 43,010–$18,494) = $24,516
Working capital on December 31, 1973 ($ 42,224–$20,154) = $22,070
                    Increase in Funds $ 2,446

If funds are defined as working capital, it is necessary to show the changes that have affected individual working capital items on a separate schedule. This is done by subtracting the beginning balance from the ending balance for each item of working capital. An increase in a current asset represents an increased investment in working capital and a decrease in a current asset is a decreased investment in working capital. Conversely, an increase in a current liability reduces the amount of investment in working capital and a decrease in a current liability increases the investment in working capital. An analysis of changes in working capital for the Atax Company would be as follows:

ANALYSIS OF CHANGES IN WORKING CAPITAL
Increases in Working Capital

Increase in Accounts Receivable	$2,560
Increase in Inventories	1,039
Decrease in Notes Payable	3,000
Decrease in Taxes Payable	442

Total Increases in Working Capital	$7,041

Decreases in Working Capital

Decrease in Cash	($2,813)
Increase in Accounts Payable	(1,782)
Total Decrease in Working Capital	(4,595)
Net Change in Working Capital	$2,446

If the investment in working capital is higher at the end of a period than it was at the beginning, this represents a *use* of funds. Some of the funds provided to the business have been used to increase the working capital. Conversely, lower working capital at the end of a period than at the beginning means that funds have been freed for other uses. This is a *source* of funds. We will turn now to a description of other major sources and uses of funds.

For any business, in the long run there are only three sources of funds: investment by shareholders, borrowings, and operations. In the long run, there are also only three uses: payment of dividends, investment in non-current assets, and investment in working capital. In any one period, however, any of these items can represent either a source or a use of funds, depending on whether the amount goes up to down.

Sources of Funds

Funds Generated from Operations. The earnings of a business represent one of the principal sources of funds. The amount of funds generated from operations is not the net income shown on the income statement, however, because some of the expenses, principally depreciation and amortization, do not involve the expenditure of funds. For example, the expenditure of funds for equipment was made when the equipment was purchased. The subsequent writing off of this equipment as it is used up is an accounting transaction and the related expense (depreciation) does not involve an outflow of funds. Consequently, any expense that represents a write off of a non-current asset should be added back to net income in calculating the source of funds from operations. Such items were deducted in computing net income but they did not involve an outflow of funds.

Another item that is eliminated is any profit or loss from the sale of property assets. *Proceeds* from such sales are a source of funds. However, the *profit* or *loss* on the sale is merely an adjustment between the undepreciated cost and the proceeds. It does not involve a flow of funds. For example, suppose that an asset with a net book value of $750 was sold for $1,000. The income statement shows a profit of $250. On another part of the funds flow statement the sale of property assets would be shown as a source of $1,000. The profit of $250 is not really a source of funds—the total proceeds are only $1,000. Consequently, all profit or loss from the sale of non-current assets is eliminated from the net income in calculating the funds generated from operations.

There are two techniques for calculating the funds generated from operations.

One way is to subtract from the sales revenue those expenses that represent an expenditure of funds. The second way is to start with the net income and adjust for the "non-fund" items. The latter technique is usually easier because there are frequently only a few "non-fund" items.

For example, consider the following income information:

Figure 3-2

Sales	$10,469
Cost of Sales	5,432
Gross Margin	5,037
Administrative Salaries	320
Sales Salaries	1,460
Depreciation	520
Amortization of Patents	310
Telephone and Telegraph	50
Utilities	20
Total Expenses	2,680
Operating Profit	2,357
Loss on Sale of Property Assets	150
Profit before Taxes	2,207
Taxes	1,100
Net Income	$ 1,107

The amount of funds generated from operations could be calculated in either of the two following ways:

Method 1:

Sales		$10,469
Expenses requiring Outlay of		
Working Capital:		
Cost of Sales	$5,432	
Administrative Salaries	320	
Sales Salaries	1,460	
Telephone and Telegraph	50	
Utilities	20	
Income Taxes	1,100	8,382
Source of Funds from Operations		$ 2,087

Method 2:

Net Income per Income Statement	$ 1,107
Add Expenses Not Requiring an Outlay of	
Working Capital in This Period:	
Depreciation	520
Amortization of Patents	310
Loss on Sale of Property Assets	150
Source of Funds from Operations	$ 2,087

Increase in Long-term Liabilities. A second source of funds is long-term borrowing. (Notice that short-term borrowing does not affect total working capital. The increase in cash is offset by the increase in current liabilities.) The change in the amount of funds from long-term borrowing can be calculated by subtracting the balance at the end of the period from the balance at the beginning of the period. If the difference is a positive number (i.e., liabilities have increased), it is a source of funds; if long-term liabilities have decreased, it is a use of funds.

Increase in Capital Stock. If a business has sold capital stock during a period, the amount for which the stock was sold is a source of funds.

Sale of Non-current Assets. The sale of non-current assets will be another source of funds equal to the net proceeds from the sale. As indicated previously, profit or loss from the sale of non-current assets is neither a source nor use of funds.

USE OF FUNDS

Purchase of Non-current Assets. One of the major uses of funds is the purchase of non-current assets, principally property assets, investments, and intangible assets. The amount of funds used to purchase property assets cannot be calculated by taking the difference between net property assets at the beginning and end of the year. Property asset accounts are affected not only by purchases, but also by the amount of depreciation taken during the year and the sale or disposition of assets during the year. Consequently, it is necessary to have information on all of these three items. The method for calculating the amount of property assets purchased will be described later in the chapter.

Dividends. A second major use of funds is the payment of dividends to stockholders. Notice that dividends become a use of funds when they are declared. (A declaration is a statement by the board of directors to the stockholders that they intend to pay a dividend of a given amount on a given date.) Dividends become a legal current liability (and, consequently, a reduction of funds) when they are declared.

Decrease in Non-current Liabilities. Funds may be used to pay off non-current liabilities. The amount of funds used for this purpose can be calculated by subtracting the balance of the non-current liabilities at the beginning of the period from the balance at the end of the period. A decrease in non-current liabilities is a use of funds. An increase in non-current liabilities is a source of funds. If there are different types of non-current liabilities and the amounts are significant, it is usual to show each type as a separate item.

Purchase of Capital Stock. As described in Chapter 7, sometimes a company will buy back some of its own capital stock. If a company repurchases its own capital stock, it is a use of funds.

Example of Statement of Changes in Financial Position

Figure 3-3

THE ACME COMPANY
Statement of Changes in Financial Position
Year Ending December 31, 1974
($000)

Source of Funds

Funds from Operations
  Net Income per Income Statement $10,492
  Add Expenses That Did Not Require an
  Outlay of Working Capital in This Period:

    Depreciation and Amortization   3,475
    Loss on Sale of Fixed Assets   425

    Total Funds from Operations $14,392
Sale of Capital Stock   4,000
Sale of Fixed Assets   3,941
    Total $22,333

Use of Funds

Purchase of Fixed Assets $10,947
Dividends   5,439
Retirement of Bonds Payable   5,000
Investment in Working Capital   947
    Total $22,333

This statement shows that the Acme Company generated $22,333 of funds during the year. Of this amount, $14,392 came from current operations (income), $3,941 from selling property assets, and $4,000 from selling stock. These funds were used to pay dividends ($5,439), to buy property assets ($10,947), to pay off some long-term liabilities ($5,000), and to increase the investment in working capital ($947). Notice that total sources must equal total uses. Every dollar of funds provided must be used somewhere, and every dollar of funds used must have come from some source.

PREPARING A STATEMENT OF CHANGES IN FINANCIAL POSITION

In this part of the chapter, we will explain how to prepare a funds flow statement of changes in financial position from a beginning and ending balance sheet and an income statement. As with the balance sheet and the income statement, we believe that learning to prepare a funds flow statement is an efficient way of learning to understand the statement.

Figure 3-4

THE SMITH COMPANY
Comparative Balance Sheet

	December 31, 1973	December 31, 1974
Assets		
Current Assets		
Cash	$ 4,679	$ 5,433
Accounts Receivable	10,896	13,296
Inventories	34,928	33,142
Prepaid Expenses	426	389
Total	50,929	52,260
Investments	3,968	3,472
Property Assets		
Land	10,485	11,895
Buildings (net)	22,946	22,377
Equipment (net)	32,384	31,010
Total (net)	65,815	65,282
Patents (net)	4,189	1,868
	$124,901	$122,882
Liabilities and Owners' Equity		
Current Liabilities		
Accounts Payable	$ 25,986	$ 26,367
Notes Payable	5,000	4,000
Taxes Payable	5,187	6,125
Other Current Liabilities	1,643	1,439
Total	37,816	37,931
Bonds Payable	20,000	5,000
Capital Stock	50,000	60,000
Retained Earnings	17,085	19,951
	$124,901	$122,882

Figure 3-5

THE SMITH COMPANY
Condensed Income Statement for Year Ending December 31, 1974

Sales	$130,496
Cost of Sales	72,895
Gross Margin	57,601
Operating Expenses	34,982[a]
Operating Profit	22,619

Loss on Sale of Fixed Assets	($1,849)	
Patent Write off[b]	(2,000)	
Profit on Sale of Investments	594	(3,255)
Profit before Taxes		19,364
Taxes on Income		11,000
Net Income		$ 8,364

[a]Operating expenses include depreciation of buildings of $569, depreciation of equipment of $5,832, and amortization of patents of $321.

[b]A patent, carried at a value of $2,000, became obsolete during the year because of new developments.

Figure 3-6
THE SMITH COMPANY
Reconciliation of Retained Earnings, 1974

Balance—December 31, 1973	$17,085
Income for 1974	8,364
	$25,449
Dividends Paid	5,498
Retained Earnings—December 31, 1974	$19,951

Other data provided by the financial statements are as follows:

Equipment with a net book value (cost minus accumulated depreciation) of $5,982 was sold for $4,133.

Investments that cost $496 were sold for $1,090.

We are now ready to develop a funds flow statement for the Smith Company for 1974.

Calculating the Figures

In this part of the chapter, we will explain how to prepare a statement of changes in financial position. It is probably better not to worry about the statement initially. Try to calculate the various items that go on the statement and record them in memorandum form on a piece of paper. Then prepare the statement after you have obtained all of the information. As we will show, you can check to see if you have included all items by comparing your total sources and total uses—they must be the same.

It may be helpful to calculate the items in the following order:

1. Calculate the Change in Working Capital

This is simply the working capital at the beginning of the period subtracted from the working capital at the end of the period.

	December 31, 1973	December 31, 1974
Current Assets	$50,929	$52,260
Current Liabilities	37,816	37,931
Working Capital	$13,113	$14,329

Difference = 14,329 - 13,113 = $1,216 increase in
working capital. This represents a use of funds.

2. Calculate Funds Generated from Operations

Net Income		$ 8,364
Add Expenses That Did Not Require an Outlay		
of Working Capital in This Period:		
Depreciation of Building	$ 569	
Depreciation of Equipment	5,832	
Amortization of Patent	321	6,722
Loss on Sale of Property Assets		1,849
Write off of Patent		2,000
		18,935
Less Profit on Sale of Investments		594
Funds Generated from Operations		$18,341

3. Analyze Each Non-current Asset

At this point, we know the change in working capital and we know the funds that have been generated from operations. All other changes in funds must result from activities in the non-current balance sheet items. The amount of these changes can be systematically determined by analyzing each non-current item on the balance sheet to see how much it has changed during the period.

We must calculate which non-current assets have been sold and for how much and what non-current assets have been purchased at what cost. It is a good idea to reconcile completely the difference between the beginning and ending balance so that you will be sure you have omitted nothing. The recommended procedure is to analyze each non-current asset in the order that it appears on the balance sheet.

Investments

Investments have decreased from $3,968 to $3,472, or $496. We know from the information provided that investments costing $496 were sold for $1,090. We have, therefore, a source of funds—the sale of investments—of $1,090. If the information about the sale of investments had not been provided, we could have calculated it deductively. We know that the carrying value of investments has been reduced by $496. We can assume, therefore, that investments with an original cost of $496 have been sold. From the income statement we know that there was a profit from the sale of investments of $594. The investments must have been sold for $1,090 because this is the only figure that will amount to a profit of $594 on the sale of investments costing $496.

Property Assets

One of the most difficult items to reconcile is property assets. The reason for this is that there are three activities that almost always affect these items and it is necessary to know the amount of at least two of these changes before the changes can be analyzed completely. These three activities are depreciation, sale or disposition of old assets, and the purchase of new assets. In equation form,

BB-D-S+P = EB, where
BB = beginning balance of net property assets
D = the amount of depreciation taken during the period
   (i.e., the amount included in the income statement)
S = the net book value of the assets sold or otherwise
   disposed of during the period
P = the cost of the new assets purchased during the period
EB = ending balance of net property assets

Land has changed from \$10,485 to \$11,895, for an increase of \$1,410. In the absence of any other information, we can assume that land costing \$1,410 has been purchased. (Remember, land does not depreciate.) We have, therefore, a use of funds–the purchase of land for \$1,410.

Buildings have changed from \$22,946 to \$22,377, or a decrease of \$569. Since this is the amount of depreciation, we can conclude that there have been no sales or purchases of buildings during the year.

Equipment has changed from \$32,384 to \$31,010, or a decrease of \$1,374. We know, however, that there has been both depreciation and sales of old equipment. Depreciation was \$5,832 and the book value of equipment sold was \$5,982. Since the total reduction was only \$1,374, this means that some equipment must have been purchased. To calculate the amount of new equipment purchased, we use the equation described earlier:

$$BB\text{-}D\text{-}S\text{+}P = EB$$

Filling in the figures that we know:
$$32{,}384 - 5{,}832 - 5{,}982 + P = 31{,}010$$
$$P = 31{,}010 - 20{,}570$$
$$P = \$10{,}440$$

We have a use of funds, purchase of equipment, of \$10,440.

We also have a source of funds, sale of old equipment, of \$4,133.

Patents have changed from \$4,189 to \$1,868, or a decrease of \$2,321. We can see from the income statement that a patent valued at \$2,000 was written off. This is not a source of funds because it was simply a bookkeeping transaction. The patent was not *sold*; it simply became obsolete. From the income statement, we can see that patent amortization was \$321. Therefore, the reduction in patents was due to writing off a \$2,000 patent and taking \$321 amortization on the remaining patents.

No patents were bought or sold; therefore, there has been no source or uses of funds from the activities in patents.

4. Analyze Non-current Liabilities

We want to find out if we have borrowed more money (a source of funds) or reduced our long-term debt (a use of funds). We do this by calculating the change in the non-current liabilities. (Notice that we ignore the changes in current liabilities because they have already been taken into account in the change in working capital.)

The only non-current liabilities are bonds payable. These have decreased by $15,000. This amount represents a use of funds.

5. Analyze the Changes in Owners' Equity

Capital stock has increased $10,000. In the absence of other information, we can conclude that additional stock was sold. This $10,000 is a source of funds.

Retained earnings have increased from $17,085 to $19,951. From the reconciliation of retained earnings, we know this change was due to: (1) income of $8,364, and (2) dividends paid of $5,498. We have already taken the income into account. The only item left is dividends. This amount, $5,498, is a use of funds.

We are now ready to put all of these figures together in a statement of changes in financial position.

Preparing the Statement of Changes in Financial Position

There is no set format for a statement of changes in financial position. We recommend that you show sources of funds first and the use of funds next. List the sources and uses of funds in the general order of magnitude, except that the first item under sources should be income from operations and the last item should be "changes in working capital." If the working capital has decreased, it is a source of funds; if it has increased; it is a use of funds. Putting together the figures that we have calculated, we get a statement as shown in Figure 3-7. If you have left out an item, classified anything incorrectly, or made mistakes in calculation, your statement will not balance. If you do balance, it does not mean that everything is correct (e.g., you could have offsetting errors), although there is a resonable assumption that it is.

Figure 3-7

THE SMITH COMPANY
Statement of Changes in Financial Position,
Year Ending December 31, 1974

Sources of Funds

Funds from Operations:		
Net Income after Taxes	$8,364	
Add Expenses Not Requiring		
Outlay of Working Capital		
in Current Period:		
Depreciation	6,401	
Patent Amortization	321	
Loss on Sale of Property Assets	1,849	
Write off of Patent	2,000	
Less Profit on Sale of Investments	(594)	
Total Funds from Operations		$18,341

Sale of Capital Stock	$10,000
Sale of Property Assets	4,133
Sale of Investments	1,090
	$33,564

Uses of Funds

Retirement of Bonds	$15,000
Purchase of Equipment	10,440
Dividends Paid	5,498
Purchase of Land	1,410
Investment in Working Capital	1,216
	$33,564

Analysis of Changes in Working Capital

Increases

Increase in Cash	$ 754
Increase in Accounts Receivable	2,400
Decrease in Notes Payable	1,000
Decrease in Other Current Liabilities	204
Total Increases	$4,358

Decreases

Decrease in Inventories	$1,786
Decrease in Prepaid Expenses	37
Increase in Accounts Payable	381
Increase in Taxes Payable	938
Total Decreases	$3,142
Net Increases in Working Capital	$1,216

Some companies present the information shown in the preceding statement in a format similar to the following:

Working Capital—December 31, 1973	$13,113
Add: Sources of Working Capital	33,564
Deduct: Uses of Working Capital	(32,348)
Working Capital—December 31, 1974	$14,329

We believe that a format like this is misleading because it suggests that working capital is a residual and, consequently, that changes in working capital are the passive result of non-working capital funds flow. This is simply not true. Decisions to invest or disinvest in individual working capital items are just as conscious decisions by management as are decisions that apply to any other item of funds flow. To emphasize this in a funds flow statement, we believe that the proper format is one that shows total sources of funds and total uses of funds, with the change in working capital shown as a source or use, depending on whether the change is negative or positive.

OTHER THAN WORKING CAPITAL CHANGES

There are changes in financial position that do not affect funds flow, yet should be included in the funds flow statement. These changes result from such transactions as exchanges of bonds or capital stock for property assets or exchanges of capital stock for bonds. For example, assume that a company needed money to expand its physical facilities and wished to borrow the money. One procedure would be to sell bonds (a source of funds) and use the funds to purchase the physical equipment (a use of funds). If, instead, the company exchanged the bonds directly with the owner of the acquired facilities, the net result would be precisely the same. Yet, in this instance, there would have been no funds flow because the bonds were never sold for cash. In cases like this, we assume an implicit funds flow. As a general rule, any time long-term debt or capital stock is exchanged, it should appear on the funds flow statement.[3]

FUNDS DEFINED AS CASH

Some companies define funds as cash, a perfectly permissible procedure. When companies follow this procedure, the statement of changes in financial position will be the same as described except that the analysis of changes in working capital will be included in the body of the statement instead of in a separate schedule. The following demonstrates the Smith Company's statement of changes in financial position, had funds been defined as cash.

Figure 3-8

THE SMITH COMPANY
Statement of Changes in Financial Position,
Year Ending December 31, 1974

Sources of Funds

Funds from Operations

Net Income after Taxes	$8,364
Add Expenses Not Requiring Outlay of Working Capital in Current Period:	
Depreciation	6,401
Patent Amortization	321
Loss on Sale of Property Assets	1,849
Write off of Patent	2,000
Less Profit on Sale of Investments	(594)
	$18,341

---

[3]For this reason, the term "funds flow statement" is technically incorrect. In practise, however, it is used interchangeably with the term "statement of changes in financial position," and we have so used it in this chapter.

Decrease in Inventories	1,786
Decrease in Prepaid Expenses	37
Increase in Accounts Payable	381
Increase in Taxes Payable	938
Sale of Capital Stock	10,000
Sale of Property Assets	4,133
Sale of Investments	1,090
Total Source of Funds	$36,706

Uses of Funds

Increase in Accounts Receivable	$ 2,400
Decrease in Notes Payable	1,000
Decrease in Other Liabilities	204
Retirement of Bonds	15,000
Purchase of Equipment	10,440
Dividends Paid	5,498
Purchase of Land	1,410
Increase in Cash	754
	$36,706

MANAGEMENT CONSIDERATIONS

There are two principal uses of a funds flow statement. First, it is used by people both outside and inside a company to review a company's investment and financing decisions. Second, it helps people inside the company to plan for funds needs. As you can see, the statement facilitates the projection of future funds requirements. In fact, it would be very difficult to forecast something like working capital requirements without a device similar to this statement.

Many people believe that the most important value of this statement is that it is largely unaffected by accounting principles or conventions. As we shall explain later in the book, there is a range of choices open to a business in handling certain types of transactions. These choices can have the effect of showing a quite different profit for any given year for two hypothetically identical companies. As a result, accounting profits are subject to a degree of manipulation. The funds flow statement, however, represents discrete activities (expenditure and receipt of funds) that can be measured reasonably accurately and are relatively unaffected by accounting principles or conventions. As a result, identical companies will be more likely to show identical funds provided by operations and, conversely, differences among companies will be reflected in different funds flow statements.

The funds flow statement is not, however, intended to show operating performance during a period, as is the income statement. It shows only the amount of funds generated from operations. Even though the annual depreciation expense does not involve an outflow of funds, it is a legitimate charge against sales revenue in measuring operating performance. The economic value of the physical plant is being gradually consumed in the process of manufacturing and selling a product, and this cost must be acknowledged. Such terms as "cash earnings" or "cash flow," which are nothing more than net earnings plus depreciation, are sometimes highlighted by companies as measures of their economic performance. This practice can be very misleading. It unfairly isolates and highlights one aspect of an overall funds flow analysis. Furthermore, net earnings is a measure of return *on* investment, whereas depreciation is a measure of the return *of* investment. Adding the two together is an example of the proverbial apples and oranges problem.

Although funds flow concepts should not be used as surrogates for net earnings in evaluating management performance, it is generally true that an overall analysis of funds flows, particularly over a period of several years, can present a very useful picture of what has been happening to the company. A similar analysis of comparative income statements is also very useful, but there is less chance with the funds flow analysis that a faulty operating situation can be disguised by such potential cosmetic devices as cost deferrals or revenue accruals. These "quality of earnings" issues will be treated in more depth in Chapter 12.

QUESTIONS

1. If the statement of changes in financial position is merely a restatement of the information included on the balance sheet and income statement, why should it be required?

2. Why are funds usually defined as working capital rather than cash?

3. Why are funds generated from operations different from net profit?

4. Why are profits from the sale of non-current assets eliminated from net income and losses on the sale of non-current assets added to net income when calculating the amount of funds generated from operations?

5. Explain how a statement of changes in financial position, in which funds are defined as cash, will differ from one in which funds are defined as working capital.

6. What is the rationale behind including an exchange of capital stock or bonds for a non-current asset in the statement of changes in financial position?

7. What type of things would you expect to learn from analyzing a statement of changes in financial position that would not be readily evident from the balance sheet and the income statement?

8. Name some of the instances in which two identical companies could show different net profits but the same funds generated from operations.

9. Company A and Company B are identical except that A uses FIFO* in valuing its inventories and B uses LIFO.* A's ending inventories are recorded at $7,500,000; B's ending inventories are recorded at $5,000,000. A's beginning inventories are recorded at $6,000,000; B's beginning inventories are recorded at $4,800,000. How much different would A's profits before taxes be from B's,

assuming everything else was the same? What is the relationship between funds generated by operations and investment in inventory for firms A and B?

10. Explain how a statement of changes in financial position is necessary (or, at least, very useful) in long-range cash planning.

Problem 3-1

Listed below are several financial transactions. For each, explain whether or not it will affect the flow of funds. If it should be included in the statement of changes in financial position, is it (1) part of the funds generated from operations, (2) another source of funds, or (3) a use of funds?

1. Equipment was purchased for $16,000.

2. Bonds were sold to the general public. The net proceeds were $25,000.

3. Capital stock was sold for $50,000.

4. Equipment with a book value of $5,000 was scrapped. The proceeds from the sale of scrap just equaled the cost of dismantling the equipment.

5. Investments that had cost $10,000 were sold for $8,000.

6. A total of $3,000 was borrowed from the bank. The bank was given a 90-day note to cover the loan.

7. A total of $50,000 was borrowed from an insurance company. The loan, which was secured by a mortgage on the building, is due in 5 years.

8. Inventory, costing $5,000, was sold on open account for $10,000.

9. A stock dividend of 10 per cent was given to the stockholders. (A stock dividend means that shareholders are given additional shares of stock instead of cash. In the above example, if a stockholder owned 100 shares, he would receive an additional 10 shares.)

10. A total of $10,000 was received from customers in payment of open accounts.

11. Inventory of $5,000 was purchased on open account.

12. Goodwill of $20,000 was written off against retained earnings. (This means that goodwill and retained earnings were both reduced by $20,000.)

13. Salaries of $5,000 were paid to administrative employees.

14. Federal income taxes of $20,000 were incurred on the current year's income.

15. Cash dividends of $20,000 were declared on December 15, 1973. These dividends were paid on January 15, 1974. (How does this affect 1973? 1974?)

16. The value of land that was carried at cost ($5,000) was written up to estimated market value ($10,000).

17. The company was given a piece of land by the city as a site for a new factory. The land had an estimated market value of $20,000.

*These terms are defined in chapter 5. For purposes of this question you need be concerned only with the numerical differences between these methods.

Problem 3-2

Calculate the funds generated from operations in each of the following cases:

	A	B	C	D	E
Sales	$10,000	$20,000	$30,000	$40,000	$50,000
Cost of sales	5,000	15,000	20,000	30,000	25,000
Administrative Salaries	1,000	500	2,000	5,000	5,000
Sales Salaries	500	1,000	1,000	4,000	10,000
Depreciation—Equipment	300	600	500	1,000	3,000
Depreciation—Building	100	100	300	500	1,000
Interest Income	50	—	100	—	500
Income Tax	1,000	500	2,000	—	2,000
Loss on Sale of Property Assets	60	—	500	1,000	500
Profit on Sale of Property Assets	—	60	—	—	300
Profit on Sale of Investments	—	70	—	3,000	200
Patent Amortization	10	—	100	500	600
Dividends Paid	100	500	1,000	—	1,000
Write off of Goodwill	50	—	300	—	500

Problem 3-3

In each of the following cases calculate the missing item:

Equipment—Net Book Value

Activity during Year

	Beginning Balance	Depreciation	Net Book Value of Sales and Disposals	Purchases of New Equipment	Ending Balance
a.	$10,500	562	100	1,000	?
b.	20,590	1,046	500	?	24,842
c.	32,649	?	1,000	5,000	35,486
d.	41,496	2,321	?	6,000	43,437
e.	?	3,698	2,437	8,928	54,372

Problem 3-4

Prepare a statement of changes in financial position from the following data:

THE DALONE COMPANY
Income Statement for Year Ending December 31, 1974
($000)

Sales		$46,398
Cost of Sales		20,432
Gross Margin		25,966
Salaries and Wages	$8,496	
Utilities	1,489	
Supplies	536	
Depreciation—Building	609	
Depreciation—Equipment	2,340	13,470

Net Operating Profit	$12,496
Write off of Goodwill	2,500
Income before Taxes	9,996
Income Taxes	6,300
Net Income	$3,696

THE DALONE COMPANY
Comparative Balance Sheet
($000)

	December 31 *1973*	*December 31* *1974*
Assets		
Cash	$10,436	$ 9,438
Accounts Receivable	12,398	13,825
Inventories	22,136	24,419
Total Current Assets	44,970	47,682
Land	1,396	1,679
Building (net)	7,432	6,823
Equipment (net)	12,320	15,491
Total Property Assets	21,148	23,993
Goodwill	6,390	3,890
	$72,508	$75,565
Liabilities and Owners' Equity		
Accounts Payable	$15,429	$16,492
Notes Payable	5,000	6,000
Taxes Payable	1,500	1,798
Total Current Liabilities	21,929	24,290
Bonds Payable	10,000	—
Capital Stock	30,000	40,000
Retained Earnings	10,579	11,275
	$72,508	$75,565

THE DALONE COMPANY

Reconciliation Retained Earnings,
Year Ending December 31, 1974
($000)

Retained Earnings—December 31, 1973	$10,579
Plus: Earnings for 1974	3,696
	14,275
Less: Cash Dividends	3,000
Retained Earnings—December 31, 1974	$11,275

Note: No fixed assets were sold or otherwise disposed of during the year.

Problem 3-5

The balance sheet as of December 31, 1975, and the results of operations for 1975 for the Dalone Company (see Problem 3-4), are reproduced below. Prepare a statement of changes in financial position from these data.

THE DALONE COMPANY
Income Statement for Year Ending December 31, 1975
($000)

Sales		$54,896
Cost of Sales		23,649
Gross Margin		31,247
Salaries and Wages	$9,438	
Utilities	1,503	
Supplies	439	
Depreciation—Building	609	
Depreciation—Equipment	2,582	14,571
Net Operating Profit		16,676
Write off of Goodwill		3,890
Net Profit before Taxes		12,786
Income Taxes		8,300
Profit after Taxes		$ 4,486

THE DALONE COMPANY
Balance Sheet as of December 31, 1975

Assets

Cash	$ 8,496
Accounts Receivable	15,214
Inventories	26,472
Total Current Assets	50,182
Land	1,679
Buildings (net)	6,214
Equipment (net)	25,520
	$83,595

Liabilities and Owner's Equity

Accounts Payable	$17,436
Notes Payable	7,000
Taxes Payable	1,898
Total Current Liabilities	26,334
Common Stock	45,000
Retained Earnings	12,261
	$83,595

Reconciliation of Retained Earnings

Retained Earnings 1/1/75	$11,275
Income for Year	4,486
Cash Dividends	(3,500)
Retained Earnings 12/31/75	$12,261

Note: No fixed assets were sold or otherwise disposed of during 1975.

Problem 3-6

Prepare a statement of changes in financial position from the following data:

THE FALONE COMPANY
Comparative Balance Sheet
($000)

Assets	December 31 1973	December 31 1974
Cash	$ 25,496	$ 30,420
Accounts Receivable	40,430	35,690
Inventories	52,620	55,330
Total Current Assets	118,546	121,440
Investments (at cost)	25,400	22,400
Land	1,596	2,069
Building (net)	30,435	27,003
Equipment (net)	110,590	165,490
Patents	25,000	22,500
	$311,567	$360,902

Liabilities and Owners' Equity

Accounts Payable	$ 36,595	$ 38,940
Notes Payable	20,000	22,000
Accrued Liabilities	10,450	14,735
Total Current Liabilities	67,045	75,675
Mortgage Payable	—	50,000
Bonds Payable	150,000	40,000
Capital Stock	50,000	151,500
Retained Earnings	44,522	43,727
	$311,567	$360,902

THE FALONE COMPANY
Income Statement for Year Ending December 31, 1974
($000)

Sales		$205,430
Cost of Sales		138,395
Gross Margin		$ 67,035
Salaries and Wages	$25,496	
Utilities	3,985	
Supplies	1,436	

Telephone and Telegraph	$ 496	
Depreciation—Building	3,432	
Depreciation—Equipment	18,396	
Amortization of Patents	2,500	$55,741
Operating Profit		$11,294
Interest Expense		4,000
Loss on Sale of Equipment		1,632[a]
		$ 5,662
Profit on Sale of Investments		1,043
Profit before Taxes		$ 6,705
Federal and State Income Taxes		2,500
Net Income		$ 4,205

[a]Equipment with a net book value of $3,439 was sold for $1,807.

THE FALONE COMPANY
Reconciliation of Retained Earnings
Year Ending December 31, 1974

Retained Earnings, December 31, 1973		$44,522
Net Profit for Year		4,205
		$48,727
Less: Cash Dividends	$3,500	
Less: Stock Dividends	1,500	5,000
Retained Earnings—December 31, 1974		$43,727

Note: A stock dividend means that capital stock has been given to shareholders instead of cash. From an accounting point of view, this results in capital stock being increased and retained earnings being decreased by the amount of the stock dividend.

Problem 3-7

Reproduced below are the 1973 balance sheet and income statement of Dan River, Inc. In addition, the following information on property, plant and equipment is provided:

1. Depreciation and amortization taken during 1973 was $11,707.

2. Additions to Property, plant, and equipment were $14,052.

3. Property, plant and equipment that had originally cost $5,012 and that had accumulated depreciation of $4,779 was sold for $1,038.

Required:

Prepare a statement of changes in financial position for Dan River, Inc., for 1973. (For purposes of this problem, treat "deferred items" under non-current liabilities as simply a long-term liability.)

DAN RIVER, INC., AND SUBSIDIARY COMPANIES
Consolidated Balance Sheet
December 29, 1973 and December 30, 1972

Assets	1973	1972
	amounts in thousands	
Current assets:		
Cash	$ 8,472	7,876
Notes and accounts receivable:		
Trade	51,716	50,362
Due from factor	19,450	11,157
Other	8,673	3,456
	79,839	64,975
Less allowance for discounts, interest and doubtful receivables .	2,007	1,329
Net notes and accounts receivable	77,832	63,646
Inventories:		
Finished goods	39,868	44,057
Work in process	41,391	38,219
Raw materials	35,466	19,013
Supplies	5,426	4,469
Total inventories	122,151	105,758
Prepaid expenses	1,999	1,286
Total current assets	210,454	178,566
Property, plant and equipment:		
Land	3,310	3,318
Buildings	86,455	84,624
Machinery and equipment	195,016	190,812
Construction in progress	4,222	1,209
	289,003	279,963
Less accumulated depreciation and amortization	191,910	184,982
Net property, plant and equipment	97,093	94,981
Non-current receivables and other assets, less allowance for interest and doubtful receivables of $397,000 ($638,000 in 1972)	2,650	2,719
	$310,197	276,266

Liabilities and Stockholders' Equity	1973	1972
	amounts in thousands	
Current liabilities:		
Notes payable	$ 26,847	33,571
Long-term debt due currently	1,727	4,467
Accounts payable	22,464	17,720
Accrued expenses	13,660	9,087
Dividends payable	918	80

Accrued income taxes	$ 7,697	$ 2,100
Total current liabilities	$73,313	$67,025
Non-current liabilities:		
Long-term debt	82,171	62,957
Deferred items	10,316	8,883
Total non-current liabilities	$92,487	$71,840

Stockholders' equity:
Preferred stock of $5 par value per share.
  Authorized, 2,000,000 shares issuable in series:
    $1.10 Cumulative Convertible Series.
      Authorized 292,552 shares, issued outstanding

289,615 shares	1,448	1,448

Common stock of $5 par value per share. Authorized,
  10,000,000 shares; outstanding 5,589,092 shares
  (5,631,053 in 1972) after deducting 61,518 shares

(19,557 shares in 1972) held in treasury	27,945	28,155
Capital in excess of par value	28,760	28,952
Retained earnings	86,244	78,846
Total stockholders' equity	144,397	137,401
	$310,197	276,266

DAN RIVER, INC., AND SUBSIDIARY COMPANIES
Consolidated Statement of Earnings
Years ended December 29, 1973 and December 30, 1972
(Amounts in thousands except per share data)

	1973	1972
Net Sales	$423,189	366,616
Cost of sales	362,442	324,712
	60,747	41,904
Selling, general and administrative expenses	33,792	29,424
	26,955	12,480
Other income—net	925	1,376
	27,880	13,856
Interest expense	8,524	7,310
Earnings before income taxes and extraordinary gain	19,356	6,546
Provision for income taxes	8,975	2,565
Earnings before extraordinary gain	10,381	3,981
Extraordinary gain from sale of factoring business, net of $840 income taxes	—	1,160
Net earnings	$ 10,381	$ 5,141

Consolidated Statement of Retained Earnings
Years ended December 29, 1973 and December 30, 1972
(Amounts in thousands)

	1973	1972
Retained earnings at beginning of year	$ 78,846	74,182
Add net earnings	10,381	5,141
	89,227	79,323
Deduct cash dividends:	318	477
Preferred stock	2,665	—
Common stock	2,983	477
Retained earnings at end of year	$ 86,244	78,846

Problem 3-8

Reproduced below are the 1973 balance sheet and income statement of Hercules, Inc. In addition, the following information is provided:

Property, Plant and Equipment	
Additions during 1973	$146,646
Sales during 1973:	
Sales Amount	4,756
Cost of Assets Sold	21,960
Accumulated Depreciation	
on Assets Sold	17,489
Cash Dividend Paid	29,656

Required:

Prepare a statement of changes in financial position for 1973. (For purposes of this problem, treat reserves in the same way as you treat long-term liabilities. Treat the change in deferred taxes ($10,238) as a source of funds from operations. Deferred taxes are explained in Chapter 9.)

HERCULES,INC.
Consolidated Statement of Income

	(Thousands) Year Ended	
	Dec. 31, 1973	Dec. 31, 1972
Net Sales and Operating Revenues	$1,154,775	$972,267
Cost of goods sold and operating expenses	836,258	696,925
Selling, general and administrative expenses	155,862	136,403
	992,120	833,328
Profit from Operations	162,655	138,939
(After depreciation and amortization: 1973—$68,918,000: 1972—$63,414,000)		
Other income—net	2,786	537
Interest and debt expense	(16,334)	(10,437)

Equity in net income of affiliated companies	$ 8,248	$ 3,188
Income Before Taxes on Income	157,355	132,227
Provision for taxes on income	66,244	59,001
Net Income	$ 91,111	$ 73,226
Earnings per Share of Common Stock	$ 2.18	$ 1.77

(Weighted average share outstanding: 1973—41,705,669;
1972—41,479,238)

HERCULES, INC.
Consolidated Balance Sheet

Assets
Current Assets

	(THOUSANDS)	
	Dec. 31, 1973	Dec. 31, 1972
Cash and time deposits	$ 24,736	$ 9,441
Marketable securities	3,778	17,703

(At cost and accrued interest which approximates market)

Accounts and notes receivable
(Less allowances for doubtful accounts)
1973—$1,626,000; 1972—$1,510,000)

Trade	181,954	156,364
Other	9,811	10,672

Inventories
(At lower of average cost or market)

Finished products	98,197	100,678
Materials, supplies and work in process	82,576	64,331
Total Current Assets	401,052	359,189

Property, Plant and Equipment—at cost		
Land	17,342	16,186
Buildings and equipment	1,059,880	936,350
	1,077,222	952,536
Accumulated depreciation and amortization	554,766	503,337
Net Property, Plant and Equipment	522,456	449,199

Investments and Advances		
Affiliated companies—at equity	65,921	54,374
Other—at cost or less	9,519	14,688
Total Investments and Advances	75,440	69,062

Goodwill	12,003	11,893
Deferred U. S. and Foreign Taxes on income	—	4,704
Deferred Charges and Miscellaneous Assets	25,353	17,522
	$1,036,304	$911,569

HERCULES, INC.
Consolidated Balance Sheet

(THOUSANDS)

	Dec. 31, 1973	Dec. 31, 1972
Liabilities and Stockholders' Equity		
Current liabilities		
Accounts payable and accrued expenses ....$	110,501	$ 97,269
Notes payable and current maturities of long-term debt	53,815	54,318
U.S., foreign and state taxes on income	38,380	44,490
Total Current liabilities	202,696	196,077
Long-Term Debt	177,222	126,443
Deferred U. S. and Foreign Taxes on Income	5,534	—
Reserves		
Pensions	37,435	39,405
Insurance	15,900	16,006
Total Reserves	53,335	55,411
Stockholders' Equity		
Series preferred stock	—	—
(Without par value, issuable in series: authorized 2,000,000 shares)		
Common stock	21,745	21,679
($$25_{48}$$ stated value: authorized 75,000,000 shares, reserved for sale to employes 145,472 shares; issued. 1973 —41,751,255 shares, 1972—41,622,809 shares)		
Paid-in surplus	70,864	68,509
Retained earnings	505,223	443,768
	597,832	533,956
Stock reacquired by company—at cost	315	318
(Common stock, 1973—19,061 shares, 1972—19,261 shares)		
Total Stockholders' Equity	597,517	533,638
	$1,036,304	$911,569

Problem   3-9

This graph is taken from the 1962 annual report of the Automatic Canteen Company of America.

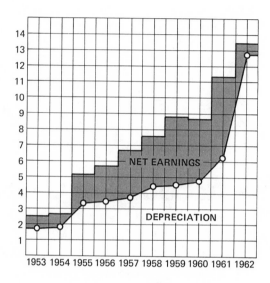

Required:

Does this graph represent "good" performance or not? Why?

The Accounting Cycle

Procedures or Principles?

The reason for [the] failure of [mathematics] to live up
to its reputation is that its fundamental ideas are not
explained to the student disentangled from the technical
procedures which have been invented to facilitate their
exact presentation in particular instances. Accordingly, the
unfortunate learner finds himself struggling to acquire a
knowledge of a mass of details which are not illuminated by
any general conception. Without a doubt, technical facility
is a first requisite to appreciate the rhythm of Milton, or
the passion of Shelly, so long as we find it necessary to spell
the words and are not quite certain of the forms of the
individual letters. In this sense there is no royal road to
learning. But it is equally an error to confine attention to
technical processes, excluding consideration of general
ideas. Here lies the road to pedantry.

Alfred North Whitehead

4

BOOKKEEPING

We stated in Chapter 1 that it is necessary to have some systematic process for keeping track of what is happening to the financial aspects of a business and that this process is called "bookkeeping." Bookkeeping is that part of accounting that is concerned with maintaining the financial records of the company. The name is derived from the fact that accounting transactions used to be recorded in various bound books and the person responsible for making entries in these books was, therefore, the bookkeeper. Modern record keeping has changed so drastically in the past few years that the process of bookkeeping in the old sense on longer exists in most businesses; it has given way to automatic data processing. Nevertheless, the general process is still the same.

In order to understand the accounting cycle, it is necessary to have some idea of the bookkeeping process. In this chapter, we will describe the bookkeeping process more in terms of how it used to exist than how it exists at present. The old bookkeeping process gives a clear picture of the accounting cycle. At this point, introducing modern data processing techniques would add undue complications and would not necessarily increase your understanding of the accounting cycle.

ACCOUNTING RECORDS AND BOOKS

Original Documents

Accounting transactions originate from three principal sources: (1) the receipt of some information from outside the company indicating that something affecting the financial status of the business has occurred; (2) the receipt of information generated within the company indicating that something affecting the financial status of the business has occurred; and (3) information contained within the accounting department indicating that changes in the financial status of the business have occurred. Each of these is discussed in this part of the chapter.

External Information. Most businesses receive literally thousands of pieces of information daily, many of which indicate that something has happened that affects the financial status of the business. For example, sales orders are received, invoices are received indicating the receipt of purchased goods, bills are received for expenses that have been incurred, money is received from customers, and so forth. Most of this information comes to the business through the mails, although there are many other sources. For example, sales orders may be telephoned or, in a retail store, the customer comes personally and carries away the goods that he purchases. In addition, a business receives a great deal of information that will have no direct impact on the financial statements—for example, the receipt of a job application or a letter of complaint. Other information may have an impact on the financial status but not immediately on receipt of the information. For example, the receipt of a sales order will not affect the financial status until the order has been filled. Yet other information will immediately affect the financial status of a business—for example, the receipt of a bill for utilities.

Some method must be installed for processing this incoming information to be sure that the accounting department is notified promptly of those transactions that will affect the financial status of the business. In its simplest form, the original documents are sent directly to the accounting department. In most companies, however, much more sophisticated methods of processing these data are employed. For example, all sales orders might be recorded on magnetic tape and the processing done entirely electronically. You need not be concerned about automatic data processing at this time. These techniques merely handle the data more cheaply, speedily, and accurately. The net result is exactly the same. The incoming information is examined, classified, and transmitted to the people who need the information.

To summarize, from an accounting point of view, the information received on a day-to-day basis from outside the business will consist principally of the following:

1. Money received in payment of goods and services;
2. Sales orders;
3. Invoices indicating the receipt of purchased material;
4. Bills for goods or services provided to the business.

Internal Information. Much information is generated within the company. For example, the payment of bills, invoices, and payrolls; the accumulation of payroll information (hours worked, salaries due, etc.); the amount of inventory on hand; and property assets scrapped or sold. A system must also be developed to process these data. The purpose of this system is to notify the accounting department of the transactions that have occurred within the company that have an effect on the financial status of the business.

Accounting Information. Some accounting transactions are generated from information contained in the accounting department itself. For example, property assets records are normally maintained by the accounting department, and each month the accounting department will reduce the value of such assets for the depreciation incurred during the period. The same applies to accrued interest, either payable or receivable, and to prepaid expenses or prepaid income. Almost all the adjustments that are made at the end of an accounting period are made from information generated within the accounting department.

Summary. In the typical business, thousands of transactions that affect the financial status of a business occur every day. The data that provide evidence that these events have occurred may come from outside the company or they may be generated inside the company. It is one of the functions of the accounting system to be sure that these data are made available to the accounting department promptly. The accounting department, then, records these data so that the indicated changes are reflected in the accounting statements. The next two sections of this part of the chapter describe how this is done.

Journals

As data concerning financial changes are submitted to the accounting department, the accountant or bookkeeper records these data in the order in which they are received. In other words, he makes a chronological record of the financial transactions. The books where the information is initially recorded are called journals. (The word "journal" is defined as a "daily record.") Journals are called the "books of original entry" because in them the financial changes that are occurring in the business are first recorded.

Ledger

The ledger is a book that is classified by type of information. For example, there would be a page for "cash," a page for "accounts receivable," a page for "notes receivable," and so forth. Each of these classifications is called an "account." Every item that appears on the financial statements has an account in the ledger. The ledger provides a means for systematically recording the changes in the items that make up the financial statements. The information that has first been recorded in the journal is rerecorded (this process is called "posting") in the ledger. For example, suppose that a customer paid $100 cash in payment of his account on January 2. The journal entry for January 2 would indicate that a transaction occurred that resulted in a $100 increase of cash and a $100 decrease in accounts receivable. Subsequently, the cash account in the ledger would be increased by $100, and the accounts receivable account, decreased by $100. This is essentially the bookkeeping process. The information on financial changes is received by the accounting department. The changes are recorded first chronologically in a journal and, subsequently, by type of activity, in the ledger. After all journal entries have been posted, the ledger accounts reflect the balances that appear on the financial statements. In other words, the bookkeeping process systematizes the plusing and minusing that we did in chapters 1 and 2 to reflect changes in the financial statements.

DEBITS AND CREDITS

Before we can describe the specific operations of the journal and the ledger, it is necessary to describe the method that is used to record the changes in the accounts—i.e., the system for increasing and decreasing the items appearing in the financial statements. The purpose of this part of the chapter is to describe this system.

The Account

The traditional account looks somewhat as follows:

Figure 4-1

Account Number: 100   Account Name: Cash

Date	Explanation	Ref.	Amount	Date	Explanation	Ref.	Amount
Jan. 1	Balance		$1,432.69	2	Accounts Payable		$268.45
2	Cash Sales		496.21				
2	Accounts Receivable		329.64				
3	Notes Payable		3,000.00				
3	Balance		$4,990.09				

The account provides a record of the transactions that have occurred with respect to a given financial statement item; it is a place in which to record each increase or decrease in this item. In the example given above, a record is kept of the date of the change, the reason for the change, and the amount of the change. (The Ref. is used to cross-reference the book of original entry in which the change was first recorded; this is a record-keeping device that need not concern us here.) Notice that the account is divided into two parts to form a "T" and, for this reason, it is called a "T" account. The left-hand side of the account is called the "debit" side. When we make an entry to the left-hand side of an account, we "debit" the account. (When referring to the process of debiting an account, some accountants use the term "charge.") In the example given above, on January 3 we debited (or charged) cash for $3,000. The right-hand side of the account is called the credit side. In the example above, we credited cash on January 2 for $268.45. The balance of an account is the difference between the total debits and total credits. If the debits are larger, there is a "debit balance"; if the credits are larger, there is a "credit balance." In the example given above, the cash account has a debit balance of $4,990.09.

All this apparent "mumbo-jumbo" is only a device for maintaining a record of the changes that are occurring in the financial status of a business. You start with the beginning balance sheet and set up an account for each asset. Since assets are shown on the left side of the balance sheet, you record the balance of each asset on the left, or *debit*, side of the appropriate account. Next, you set up an account for each liability, for capital stock, and retained earnings. Since these items appear on the right side of the balance sheet, you record these amounts on the right, or *credit*, side of the appropriate accounts. The total debits in the ledger are, therefore, equal to the total credits. The books are said to be "in balance." They should always remain in balance after each financial transaction because each transaction involves both a debit and a credit in equal amounts.

The decision to show assets on the left side of a balance sheet and liabilities and owner's equity on the right side is purely arbitrary. The decision to call left-side entries debits and right-side entries credits is also arbitrary. Consequently, you should not try to find a logical support for these conventions. Once they are established, however, all the other accounting mechanics follow logically. These mechanics were well known as early as the 1500s and have not changed significantly since.

Changes in Accounts

If you wish to increase an asset, you debit it (left-side entry) because assets appear on the left side of the basic accounting equation. (This is like adding a positive number to a positive number.) If you wish to decrease an asset, you credit it because a right-side entry reduces the balance of a left-side account. To increase a liability, on the other hand, you credit it (right-side entry) because it appears on the right side of the accounting equation. To decrease a liability, you debit it. In this regard the capital stock and retained earnings accounts are the same as a liability account. A credit will increase them; a debit will decrease them. You probably should reread this paragraph several times until you are sure that you understand it. The ideas follow directly from the preceding section of the chapter, but they are not easy to grasp at first exposure.

The retained earnings account is not normally used to record day-to-day changes in owners' equity. For these, we use the income accounts. This is to say, an account is set up for each item on the income statement and, as sales are made and expenses incurred, they are recorded in these accounts rather than directly in the retained earnings account. The income statement accounts, however, are merely extensions of the retained earnings account. Sales and other revenue items *increase* retained earnings and, therefore, carry credit balances; expenses *decrease* retained earnings and, therefore, have debit balances. Consequently, to increase revenue, you credit the appropriate revenue account; to decrease revenue, you debit the account. Expenses are just the opposite; a debit will increase them and a credit will decrease them.

The following table summarizes the impact of debits and credits on the various types of accounts. Study it carefully.

Type of Account	To Increase	To Decrease
Asset	Debit	Credit
Liability	Credit	Debit
Net Worth	Credit	Debit
Revenue	Credit	Debit
Expense	Debit	Credit

Example

This may all appear to be very confusing. Remember that all we are doing is developing a systematic means for recording changes in the financial statement items. You recorded these changes in chapters 1 and 2 by increasing or decreasing the financial statement balances, which is *all* the system of debits and credits is designed to do. It has, however, some advantages that plusing and minusing do not have and these advantages will be explained later in the chapter. To show how debits and credits operate, let us take the first example given in Chapter 1.

The ABC Corporation starts business on January 1, 1974. It has a capital of $100,000, which was raised through the cash sale of stock. The balance sheet on January 1 is:

	Assets		Owners' Equity	
Cash	$100,000	Capital Stock		$100,000

Let us start our ledger with two accounts: cash and capital

Figure 4-2

CASHa			CAPITAL STOCKa	
Jan. 1 Bal. $100,000			Jan. 1 Bal. $100,000	

aFor purposes of demonstrating ledger accounts, we usually use just a "T," as shown here.

On January 3, the manager of the company did the following things:

1. He purchased $25,000 worth of inventory on open account.

2. He leased a building, paying 1 year's rent in advance in cash. The annual rent is $12,000.

3. He purchased $30,000 worth of equipment for cash.

The first task is to record these transactions in a journal. We will record these transactions in a general journal, which shows the following: the date, the transaction number, the account to be debited, the amount of the debit, the account to be credited; and the amount of the credit. In the general journal, these transactions will look like those on page 83.

Notice that the debit comes first and the amount is recorded to the left. The credit comes second, it is indented, and the amount appears to the right of the debit. General journal paper has two money columns on the right-hand side of the page. The left-hand money column is used to record the amount of the debit; the

January 3, 1968

		DR[a]	CR.[a]
	(1)		
Inventory		25,000	
Accounts Payable			25,000
	(2)		
Prepaid Rent		12,000	
Cash			12,000
	(3)		
Equipment		30,000	
Cash			30,000

[a]The term "debit" is abbreviated "DR." because it is derived from the latin term "debitor." The term credit is abbreviated "CR." for a similar reason.

Figure 4-3
ABC COMPANY
General Journal

page 1

Date		Account Title and Explanation	Folio	Debit	Credit
Jan.	3	Inventory		25,000	
		Accounts Payable			25,000
		To Record the Purchase of			
		Inventory for Credit			
	3	Prepaid Rent		12,000	
		Cash			12,000
		To Record the Payment of 1			
		Year's Lease on the Building in			
		Advance in Cash			
	3	Equipment		30,000	
		Cash			30,000
		To Record the Purchase of			
		Equipment for Cash			

right-hand money column is used to record the amount of credit. Figure 4-3 is an example of the traditional general journal format. Each entry is identified by date and an explanation accompanies each entry. The folio column indicates the page in the ledger to which the amount was posted. For our purposes, we will follow the simplified general journal format demonstrated by entries (1), (2), and (3), above. We will leave out the explanations and identify each entry by a consecutive number rather than by a date.

In *transaction 1*, $25,000 worth of inventory was purchased on account. This increases the amount of inventory, which is an asset. To increase an asset, you debit it. Therefore, the debit is to inventory. You have also increased the amount of accounts payable. Accounts payable is a liability. In order to increase a liability, you credit it. Therefore, the credit is to accounts payable.

In *transaction 2*, a year's rent was paid in advance. Prepaid rent is an asset and, to increase an asset, you debit it. Therefore, the debit is to prepaid expense. Cash is decreased. To decrease cash, you credit it. Therefore, the credit is to cash.

In *transaction 3*, $30,000 worth of equipment was purchased for cash. Equipment is an asset and, since it has been increased, you debit it. As in transaction 2, cash is being decreased so you credit it.

Let us now set up accounts for the new items in our ledger. The ledger will look as follows:

Figure 4-4

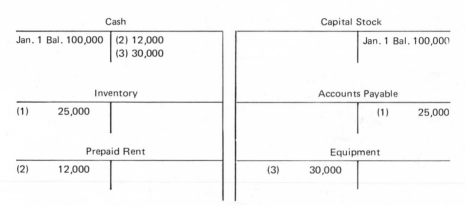

During the remainder of January, the following transactions occurred: Sales were made as follows:

1. Inventory that cost $5,000 was sold for $7,500 on open account.

2. Inventory that cost $3,000 was sold for $4,000 in cash.

A sum of $10,000 was borrowed on a 60-day, noninterest-bearing note. The manager paid himself a salary of $1,000 for the month of January. The life of the equipment is estimated to be 10 years. These transactions are entered in the journal as follows:

	(4)	
Accounts Receivable	$7,500	
Sales		7,500
	(5)	
Cost of Sales	5,000	
Inventory		5,000

The sale of goods involves two journal entries. The first sets up the asset (accounts receivable) and records the increase in revenue (sales). The amount of this entry is the *selling price* of the goods sold. The second entry sets up the cost of the sale as an expense and reduces the amount of inventory. The amount of this entry is the *cost* of the goods sold.

	(6)	
Cash	4,000	
Sales		4,000
	(7)	
Cost of Sales	3,000	
Inventory		3,000

Entries 6 and 7 identical to 4 and 5 except that the cash is debited instead of accounts receivable, because this was a cash sale.

	(8)	
Cash	10,000	
Notes Payable		10,000

Cash is increased; therefore, it is debited. Notes payable (a liability) is increased; therefore, it is credited.

	(9)	
Administrative Expense	1,000	
Cash		1,000

An expense has been increased by $1,000; therefore, it is debited. (Notice that you could have used some other expense title if you had wished. For example, "salary expense" or "manager's salary.") Cash is decreased; therefore, it is credited.

	(10)	
Depreciation Expense	250	
Equipment		250

This entry records 1 month's depreciation of equipment. The equipment cost $30,000 and has an estimated life of 10 years. It will be depreciated, therefore, at $3,000 a year (30,000 ÷ 10), or $250 a month (3,000 ÷ 12). Expenses are increased by $250 and the value of the equipment is reduced by $250.

	(11)	
Rent Expense	1,000	
Prepaid Rent		1,000

This entry records the 1 month's rent that has been used up. Expense is increased by $1,000 and prepaid expenses are decreased by a like amount.

Notice that entries (10) and (11) are not triggered by anything that happened outside the accounting department: The transactions occur because someone in the accounting department recognizes that the equipment asset account and the prepaid rent account must be adjusted before accurate financial statements can be prepared. Such entries are called "adjusting" entries. We will discuss adjusting entries later in the chapter.

Our ledger now looks as follows:

Figure 4-5
THE ABC COMPANY
General Ledger

	Cash					Capital Stock		
Jan. 1 Bal.	100,000	(2)	12,000				Jan. 1 Bal.	100,000
(6)	4,000	(3)	30,000					
(8)	10,000	(9)	1,000					

	Inventory					Accounts Payable	
(1)	25,000	(5)	5,000			(1)	25,000
		(7)	3,000				

	Prepaid Rent					Equipment	
(2)	12,000	(11)	1,000		(3)	30,000	(10)	250

	Accounts Receivable				Sales	
(4)	7,500				(4)	7,500
					(6)	4,000

	Cost of Sales				Notes Payable	
(5)	5,000				(8)	10,000
(7)	3,000					

	Administration Expense				Depreciation Expense	
(9)	1,000			(10)	250	

	Rent Expense	
(11)	1,000	

Closing Entries. At this point we are ready to prepare financial statements similar to the ones shown in Chapter 1. In preparing financial statements, it is necessary to transfer the values from the income statement accounts to the retained earnings account. We make this transfer for two reasons:

1. To bring the retained earnings account up to its correct balance.
2. To close out (reduce to zero value) the income statement accounts. Income is measured over a period of time. Consequently, it is necessary to begin each period with no balances in the income statement accounts. Otherwise, you would be obtaining cumulative amounts. For example, if you did not close out sales at the end of January, the account at the end of February would include both January and February.

The process of closing an account is very simple. If it has a debit balance, you credit it for the amount of that balance. If it has a credit balance, you debit it for the amount of that credit balance. (This will give the account a zero value.) The opposite entry is to retained earnings. In the example given above, the closing entries are:

Sales	11,500	
Retained Earnings		11,500
Retained Earnings	8,000	
Cost of Sales		8,000
Retained Earnings	1,000	
Administrative Expense		1,000
Retained Earnings	250	
Depreciation Expense		250
Retained Earnings	1,000	
Rent Expense		1,000

In actual practice, it is simpler to make a *combined* entry to close out the income statement accounts. We debit the income accounts and credit the expense accounts and then credit retained earnings for the difference (which is, of course, the net profit). In this example, the entry would be as follows:

(12)

Sales	11,500	
Cost of Sales		8,000
Administrative Expense		1,000
Depreciation Expense		250
Rent Expense		1,000
Retained Earnings		1,250

Notice that this entry accomplished exactly the same thing as the multiple entries shown just before.

After closing the books, the ledger of the ABC Company will look as follows: (At this point we have also placed the accounts in the order that they appear on the financial statements, which is the usual way they appear in a ledger.)

Figure 4-6

Cash			
Jan. 1 Bal. 100,000	(2)		12,000
(6) 4,000	(3)		30,000
(8) 10,000			1,000
Feb. 1 Bal. 71,000			

Accounts Receivable			
(4)	7,500		
Feb. 1 Bal.	7,500		

Inventories			
(1) 25,000	(5)		5,000
	(7)		3,000
Feb. 1 Bal. 17,000			

Prepaid Rent			
(2)	12,000	(1)	1,000
Feb. 1 Bal.	11,000		

Equipment			
(3) 30,000	(10)		250
Feb. 1 Bal. 29,750			

Accounts Payable			
		(1)	25,000
		Feb. 1 Bal.	25,000

Notes Payable			
	(8)		10,000
	Feb. 1 Bal.		10,000

Capital Stock			
		Jan. 1 Bal.	100,000
		Feb. 1 Bal.	100,000

Retained Earnings			
	(12)		1,250
	Feb. 1 Bal.		1,250

Sales			
(12)	11,500	(4)	7,500
		(6)	4,000

Cost of Sales			
(5)	5,000	(12)	8,000
(7)	3,000		

Administrative Expense			
		(12)	1,000
(9)	1,000		

Depreciation Expense			
(10)	250	(12)	250

Rent Expense			
11)	1,000	(12)	1,000

Notice that it is customary each month to bring the balances of the balance sheet items forward. A double line means that a balance has been taken at that point so that entries above this line should be ignored when the next balance is taken. This is purely for bookkeeping expediency. Once having calculated the balance of an account, it is more efficient to start from this balance the next time.

Otherwise, you would keep adding the same figures again and again. The balance sheet accounts are called "real" accounts because they are carried forward from period and period. The income statement accounts are called "nominal" accounts because they are part of the retained earnings account and are closed out at the end of each period.

February Transactions. The February activities of the ABC Company are listed below. For further clarification of the ideas that we have been discussing, we will (1) prepare the journal entries necessary to (a) record the activities described; (b) adjust the accounts at the end of the month; and (c) close the nominal accounts; and (2) post these entries to the ledger. At this point, you might want to prepare your own solution and then compare it with the one provided below.

February Transactions

1. Inventory worth $15,000 was purchased on account.

2. Suppliers were paid $20,000.

3. Sales were made as follows:
   (a) Inventory costing $10,000 was sold on open account for $15,000.
   (b) Inventory costing $5,000 was sold for $8,000 cash.

4. A total of $5,000 was collected from customers.

5. The manager received $1,000 in salary.

6. A dividend of $500 was paid to the stockholders.

Journal Entries

(13)

Inventories	15,000	
Accounts Payable		15,000

(14)

Accounts Payable	20,000	
Cash		20,000

(15)

Accounts Receivable	15,000	
Sales		15,000

(16)

Cost of Sales	10,000	
Inventories		10,000

(17)

Cash	8,000	
Sales		8,000

(18)

Cost of Sales	5,000	
Inventories		5,000

(19)

Cash	5,000	
Accounts Receivable		5,000

(20)

Administrative Expense	1,000	
Cash		1,000

(21)

Dividends Paid	500	
Cash		500

Adjusting Entries

(22)

Depreciation Expense	250	
Equipment		250

(23)

Rent Expense	1,000	
Prepaid Rent		1,000

Closing Entries

(24)

Sales	23,000	
Cost of Sales		15,000
Administrative Expense		1,000
Depreciation Expense		250
Rent Expense		1,000
Retained Earnings		5,750

(25)

Retained Earnings	250	
Dividends Paid		250

Figure 4-7

Cash				Accounts Receivable			
Feb. 1 Bal.	71,000	(14)	20,000	Feb. 1 Bal.	7,500	(19)	5,000
(17)	8,000	(20)	1,000	(15)	15,000		
(19)	5,000	(21)	500	Mar. 1 Bal.	17,500		
Mar. 1 Bal.	62,500						

Inventories				Prepaid Rent			
Feb. 1 Bal.	17,000	(16)	10,000	Feb. 1 Bal. 11	11,000	(23)	1,000
(13)	15,000		5,000	Mar. 1 Bal.	10,000		
Mar. 1 Bal.	17,000						

Equipment				Accounts Payable			
Feb. 1 Bal.	29,750	(22)	250	(14)	20,000	Feb. 1 Bal.	25,000
						(13)	15,000
Mar. 1 Bal.	29,500					Mar. 1 Bal.	20,000

Notes Payable		
=====	Feb. 1 Bal.	10,000
	Mar. 1 Bal.	10,000

Capital Stock		
==	Feb. 1 Bal.	100,000
	Mar. 1 Bal.	100,000

Retained Earnings			
(25)	500	Feb. 1 Bal.	1,250
			5,750
		Mar. 1 Bal.	6,500

Sales			
		(15)	15,000
(24)	23,000	(17)	8,000

Cost of Sales			
(16)	10,000		
(18)	5,000	(24)	15,000

Administrative Expense			
(20)	1,000	(24)	1,000

Depreciation Expenses			
(22)	250	(24)	250

Rent Expense			
(23)	1,000	(24)	1,000

Dividends Paid			
(21)	500	(25)	500

Some Aspects of Debits and Credits

Advantages. The principal advantage of being able to think of accounting transactions in terms of debit and credit is that it is a convenient shorthand, not unlike using mathematical symbols. The theory provides, in effect, a sort of algorithm for determining the impact of various financial events on the financial statements of a business.

At first, many students find it very difficult to express financial transactions in terms of debits and credits, even though they had no trouble using pluses and minuses. Pluses and minuses are all right for simple transactions but they can be very confusing if the transactions become complex. Furthermore, it becomes very awkward for us to explain certain things in accounting without expressing them in terms of debits and credits. In other words, we need this shorthand to explain certain types of more complex transactions concisely.

Notice that there is nothing either mysterious or arbitrary about the fact that the debits always equal the credits. (The only arbitrary thing about the entire process is that debits are *on the left*. In some foreign countries, debits are entered on the right-hand side of the page and credits are recorded on the left.) It is merely an extension of the accounting equation—Assets = Liabilities + Owner's Equity—to *every* transaction. Consequently, every transaction *must* affect two items. For example, an increase in an asset must come from somewhere. It must result from a decrease in another asset, an increase in a liability or, if neither of these, it must represent an increase in owner's equity. It is important to understand this point. Debits and credits are merely a way of expressing the fact that assets will always equal liabilities plus owner's equity, no matter what happens in a business. This is true by definition.

A second advantage of using debits and credits is that it provides a check on the accuracy of the books of account. However, just because the books balance does not mean that they are correct. There could be offsetting errors or information could have been recorded in incorrect accounts. If the books do *not* balance, however, we know that a mistake has been made. This advantage has become less important with the development of modern data processing equipment, which provides extensive checks on clerical accuracy.

Technique for Analyzing Transactions. For each transaction, you have four things to decide: the two items that are affected by the transactions, which item to debit, and which item to credit. Really, however, you have to decide only three things because, if you can decide which item to debit, the other entry must be a credit, and vice versa. Consequently, you will find that the easiest approach is to pick out the most obvious item and, once you have decided whether this should be debited or credited, the other item must be the opposite. Following are some guidelines for analyzing transactions:

1. For anything that involves cash, you simply decide whether you are receiving money or spending it. If you are receiving it, it is a debit to cash and a credit to the source from which it comes. If you are spending cash, it is a credit to cash and a debit to the item for which you are spending the cash.

2. Every sale of goods involves two entries: a debit to cash, accounts receivable, or whatever asset is being given; and a credit to sales for the selling price of the goods. The second entry is a debit to cost of sales and a credit to inventory for the cost of the goods. Thus, the entry for every sale will be identical except for the asset received in exchange for the goods. For practical purposes, this will just about always be either cash or accounts receivable.

3. Any time you incur an expense, you debit the expense for the amount incurred.

4. Any time you earn income, you credit the income account for amount earned.

THE ACCOUNTING CYCLE

We are now ready to describe the entire accounting cycle and to expand some of the explanations that were given earlier.

Recording Daily Transactions

Each day it is necessary to record in transaction form the events that have occurred that affect the financial status of the business. Most of these are routine and can be handled by clerks. Many, however, require accounting judgment because it is at this point that the determination is made about what item to debit and what item to credit. In the day-to-day operations of an accounting system, therefore, this is the crucial point because it is the one at which accounting judgment must be used. Once the accounting treatment of an item has been determined, all the rest is clerical. Consequently, all good accounting systems provide for careful control of the decision-making process. Routine entries (sales, payment of accounts payable, etc.) are covered by instructions to the clerks who record these transactions. Non-routine decisions are referred to the appropriate accountant.

Specialized Journals. We have been recording transactions in the general journal and, for convenience, we will continue to do so. You can see, however, that this would be quite inefficient in actual business situations. For example, suppose that you had 1,000 sales transactions per day; writing 2,000 separate entries (remember, there are two entries for each sale) and then posting them to a ledger would be very time consuming and also subject to extensive clerical error. Consequently, even the smallest businesses keep specialized journals to record recurring types of transactions. Typical special journals would include a sales journal, cash receipts journal, cash disbursement journal, payroll journal, and purchases journal. The purpose of these specialized journals is solely to reduce clerical effort. The nature of these journals need not be of concern to you here; they are simply data processing devices. It is important, however, for you to understand that the general journal is used only for non-routine entries in actual business practice.

Data Processing Equipment. In all but the smallest businesses, daily transactions tend to be recorded using special bookkeeping machines, punched card equipment, or computers. Consequently, if you were to observe the prcedure in most businesses, you would not recognize it as the processes we have described in this chapter. Nevertheless, the results are exactly the same; it is merely the process of obtaining these results that differs.

The Ledger

The posting of the daily transactions to the ledger goes on concurrently with keeping up the journals. The decision on what accounts to debit and credit was made as part of journal-keeping process. Posting these entries is a routine clerical operation.

The composition of the ledger is the key to the adequacy of the accounting system. The number and type of accounts that are contained in the ledger determine the information that will be available to management on a recurring basis. For example, it would be possible to keep a ledger that contained only three accounts—assets, liabilities, and owner's equity. Such a ledger, however, would provide little information to management. It is necessary, therefore, to decide the amount and type of information that you will need for adequate financial statements, as well as for additional management needs. Your ledger should be designed accordingly. The more accounts that your ledger contains, the more information will be available; however, the more accounts that are maintained, the higher will be the cost of maintaining your accounting systems. Consequently, the key consideration in the design of a ledger is to increase the number of accounts only to the point that the resulting additional information is worth the additional cost of obtaining it. The listing of ledger accounts for a business is called the "chart of accounts."

The Ledger and the Financial Statements. In most businesses, the ledger contains many more accounts than the items included on the financial statements. For example, you might have in your income statement an account called "administrative expense." In the ledger you might have accounts for each type of administrative expense (e.g., professional salaries, clerical salaries, supplies, travel, rent, depreciation of equipment, etc.) as well as a breakdown according to the organizational component spending the money (e.g., finance, industrial relations, president's office, etc.). Management needs this detail to control these expenses, but on the published financial statements they are included as a single item. In fact, in most medium- to large-sized businesses, every item on the financial statements will represent several accounts in the ledger. The principle, however, is exactly the same as we have described. It is simply that as a business gets larger and more complex, management needs to have more detail than what is included in the financial statements. This detail is provided by expanding the size of the ledger.

Subsidiary Ledgers. The ledger with which we have been working is called a "general ledger" because it contains the major account classifications. Behind this general ledger are a number of subsidiary ledgers that provide additional detail required to run the business. For example, the accounts receivable account could represent money owed from literally thousands of customers. It is not enough to know that accounts receivable total $1,496,321.62, for example. You must know *who* owes how much money. One way would be to keep an account for each customer in the general ledger. If there are many customers, however, this creates record-keeping problems. Consequently, a single account, accounts receivable, is established in the general ledger and a separate ledger is maintained that has an account for each customer. The general ledger account is called a "control" account; the accounts receivable ledger is called a "subsidiary" ledger. The total of the balances in the subsidiary ledger must equal the balance in the control account.

The mechanics for processing data through the subsidiary ledger need not concern you here because this is only a data processing device for handling large amounts of information that cannot be conveniently dealt with through the general ledger alone. The principle, however, does not change. The accounts receivable account means precisely the same whether it includes a few customers or several thousand. It is only the means of handling the data that must change as the business becomes larger.

The Account. Earlier in the chapter, we showed a picture of a typical "T" account. We will continue to use "T" accounts throughout this book when we are describing the flow of information through the ledger. In actual practice, however, the "T" account is used only in smaller companies. More often the ledger is maintained on punched cards, magnetic tape, or, with increasing frequency, on random access computers. The point is that, in actual business situations, the ledger, like the journal, may bear no apparent resemblance to the things described in this chapter. This should not disturb you, however, because, again, these differences result from the necessity of handling large amounts of data. They are doing exactly the same thing with the computers that we are doing with simple transactions. The results are the same; only the methods are different.

The Trial Balance

The financial transactions are posted daily from the journals. At the end of the month, before beginning the preparation of financial statements, it is customary to prepare a trial balance.[1] A trial balance is simply a listing of the balances of all of the accounts in the ledger to be sure that the total debits equal the total credits. If they do not, this means that some mistakes have occurred and these must be corrected before the accountant can continue with the preparation of the financial statements.

Adjusting Entries

The next step after the trial balance is prepared is to make the adjusting entries. Adjusting entries were introduced in Chapter 2. In this part of the chapter we will summarize the different types of adjusting entries.

Adjusting entries are designed to adjust the books for the following:

1. Items of expense or income that occur on a continuous basis. These include: (a) the depreciation, depletion, or amortization of non-current assets; (b) interest expense or income; (c) other expenses or income that are paid for on a time basis—e.g., rent, insurance, etc.

2. Items that are measured only periodically. For example, you usually do not keep track of supplies as you use them. Instead, at the end of a period, an inventory of supplies is taken. The difference between what has been bought and what is left is the cost of the supplies used. If you started with an inventory of supplies of $100, purchased $400 worth of supplies during the month, and had $150 worth left at the end of the month, you would have an expense of $350 (100 + 400 − 150).

3. Goods or services that have been received but not billed or paid for. For example, labor is usually paid at the end of the week. If the end of the month comes in the middle of the week, you would have used two or three days' labor that would not yet have been paid. You would set up an entry as follows:

    Wage Expense   xxx
    Wages Payable   xxx

4. Goods and services that have been rendered but not billed.

5. The liability for income taxes payable. (This can only be done after you have calculated the profit before taxes.)

---

[1] In actual business practice, a trial balance might be prepared daily or even more frequently. For our purposes, however, we will assume that it is prepared monthly.

The adjusting entries, in short, are designed to bring all of the accounts up to date so that the financial statements can be prepared accurately.

The Financial Statements

After the adjusting entries have been made and posted, the financial statements are prepared. This process was discussed in detail in chapters 1, 2, and 3 and need not be repeated here.

Closing Entries

After the financial statements have been prepared, the final step is to close out the income statement accounts to the retained earnings account. This is a simple bookkeeping operation and has been described earlier in the chapter. It is necessary to close out the income statement accounts because these measure revenue and expense *over a period of time*. If they were not closed out at the end of each period, they would reflect *cumulative values*.

SUMMARY

The accounting cycle includes the following activities in the following order:

1. Recording transactions in the journal
2. Posting to the ledger
3. Taking a trial balance
4. Adjusting the books
5. Preparing the financial statements
6. Closing the books

Usually, interim (e.g., monthly) financial statements are prepared without formally adjusting and closing the books. A trial balance is taken from the books and adjustments are made to these balances outside the ledger on a paper called a "work sheet." Financial statements are then prepared directly from the work sheet. The results will be identical, however, and we need not be concerned with the mechanics of preparing interim financial statements at this point.

MANAGEMENT CONSIDERATIONS OF ACCOUNTING MECHANICS

Prior to World War II, most businesses kept their books in a manner not too dissimilar from the procedure described in this chapter, in journals in which the financial transactions were originally recorded and in ledgers in which the financial transactions were summarized according to the type of activity. Since then, record keeping has changed tremendously and these changes seem to be increasing at an increasing rate. Now, record keeping is pretty much in the hands of the data processing department. Since this requires an intimate knowledge of data processing equipment and techniques, the manager has had to delegate this responsibility. As long as the information he needs is available at a reasonable cost, he is not too concerned with the specific procedure for acquiring this information.

Nevertheless, the general manager must be able to visualize the impact of events and transactions on his financial statements. In many instances, this presents no problems. In other cases, however, in which technical accounting problems are involved, it can be quite difficult without an understanding of the accounting process. For this reason, we believe it is important that the management student be able to visualize the flow of data through the business.

The second reason why we believe it is important to understand the accounting process is that the management student should be familiar with the theory of debits and credits. This is the shorthand of the accountant and it is an important communication link with him and with relevant accounting literature that the non-accounting management student may wish to read.

QUESTIONS

1. What is bookkeeping? What purposes does it serve?

2. Describe the ways in which information concerning the financial status of a company enters the business. Give some examples.

3. Give some examples of information generated within a business that affects the financial status of the company.

4. What type of financial information is customarily maintained within the accounting department?

5. What is the purpose of a journal?

6. What is the purpose of a ledger?

7. What is an account? What is its purpose?

8. What is a debit? What is a credit?

9. Why must debits always equal credits in the ledger?

10. Why must the debits equal the credits in every accounting transaction?

11. Why do debits increase the amount of an asset? Why do credits increase the amount of a liability? Why do expenses normally have a debit balance? Why do items of income have credit balances?

12. Of what advantage is it to the manager to understand debits and credits?

13. If the books do not balance, why does this indicate that a mistake has been made? If they do balance, why does this *not* mean that the books are necessarily correct?

14. Why are journal entries so critical in the accounting procedure?

15. What are the characteristics of a good ledger?

16. What is a subsidiary ledger? A control account?

17. What is the trial balance? What is its purpose?

18. What are the types of activities that are recorded in adjusting entries?

19. What are closing entries? Why do the income statement accounts need to be closed at the end of each period?

PROBLEMS

For each of the problems listed below, do the following:

a. Set up a general journal and record the daily transactions;

b. Set up a general ledger, record the beginning balance, and post the transactions to the ledger;

c. Prepare a trial balance;

d. Prepare adjusting entries and post them to the ledger;

e. Prepare financial statements, if you have not already done so previously. If you have already prepared financial statements, compare the balances in the accounts with these statements.

f. Prepare closing entries and post them to the ledger

Problem 4-1

Problems 1-5 and 1-6 on pages 18 and 19.

Problem 4-2

Problems 1-7 and 1-8 on pages 19 to 20.

Problem 4-3

Problem 2-3 on pages 37 to 38.

Problem 4-4

Problem 2-4 on pages 38 and 39.

Problem 4-5

Problem 2-5 on pages 39 to 40.

Problem 4-6

Problem 2-6 on pages 41 and 42.

Problem 4-7

Problem 2-8 on pages 43 and 44.

Problem 4-8

Problem 2-9 on pages 44 to 45.

Problem 4-9

The post closing trial balance (a trial balance taken after the closing entries have been posted) of the Kennett Corporation as of December 31, 1974, is as follows:

Account	($000) Debit	Credit
Cash	$ 329	
Accounts Receivable	540	
Notes Receivable	100	
Accrued Interest Receivable	3	
Inventories	982	
Supplies	15	
Land	150	
Building	785	
Equipment	1,063	
Accounts Payable		$ 730
Accrued Interest Payable		15
Taxes Payable		125
Mortgage Payable		1,000
Capital Stock		1,500
Retained Earnings		597
	$3,967	$3,967

Notes:

1. The note receivable is a 6-month note due April 1 with interest at 12 per cent.

2. The building originally cost $960 and has an estimated life of 20 years. The equipment originally cost $1,800 and has an estimated life of 10 years.

3. The mortgage is due in 10 years. Interest of 6 per cent is payable on October 1 and April 1.

Transactions During January 1975

1. Goods costing $285 were sold on open account for $406.

2. Goods costing $356 were purchased on open account.

3. A total of $304 was collected from customers.

4. Suppliers were paid $256.

5. The taxes payable of $125 were paid in cash.

6. A piece of equipment costing $240 was purchased on January 15. It is estimated that this equipment has a 10-year life.

7. On January 15 a bank loan of $200 was taken on a 60-day note, bearing interest at 12 per cent.

8. Supplies worth $10 were purchased during the period for cash.

9. The following expenses were paid in cash during January:

Salesmen's Salaries	$28
Advertising	12
Administrative Salaries	15
Utilities	6
Telephone and Telegraph	3

10. At the end of January, the following salaries had been earned but not yet paid:

Salesmen's Salaries	$ 3
Administrative Salaries	2

11. An inventory of supplies indicated that $12 worth were on hand at the end of January.

12. The company pays income taxes equal to 50 per cent of income before taxes.

Required:

1. Set up a ledger and enter the beginning balances.

2. Enter in the journal and post transactions 1-9.

3. Take a trial balance.

4. Prepare adjusting entries and post them to the ledger.

5. Prepare financial statements.

6. Prepare closing entries and post them to the ledger and close the ledger accounts.

Problem 4-10

Record the following transactions in the journal. (Treat each entry as a separate transaction, not related to the others.)

1. The XYZ company was started by selling $500,000 worth of capital stock for cash.

2. The company purchased a patent for $50,000.

3. Land costing $30,000 was purchased for cash. A building costing $50,000 was erected on this land. The company borrowed $30,000 of this amount from the bank on a mortgage. Equipment worth $100,000 was purchased. The company paid $20,000 in cash and gave a 5-year note for the remainder.

4. A dividend of $10,000 was declared on January 15. It was paid on February 15.

5. Office supplies on hand at the beginning of the month were worth $3,600. During January, $2,000 worth of supplies were purchased. An inventory at the end of January indicated that $3,200 worth of office supplies were on hand. Make the adjusting entry at the end of January.

6. On January 15, the company borrowed $3,000 from the bank on a 60-day, 6 per cent note. The bank took out the interest of $30 in advance, giving the company $2,970. Make the entry on January 15, on January 31, on February 29, and on March 15.

7. On February 15, the company lent an employee $1,000 on a 90-day note, with interest of 6 per cent to be paid when the note becomes due. Make the entry for February 15, February 28, March 31, April 30, and May 15.

8. The company sold equipment with a net book value of $1,500 for $600.

9. The company rented office space to an outside firm. On March 15, they received $3,000 (three months' rent) in advance. Make the entries for March 15 and March 31.

10. The company purchased a 2-year fire insurance policy for $340 on April 15. Make the entries for April 15 and April 30.

Accounts Receivable
and
Inventories

The Hardship of Accounting

Never ask of money spent
Where the spender thinks it went.
Nobody was ever meant
To remember or invent
What he did with every cent.

Robert Frost

5

The purpose of this chapter is to describe the accounting treatment of accounts receivable, inventories, and long-term receivables.

ACCOUNTS RECEIVABLE

In general, the accounting for accounts receivable is straightforward. When goods are sold on open account, the customer's account is debited for the amount of the sale; when payment is received, the customer's account is credited with the amount of the payment. The total amount of accounts receivable is equal to the sum of the net amount in the customers' accounts. There are, however, two special problems that require deviations from these straightforward accounting procedures: (1) discounts, and (2) bad debts. These two problems are discussed in this part of the chapter.

Discounts

There are two important types of discounts. One is called a "trade" discount; the other is called a "cash" discount. Each is discussed below:

Trade Discount. A trade discount is simply a reduction from a list price. Typically, a company will publish a catalog of prices and then offer discounts to different classes of customers. For example, the retail customer may pay the list price; the wholesale customer may pay the list price minus 10 per cent; the distributor (one who services several wholesalers) may pay the list price less discounts of 10 per cent and 5 per cent. Assume that a product carries a catalog price of $100. The retail customer pays $100; the wholesaler pays $90; the distributor pays $85.50. Notice that trade discounts are taken sequentially on the net amount after taking the preceding discount. For example, discounts of 10 per cent, 5 per cent, and 10 per cent on a $100 price would be calculated as follows:

$$100 - .10 (100) = 90 - .05 (90) = 85.00 - .10 (85.50) = \$76.95$$

For accounting purposes, trade discounts are treated as a mechanism for calculating the price. Both the debit to accounts receivable and the credit to sales are at the *net* amount. The catalog price is used only as a basis for calculating the final price. For example, goods are sold at a catalog price of $1,000 subject to trade discounts of 5 per cent and 10 per cent. The accounting entry will be a debit to accounts receivable and a credit to sales of $855 ($1,000 minus $50 minus $95).

Cash Discounts. A cash discount, as the name implies, is a discount for paying cash. Essentially, it is a discount given if a company pays a bill before it is due. For example, a typical cash discount is expressed as follows: 2 per cent, 10 days; net 30. This means that a discount of 2 per cent will be allowed if the bill is paid within 10 days of its receipt. If the discount is not taken, the bill should be paid within 30 days.

There are two principal methods for handling cash discounts. One is to treat them like trade discounts and debit accounts receivable. and credit sales for the net amount. The other method is to enter the transaction at the gross amount and treat the cash discount as an expense when it is taken.

Cash discounts differ from trade discounts in that cash discounts are not always taken. (Trade discounts, of course, always are.) The theory for treating cash discounts like trade discounts is that, for practical purposes, they are really discounts from the quoted price in those instances in which there is a high rate of return on the money paid—for example, the terms 2 per cent, 10 days, net, 30. A company can save 2 per cent by paying in 10 days instead of 30. This means that the company is paying 2 per cent for using the money an extra 20 days before paying. The interest rate on an annual basis is 36 per cent (360/20 X 2 per cent).[1] Clearly, money can usually be borrowed for much less than 36 per cent. Even if a company were short of cash, it would be more economical to borrow money from the bank and pay within the discount period. Because of the disparity between the bank's borrowing rate and the typical cash discount, it can logically be assumed that the discount is *not* given in consideration of early payment. It usually represents a trade practice and, in fact, is really more of a penalty for late payment. For this reason, cash discounts should normally be treated like trade discounts and the accounting entry should be made for the net amount. For example, if a sale of $100 was made subject to a cash discount of 2 per cent, 10 days; net 30, the accounting entry at the date of sale would be:

Accounts Receivable	98	
Sales		98

On the date of payment, the entry would be:

Cash	98	
Accounts Receivable		98

[1] This is an approximation. Calculated using more precise mathematics, the annual interest equivalent of 2 per cent in 20 days is in excess of 40 per cent.

If, by some chance, the customer did not pay within the 10 days, the entry would be:

Cash	100	
Accounts Receivable		98
Cash Discounts Not Taken*		2

*This would be a miscellaneous income account.

The second way of handling cash discounts is as follows: In the above example, the initial entry would be:

Accounts Receivable	100	
Sales		100

When the bill was paid within the discount period, the entry would be:

Cash	98	
Cash Discounts*	2	
Accounts Receivable		100

*This account is usually treated as a miscellaneous expense on the income statement.

This treatment is correct *if* the cash discount actually represents a payment for the early receipt and, therefore, bears some approximation to the current rate of interest. If this is not true, the accounts receivable are overstated if they are included on the balance sheet at the gross amount.

Summary. The accounting treatment of trade and cash discounts are not of great importance to the manager. It is useful that he have some understanding of them, however, because often these items will appear on the financial statements. The following considerations are particularly significant to the manager:

1. If cash discounts are high in relation to interest rates, accounts receivable may be overstated if they are included at the gross amount. Since the customer will almost always take advantage of the discount, the company will receive only the net amount.

2. If cash discounts are high in relation to the interest rates, businesses that do not take advantage of cash discounts may be having financial problems. In evaluating potential bad debts (discussed in the next part of the chapter), this could be significant.

3. If trade discounts are given, the list price has really no significance. For example, if an item lists for $100 and you sell it for $90, you are *not* selling a $100 item for $90. You are selling a $90 item for $90. In other words, what you sell an item for represents its sales value.

Although this discussion has been limited to sales, exactly the same principles apply to purchases. The cost of anything that is purchased is the amount paid. Inventories and property assests that are purchased subject to trade discounts should be entered on the books at the *net* amount. If cash discounts are high in relation to interest rates, the purchase should be entered into inventory at the net amount.

Bad Debts

Almost any company that sells goods or services on credit will have difficulty in collecting from some customers. When it becomes evident that a customer cannot pay his bill, the amount is written off and charged to an expense account called "bad debts." There are two accounting problems associated with the treatment of bad debts. First, the gross value of the accounts receivable appearing on the books of account will, in most instances, be overstated because a certain number of these accounts will prove to be uncollectible. For balance sheet purposes, some adjustment must be made to the total gross value of the accounts receivable to reflect this situation. Second, the determination that a debt is uncollectible may occur at a time subsequent to the date of sale. If we are to follow the principle of matching costs against revenues, bad debt expense should be reflected at the time the sale was made. Some allowance, therefore, for the potential bad debt expense incurred during a period should be made at the end of that period. There are two principal methods for handling these two problems: the percentage of accounts receivable method and the percentage of sales method. These methods are described in this part of the chapter.

Percentage of Accounts Receivable. At the time a balance sheet is prepared, the accountant knows from experience that all accounts are not collectible, but he does not know *which* particular accounts are uncollectible. (If he did, there would be no problem; he would simply write off the uncollectible accounts.) He, therefore, estimates what percentage of the accounts are uncollectible. He usually obtains this percentage by calculating the historical relationship between bad debts and accounts receivable and applies this percentage to the amount of accounts receivable. For example, assume that the total amount of accounts receivable on December 31, 1973, was $25,500 and that for the past 3 years the relationship between accounts receivable and bad debts has been as follows:

Year	Average Amount of Accounts Receivable	Amount of Bad Debts	BD/AR
1970	$27,600	$500	1.8%
1971	24,900	475	1.9
1972	25,200	500	2.0

The accountant would probably use 2 per cent of accounts receivable as an allowance for bad debts, unless he knew of some unusual circumstance that would invalidate the historical relationship.[2] The procedure for doing this is as follows:

1. Bad debt expense is debited and an account called "allowance for doubtful accounts" or, sometimes, "reserve for bad debts" is credited for the estimated amount of uncollectible accounts. This is an adjusting entry made before financial statements are prepared. In the example given above, the entry would be:

Bad Debt Expense	510	
Allowance for Doubtful Accounts		510

    The allowance for doubtful accounts is *subtracted* from the gross amount of accounts receivable on the balance sheet. The bad debt expense appears on the income statement, usually as a selling expense.

2. When it is determined that an account is uncollectible, the allowance for doubtful accounts is debited and accounts receivable is credited for the amount that is uncollectible. For example, suppose that a customer went bankrupt owing $200, none of which was collectible. The entry would be

Allowance for Doubtful Accounts	200	
Accounts Receivable		200

    The allowance for doubtful accounts is debited because we have already taken the bad debt expense on the first entry. This entry indicates that what we previously estimated would happen (i.e., not all accounts would be paid) has happened.

3. If the estimate had been equal to the bad debts incurred during the period, there would be no balance in the allowance for doubtful accounts at the end of the period. Since such a situation is unusual, there will usually be a balance at the end of the period. (This balance can be either a debit or a credit.) In making the entry for the following year, we take into account whatever balance is in the account.

    For example, suppose that:

    (a) the gross amount of accounts receivable is $50,000

    (b) the estimated amount of bad debts is 2 per cent of accounts receivable

    (c) there is a credit balance of $100 in the allowance for doubtful accounts

    The entry would be:

Bad Debt Expense	900	
Allowance for Doubtful Accounts		900

---

[2] A more accurate way of estimating bad debts is to "age" the accounts receivable; that is, to classify them by the length of time they have been outstanding. For example: current; 1 month old; 2-3 months old; 4-6 months old; over 6 months. A separate percentage, based on historical experience, is applied to each group. (Clearly the older the group, the higher would be the percentage.)

This will bring the allowance for bad debts up to 2 per cent of accounts receivable, or $1,000. If there had been a $100 *debit* balance in the allowance for doubtful accounts, the entry would have been:

Bad Debt Expense	$1,100	
Allowance for Doubtful Accounts		$1,100

4. If an account, which had been written off as a bad debt, is subsequently paid, the usual procedure is to debit cash and credit the allowance for doubtful accounts, even though the account had been written off in a past period.

Percentage of Sales. A second method of estimating potential bad debts is to use credit sales as the base for the calculation. For example, assume that bad debts averaged historically 1/2 of 1 per cent of credit sales. If a company had annual sales of $1,000,000, the accountant would debit bad debt expense and credit allowance for doubtful accounts for $5,000. The entries are identical to those described in the preceding section except that the balance in the allowance for doubtful accounts is not taken into consideration in making the adjusting entry. In the example above, the amount would be $5,000 regardless of the balance in the allowance for doubtful accounts. (Of course, if this account appears to be out of line, it will be adjusted.)

Summary of Bad Debts.

1. The percentage of accounts receivable method places primary importance on the balance sheet valuation of accounts receivable.

2. The percentage of sales method places primary importance on matching costs against revenues. For practical purposes, either method will be satisfactory since the difference between the two should almost always be small.

3. Both methods are based on estimating from historical patterns. It is necessary to be sure, therefore, that no changes have occurred that will result in a change from the historical pattern. For example, if a change in credit terms has been made during a period, the historical data would have to be adjusted for the effect of this change.

INVENTORIES

As stated earlier, inventories are goods held for resale. There are three types of inventories: (1) raw materials and purchased parts that will eventually be processed into manufactured goods; (2) work in process that represents partially finished manufactured goods; (3) finished goods, which are completed goods or goods purchased for resale. In other words, finished goods are those items that are in a form to be sold to a customer. Notice that finished goods to one manufacturer could be raw material to another. For example, transistors would be finished goods to a transistor manufacturer, but raw material to a radio manufacturer. Manufacturing companies maintain all three types of inventories. Merchandising companies (e.g., a wholesaler or retailer) would keep only finished good inventories.

There are two principal accounting problems involved with inventories. The first is the method of valuation. The second is the method of applying this valuation to identical units of inventory. Each of these problems is discussed in this part of the chapter.

Valuation

Following the accounting principle that an asset is recorded on the books at the price that was paid to acquire it, most inventories are valued at cost. Raw material and other purchased goods are valued at the price paid to obtain them. Manufactured goods (both work in process and finished goods) are valued at their cost of manufacture.

There are two general exceptions to using cost as a value for inventory. First, obsolete or damaged goods should be written down to their net realizable value.[3] Second, most companies value inventory at "the lower of cost or market." The market value is the price for which the goods can be bought by the company that holds the inventory (i.e., the replacement cost). It does not mean the price for which the company can sell the item.

Under some circumstances, however, replacement cost is not used as "market" for purposes of a lower of cost or market computation. Specifically, replacement cost can never be higher than net realizable value nor lower than net realizable value less a normal profit margin. Valuing inventory in excess of net realizable value would violate the principle of conservatism—i.e., provide for all known losses. Writing inventory down to an amount below net realizable value less a normal profit margin would create losses in the current period that are offset by abnormal profits in a subsequent period when the item was sold. Neither of these situations represents "good" accounting. In short, for purposes of the lower of cost or market test, market is defined as replacement cost subject to a ceiling value of net realizable value and a floor value of net realizable value minus a normal profit margin. The following example illustrates this procedure:

Cost	Replace- ment Cost	Net Real- izable Value	Net Realiz- able Value Less Normal Profit Margin	Indi- cated Market Value	Lower of Cost or Market
$10	$12	$13	$8	$12	10
10	9	13	8	9	9
10	14	13	8	13	10
10	7	13	8	8	8

Step 1: Compute net realizable value (selling price minus costs to complete and sell). This is the ceiling on market value.

Step 2: Compute net realizable value less a normal profit margin. This is the floor on market value.

Step 3: Compute market value. This is replacement cost unless replacement cost is above net realizable value (in which case market = the ceiling value), or unless

[3] Net realizable value is the net amount that is expected to be realized after deducting the costs of disposition.

replacement cost is below net realizable value less a normal profit margin (in
which case market = the floor value).
Step 4: Compute lower of cost or market.

Inventory records are usually maintained at cost and written down to the lower
of cost or market for balance sheet purposes.

Application of Cost to Identical Items of Inventory

The application of the cost principle to inventories is complicated because
identical items of inventory will be purchased or manufactured at different costs.
All of the units of an item of inventory, containing several lots purchased at
different prices, may be stored in the same place. The question is which of the
several prices should be applied to a given item of inventory when it is sold. There
are three principal methods for determining the cost of a particular item of
inventory: first-in-first-out (FIFO), average, and last-in-first-out (LIFO).[4]

First-in-first-out. First-in-first-out, as the name implies, values inventories in the
chronological order of purchase. When inventory is used, it is costed at the price of
the oldest items. Assume the following conditions with respect to an item of
inventory:

Transaction	Date of Purchase or Sale	Amount in Units	Cost Per Unit	Total Inventory
Beginning Inventory	Feb. 1	100	$ .90	100
Purchase	Feb. 15	50	1.00	150
Purchase	March 5	100	1.05	250
Sale	March 15	50		200
Purchase	March 18	40	1.10	240
Sale	March 28	150		90

The problem is to place a value on the items that were sold on March 15 and
March 28, and thus obtain a value for the inventory of ninety items at the end of
the period. Using FIFO, it is assumed, for valuation purposes, that the first items
purchased are the first sold. In the example, the oldest items were those purchased
prior to February 1 for $.90 a unit. The cost of the March 15 sale would be,
therefore, $.90 a unit, or $45.00. This is the amount that would be debited to cost
of sales and credited to the inventory. The sale on March 28 would be the final fifty
units purchased on February 1 valued at $45.00; the fifty units purchased on
February 15, valued at $50.00; and fifty of the units purchased on March 5, valued
at $52.50. The total cost of sales, therefore, is $147.50.

---

[4] The discussion in this chapter is concerned solely with the *valuation* of inventory. It has
nothing to do with the physical handling of inventory. This is determined by the type of
inventory and the facilities used to store the inventory. The physical handling and the valuation
of inventory are completely independent. The former is an engineering problem; the later is an
accounting problem.

The value of the ninety units left in inventory will be $44.00 for the units bought on March 18 and $52.50 for fifty of the units purchased on March 5, or a total of $96.50.

Average. The average method of inventory valuation maintains the inventory at the moving average of the purchases. When the inventory is sold or used, the inventory account is credited for an amount equal to the average purchase price at the date of sale multiplied by the number of units sold. In the preceding example, this would be as follows:

Transaction	Date of Purchase of Sale	Amount in Units	Cost/Sale Per Unit	Units	Inventory Total Amount	Per Unit
Beginning Inventory	Feb. 1	100	$ .90	100	$ 90	$ .90
Purchase	Feb. 15	50	1.00	150	140	.933
Purchase	March 5	100	1.05	250	245	.98
Sale	March 15	(50)	.98	200	196	.98
Purchase	March 18	40	1.10	240	240	1.00
Sale	March 28	(150)	1.00	90	90	1.00

Using the average method, the March 15 sale would have cost $49 (50 × $.98) and the March 28 sale $150 (150 × $1.00). The value of the inventory at the end of the month would be $90.

Last-in-first-out. Last-in-first-out, as the name implies, assumes that the last units purchased will be the first to be sold. In the preceding example, the cost of the March 15 sale of fifty units would be $52.50 (50 × $1.05 [the March 5 purchase]). The cost of the 150 units sold on March 28 would be as follows:

Number of Units	Date of Purchase	Unit Cost	Total Cost
40	March 18	$1.10	$ 44.00
50	March 5	1.05	52.50
50	March 15	1.00	50.00
10	March 1	.90	9.00
			$155.50

The ninety units left in inventory would be valued at $.90 a unit, or $81.00.

Comparison of Methods. The three methods can be compared as follows:

Cost of Sales	FIFO	Average	LIFO
March 15	$ 45.00	$ 49.00	$ 52.50
March 28	147.50	150.00	155.50
Total	$192.50	$199.00	$208.00
Value of Ending Inventory	$ 96.50	$ 90.00	$ 81.00

Which Valuation Method to Use?

For all practical purposes, average and FIFO yield virtually the same inventory values. In a rising market, average inventory values will be somewhat lower than FIFO values but not enough to make any material difference. Consequently, the decision whether to use FIFO or average is one of clerical expediency. Generally, the average method requires a little less clerical effort. The important management decision, therefore, is between FIFO[5] or average and LIFO.

Implications of FIFO. Under FIFO, inventories are costed at the most recent acquisition prices. As a result, the cost of sales reflects the prices in effect during some previous period. In an inflationary economy, therefore, the cost of sales could be considerably below and replacement cost of the items sold. Many accounting theorists believe that the difference between the cost of sales as calculated on the FIFO basis and as calculated at replacement cost is inventory holding profits, rather than operating profits, and should be so designated. Furthermore, these theorists point out that this profit will be unrealized as long as the business is operating, since the profit cannot be realized without liquidating the inventory. For example, suppose that a business has a physical inventory of 1,000 units at the beginning of the year that has cost $1 per unit. During the year, 1,000 units are sold for $3 a unit and 1,000 units are purchased for $2 a unit. On the FIFO basis, the profit would be calculated as follows:

Sales	$3,000
Cost of Sales	1,000
Profit before Taxes	2,000
Taxes	1,000
Profit After Taxes	$1,000

The cash inflow is just enough to replace the inventory ($3,000 revenue minus $1,000 in taxes). Consequently, this transaction has resulted in no cash flow but an increase in inventory values of $1,000. In other words, everything is the same as if nothing had been sold, but the inventories are $1,000 higher and the retained earnings are $1,000 higher. Although the example may be exaggerated, it demonstrates the problem with using FIFO. The economic value of an item of inventory is the replacement cost (assuming, of course, that you are going to replace it). The difference between the FIFO cost of goods sold and the replacement cost of goods sold is unrealized profits in inventories. The larger the inventory and the greater the degree of inflation, the larger will be these unrealized profits.

FIFO inventories, however, reflect the latest purchase prices and, consequently, more closely approximate replacement costs than do LIFO inventories.

Features of LIFO. Before discussing LIFO, two points regarding this valuation technique must be described.

First, if you use LIFO for income tax purposes, you must also use it in your

---

[5] Throughout this part of the chapter, we will use the term FIFO to refer to both the FIFO and the average method.

financial reporting. (This is one of the very few instances in which the tax law specifically prescribes consistency between the tax accounting and financial reporting.) Since LIFO results in lower profits than FIFO in an inflationary economy, the use of LIFO represents real cash savings from lower taxes.

Second, all companies maintain their inventory records on either a FIFO or average basis. These inventories are converted to a LIFO basis by means of a LIFO reserve. The LIFO reserve is the difference between the inventory as valued on the inventory records and what the value would be on a LIFO basis. The calculation of this reserve is quite technical and need not concern you here. However, there are two things you should know about it.

1. It is an *additional* calculation that is not required if you use FIFO or average, and, as mentioned, this calculation can be quite complex.
2. There are two basic methods for calculating the LIFO reserve. One is based on actual historical prices for the items in inventory. The other is a statistical calculation based on price level changes. The former is usually used if specific items of inventory can be readily identified (e.g., gallons of gasoline). The latter is used if the type of inventory changes, such as in a retail store or in a company that makes annual model changes. In both instances, however, the LIFO reserve is a total amount applied to the entire inventory. The individual items in the inventory are not adjusted. The net result of these alternative methods for calculating LIFO is that almost any business can use LIFO if it wishes to.

Implications of LIFO. Perhaps the most important implication of LIFO is that it can result in substantial tax savings for most companies.[6] Consequently, this becomes a management decision rather than an accounting decision. The decision whether to adopt LIFO revolves around the trade-off between lower taxes on one hand and lower reported earnings and inventory values on the other. Also involved is the additional cost of making the LIFO calculation. Many managers evidently would rather pay the additional tax than show the lower reported earnings.

The following are the principal implications of LIFO inventories:

1. Inventories tend to be seriously undervalued. Many companies adopted LIFO as early as 1946. If these companies produced at least as much as they sold (and many of them have), part of their inventories are valued at 1946 price levels. This is because, if inventories are not depleted, they will always be valued at the price in effect when LIFO was first adopted.

2. In instances wherein a company is required to deplete its inventories (as in the case of a strike), there can be some peculiar profit situations. For example, one company used up most of its inventories during a strike in 1964. The company had been using LIFO since 1946 and much of these inventories were at 1946 price levels. The strike resulted in the company earning record profits because of the low value of the inventories that were sold.

___

[6]Throughout this discussion we are assuming that the United States will continue to experience inflation.

3. The management of any company not using LIFO should be able to justify this situation to its stockholders. It should be able to show that unnecessary income taxes were not paid. Or, if unnecessary taxes were paid, management should be able to show that the benefits were worth at least as much as the excess tax payments.

Summary. FIFO results in higher profits, higher inventory values and higher income taxes than LIFO. Most managers will make the decision between the two techniques on the basis of these considerations. Many accounting theorists, however, believe that the FIFO method overstates profits in an inflationary economy and, consequently, prefer the use of LIFO, not because it saves taxes, but because it reflects more accurate profit figures.

Other accounting theorists believe that neither LIFO nor FIFO is preferable. These theorists recommend that three actions be taken with respect to inventory values:

1. The tax treatment should be separated from the accounting treatment. The rationale is that LIFO is correct for tax purposes because it is consistent with the ability to pay. They contend that LIFO is not reliable for accounting purposes, however.

2. Inventories should be stated at current replacement costs. The differences between historical cost and replacement cost would be credited to an account called "reserve for unrealized profit in inventory."

3. The treatment of inventory described in 2, above, should be mandatory for all companies. In short, the LIFO-FIFO option should no longer be available.

The LIFO-FIFO problem is treated in more detail in chapters 9 and 12.

Periodic Inventories

So far in this book, we have assumed that perpetual inventory records were maintained. A perpetual inventory is one in which a record of all purchases and sales is maintained so that the amount of inventory that should be on hand is known at all times. With a perpetual inventory, the cost of sales can be calculated for each sale made. Many companies (particularly retail stores) do not maintain a perpetual inventory and, consequently, can calculate the cost of sales only after taking a physical inventory. If perpetual inventories are not maintained, the cost of sales is calculated as follows:

1. The goods purchased during the period are added to the inventory at the beginning of the period. This is the cost of the goods that were available for sale during the period.

2. The ending inventory is subtracted from the cost of goods available for sale. This is the cost of goods sold. For example, assume that a company has an inventory of $116,900 at the beginning of January and purchased $562,391 during January. A physical inventory indicates that the

inventory on hand at the end of January is worth $109,462. The cost of sales for January is calculated as follows:

Beginning Inventory	$116,900
Plus Purchases	562,391
Goods Available for Sale	679,291
Less Ending Inventory	109,462
Cost of Goods Sold	569,829

If perpetual inventories are not maintained, the day-to-day accounting differs from that described in Chapter 4 in the following ways:

1. When a sale is made, accounts receivable is debited and sales is credited for the amount of the sale. No entry is made for the cost of goods sold or for the reduction in inventory.

2. When goods are purchased, an account called "purchases" is debited and accounts payable is credited for the amount of the purchase.

3. A physical inventory is taken at the end of each period and the cost of goods sold is calculated as described above.

Better control over the inventory is maintained if a perpetual inventory system is system is used. When a physical inventory is taken, the book inventory is compared to the actual inventory on hand. If, for example, someone has been stealing from inventory, a perpetual inventory would reveal the theft. A perpetual inventory system also provides more current information on the status of the inventories. Offsetting these two advantages is the cost of maintaining the additional records. The advantages of a perpetual inventory are sufficiently great that most companies maintain this type of system. It is still necessary to take a physical inventory periodically, however, to verify the accuracy of the records.

Inventory Reserves

It is customary, particularly in companies that carry significant amounts of inventories, to set up *reserves* that are subtracted from the gross inventory values. These reserves are somewhat similar to the allowance for doubtful accounts. One of the principal reasons for setting up such a reserve is to provide for potential obsolescence or deterioration of the inventories. At the time the inventory is taken, obsolete or deteriorated items are written down to their net realizable value. Others however, that are not currently obsolete may become so before they are sold or used. Also, items that are in good physical condition on the date that the inventory is taken may deteriorate before they are sold or used. In short, the inventory reserve is used to anticipate obsolence or deterioration in somewhat the same way that the allowance for doubtful accounts is used to anticipate the uncollectibility of some of the accounts receivable.

One of the important considerations of inventory reserves is that they are subject to a considerable amount of managerial judgement. Whereas potential bad debts can be supported statistically, this is not always the case with obsolete inventories. As a result, it is more difficult for the public accountant to verify inventory reserves. Consequently, these reserves are subject to manipulation at least to a degree. In profitable years, high inventory reserves often, will be established. These are lowered in less profitable years.

Another type of inventory reserve maintained by many companies is a LIFO reserve, previously described.

Inventories as Current Assets

Current assets are those assets that are expected to be converted into cash during the normal operating cycle of a business. If there is more than one operating cycle in a year, current assets are those that are expected to be converted into cash within a year. In those instances in which the normal operating cycle is longer than a year (e.g., tobacco or liquor) inventories are treated as current assets even though they will not be converted into cash in a year or less.

Occasionally, a company might find itself carrying more than a year's supply of inventories, even though its operating cycle is a year or less, if, for example, there was a significant and unexpected drop in the demand for an item of inventory. Assume that a company found itself with 3 year's supply of an item of inventory that normally turned over every 3 months. The company could do one of two things. First, it could write down the inventory to the net value that could be realized if the inventories had to be liquidated during the year. (In other words, the inventory is valued at its net realizable value under a forced sale.) Second, it could treat the amount of inventory in excess of 1 year's supply as a non-current asset.

Such actions would apply only to inventories in which the supply is greater than that which is expected to be sold or used in the normal operating cycle or in 1 year, whichever is longer. Some companies maintain several year's supplies of replacements parts because the economic order quantity is greater than a year's supply. In this case, the economic order quantity would establish the normal operating cycle. These items of inventory would, therefore, be treated as current assets.

LONG-TERM RECEIVABLES

In this section of the chapter we will describe and illustrate the current accounting rules for long-term receivables. The rules for recording long-term receivables (and payables as well) were changed significantly in 1971. To understand the significance of these changes, however, it is useful to begin with an example of accounting for long-term receivables before these changes were made.

Assume that Company A owns a piece of land that cost $5,000. It agrees to sell it to Company B for $10,000. The terms are *no* cash down and a note requiring payments of $1,000 per year for 10 years. Also assume for the moment that no interest will be charged on the note. Before 1972, this transaction would have been recorded as follows:

At Date of Sale

Dr. Note Receivable	$10,000	
Cr. Land		$5,000
Gain on Sale of Land		5,000

Each Year Thereafter,
for 10 Years

Dr. Cash	$1,000	
Cr. Note Receivable		$1,000

Thus, there would be $5,000 of profit and a $10,000 note receivable recorded at the date of sale; this transaction would have no effect on earnings thereafter. As each $1,000 payment was received, the note receivable would be reduced by $1,000. Many people believe that such treatment is misleading because it implies that receiving $1,000 per year for 10 years is as good as receiving $10,000 now.[7] Whether the contract specifically allows for it or not, there *is* a "time value of money." And no one who is in business to make a profit lends money interest-free. Although it may be difficult to specify the real interest rate implicit in a transaction, it is totally misleading to assume that the rate is zero.

Suppose, for example, that we knew that the cash price for which land A was selling was $6,710. Through present value tables we could find that the rate of interest implicit in the installment purchase was 8 per cent. This is the rate of interest that equates ten annual payments of $1,000 to a present value of $6,710. If $6,710 is the cash price of the land, the gain on the sale of the land is only $1,710 ($6,710-$5,000). The remainder of the profit is really interest income over the years on the unpaid note. If the cash price is not known, we cannot determine the interest rate so precisely. This doesn't mean, however, that the transaction is interest-free.

Imputed Interest—Noninterest-bearing Notes

If the equivalent cash price for an installment transaction is not determinable, a company is required under the new accounting principles for long-term receivables, to *estimate* or "impute" the rate of interest that the transaction carries. Quoting from the relevant ruling, "The objective is to approximate the rate which would have resulted if an independent borrower and an independent lender had negotiated a similar transaction under comparable terms and conditions with the option to pay the cash price upon purchase or to give a note for the amount of the purchase which bears the prevailing rate of interest to maturity."[8] Suppose, for example, that management, with the concurrence of the auditor, were able to decide that 10 per cent is a reasonable approximation of the appropriate interest rate for the hypothetical transaction we have been discussing, considering both its riskiness and the prevailing rates of interest on installment debts. Then, the imputed cash price would be $6,145, which is the present value of the ten annual payments of $1,000 discounted at 10 per cent. The total profit of $5,000 on the transaction is split into two parts. The real estate profit is $6,145-$5,000, or $1,145. This profit should be recognized at the time of sale. The balance of the profit, $5,000-$1,145, or $3,855,

---

[7] The appendix to this chapter explains present value for those who are not already acquainted with this concept.

[8] This quote is from paragraph 13 of Opinion Number 21 of the Accounting Principles Board. The subject of Accounting Principles Board opinions is discussed in Chapter 8.

is interest income. This amount should be spread over the life of the note. The transaction would be recorded as follows:

Dr. Note Receivable	$6,145	
Cr. Land		$5,000
Gain on Sale of Land		1,145

The note receivable reflects the present value of the future payments to be received, discounted at the assumed rate of interest. This accounting principle thus provides a way for valuing an asset that represents a future claim to cash. Such an asset should be shown on the balance sheet at the present value of the cash payments to be received.

Interest income in year 1 would be equal to 10 per cent times the carrying value of the note ($6,145), or $615. Of the first year's payment of $1,000, since $615 is interest income, only $385 ($1,000-$615) goes to reduce the note receivable. The journal entry is as follows:

Dr. Cash	$1,000	
Cr. Interest Income		$615
Note Receivable		385

The note thus carried a balance of $5,760 ($6,145–$385) into year 2. Notice that $5,760 is the present value at 10 per cent of the remaining nine annual payments of $1,000. Similarly, interest income in year 2 would be 10 per cent times $5,760, or $576. Thus, in year 2, $424 of the $1,000 payment goes for principal reduction, leaving a note receivable balance of $5,336 at the beginning of year 3. The following table illustrates this approach over the full 10 years of the note:

Time	Cash Payments Received	Interest Income	Paid on Principal	Ending Note Receivable Balance[b]
0	$	$	$	$6,145
Year 1	1,000	615	385	5,760
2	1,000	576	424	5,336
3	1,000	534	466	4,870
4	1,000	487	513	4,357
5	1,000	435	565	3,792
6	1,000	379	621	3,171
7	1,000	317	683	2,488
8	1,000	249	751	1,737
9	1,000	174	826	911
10	1,000	89[a]	911	0
Totals	$10,000	$3,855	$6,145	

[a] Adjusted for rounding errors.
[b] This balance is always the present value at 10 per cent of the remaining payments to be received.

From an accounting standpoint, the significant result is that profit recognized at the time of sale is only $1,145 instead of $5,000. The remaining $3,855 flows through earnings in a decreasing pattern over the following 10 years.

If the cash price is known with more certainty than the implicit interest rate, this price is used to impute an interest rate. From this point on, the procedure would be exactly as above. In short, one or the other of two approaches is adopted. Either an assumed cash price is used to impute an interest rate or an assumed interest rate is used to impute a cash price. Then, present value methods are used to amortize the note.

This procedure would be exactly reversed on the books of Company B. The land would be carried at $6,145, the cash equivalent purchase price. A 10-year note payable for $6,145 would be set up. The note would reduce to zero over 10 years with total interest costs of $3,855. Interest expense each year for B would be the same as interest income for A. In short, this imputed interest principle applies to *both* long-term payable *and* receivables.

Imputed Interest on Interest-bearing Notes

If the note in our hypothetical example had carried interest at some rate that was clearly below a "fair" rate, the imputed interest principle still required the company to approximate a "fair" rate and to reflect income from the transaction in terms of this "fair" rate. Although the mechanics are more complicated, the result is still the same: to transform part of the real estate profit into interest income and to defer its recognition over the life of the note. We will illustrate this situation because it is the most common one in which the imputed interest principle is applied.

Suppose that the $10,000 note carried interest at a token rate of 4 per cent. Then, the level payments each year would be $1,233. According to standard present value tables, ten annual payments of $1,233 will just liquidate a $10,000 note plus compound interest at 4 per cent. Under pre-1972 accounting, Company A would still record $5,000 of profit and a $10,000 note receivable at the time of sale. In year 1, interest income would be 4 per cent times $10,000, or $400. Thus, of the $1,233 payment, $833 would go toward principal reduction, leaving a balance of $9,167 on the note at the beginning of year 2. Notice that $9,167 is the present value *at 4 per cent* of nine annual payments of $1,233. Interest in year 2 would be 4 per cent times $9,167, or $367, and so on. After 10 years the note would be reduced to zero. Total interest income over the 10 years would be $2,330. (10 times $1,233 = $12,330. $12,330-$10,000 = $2,330.)

Under imputed interest accounting, using 10 per cent as the "fair" rate of interest, the "cash equivalent" price for the land is $7,577, which is the present value at 10 per cent of ten annual payments of $1,233. Thus, following the same procedure we outlined earlier, real estate profit would be $7,577 − $5,000, or $2,577, and it would be recognized at the time of sale. Interest income in year 1 would be 10 per cent of $7,577, or $758, and so on. The results over the full 10 years are as follows:

Time	Cash Payments Received	Interest Income	Paid on Principal	Ending Note Receivable Balance
0	$	$	$	$7,577
Year 1	1,233	758	475	7,102
2	1,233	710	523	6,579

3	$ 1,233	$ 658	$ 575	$6,004
4	1,233	600	633	5,371
5	1,233	537	696	4,675
6	1,233	468	765	3,910
7	1,233	391	842	3,068
8	1,233	307	926	2,142
9	1,233	214	1,019	1,123
10	1,233	110[a]	1,123	0
Totals	$12,330	$4,753	$7,577	

[a]Adjusted for round errors.
Again, the results would be exactly reversed for Company B.

The Impact of Imputing Interest

The last hypothetical transaction described in the preceding section reveals the impact of this new accounting principle. Under pre-1972 accounting procedures, there is $5,000 of real estate profit, which is recognized immediately. There is $400 of interest income in year 1, $367 of interest in year 2, and so on, for a total of $2,330. Total profit over the 10 years is $7,330 ($5,000 of real estate profit and $2,330 of interest income). Under post-1972 accounting principles, there is still $7,330 of total profit over the 10 years. (*Total* profit must equal *total* proceeds [$12,330] less cost [$5,000] under *any* accounting approach.) In the new approach, however, the timing is much different. There is only $2,577 of real estate profit to be recognized immediately. There is $758 of interest income recognized in year 1, $710 of interest income recognized in year 2, and so on, for a total of $4,753 over the 10 years. In short, imputed interest accounting postpones recognition of a larger share of the profit. Notice also that the split between operating and financing income is much different. Instead of $5,000 of operating profit and $2,300 of interest, Company A will now show $2,577 of operating profit and $4,753 of interest.

In adopting this new principle, the accounting profession was careful to point out that it was not intended as a major move toward "present value" accounting. It was intended as a *minor* move to correct abuses in the narrow area of profit recognition on transactions involving long-term payables and receivables. Many observers, however, including the authors, consider the new principle to be *very significant*. It establishes a framework that is just as applicable to other assets or liabilities as it is to the specific items singled out for present value treatment. In our view, it represents a major breakthrough in acknowledging formally that economic substance should take precedence over "facts" (a zero interest note, for example) in accounting, even if this involved estimates of what the substance is. The accounting profession had decided in at least this one instance that it is better to be vaguely right than precisely wrong.

CHAPTER 5 — APPENDIX

Present Value

The Concept of Present Value. Present value is based on the mathematics of compound interest. For example, suppose that $1,000 is invested in a bank that

Table B

PRESENT VALUE OF $1 RECEIVED ANNUALLY FOR N YEARS

Years (N)	1%	2%	4%	6%	8%	10%	12%	14%	15%	16%	18%	20%	22%	24%	25%	26%	28%	30%	35%	40%	45%	50%
1	.990	.980	.962	.943	.926	.909	.893	.877	.870	.862	.847	.833	.820	.806	.800	.794	.781	.769	.741	.714	.690	.667
2	1.970	1.942	1.886	1.833	1.783	1.736	1.690	1.647	1.626	1.605	1.566	1.528	1.492	1.457	1.440	1.424	1.392	1.361	1.289	1.224	1.165	1.111
3	2.941	2.884	2.775	2.673	2.577	2.487	2.402	2.322	2.283	2.246	2.174	2.106	2.042	1.981	1.952	1.923	1.868	1.816	1.696	1.589	1.493	1.407
4	3.902	3.808	3.630	3.465	3.312	3.170	3.037	2.914	2.855	2.798	2.690	2.589	2.494	2.404	2.362	2.320	2.241	2.166	1.997	1.849	1.720	1.605
5	4.853	4.713	4.452	4.212	3.993	3.791	3.605	3.433	3.352	3.274	3.127	2.991	2.864	2.745	2.689	2.635	2.532	2.436	2.220	2.035	1.876	1.737
6	5.795	5.601	5.242	4.917	4.623	4.355	4.111	3.889	3.784	3.685	3.498	3.326	3.167	3.020	2.951	2.885	2.759	2.643	2.385	2.168	1.983	1.824
7	6.728	6.472	6.002	5.582	5.206	4.868	4.564	4.288	4.160	4.039	3.812	3.605	3.416	3.242	3.161	3.083	2.937	2.802	2.508	2.263	2.057	1.883
8	7.652	7.325	6.733	6.210	5.747	5.335	4.968	4.639	4.487	4.344	4.078	3.837	3.619	3.421	3.329	3.241	3.076	2.925	2.598	2.331	2.108	1.922
9	8.566	8.162	7.435	6.802	6.247	5.759	5.328	4.946	4.772	4.607	4.303	4.031	3.786	3.566	3.463	3.366	3.184	3.019	2.665	2.379	2.144	1.948
10	9.471	8.983	8.111	7.360	6.710	6.145	5.650	5.216	5.019	4.833	4.494	4.192	3.923	3.682	3.571	3.465	3.269	3.092	2.715	2.414	2.168	1.965
11	10.368	9.787	8.760	7.887	7.139	6.495	5.938	5.453	5.234	5.029	4.656	4.327	4.035	3.776	3.656	3.544	3.335	3.147	2.752	2.438	2.185	1.977
12	11.255	10.575	9.385	8.384	7.536	6.814	6.194	5.660	5.421	5.197	4.793	4.439	4.127	3.851	3.725	3.606	3.387	3.190	2.779	2.456	2.196	1.985
13	12.134	11.343	9.986	8.853	7.904	7.103	6.424	5.842	5.583	5.342	4.910	4.533	4.203	3.912	3.780	3.656	3.427	3.223	2.799	2.468	2.204	1.990
14	13.004	12.106	10.563	9.295	8.244	7.367	6.628	6.002	5.724	5.468	5.008	4.611	4.265	3.962	3.824	3.695	3.459	3.249	2.814	2.477	2.210	1.993
15	13.865	12.849	11.118	9.712	8.559	7.606	6.811	6.142	5.847	5.575	5.092	4.675	4.315	4.001	3.859	3.726	3.483	3.268	2.825	2.484	2.214	1.995
16	14.718	13.578	11.652	10.106	8.851	7.824	6.974	6.265	5.954	5.669	5.162	4.730	4.357	4.033	3.887	3.751	3.503	3.283	2.834	2.489	2.216	1.997
17	15.562	14.292	12.166	10.477	9.122	8.022	7.120	6.373	6.047	5.749	5.222	4.775	4.391	4.059	3.910	3.771	3.518	3.295	2.840	2.492	2.218	1.998
18	16.398	14.992	12.659	10.828	9.372	8.201	7.250	6.467	6.128	5.818	5.273	4.812	4.419	4.080	3.928	3.786	3.529	3.304	2.844	2.494	2.219	1.999
19	17.226	15.678	13.134	11.158	9.604	8.365	7.366	6.550	6.198	5.877	5.316	4.844	4.442	4.097	3.942	3.799	3.539	3.311	2.848	2.496	2.220	1.999
20	18.046	16.351	13.590	11.470	9.818	8.514	7.469	6.623	6.259	5.929	5.353	4.870	4.460	4.110	3.954	3.808	3.546	3.316	2.850	2.497	2.221	1.999
21	18.857	17.011	14.029	11.764	10.017	8.649	7.562	6.687	6.312	5.973	5.384	4.891	4.476	4.121	3.963	3.816	3.551	3.320	2.852	2.498	2.221	2.000
22	19.660	17.658	14.451	12.042	10.201	8.772	7.645	6.743	6.359	6.011	5.410	4.909	4.488	4.130	3.970	3.822	3.556	3.323	2.853	2.498	2.222	2.000
23	20.456	18.292	14.857	12.303	10.371	8.883	7.718	6.792	6.399	6.044	5.432	4.925	4.499	4.137	3.976	3.827	3.559	3.325	2.854	2.499	2.222	2.000
24	21.243	18.914	15.247	12.550	10.529	8.985	7.784	6.835	6.434	6.073	5.451	4.937	4.507	4.143	3.981	3.831	3.562	3.327	2.855	2.499	2.222	2.000
25	22.023	19.523	15.622	12.783	10.675	9.077	7.843	6.873	6.464	6.097	5.467	4.948	4.514	4.147	3.985	3.834	3.564	3.329	2.856	2.499	2.222	2.000
26	22.795	20.121	15.983	13.003	10.810	9.161	7.896	6.906	6.491	6.118	5.480	4.956	4.520	4.151	3.988	3.837	3.566	3.330	2.856	2.500	2.222	2.000
27	23.560	20.707	16.330	13.211	10.935	9.237	7.943	6.935	6.514	6.136	5.492	4.964	4.524	4.154	3.990	3.839	3.567	3.331	2.856	2.500	2.222	2.000
28	24.316	21.281	16.663	13.406	11.051	9.307	7.984	6.961	6.534	6.152	5.502	4.970	4.528	4.157	3.992	3.840	3.568	3.331	2.857	2.500	2.222	2.000
29	25.066	21.844	16.984	13.591	11.158	9.370	8.022	6.983	6.551	6.166	5.510	4.975	4.531	4.159	3.994	3.841	3.569	3.332	2.857	2.500	2.222	2.000
30	25.808	22.396	17.292	13.765	11.258	9.427	8.055	7.003	6.566	6.177	5.517	4.979	4.534	4.160	3.995	3.842	3.569	3.333	2.857	2.500	2.222	2.000
40	32.835	27.355	19.793	15.046	11.925	9.779	8.244	7.105	6.642	6.234	5.548	4.997	4.544	4.166	3.999	3.846	3.571	3.333	2.857	2.500	2.222	2.000
50	39.196	31.424	21.482	15.762	12.234	9.915	8.304	7.133	6.661	6.246	5.554	4.999	4.545	4.167	4.000	3.846	3.571	3.333	2.857	2.500	2.222	2.000

to use Table A-2 than to calculate the present value for each year and add them up. For example, suppose that you were to be paid $10,000 a year for 10 years and that money is worth 10 per cent. If you wish to find the present value of this amount, it is easier to look it up in Table A-2 (10,000 × 6.145 = $6,145) than to calculate the present value for each year and add these amounts.

Calculating the Time-Adjusted Rate of Return. You know the amount of proposed investment, the amount of anticipated earnings from this investment, and the timing of these earnings. You wish to know the rate of return (time adjusted) that is expected from the investment. Suppose that the proposed investment is $3,000 and the anticipated earnings are $1,000 a year for 5 years. (In this instance, assume that the earnings are received at the end of the year.) One way to find the rate of return is to discount the earnings (find their present value) at various rates until a rate is found that equates the present value of the earnings to the amount of investment. For example:

	10%	20%	30%
Year 1	$ 909	$ 833	$ 769
2	826	694	592
3	751	579	455
4	683	482	350
5	621	402	269
	$3,790	$2,990	$2,435

This shows that earnings of $1,000 a year for 5 years on an investment of $3,000 will earn slightly less than 20 per cent. It may be more meaningful to look at it this way. The process of discounting (i.e., finding present value) means that the amount of cash flow is reduced by the interest; the remainder, therefore, is the return of principal. If the discounted cash flow adds up to the principal, this means that you are earning the interest rate that was used to calculate the discounted cash flow. In the above example, at the 10 per cent rate, the return of principal is $3,790. This means that you earn 10 per cent + $790, which is obviously more than 10 per cent. On the other hand, if the earnings are discounted at 30 per cent the return of principal is only $2,435, or $565 less than the $3,000 investment. This means that you earn 30 per cent minus $565, or less than 30 per cent.

If the cash flow is equal for all years, there is a short-cut method for obtaining the time-adjusted rate of return. This method is as follows.

1. Divide the annual cash flow into the investment (investment/earnings).

2. From Table A-2 pick out the line for the number of years you will receive the cash flow.

3. Move across this line until you find a figure nearly equal to the amount calculated in 1. The rate indicated by this column is the time-adjusted rate of return.

In the example given above, 3,000/1,000 = 3.000. Looking at Table A-2 and moving across the 5-year line, you can see that 2.991 is the closest to 3.000. This is

Problem 5-5

Make the appropriate journal entries in the books of the XYZ Company, assuming that cash discounts are *not* deducted from the selling price.

Problem 5-6

Make the appropriate journal entries in the books of the ABC Company, assuming that cash discounts are *not* deducted from the purchase price.

Problem 5-7

Make journal entries reflecting the following transactions (make calculations to the nearest dollar):

1. On December 31, 1973, the XYZ Company had accounts receivable with a gross value of $193,486. It was estimated that 2 per cent of these would eventually prove to be uncollectible. There was a credit balance in the allowance for bad debts account of $500.

2. During the year, accounts worth $4,150 proved to be uncollectible and were written off.

3. A payment of $250 was received from an account that had been written off as uncollectible in 1972.

4. On December 31, 1974, accounts receivable had a gross value of $269,496. It was estimated that 2 per cent of these accounts were uncollectible.

Problem 5-8

Make the journal entries reflecting the following transactions:

1. The ABC Company estimates that bad debts average 1/4 of 1 per cent of credit sales. The credit sales during 1973 were $3,426,818. There was a credit balance in the allowance for doubtful accounts of $350.

2. During the year $9,463 worth of accounts were written off as uncollectible.

3. A payment of $400 was received on an account written off as uncollectible in 1965.

4. The credit sales for 1974 were $4,982,647. The ABC Company estimates that bad debts will equal 1/4 of 1 per cent of credit sales.

Problem 5-9

Below are the transactions that occurred on an item of inventory during 1974:

Date	Type of Activity	Number of Units	Unit Purchase Price
1-1	Beginning Inventory Purchased on October 1, 1973	100	$ .90

	Purchased on November 30, 1973	50	1.00
1-31	Purchase	100	1.10
2-15	Sale	50	
4-20	Purchase	50	1.15
5-10	Purchase	50	1.20
6-15	Sale	140	
7-15	Purchase	90	1.25
8-10	Sale	40	
9-15	Purchase	100	1.30
10-15	Sale	200	

Calculate the cost of each sale and the value of the ending inventory using FIFO, average, and LIFO. Compare the results.

Problem 5-10

Below are the transactions that occurred on an item of inventory during 1975:

Date	Type of Activity	Number of Units	Unit Purchase Price
1-1	Beginning Inventory		
	Purchased October 16, 1974	50	$1.30
	Purchased December 8, 1974	100	1.25
1-15	Purchase	50	1.20
2-16	Purchase	100	1.15
3-1	Sale	150	
4-15	Purchase	50	1.10
5-15	Sale	40	
6-17	Sale	60	
7-16	Purchase	200	1.05
8-17	Purchase	150	1.00
9-20	Sale	170	

Calculate the cost of each sale and the value of the ending inventory using FIFO, average, and LIFO. Compare results. How do these results differ from those in 5-9? Why?

Problem 5-11

Calculate the cost of sales under the following situations:

Beginning Inventory	Purchases during the Period	Ending Inventory
$ 6,982	$ 14,436	$ 10,839
53,576	25,389	50,238
117,469	1,496,325	562,874
98,367	341,372	54,119
17,369	52,175	18,117

Problem 5-12

The inventory on January 1, 1974, of the DEF Company was $98,462. The following transactions took place during the year:

1. Sales amounted to $1,964,321. (The DEF Company does not maintain a perpetual inventory; therefore, no cost of sales were available.)

2. Goods were purchased costing $1,096,420.

3. The following expenses were paid:

   a.) Selling Expenses $319,469
   b.) Administrative Expenses   214,379

4. Depreciation of $182,344 was incurred.
5. Bad Debts expense is expected to equal 1/2 of 1 per cent Sales.

6. Income taxes are 50 per cent of the profits before taxes.

7. The inventory on December 31, 1974, was $103,496.

Required:

Prepare an income statement for the DEF Company for 1974.

Problem 5-13

Following is certain financial data for the GHI Company:

	1970	1971	1972	1973	1974
		($000)			
Inventory 1/1					
FIFO	$ 10,000	$ 12,000	$ 15,000	$ 20,000	$ 28,000
LIFO	10,000	10,000	11,000	14,000	16,000
Purchases	40,000	42,000	46,000	50,000	55,000
Operating Costs	60,000	65,000	70,000	72,000	75,000
Sales	110,000	120,000	125,000	130,000	135,000

The inventories on December 31, 1974 were:

            FIFO $30,000
            LIFO $16,000

The tax rate is 50 per cent of the net profit before taxes.

Required:

1. Calculate the excess amount of tax that would be paid using FIFO instead of LIFO.

2. What balance sheet accounts would be different using LIFO instead of FIFO and by how much?

Problem 5-14

Inventory Values

Item No.	Cost	Replacement Cost	Net Realizable Value	Net Realizable Value Minus Normal Margin
101	$100	$101	$110	$ 99
102	50	48	52	49
103	10	8	9	7
104	20	23	25	20
105	25	20	27	22
106	5.00	5.50	6.00	5.25
107	1.00	.90	.80	.70
108	.50	.40	.30	.25
109	.10	.07	.11	.09
110	.0270	.0250	.0300	.0290

Required:

For each of the above items, determine the lower of cost or market.

Problem 5-15

1. Calculate the present value of $100 under the following conditions:

Length of Time Until Paid	Interest Rate
4 years	6%
5 years	10
10 years	4
15 years	15
20 years	20
25 years	2

2. You are told that the present value of $1,000 to be paid in 20 years is $37. What interest rate is assumed? What interest rate would be assumed if the present value were $312? $104?

3. You are told that money is worth 6 per cent and that the present value of $1,000 is $747. What time period is assumed? What time period would be assumed if the present value were $592? $394?

Problem 5-16

Calculate the even annual payments necessary to liquidate a debt under the following conditions:[a]

Amount of Debt	Time Period	Interest Rate
$ 100,000	10 years	10%
500,000	4 years	4
1,500,000	8 years	8
300,000	6 years	15
50,000	10 years	15
120,000	12 years	12

[a]In order to calculate the amount of even annual payments, go to Table A-2 and look up the present value factor for the time period and interest rate involved. This is divided by the principal to be repaid. For example, in (a) the first condition above, the PV factor for 10 per cent for 10 years is 6.145. Consequently, the amount of even payments required to liquidate a debt of $100,000 in 10 years at an interest rate of 10 per cent is 100,000 ÷ 6.145, or $16,273.

Problem 5-17

The Delta Company sold a piece of land to the Gamma Company for $150,000 on January 1, 1974. This land had cost the Delta Company $100,000. The Gamma Company gave a noninterest-bearing note with a face amount of $150,000. This note was to be paid off in five equal annual installments, beginning January 1, 1975.

Required:

1. Record all the journal entries that would be entered on the books of the Delta Corporation:
   (a) Using the accounting rules in effect before 1971.
   (b) Using the accounting rules in effect after 1971, assuming:
      (1) an implicit interest rate of 10 per cent; and
      (2) a cash value of land equal to $119,800.
2. Record the journal entries on the Gamma Company books using the same assumption as in Question 1 above.
3. Record the journal entries for Question 1 above, assuming that the note receivable carried an interest rate of 4 per cent and that a "fair market" rate was 10 per cent.

Problem 5-18

A new business was started with an investment of $15. Part of the cash was used to buy a keg of nails for $12. At this point (January 1) the balance sheet was as follows:

Balance Sheet at January 1

Cash	$ 3		$
Inventory	12	Capital	15
	$15		$15

The keg was sold for $17 and another keg was purchased on the last day of the year for $14.

Required:

1. Prepare income statements for the year under LIFO, FIFO, and average cost assumptions. You may ignore taxes.

2. Prepare balance sheets as of December 31 for each of the three income statements in Question 1.

3. Assuming that you want to maintain the business as a "going concern" but that you want to spend *all* the income, how much of a dividend could be paid for the year?

Non-Current Assets

Logic or good sense?

...the whole outline of the law, as it stands today, is the resultant of a conflict between logic and good sense—the one striving to carry fictions out to consistent results, the other restraining and at last overcoming that effort when the results become too manifestly unjust.

...the logical method and form flatter that longing for certainty and for repose which is in every human mind. But certainty is illusion, and repose is not the destiny of man.

Oliver Wendell Holmes

6

The purpose of this chapter is to describe the accounting treatment of the most common types of non-current assets. Because of their relative importance, however, most of the chapter is devoted to property, plant, and equipment.

PROPERTY, PLANT, AND EQUIPMENT

As stated earlier, so-called "property" assets consist of land and long-lived physical goods that are purchased for use by a company in carrying out its business. There are two principal problems in accounting for such assets. The first is to determine the gross amount at which a property asset should be recorded on the books; the second is to determine how this amount should be written off over the life of the asset. In this part of the chapter we will describe the accounting principles and techniques for solving these two problems. In addition, we will consider some of the problems resulting from changes in price levels.

VALUATION

The general principle is that property assets are recorded on the books of account at their cost of acquisition. There are two problems that arise in applying this principle. The first is to define what constitutes the cost of acquisition. The second is to decide to what extent expenditures on property assets, made subsequent to their acquisition, should be added to the original cost.

Cost of Acquisition

The cost of acquisition includes the purchase price, the delivery costs, and the installation costs. The general principle is that all costs incurred up to the point that the asset is ready for normal use should be capitalized.[1] For the most part, few problems arise in applying this principle; however, following are some special points concerning its application.

Cash Value of Assets. The purchase price of a property asset is the cash amount that it would cost to acquire it. There are two common situations, however, that may obscure the cash price: (1) when payment is deferred, and (2) when a trade-in is involved in the acquisition. Each is discussed below:

Deferred Payment. If payment is not required at the time of acqusition, and no interest (or interest at less than the normal market rate for such a transaction) is charged on the outstanding balance, the purchase price includes an implicit interest charge. As described in Chapter 5, the cost of the asset and the related liability are less than the listed purchase price. The implicit interest charge should be separated from the cost of the property asset. For example, assume that a company purchased a building for $100,000, to be paid in five annual installments of $20,000 each. Assume, also, that if the building had been purchased for cash, it would have cost only $85,000. For accounting purposes, the cost of the building is $85,000. The $15,000 represents the interest charges for extending the payment over 5 years. Even if the cash price for the building were not known, it would be possible to estimate it by subtracting the interest that would normally be charged on the outstanding balance over the period. Clearly, discretion should be used in applying this principle. If the time period is relatively short, it may be ignored. Notice that this principle applies only to the purchase of a completed asset. For some property assets (e.g. buildings), the interest charged during construction is capitalized as a necessary costs of constructing an asset.

Trade-In. If a new asset is partially paid for by trading-in an old asset, the cost of the new asset is the price that would have been paid if it had been purchased entirely for cash. Looking at it another way, the value of the trade-in reflected on the accounting records should be the cash value of the asset traded. For example, a company purchases a new truck with a list price of $5,000. An allowance of $2,000 is given for a used truck that is being traded-in. If the company could have purchased the new truck for $4,000 cash, the truck should be recorded on the books at $4,000. The cash value of the trade-in was $1,000; therefore, an overallowance of $1,000 has been given on the trade-in. (Otherwise, why would the cash price have been $1,000 less than the price with the trade-in?) In applying this rule, you would, of course, be concerned only with cases in which the difference between the cash value and the trade-in allowance is material. In many types of business, it is not the custom to provide overallowances on trade-ins. In these cases, the list price can be accepted as the cost. In other businesses (e.g., automobiles and trucks), it is usual to give overallowances and, often, the list price is the price from which negotiations *start*. In these instances, it is necessary to look beyond the list price to see how much is really being paid for the asset. This is the amount that should be capitalized.

---

[1] The term "capitalization" means to record an expenditure as an asset. Thus, all necessary expenditures associated with a property asset up to the time it is ready for normal use should be included in the gross book value of the asset.

Valuations of Land and Land Improvements. When land is purchased, the cost of bringing the land to the point where it can be used is capitalized. For example, the cost of removing existing structures would be included in the cost of the land. If the change is permanent (e.g., demolishing existing buildings), the cost is added to the price paid for the land. If the change is subject to physical deterioration (e.g., water mains or landscaping), the cost is included in an account called land improvements. The reason for segregating these two is that the land is not depreciated but land improvements are. In other words, all the money spent on preparing the land for use is divided into two parts: those improvements that are permanent and those improvement that will deteriorate over time. The former is added to the purchase price of the land; the latter is debited to the land improvements account.

Costs Subsequent to Acquisition

Usually, some expenditures on property assets are made during the time they are being used. Most of these expenditures represent maintenance or repairs and are treated as operating expenses. When extensive maintenance work is undertaken, the cost of this work should be capitalized in some instances. The general rule is that part of the maintenance costs should be capitalized if:

1. The asset is improved over its original capabilities; or

2. The original life of the asset is extended.

An example of the first would be maintenance work that increased the capacity of a machine beyond its original capabilities. The cost of increasing the capacity would be capitalized by adding it to the original cost of the equipment. The portion of the cost that was incurred to maintain the machine at its present capacity would be expensed.

An example of the second would be a major overhaul that extends, to 15 years, the life of an asset that normally would be scrapped in 10 years. In this case, it is usual to recognize the extended life by decreasing the accumulated depreciation account for the amount spend to extend the life.

It is often quite difficult to separate maintenance expenditure into the portion that should be capitalized and the portion that should be expensed. In fact, it is sometimes even difficult to tell whether the equipment has been improved or the life extended. Consequently, many companies set arbitrary rules for making these decisions. For example, one company capitalizes maintenance projects that amount to 50 per cent or more of the original cost of the equipment that is being maintained. Anything less than 50 per cent is expensed. The decision on how much to capitalize is largely one for the accountant and engineer and need not be of great concern to the manager. As long as maintenance expenditures are capitalized with a reasonable degree of common sense and consistency, they present no important management problems.

Notice that expensing a maintenance expenditure rather than capitalizing it results in an immediate reduction in profits. If it is capitalized, the expenditure will be expensed over the remaining life of the asset. Consequently, most companies expense those expenditures if there is a reasonable doubt about whether the asset has been improved or the life extended. In fact, many companies arbitrarily expense all maintenance costs, although this practice is theoretically incorrect.

DEPRECIATION

As explained earlier, property assets are written off over their useful life to match costs with the revenues they produce. Since property assets are used up over several accounting periods, we try to allocate the cost of these assets to the periods that benefited from their use. In order to do this we need to know, in addition to the cost of the asset: (1) its useful life, and (2) its salvage value, if any. Furthermore, we must decide on a method for allocating the cost minus the salvage value to the appropriate periods. Determining the life and the salvage value of an asset involves largely technical considerations and need not concern us here except for one thing. The life of an asset, for depreciation purposes, is not necessarily its physical life; it is the length of time the company expects to keep it. An asset may be scrapped before it is worn out for several reasons. For example, a better piece of equipment may be developed, or the product that a piece of equipment produced may be discontinued.

The accounting problem is to decide on a method for writing off the depreciable value (cost less salvage value). Before considering this problem, however, let us consider the accounting technique for recording these write offs.

Accumulated Depreciation

So far in this book, we have usually subtracted depreciation directly from the property asset account. For example, if the monthly depreciation of machinery and equipment were $10,000, we have made the following entry:

Depreciation Expense—Machinery and Equipment	10,000	
Machinery and Equipment		10,000

In nearly all accounting systems, however, there are two accounts in the general ledger for each property asset classification: an account in which the cost of the assets is recorded and an account in which the depreciation is accumulated. For example, there would be two accounts for machinery and equipment: one called machinery and equipment, the other called accumulated depreciation—machinery and equipment.[2] Transactions reflecting the purchase, sale, or capitalized maintenance of machinery and equipment are entered in the machinery and equipment account. The balance in the account is the cost (gross book value) of the machinery and equipment being used by the company. The balance in accumulated depreciation account represents the accumulated depreciation that has been charged off against the machinery and equipment included in the machinery and equipment account.

---

[2] Another title for the accumulated depreciated account is reserve for depreciation. This means exactly the same as accumulated depreciation. The word "reserve," however, is misleading to the layman. Many think that it represents a cash reserve to replace the asset. Consequently, this term is used less frequently now than in the past.

One of the reasons for using two accounts is that information on both the gross book value and the accumulated depreciation is often shown on the balance sheet. Consider, for example, two firms, each of which lists net property assets of $2,000,000. Suppose that the first firm has property assets with a gross cost of $50,000,000 and accumulated depreciation of $48,000,000. The second firm has property assets with a gross cost of $2,500,000 and accumulated depreciation of $500,000. Clearly, the two firms are not comparable. Showing gross cost and accumulated depreciation separately allows the reader of financial statements to see how much of the gross investment in property assets has been written off.

There are other reasons for separating the gross book value and the accumulated depreciation but these involve record-keeping expediency and need not concern you here.

Examples. Following are some examples of transactions involving property asset and accumulated depreciation accounts.

1. *Acquisition of an Asset* Machinery and equipment, costing $15,000, and delivery equipment, costing 10,000, was purchased on January 1, 1974.

January 1

Machinery and Equipment	15,000	
Cash		15,000
Delivery Equipment	10,000	
Cash		10,000

Notice that this is exactly the same journal entry that we have made previously in the book.

2. *Depreciating the Property Assets* The machinery and equipment purchased above is estimated to have 10-year life; the delivery equipment is estimated to have a 5-year life. Neither asset will have any salvage value. The entries on December 31, 1974, would be as follows:

December 31

Depreciation Expense—Machinery and Equipment	1,500	
Accumulated Depreciation—Machinery and Equipment		1,500
Depreciation Expense—Delivery Equipment	2,000	
Accumulated Depreciation—Delivery Equipment		2,000

3. *Disposal of Property Assets* A machine with an original cost of $5,000 and accumulated depreciation of 4,000 was scrapped:

Accumulated Depreciation—Machinery and Equipment	4,000	
Loss on Disposal of Property Assets	1,000	
Machinery and Equipment		5,000

4. *Sale of Property Assets* Assume that the facts are the same as in (3), above, except that the machine was sold for $2,000. The entry would be:

Cash	2,000	
Accumulated Depreciation—Machinery and Equipment	4,000	

| Machinery and Equipment | $5,000 | |
| Gain on Disposal of Property Assets | 1,000 | |

5. *Trade-In of a Property Asset*   Assume that the facts are the same as in 3, above, except that the machine was traded in on a new machine that cost $10,000. A trade-in allowance of $2,000 was given on the old machine and this was the amount that the old machine could have been sold for on the open market. The entry is:

Machinery and Equipment[a]	$10,000	
Accumulated Depreciation—Machinery and Equipment[b]	4,000	
Cash[c]		$8,000
Machinery and Equipment[b]		5,000
Gain on Disposal of Property Assets		1,000

[a]This records the new machine on the books.
[b]This removes the old equipment and related accumulated depreciation from the books.
[c]This is the difference between the cost of the new machine and trade-in allowance.

Methods of Depreciation

The purpose of this part of the chapter is to describe the most common methods for depreciating property assets.

Straight-Line.   So far in this book, we have been using straight-line depreciation. Straight-line depreciation is calculated as follows:

The amount of straight-line depreciation for any period is equal to the cost minus the salvage value divided by the number of periods in the life of the asset.

In short, the same depreciation amount is assigned to each period. The method is called straight-line because the asset value is reduced evenly (or in a straight line) over its life.

For example, an asset costs $30,000 and has an estimated life of 10 years. At the end of 10 years, its salvage value is estimated to be $6,000. The calculation of depreciation is as follows:

$$\text{Annual Depreciation} = \frac{(30,000 - 6,000)}{10} = \frac{24,000}{10} = \$2,400$$

$$\text{Monthly Depreciation} = \frac{(30,000 - 6,000)}{240} = \$200$$

or

$$\text{Monthly Depreciation} = \frac{\text{Annual Depreciation}}{12} = \frac{2,400}{12} = \$200$$

The principal advantages of the straight-line method of depreciation are (1) it is simple, and (2) costs are distributed evenly over the life of the assets. However, according to the proponents of accelerated depreciation (described below), the second advantage really is a disadvantage.

Accelerated Depreciation. Accelerated depreciation results in writing off a greater portion of the cost of an asset in the early years than straight-line depreciation does. Before World War II, straight-line depreciation was used almost universally. After the end of World War II, a growing number of companies began to use some form of accelerated depreciation. In 1954, the Internal Revenue Service authorized certain types of accelerated depreciation techniques for income tax purposes. Consequently, most companies now use accelerated depreciation for tax purposes because it results in lower taxes. Although a company is not required to use the same method of depreciation for both accounting and tax purposes (as in LIFO), many companies do so. As a result, accelerated depreciation is used by many businesses for accounting purposes.

There are three main advantages cited for accelerated depreciation:

1. As assets become older, the cost of maintenance becomes greater. By taking a higher depreciation in the early years and reducing the amount as the asset becomes older, the total cost of maintenance and depreciation will tend to even out.[3]

2. It is becoming increasingly difficult to predict the life of an asset because of technological innovations. Accelerated depreciation will result in more depreciation being taken during the early life when uncertainty is less. If the asset should become obsolete earlier than expected, a greater proportion of its costs will already have been written off.

3. In some instances (for example, a new product introduction) prices will be higher in the earlier years. If the equipment required to produce this product is depreciated more in the earlier years, it will help to level out profits.

Perhaps a more important reason for adopting accelerated depreciation is that it will result in higher immediate depreciation costs. Depreciation based on acquisition cost will usually be less than depreciation based on replacement cost because the original acquisition cost will normally be less than the replacement cost. If one believes that depreciation should be measured in terms of what it will cost to replace the facilities being used, accelerated depreciation is preferable to straight-line in the early years of an asset's life and is always preferable to straight-line for growing businesses. Accelerated depreciation is not a substitute for replacement depreciation, however, because over the life of the asset only the total cost (less salvage value) will be taken as depreciation, just as with the straight-line method.

Whatever the reasons, accelerated depreciation is now used almost exclusively for tax purposes and also by a large number of firms for accounting purposes. Following is a description of the two most commonly used methods of accelerated depreciation: declining balance and sum-of-the-year's digits.

In the *declining balance* method, depreciation is calculated by taking a constant percentage of the undepreciated value (net book value). Thus, the amount of depreciation will decline each year. The percentage that is usually used is twice the

---

[3] Although this argument sounds logical, the studies that we have seen on actual manufacturing facilities do not bear out this conclusion. Maintenance does not necessarily increase with age, particularly if a well-designed program of preventive maintenance is in effect.

straight-line rate. (This is the rate allowed for tax purposes for new assets.) This rate will result in writing off about one-half of the cost of the asset during the first third of its life and about two-thirds of its cost during the first half of its life. Take, for example, an asset that costs $10,000 and has an expected life of 10 years, with no salvage value. Declining balance depreciation is calculated by taking annually 20 per cent (twice the straight-line rate of 10 per cent) of the undepreciated value of the asset, as follows:

Year	Net Book Value at Beginning of Year	Depreciation Taken during Year	Net Book Value at End of Year
1	$10,000	$2,000	$8,000
2	8,000	1,600	6,400
3	6,400	1,280	5,120
4	5,120	1,024	4,096
5	4,096	819	3,277
6	3,277	655	2,622
7	2,622	524	2,098
8	2,098	420	1,678
9	1,678	336	1,342
10	1,342	268	1,074

Notice that although one-half of the value was written off in the first 3 years, there still remained a net book value of $1,074 at the end of 10 years. This is because the depreciation declines sharply in the final years. In fact, it is mathematically impossible to ever reach a zero net book value using this method because each year the expense is 20 per cent of the remaining value, leaving 80 per cent undepreciated. If, however, we were to use a rate high enough to make the net book value low at the end of 10 years, it would result in taking higher depreciation in the early years than is allowed for tax purposes. Consequently, companies that use declining balance depreciation normally change to straight-line at the point at which the straight-line depreciation will yield a higher amount.[4] (You may change to straight-line at any time during the period for tax purposes.) If the company had changed to straight-line depreciation at the end of 5 years, the depreciation schedule would be as follows:

Year	Net Book Value at Beginning of Year	Depreciation Taken during Year	Net Book Value at End of Year
1	$10,000	$2,000	$8,000
2	8,000	1,600	6,400
3	6,400	1,280	5,120
4	5,120	1,024	4,096
5	4,096	819	3,277
6	3,277	655	2,622
7	2,622	655	1,967
8	1,697	655	1,312
9	1,312	655	657
10	657	657	

[4] Notice that the straight-line method is applied to the undepreciated amount of the fixed assets, *not* to its original cost.

If the salvage value of a piece of equipment was expected to be about 10 per cent of its original cost, the declining balance method, using double the straight-line rate, would depreciate the asset down to its salvage value.

The *sum-of-the-year's* digits method is as follows:

1. Calculate the total of an arithmatic series that starts with 1 and has an increment of 1 up to the life of the asset. For example, if the asset had a 5-year life, the sum-of-the-year's digits would be $1 + 2 + 3 + 4 + 5$, or 15. The formula for calculating the sum-of-the-year's digits is:

$$S = \frac{n}{2}(1 + n)$$

where

s = the sum-of-the-year's digits
and
n = the life of the asset in years

2. For each year, calculate a fraction, as follows: the numerator is the remaining life of the asset at the beginning of the year. The denominator is the sum-of-the-year's digits. In the example above, the fractions for the various years would be as follows:

Year	Fraction
1	5/15
2	4/15
3	3/15
4	2/15
5	1/15

3. The depreciation for each year is the cost of the asset (minus salvage value, if any) multiplied by the fraction for that year.

In the example given previously for declining balance, the calculations are as follows:

Year	Fraction[a]	Amount	Net Book Value at End of Year
1	10/55	$1818	$8,182
2	9/55	1636	6,546
3	8/55	1455	5,091
4	7/55	1273	3,818
5	6/55	1091	2,727
6	5/55	909	1,818
7	4/55	727	1,091
8	3/55	545	546
9	2/55	364	182
10	1/55	182	0

[a]$S = 10(10 + 1) = 5 \times 11 = 55$

A comparison of straight-line, declining balance, and sum-of-the-year's digits is as follows:

	Straight-Line		Declining Balance[a]		Sum-of-the-Year's Digits	
Year	Amount of Depreciation	Year-End Balance	Amount of Depreciation	Year-End Balance	Amount of Depreciation	Year-End Balance
1	$1,000	$9,000	$2,000	$8,000	$1,818	$8,182
2	1,000	8,000	1,600	6,400	1,636	6,546
3	1,000	7,000	1,280	5,120	1,455	5,091
4	1,000	6,000	1,024	4,096	1,273	3,818
5	1,000	5,000	819	3,277	1,091	2,727
6	1,000	4,000	655	2,622	909	1,818
7	1,000	3,000	655	1,967	727	1,091
8	1,000	2,000	655	1;312	545	546
9	1,000	1,000	655	675	364	182
10	1,000	0	657	0	182	0

[a]Using straight-line for the last 5 years.

Units of Production Method.   There are several methods of depreciation based on the extent to which an asset is used. For example, an airplane engine might be depreciated on the basis of the number of hours actually used, or a machine may be depreciated on the basis of the number of units produced. To calculate the unit depreciation, the lifetime usage of the equipment is estimated and then divided into the cost minus salvage value. This gives a cost per unit. Each accounting period, this cost per unit is multiplied by the actual usage. For example, suppose that a machine was purchased for $10,000. It was estimated that the lifetime output for this machine was 10,000,000 units. The cost per unit is, therefore, $\frac{\$10,000}{10,000,000}$, or $.001. If, in 1975, the actual output of the machine was 1,500,000 units, the depreciation charged would be $1,500.

This method is useful if the life of an asset is dependent principally on the extent to which it is used. If the life of a piece of equipment is determined largely by the passage of time, the use of this method could provide management with misleading information. Depreciation methods based on the amount of usage tend to make depreciation expense variable with the amount of production. If the depreciation is really variable (this would be true when the amount of use determined the life of the equipment), this method provides relevant information. If, however, the life of a property asset is determined by the passage of time, treating depreciation as a variable cost[5] could be misleading.

Management Implications of Methods of Depreciation

The acquisition of a property asset is a discrete event that must be recorded on the books of account when it occurs. The accounting principles applicable to the recording of this purchase are reasonably clear and well established so there is little room for differences with respect to the amount to be capitalized and the timing of

---

[5] A variable cost is one that varies directly and proportionately with production.

the transaction. Estimates of the salvage value and economic life of a property asset require technical judgement. It is only through the method of depreciation that the manager or the accountant can effect the timing of profits.[6] There is considerable latitude in regard to the depreciation method that a company can employ. Different companies can and do use different methods for identical assets. The question, therefore, is which method should be used? The method of depreciation that is used will affect the reported earnings of a company. Since generally accepted accounting principles allow the use of different methods, the decision about which depreciation method to use becomes a managerial decision rather than an accounting decision. The question is, which method best implements management's strategy?

First, we wish to make it clear that in this part of the chapter we are considering the depreciation method to be used for accounting purposes, *not* for tax purposes. For tax purposes, a company would normally use the method that results in the lowest tax. Since there is no requirement for consistency between tax depreciation and accounting depreciation, the depreciation method to be used for accounting purposes is a separate issue.

The alternative facing most managers is straight-line versus some form of accelerated depreciation. If older assets are subject to higher maintenance costs or if revenues decline in the later years of the life of an asset, accelerated depreciation would tend to smooth the stream of earnings. If, however, there was no significant change in costs and revenues as assets became older, earnings would be smoothed through the use of straight-line depreciation.

Regardless of the pattern of maintenance costs or revenues, the net effect of adopting accelerated depreciation will always be to reduce income and net book value below the level that would have existed had straightline depreciation been used. This reduction will be permanent as long as a company does not curtail its investment in property assets. Furthermore, the accumulated difference between accelerated and straight-line depreciation will continue to increase as long as the company continues to expand its property assets. (This point is demonstrated in Chapter 9. For now, simply accept this statement.) This means that the decision whether to use straight-line or accelerated depreciation often boils down to the degree of conservatism management wishes to reflect in the financial statements. It is our belief that this consideration is the dominant one in, for example, a company's decision to change from accelerated to straight-line depreciation. Management simply wants to increase reported earnings. For example, in the 1968 annual report of U.S. Steel Corporation the following statement was made concerning a change from accelerated depreciation to straight-line depreciation. (A change was also made in the method for handling the investment credit. The investment credit is explained in later chapters.)

U.S. Steel considered the procedures it previously followed in connection with depreciation and the investment credit preferable to other methods of reporting results of operations. However, to enhance the comparability of financial statements in the steel industry and to bring depreciation and investment credit accounting more in line with methods followed by U.S. business in general, U.S.

---

[6] It could be argued that managerial judgment can be applied to the estimated life of the property asset. If the probable life is uncertain, this judgement could be biased.

Steel, for financial reporting purposes, revised lives of certain properties and changed its method of recording depreciation and investment credit for the year 1968 to a straight-line basis and a flow-through basis, respectively. The effect of these changes was to increase reported income for the year 1968 by $94.0 million or $1.24 per share of common stock.

Annuity Depreciation

If used under the appropriate conditions, either straight-line or accelerated depreciation will help to smooth reported earnings. Neither, however, will smooth return on investment. In fact, both create distortions in return on investment. Take, for example, a property asset that costs $10,000 and is expected to earn a gross cash inflow of $3,000 a year for 5 years. If the cash flow is spread evenly throughout the period, the return on this investment is about 17.5 per cent over the 5 years. (This can be obtained from the present value tables in Chapter 5.) Let us look at how this return on investment will look, using either straight-line or sum-of-the-year's digits depreciation.

Return on Investment—Straight-line Depreciation

Year	Beginning of Year	Book Value End of Year	Average	Profit after Depreciation[a]	Rate of Return
1	$10,000	$8,000	$9,000	$1,000	11.1%
2	8,000	6,000	7,000	1,000	14.3
3	6,000	4,000	5,000	1,000	20.0
4	4,000	2,000	3,000	1,000	33.3
5	2,000	0	1,000	1,000	100.0
Average			$5,000	$1,000	20%

[a]Represents $3,000 gross cash inflow minus $2,000 depreciation. (For these examples, income taxes have been ignored.)

The rate of return increased from 11.1 per cent to 100 per cent and averaged 20 per cent.

Return on Investment—Sum-of-the-Year's Digits

Year	Beginning of Year	Investment End of Year	Average	Profit after Depreciation[a]	Rate of Return
1	$10,000	$6,667	$8,334	$ (333)	(4.0)%
2	6,667	4,000	5,333	333	6.2
3	4,000	2,000	3,000	1,000	33.3
4	2,000	667	1,333	1,667	125.1
5	667	0	334	2,333	698.5
Average			$3,667	$1,000	27.3%

[a]Year

	Gross Cash Inflow	Depreciation	Profit after Depreciation
1	$3,000	$ 3,333	(333)
2	3,000	2,667	333
3	3,000	2,000	1,000
4	3,000	1,333	1,667
5	3,000	667	2,333
Total	$15,000	$10,000	$5,000

As you can see, using the sum-of-the-year's digits depreciation, the return on investment goes from a loss of 4 percent to a profit of nearly 700 per cent, with an average of 27 per cent.

There are two problems with this situation:

1. The return on investment increases merely by the passage of time.

2. The average rate of return is higher than the rate of return calculated on the basis of financial tables. (This is the correct return.)

Both of these problems can be corrected by using annuity depreciation. Annuity depreciation is the reverse of accelerated depreciation. Under annuity depreciation, the depreciation is low in the early years when the investment is high and high in the later years when the investment is low. The return on investment is kept constant. For example:

TABLE A

Year	Beginning	End	Average	Profit after Depreciation	Return on Investment
1	$10,000	$8,630	$9,315	$1,630	17.5%
2	8,630	6,997	7,814	1,367	17.5
3	6,997	5,051	6,024	1,054	17.5
4	5,051	2,732	3,892	681	17.5
5	2,732	0	1,366	268	19.6[a]
Average			5,682	1,000	17.5

TABLE B

Year	Cash Flow	Depreciation	Profit[b]
1	$3,000	$1,370	$1,630
2	3,000	1,633	1,367
3	3,000	1,946	1,054
4	3,000	2,319	681
5	3,000	2,732	268

[a]Due to rounding.

[b]Profits are calculated first to yield 17.5 per cent. Then, depreciation is the difference between the cash flow and the profit. The formula to find the amount of profit is: profit = .1918 X the beginning balance minus 288. See if you can derive this formula.

As you can see, annuity depreciation not only maintains a constant return on investment, but also results in a financially correct rate of return. In fact, it can be argued that annuity depreciation is the correct financial method. A company invests a given amount of money in various assets. From these assets, the company receives a flow of cash. This cash flow includes both return *on* the investment and a return *of* the investment in exactly the same way that a bank receives payments on a loan or mortgage. In this situation, with each payment, the interest is calculated first and anything in excess of interest is used to reduce the outstanding amount of the loan. This, in effect, is what annuity depreciation does.

In spite of its theoretical consistency, no company to our knowledge uses it. There are several reasons for this.

1. Management tends to think of depreciation as a wearing out of assets. Straight-line or accelerated depreciation is more consistent with this concept.

2. Most managers are more concerned with smoothing earnings than the return on investment.

3. It is less conservative than traditional methods.

We believe that annuity depreciation will continue to be of little more than academic interest.

Unit and Composite Depreciation

There are two basic methods of applying depreciation rates. One method, called "unit" depreciation, is to calculate depreciation and to maintain a record of accumulated depreciation for each individual asset. So far, in the examples given in this book, we have been using unit depreciation. That is, we have been calculating the gross book value and the accumulated depreciation for each asset separately. When an asset is disposed of, we have had a gain or a loss, depending on whether the net book value is less than or greater than the disposal price.

Another method called "composite" or "group" depreciation, is to calculate depreciation by group of assets. The rationale behind composite depreciation is that the average life of a group of similar assets can be estimated more accurately than the life of any one of these assets. For example, assume that a company had 100 milling machines. Even though the average life of these machines is estimated to be 10 years, the life of any one machine might vary from 5 to 20 years. By treating the 100 milling machines as a group for depreciation purposes, it is possible to offset the loss from retiring the shorter-lived machines against the gain from retiring the longer-lived machines.

The unique feature of composite depreciation is that no gain or loss is taken on the disposition of individual assets. In the example above, no loss would be taken if a milling machine were scrapped after 5 years. It would be assumed that some other machine would last 15 years, so that this extra depreciation would offset the depreciation not taken on the machine that was scrapped after only 5 years.

Composite depreciation is generally applicable to companies that have large amounts of machinery and equipment. In these cases, equipment is constantly being disposed of and newer equipment purchased. If unit depreciation were used, there would be gains or losses from the disposal of equipment in each accounting period. Such gains or losses are really just adjustments to depreciation expense because either too much or too little depreciation was taken in the preceding periods. Furthermore, the gains and losses should offset over a period of time. Consequently, composite depreciation eliminates these temporary distortions from the income statements. If composite depreciation is used, it is necessary to review the property asset accounts regularly to be sure that the accumulated depreciation is in line with the estimated remaining life of the equipment. Also, when large dispositions are made (e.g., the disposal of an entire plant), it is usual to show the difference between the salvage value and the net book value as a gain or loss.

Examples. 1. A machine costing $10,000 was scrapped after 5 years. This machine was part of the group of machines that were being depreciated on the basis of a composite, straight-line rate of 10 per cent a year. The entry would be:

Accumulated Depreciation—Machinery and Equipment	10,000	
Machinery and Equipment		10,000

2. The above machine was *sold* for $1,000 at the end of 5 years. The entry would be:

Cash	1,000	
Accumulated Depreciation—Machinery and Equipment	9,000	
Machinery and Equipment		10,000

Even when the equipment is sold, no gain or loss is shown. The proceeds from the sale reduce the amount of accumulated depreciation that is debited. In other words, it is assumed that each piece of equipment has been depreciated down to its salvage value as of the date of disposal.

Depletion

Depletion is the using up of a "wasting" asset—e.g., a coal mine or a marble quarry. From an accounting point of view, depletion is handled like depreciation. That is to say, each accounting period there will be a debit to depletion expense and a credit to allowance for depletion. On the balance sheet, the allowance for depletion is subtracted from the asset account.

Depletion is usually taken on the basis of the number of units produced. The estimated number of units available, (e.g., tons of coal in a mine) is divided into the cost of the asset. Each accounting period, the amount of depletion is calculated by multiplying this amount by the number of units produced. Depletion is thus very similar to the units of production method used in depreciating property assets.

Leasehold Improvements

Sometimes a company will make improvements to leased property. Usually these improvements will legally revert to the owner of the property at the end of the lease. In these instances, it is necessary to write off leasehold improvements over the period of time the company expects to maintain its lease. Often this time period is easy to determine. If the lease has a number of years to run and there is no expectancy of renewal, the leasehold improvements would be written off over the remaining life of the lease. In some instances, however, the lease is renewable and there is reasonable expectancy of renewal. In this case, the leasehold improvements are usually written off over the remaining life of the lease plus one renewal.

For example, a company installs central air conditioning in a leased building for

$150,000. The lease has 5 years yet to run with the option of renewing the lease for an additional 10 years. The company expects to renew the lease at the end of 5 years. The accounting entries would be as follows:

On the date of installation:

Leasehold Improvements	150,000	
Cash		150,000

Each year thereafter:

Amortization of Leasehold Improvements	10,000	
Leasehold Improvement		10,000

Depreciation on Replacement Cost

In an inflationary economy, depreciation based on original cost is less than the cost of replacing the asset being depreciated. As we pointed out earlier, many accounting theorists do not believe that a trading profit has been earned until sales revenue has been reduced by the costs necessary to replace the item being sold. Consequently, many businessmen and accountants argue that depreciation should be based on replacement value rather than original cost.

Under any depreciation system, the allowance for depreciation does not reflect the amount of cash available for reinvestment. The availability of cash is reflected in the cash account. The accumulated depreciation account shows only the accumulated amount that has been charged against earnings. If depreciation is based on historical costs, however, it may be necessary to set aside some of the earnings in order to have sufficient funds to replace assets. If all earnings were paid out in dividends, a company would have to borrow money or sell new stock to finance its replacement of fixed assets. Most companies have systems of cash planning that provide, among other things, for replacing assets. These plans are based on a projection of the sources and uses of funds described in Chapter 3.

Support for depreciation based on replacement costs is based on the concept that, for an ongoing business, profit is equal to sales revenue minus the cost of replacing those assets that were used up in generating the sale. In this vein, there are two problems with basing depreciation on historical cost:

1. Product costs are understated, and
2. Profits are overstated.

The first problem can be overcome by adding an allowance for replacement costs through the cost accounting system. Since the internal costs are a matter of concern only to the company, the cost accounting system can provide whatever information management wants.[7] We can conclude, therefore, that this is not a valid argument for using replacement costs for financial statement purposes.

The second argument, however, does have some validity. The profit shown in the income statement may not really be available to stockholders, to the extent that the depreciation does not cover the cost of replacement. This may not be a great problem in most companies because few companies pay out all of their profits in

[7] A company using replacement cost internally will have to remove these costs from the inventory value for financial statements. This can be done quite simply, however.

dividends. Furthermore, stockholders are usually not able to insist on a given level of dividend payments. Management can simply plan to withhold enough reported profits to cover replacement costs. Stockholders or potential stockholders, however, may be misled into believing that a company is more profitable.

The real problem is caused by the income tax. With nearly a 50 per cent tax rate, a company must pay with after-tax dollars. The amount by which replacement costs exceed depreciation based on historical cost. Since it seems very unlikely that the tax law will be changed in the foreseeable future to allow depreciation on replacement costs, it appears that business will have to continue to live with this situation.

In summary, then, depreciation following traditional methods will not equal replacement costs and, if this difference is significant, management should take it into account in internal cost accounting and cash planning. The problems of price level accounting are discussed in detail in Chapter 13.

DEFERRED CHARGES

Deferred charges are expenses paid in advance. In general, there are two types of deferred charges. First, there are prepaid short-term costs, such as insurance or taxes. Traditionally, these are treated as current assets and usually called "prepaid expenses." The rationale for treating these costs as current assets is that they will save an expenditure of cash during the current year. Looked at another way, a company that pays its insurance in advance is in the same financial condition as an identical company that does not. The company that has paid its insurance in advance will have less cash on hand, but it will also have to pay out less cash in the coming year.

If the benefit from the prepaid expense covers a period longer than a year, it is treated as a non-current asset, usually called a "deferred charge."

INTANGIBLE ASSETS

Intangible assets are assets that are used in a business but which have no physical form, except perhaps a piece of paper attesting to their existence. Intangible assets are usually of two types. One type represents the right to use something of value, such as a patent, copyright, or franchise. The second type of intangible asset is goodwill. This results when one business, in acquiring all or part of another business, pays a price greater than the fair value of the net assets that are acquired. It is assumed that the payment in excess of fair value is for benefits that will result from such things as customer acceptance, an established location, or an effective organization. This is the goodwill that the original business has developed.

Intangible assets, like fixed assets, must be recorded on the books at *cost* and they must be written off over their expected useful life on a systematic basis. The useful life of many intangible assets is fairly easy to estimate. For example, a patent has a legal life of 17 years. Some intangible assets, such as goodwill, however, may have an indefinite life. Until November 1, 1970, goodwill could be maintained indefinitely on the books. Goodwill acquired after this date must be written off over a period not to exceed 40 years. (This is described in Chapter 12.)

Goodwill can appear on the financial statements only if it has been purchased.

Internally generated goodwill may not be capitalized. The same is true of patents. A patent may be capitalized only if it has been purchased. Only the cost of obtaining the patent may be capitalized if the invention is developed internally. The actual costs of developing the invention may not be included in the capitalized value of the patent.

QUESTIONS

1. What is the reason for capitalizing all the expenditures for a property asset up to the point that it is ready for normal use?

2. What is the logic in ignoring the trade-in value of an asset if this value is different from the cash disposal price?

3. What is the logic behind *adding* the cost of demolishing an existing building to the price paid for a piece of property?

4. Describe some circumstances in which the depreciable life would be less than the physical life.

5. What is the accumulated depreciation account? What are its purposes?

6. What is the difference between straight-line and accelerated depreciation? What are the advantages and disadvantages of each?

7. What type of assets might most logically be depreciated on a straight-line basis? On an accelerated basis?

8. Explain the logic behind composite depreciation.

9. Why do you think that accountants show property assets at their historical costs even where these are clearly different from their current value?

10. Explain the concept of goodwill. How would you decide the method and time period for writing it off? Why do you suppose internally generated goodwill may not be capitalized?

11. What is annuity depreciation? How do you set up a depreciation schedule based on this method? What are its advantages? What are its disadvantages?

12. Why would a manager want to show lower reported earnings by using accelerated depreciation?

PROBLEMS*

Problem 6-1

Make the general journal entries to record the following transactions.

1. A machine is purchased for $15,000 cash. The delivery costs were $300 and the installation costs were $200.

2. A machine is purchased for $15,000 cash. The delivery costs were $300 and the installation costs were $500. Of the $500, $300 were spent to replace a part that was inadvertently broken while the machine was being installed.

*Unless otherwise indicated, use the straight method of depreciation applied on a unit basis.

3. A machine that 7 years ago cost $10,000 is completely overhauled at a cost of $4,000. The original life of the machine was estimated to be 10 years. It is believed the machine will last 7 years from the date of overhaul. To repair the machine without adding to its life would have cost $2,000.

4. A building is purchased for $300,000, to be paid in three equal annual installments. The first installment is to be paid 1 year from the date of occupancy. The current bank rate for borrowing money is 6 per cent.

5. Land is purchased for $20,000. It costs $2,000 to remove a building from the plot, $1,000 to grade the land, and $6,000 for installing water mains and landscaping.

Problem 6-2

Make the journal entries to record the following acquisitions of machinery involving trade-ins. The acquisitions are all made for cash.

	a	b	c	d	e
List Price of New Machine	$10,000	$10,000	$10,000	$25,000	$20,000
Old Machine:					
Gross Book Value	8,000	8,000	8,000	12,000	15,000
Accumulated Depreciation	6,000	6,000	6,000	6,000	14,000
Trade-In:					
Amount Allowed from List Price	2,000	3,000	4,000	8,000	4,000
Fair Market Value of Old Machine	2,000	1,000	3,000	4,000	4,000

Problem 6-3

The following are some facts concerning the acquisition and disposition of certain machinery:

	a	b	c	d	e
Date of Acquisition	1/1/64	1/1/65	3/21/66	12/1/66	7/31/67
Date of Disposition	12/31/73	12/31/73	9/30/73	3/17/73	7/31/73
Original Cost	$10,000	$20,000	$30,000	$40,000	$50,000
Selling Price	$ 1,000	$ 2,000	$10,000	$10,000	$25,000
Estimated Life	10 years	10 years	10 years	10 years	10 years

No salvage was included in the depreciation schedule.

Required:

1. Make the journal entries to record the disposition of each of these property assets assuming:

   a. Straight-line depreciation
   b. Unit depreciation
   c. The company follows the policy of taking a full year's depreciation in the year that it acquires an asset and no depreciation in the year that it disposes of an asset.

2. How would your answers differ if company policy was to take a full year's

depreciation in the first year if the assets were acquired before July 1 and no depreciation if the asset were acquired on or after July 1? In the year of disposition, the company takes no depreciation if the asset were disposed of before July 1 and a full year's depreciation if the asset were disposed of on or after July 1.

3. How would your answers differ if the company's policy was to take depreciation on a monthly basis? Assets acquired or disposed of by the 15th of the month were considered to be acquired as of the 1st of that month. Assets acquired or disposed of after the 15th were considered to be acquired or disposed of as of the 1st of the following month.

Problem 6-4

How would your answer to 6-3 differ if composite depreciation had been used?

Problem 6-5

How would your answer to Question 6-3 (1) and (2) differ if the sum-of-the-year's digits depreciation had been used?

Problem 6-6

A fixed asset costing $400,000 was acquired on January 1, 1973. The asset has an estimated life of 8 years with no salvage value at the end of that time. Develop a depreciation schedule for this asset assuming:

1. Straight-line depreciation
2. Sum-of-the-year's digits depreciation
3. Declining balance depreciation using double the straight-line rates.

Problem 6-7

The Sanbo Company has the following depreciable fixed assets on its books on December 31, 1974.

Asset	Date Acquired	Estimated Life	Original Cost
A	1/1/60	20	$ 50,000
B	1/1/64	20	100,000
C	1/1/68	10	120,000
D	1/1/72	10	80,000
E	1/1/74	10	150,000

Required:

1. For the years 1974 and 1975, estimate the amount of depreciation expense: (a) using straight-line depreciation; (b) using the sum-of-the-year's digits depreciation. (Assume that there will be no salvage value.)

2. What would be the difference between the accounted income and the taxable income assuming that straight-line depreciation was used for accounting purposes and the sum-of-the-year's digits was used for tax purposes? When, if ever, would this difference be made up?

3. What would be the difference in income taxes between the two methods, assuming that the tax rate is 50 per cent of net income?

Problem 6-8

The Insta Corporation decided to defer 50 per cent of its research and development costs and write off these deferred costs equally over a 4-year period. In each case, the first write off of the deferred expenditure would be in the year following the expenditure. The policy went into effect on January 1, 1970. Research and development expenditures for the year 1970-1973 are as follows:

1970	$100,000	1972	$160,000
1971	120,000	1973	200,000

For tax purposes, of course, the Insta Company wrote off its research and development costs in the year in which they were incurred.

Required:

1. Calculate the difference between the taxable expense and the accounted expense for 1970 through 1973.

2. How much is the deferred research and development on December 31, 1973? Where will this account appear on the balance sheet?

3. In which year will the taxable expense be less than the accounted expense?

Problem 6-9

On December 31, 1973, the ABC Company acquired the DEF Company by purchasing all of its stock for $15,000,000 in cash and then retiring the stock. The DEF Company became a division of the ABC Company at that time. The books of the DEF Company showed the following account balances on the date of acquisition.

DEF COMPANY ($000)

Assets			
Cash	$ 490	Payables	$ 3,900
Receivables	1,760	Capital Stock	5,000
Inventories	2,490	Retained Earnings	1,650
Property Assets (net)	5,810	Total Equities	$10,550
Total Assets	$10,550		

An examination of the company's assets and liabilities revealed the following:

1. The inventories were valued on a LIFO basis. The current value of these inventories was $3,500,000.

2. The company held a patent that had a fair market value of $1,000,000. Since this patent was developed internally, it did not appear on the books as an asset.

3. The fair market value of the property assets were $7,000,000.

Required:

1. Make the journal entry to record the acquisition of the DEF Company by the ABC Company.

2. Where will goodwill appear on the books of the ABC Company?

3. What will happen to the goodwill in 1974 and subsequent years?

Problem 6-10

Property assets were acquired on the following dates:

Date	Cost ($000)
1/1/66	5,000
1/1/68	3,000
1/1/70	2,000
1/1/72	2,000
1/1/73	4,000

Straight-line depreciation over a 10-year life was used for all assets.

It has been estimated that on December 31, 1973, the price level of property assets had changed as follows:

	% Increase in the Price of Assets between the Year Indicated and 1973
1966	30%
1967	28
1968	26
1969	23
1970	18
1971	14
1972	08
1973	00

Required:

For 1973 calculate the depreciation based on historical costs and the depreciation based on replacement costs, using the table above to convert historical costs into replacement costs.

Problem 6-11

An asset is purchased on January 1, 1974, for $100,000 and is expected to have a life of 5 years. This asset is expected to produce a cash income before depreciation of $30,000 a year. Develop an annuity depreciation schedule that will result in a constant rate of return on investment during its 5-year life. (Hint: Find out from Schedule B in the Appendix to chapter 5 what rate of return will convert five equal payments of $30,000 into a present value of $100,000. Then, make the depreciation each year equal to this amount of interest on the outstanding balance. For purposes of this problem, assume the $30,000 is received at the end of each year.)

Problem 6-12

An asset is purchased on January 1, 1974, for $653,250 and is expected to have a life of 6 years. This asset is expected to produce a cash income before depreciation of $150,000 a year over its life. Develop an annuity depreciation schedule that will result in a constant rate of return on investment. (Assume that the cash income is received at the end of each year.)

Equities

7

This chapter discusses the right side of the balance sheet. The right side of the balance sheet discloses how a business is financed—i.e., the sources of the money that has been invested in the business. The general term for such sources is "equities." This term encompasses both borrowed funds (liabilities) and funds invested by owners (owners' equity). There are many different and complex ways to finance a business, and the type and nature of these financing arrangements are normally treated in finance courses. Nevertheless, an understanding of the accounting concepts of liabilities and ownership is necessary for an understanding of financial statements. In this chapter, we emphasize the accounting aspects of these financing sources, rather than how, why, and where they are used.

LIABILITIES

As we indicated in Chapter 1, liabilities generally represent monetary claims against a company. These claims can be actual debts, such as accounts payable, or they can be potential future claims, such as expected warranty payments on products for which the warranty period has not yet expired. Liabilities can be currently due, due in the near future, or not due for a period of years. On the balance sheet, the liabilities are separated into current and non-current. Each is discussed in this part of the chapter.

Current Liabilities

Current liabilities are liabilities that have arisen in the business as a result of its normal operating cycle. These include accounts payable for goods or services rendered and debts that arise from operations such as accrued salaries, taxes, and so forth. In addition, any debt that is due within a short period of time, usually 1 year, is also included in current liabilities. Current liabilities, therefore, are those that will normally be liquidated out of current assets. For practical purposes, current liabilities are those that are due within 1 year, although occasional exceptions occur when a liability with a maturity longer than 1 year is incurred as part of the operating cycle.

Non-current Liabilities

In general, non-current liabilities are liabilities that are not due until more than a year from the balance sheet date. Non-current liabilities are usually part of the long-run financial structure of the company. The more common types of non-current liabilities are described in this part of the chapter.

Term Loans. Term loans are loans, usually from banks, that are due within a period longer than 1 year. Term loans are often accompanied by agreements between the company and the loaning institution that limit company action. For example, working capital may have to be maintained at a given level or dividend payments may be restricted.

Mortgage Loans. A mortgage loan covers a debt secured by property. This means that if the company defaults on the loan, the mortgaged property may be taken by the lender and sold to satisfy the debt. A lender, holding a mortgage, therefore, has prior rights over other creditors to the specific property mortgaged. For example, Bank A loans $1,000,000 to Company X, and Company X secures the loan with a mortgage on its manufacturing plant. If Company X defaults on the loan, Bank A can foreclose and sell the manufacturing plant to discharge the debt. If Company X goes into bankruptcy, Bank A will have prior rights to the proceeds from the sale of the manufacturing plant. For accounting purposes, a mortgage loan is treated exactly like any other loan.

Bonds. The most common form of long-term debt financing is the bond. The advantage of the bond is that a large number of people or institutions can participate in the financing. Thus, no one person or institution has to provide the entire amount of a loan. When a company decides to issue bonds, it first determines the amount it wishes to borrow. This total amount is divided into a number of parts, called bonds, usually in multiples of $1,000. (Bonds, however, are always quoted on the securities exchanges as having a face value of $100.) These bonds are then sold to the public. Thus, a large number of people normally share in a given bond issue. The methods of sale and the legal documents that accompany such sales are properly in the area of finance and need not concern us here. It is enough to understand that as a result of this process, the company ends up with an amount of cash from the sale of the bonds. In exchange for this cash, the company assumes a legal obligation to pay a set interest rate (usually semi-annually) on the face value of the outstanding bonds and to retire (pay back) the bonds on a given date or series of given dates in the future.

Example 1 The company sells bonds with a face value of $1,000,000 for $1,000,000 on January 1, 1973. (When the amount of cash received is equal to the face value, the bonds are said to be issued "at par.") The bonds bear a 6 per cent annual interest rate and they are to be retired on January 1, 1983. The accounting entries to record the transactions are as follows:

(a)   On January 1, 1973
    Cash $1,000,000
    Bonds Payable $1,000,000

(b) On June 30 and December 31 of each year the bonds are outstanding:
    Interest Expense $ 30,000
    Cash $ 30,000

(c)   On January 1, 1983
    Bonds Payable $1,000,000
    Cash $1,000,000

Example 2 Assume the same facts as in Example 1 except that the bonds sold for only $864,000. A company may receive less than the face amount of the bonds when they are sold for two reasons. First, the investment banking firm that sells these bonds to the public incurs costs in making the sale. It also charges a fee for its services. Consequently, the company issuing the bonds will always receive less than the amount paid by the public. Second, the interest rate on the face of the bond (called the "coupon" rate) may be less than the going interest rate for comparable bonds at the time of sale. As a result, buyers would be unwilling to pay the face amount. For example, suppose that a bond, with an interest rate of 6 per cent, was offered for sale. Also, assume that the going rate for comparable bonds was 8 per cent at the time the bonds went on sale. Buyers would be unwilling to pay $1,000 for a bond that yielded only 6 per cent. Buyers would, however, be willing to pay a sufficiently lower price for the bonds so that the net return to the buyer over the 10 years would be 8 per cent. If the bond sold for $864, an investor would have to invest only $864. For this investment, he would receive $60 in interest per year plus $1,000 when the bond matured. Thus, the effective interest on his investment would be 8 per cent higher than 6 per cent. In this case, it would be 8 per cent. Stated another way, the present value of $60 per year for 10 years and $1,000 at the end of year 10 is $864. This is the way bonds are sold. The prices of bonds reflect the present value of the stream of payments the issuer agrees contractually to make, discounted at a rate of interest the purchaser considers to be fair given "money market" conditions and the perceived riskiness of the contract.

When a company receives less cash than the face value of the bonds, the difference is called "bond discount." Since the issuer receives only $864,000 but agrees to repay $1,000,000 after 10 years, it is clear that the cost of using the money over the 10 years is more than the $60,000 per year of interest paid in cash. In fact, over the 10 years, the additional cost of using the money is equal to $136,000 ($1,000,000–$864,000), which is the amount of the discount. The discount thus represents extra interest cost over the life of the bonds. It is the adjustment necessary to reflect the fact that although the bonds carry a 6 per cent coupon, the purchasers of the bonds require an 8 per cent rate of return. The discount arises because the rate of interest on the face of the bond is lower than the market rate at the date of issue. If the bond had carried the higher coupon rate of 8 per cent there would be no discount. Consequently, the discount represents implicit interest cost.

There are three methods of accounting for bond discount.

METHOD 1

(a)   **On January 1, 1973**
    Cash $864,000
    Bond Discount   136,000
      Bonds Payable $1,000,000

(b) On June 30 and December 31 of each year that the bonds are outstanding
    Interest Expense $ 30,000
      Cash $ 30,000
    Interest Expense   6,800
      Bond Discount   6,800

(c)   **On January 1, 1983**
    Bonds Payable $1,000,000
      Cash $1,000,000

This method is very common in practice. It considers the bond discount to be a prepaid expense that is written off over the life of the bonds using the straight-line method. Since no actual prepayment has been made, many accountants question the inclusion of bond discount among the assets of the firm.

An approach that is similar to Method 1 but avoids showing bond discount as an asset is the following:

METHOD 2

(a)   **On January 1, 1973**
    Cash $ 864,000
      Bonds Payable $ 864,000

(b) One June 30 and December 31 of each year that the bonds are outstanding
    Interest Expense $ 30,000
      Cash $ 30,000
    Interest Expense $ 6,800
      Bonds Payable $ 6,800

(c)   **On January 1, 1983**
    Bonds Payable $1,000,000
      Cash $1,000,000

This method is also commonly encountered in practice. It too uses a straight-line approach in charging off the bond discount over the life of the bonds, but it avoids the misleading inference that bond discount is in some sense an asset. The question raised by this method is the way the bonds payable liability is shown. The amount starts at $864,000 when the bonds are issued, which equals the amount of cash received. It rises to $1,000,000 at the date of maturity, which equals the amount of cash that must be paid out at that time. But what about the amounts that show in the interim ($870,800 after 6 months, $877,600 after 1 year, etc.)? They seem to have no particular significance at all.

This raises the very fundamental issue of what *should* show on a balance sheet for a liability. Generally accepted accounting principles define liabilities as economic obligations and state that such obligations should be reflected at the present value of the amounts to be expended in extinguishing the obligations. For current liabilities, discounting of amounts due in order to reflect present values is not deemed necessary since discounted amounts would not be materially different from the undiscounted sums. For long-term liabilities, however, GAAP requires that present values be used. What does this mean for the question of showing the bonds payable liability?

In answering this question, go back for a minute to Example 1 in which the bonds were issued at par. Notice that the bonds payable liability was $1,000,000 at the date of issue and remained $1,000,000 until the bonds matured. In that case, the amount of cash received and the amount due at maturity were both $1,000,000. Under GAAP as outlined above, however, neither of these factors (amount of cash received or amount due on maturity) explain why the liability is shown at $1,000,000. The reason $1,000,000 shows as the liability throughout the life of the bonds is that at any point in time prior to maturity the present value of the future payments the company has agreed contractually to make is $1,000,000. At the date of issue, the present value at 6 per cent of twenty semi-annual payments of $30,000 and a terminal payment of $1,000,000 after 10 years is $1,000,000. Six months later, the present value at 6 per cent of 19 semi-annual payments of $30,000 and a terminal payment of $1,000,000 after 9 1/2 years is $1,000,000. Nine years later, the present value at 6 per cent of one interest payment of $30,000 in 6 months and a principal payment of $1,000,000 at the same time is $1,000,000.

If you think $1,000,000 shows as the liability because it is the principal amount due at maturity, ask yourself why the contractual obligation for this payment would be shown but not the other contractual obligations (namely, the interest payments). The answer, of course, is that *all* future contractual obligations (both principal and interest) are shown *at their present value.*

This concept of a liability suggests a third method of accounting for bond discount. Specifically, it suggests a method such that the values that show in the balance sheet for bonds payable over the life of the bonds are consistent with the theoretical definition of a liability. Such a method is the following.

Method 3
On January 1, 1973

(a)

Cash	$ 864,000	
Bonds Payable		$ 864,000

(b)
On June 30, 1973

Interest Expense	$ 34,560	
Cash		$ 30,000
Bonds Payable		$ 4,560

On December 31, 1973

Interest Expense	$ 34,742	
Cash		$ 30,000
Bonds Payable		4,742

(c)
On January 1, 1983

Bonds Payable	$1,000,000	
Cash		$1,000,000

Interest expense for each 6-month period is equal to 4 per cent (one-half the effective annual rate) times the outstanding bond liability at the beginning of the period. The difference between the cash interest payment and the true interest cost is credited to the bond liability account. Under this method the bond liability at any point in time reflects the present value of all the future contractual payments (*principal and interest*) discounted at the effective interest rate on the bonds.

This method as applied over the full 10 years is shown in Figure 7-1 at the date of issue.

Method 3 differs from method 2 in that the bond discount is written off under a compound interest approach rather than a straight-line approach. This is the only conceptually sound method because it accurately reflects interest cost each period and also accurately states the bond liability at the present value of all future contractual payments, both interest and principal. Method 2 is only an approximation to method 3 and its sole justification is simplicity of computation. Method 1 is no longer considered good accounting although many firms still use it.

Figure 7-1

Time	Principal Payments	Cash Interest Payment	Amortization of Bond Discount	Bond Liability
January 1, 1973		$ —	$ —	$ 864,000
June 30, 1973		30,000	4,560	868,560
December 31, 1973		30,000	4,742	873,302
June 30, 1974		30,000	4,932	878,234
December 31, 1974		30,000	5,129	883,363
June 30, 1975		30,000	5,335	888,698
December 31, 1975		30,000	5,548	894,246
June 30, 1976		30,000	5,770	900,016
December 31, 1976		30,000	6,001	906,017
June 30, 1977		30,000	6,241	912,258
December 31, 1977		30,000	6,490	918,748
June 30, 1978		30,000	6,750	925,498
December 31, 1978		30,000	7,020	932,518
June 30, 1979		30,000	7,301	939,819
December 31, 1979		30,000	7,593	947,412
June 30, 1980		30,000	7,897	955,309
December 31, 1980		30,000	8,212	963,521
June 30, 1981		30,000	8,541	972,062
December 31, 1981		30,000	8,882	980,944
June 30, 1982		30,000	9,238	990,182
December 31, 1982		30,000	9,818[a]	1,000,000
January 1, 1983	-1,000,000	—	—	0
	$600,000		$136,000	

[a]Adjusted for rounding errors.

Most firms today use method 2, but it is important to understand why method 3 is the conceptually correct approach if one is to understand the problems related to liability valuation in financial statements. A bond liability should reflect the present value of *all* future contractual payments, both principal *and* interest. Method 3 preserves this relationship so that it is correct at all intermediate dates. (Method 2 is correct only at date of issue and date of maturity.)

Example 3. Assume the same facts as in Example 1 except that the bonds were sold for $1,164,000. The excess of proceeds over the face value is called "bond premium." The reason why a bond sells for a premium is that the coupon rate is higher than the market rate for comparable bonds. For example, suppose that the going market rate for a particular type of bond was 4 per cent. If a bond of this type were issued with a coupon interest rate of 6 per cent, buyers would be willing to pay more than the face amount of the bond. Specifically, they would be willing to pay $1,164 for a $1,000 bond because $1,164 represents the present value at 4 per cent a year of twenty semi-annual payments of $30 and a maturity payment of $1,000. The conceptually correct accounting entries for these bonds are as follows:

(a)
On January 1, 1973

Cash	$1,164,000	
Bonds Payable		$1,164,000

(b)
On June 30, 1973

Interest Expense	$ 23,280	
Bonds Payable	6,720	
Cash		$ 30,000

On December 31, 1973

Interest Expense	$ 23,146	
Bonds Payable	6,854	
Cash		$ 30,000

(c)
On January 1, 1983

Bonds Payable	$1,000,000	
Cash		$1,000,000

Interest expense for any 6-month period equals 2 per cent times the outstanding bond liability at the beginning of the period. The bond liability always reflects the present value of all future payments discounted at the effective annual rate of 4 per cent.

A summary of the entries over the 10-year live of the bonds is shown in Figure 7-2. Notice that for premium bonds, the effective cost of using the borrowed funds over the 10 years is less than the coupon rate of interest. Part of each so-called interest payment, therefore, is really a return of part of the borrowed capital. This is reflected in the net interest expense calculations.

Bond premium can also be treated in ways that parallel the first two methods we discussed for bond discount. Such methods are not conceptually sound.

Bond Accounting—Other Issues. If market rates of interest change subsequent to the issuance of the bonds, the interest expense calculations outlined above will not be affected. The effective rate of interest to the issuer on the borrowed funds is established at the date of issue and does not change thereafter unless the bonds are refinanced or retired before maturity.

If the bonds are extinguished before maturity, any unamortized bond discount or premium is written off at that time and any gain or loss from early extinguishment is taken into income in the year the bonds are retired.

Figure 7-2

Time	Principal Payments	Cash Interest Payments	Amortization of Bond Premium	Bond Liability
January 1, 1973	$+1,164,000	$ —	$ —	$1,164,000
June 30, 1973		30,000	6,720	1,157,280
December 31, 1973		30,000	6,854	1,150,426
June 30, 1974		30,000	6,991	1,143,435
December 31, 1974		30,000	7,131	1,136,304
June 30, 1975		30,000	7,274	1,129,030
December 31, 1975		30,000	7,419	1,121,611
June 30, 1976		30,000	7,568	1,114,043
December 31, 1976		30,000	7,719	1,106,324
June 30, 1977		30,000	7,874	1,098,450
December 31, 1977		30,000	8,031	1,090,419
June 30, 1978		30,000	8,192	1,082,227
December 31, 1978		30,000	8,355	1,073,872
June 30, 1979		30,000	8,523	1,065,349
December 31, 1979		30,000	8,693	1,056,656
June 30, 1980		30,000	8,867	1,047,789
December 31, 1980		30,000	9,046	1,038,743
June 30, 1981		30,000	9,225	1,029,518
December 31, 1981		30,000	9,410	1,020,108
June 30, 1982		30,000	9,598	1,010,510
December 31, 1982		30,000	10,510[a]	1,000,000
January 1, 1983	-1,000,000	—	—	0
Totals	$600,000		$164,000	

[a]Adjusted for rounding errors.

Convertible Debentures. Sometimes bonds are issued with a provision that they may be converted into stock at some future date. These are called "convertible debentures." (A debenture is just another name for an unsecured bond.) For example, a bond may be sold with the provision that, after 5 years, the bond can be converted into three shares of common stock for each $100 in face value. If, at some time after 5 years, the stock of the company is selling for higher than $33.33, the bonds would sell on the open market at a premium since they would be worth, at a minimum, the value of the common stock into which they are convertible. The bondholder might continue to hold the bonds rather than convert them if the bond coupon payment per $100 is greater than the dividend income from three shares of common stock. He may sell the bonds on the open market if he believes that he can earn a higher rate of return with the money elsewhere. Or he may convert the bonds into common stock. If he converts the bonds into stock, the accounting entry is:

Bonds Payable	$100	
Capital Stock		$100*

*This assumes that the bonds are being carried on the books at their par value. If there was any discount or premium, this would be written off at this time. The other account affected would be paid-in capital.

Market Value of Bonds. Corporate bonds can have a market value considerably different from their carrying value on the books of the corporation. This could be caused by changes in interest rates since the date of issue or by changes in the investment status of the bonds. (For example, if a company runs into financial difficulty, the market price of its outstanding bonds usually drops. The greater the financial difficulty, the greater tends to be the drop in prices.) However, bonds are carried on the balance sheet at face value adjusted for unamortized discount or premium, regardless of the current market price.

Other Types of Liabilities

In general, liabilities represent the amount of money that a business owes. This is not true of all liabilities, however. There are types of liabilities that do not fit this definition very well. On one hand, there are liabilities that may never require payment. On the other hand, there may be financial obligations that a company does not reflect on its balance sheet. The purpose of this part of the chapter is to describe some of the exceptions to the rule that liabilities represent the indebtedness of a company.

Liabilities That May Not Require Payment. Several types of liabilities are listed on the balance sheet that may never require payment. For example, some companies set up reserves to cover anticipated future losses. This occurs, for example, if a company decides to discontinue certain operations. In the year that management decides to discontinue these operations, the following entry is made:

Loss on Discontinuance of Certain Operations	XXX	
Allowance for Discontinuation of Certain Operations		XXX

The allowance for discontinuance of certain operations is included in the balance sheet as a liability. After this reserve is established, all the costs associated with the discontinued operations are charged against this account. The effect is to reduce income in the year the decision was made to discontinue the operations. If this entry had not been made, the loss would have been recognized in the period when the operations were actually being sold or scrapped. This situation is discussed in more detail in later chapters.

In addition to "reserves" or "allowances," there are two other types of liabilities commonly found on balance sheets that do not represent debts of the company. These are "deferred taxes" and "minority interests." Both of these also are described in detail in later chapters.

Obligations Not Included on the Balance Sheet. There are certain obligations or potential obligations that are not included in the balance sheet figures. A discussion of the three most common types follows.

Executory Contracts Executory contracts are agreements to perform a future service. The rights and obligations related to unperformed executory contracts are not recognized under generally accepted accounting principles. These rights and obligations are disclosed in separate schedules or notes to the financial statements if the omission of this information would tend to make the financial statements misleading.

Two of the most common types of executory contracts are leases and employment contracts. For example, assume that a company enters into an agreement to lease a building for 10 years at $10,000 a year. This will not appear as a liability until the lease payments are actually due. The rationale behind this is that there is no liability until the service has been rendered. If the lease payments are due in advance, the amount of advanced payment will appear as an asset, exactly like prepaid rent. The lease expense appearing on the income statement will be the amount applicable to the period covered by the income statement. Again, this is precisely like the treatment of rent. (Certain types of leases are treated differently and these are explained in the next part of this chapter.)

Another example of an executory contract is an agreement to pay a company's president $100,000 a year for 10 years. This amount is not reflected as a liability on the balance sheet. The rationale for this is similar to that for leases. The liability is not incurred until the service is rendered. The existence of an employment contract, therefore, is not reflected in the accounting records. A liability will be shown only for the salary earned but unpaid at the balance sheet date. As in leases, an employment contract is disclosed by a footnote if it is material.

Pension Liabilities There is a good deal of flexibility under present accounting rules regarding the treatment of a company's liability for pensions due to its employees. In many instances a liability exists, but this is disclosed in the financial statements only in a footnote, if at all. (Chapter 12 explains the accounting for pension costs.)

Contingent Liabilities Suppose that a company is being sued for $100,000 for breach of contract. The outcome of the suit is unknown for it has not yet come to trial. This is a contingent liability. Contingent liabilities are also disclosed in a footnote, where material. They do not normally appear in the liability section of the balance sheet.

Below is the liability side of the balance sheet of the Budd Company in 1971.

Liabilities and Shareholders' Equity

	December 31	
	1971	1970*
CURRENT LIABILITIES: Notes payable	$ 38,367,340	$ 80,148,000
Accounts payable	22,843,298	42,324,942
Accrued payroll, taxes, interest, etc.	30,688,458	25,869,470
Current portion of long-term debt	6,018,216	6,583,768
Income taxes	5,553,911	6,729,848
TOTAL CURRENT LIABILITIES	$103,471,223	$161,656,028

LONG-TERM LIABILITIES AND RESERVES:

Long-term debt	$125,827,931	$114,005,615
Deferred income taxes	8,642,755	3,495,352
Provision for discontinuance of certain operations	12,518,713	19,785,290
Provision for extended product warranties	880,548	1,113,602
Minority interest	3,788,457	3,381,254
TOTAL LONG-TERM LIABILITIES AND RESERVES	$151,658,404	$141,781,113

The following footnote accompanied the financial statements:

Contingencies In July 1971 the Federal Trade Commission issued a complaint against the company alleging that the acquisition of Gindy Mfg. Corporation and subsidiaries violated Section 7 of the Clayton Act. The complaint seeks the divestiture of the acquired companies if the alleged violation is established. The company has filed its answer to the complaint in which it denies that any violation of Section 7 of the Clayton Act has occurred. The outcome is not known at this time. Sales of Gindy accounted for less than 10% of consolidated sales in both 1971 and 1970.

Contingent Liabilities vs. Estimated Liabilities A *contingent* liability is one for which the existence of the liability is uncertain. An *estimated* liability is one for which the existence of the liability is certain but the amount is uncertain. An allowance for product warranties is an example of an estimated liability. We know that the firm is definitely liable for product defects that might occur in the future during the warranty period, but we must estimate the dollar impact of warranty claims. GAAP requires that such estimates be made so that balance sheets will reflect all known liabilities. Contingent liabilities may involve a very specific sum. For example, Company A co-signs a note payable of Company B for $1,000,000. If Company B defaults, Company A is liable for $1,000,000. The amount is known with certainty. However, such a situation would not normally be shown on a balance sheet because the liability itself is only a contingent one.

Leases

A lease is an agreement whereby the lessor agrees to allow the lessee to have physical possession and use of an asset owned by the lessor in return for a series of specified payments. Leases may range from short-term, easily cancellable leases (e.g., a leased automobile) to a long-term, non-cancellable lease (e.g., a 25-year lease on a new office building).

Most leases are treated as executory contracts and are disclosed on the financial statements in a footnote, if at all. Certain long-term, non-cancellable leases, however, must be included in the body of the financial statements. These are leases in which the lessee is, for practical purposes, the owner of the property.

For example, assume that a company wishes to have a new office building and that this building will cost $1,000,000. The company wishes to finance the new building by borrowing the $1,000,000. One way to finance the building would be to borrow the money from a bank and place a mortgage on the building. Under these circumstances, the company would have an asset on its balance sheet of $1,000,000 and a liability equal to the outstanding amount on the mortgage loan.

Another alternative would be to build the office building and then sell it on a sale and leaseback agreement. In this type of contract, a leasing (or finance) company would buy the building for $1,000,000 and lease it back to the company for a given number of years (say 25) at a rate that would cover the interest on the outstanding amount of the $1,000,000 plus the return of the million dollars. At the end of the 25 years, the lessor would have his $1,000,000 back plus interest for the period. At that time, the ownership of the building would revert to the lessee. The lessee would be responsible for maintenance, taxes, and so forth. As you can see, there is no difference between these two arrangements except that the building legally belongs to the company that occupies it if the money is borrowed and to the lessor under the sale and leaseback arrangement. Under these circumstances, it is necessary to ignore the legal differences and treat both financing arrangements in the same manner. In this case, it is necessary to show the building as an asset and the unpaid balance of the million dollars as a liability. Specificially, accounting rules require that leases that are clearly in substance installment purchases of property should be recorded as purchases. Both the property and the liability should be disclosed on the balance sheet.

It is necessary to disclose the details of all lease agreements in footnotes to the financial statements if these agreements are material, although such disclosure tends to be minimal at best.

Deferred Credits. Another kind of item that sometimes appears on the right side of balance sheets is the so-called deferred credit. You will remember that in Chapter 1 we defined deferred charges as costs incurred that benefit future periods, such as prepaid insurance premiums. In effect, deferred charges are costs that have not yet been recognized as expenses. Similarly, deferred credits represent sums of money received by the business that will not be counted as revenue until some future period. They are receipts that have not yet been recognized as revenues. A good example is the proceeds from a 3-year magazine subscription. When the cash is collected, the magazine sets up a deferred credit called "unearned subscription revenue." Each year, one-third of the amount is transferred to sales revenue as it is earned. Another example would be advance deposits from customers.

Deferred credits are shown between the liabilities and owners' equity sections of the balance sheet. They are not liabilities because they will not involve any future outflow of funds. Nor, are they part of owners' equity since they relate to revenues that have not yet been earned.

OWNERS' EQUITY

The Corporation

A business corporation is a legal entity authorized by the state that issues the charter to carry on a particular business. (The legal document creating a corporation is called the "articles of incorporation.") The corporation has two important legal characteristics. First, the owners (stockholders) have only limited liability for the debts of the corporation. For the most part they are liable only for the amount they have invested. Second, a corporation is taxed separately on its profits. Stockholders pay taxes only on the dividends that they receive. In other words, a corporation is treated as a legal entity for tax purposes.

The ownership of a corporation is represented by shares of stock. As in the case of bonds, the division of ownership into shares allows a large number of people to participate in financing a single company. For any individual, this participation may be large or small. The rights of each shareholder depend on the type of stock he holds. His relative interest in the company depends on the number of shares he holds in relation to the total shares outstanding.

The owners' equity of a corporation comes from two sources: (1) the money invested by the owners in the business, and (2) the money earned by the business but not paid out in dividends. The first is called "paid-in capital" and the second is called "retained earnings."

Paid-In Capital

Paid-in capital may be divided into two parts: the par value of capital stock and payments in excess of par value of capital stock. Capital stock may be divided into common stock and preferred stock. A discussion of these three subjects follows.

Common Stock. All corporations issue common stock. All common stockholders have four basic rights:

1. To share in the earnings of the corporation in proportion to their relative shareholding.

2. To share in the net proceeds of the corporation in case of liquidation in proportion to their relative shareholding.

3. To participate in any new stock issue in .proportion to their relative stockholding. (In other words, a stockholder's percentage of ownership may not be diluted unless he does not wish to buy additional shares.)

4. To vote for the directors of the corporation who will in turn elect the officers who will run the corporation.

Sometimes common stock is divided into classes—e.g., Class A and Class B, usually to represent a difference in voting rights. If there is only one class of common stock, each share is entitled to one voter in electing the board of directors.

Common stock normally carries a par value. The par value of common stock really has very little significance today. Some states (for example, Michigan) levy personal property taxes that are, in part, based on the par value of the stock. Also, some states base the incorporation tax on the par value of the stock. In some states a stockholder is liable for any excess of the par value of the stock over the amount originally paid to the corporation for it. As a consequence, the par value of most common stock tends to be very low and bears no relation to either its accounting book value or its market value. For accounting purposes, the only significance of par value that it is the amount shown on the balance sheet as representing the dollar amount of common stock outstanding. Some companies issue "no par" value stock. In this case, the stock is given a "stated" value, which is the amount shown in the capital stock account on the balance sheet.

When a company incorporates, the articles of incorporation authorize a number of shares of common stock to be issued. When some of these shares are sold, they become issued shares. The difference between the number of shares authorized and the number of shares issued is called "authorized but unissued." This simply means that the corporation can sell that many more shares without changing the articles of incorporation.

Preferred Stock. Preferred stock is capital stock that has preferential treatment over the common stock in one or more respects. Usually, a share of preferred stock will carry a specific dividend—for example, $1 a share on January 1, March 1, July 1, and October 1 of each year. The preferred dividend must be paid before any common stock dividends are paid. (The corporation, however, is not legally required to pay *any* dividend.) If the preferred stock is cumulative, no common stock dividend may be paid until all preferred dividends in arrears have been paid. If it is noncumulative, the restriction on dividends is applied each year. In this case, if the preferred dividend is not paid in a given year, it is lost to the preferred stockholder because there is no obligation to pay it in subsequent years. Preferred stock is also usually given preference in liquidation. That is, the preferred stockholders are entitled to the par value of their shares before any payment is made to the common stockholders. Preferred stock may also be convertible into common stock at a prescribed ratio. For example, a share of preferred stock might be convertible into five shares of common stock. (This is similar to convertible bonds.)

Par value is the monetary value printed on the share of stock. Preferred stock usually carries a par value of $100. The par value of preferred stock has legal significance in that it may be the amount of money to which the shareholder is entitled on liquidation. Also, preferred dividends are sometimes expressed as percentages. These percentages apply to the par value of the stock. For example, a 6 per cent preferred dividend would mean $6 per share of stock.

Preferred stock usually does not carry voting rights.

Payment in Excess of Par Value. Since the par value of common stock tends to be nominal, the sale of common stock by a corporation is almost always at a price in excess of its par value. The difference between the par value and the amount paid is credited to an account called "additional paid-in capital," "amount paid in excess of par value of capital stock," "paid-in surplus" or "capital surplus." The total of the capital stock account and the additional paid-in capital account generally reflects the amount that the stockholders have paid to the corporation for the capital stock. (An exception to this generalization occurs when a company pays a stock dividend, described below.)

Retained Earnings

In addition to selling stock, a corporation can increase the investment by the stockholder through reinvesting earnings. This occurs when the dividends paid are less than the net income. Retained earnings are the total earnings of a corporation minus the total dividends paid. Retained earnings are important because, under some state laws, dividends cannot be declared unless there is an amount in retained earnings sufficient to cover the dividends. Also, loan agreements sometimes require that dividends cannot be paid if retained earnings are less than a specified amount.

Common stock cash dividends are simply a distribution of corporate earnings. Usually each quarter the board of directors will declare a dividend of a certain amount per share to stockholders of record as of a given date. This means that persons owning the stock on the specified date will receive an amount of cash equal to the number of shares they hold multiplied by the dividend per share. The dividend becomes a liability to the company on the day that it is declared. The subsequent payment eliminates this liability.

Notice that the financial ability to pay dividends has nothing to do with the amount of retained earnings. The ability to pay dividends is determined by the availability of cash. For example, suppose that over a period of several years a company earned $5,000,000, of which $2,500,000 was paid in dividends and $2,500,000 was invested in plant and equipment. The retained earnings would show a balance of $2,500,000 but this balance would not be available for dividends. It has already been invested in property assets.

To show that retained earnings are not available for dividends, companies will sometimes declare stock dividends. That is, each shareholder is given additional stock instead of cash. This reduces the retained earnings and increases capital stock. For example, assume that a company has $10,000,000 in its capital stock account that represents 1,000,000 shares with a par value of $10 per share. (The fair market value of the stock is currently $20 a share.) It has $5,000,000 in retained earnings. The company declares a stock dividend of 10 per cent. Each shareholder receives an additional one-tenth of a share for each share he holds. The outstanding capital stock is thus increased by 100,000 shares. The accounting entry to reflect this stock dividend would be as follows.

Retained Earnings	$1,000,000	
Capital Stock		$1,000,000

A stock dividend indicates to stockholders that a given amount of the retained earnings has been permanently reinvested in the company. Notice that the stockholder is no better off after the stock dividend. He owns 10 per cent more shares but so do all other stockholders. He still owns the same percentage of the company that he did before the stock dividend.

Sometimes the retained earnings account is reduced by the current market value of the new shares issued. In this case, capital stock is credited for the par value and additional paid-in capital is credited for the difference. In the preceding example, for instance, retained earnings would be debited for $2,000,000, capital stock would be credited for $1,000,000, and additional paid-in capital would be credited for $1,000,000.

To prevent stockholders' misunderstanding with respect to retained earnings, some companies use a title similar to "earnings reinvested in the business." The term "earned surplus" is also used to mean retained earnings in some instances. This term is now considered old-fashioned because the word "surplus" is meaningless and even misleading in this context.

Stock Splits

Sometimes a company will split its stock. For example, management might decide to make a three-for-one stock split. This means that for every share of stock that is currently held, the shareholder will receive two additional shares. Thus, each shareholder will have three times his original number of shares. These shares, however, will represent the same relative ownership in the corporation and, consequently, the same total value.

The market value of the shares will normally reflect the fact that there are now three times as many shares representing the total value. For example, if the market price were $120 per share before the split, it would fall to $40 per share after the split. Companies usually split their stock to reduce the market value per share in the belief that a lower-priced stock will be traded more widely.

A stock split has no effect on the balance sheet except to increase the number of outstanding shares shown parenthetically for the capital stock.

Book Value of Common Stock

Financial analysts often calculate the book value of a share of common stock. This is done by adding the common stock account, the paid-in capital, and retained earnings and dividing this sum by the number of shares of common stock outstanding. Sometimes the analyst will subtract intangible assets before making the calculation. The comparison of the net book value of a stock with the market price provides some insights into the investing public's opinion of the accounting value of the company's assets. A high market value relative to book value could indicate that the company's earning potential is not reflected in the accounted value of its assets.

Treasury Stock

When a company repurchases its own stock, the reacquired shares are called "treasury stock." There are several reasons why a company might purchase its own shares. It might need them for executive stock option plans or employee stock purchase plans. In some instances, management believes that the purchase of the company's stock is the best investment available for surplus funds.

There are two principal methods for recording the purchase of treasury stock. One method simply records the treasury stock at the price that was paid for it. For example, assume that a company bought 1,000 shares of its own stock for $50,000. The accounting entry would be

Treasury Stock	$50,000	
Cash		$50,000

The treasury stock as shown on the balance sheet is subtraction from the owners' equity. (See the example on page 173). This is the usual way of treating treasury stock when it is being held for reissue.

The alternative way of recording the purchase of treasury stock is as follows:

1. Debit the capital stock account for the par value of the stock

2. Debit the paid-in capital account for the average paid-in capital per share multiplied by the number of shares bought.

3. Debit retained earnings for the difference between the purchase price and the total of (1) plus (2).

4. Credit cash for the purchase price.

For example, assume that the stock purchased in the preceding example had a par value of $5 per share and the paid-in capital was equal to $20 per share on average. The entry would be as follows:

Capital Stock	$ 5,000	
Paid-in Capital	20,000	
Retained Earnings	25,000	
Cash		$50,000

This method is usually used when the treasury stock is to be retired.

Example of Owners' Equity

Below is the owners' equity portion of the 1971 balance sheet of the Budd Company, together with the reconciliation of retained earnings.

SHAREHOLDERS' EQUITY: Preferred shares, without par value: Authorized 188,306 shares; issued 106,500 shares designated $5 cumulative preferred		
Less 7,375 shares in treasury	$10,650,000	$10,650,000
	737,500	737,500
Preference shares, without par value:	$ 9,912,500	$ 9,912,500
Authorized 5,000,000 shares; issued none	———	———
Common shares, $5 par value: Authorized 10,000,000 shares; issued 5,990,732 shares		
Capital surplus	$29,953,660	$29,953,660
Earnings reinvested in the business	17,617,162	15,894,826
Less 9,752 common shares in treasury, at cost	95,413,079	90,227,665
TOTAL SHAREHOLDERS' EQUITY	(116,190)	(116,190)
	$152,780,211	$145,872,461

Earnings Reinvested in the Business

BEGINNING OF YEAR—Previously reported	$89,008,425	$112,595,797
Retroactive restatement to reflect cumulative effect of change in accounting method of valuing inventories, net of tax effect	1,219,240	1,223,474
Restated balance	$ 90,227,665	$113,819,271
Net earnings (loss) for the year	5,681,039	(20,557,540)
DEDUCT CASH DIVIDENDS:		
Preferred shares—$5 per share	(495,625)	(495,625)
Common shares—$.45 per share, 1970	—	(2,538,441)
END OF YEAR	$95,413,079	$90,227,665

OTHER FORMS OF ORGANIZATION

So far in this book we have considered only the corporate form of organization. Businesses may also be organized as individual proprietorships or partnerships.

Individual Proprietorships

An individual proprietorship is an unincorporated business. From an accounting point of view, instead of a capital stock account the owner's investment is represented by an account called John Jones, Capital, or John Jones, Proprietorship. This account is credited for any investment in the business made by the owner. It is credited with the business's net profit. It is debited with any money that the proprietor withdraws. In short, the proprietorship account serves an identical function to the capital accounts in a corporation.

There are some legal differences between an individual proprietorship and a corporation. First, the earnings of a proprietorship are personal income to the proprietor for income tax purposes. The business, as such, is not taxed. Consequently, income taxes are not shown on the proprietorship's books. Second, the proprietor is personally liable for the debts of the business. If the business goes bankrupt, he must satisfy the creditors from his personal wealth.

Partnerships

A partnership is an unincorporated business consisting of more than one proprietor. Partnerships are similar to individual proprietorships legally. The partnership is not taxed but each partner is taxed on his share of the partnership profits. Also, at least one partner must have unlimited liability for the debts of the partnership,

From an accounting point of view, partnerships are treated similarly to individual proprietorships except that a capital account is maintained for each partner. When a partner invests money, his account is credited. When he withdraws money, his account is debited. Periodically, each partner's account is credited with his share of the partnership's profits.

QUESTIONS

1. In what situations, if any, could a liability that was not due for 2 years be treated as a current liability?

2. What is the reason for separating liabilities into current and long-term?

3. What is a mortgage? What is the advantage to a lender of obtaining a mortgage?

4. What is a bond? Explain why bonds sell at a discount. Why is bond discount treated as interest?

5. Explain why the compound interest method of amortizing bond discount is superior to the straight-line method.

6. What is the advantage of a convertible debenture? To the bond holder? To the company?

7. Explain why lease agreements and employment contracts are not treated as liabilities.

8. Why would a company issue preferred stock?

9. Why would a company issue more than one class of common stock?

10. What is a cash dividend? What is a stock dividend? Why, other than the reason given in the text, would a company declare a stock dividend?

11. Why would a company use the partnership form of organization rather than the corporate form?

Problem 7-1

Exhibit 1 shows the balance sheet items of a company as of December 31, 1972.

Required:

Reconstruct the company's balance sheet. (Round to the nearest million dollars.)

EXHIBIT 1

Accounts Payable	$ 418,805,000
Dividends payable to Shareowners	58,718,000
Cash on Hand and in Banks	285,580,000
Marketable Securities	87,745,000
Short-term Borrowings	280,600,000
Plant and Equipment—Less Accumulated Depreciation	1,677,651,000
Other Assets (long-term receivables, etc.)	401,416,000
Receivables	1,455,685,000
Inventories	1,482,108,000
Investment and Advances (mainly securities of wholly owned companies not consolidated plus loans to them)	353,589,000
Taxes Accrued	216,542,000
Other Costs and Expenses Accrued	601,435,000
Long-term Borrowings	749,075,000
Other Liabilities (largely long-term borrowings by foreign affiliates)	227,155,000
Miscellaneous Reserves (provisions for future payments of costs incurred to date)	129,675,000
Interest of Other Shareowners in Equity of Affiliates (minority interest)	40,140,000
Collections from Customers on Contracts in Progress and Anticipated Price Adjustments on Contracts	528,181,000
Common Stock (issued shares, $5 par value)	458,324,000
Amounts Received for Stock in Excess of Par Value	296,880,000
Retained Earnings	1,738,244,000

Problem 7-2

The following transactions occurred with respect to the long-term debt of the Odelta Corporation:

1. On January 1, 1970, the company borrowed $100,000 on a 4-year term loan. The loan was to be paid back in four equal installments beginning January 1, 1971. Interest of 5 per cent on the outstanding balance was due annually, beginning on January 1, 1971.

   Make the journal entries to record the transactions that occurred from January 1, 1970, through 1974,

2. On January 1, 1968, the company sold bonds with a face value of $10,000,000 for $9,500,000. The bonds were due in 10 years. Annual interest of 5 per cent was payable semi-annually. On January 1, 1974, the bonds were retired. To retire the bonds early, the company had to pay a premium of $200,000 over the face value.

   Make all the journal entries to reflect these transactions. (Assume that the bond discount was written off on a straight-line basis.)

3. On January 1, 1967, the company sold bonds with a face value of $5,000,000 for $5,200,000. The bonds were due in 20 years. Annual interest of 7 per cent was payable semi-annually, on July 1 and January 1. On January 1, 1970, the company repurchased the bonds for $4,900,000.

   Make the journal entries to reflect these transactions. (Assume that the bond premium is written off on a straight-line basis.)

4. On January 1, 1970, the company sold $1,000,000 of 5 per cent convertible debentures, due in 10 years, for $1,100,000. Each $100 debenture was convertible into four (4) shares of common stock, par value $5.00 a share, after January 1, 1973. On January 1, 1973, one-half of the bonds were converted. Make the journal entries to reflect these transactions. (Assume that the bond premium is written off on a straight-line basis.)

Problem 7-3

Each of the numbered items below is a description of a transaction or transactions. Each item is unrelated to the others. *Analyze these transactions and prepare journal entries to record them.*

1. The Tudor Company was organized on January 1, with authorized capital stock of 1,000 shares, par value $100 per share. On February 1, 800 shares were subscribed for at $110 per share. On February 2, 100 shares were issued to Mr. A. B. Smith in payment of a patent. On March 1, the subscribers paid cash for one-half of their subscription. On April 1, the remaining half of the subscription was paid and the stock was issued.

2. The Thredor Corporation was organized on January 1 with authorized capital stock of 10,000 no-par value shares. On February 1, 8,000 shares were sold for $80,000. An additional 1,000 shares were issued to the founder, Mr. A. J. Thredor, for his effort in organizing the corporation.

3. The Fordor Corporation was organized on January 1 with authorized no-par value capital stock of 20,000 shares. The stock had a stated value of $10 a share. On February 1, 10,000 shares were sold for $120,000. Mr. D. Z. Fordor received 5,000 shares in payment of a building taken over by the new corporation.

Problem 7-4

The owners' equity section of the balance sheet of the Fivdor Corporation on December 31, 1973, was as follows, prior to the events listed below:

Preferred Stock (10,000 shares, par value $100)	$ 1,000,000
Common Stock (1,000,000 Shares, no par value)	5,000,000
Retained Earnings	4,000,000
Total Owners' Equity	$10,000,000

The Board of Directors took the following action:
December 31, 1973:

1. A three-for-one split of common stock was declared.

2. A total of 5,000 shares of outstanding preferred stock were purchased for $120 per share.

January 1, 1974:

1. The quarterly preferred dividend of 1.5 per cent was declared.

2. A cash dividend of $.10 a share on common stock was declared.

3. A stock dividend of one-tenth of a share was declared on the common stock.

February 1, 1974:

The dividends declared in January were paid.

Required:

1. Make the journal entries to reflect the transactions indicated above.

2. Show how the owners' equity section of the balance sheet would look on January 2, 1974.

Problem 7-5

On January 1, 1974, the partnership of Sixdor and Sevdor was organized as the SixSev Corporation. The accounts of the partnership as of December 31, 1973, showed the following balances:

Cash	$ 5,420	Accumulated Depreciation	$15,700
Receivables and Accruals	9,832	Payables	14,946
Inventory	16,985	Sixdor, Capital	10,285
Fixed Assets (gross)	24,398	Sevdor, Capital	15,704
	$56,635		$56,635

The authorized capital stock of the new corporation was 40,000 shares of $1 par value. The partnership agreed to accept payment for their interest in the partnership for the stock.

Required:

1. Make the journal entries to close out the partnership books.

2. Make the journal entries to open the books of the new corporation.

Problem 7-6

Exhibit 2 summarizes the long-term debt and capital structure of the Sherwood Company as of December 31, 1973.

The following events took place during the first half of 1974.

1. On January 15, the company made the semi-annual interest payment to its bondholders.

2. On January 29, the board of directors declared a cash dividend on the preferred stock to cover the amount of dividend payments that were in arrears. This dividend was paid on February 15.

3. On February 1, Sherwood Company bonds, with a maturity value of $106,000, were purchased by the company on the open market for $108,932.

4. On February 29, a cash dividend for the first quarter of 1974 was declared on the preferred stock. It was paid on March 10.

5. On February 29, a cash dividend of $.25 a share was declared on the common stock. It was paid on March 10.

6. On March 15, a stock dividend of one share of preferred stock for each 100 shares of common stock was declared; the new stock was issued on March 31.

7. On April 15, a three-for-one stock split was declared. On May 2, the additional stock was issued.

8. On April 20, employees were sold 1,325 shares of common stock at $50 a share.

9. On April 21, company executives bought 2,650 shares of common stock at $10 a share in the exercise of a stock option agreement.

10. The bondholders had the option of exchanging their bonds for preferred stock. The bondholders would receive preferred stock with a total par value equal to the maturity value of the bonds exchanged. Bonds with a maturity value of $426,000 were exchanged for preferred stock on April 29.

Required:

1. Make the necessary journal entries to record the event listed above.

2. Prepare a schedule showing the long-term equity section of the balance sheet after the journal entries have been posted.

EXHIBIT 2

SHERWOOD COMPANY
Long-term Equities as of December 31, 1973

Bonds Payable (6 percent interest rate)	$ 1,000,000
Preferred stock (32,420 shares at par value of $100; 6 per cent cumulative; dividends in arrears, $90,000)	3,242,000
Common Stock (479,600 no-par value shares)	24,627,385
Retained Earnings	3,483,162
Total Long-term Equities	$32,352,547

Problem 7-7

In 1963, Fred Bennett resigned his job as plant superintendent for a large automobile company and went into business for himself, producing metal stamping parts in a small plant on the outskirts of Detroit. The new business was financed as follows:

> Fred Bennett contributed $10,000.
> Joseph McDonald, Fred's brother-in-law, contributed $20,000.
> James McDonald, Fred's father-in-law, allowed them to use, rent free, a building that he owned.

Fred Bennett and Joseph McDonald were to be equal partners; that is, each was to receive one-half of the profits. Fred was to work full time for the partnership. Joseph was to work little or no time on partnership business. With the money that the partners had put up and with funds borrowed from the bank, Fred purchased equipment, had it installed in his father-in-law's building, hired workers, obtained several contracts, and started to produce metal stampings.

The partnership prospered and the partners "plowed back" much of the profits into the business. By 1973, they decided that it was time to incorporate. Accordingly, they hired an attorney and made plans to organize the Bennett Stamping Corporation as of January 1, 1974.

Exhibit 3, following, is the partnership's balance sheet as of December 31, 1973, prior to the adjustments described below.

The Bennett Stamping Corporation was to be incorporated with an authorized capital of 50,000 shares at $5 per share par value. The new corporation was to take over the assets and liabilities of the partnership. Stock was to be issued to the partners, at par value, based on their share of the book value in the partnership. Before transferring the assets to the new corporation, it was decided to adjust the value to realistic market values. Accordingly, the following adjustments were made to the partnership assets:

1. An allowance for bad debts of $1,250 was established.

2. Obsolete inventory worth $4,680 was written off.

3. The net book value of the machinery and equipment was increased by $14,700 by debiting the accumulated depreciation account.

James McDonald agreed to accept $19,500 worth of stock for the land and building that the partnership had been using.

The note payable was held by the Johnson Corporation, a customer of the partnership. Mr. Johnson, president of the Johnson Corporation, agreed to accept $10,000 worth of stock at par in partial payment of the note.

Thomas Moore, a local businessman, offered to pay $6,500 for 1,000 shares of stock. The offer was accepted and Mr. Moore purchased the stock.

Organizational expenses amounted to $498; this amount was treated as an asset.

Required:

1. Make the necessary journal entries to close the partnership books. (Assume that all transactions took place on December 31, 1973.)

2. Make the necessary entries to open the books of the new corporation. (Assume that all transactions took place on January 1, 1974.)

3. Prepare a balance sheet for the Bennett Stamping Corporation after the above entries have been made.

4. Prepare a schedule showing the shares held by each stockholder.

EXHIBIT 3

THE BENNETT-McDONALD PARTNERSHIP
Balance Sheet as of December 31, 1973

Assets

Cash		$ 14,342
Accounts Receivable		10,930
Inventory		28,482
Machinery and Equipment	$175,681	
Accumulated Depreciation	80,419	
Net Machinery and Equipment		95,262
Total Assets		$149,016

Equities

Accounts Payable	$ 9,696
Note Payable	20,000
Bennett, Partner	71,430
McDonald, Partner	47,890
Total Equities	$149,016

Problem 7-8

Calculate the net book value per share of common stock in each of the following cases:

1. *Stockholders' Equity ($000)*

$5 Series A Cumulative Convertible Preferred	$ 2,560
Special Stock, Class AA Convertible	862
Common Stock (par value $.50)	1,036
Capital Surplus	130,078
Retained Earnings	40,917
Total Owner's Equity	$175,453

2. *Stockholders' Equity ($million)*

Preferred Stock (without par value)	$ 238.9
Common Stock ($5 par value)	235.4
Paid-in Capital	139.3
Reinvested Earnings	2,071.0
	$2,684.6

3. The stockholders' equity section of the General Motors Corporation balance sheet as of December 31, 1973, was as follows:

Preferred Stock	$ 283,564,400
Capital Stock (287,617,041 shares)	479,361,735
Capital Surplus	766,979,178
Earnings Retained in the Business	11,036,871,314
Total Owner's Equity	$12,566,776,627

The market price of General Motors stock in March 1974 was about $50 a share. How can you account for the difference between the market price and the book value per share? How does it happen that over $11 billion of GM's stockholders' equity is in retained earnings? Where is the money now?

Problem 7-9

The balance sheet for the XYZ partnership as of January 1, 1973, was as follows:

Assets

	($000)
Cash	$ 500
Receivables	1,430
Inventories	4,260
Fixed Assets (gross)	8,920
Less Accumulated Depreciation	(5,240)
Net Fixed Assets	3,680
Deferred Research and Marketing Costs	149
Total Assets	$10,019

Equities

Accounts Payable	$ 1,485
Notes Payable	300
Taxes Payable	565
Long-term Debt	6,000
X's Capital	943
Y's Capital	522
Z's Capital	204
Total Equities	$10,019

X, Y, and Z are equal partners and share profits or losses equally. On January 1, 1973, they decided to liquidate the business. X agreed to perform the liquidation, for which he was to be paid $10,000. During the first 6 months of 1973, X completed the liquidation of the business and, on July 1, 1973, the partners were ready for the final distribution. The liquidation process was as follows:

1. Of the accounts receivable, $300 proved to be uncollectible,

2. The inventory was sold for $3,940.

3. The fixed assets were sold for $3,500.

4. Nothing was obtained from the deferred research and marketing expenses.

Make the journal entries that reflect the liquidation transactions. Show how much each partner should have received on July 1, 1973,

Problem 7-10

In 1974, the General Electronics Corporation decided to dissolve one of its divisions because it had been losing money. Because of certain contractural requirements, it was necessary for this division to remain partially in business for the next 3 years. Over the next 3 years, the company estimated that the division would lose $9,500,000 before the dissolution could be completed. It was decided to write off the entire loss in 1973. This was done and the subsequent losses were as follows:

(In $thousands)

	1974	1975	1976	Total
Revenues	$3,426	$2,130	$ 490	$6,046
Costs	5,632	4,980	3,270	13,882
Net Operating Loss	$2,206	$2,850	$2,780	$7,836
Loss on Sale of Assets	150	400	1,620	2,170
Total Expected Loss	$2,356	$3,250	$4,400	$10,006

Required:

1. Make the journal entries reflecting the transactions above.

2. Do you agree with the company's actions in writing off the entire loss in 1973?

3. What type of liability was set up in 1973? How does this differ from other liabilities—e.g., notes payable?

Problem 7-11

For each of the following conditions, calculate the selling price of bonds with a face value of $1,000,000, due in 10 years, interest payments to be made semi-annually.

1. coupon rate 4 per cent, to be sold to yield a rate of 8 per cent,

2. coupon rate 8 per cent, to be sold to yield a rate of 4 per cent;

3. coupon rate 5 per cent, to be sold to yield a rate of 8 per cent;

4. coupon rate 10 per cent, to be sold to yield a rate of 8 per cent;

5. coupon rate 6 per cent, to be sold to yield a rate of 12 per cent.

An Introduction
to
Financial Reporting

On legislating truth

*First Umpire: Some 'r balls and some 'r strikes, and
I calls 'em as I sees 'em.*

*Second Umpire: Some 'r balls and some 'r strikes, and
I calls 'em as they 'r.*

*Third Umpire: Some 'r balls and some 'r strikes, but
none of 'em ain't nothin' 'til I calls 'em.*

8

In the first seven chapters of the book, we have concentrated on the three basic financial statements—the balance sheet, the income statement, and the statement of changes in financial position. The emphasis was placed on the *preparation* of these financial statements. Consequently, in most instances, we were looking at the financial statements from the point of view of someone *inside* the company for whom the statements were prepared. In this part of the book, the emphasis will be changed. We will be looking at financial statements from the point of view of someone *outside* the company for whom the statements were prepared. Our objective is to provide enough understanding of financial accounting and reporting to allow you to read almost any set of financial statements intelligently. To this end, we will be primarily concerned with those aspects of financial accounting that are important to the outside user of financial statements. To the extent feasible, we have eliminated those aspects of financial accounting that are of primary concern only to the preparer of the statements.

A word of caution is perhaps in order here. It is impossible to condense all of the annual economic activities of a complex business down to the few pages that make up the financial statements. As a consequence, no set of financial statements will disclose the economic effects of everything important that has happened during the year. In many cases, the economic effects of certain events are unknown and must be estimated. In other cases, events may not have an immediate monetary impact and so, for accounting purposes, they are ignored. In addition to these limitations, it is sometimes impossible for even an experienced accountant to interpret the meaning of every item that has been included in the financial statements. For example, often some of the footnotes, presumably provided to clarify items on the financial statements, are all but unintelligible. As a consequence, no set of rules for preparing and interpreting financial statements will ever be wholly satisfactory.

OBJECTIVES OF FINANCIAL REPORTING

Prior to the nineteenth century, companies largely were closely held and internally financed. Consequently, the financial statements (to the extent they were prepared at all) were for internal use by management. Outsiders had little or no interest in the financial affairs of most businesses. Subsequently, as borrowed money became important, two parties were involved—the owners and the creditors. At this time, financial statements were used as a basis for granting credit or making loans. The emphasis was on the balance sheet. Also, it was within this climate that the principle of conservatism evolved. The value of assets should be at least equal to the amount indicated on the balance sheet. An understatement of asset values could do no harm to the potential creditor, but an overstatement could. As a result, conservative accounting was considered to be good accounting.

With the development of the corporation, a new group of people became interested in the financial affairs of business—the stockholders. In the United States the growth of the corporate form of organization has continued until today there are thousands of publicly held corporations owned by millions of stockholders. In most cases, the management of these public corporations is almost completely divorced from the ownership. As a result, the number and type of people interested in financial statements have changed radically from their early beginnings. Financial statements are necessary for stockholders and potential stockholders, in addition to management and creditors. Also, the following groups have a direct interest in the financial affairs of publicily held corporations: suppliers and potential suppliers, taxing authorities, employees, and customers. The following users have an indirect interest in the financial affairs of the publicly held corporation: financial analysts and advisors, stock exchanges, lawyers, regulatory authorities, the financial press, trade associations, and labor unions.

The Accounting Principles Board (described below) lists the general objectives of financial statements as follows:

1. To provide reliable financial information about economic resources and obligations of a business enterprise.

2. To provide reliable information about changes in net resources (resources less obligations) of an enterprise that result from its profit-directed activities.

3. To provide financial information that assists in estimating the earning potential of a business.

4. To provide other needed information about changes in economic resources or obligations.

5. To disclose, to the extent possible, other information related to the financial statements that is relevant to the statement users' needs.

Clearly, objectives as comprehensive as these are extremely difficult to implement. As might be expected, there is a great deal of disagreement, both inside and outside of the accounting profession, about the best means for meeting these objectives. (For that matter, there is considerable disagreement on what the objectives should be.) Given the fact that there are a large number of outside owners (the stockholders) who require financial information about the companies in which they own an interest, meeting the above objectives requires at least two things:

1. A set of guidelines that must be followed in preparing financial statements to ensure consistency, completeness, and fairness. These guidelines are called "generally accepted accounting principles" (GAAP).

2. An independent review of the financial statements to make sure that GAAP has been followed such that the resulting statements present fairly the financial condition of the company. This is the function of the auditor.[1]

Generally Accepted Accounting Principles

Although the term "generally accepted accounting principles" has been used for years, *there is no official list of such principles*. The reason is that accounting principles have evolved over the years. What the accounting profession was doing at any particular time became the "accepted" principle or practice for that time. The Accounting Principles Board (to be described later in the chapter) defines generally accepted accounting principles as follows:

"Generally accepted accounting principles encompass the conventions, rules, and procedures necessary to define accepted accounting practice at a particular time. The standard of 'generally accepted accounting principles' includes not only broad guidelines of general application, but also detailed practices and procedures." The board goes on to explain that "they become generally accepted by agreement rather than by formal derivation. The principles have developed on the basis of experience, reason, custom, usage, and, to a significant extent, practical necessity." In some respects, the process was similar to the development of the common law.

The American Institute of Certified Public Accountants. The American Institute of Certified Public Accountants (AICPA) is the national organization of certified public accountants (CPA's). As we shall explain in the next part of the chapter, the CPA is an independent accountant who attests to the fairness of the financial statements of a company after an appropriate examination. The AICPA has been the body most responsible for developing generally accepted accounting principles. Between 1939 and 1959, the AICPA worked through a group called the Committee on Accounting Procedure (CAP). The CAP functioned as a part-time quasi--legislative body of about eighteen members whose composition was changed every year. The CAP published 51 accounting research bulletins and 4 accounting terminology bulletins in this 20-year period. These bulletins were *not binding* on

---

[1] Throughout this part of the book, we will be using two expressions frequently. One is that the statements "present fairly" the financial condition of the company. The other is that disclosure is "complete." Both these expressions are always subject to qualification. The term "fairly" means that the statements are fairly presented in accordance with generally accepted accounting principles. To the extent that GAAP might not be fair (and many believe there are instances in which they are not), the statements may not present the financial condition fairly. The term "complete" when used in connection with disclosure in financial statements does not mean that everything is disclosed. It means that no financial facts have been omitted which, if included, would lead the reader to a different conclusion concerning the financial condition of the company.

the CPA. He could deviate from these recommendations if he believed that another accepted accounting principle was more appropriate.

The Accounting Principles Board. Because of the continuing dissatisfaction with the looseness with which accounting principles were applied, the AICPA established the Accounting Principles Board (APB) in 1959. The APB (which went out of existence in 1973) published 31 serially numbered opinions on controversial accounting issues. These opinions are binding on the CPA. If a company does not use the accounting principle designated in these opinions, the CPA must qualify his opinion about the fairness of the financial statements involved. (This situation is described in the next part of the chapter.) The effect of these opinions has been to reduce the available alternatives in preparing financial statements. (Many of these opinions will be described later in the book.) Although the APB reduced significantly the available alternatives, there are still many cases in which different accounting principles may be applied in identical situations.

In addition to issuing opinions, the APB issued four statements. (Statements are not official pronouncements.) The most complete description of generally accepted accounting principles is APB Statement Number 4, *Basic Concepts and Accounting Principles Underlying Financial Statements of Business Enterprises.*

The Financial Accounting Standards Board (FASB). In 1973, the Accounting Principles Board was replaced by the Financial Accounting Standards Board. The FASB is smaller than the APB (seven members instead of eighteen). The seven members are full-time employees of the FASB and have severed their connections with other employers. (The APB membership was part time and members were still employed by their firms.) Finally, the FASB is not completely controlled by the AICPA. The Board of Trustees includes representatives from industry, the security analysts, and so forth. The work of the FASB is the same as that undertaken by the APB. That is, its function is to conduct research and issue opinions that will improve financial reporting. Because the FASB had just started to issue opinions, the major basis for GAAP as this book went to press is still the set of opinions issued by the APB and the earlier Accounting Bulletins.

The Auditor

The management of a company is responsible for keeping proper accounting records and for issuing periodic financial reports to parties with a current or potential interest in the company. Since management is a party at interest, some independent opinion is required to attest to the fairness of the statements. This is the function of the auditor (the independent CPA). An auditor is necessary not only to prevent deliberate misstatement of facts. Judgment is required in many instances and the auditor is relied on for assurance that these judgments are not unduly biased in favor of management. In addition, the auditor makes sure that the financial records are dependable, that GAAP have been followed consistently, and that the disclosure is complete.

The Certified Public Accountant. The Certified Public Accountant (CPA) examines the financial statements and the supporting evidence and attests to the fairness of the financial statements. The CPA is licensed by the state or territory in which he practices. In general, a license is obtained by passing an examination, fulfilling an education requirement, and fulfilling an experience requirement. The examination is uniform for all states and territories. The education and experience requirements, however, differ by state or territory. Also, a few states supplement the uniform CPA examination with special subject examinations—e.g., on state taxes or economics.

Most CPA's, like lawyers, work in firms, although there are many who work for themselves. There are about 150,000 CPA's in the United States.

The Audit. A CPA attests to the fairness of a set of financial statements by issuing an opinion (discussed below). Before he can issue such an opinion he must have satisfied himself that the statements fairly reflect the financial situation of the company. The process for obtaining this assurance is called an "audit." The CPA must conduct an audit before issuing an opinion.

The audit consists of a review of the balance sheet, income statement, and statement of changes in financial position, together with the underlying documents supporting the information given in these financial statements. He must be assured that the assets shown on the balance sheet really exist. For example, he conducts an independent check of accounts receivable by asking the firm's customers to verify the balances shown in their accounts. He will review the inventory records and observe the inventory-taking process. He will verify the existence of securities. He will review the basis for the various estimates that must be made—for example, the time period over which fixed assets are depreciated. He will sample the accounting records to assure himself of their completeness and accuracy. In short, he will take whatever steps he believes are necessary to confirm the accuracy of the financial data.

It is not the auditor's main task to detect fraud. Consequently, an auditor's opinion does not assure management that no fraud or embezzlement exists. As part of his examination, the auditor reviews the "internal control" system of the company. Internal control systems are those that are designed to protect the assets of the company. Examples of internal control systems are (1) the separation of the billing function from the cash collection function, (2) the maintenance of a perpetual inventory system, or (3) the countersigning of checks. If the auditor finds the internal control systems inadequate, he will inform management of this fact. If the internal control system is so inadequate that he cannot assure himself of the accuracy of the financial statements, he may refuse to issue an opinion.

On very rare occasions the CPA may believe that using an accounting method *not* sanctioned by GAAP would produce fair financial statements but that the use of GAAP for the item at issue would not produce fair statements. In such a case, the CPA must require that the statements be prepared using the non-sanctioned accounting method. The auditor's opinion would then explain the situation. In short, GAAP should not be used in those situations in which their use results in unfair financial statements.

The auditor is also responsible, of course, for reviewing the accounting principles that are used to be sure that they conform to generally accepted accounting principles and that these are applied on a basis consistent with preceding years. In conducting his audit, the CPA uses generally accepted auditing standards that have been established by the AICPA.

The Audit Report—The Unqualified Opinion. When the audit is completed, the auditor will give the company an unqualified opinion if he believes that everything is satisfactory. In this case, he would normally use the short opinion, as follows:

Exhibit 1
REXNORD, INC.

Report of Independent Public Accountants

To the Board of Directors
and the Shareholders of
Rexnord Inc.

We have examined the consolidated balance sheets of REXNORD INC. (a Wisconsin Corporation) and subsidiaries as of October 31, 1972 and 1973, and the consolidated statements of income and retained earnings and changes in financial position for the years then ended. Our examinations were made in accordance with generally accepted auditing standards, and accordingly included such tests of the accounting records and such other auditing procedures as we considered necessary in the circumstances.

In our opinion, the consolidated financial statements referred to above present fairly the financial position of REXNORD INC. and subsidiaries as of October 31, 1972 and 1973, and the results of their operations and changes in their financial position for the years then ended, in conformity with generally accepted accounting principles consistently applied during the periods.

Milwaukee, Wisconsin
November 23, 1973

ARTHUR ANDERSEN & CO.

There are a few things that you should note about the audit report.

1. The auditor does not certify the statements. He expresses an opinion concerning their fairness and he confirms that generally accepted accounting principles were followed and consistently applied. Fairness means two things: first, that the statements are free of bias or dishonesty; second, the information presented is complete.

2. The financial statements are the responsibility of the company's management. The auditor cannot change them in any way. If the auditor and management disagree about the treatment of some item, management must agree to change the statements if they are to be changed.

3. An unqualified opinion does not mean that the company is in satisfactory financial condition. The financial condition of the company must be determined by an analysis of the statements. If, however, the company was in such bad financial condition that it was in danger of bankruptcy, the auditor would probably disclaim an opinion on the grounds that the "going concern" concept would not apply.

The Qualified Opinion. If an auditor cannot give a company a completely "clean bill of health" he may give a qualified opinion. Qualified opinions are of various degrees of seriousness, but any time the auditor's opinion differs from the standard two-paragraph form shown in Exhibit 1, the reader of the statements should be aware that a red flag is being waved. The least serious qualification is one in which a company changes from one generally accepted accounting principle to another, which the auditor agrees is preferable. An example would be a change from the LIFO to the FIFO inventory method. For practical purposes this type of qualification does not affect the acceptability of financial statements. Exhibit 2 is an example of such a qualification, which is usually called a "consistency exception."

A more serious qualification is the "subject to" qualification. In this type of an opinion, the auditor attests to the fairness of the financial statements "subject to" one or more items that the auditor was unable to verify—for example, the outcome of a pending law suit. The seriousness of this type of qualification depends on the relative size of the unverified items. Exhibit 3 is an example of a "subject to" qualification. Bascially, a "subject to" opinion means that the financial statements contain some significant item that management believes has been treated fairly but which the auditor can neither accept nor reject. In effect, the auditor expresses no opinion at all about this item. The item in question, however, cannot be major enough to distort the overall fairness of the financial statements.

Exhibit 2
CHRYSLER CORPORATION

Reductions in taxes resulting from the investment credit provisions of the Internal Revenue Code are being taken into income over the estimated lives of the related assets. The amounts of such credits which were reflected in net earnings were $6,300,000 in 1970 and $5,400,000 in 1969.

TOUCHE ROSS & CO.
Detroit, Michigan

February 9, 1971

Shareholders and
Board of Directors
Chrysler Corporation
Detroit, Michigan

We have examined the accompanying consolidated balance sheet of Chrysler Corporation and consolidated subsidiaries as of December 31, 1970 and 1969, and the related statements of net earnings, net earnings retained for use in the business, additional paid-in capital and source and application of working capital for the years then ended. Our examination was made in accordance with generally accepted auditing standards, and accordingly included such tests of the accounting records and such other auditing procedures as we considered necessary in the circumstances. We performed similar examinations of the balance sheets of Chrysler Financial Corporation and consolidated subsidiaries and Chrysler Realty Corporation, and the related statements of net earnings, net earnings retained for use in the business, additional paid-in capital and source and application of funds for the years then ended (not shown here).

In our opinion, the financial statements referred to above
present fairly the financial position of Chrysler Corporation
and consolidated subsidiaries, Chrysler Financial Corporation
and consolidated subsidiaries and Chrysler Realty
Corporation at December 31, 1970 and 1969, the respective
results of their operations and the source and application
of funds for the years then ended, in conformity with
generally accepted accounting principles applied on a
basis consistent with that of the preceding year, after giving
retroactive effect in the financial statements of Chrysler
Corporation and consolidated subsidiaries to the change
in inventory valuation, which we approve, described
in the notes to financial statements.

TOUCHE ROSS & CO.
Certified Public Accountants

Exhibit 3
B.F. GOODRICH COMPANY

Accountants' Report

**To the Board of Directors and Shareholders of
The B.F.Goodrich Company**

We have examined the balance sheet of The
B.F.Goodrich Company and subsidiaries as of
December 31, 1972 and 1971, and the related
statements of income, shareholders' equity and
changes in financial position for the years then
ended. Our examinations were made in accordance with generally accepted auditing standards, and accordingly included such tests of
the accounting records and such other auditing
procedures as we considered necessary in the
circumstances.

In our opinion, subject to the effect on the
financial statements of any adjustments which
may result from the ultimate disposition of the
reserves for redeployment of assets (see Note
E), the accompanying financial statements
identified above present fairly the consolidated
financial position of The B.F.Goodrich Company and subsidiaries at December 31, 1972
and 1971, and the consolidated results of their
operations, and changes in shareholders' equity
and financial position for the years then ended,
in conformity with generally accepted accounting principles applied on a consistent basis.

Ernst & Ernst

Cleveland, Ohio
February 14, 1973

Finally, the auditor may be unable to give an unqualified opinion because he disagrees with management about the use of some accounting principle or the amount of some estimate. In these instances, he will issue an "except for" qualification. This qualification states that the financial statements are fairly presented except for the item in question, which, is not fairly presented in the auditor's opinion. Most companies try to avoid such qualifications because the credibility of the financial statements is thus considerably reduced. The New York Stock Exchange will not trade a security whose financial statements contain an "except for" opinion. Similarly, the Securities and Exchange Commission will not allow public trading of a company's securities if the financial statements contain an "except for" opinion. Exhibit 4 is an example of an "except for" qualification.

Exhibit 4
SOUTHERN RAILWAY COMPANY*

Opinion of Independent Accountants

Board of Directors and Shareholders
Southern Railway Company

We have examined the consolidated balance sheets of Southern Railway Company and subsidiaries as of December 31, 1972 and December 31, 1971 and the related statements of consolidated income, income retained in the business, and changes in financial position (pages 24 through 30) for the years then ended. Our examinations were made in accordance with generally accepted auditing standards and accordingly included such tests of the accounting records and such other auditing procedures as we considered necessary in the circumstances.

As explained in Note 3, the accompanying financial statements vary from generally accepted accounting principles in that they do not include provisions for deferred income taxes.

In our opinion, except for the matter outlined in the preceding paragraph, the consolidated financial statements referred to above present fairly the financial position of Southern Railway Company and subsidiaries at December 31, 1972 and December 31, 1971, the results of their operations and the changes in their financial position for the years then ended, in conformity with generally accepted accounting principles consistently applied.

Washington, D. C.   *Price Waterhouse & Co*
January 23, 1973

Disclaimer of Opinion. In some instances, the auditor is unable to express any opinion at all and must, therefore, make a disclaimer. A disclaimer, as the term implies means that the auditor has not been able to evaluate the fairness of the financial statements taken as a whole. A disclaimer may be necessary if the underlying accounting records are so inadequate that the auditor cannot verify the accuracy of the financial statements. Another reason could be uncertainty concerning some very major item e.g., a pending law suit. In this regard, a disclaimer is the appropriate response by the auditor when a "subject to" opinion would not really reflect the major significance of the item about which he cannot form an opinion. An example of a disclaimer of opinion is shown in Exhibit 5.

*Because the company's accounting policy in this case, which differs from GAAP, does represent "good accounting" according to the regulatory body that prescribes railroad accounting–the Interstate Commerce Commission–the New York Stock Exchange and the SEC do permit the company's stock to trade even though the financial statements violate GAAP.

Exhibit 5

TELECHECK INTERNATIONAL, INC.

PEAT, MARWICK, MITCHELL & CO.

CERTIFIED PUBLIC ACCOUNTANTS
FINANCIAL PLAZA OF THE PACIFIC
P. O. BOX 4150
HONOLULU, HAWAII 06813

The Board of Directors and Stockholders
Telecheck International, Inc.:

We have examined the consolidated balance sheets of Telecheck International, Inc. and subsidiaries as of May 31, 1971 and 1970 and the related statements of operations and deficit for the respective years then ended. Our examination was made in accordance with generally accepted auditing standards, and accordingly included such tests of the accounting records and such other auditing procedures as we considered necessary in the circumstances.

As set forth in note 2 to financial statements, the Company has recorded estimated future income tax benefits of $1,615,000. We are unable to support this accounting which is based on the opinion of management that realization is assured beyond any reasonable doubt. Also the ultimate disposition or realization of the following items reflected in the accompanying financial statements is not determinable at this time: the lawsuit and recovery of related expenditures as described in note 4; the patent applications and other intangibles and deferred charges in the accompanying balance sheets; and the absence of provision for retirement benefits as described in note 15.

Because of the materiality of the matters discussed in the preceding paragraph, the degree of uncertainty associated with them and their related effect on financial position and results of operations, we express no opinion on the above mentioned financial statements for the years ended May 31, 1971 and 1970, as restated. Under date of August 27, 1970, we previously reported, with certain qualifications, on the financial statements for the year ended May 31, 1970 before restatement.

Adverse Opinion. In rare instances, the auditor may issue an adverse opinion. An adverse opinion means that the auditor believes that the financial statements *unfairly* reflect the financial condition of the company. (This is different from the disclaimer, wherein the auditor does not have an opinion whether the financial statements are fair or not.) As should be obvious, situations in which the auditor believes the statements are unfair usually get resolved in some way other than by issuing the statements along with an "adverse" opinion. Typically, either the statements are changed to make them fair or the auditor quits or is fired.

THE SECURITIES AND EXCHANGE COMMISSION

This part of the chapter describes the financial reporting structure administered by the Securities and Exchange Commission (SEC). The structure has evolved primarily from two statutes: The Securities Act of 1933 and The Securities Exchange Act of 1934.

The Securities Act of 1933, the first securities law enacted after the 1929 stock market crash, was designed to curb a multitude of fraudulent practices. Basically, the law requires users to register securities with the SEC prior to a public offering. In order for a security issue to be exempt, it must be under $500,000 or qualify as a "private placement", which requires meeting several stringent tests.

The Securities Exchange Act of 1934 created the Securities and Exchange Commission. The act provides for registration of all securities listed on exchanges, for certain broker-dealers, and regulation of the exchanges themselves. Also included are powers governing security credit requirements, insider trading rules, proxy solicitations, and broker-dealer borrowings.

Registration Under the 1933 Act.

The law provides for the use of various "forms" in complying with the registration provision, each of which requires a different set of information to be supplied. The general form S-1 requires the most data. (Other documents range from Form S-2 to S-14, inclusive, S-16, and N-5.) The S-1 must include 3 years of at least the following consolidated financial statements: balance sheets, income statements, statements of additional paid-in capital, retained earnings statements, and statements of changes in financial position. Because accountants' opinions are usually required to be unqualified, these financial statements must be prepared in accordance with generally accepted accounting principles (GAAP).

Current Reporting Under the '34 Exchange Act

Annual Reports. Every corporation whose securities are registered must file an annual report each fiscal year. Again, there are a variety of forms involved. The general report form, 10-K, is designed to keep current the information given in the previous forms. (Analysts often use this document because it requires extensive operating disclosures.) Exhibit 6 provides a listing of the contents of a 10-K report.

Quarterly Reports. Every registrant required to file an "annual report" must also file a Form 10-Q each quarter. It contains comparative quarterly income statements, statements of capitalization and stockholders equity, and data on sales of unregistered securities.

Current Reports. A registrant is required to file a report on Form 8-K if any of several specified events occur. These include, for example, changes in control, changes in auditors, new legal proceedings. The report must be rendered within 10 days after the close of the month in which the event occurred. This report's timeliness and contents are significant and, accordingly, Exhibit 7 lists the specified "events."

Exhibit 6

FORM 10-K DISCLOSURES REQUIRED

Part I

Item

1. Products produced, services rendered, and markets for each
   Changes in these areas since last year
2. Summary of operations for at least the last 5 years
3. A physical and geographical description of important properties
4. Parents and subsidiaries
5. Pending legal proceedings
6. Increases and decreases in outstanding securities
7. Numbers of equity security holders by class
8. Officers
9. Indemnification of directors and officers
10. List of financial statements and exhibits filed

Part II

11. Principal security holders and management holdings
12. Directors of registrant
13. Remuneration of directors
14. Options granted to management to purchase securities
15. Interest of management and others in certain transactions

Instructions as to Financial Statements

1. Balance sheets—certified, 2 years
   Profit and loss statement—certified, 2 years
   Source and application of funds statements—certified, 2 years
2. Consolidated statements of each in 1 above
   (file under 1 or 2 above, not both)
3-9 Certain other statements, e.g., affiliates, subsidiaries, etc.
   — (The schedules required by Regulation S-X)

Exhibit 7

EVENTS THAT MUST BE REPORTED ON FORM 8-K

Item

1. Changes in control of registrant
2. Acquisition or disposition of assets
3. Legal proceedings
4. Changes in securities
5. Changes in security for registered securities
6. Defaults upon senior securities
7. Increase in amount of securities outstanding
8. Decrease in amount of securities outstanding
9. Options to purchase securities
10. Extraordinary item changes and credits, other material

       charges and credits to income of an unusual nature, material
       provisions for loss, and restatements of capital share
       account

11.   Submission of matters to a vote of security holders
12.   Changes in registrant's certifying accountant
13.   Other materially important events

Other Reports. The act also requires public disclosure by corporations of those individuals controlling 5 per cent or more of any class of equity security. Officers, directors, and these 5 per cent individuals are required to disclose personal transactions in the related company's securities. There are also a number of additional requirements and reports not related to financial reporting.

Regulation S-X

This regulation is a blanket provision applicable under both of the previously mentioned acts. It states requirements governing the "form and content of all financial statements" that are to be filed. (The term "financial statements" is defined to include the footnotes and all related schedules.)

Each form states which financials are to be filed with it. Regulation S-X then decrees the format to be used and the minimum disclosure necessary to make them "not misleading" (footnotes, specific supplemental schedules, etc.)

The regulation's first section governs the opinions, independence, and qualifications of the outside accountants. The next sections cover accounting definitions and terminology and certain types of statements. The remaining sections each concern an individual type of company.

Each of these "company" sections explains four basic requirements: When does the section apply, what is to be shown on or disclosed about the balance sheet, what is to be shown on or disclosed about income statements, and which supplemental schedules are to be filed.

The most generally applicable section (Article 5) is to be used by "Commercial and Industrial Companies." The section first explains what the company must disclose for each of possible balance sheet line items. Next comes similar treatment for income statement items.

Accounting Series Releases

These releases are commission-approved opinions of the SEC's chief accountant on specific accounting matters and have statutory powers equivalent to Regulation S-X. An examination of these releases indicates how rapidly requirements have changed in recent years. At least 25 of the 150 releases to date have been issued in the last 3 years of the Commission's 40-year history. These 25 also contain the most controversial topics, such as expanded disclosure for leases, income taxes, product line information, and financing arrangements.

Impact of These Acts, Forms, and Rules

Public Availability. The reports that companies file with the SEC are available in several places. The regional SEC offices contain most forms for any company headquartered within that district. An investor can use these documents on the premises or copy them for $.10 per page.

The public can also get copies by visiting or writing the main office annex at 1100 L. Street, N.W., Washington, D.C. Mail orders have various timing and pricing schedules, one of which is the minimum no-rush treatment for $.25 per page. This expense can be significant considering that many 10-K's exceed 100 pages.

The reports are now being microfilmed by Leasco Services for public distribution. Many major libraries have installed this service.

The required disclosures obviously aid investors in evaluating and understanding a company's performance. Unfortunately, most investors do not take advantage of their availability. Realizing this, the commission in January 1974 proposed that annual reports to shareholders include much of the 10-K disclosure. In addition they proposed that proxy statements contain a form for shareholders to use in requesting the company to send them (free) the latest 10-K.

Penalties and Liabilities. Failure to comply with the reporting requirements results in a 10-day renewable trading suspension. This means that no stock can be sold or purchased, nor options fulfilled. The ramifications of a suspension can obviously be severe.

A second form of suspension is levied against accountants and attorneys. They are temporarily prohibited from "practice in front of the Commission." Any of their clients who are at that time working with the SEC must find new "experts" or wait. The impact on "experts" particularly if a new issue is being sold, is obvious.

A final form of penalty is the after-the-fact lawsuit. The SEC works to prove guilt regarding fraudulent financial statements and may attempt to secure censures, fines, or jail terms. Once guilt is proven on criminal charges, investors have a better chance of recouping their losses through civil suits. Suits can entail substantial legal costs, large settlements, and extensive adverse publicity.

Role in Setting Accounting Standards. The SEC has statutory authority under the 1934 act to prescribe all financial reporting practices for publicly held companies. Prior to about 1972, however, the commission exercised very little initiative in this regard preferring to leave the job of determining accounting standards to the private sector. Thus for all practical purposes, between 1934 and 1972 full responsibility for accounting practices devolved to the public accounting profession.

Since 1972, however, the commission has been taking a much more active role in the development of accounting standards. As noted earlier, ASR's are being issued at about twice the previous rate. They are now also much more substantive than those issued in earlier years. The commission has stated that it views the FASB as being responsible for "measurement" problems in accounting; whereas, the SEC is responsible for "disclosure" problems. This is a very "soft" distinction, however. Many observers believe that the SEC will continue to play a more active role in accounting procedure matters in the future.

The extent to which the private sector will continue to play the dominant role, or even a major shared-responsibility role, hinges on the success of the FASB in dealing with the major accounting issues of the 1970s.

SOME AREAS OF DISAGREEMENT

Flexibility vs. Uniformity

One of the principal criticisms of the accounting profession is the amount of flexibility still possible in preparing financial statements. The argument for flexibility is that all companies are different and may need different accounting practices to disclose fairly their financial position. Uniformity of accounting practices, therefore, could make financial statements less useful. The argument against flexibility is that companies use those accounting principles that reflect what management wants the reader to see. It is true that two identical companies should not be permitted to appear to be different through the adoption of different accounting methods. The authors, however, have never seen two identical companies. Furthermore, it is also true that two unlike companies should not be made to appear alike by the requirement of uniform accounting procedures.

Three things seem to us to be inevitable in the next few years:

1. The FASB will continue to limit the accounting alternatives that are available. However, there will still be areas in which different accounting principles can be used for identical transactions.

2. As long as alternative accounting treatment is permitted, some companies will use the alternatives that best reflect what management wishes the public to see and these may not be the alternatives that best reflect the financial position of the company.

3. A trend toward fuller disclosure is developing, which means that the sophisticated reader of financial statements will be able to discern the impact of particular accounting methods on reported results and adjust his or her evaluation accordingly.

Chapter 12 contains a description of the principal areas of alternative accounting practices.

Theory vs. Practice

As we explained earlier, generally accepted accounting principles have evolved from the practice of accounting. One advantage of this is that acceptability by the business community is assured because GAAP represent what is actually being done. A disadvantage with this arrangement is that it can result in financial reporting that may be misleading and inconsistent. An alternative would be to develop a theory of accounting and develop a set of principles from this theory in somewhat the same way that Euclidean geometry was developed. Such an approach would assure internal consistency, consistency of means to objectives, and consistency with other fields of knowledge, principally economics. The American Accounting Association (essentially the organization of accounting professors) has officially adopted the position that accounting principles should be developed from such a theory. As indicated earlier, the AICPA takes the position that accounting principles should evolve through practice.

Because the AICPA has the responsibility for implementing generally accepted accounting principles, it appears unlikely that there will be any significant change in the current approach to establishing GAAP. This does not mean that the advocates of a more theoretical approach have not had significant influence on GAAP. Many of the APB opinions that we shall describe in the following chapters have resulted from research done by accounting theoreticians.

Cost vs. Fair Value

Perhaps the greatest criticisms leveled at generally accepted accounting principles revolve around the use of the cost principle as a basis for balance sheet values and income determination. The alternative to cost would be some form of "fair value." This area of disagreement is discussed in detail in Chapter 13.

QUESTIONS

8-1. List some of the generally accepted accounting principles that were described in chapters 1 through 7.

8-2. Name some events that might materially affect the future of a company and yet would not be reflected in the current year's financial statements.

8-3. How would you describe generally accepted accounting principles to someone who knew little or no accounting—e.g., a doctor?

8-4. How does the FASB differ from the APB? What do you think are the reasons for these differences?

8-5. Why is it necessary for the state to control the public accounting profession by requiring a license to practice?

8-6. What are some of the things that an auditor might do in conducting his audit?

8-7. What is an unqualified auditor's opinion? Under what circumstance would it be issued?

8-8. What is a qualified auditor's opinion? Name some of the situations in which an auditor might issue a qualified opinion.

8-9. What is an auditor's disclaimer? Name some of the situations that might require an auditor to make a disclaimer.

8-10. The "consistency exception" shown in Exhibit 2 contains the two words "except for." Do these words mean the same thing as the "except for" opinion shown in Exhibit 4? How do these two uses of the two words "except for" differ?

8-11. It has been observed that a "subject to" opinion is to a "disclaimer of opinion" as an "except for" opinion is to an "adverse" opinion. Do you believe that this analogy is fair?

8-12. Do you believe that some companies use flexibility in accounting principles to show a less accurate financial picture? Why or why not?

Income Tax Issues
In
Accounting

On inevitabilities

"When there is an income tax, the just man will pay more and the unjust less on the same amount of income."

Plato

9

"Remember, what you render unto God is deductible from what you render unto Caesar."

Cartoon in the *New Yorker*

The income tax law is complex and an expert opinion is required for most business decisions involving tax considerations. Income taxes, however, take up a considerable share of corporate profits and, consequently, are of great importance to management. Furthermore, it is necessary to understand certain aspects of the income tax law in order to interpret financial statements correctly. In the past few years, accounting for income taxes has been changing significantly and the impact of these changes is being reflected in current financial statements. It is, therefore, necessary for the student of management to have some understanding of income tax law as it affects management decision making and as it affects financial statements.

TAX MINIMIZATION

The corporation federal income tax rates are 22 per cent of all taxable income up to and including $25,000 and 48 per cent of all income in excess of $25,000. (Long-term corporate capital gains are taxed at a maximum rate of 30 per cent.) Since, for practical purposes, these rates are fixed, the key to minimizing income taxes is to minimize taxable income. This can be done in several ways. One way is to increase receipts that are not considered to be income and, therefore, not subject to tax. Another way is to maximize tax deductible expenses. A third way is to defer paying taxes until some future period, if possible. It is one of the duties of the tax specialists to advise managers on ways to reduce income taxes. It is one of management's obligation to its stockholders to pay the legally minimum income tax and to defer the payment of these income taxes as late as possible.[1] Income taxes are like any other expense, and the payment of excess taxes can make a company noncompetitive in the same way that the payment of any other excess costs can.

[1] The Supreme Court ruled in Gregory v. Helvering that: "The legal right of a taxpayer to decrease the amount of what otherwise would be his taxes, or altogether avoid them, by means which the law permits cannot be doubted."

Reasons for Differences
Between Accounting Principles and Tax Laws

Accounting statements and tax returns serve different objectives and, consequently, it is logical that each should be determined by different rules. There are very few instances in which the tax law requires a company to use the same accounting practice for financial statement purposes that it uses for tax purposes. One case is the LIFO inventory method. A company using LIFO inventory for tax purposes *must* also use LIFO in its published accounting statements. (This point was discussed briefly in Chapter 5.) Legally, at least, there need be no consistency between tax accounting and the financial statements issued to the public in most instances. For practical purposes, however, there may be reasons why, a company will allow its tax situation to dictate its accounting practices. If, for example, a company was proposing to use a disputed tax practice, it might create problems if a different practice were used for accounting purposes. The Internal Revenue agent could point out, in questioning the practice, that the company did not believe in its own arguments sufficiently to use this practice for accounting purposes.

The principal reasons for differences in taxable income and accounted income are:

1. The goal of accounting income is to measure as precisely as possible the change in the economic worth of a company over a period of time. To the extent possible, income is recognized when it is earned. On the other hand, measurement of taxable income is usually influenced by the "ability to pay" criterion. The time income is earned and the time it is realized may be considerably different. For example, an installment sale is income for accounting purposes on the day the sale is made. The ability of a company to pay a tax on that income, however, depends on collecting the installment accounts receivable. For tax purposes, therefore, the income is counted only as it is received.

2. The income tax policy frequently involves social and economic goals. For example, rapid depreciation was allowed during the Korean War for certain types of defense facilities in order to encourage companies to build that type of facility. The investment credit (discussed later in the chapter) is designed to encourage business investment. Public policy goals are a legitimate aspect of tax law, but they should not interfere with fair presentation of published financial statements.

3. In tax law, flexibility is frequently sacrificed to expediency. Since the objective of good tax management is to minimize taxable income, alternative practices will induce each company to use the practice that minimizes its taxable income. On the other hand, alternative accounting rules should result in a company using that practice that most fairly reflects its performance for the period.

4. To increase predictability and to reduce administrative burdens, including the cost of litigation, allowable tax practices are frequently codified. For example, depreciation guidelines are provided so that companies using such guidelines will not have to defend their depreciation practices. For somewhat the same reason, many accruals are not allowed for tax purposes because of their uncertainty. Such codification does not imply

that the permissible practices are "right." What is "allowable" under the revenue code, therefore, has no bearing on what is "appropriate" for financial reports.

DIFFERENCES BETWEEN ACCOUNTING AND TAXABLE INCOME

There are two major reasons why taxable income in any year might differ from accounting income:

1. The tax laws and accounting practices may differ with respect to recognizing certain revenues and expenses. These are permanent differences between tax and accounting income.

2. The tax laws and accounting practices may differ with respect to the timing of revenues and expenses.

Permanent Differences

In this part of the chapter the principal ways in which taxable income can differ permanently from accounting income are described. In general, some expenses are deductible for income statements but not for taxes; some expenses are deductible for taxes but not for income statements; some revenues are counted for income statements but not for taxes; and some revenues are counted for taxes but not for income statements.

Expense Differences. Depletion Allowance. Depletion was described in Chapter 6 as using up "wasting" assets. Depletion, thus, is to the extractive industries as depreciation is to the manufacturing industries. Depletion expense is generally calculated in a way similar to the units of production method of depreciation. The cost of the depleting asset (e.g., mine, quarry, or oil well) is divided by the expected yield to obtain the depletion cost per unit. Then, each period, the actual yield is multiplied by the depletion per unit. This amount is charged against income and the asset account is reduced by a like amount. As you might expect, there are some very sophisticated ways of calculating depletion, especially if the product differs in quality. They all have the same characteristics, however, in that the cost of the asset is written off in proportion to the amount and type of product that is extracted.

For tax purposes, in just about all extractive industries, the depletion allowance may be based on a percentage of gross revenue. (The alternative of using cost-based depletion is also available but it usually results in a lower tax deduction.) These percentages vary from 22 per cent to 5 per cent, depending on the type of material being extracted.[2] This means that, if a company uses the percentage depletion method (called the "statutory" method), its tax depletion may be considerably higher than its accounting depletion and this difference is permanent. As long as the mine or well is productive, the company may take the statutory depletion allowance for tax purposes, even though the total depletion allowance may have exceeded the original cost.

---

[2] There are some limitations on the total amount of depletion. For example, the percentage depletion may not exceed 50 per cent of the taxable income attributed to the property.

Non-deductible Expenses. There are several types of expenses shown in financial statements that may not be fully deductible for tax purposes. For example, there are limitations on charitable deductions and officers' salaries. Premiums paid on life insurance for which the company is beneficiary are not deductible. Also, the write off of certain intangible assets (e.g., goodwill) is not deductible.

Revenue Differences. *Dividends* Eighty-five per cent of most dividends received by one corporation from another are excludable in computing taxable income. In instances wherein the parent company owns 80 per cent of the stock of a subsidiary, 100 per cent of the dividends are excludable, if the members of the affiliated group elect to be treated as one taxpayer. (As described in Chapter 11, no tax is paid on dividends if a consolidated tax return is filed.) This dividend exclusion reduces (85 per cent) or eliminates (100 per cent) the double taxation that would result if earnings on which the subsidiary company has already paid income taxes were fully taxable again to the parent corporation when received as dividends.

Other Tax-Exempt Income Some types of receipts are completely exempt from the income tax. Major examples are interest on municipal bonds and proceeds from life insurance policies on which the corporation is the beneficiary.

Non-Revenue Taxable Receipts There are a few items that are considered to be taxable income by the IRS but that are not included in income statements. One primary example concerns proceeds received from the sale of warrants for the purchase of common stock that expire without being exercised. This area is very technical and thus is beyond the scope of this book.

Foreign Business. As you might expect, the tax regulations on the various types of foreign business in which a company may engage are exceedingly diverse and complex. Some of these regulations can result in some fairly significant differences between accounting income and taxable income. These differences, too, are beyond the scope of this book.

Timing Differences

The most important differences between taxable and accounting income in any one year result from differences in timing. That is, an item of revenue or expense may be taken in one time period for tax purposes and in another time period for accounting purposes. This part of the chapter describes the principal items to which this condition applies.

Installment Sales. When a company sells products on the installment plan, the profit is recognized for financial statement purposes in the period when the sale is made.[3] For tax purposes, the profit may be deferred until the periods in which the installments are collected. The following example illustrates the differences in tax and accounting income for installment sales.

---

[3] If the collection of the installments is considered to be uncertain, the income may be deferred until collection is made. This, however, is the *exception*. The general rule is as stated above.

Figure 1
Assumptions

	Year 1	Year 2	Year 3	Year 4	Year 5
Sales	$100,000	$120,000	$130,000	$150,000	$180,000
Accounts Receivable					
January 1	$ 0	$ 10,000	$ 12,000	$ 13,000	$ 15,000
December 31	10,000	12,000	13,000	15,000	19,000
Gross Margin on Sales					
Made during Year	40%	42%	45%	45%	50%
Period Costs	$ 20,000	$ 21,000	$ 23,000	$ 25,000	$ 30,000
Tax Rate	50%	50%	50%	50%	50%

Figure 2
Accounting Method
(Income recognized at time of sale)

	Year 1	Year 2	Year 3	Year 4	Year 5
Sales	$100,000	$120,000	$130,000	$150,000	$180,000
Cost of Sales	60,000	69,600	71,500	82,500	90,000
Gross Margin	$ 40,000	$ 50,400	$ 58,500	$ 67,500	$ 90,000
Period Costs	20,000	21,000	23,000	25,000	30,000
Profit before Taxes	$ 20,000	$ 29,400	$ 35,500	$ 42,500	$ 60,000
Income Tax	10,000	14,700	17,750	21,250	30,000
Profit after Taxes	$ 10,000	$ 14,700	$ 17,750	$ 21,250	$ 30,000

Figure 3
Tax Method
(Income recognized at time of payment)

Sales	Year 1	Year 2	Year 3	Year 4	Year 5
Sales Contracted for	$100,000	$120,000	$130,000	$150,000	$180,000
Less Uncollected 12/31	10,000	12,000	13,000	15,000	19,000
Sold and Collected	$ 90,000	$108,000	$117,000	$135,000	$161,000
Previous Year's Collections	—	10,000	12,000	13,000	15,000
Total Collections	$ 90,000	$118,000	$129,000	$148,000	$176,000
Gross Margin					
Last Year's Sales	—	4,000	5,040	5,850	6,750
Current Year's Sales	36,000	45,360	52,650	60,750	80,500
Total	$ 36,000	$ 49,360	$ 57,690	$ 66,600	$ 87,250
Period Costs	20,000	21,000	23,000	25,000	30,000
Profit before Taxes	$16,000	$28,360	$34,690	$41,600	$57,250
Income Tax	8,000	14,180	17,345	20,800	28,625
Profit after Taxes	$ 8,000	$ 14,180	$ 17,345	$ 20,800	$ 28,625

Figure 4
Comparison of Two Methods

Income Taxes Using the Accounting Method	$ 10,000	$ 14,700	$ 17,750	$ 21,250	$ 30,000
Income Taxes Using the Installment Method	8,000	14,180	17,345	20,800	28,625
Savings from Installment Method:					
In Year	$ 2,000	$ 520	$ 405	$ 450	$ 1,375
Cumulative	2,000	2,520	2,925	3,375	4,750

Notice that the use of the installment method results in the payment of $4,750 less income tax over the 5 years than would have been paid using the accounting method. Even more important, however, is that this saving will continue to grow as long as the accounts receivable continue to grow. If the company stops growing (for example, if sales level off at $180,000 and accounts receivable at $19,000), there would be no *additional* tax savings. However, the company would *never* have to pay back to the government any part of the saving of $4,750 until the business contracts. At any point in time, the cumulative tax savings from the installment method is equal to the ending accounts receivable times the gross margin percentage times the tax rate. The implication to management is clear. If you can defer your income tax payments, you should do so. The savings are not just in the timing of the payments; for growing businesses, they will usually represent permanent tax reductions. Failure to take advantage of tax deferments means incurring unnecessary costs.

Completed Contract Method. Many firms work under long-term, fixed price contracts for the construction of such things as dams, hydroelectric plants, or defense hardware. These contracts may require several years to complete. There are two basic methods of accounting for long-term contracts: the completed contract method and the percentage completion method. In the *completed contract method*, income from the contract is recognized in the year that the contract is completed. Costs are capitalized in an asset account during the life of the contract and charged to cost of sales in the period when the contract is completed. It is usual for a company engaged in a long-term contract to receive partial payments during the period. Under the completed contract method, these payments are credited to a liability account until the contract has been completed. (On the balance sheet, this account is often subtracted from the asset account to which the costs have been debited.) Although the actual accounting practices can vary, the results of these different practices are precisely the same. Costs are capitalized as incurred, and payments received are deferred in a balance sheet account during the life of the contract. When the contract is completed, the costs are charged to cost of sales, the proceeds are credited to a revenue account, and the entire profit is recognized.

Using the *percentage completion* method, part of the profit on a long-range contract is recognized each accounting period based on the amount of work that has been completed during that period. Again, there are several methods involved.

The usual method is, at the end of each period, to estimate the cost to complete and the total gross margin on the completed contract. Cumulative gross margin earned at any point in time will be an amount equal to the estimated total gross margin multiplied by the fraction of expected total costs that have already been incurred. Gross margin earned for any given period is equal to gross margin earned at the end of the period less gross margin earned at the beginning of the period.

For example, assume that a fixed-price contract of $500,000 was obtained by a company to build a small dam. The contract starts on July 1, 1972, and is expected to be completed in 1975. At the end of 1972, the following conditions existed:

1. Spent to date	$ 50,000
2. Estimated cost to complete	350,000
3. Estimated total gross profit	100,000
4. Percentage completed (50 ÷ 400)	12.5%
5. Earned in 1972	12,500

At the end of 1973, the following conditions existed:

1. Spent to date	$200,000
2. Estimated cost to complete	220,000
3. Estimated gross profit	80,000
4. Percentage completed (200 ÷ 420)	47.6%
5. Earned to date	38,080
6. Recognized in 1973 (38,080–12,500)	25,580

At the end of 1974, the following conditions existed:

1. Spent to date	$350,000
2. Estimated cost to complete	80,000
3. Estimated gross profit	70,000
4. Percentage completed (350 ÷ 430)	81.4%
5. Earned to date	56,980
6. Recognized in 1974 (56,980–38,080)	18,900

In 1975, the contract was completed as follows:

1. Revenue from contract	$500,000
2. Cost of contract	440,000
3. Gross profit	$ 60,000
4. Earned in prior years	56,980
5. Recognized in 1975	$ 3,020

In the example above, the percentage completion was determined by the amount spent in relation to the total amount expected to be spent. This is the usual method of determining the percentage of completion. There are, however, other ways, such as basing the percentage of completion on an architect's estimate of the percentage of physical completion. Regardless of the actual methods used, the principles are identical. The income is recognized over the period of construction instead of when the contract is completed.

It is usual in the construction industry to use the percentage of completion method for accounting statements and the completed contract method for tax purposes. The percentage of completion method is favored for accounting purposes if the estimates are reasonably reliable. If reasonably reliable estimates are not available, however, the completed contract method is favored. For tax purposes, it is clearly to the taxpayer's advantage to use the completed contract method as long as he is earning a profit. In the example above, the two methods are contrasted with respect to tax payments.

Figure 5

	1972	1973	1974	1975
Percentage Completion:				
Profits	$12,500	$25,580	$18,900	$ 3,020
Tax	6,250	12,790	9,450	1,510
Completed Contract:				
Profits				60,000
Tax				30,000
Tax Savings:				
In Year	6,250	12,790	9,450	(28,490)
Cumulative		19,040	28,490	—

Since we are looking at a single contract, the tax benefits of deferment are offset in 1975. In a going concern, however, with a number of different contracts, some of which are always open at any year's end, there will always be accumulated tax saving from using the completed contract method as long as the company is profitable. New contracts (and, consequently, new "deferred taxes") will offset the taxes due on completed contracts. If the company is growing, the tax savings will grow proportionately. Even when tax differences do ultimately reverse, the company has had the use of the funds, interest free, over the period. This alone can be a significant economic saving.

Depreciation. As you will remember from Chapter 6, the amount of annual depreciation taken on a given asset depends on two things: the depreciable life of the asset and the depreciation method used. The tax code provides depreciation guidelines for depreciable assets. These guidelines indicate the acceptable life for tax purposes of many different classes of assets. As long as the taxpayer uses these guidelines, he need not justify the depreciable life of his assets. (If he uses a shorter life than indicated in the guidelines, he will have to justify it.) To encourage business investment, the guideline lives tend to be very liberal (i.e., short) so that the taxpayer can write off his assets fairly quickly. In addition to relatively short lives, the tax code also allows the taxpayer to use accelerated depreciation—either declining balance or the sum-of-the-year's digits. (See Chapter 6.) The combination of the guideline life and accelerated depreciation allows a taxpayer to write off property assets for tax purposes more quickly than he may wish to do for accounting purposes. Consequently, many companies distinguish between tax depreciation and accounting depreciation. For example, assume that a company uses straight line depreciation on a 10-year life for accounting purposes and the sum-of-the-year's digits depreciation on a 5-year life for tax purposes. The following schedule shows the difference in depreciation on a $90,000 piece of equipment.

Figure 6

Year	(1) Accounting Depreciation	(2) Tax Depreciation	(3) (2) Greater (Less) Than (1)	(4) Tax Effects Fav. (Unf.)
1	$9,000	$30,000	$21,000	$10,500
2	9,000	24,000	15,000	7,500
3	9,000	18,000	9,000	4,500
4	9,000	12,000	3,000	1,500
5	9,000	6,000	(3,000)	(1,500)
6	9,000		(9,000)	(4,500)
7	9,000		(9,000)	(4,500)
8	9,000		(9,000)	(4,500)
9	9,000		(9,000)	(4,500)
10	9,000		(9,000)	(4,500)
TOTAL	$90,000	$90,000	0	0

Because we are looking at a single asset, the lower taxes in the early years are offset by higher taxes in later years. In a going concern, however, this reversal of tax advantage may not occur because new assets at higher depreciation rates are often purchased as old assets are retired. In a static concern (i.e., replacement equal to retirements), an equilibrium would eventually be reached at which the taxable depreciation and the accounting depreciation would be equal. The previous savings in taxes, however, would not be reversed unless the property asset base declined. In a growing company, the amount of tax advantage usually will continue to increase indefinitely.

Deferrals. Some expenses are capitalized for accounting purposes but expensed as incurred for tax purposes. For example, some companies defer part of their marketing for accounting purposes. For tax purposes, however, they are written off in the year that they are incurred.

Accruals. Most accrued expenses that do not represent specifically identifiable liabilities are not allowable for tax purposes. For example, for accounting purposes, a company may wish to set up a provision for warranty payments on products sold to customers. This accrual would be an expense for accounting purposes in the year that the accrual was made. It would not be an expense for tax purposes until the warranty costs were actually incurred. Similarly, a contribution to a pension fund is only deductible for tax purposes when actually paid, not when accrued.

Management Considerations. The important point for management to realize is that deferring tax payments actually reduces tax payments in most instances. Even when it does not permanently reduce total taxes it involves an interest-free loan from the government. Consequently, it is important for management to take advantage of any acceptable opportunities to defer tax payments (assuming, of course, that the company is earning a profit).

ACCOUNTING FOR DEFERRED INCOME TAX

Deferred taxes result from differences in *timing* between accounting income and taxable income. The theory is that if taxable income is less than accounting income in the current year, it will be more than accounting income in some future year. Consequently, the tax that you save today will have to be paid in the future and this represents a liability to the company. In the examples given in the preceding section, the difference between the tax that would have been paid if the accounting statement methods had been used for tax purposes and the tax that was actually paid is a liability. This liability is called "deferred taxes." The purpose of this part of the chapter is to describe the accounting for deferred taxes. APB opinions 11 and 23 cover the rules for deferred tax accounting. The following quotation is from APB Opinion 11.

> The Board has considered the various concepts of accounting for income taxes and has concluded that comprehensive interperiod tax allocation is an integral part of the determination of income tax expense. Therefore, income tax expense should include the tax effects of revenue and expense transactions included in the determination of pretax accounting income.

This means simply that the income tax expense shown on the financial statements is *not* necessarily the tax paid to the government. It is the tax that would have been paid if the tax returns had reflected the same timing of expenses and revenues as the financial statements. Notice that the rule applies only to *timing* differences. There is no adjustment for *permanent* differences because they do not involve a *future* tax liability or benefit.

Accounting Entries

Let us consider the example given in figures 1, 2, 3, and 4 in which the installment method was used for tax purposes.

The profits on the financial statements would have been as follows, if the actual tax payments were recorded as the total tax expense:

Figure 8

Year	Profit before Taxes (Figure 2)	Taxes (Figure 3)	Profit after Taxes	Implicit Tax Rate
1	$20,000	$ 8,000	$12,000	40%
2	29,400	14,180	15,220	48
3	35,500	17,345	18,155	49
4	42,500	20,800	21,700	49
5	60,000	28,625	31,375	48

According to APB 11, however, a company cannot use the actual tax payments as the total tax expense if the accounting income reflects differences in timing from the taxable income. In this case the tax expense shown on the financial statements should be the amounts shown in Figure 2, which are equal to 50 per cent of the accounting income. Consequently, tax expense is debited and deferred taxes is credited for the difference between the tax actually due and the tax that would have been due if the taxable income had been the same as the accounting income. These amounts are shown in Figure 4 and the accounting entries would be as follows:

	Year 1		
Income Tax Expense		8,000	
Cash			8,000
Income Tax Expense		2,000	
Deferred Taxes			2,000
	Year 2		
Income Tax Expense		14,180	
Cash			14,180
Income Tax Expense		520	
Deferred Taxes			520
	Year 3		
Income Tax Expense		17,345	
Cash			17,345
Income Tax Expense		405	
Deferred Taxes			405
	Year 4		
Income Tax Expense		20,800	
Cash			20,800
Income Tax Expense		450	
Deferred Taxes			450
	Year 5		
Income Tax Expense		28,625	
Cash			28,625
Income Tax Expense		1,375	
Deferred Taxes			1,375

Suppose that in Year 6 the company had a reduction in installment sales and accounts receivable, and, consequently, the taxable income was $32,000 whereas the accounting income was only $30,000. In this instance a tax of $16,000 would be paid; however, tax expense for accounting purposes would be only $15,000. The accounting entry would be as follows:

Income Tax Expense	15,000	
Deferred Taxes	1,000	
Cash		16,000

Deferred Taxes on the Balance Sheet

The deferred tax account is shown on the balance sheet partly as a current and partly as a non-current liability. That part of the deferred taxes that applies to current assets is treated as a current liability. For example, the income tax deferred from using the installment method of income recognition is a current liability because it results from deferring income represented by accounts receivable, which is, of course, a current asset. On the other hand, the deferred taxes resulting from timing differences in depreciation is treated as a non-current liability.

Paragraph 57 of APB Opinion 11 reads as follows:

> They [deferred taxes] should be classified in two categories—one for the net current amount and the other for the net noncurrent amount. The presentation is consistent with the customary distinction between current and noncurrent categories and also recognizes the close relationship among the various deferred tax accounts, all of which bear on the determination of the income tax expense. The current portions of such deferred charges and credits should be those amounts which relate to assets and liabilities classified as current. Thus, if installment receivables are a current asset, the deferred credits representing the tax effects of uncollected installment sales should be a current item; if an estimated provision for warranties is a current liability, the deferred charge representing the tax effect of such provision should be a current item.

In instances where accounting expense is more than taxable expense (e.g., warranty expense), the deferred tax would appear as an asset on the balance sheet.

Deferred Tax as a Liability. There is a considerable difference of opinion among accounting theorists about whether deferred taxes are a liability or not. Certainly no contractual obligation exists, as is true for current taxes payable. As we pointed out earlier, the deferment will be permanent as long as the business does not contract. Furthermore, even if the business began to shrink, the deferred taxes would be payable only if the business continued to show profits. A more normal condition is for a business contraction to be coupled with operating losses, in which case no taxes at all would be due. Accountants who favor treating deferred taxes as a liability point out that *no* liabilities (e.g., accounts payable) are ever reduced to zero in a going concern. As one account is paid, another purchase is being made on credit. Thus, the overall amount remains constant and, in fact, increases as the business grows. They go on to point out that the same condition applies with deferred taxes. In the installment sales method, for example, taxes are paid this year on last year's uncollected installment accounts receivable, but taxes are not paid on this year's sales that are uncollected at the end of the year. Although the overall amount of deferred tax may be constant or growing, it applies to different specific accounts receivable. This is called the "roll-over" argument.

For accounting purposes, deferred taxes must be treated as described above because the APB feels that income tax expense should reflect the tax effect of all items counted in the income statement, regardless of the timing of the tax effect. It is important, however, that you understand that a deferred tax liability is different from a liability representing a contractual debt such as long-term bonds. Two conditions are necessary before most deferred tax liabilities must be paid. (1) The business must contract; and (2) there must be a taxable profit. This second consideration is especially important with respect to non-current deferred taxes, particularly those created by differences in the timing of depreciation. Before this liability must be paid, essentially the company must at least partially go out of business. A company going out of business is rarely profitable. Consequently, we believe that, in analyzing financial statements, you should take account of the fact that there *is* a difference between a deferred tax liability and a liability representing a contractual debt.

Even if one accepts the roll-over argument to support showing the deferred tax liability, it is possible to argue that the liability should be shown at its discounted present value rather than the gross amount. This practice would be more in keeping with the general concept of a liability espoused by the APB.

Some authorities think that it is most useful to think of deferred taxes as a source of funds—a long-term, interest-free loan from the government. This does not, however, resolve the issue of whether these funds ever will be repaid. If not, they are more properly shown as part of owners' equity than as a liability. If deferred tax expense is not recorded, net income is higher and retained earnings are higher. This would be appropriate if the deferral is permanent.

LOSS CARRYBACK AND CARRYFORWARD

One important feature of the income tax law with which you should be familiar is the operating loss carryback and carryforward provision. If a company incurs a taxable loss in any year, it may apply this loss against taxable profits reported in the preceding 3 years by recalculating the tax liability beginning with the third prior year. The tax liability is recalculated by reducing taxable income by the amount of the loss. If the loss is greater than the profits of year 3, the difference is applied to the second prior year. If the loss is greater than the total of the third-and second-year profits, the remainder is applied to profits of the immediately preceding year. The difference between the actual taxes paid and the taxes that have been calculated using the loss carryback are refunded to the company by the government. For example, assume the following:

	1970	1971	1972
Taxable Income	$10,000	$20,000	$30,000
Tax	5,000	10,000	15,000
After-tax Income	$ 5,000	$10,000	$15,000

If, in 1973, the company had a taxable loss of $40,000, this loss would be applied against the preceding years' profits as follows:

	1970	1971	1972	Total
Taxable Income before Carryback	$10,000	$20,000	$30,000	
Carryback	10,000	20,000	10,000	
Adjusted Taxable Income	—	—	$20,000	
Adjusted Tax Liability	—	—	10,000	
Tax Refund	$ 5,000	$10,000	$ 5,000	$20,000

The income statement for 1973 would show the following:

Net Loss before Taxes	$40,000
Less Income Tax Refund Applicable to Loss	20,000
Net Loss after Taxes	$20,000

In other words, the current loss is reduced by the refund for recoverable prior period income taxes.

Suppose, however, that the loss in 1973 has been $100,000. Since the entire income for the past 3 years was only $60,000, the maximum recovery from the loss carryback provision is $30,000. The remaining $40,000 in losses, which cannot be carried back, can be carried forward for the next 5 years. The loss can be used to reduce taxable income earned during the next 5 years. If the company earned no profits for the next 5 years, the carryforward loss could not be used. In most instances of tax loss carryforwards, the potential benefit of the lower taxes is not shown until the year in which the loss is actually used to reduce the income tax liability.

To summarize the accounting treatment:

1. The tax benefits of a loss carryback are reflected in the income statement of the year the loss was incurred.

2. In most cases the tax benefits of a tax loss carryforward are reflected in the periods that such carryforward is realized.

3. In the unusual case when the realization of the tax benefits of a loss carryforward is *assured*, the benefits may be taken in the period of the loss by debiting a non-current asset and crediting the tax refund account. The Allis-Chalmers case at the end of the next chapter deals with this situation.

Except in (3), the existence of a tax loss carryforward is disclosed in the financial statements only in the footnotes.

INVESTMENT CREDIT

To encourage business expansion, the government grants a tax reduction called an "investment credit" for investment in some types of facilities. The regulations concerning eligibility for the investment credit, restrictions on the amount taken, and methods of calculation are very complex and need not concern you at this point. For purposes of this book you can think of the investment credit as a direct offset to the tax bill equal to 7 per cent of investment in new facilities. The investment credit does not affect the amount of depreciation that can be taken on the facilities for which the investment credit was granted. For example, assume that a company purchased facilities in 1973 for $1,000,000 that qualified for the investment credit. The company would be given a tax credit in 1973 of $70,000. It would depreciate the entire $1,000,000 over the taxable life of the equipment. If the company does not have any taxable profit in 1973, the credit may be carried back 3 years and forward 7 years.

There are two ways of accounting for the investment credit. The first way is the so called "flow through" method. Under this method, the current year's tax expense is simply reduced by the amount of the investment credit. Notice that, under the flow through method, the after-tax income of a company can be increased merely by investing in facilities.

The second method is to defer the tax saving and amortize it over the life of the asset. There are several ways of doing this. One is to debit the tax liability and credit the property asset account by the amount of the investment credit. Then, the investment credit is recognized for accounting purposes over the life of the asset via a reduction in depreciation expense. Another way is to set up the investment credit as a deferred credit and recognize it as income over the life of the asset. Regardless of how it is handled, the deferral method spreads the accounting benefits over the life of the asset that provides the investment credit.

The accounting profession generally believes that the deferred method should be used to account for the investment credit. This belief is based on the idea that profits are earned by *using* assets, not by *buying* them. However, Congress in 1972 wrote into the tax law a provision that prevents the APB or any other professional accounting body from prescribing the deferral method exclusively. Consequently, either the flow through or the deferral methods are acceptable for financial statement purposes. Given this choice, most firms adopt the flow through method because it allows more flexibility to manipulate reported earnings.

Congress acted in this case because the Administration wanted the results of the investment tax credit to show up as an immediate boost in reported earnings as well as a tax savings. This illustrates the role of public policy in the setting of accounting principles. Some people believe that accounting principles should be above governmental policy. Others feel that this stance is naive and that accountants must always be sensitive to the public policy implications of their actions.

LIFO INVENTORY METHOD

A company may use either the LIFO, FIFO, or average method of valuing inventory for either tax or accounting purposes. However, if a company uses LIFO for tax purposes, it must also use LIFO for accounting purposes. In an inflationary economy, LIFO will result in lower (relative to FIFO or average) ending inventories, higher cost of sales, and, consequently, lower profits. This, of course, results in a tax saving. This tax saving will be permanent as long as the inventory is not reduced in size. It will grow as long as the inventory grows as a result of either an increase in physical size or an increase in the level of prices. To illustrate, assume that a company starts out with an inventory of $1,000,000 in 1960. Assume that the inventory increases $100,000 a year as a result of sales growth and 5 per cent a year as the result of inflation. The inventory values for a 10-year period would be as follows:

Year	LIFO Inventory	FIFO Inventory*	Difference
1960	$1,000,000	$1,000,000	—
1961	1,100,000	1,150,000	$50,000

1962	$1,200,000	$1,307,500	$107,500
1963	1,300,000	1,472,875	172,875
1964	1,400,000	1,646,519	246,519
1965	1,500,000	1,828,845	328,845
1966	1,600,000	2,020,287	420,287
1967	1,700,000	2,221,301	521,301
1968	1,800,000	2,432,366	632,366
1969	1,900,000	2,653,984	753,984

*For simplicity, it has been assumed that the 5 percent increase in the cost of inventory applies only to the amount of inventory at the beginning of the year.

Thus, over the 10-year period, taxable income using LIFO would be about $750,000 less than that using FIFO and this would result in a tax savings of about $375,000. This tax savings will be permanent unless the inventories are subsequently reduced. On the financial statements, the inventory values are $750,000 lower than they would be under FIFO and the net profits over this 10-year period would be $375,000 less, thus reducing retained earnings by this amount. The difference is the increase in cash as a result of lower income taxes.

One recent survey showed that less than 15 per cent of manufacturing inventories in the United States are based on LIFO. This means that most of the companies surveyed are not taking advantage of the lower tax rates that LIFO offers. For companies that are earning no profits or are in industries where there is little or no inflation (how many such industries can there be?), this may be the correct economic decision. For most companies, however, it seems clear to us that they are paying unnecessary income taxes.

Many companies have been reluctant to adopt LIFO because of the depressing effect it has on reported profits and working capital. (Remember, LIFO inventory values on the balance sheet may reflect prices in effect dozens of years ago.) In fact, in recent years, several companies have changed from LIFO to FIFO or average just to increase their accounting profits and reported working capital. But they have had to pay the government the accumulated tax savings as well as higher taxes each subsequent year. This is the dilemma in which some managers find themselves. To increase inventory values on the balance sheet, it may cost one-half of the increase in out-of-pocket tax expense. So, although the balance sheet may look better, in reality nothing has happened except the cash is smaller by the amount of the tax.

We believe that it is important in analyzing financial statements to examine the method of valuing inventories. If LIFO is not being used, there should be a logical explanation. Particularly, if a company changes from LIFO to FIFO or average, the reasons for the change should be well documented.

SUMMARY

Some of the important considerations of income taxes are:

1. It is important that a company take full advantage of the tax laws to minimize its taxes. In particular, most tax provisions that allow a taxpayer to defer tax payment until some future period will provide a *permanent* deferment of tax expense for most companies.

2. The deferred tax liability is really a different type of liability from one represented by a contractual debt. In particular, non-current deferred income taxes resulting from using different depreciation methods and asset lives are really not liabilities at all in the usual sense. Furthermore, this type of deferred tax is growing in size in many companies. It is important in analyzing a company's financial statements to recognize this situation.

3. Because of the carryback and carryforward features of the tax laws, a company must be in a long-run loss position before income taxes are not an important consideration. Consequently, even if a company loses money in several years, it is still important to minimize the taxable income. Only when a company has a tax loss carryforward that it cannot use in the time provided does the minimization of taxable income become unimportant. In fact, at that point, it is most useful to have the *maximum* taxable income (or minimum taxable loss). In this way, expenses can be written off for tax purposes now, thus reducing taxable income in future and, hopefully, more profitable years.

QUESTIONS

1. Give examples of specific tax laws that are designed to accomplish social or economic objectives.

2. Explain why the use of the installment method of income recognition will result in a permanent saving in income taxes for a growing business.

3. Why do you think that the accounting profession favors the use of the percentage completion method of income recognition if the results are reasonably predictable? Why is the completed contract method favored if the results are uncertain?

4. Describe some circumstances in which deferred taxes from timing in depreciation expense will completely reverse itself? (That is, will be reduced to zero.)

5. Explain why deferred taxes should be shown as a liability on the balance sheet? How else could deferred taxes be handled on financial statements?

6. Give some specific pattern of earnings (or lack of earnings) that would negate the economic effect of the income tax on a company.

7. Why do you think that the income tax law allows carrybacks and carry-forwards? Is this reasonable from a social and economic point of view?

8. Do you agree with the investment credit? (Remember that if one group pays less income tax, another group must pay more.) Do you approve of Congress' action in making it impossible for the accounting profession to proscribe the flow through method of accounting for the investment credit?

9. Explain the advantages and disadvantages of the LIFO method of inventory valuation? Under what circumstances would you recommend it? Under what circumstances would you recommend FIFO or average?

10. Explain why a timing difference in the recognition of income or expense for tax purposes will result in a permanent saving in income taxes. What are some exceptions?

Problem 9-1

The Silver Company sells goods on the installment plan. The sales, accounts receivables, and gross profit percentage for 1969 through 1973 are listed below:

	($000)				
	1969	*1970*	*1971*	*1972*	*1973*
Sales	$1,060	$1,920	$2,080	$1,420	$1,880
Installment Receivable:					
January 1	0	100	180	220	150
December 31	100	180	220	150	190
Period Costs	210	220	230	240	250
Gross Margin as a Percentage					
of the Sales	30%	35%	35%	40%	35%

(Tax rate = 50 per cent of profits each year.)

Required:

1. Calculate the income tax that would have to be paid each year if revenues were recognized when the sale was made.

2. Calculate the income tax that would have to be paid each year if revenues were recognized in the period when payment was received. (Assume that all installments are collected when due.)

3. If the Silver Company can earn 5 per cent annually on its money after taxes, how much better off would the company be in 1973 if it had used the installment method of revenue recognition for tax purposes during this period instead of recognizing revenue at the date of sale? (Assume that the company pays its income tax at the end of the year.)

Problem 9-2

The Copper Company is a construction contractor. The company has three fixed-price contracts that it worked on from 1970 through 1973. Following are the details of these contracts:

	Contract A	*Contract B*	*Contract C*
Year Started	1970	1971	1972
Year Completed	1971	1973	1973
Fixed-price Contract	$100,000	$150,000	$200,000
Amount Spent through 1970	40,000		

	Contract A	Contract B	Contract C
Estimated Cost to Complete in 1970	$40,000	$	$
Amount Spent through 1971	86,000	65,000	
Estimated Cost to Complete in 1971	(c)	65,000	
Amount Spent through 1972		90,000	80,000
Estimated Cost to Complete in 1972		30,000	80,000
Amount Spent through 1973		125,000	160,000
Estimated Cost to Complete in 1973		(c)	(c)

(c) Contract completed before end of year.

Required:

1. Calculate the income tax payable for years 1970-1973 using the percentage completion method.

2. Calculate the income tax payable for years 1971-1973 using the completed contract method.

Problem 9-3

The Brass Company has the following investment in fixed assets:

Acquired January 1	Cost
1973	$15,000
1972	14,000
1971	12,000
1970	8,000
1969	10,000
1968	8,000
1967	6,000
1966	6,000
1965	5,000
1964	5,000
Total	$89,000

The Brass Company uses a 5-year life and sum-of-the-year's depreciation for tax purposes. It uses a 10-year life and straight-line depreciation for accounting purposes.

Required:

1. Calculate the amount of tax depreciation and the amount of accounting depreciation for the calendar year 1973.

2. Calculate the net book value of the assets for tax purposes and the net book value for accounting purposes as of December 31, 1973.

3. How much income tax has the Brass Company saved over the last 10 years by using the more liberal tax depreciation? (Assume a 50 per cent tax rate.)

Problem 9-4

Make the journal entries to record the tax expense in each of the following:

1. Problem 9-1 for years 1969 through 1973, assuming that the installment method was used for tax purposes and the revenue was recognized at the date of sale for accounting purposes.

2. Problem 9-2 for years 1970 through 1973, assuming that the completed contract method was used for tax purposes and the percentage completion method was used for accounting purposes.

3. In Problem 9-3 what is the amount of deferred taxes as of December 31, 1973?

Problem 9-5

The Zinc Company decided to defer 40 per cent of its expenditures for research and development beginning in 1969. Beginning in 1972, 25 per cent of the balance in the deferred research account at the end of the year was written off. The actual expenditures for research and development were as follows:

1969	$1,500,000
1970	1,670,000
1971	1,780,000
1972	1,400,000
1973	2,000,000

For tax purposes, research and development costs were expensed as incurred.

Required:

1. Make the journal entries each year to record research and development costs and the related deferred tax liability.

2. Show for each year and on a cumulative basis how much more after-tax profits were earned than would have been true had the Zinc Company continued to expense research and development costs as they were incurred.

Problem 9-6

For accounting statement purposes, the 1973 income before taxes for the Lead Company was $32,490,000. Following is a list of items that were included in this income:

1. Depreciation was calculated using the straight-line method on the basis of an average life of 8 years. For tax purposes, a 5-year life using the double declining balance method is used. The tax method would result in $1,840,000 more depreciation in 1973.

2. Revenue on installment sales has been recognized when the sale was made. For tax purposes, however, the Lead Company recognizes revenue when the installment receivable is collected. For 1973, there was a beginning

installments accounts receivable of $3,267,840 and an ending installments accounts receivable of $2,490,000. Gross profit is 30 per cent on both beginning and ending receivables.

3. Income from long-range fixed-price contracts was recognized on a percentage completion basis. For tax purposes, it is recognized on a completed contract basis. The completed contract basis would have resulted in $349,000 more income in 1973.

4. Research and development costs of $1,560,000 were capitalized during the year. (This was the first year these costs had been capitalized.)

5. Dividend income of $2,960,000 was received from other corporations. (The Lead Company held less than 80 per cent of the stock of these companies.)

6. On December 31, the Lead Company accrued $1,836,000 to cover product warranties that are expected to be paid in 1974. At the beginning of the year, there was $1,320,000 in the accrued warranty liability.

7. Tax-free interest from municipal bonds was $429,000.

Before taking account of the above factors, there was $3,427,000 in a current deferred tax liability account and $6,492,000 in a non-current tax liability account. The tax rate is 50 per cent.

Required:

1. Calculate the amount of income tax that the Lead Company would pay for 1973.

2. Calculate the tax expense that would appear on the 1973 financial statements.

3. Calculate the amount of current and non-current deferred taxes that would appear on the Lead Company's balance sheet as of December 31, 1973.

Problem 9-7

Listed below is the taxable income for the three companies for the past 4 years:

Year	*Taxable Income/(Loss)* *Company A*	*($000)* *Company B*	*Company C*
1970	$1,480	$ 340	$1,880
1971	1,680	180	2,860
1972	2,360	400	3,400
1973	(500)	(600)	(10,200)

Required:

1. For companies A and B, calculate the profit after taxes that should be shown on the 1973 income statements. (Assume that accounting income before taxes is the same as taxable income and that a 50 per cent tax rate was in effect throughout this period.)

2. For Company C:

(a) Calculate the profit after taxes that should be shown on the 1973 income statements, assuming that future profitability is uncertain.

(b) Make the journal entry to record the tax refund. (Assume that it has not been paid by December 31, 1973.) Where would the refund appear on the balance sheet? Where would the operating loss carryforward appear on the balance sheet?

3. Answer Question 2 assuming that a $10 million profit was virtually certain in 1974.

4. In 1974, the C Company earns a taxable and accounting profit before taxes of $8 million. What income would be reflected on the income statement for 1974 under situation 2, above? Under situation 3, above? Make the journal entries to record the income tax expense.

Problem 9-8

If one company (Company A) acquires another company (Company B) that has an unused operating loss carryforward, the new company (Company AB) can use that entire operating loss carryforward only if the stockholders of Company B end up owning 20 per cent of Company AB. The fraction of the loss carryforward that can be used if the former B stockholders own less than 20 per cent of Company AB is calculated as follows: percentage ownership of AB held by former stockholders of B divided by 20 per cent.

Required:

Fill in the blanks for each of the cases listed below:

			(000)		
	A	*B*	*C*	*D*	*E*
Operating Loss Carryforward	$1,000	$2,000	$4,000	$5,000	$?
Total Shares in Company AB	100	500	1,000	?	5,000
Shares of AB held by former Shareholders in B	50	100	?	50	50
Usable Operating Loss Carryforward by AB	?	?	2,000	1,250	100
Tax Savings (50 per cent rate)	?	?	1,000	625	50

Problem 9-9

Following are some financial data for the Iron Company for years 1970 through 1974.

	1970	*1971*	*1972*	*1973*	*1974*
Profit before Taxes	$1,000	$1,200	$1,500	$1,400	$1,800
Facilities Acquired That Are Eligible for the Investment Credit	2,500	3,600	1,800	4,000	7,200

All facilities acquired during this period had an expected life of 10 years. The income tax rate has been 50 per cent of before-tax profits during this period.

Required:

Calculate the profits after taxes for the Iron Company for the years 1970 through 1974:

1. Using the flow through method of accounting for the investment credit; and

2. Using the deferred method of accounting for the investment credit. (Assume that the facilities were acquired on July 1.)

Problem 9-10

In 1969, the Steel Company had $10 million in inventories and was using the FIFO method of inventory valuation. At the time, the company considered adopting LIFO but rejected the idea. By 1973, inventories had increased to $18 million. Part of the increase was due to increasing price levels and part was due to an expansion of sales. In December 1973, a study was made to measure the financial impact of the Steel Company's failure to adopt LIFO in 1969. Tax rates were 50 per cent throughout the period. It is estimated that the Steel Company could have earned 4 per cent after taxes on money during this period. These earnings would have started in the year following the tax savings.

Listed below are the Steel Company's inventories at LIFO and FIFO for 1969 through 1973.

December 31	Inventories FIFO	Inventories at LIFO
1969	$10,000	$ 9,800
1970	12,000	11,200
1971	15,000	13,400
1972	17,000	14,400
1973	18,000	14,500

Required:

1. Calculate the extra income taxes that the Steel Company paid over this period.

2. Given the assumptions above, what is the total financial impact of the failure to adopt LIFO in 1969?

3. How would the balance sheet of the Steel Company be different as of December 31, 1973, if LIFO had been adopted in 1969?

Results of Operations
and
Earnings Per Share

Flexibility or Uniformity?

Manager: What is two plus two?

Accountant: What did you have in mind?

10

As we explained in Chapter 8, when accounting principles were first developed, the emphasis was placed almost entirely on the balance sheet because the outsider most likely to have a financial interest in a company was a potential lender, such as a bank. An investor was almost always an insider who had an insider's knowledge of operations. Consequently, published income statements were not necessary to keep the investor informed. All of this, of course, has changed. In recent years, particularly, the balance sheet is often all but ignored by potential investors (although not by potential lenders). The income statement and, particularly, earnings per share have become the most widely accepted indicators of a company's value on the stock market.

The most important single factor in the market value of most stocks is the projected earnings per share (eps). This projection is generally based on the growth in earnings over a period of time. (Of course, the prices of many so-called "glamour stocks" are based on projected *potential* profit, because there is no historical pattern of actual earnings.) During the 1960s, many companies were growing through acquisitions. These acquisitions were made either for cash or for an exchange of stock. In either case, the company with the highest-priced stock, relative to earnings, was in the most favorable position to acquire additional companies. The higher the price of the acquiring company's stock, the fewer shares need be given to meet a given price for the acquired company. As a result, the maintenance of a rising and steady pattern of earnings per share became an important element in corporate strategy for many managements. To the extent that earnings per share could be influenced by accounting methods, accounting policy became a matter of corporate strategy.

To illustrate how earnings per share can be increased by acquiring another company, consider the following example in which Company A acquires Company B by giving the shareholders of B one share of A stock for each four shares of B stock they hold:

	Company A	Company B	Company A after Acquiring B
Earnings	$10,000	$5,000	$15,000
Shares Outstanding	5,000	4,000	6,000[a]
Earnings per Share	$ 2.00	$ 1.25	$ 2.50
Market Price per Share	$ 60.00	$12.50	

[a]Includes 5,000 original shares plus 1,000 shares issued to the owners of B. Notice that A has paid $60,000 (1,000 shares worth $60 each) for the stock of B, which had a total market value of only $50,000 (4,000 shares times $12.50 each). This 20 per cent premium over market value should make the owners of B happy to exchange their shares.

For the investor who does not analyze *why* financial results are as they are, this increase of 25 per cent in the earnings per share of A may be cause to bid the stock price even higher than $60 per share.

The accounting principles and practices used in developing the income statement came under close scrutiny by the Accounting Principles Board during the 1960s. As a result, the APB published several opinions that have had an important effect on reported earnings per share. Two of the most important were APB Opinion 9, "Reporting the Results of Operations," and APB Opinion 15, "Earnings Per Share." Opinion 30 modified some parts of Opinion 9. These changes will be noted where appropriate. Two other opinions that effect earnings per share—APB Opinion 16, "Business Combinations," and APB Opinion 17, "Intangible Assets"—are discussed in Chapter 11. This chapter summarizes the main parts of opinions 9, 15, and 30.

REPORTING THE RESULTS OF OPERATIONS

Changes in the owners' equity of a business enterprise over a period of time may be divided into three different kinds:

First, and by far the most important, are the results of normal business operations.

Second are extraordinary items: for example, an uninsured casualty loss. Extraordinary items are those that are both non-recurring and not part of the normal business operations.

Third are items that are associated with specific previous periods, but which were not recorded at that time. For example, an unfavorable judgment in a law suit would be applicable to the period in which the action causing the law suit occurred, but it may not have been recognized until the suit was finally adjudicated.

As you can see, it is useful to the user of a financial statement to have these three types of economic changes isolated. If a loss in a particular year is caused by an extraordinary write off, the implications of this loss are generally less serious than if it had resulted from normal operations and, thus, might be expected to continue into future years. Also, a loss applicable to a past period would tend to distort current performance if it were not isolated.

Until December 1966, there was considerable latitude regarding what items would be treated as extraordinary and what items would be treated as applicable to prior periods. Also, there was some flexibility whether to charge or credit items applicable to prior periods directly to retained earnings or whether to treat them as part of the current income statement. Thus, it was permissible for companies to treat similar items differently, with resulting confusion in interpreting reported financial information. The purpose of Part 1 of APB Opinion 9 was to ensure consistency among companies in reporting the results of operations. The remainder of this part of the chapter describes some of the principal features of this opinion.

Part 1—APB Opinion 9

Part 1 of APB Opinion 9 accomplished two principal things. First, it made it mandatory for extraordinary items to be disclosed separately on the financial statements. Second, it provided guidelines to what could be considered extraordinary items and what could be treated as an adjustment to prior periods' income. Thus, Opinion 9 defined what should be included in income from normal operations by defining what items might be excluded.

Income Statement Presentation. The income statement must disclose (1) income before extraordinary items (2) extraordinary items (less applicable tax), and (3) net income.

The significance of this part of the opinion is that, if a company has material extraordinary items, they must be disclosed separately on the income statement. Extraordinary items may not be buried in normal operating results or charged directly to retained earnings. The amount of income tax applicable to extraordinary items must also be disclosed in the financial statements.

Criteria for Prior Period Adjustments. A company can increase its reported earnings per share by charging certain costs directly to retained earnings. For example, assume that a company deferred part of its research expense over a period of years, say 1970 through 1974. At the end of 1974, the company decided to change its policy and charge research costs to expense as they are incurred. Prior to Opinion 9, the amount of deferred research could be considered as a prior period expense and charged off directly against retained earnings. Thus, the deferred research cost would never have affected earnings per share. As you can see, one way to increase earnings per share would be to charge as much expense as possible directly to retained earnings. For instance, if a company understated depreciation on its property assets and then wrote off the losses from disposition against retained earnings, the true depreciation would never be reflected in earnings per share. The APB has, consequently, restricted very carefully those items that can be treated as prior period adjustments.

APB 9 has this to say about the items that can be treated as a prior period adjustment:

> 23. Adjustments related to prior periods—and thus excluded in the determination of net income for the current period—are limited to those material adjustments which (a) can be specifically identified with and directly related to the business activities of particular prior periods, and (b) are not attributable to economic events occurring subsequent to the date of the financial statements for the prior period, and (c) depend primarily on

determinations by persons other than management and (d) were not susceptible of reasonable estimation prior to such determination. Such adjustments are rare in modern financial accounting. They relate to events or transactions which occurred in a prior period, the accounting effects of which could not be determined with reasonable assurance at that time, usually because of some major uncertainty then existing. Evidence of such an uncertainty would be disclosure thereof in the financial statements of the applicable period, or of an intervening period in those cases in which the uncertainty became apparent during a subsequent period. Further, it would be expected that, in most cases, the opinion of the reporting independent auditor on such prior period would have contained a qualification because of the uncertainty. Examples are material, nonrecurring adjustments or settlements of income taxes, or renegotiation proceedings or of utility revenue under rate processes. Settlements of significant amounts resulting from litigation or similar claims may also constitute prior period adjustments.

This paragraph just about restricts prior period adjustments to costs (or revenues) that have resulted from some type of adjudication process. (The major exception is the recognition of accounting errors.) All other items of expense and revenue must be included in the income statement in the period in which they are recognized in the books of account.

In Opinion 20, the Accounting Principles Board modified somewhat this restriction on prior period adjustments to cover certain changes in *accounting principles*. It was the belief of the APB that the advantages of retroactive treatment in prior period reports (better comparability of interperiod data) outweighed the disadvantages in the following cases:

1. A change from the LIFO method of inventory pricing to another method;

2. A change in the accounting for long-term construction-type contracts; and

3. A change to or from the "full cost" method of accounting that is used in the extractive industries.

4. A change required by a specific APB Opinion.

When a company makes a prior period adjustment for one of the changes in accounting principles described above, the nature and justification must be disclosed and the effect on income before extraordinary items, extraordinary items, and earnings per share for all periods affected must be shown. Figure 1 shows how a prior period adjustment for inventory valuation was shown in the 1971 financial statements of the Budd Company.

Figure 1

Earnings Reinvested in the Business

BEGINNING OF YEAR—Previously reported	$89,008,425	$112,595,797
Retroactive restatement to reflect cumulative effect of change in accounting method of valuing inventories, net of tax effect	1,219,240	1,223,474
Restated balance	90,227,665	113,819,271
Net earnings (loss) for the year	5,681,039	(20,557,540)

DEDUCT CASH DIVIDENDS:

Preferred shares—$5 per share	(495,625)	(495,625)
Common shares—$.45 per share, 1970	–	(2,538,441)
END OF YEAR	$95,413,079	$ 90,227,665

The following paragraph was included in a footnote on "inventories":

> Effective January 1, 1971, the company changed its method of pricing that portion of its inventories previously stated on the last-in, first-out cost basis (Lifo) to the lower of average cost or market. As a result of this change, net earnings in 1971 were increased by approximately $450,000 (7¢ per share). The use of the Lifo inventory method was discontinued because (a) the Lifo values were not used in determining product selling prices or in measuring divisional operating results and (b) fourth-quarter earnings were distorted since adjustments to the Lifo reserve for the year normally had been provided in that quarter. The financial statements for 1970 have been restated for the resultant increase in 1970 inventories of $2,438,000; the effect on the loss for 1970 was negligible.

APB Opinion 20 also grants a special exemption to companies when they offer their stock to the public for the first time. In these cases, a company may restate its financial statements retroactively in accordance with the accounting policies it will follow as a publicly owned company.

To summarize, then, prior period adjustments are, for practical purposes, restricted to cases involving adjudication, accounting errors, and the few cases of accounting changes described above. (Prior period adjustments may also be made for acquired earnings under the pooling of interest method. This procedure is described in Chapter 11.) When a prior period adjustment is made, full disclosure of that adjustment (both gross and net of applicable income tax) must be made in the financial report for the year in which the adjustment is made. If more than one period is included in the financial report, the effect of the adjustment on all periods must be disclosed.

Criteria for Extraordinary Items. In establishing the criteria for extraordinary items, the APB left more to individual judgment than it did in establishing criteria for prior period adjustments. Nevertheless, the guidelines laid down are fairly specific. The general rule as laid down in Opinion 30 is that for an event or transaction to be treated as extraordinary it must have resulted from circumstances that are significantly *different* from the typical or customary business activities of the entity. Accordingly, they would not be transactions or events that would be expected to occur *frequently*. In short, an item must be both non-recurring and not related to the business before it can be considered extraordinary. Some examples of extraordinary items include material gains or losses from:

1. Sale or abandonment of a significant "segment" of the business (eliminating an entire product line would be extraordinary, but eliminating part of a continuing product line would not be);

2. A natural calamity that could not be reasonably anticipated.

Regarding item 1 Opinion 30 provides the following examples of events that would and would not qualify as extraordinary:

Qualifies as Disposal of a Segment of a Business

1. Sale by diversified company of major division which represents its only activities in electronics industry.

2. Sale by meat packing company of 25 per cent interest in professional football team (on equity method).

3. Sale by communications company of all radio stations with television and publishing company continuing.

4. Food distributor sells wholesale to supermarket chains and through fast food restaurants (two major classes of customers) and decides to discontinue the division which sells to one of the two classes of customers.

Does Not Qualify as Disposal of a Segment of a Business

1. Sale of foreign subsidiary engaged in silver mining and seller continues to engage in silver mining.

2. Sale by petrochemical company of 25 per cent interest in petrochemical refinery (on equity method) while remaining business continues in petrochemicals.

3. Manufacturer of children's wear discontinues its operations in Italy but not elsewhere.

4. Sale by diversified company of subsidiary which manufactures furniture while retaining other furniture manufacturing subsidiary.

5. Sale of all assets (including plant) related to manufacture of woolen suits to concentrate on suits made of synthetic products.

The APB has provided a list of other items that can *not* be considered extraordinary. These are:

1. Write downs of receivables, inventories, property assets, and deferred research and development costs;

2. Adjustments of accrued contract prices;

3. Gains or losses from fluctuations of foreign currency;

4. Sale or abandonment of a plant.

To summarize, then, the key to an item being treated as extraordinary is that it results from events different from the typical business activity and, consequently, such an event would be expected to occur only rarely.

The following excerpts from the 1973 annual report of Genesco, Inc. illustrate the treatment of extraordinary items and of items that are special or non-recurring but not extraordinary.

Exhibit 10-1

Genesco, Inc. 1973 Annual Report

CONSOLIDATED EARNINGS Year ended 31 July	1973	1972 Restated
Net sales	$1,410,503,000	$1,395,403,000
Discontinued operations	185,953,000	236,470,000
Net sales from continuing operations	1,224,550,000	1,158,933,000
Cost of sales	855,320,000	786,121,000
Non-recurring inventory writedowns	–	8,400,000
Selling, administrative and general expenses	321,049,000	309,939,000
Equity in losses of nonconsolidated companies	1,547,000	2,614,000
Interest expense	17,299,000	15,062,000
	1,195,215,000	1,122,136,000
Earnings from continuing operations before taxes	29,335,000	36,797,000
Minority interest	337,000	173,000
Federal, state and Canadian income taxes	14,507,000	16,487,000
Earnings from continuing operations after taxes	14,491,000	20,137,000
Operating loss from discontinued operations net of taxes	(11,771,000)	(7,324,000)
Earnings before extraordinary loss	2,720,000	12,813,000
Extraordinary loss net of taxes	(55,623,000)	(3,909,000)
Net earnings (loss)	$(52,903,000)	$ 8,904,000

EARNINGS (LOSS) PER COMMON SHARE PRIMARY		
Continuing operations	$ .85	$ 1.31
Discontinued operations	(.94)	(.59)
Before extraordinary loss	(.09)	.72
Extraordinary loss	(4.45)	(.31)
Net	$(4.54)	$ .41

FULLY DILUTED		
Continuing operations	$ .80	$ 1.27
Discontinued operations	(.89)	(.55)
Before extraordinary loss	(.09)	.72
Extraordinary loss	(4.45)	(.31)
Net	$(4.54)	$ .41

Notice that the inventory write down and the operating losses of discontinued operations prior to discontinuance are highlighted as "special" items but they do not qualify for treatment as extraordinary items.

(11) Losses Resulting from Discontinued Companies and Operations

On 30 July 1973, the company's Board of Directors approved a formal plan to (a) close a substantial number of unprofitable stores in its S. H. Kress variety store chain and to sell the remaining stores, (b) liquidate its Italian suit manufacturing company, along with several other European companies engaged in the manufacture and sale of women's apparel in the European market, (c) liquidate and/or sell the assets of certain knitting operations, and (d) close about one-third of the stores in certain women's shoe retailing divisions. Provision for losses estimated to be incurred as a result of this action has been made in the accompanying consolidated financial statements. The effect on the consolidated balance sheet was as follows (decrease):

Assets	
Accounts receivable	$ (1,003,000)
Inventory	(12,816,000)
Fixed assets held for resale	12,567,000
Fixed assets	(30,481,000)
Investments	(18,980,000)
Future tax benefits	25,899,000
Investment in excess of equity	(780,000)
Liabilities and stockholders' equity	
Deferred credits to income	(11,785,000)
Provision for discontinued operations	
Current	25,609,000
Long-term	20,728,000
Stockholder's equity	(60,146,000)

During fiscal 1973 certain other operations were also sold or discontinued. *The consolidated earnings statement reflects the losses of all discontinued operations prior to the date of the decision to discontinue as a separate item,* net of taxes of $11,516,000 in 1973 and $5,934,000 in 1972.

	The extraordinary loss is made up of	
	1973	1972
Provision for estimated losses on sale, restructure or discontinuance of operating divisions	$ 80,745,000	$ —

Gain on divisions sold	(6,148,000)	$ –
Losses on other operating divisions discontinued	2,499,000	–
Flood damage caused by Hurricane Agnes.	–	3,784,000
Losses on disposal of operations discontinued in prior years in excess of reserve provided.	–	3,324,000
	77,096,000	7,108,000
Taxes	21,473,000	3,199,000
Net	$ 55,623,000	$ 3,909,000

EARNINGS PER SHARE

In this part of the chapter, we will summarize the present requirements for reporting earnings per share. In doing so, we have selected those features of Opinion 15 that are important to the user of financial statements. Parts of Opinion 15 are concerned with procedures for making the calculations. These, of course, are extremely important to the accountant responsible for calculating earnings per share. They are of considerably less importance to the user of financial statements. He needs only to be generally familiar with the procedures. For example, the part of the denominator of the earnings per share calculation is the *weighted average* of the shares outstanding. This is really all the user of financial statements needs to know. The details of how this weighted average is calculated are important principally to the accountant who must make the calculation.

Significance of APB Opinion 15

APB Opinion 15 (effective as of December 31, 1968) made two significant changes to the then current practice of reporting earnings per share. First, it made the earnings per share calculation a required part of financial reporting. This means not only that every company must report earnings per share, but that the earnings per share calculation is covered by the auditor's opinion and, consequently, must conform to APB opinions. Second, APB Opinion 15 provides specific rules for calculating earnings per share. These rules introduced factors into the earnings per share calculation that were rarely, if ever, shown on financial reports up to that time. The earnings per share calculation now includes not only the number of outstanding shares of stock, but "common stock equivalents" as well. Also, two earnings per share calculations are required if a company has a "complex" capital structure: (1) "primary" earnings per share, and (2) "fully diluted" earnings per share. Methods for calculating primary and fully diluted earnings per share are discussed in the section titled Complex Capital Structure. First, however, let us review the earnings per share calculation in a simple capital structure.

Simple Capital Structure

A simple capital structure is one in which there are no material amounts of potentially dilutive[1] securities, such as convertible securities, warrants, or stock options. In other words, the capital structure consists of common stock and nonconvertible bonds and preferred stock.[2] The method of calculating earnings per share is quite straightforward. The earnings are divided by the weighted average of the number of common shares outstanding during the year. Dividends on preferred stock are first subtracted from earnings to get earnings available to the common shareholders. Notice that you subtract the dividends that are payable under the preferred stock agreement, whether or not these dividends have yet been paid. Any dilution of less than 3 percent in the aggregate need not be considered.

Complex Capital Structure

A complex capital structure is one that includes material amounts of convertible securities, warrants, stock options, or stock purchase contracts. As you will remember from Chapter 7, a *convertible security* is either a bond or a share of preferred stock that may be converted into a given number of shares of common stock during some specified period of time. *Warrants* are instruments (sometimes issued along with bonds or preferred stock) that give the holder the priviledge of buying common stock at a specified price within a prescribed time period. *Options* are agreements (made usually with executives of a company) that allow the holder of the option to buy a specified number of shares of stock at a specified price within a prescribed time period. For all practical purposes a warrant is the same as an option. The Accounting Principles Board concluded that some of these securities

---

[1] A "dilutive" security is one that can be converted into shares of common stock, thus diluting the relative ownership interest of the current shareholders.

[2] There are types of preferred stock that carry participating rights in net income. This can make the problem of calculating earnings per share considerably more complex. We believe that you need not be concerned with this matter. If you are interested, see paragraphs 59 and 60 of APB Opinion 15.

were "common stock equivalents." Paragraph 15 of APB Opinion 15 describes a common stock equivalent in this way:

> A common stock equivalent is a security which is not, in form, a common stock but which usually contains provisions to enable its holder to become a common stockholder and which, because of its terms and the circumstances under which it was issued, is in substance equivalent to common stock. The holders of these securities can expect to participate in the appreciation of the value of the common stock resulting principally from the earnings and earnings potential of the issuing corporation . . . . The value of a common stock equivalent is derived in a large part from the value of the common stock to which it is related, and changes in its value tend to reflect changes in the value of the common stock.

Common stock equivalents are used in the calculation of both "primary" and "fully diluted" earnings per share. The next two parts of this chapter describe how earnings per share are calculated in a company with a complex capital structure.

Primary Earnings Per Share. The calculation of primary earnings per share allows for common stock equivalents as well as actual common stock outstanding. The following paragraphs explain how primary eps is calculated.

Convertible securities are considered common stock equivalents if, *on the date of issue*, the effective (cash) yield to the holder was less than 66 2/3 per cent of the prime bank rate at that time. The rationale behind this rule is that if the purchaser of the security is willing to accept a cash yield significantly less than the prime bank rate, an important part of the value of the security must be due to its conversion feature. The "2/3 bank prime rate yield" test is a purely arbitrary way of defining "equivalence" to common stock. This test converts what is intrinsically a subjective issue into a black-white, on-off issue. Once the determination is made that a convertible security is a common stock equivalent, it is considered to be so for as long as the issue is outstanding. Conversely, an issue of convertible securities that is not deemed a common stock equivalent when issued can never be considered one later. In calculating earnings per share, an adjustment is made to both the number of shares and the net income to simulate the conversion. The number of shares will be increased as though the security was completely converted to common stock at the beginning of the accounting period. The net income figure used will be net income *before* applicable interest expense or preferred dividends. Notice that the income statement itself is *not adjusted*. Only the income number used to calculate earnings per share.

Stock *warrants* and stock *options* are considered to be common stock equivalents at the end of any given period if the average market price of the stock during the period is higher than the exercise price of the warrants or options. Suppose, for example, that a warrant or option can be exercised to acquire one share of stock at a price of $10. If the stock is selling for $11, the warrant or option is a common stock equivalent. If the stock is selling for $9, the warrant or option is not a common stock equivalent. As a paractical matter, the board recommends that, before a warrant or option be considered a common stock equivalent, the market price of the common stock must be in excess of the exercise price for substantially all of three consecutive months. Unlike convertible securities, for which the test for common stock equivalency is made once and for all time at the date of issue, the test for common stock equivalency for warrants and options is made at the end of each accounting period. If a stock warrant or a stock option is considered to be a common stock equivalent, the procedure for calculating the impact on eps is called the "treasury stock" method. It is as follows:[3]

1. Multiply the number of warrants or option shares by the exercise price. This amount is the total proceeds the firm would receive if all warrants or options were exercised.

2. Divide the amount calculated in (1) by the average market price of the shares during the period. This represents the number of outstanding shares that could hypothetically be reacquired (treasury shares) using the total warrant or option proceeds.

3. Subtract this amount from the number of warrants or option shares. The difference is the hypothetical dilution (net additional shares) due to the exercise of the warrants or options.

4. Add this number to the shares outstanding for the period. This procedure is illustrated in the next section of the chapter.

5. The calculation is made for each quarter and the quarters are averaged. For example, if the time period is one year, the common stock equivalents for each quarter are added together and divided by four.

Implicit in this calculation is the idea that a firm uses the proceeds from the exercise of warrants or options to acquire as many of its own shares of stock as possible on the open market. The board pointed out in Opinion 15 that the rationale behind this procedure was *not* that the exercise of the stock option or warrant would be likely to result in the acquisition of treasury stock. The treasury stock method is just a means of indicating the possible effect on the present shareholders of the exercise of these warrants or options. Clearly, the greater the difference between the exercise price and the market price, the more favorable it will be for the present stockholders. Many accountants disagree with the APB on this part of the opinion. Their position is that this calculation is totally arbitrary and thus not meaningful.

Example of Calculation of Primary Earnings Per Share

Income Statement Information

Net Income before Extraordinary Items	$26,470,000
Extraordinary Loss (net of taxes)	3,360,000
Net Income	$23,110,000

---

[3] If the number of shares involved is greater than 20 per cent of the shares outstanding, there is an alternative procedure. See Problem 10-9 for an example of this procedure.

Common Stock Outstanding
Number of Shares of Common Stock

Outstanding on January 1	6,400,000
Issued on July 1	100,000
Number of Shares Outstanding on December 31	6,500,000

Preferred Stock. Throughout the year, 10,000 shares of nonconvertible preferred stock, par value $100 per share, preferred dividend $5 per share, were outstanding.

Convertible Debentures. During the year, $5 million of 3% debentures, convertible to four shares of common stock per $100 bond, were outstanding. These bonds were sold 3 years ago at par. The prime bank rate at the time of sale was 5.5 per cent. Since 3 per cent is less than two-thirds of 5.5 per cent, this issue is a common stock equivalent.

Also, $10 million of 5 per cent debentures, convertible into five shares of common stock per $100 bond, were outstanding during the year. The bonds were sold 5 years ago when the bank prime rate was 6 per cent. This issue is not a common stock equivalent.

Stock Warrants. Each share of preferred stock has a warrant to purchase one share of common stock for $30 a share.

Stock Options. Executives of the company have options as follows:

Number of Shares	Exercise Price
50,000	$20
50,000	25
100,000	30
50,000	40

Market Price. The average market price of the stock during the year was $35 per share. The price never fell below $35 or rose as high as $40 during October, November, or December.

Calculation of Average Oustanding Shares

Weighted Average of Common Stock outstanding:

Shares on January 1	6,400,000
Shares Issued during Year	
100,000 X .5 (one-half year)	50,000
3% Convertible Debentures[a]	200,000
Stock Warrants[b]	1,429
Stock Options[c]	50,000
Weighted Average of Shares Outstanding	6,701,429

[a]$5,000,000 ÷ 4 shares per $100 = 200,000 shares potentially outstanding. Since the yield of 3 per cent is 55 per cent of the prime rate at date of issue, these are considered to be common stock equivalents. The 4 per cent convertibles are not included because they yielded more than two-thirds of the bank prime rate at date of issue.

[b]10,000 warrants × $30 = $300,000 potential proceeds from the exercise of the warrants. $300,000 ÷ $35 = 8,571 shares that could be purchased at the average market price. 10,000 − 8,571 = 1,429 *increase* in common shares outstanding.

[c](50,000 × $20) + (50,000 × $25) + (100,000 × $30) = $5,250,000 proceeds. (The 50,000 shares optioned at $40 a share are not common stock equivalents when the stock price is only $35). $5,250,000 ÷ $35 = 150,000 shares. 200,000 − 150,000 = 50,000 shares increase.

In (b) and (c) above, we have used a simple calculation for the entire year for simplicity. In actual practice, these calculations would be made by quarter and the quarters averaged.

Calculation of Net Income

Net Income before Extraordinary Items	$ 26,470,000
Less: Preferred Stock Dividends	50,000
Plus: Interest on Convertible	
Debentures (3 per cent of $5 million × .5 after tax)	75,000
Net Income before Extraordinary Items for	
EPS Calculation	$26,495,000
Extraordinary Losses	3,360,000
Net Income for EPS Calculation	$23,135,000

Calculation of Primary Earnings Per Share

Net Income before Extraordinary Items:
  $26,495,000 ÷ 6,701,429 = $3.95 per share
Extraordinary Losses ($3,360,000 ÷ 6,701,429) = $.50 per share
Net Income Per Share $3.45

Fully Diluted Earnings Per Share

In theory, the purpose of including fully diluted earnings per share in the income statement is to show the eps impact if *all* potential common stock conversions were made. (As we shall see, this is not really true in practice.) Of course, any items considered to be common stock equivalents for purposes of computing primary earnings per share will also be considered such for purposes of computing fully diluted earnings per share. The principal additional items considered to be common stock for fully diluted eps are those convertible securities that did not qualify as common stock equivalents for calculating primary earnings per share. All convertible securities are considered to be converted to common stock for purposes of calculating fully diluted earnings per share, unless this assumed conversion would result in "anti-dilution"—i.e., increasing the eps.[4] Also, when calculating common stock equivalents for warrants and options, the closing market price is used if this is higher than the average.

Calculation of Fully Diluted Earnings Per Share

Calculation of Shares

Shares Per the Primary EPS Calculation	6,701,429
Shares from 4% Convertible Debentures	500,000
	7,201,429

Calculation of Earnings

From Primary EPS Calculation: Net Income before Extraordinary Items	$26,495,000
Plus: Interest on 5% Convertibles (after tax)	250,000
	$26,745,000

Fully Diluted Earnings Per Share

Before Extraordinary Items	$26,745,000 ÷ 7,201,429 = $3.71
Extraordinary Losses	$ 3,360,000 ÷ 7,201,429 = $ .47
Net Income Per Share	$3.24

Interpreting the EPS Numbers under Opinion 15. Opinion 15 was issued because it was felt that the reader of financial statements can be misled when he or she interprets eps to be simply earnings after preferred dividends divided by average shares outstanding. Such a view is clearly misleading if the capital structure of a firm includes convertible securities and other items that can potentially dilute the shareholders' equity. For companies with complex capital structures, the opinion does require two eps numbers and thus puts the statement reader on guard that no single eps number can be accepted as the "correct" answer. The problem with eps under Opinion 15 is that it is based on so many arbitrary calculations and assumptions that many people consider it to be perhaps as misleading as the naive calculation.

It is useful to think of eps as a continuum, actual shares outstanding divided by actual earnings would be the maximum number. Some minimum number at the other extreme would allow somehow for all potential common shares and their

---

[4] Suppose, for example, a firm has outstanding an issue of convertible preferred stock that pays a $5 per share dividend and converts into one share of common for each share of preferred. Suppose also that the company earns $3.50 a share before considering this preferred issue. This issue cannot be considered as common stock for either the primary or fully diluted calculation under Opinion 15. If the number of shares of this convertible stock were added to shares of common stock and the dividend were added back to earnings, the eps would go *up* from $3.50. Such anti-dilution is not permissible under the opinion. The Bunker-Ramo Corporation case at the end of the chapter illustrates this further. Also, warrants and options with exercise prices above the market price of the stock at the end of the period (as contrasted with the average price during the period) are not considered in the fully diluted calculation because applying the treasury stock method to them would result in anti-dilution.

effect on eps. Many accountants believe that Opinion 15 highlights two intermediate numbers on this continuum, neither of which has any particular significance. Primary eps is not necessarily the maximum eps number that a reader should consider. Its determination of whether a convertible security should be considered or not relates to information at date of issue of the security. Such data can get badly out of date. In our earlier example, the 5 per cent convertibles are even more like common stock today than the 3% convertibles ($20 conversion price versus $25 conversion price) but they are not counted because of the arbitrary nature of the "yield test." It is also possible for securities to go on being counted for primary eps purposes even after they have ceased to have any value at all in terms of conversion to common stock. Consider, for example, a debenture issued in 1971 that converts to three shares of common per $100 of face value. If it yielded 50 per cent of "prime" at the date of issue, it was deemed a common stock equivalent for all time. Suppose that the stock sold for $30 a share then and now sells for $5 a share. It is unlikely that anyone would still consider the security to be like common stock. Very probably, the market price now of such a bond would be based simply on the fact that it is a very low yield bond. Its conversion feature would have no particular operational significance. Furthermore, the very arbitrary nature of the "treasury stock" method can understate significantly the impact of warrant or option conversion on eps if proceeds are *not* used to purchase treasury stock.

Similarly, fully diluted eps is not the minimum number possible under conversion of all potential shares outstanding. In our earlier example the 50,000 shares optioned at $40 are not counted even though the potential dilution here is very real. Anti-dilutive securities are also not counted although they too represent potential extra shares outstanding.

In short, we believe that Opinion 15 represents a questionable attempt by the APB to "legislate truth" in a very complex and highly judgmental area. It is definitely true that naive approaches to calculating eps should be discouraged. This does not mean, however, that very complicated and arbitrary calculation rules necessarily represent an improvement over such naive calculations. We believe that anyone who is interested in trends in the earnings record of an individual share of common stock should consider very carefully the rules laid down in APB 15 and the results such rules produce.

To the extent that disclosure permits, many analysts prefer to reconstruct their own calculations, allowing however they choose for the problem of potential dilution.

QUESTIONS

1. What are the circumstances that could result in the market value of a company's stock being only a fraction of its book value? Since in many instances book value understates fair value, would it not be wise to invest in such stocks? Conversely, why would a stock sell at several times its book value? Would not this situation indicate that the stock was overpriced?

2. Why is it important that income statements be consistent with respect to extraordinary items and prior period adjustments? Why not let companies

determine for themselves how to classify items on the income statement as long as they disclose the nature of any unusual revenue or expense in a footnote?

3. Why do you think that the board has restricted the use of prior period adjustments so greatly? Do you agree? Why do you think that they made an exception when a company changes from LIFO to FIFO?

4. What is the advantage of segregating extraordinary items in the income statement? Do you agree with the board's guidelines for determining whether or not an item is extraordinary? If not, how would you change it?

5. What is the advantage of having the earnings per share calculations appear as part of the income statement? Particularly, what is the advantage of having earnings per share covered by the auditor's opinion?

6. What is a common stock equivalent? What is the rationale for including those in the earnings per share calculation? Do you agree with the Board's position on this matter?

7. How is a shareholder's interest affected adversely if some executives of the company have an option to buy common stock at substantially less than the market price?

8. What does the term "anti-dilution" mean? Under what circumstances could it occur? Why do you think the APB disallows anti-dilution?

9. Can you think of a method, other than the "treasury stock" method, for calculating the effect of outstanding stock options on the earnings per share?

10. Explain the difference between primary earnings per share and fully diluted earnings per share. Why do you think the APB requires that both be calculated?

PROBLEMS

Problem 10-1

For each of the expense and revenue items listed below indicate whether they should be:

1. Included as ordinary income;
2. Included as an extraordinary item;
3. Treated as a prior period adjustment.

(a) Sales to customers of the products produced by the manufacturing facilities.

(b) Sales to employees, at a special discount, of certain products produced by the company.

(c) A sale to an officer, at a special price, of one of the products produced by the company. This is the first time such a sale has been made.

(d) Research costs for a product that will not be produced for at least 3 years, if at all.

(e) The sale of a plant in which operations had been discontinued.

(f) A loss, in excess of insurance, resulting from a fire in one of the company's warehouses.

(g) The loss by embezzlement of a material amount of money by the company's former treasurer. The treasurer lost the money gambling on horses.

(h) The tax court upheld during the year the IRS claim that the company owed additional taxes from 3 years ago. These taxes have not yet been recognized as expenses.

(i) The company changed during the year from the completed contract method of recognizing income on long-range fixed price contracts to the percentage completion method.

(j) An employee won a suit to compensate him for an accident that occured 2 years ago.

(k) The company discovers that several fixed assets that are less than 50 per cent depreciated are nearly obsolete. The amount of depreciation on these assets is increased accordingly.

(l) A creditor who had signed a large note unexpectedly went bankrupt. This possibility had not been covered in the allowance for doubtful accounts.

(m) The company decides to stop producing an entire line of products. The estimated loss from closing down this part of the business and disposing of the assets is $3,000,000.

(n) It is necessary to make a large and unexpected write off of certain items of inventory.

Problem 10-2

The ABC Company has used the LIFO method of inventory valuation for several years. In 1973, the FIFO method of inventory valuation was adopted. The inventories on December 31, 1972, on a LIFO basis, were valued at $12,694,000. On a FIFO basis, these inventories would be valued at $16,423,000. An income tax of 50 per cent of the increase would have to be paid. The retained earnings as of December 31, 1972, were $106,370,000; earnings for the year using FIFO inventory valuation were $25,496,000, and dividends were $15,000,000.

Required:

Prepare the retained earnings statement for the year ended December 31, 1973.

Problem 10-3

The DEF Company has been using the completed contract method of accounting for its long-term construction contracts. In 1973 it decided to adopt the percentage completion method for accounting purposes. On December 31, 1972, the following contracts are in process:

	Contract 101	Contract 102	Contract 103
Price	$100,000	$200,000	$300,000
Amount Spent to Date	60,000	50,000	80,000
Expected Cost to Complete	25,000[a]	120,000[a]	180,000

[a]These contracts were completed during 1973.

As of December 31, 1972, the retained earnings had a balance of $6,497,000. Earnings for 1973 were $1,484,000 and dividends were $850,000. The tax rate was 50 per cent. No change is to be made in the taxable earnings.

Required:

Prepare the retained earnings statement for the year ended December 31, 1973.

Problem 10-4

During 1973 the AMP Company lost a dispute with the Internal Revenue Service. As a result, it was required to pay $5,467,000 for income taxes applicable to its 1970 income. As of December 31, 1972, retained earnings had a balance of $25,964,000 before recognizing the additional tax. After-tax earnings for 1973 were $4,533,000 before recognizing the additional tax, and dividends were $3,000,000.

Required:

1. How would this adverse judgment be handled on the books at the time it occurred?
2. Prepare a retained earnings summary for 1973.

Problem 10-5

Below are some financial facts concerning the earnings and capital structure of the PMD Company for 1973.

Preferred Stock:

> 100,000 shares; nonconvertible; $5 annual dividend;
> par value $10,000,000; preferred dividends paid in 1973, $500,000.

Common Stock:	Number of Shares
Outstanding on January 1	1,000,000
Additional Shares Sold during Year	
March 1	100,000
July 1	50,000
September 1	45,000

Stock Options:

> Options to buy 5,000 shares were outstanding on December 31; option price, $30 per share; average market price during year, $34.

Income:

Net Income before Extraordinary Items	$3,470,000
Extraordinary Losses Net of Tax	530,000
Net Income after Extraordinary Losses	$2,940,000

Required:

1. What is the earnings per share for the PMD Company for 1973?
2. Does the PMD Company have a simple or complex capital structure? Why?

Problem 10-6

Below are some financial facts concerning the earnings and capital structure of the ACE Company for 1973.

Preferred Stock:

> 10,000 shares; par value, $100 per share; nonconvertible; preferred dividend, $5 per share; no dividends paid in 1973; each preferred share has a warrant that entitles the owner to buy a share of common stock for $20 per share.

Common Stock:

> 50,000 shares of $5 par value were outstanding on January 1; the following sales of stock were made during the year; 5,000 on July 1 and 5,000 on October 1.

Stock Options:

> The following stock options were outstanding at the end of the year:

Number of Shares	Option Price
5,000	$20
4,000	22
6,000	25

Market Value:

> The common stock had an average market value of $40 per share during 1973.

Income:

Net Income before Extraordinary Items	$536,000
Extraordinary Loss	350,000
Net Income (loss) after Extraordinary Items	$186,000

Required:

Calculate primary and fully diluted earnings per share for 1973.

Problem 10-7

Below are some financial facts concerning the earnings and capital structure of the MNO Company for 1973.

Preferred Stock:

> 100,000 shares; par value, $100 per share; preferred dividends, $3 per share; no dividends were paid in 1973; each share convertible into four shares of common; the preferred stock was originally sold at par; prime bank rate at time of sale was 5 percent.

Common Stock:

> 1,000,000 shares outstanding throughout the year.

Bonds:

> $10,000,000 in 5% debentures. Bonds are convertible to five shares of stock for each $100 bond. The bonds were sold for par. The prime bank rate at the time of sale was 6 per cent.

Options:

> The following options are outstanding as of December 31:

Number of Shares	Option Price
10,000	$25
20,000	30
10,000	35

Market Price:

> The market price of the stock averaged $35 per share during 1973.

Earnings:

Income before Extraordinary Items	$3,496,000
Extraordinary Losses	1,327,000
Income after Extraordinary Items	$2,169,000

Required:

Calculate the primary and fully diluted earnings per share for the MNO Company for 1973.

Problem 10-8

How would your answers to problems 10-6 and 10-7 differ if the 1973 income were as follows:

The ACE Company

Net Income (loss) before Extraordinary Items	$ (536,000)
Extraordinary Income	350,000
Net Income (loss) after Extraordinary Items	$ (186,000)

The MNO Company

Net Income (loss) before Extraordinary Items	$(3,496,000)
Extraordinary Income	1,327,000
Net Income (loss) After Extraordinary Items	$(2,169,000)

Problem 10-9

APB Opinion 15 makes one modification in the use of the treasury stock method of determining common stock equivalents for stock warrants and stock options. This exception occurs if the number of outstanding warrants and options exceed 20 per cent of the number of common shares outstanding at the end of the period for which the computation is made. In this circumstance, the following procedure is followed:

1. The treasury stock method is used to simulate the purchase of 20 per cent of the outstanding shares;
2. The balance of the funds is used, first, to simulate the retirement of any short- or long-term borrowings. If there are additional funds after the borrowings have been retired, these are used to simulate an investment in U.S. government securities or commercial paper.

Below are some financial facts concerning the earnings and capital structure of the PQR Company for 1973.

Common Stock:

1,000,000 shares of common stock were outstanding during the year.

Bonds:

$1,000,000 in 6% nonconvertible mortgage bonds were outstanding during the year.

Short-term Loans:

The company held $100,000 in short-term loans on which $6,000 was paid in interest during the year.

Stock Option:

As of December 31, there were outstanding options to purchase 400,000 shares of common stock for $12 per share.

Market Price:

The market price of the stock averaged $15 per share during the year.

Earnings:

Net Income after Taxes[a] $543,000

[a]There were no extraordinary items in 1973.

Government Securities:

The company could expect to earn 4 per cent on government
securities.

Required:

Calculate the earnings per share for the PQR Company for 1973.

Problem 10-10

Below are some financial facts concerning the earnings and capital structure of
the STU Company for 1973.

Common Stock:

10,498,000 shares were outstanding during the year.

Mortgage:

The company had a 10-year loan (5 years yet to run) of
$4,000,000 with a local insurance company. The interest
rate was 7 per cent. Part of the company's fixed assets
were mortgaged as security for the loan.

Short-term Loans

As of December 31, 1973, the company had $1,000,000 in short-term
loans. The interest on these loans was $100,000 during 1973.

Stock Warrants:

As of December 31, there were outstanding warrants to purchase
3,000,000 shares of common stock at $20 per share.

Market Price:

The market price averaged $25 per share during 1973.

Earnings:

Net Income after Taxes $25,496,000

Government Securities:

The company could expect to earn 6 per cent on government securities.

Required:

Calculate the earnings per share for the STU Company for 1973.

Problem 10-11

This footnote is taken from the 1972 annual report of the Continental Can
Company.

B. Plan for Facilities Retirement and Asset Redeployment

In October 1972, the Board of Directors approved a plan for facilities retirement and asset redeployment of certain metal operations and certain other operations. The aggregate cost of $231,200,000 anticipated in connection with the plan is shown in the accompanying statement of consolidated earnings as an extraordinary charge, less related tax benefit of $111,100,000. While it is not presently possible to determine the actual cost to be incurred in connection with the plan, the following reserves have been provided:

	(In Thousands)
Fixed asset disposals, extraordinary obsolescence, etc.	$ 82,500
Pensions and group insurance, severance pay, etc.	76,400
Equipment transfer, etc.	41,700
Other	30,600
	$231,200

Question:

Which of the items mentioned would still qualify for treatment of extraordinary items after APB 30?

Problem 10-12

The following note is taken from the 1973 annual report of Pneumo Dynamics Corporation. How would the items described in this note be treated under APB 30?

NOTE I Extraordinary Items

The 1973 extraordinary credit is represented by the current year benefit resulting from the availability of the prior year operating loss carryforwards.

During 1972, the Corporation incurred the following extraordinary charges:

Loss on sale of net assets of Machine Tool Group Division	$4,012,929
Loss on discontinuance of Trans-Wheel Division	1,917,706
Consolidation of and discontinuance in use of certain Cleveland Pneumatic plant facilities and transfer of Corporate offices to Boston	1,901,327
Net loss from sales of assembly plant and airplanes and flood loss	621,988
	8,453,950
Less related income tax credit	1,921,000
	$6,532,950

Under an agreement effective November 30, 1972, the Corporation sold the net assets of the Machine Tool Group Division, except for certain finished parts inventories, and the Capital Stock of Cone Automatic Machine Company Limited, an unconsolidated British subsidiary, for $5,500,000 in cash at the closing in December, 1972, and a note receivable of $5,500,000 which was paid on November 30, 1973. The finished parts inventories at November 30, 1972, were sold in 1973 to the same buyer for their approximate carrying value.

The Trans-Wheel Division, created early in 1971, was involved in a substantial product development program for advancing technologies in hi-torque motors and hydrostatic transmission systems. In 1972, management determined not to invest additional funds and discontinued operations of the Division.

During 1972, the Corporation consolidated and discontinued use of certain of its landing gear facilities in Cleveland and transferred its Corporate office to Boston, resulting in losses on the sale of machinery and equipment and consolidation costs.

Intercorporate Investments
and
Business Combinations

Form or Substance?

*"No matter how specific and detailed the accounting
rule, the mind of the enterprising entrepreneur will
conceive a transaction consistent with the rule and
inconsistent with the spirit behind it."*

Shank's Axiom

11

When one corporation acquires stock of another corporation, the transaction results in one of several possible relationships, depending on the percentage of ownership acquired, the conditions of the acquisition, and, to some extent, the decisions of the management of the acquiring company. In this part of the chapter we will consider the accounting issues related to such intercorporate investments.

Marketable Securities

If one corporation purchases relatively small blocks of the stock of other corporations as a temporary investment in order to earn a return on excess funds that would otherwise be idle, the investments are called marketable securities and are classified as a current asset. Marketable securities also would include any other short-term holdings of income-producing securities that can readily be sold. Examples of other items are government notes or bills, commercial paper, and certificates of deposit. Because marketable securities represent temporary investments of excess cash that could readily be converted to cash, they are often termed "cash equivalents" in financial statements.

Stock of publicly traded corporations held as a marketable security is almost always carried on financial statements at the amount paid for the stock. Dividends received are treated as income. If the securities are sold, the difference between the original cost and the selling price is recognized as a capital gain or loss. This approach to accounting for marketable securities is called the "cost method." Because the market prices of common stocks fluctuate daily, the amount that could be realized through sale is usually different from the cost and is often substantially different. Under the cost method, such differences between cost and market values are usually disclosed parenthetically in the financial statements.

The principle of conservatism suggests an alternative approach to valuing marketable securities and is called the "lower of cost or market (lcm) method." The lcm method is used by a few companies. This method recognizes market price movements *downward* from cost but does not recognize price movements *upward* from cost. In other words, capital losses are recognized when they occur even if they are not realized. Capital gains, however, are recognized only when they are realized. Like the cost method, the lcm method recognizes dividends received as income.

Many people believe that marketable securities should be listed on the balance sheet at their market value. They argue that a cash equivalent should be valued at the amount of cash to which it is equivalent. Under the market value method, *both* capital gains *and* capital losses are recognized as they occur, whether or not they are realized. Income for any period under this method also includes dividends received. The market value method is used by mutual funds, investment companies, and by any other companies whose primary business is investments. It is not currently considered to be good accounting for companies whose primary business is not investments.

In terms of basic approaches to profit recognition, which were discussed in Chapter 2, the market value method measures profit as change in "wealth" between two balance sheet dates plus realized flows during the period. Wealth in this context is equal to market price, which represents the command over goods and services as of the balance sheet date. In this regard, the measurement of wealth is "objective" (in the sense that it reflects public, factual data) but not "conservative" (it counts "birds in the bush"). In contrast, the cost method focuses on realized flows during a period as the measure of performance. It deemphasizes balance sheet values as approximations of current wealth. This is more consistent with the overall character of current accounting conventions. However, to the extent that current values reflect a more desirable conceptual accounting model, many people believe that accounting should reflect such values whenever they can be objectively measured.

The following example is presented to illustrate the differences among the cost, lcm, and market value methods of valuing securities. On January 1, 1974, one share of stock in Company XYZ is purchased for $10. In June of 1974, Company XYZ pays a dividend of $1 per share. On December 31, 1974, the price of the stock is $15, but the stock is not sold. Dividends received during 1975 are again $1 per share. Market price at December 31, 1975, is $8, but the stock is not sold. Finally, the share of stock is sold in 1976 for $12 before the 1976 dividend is paid.

	Recognized	Earnings/Loss	Ending Balance Sheet Amount
Cost Method	1974	$1 (dividends)	$10
	1975	$1 (dividends)	$10
	1976	$2 (realized capital gain of 12 - 10=2)	0
	Total	$4	
LCM Method	1974	$1 (dividends)	$10
	1975	$(1) (dividends and an unrealized loss of 2)	$ 8
	1976	$4 (realized gain of 12 - 8=4)	0
	Total	$4	

Market Method	1974	$6	(dividends + un-realized gain of 5)	$15
	1975	$(6)	(dividends – un-realized loss of 15 - 8=7)	$ 8
	1976	$4	(realized gain of 12 - 8=4)	0
	Total	$4		

Notice that total earnings over the 3 years are the same under all three methods. Total earnings reflect total dividends received plus the difference between cost and selling price. You might ask yourself which of the three methods seems to you to more "fairly reflect" what has happened in each of the 3 years.

Long-term Minority Investments

Sometimes one company will acquire some of the stock of another company as a long-term investment. Such investments might be made to strengthen relationships with a customer or a supplier or just to earn a return. If the holding constitutes less than 20 per cent of the stock of the investee, GAAP requires that the investment be carried under the cost method and shown under long-term investments on the balance sheet.

If the holding constitutes 20 per cent or more of the investee's stock, GAAP normally requires that the investment be carried under what is called the "equity method." Under this method the investing company counts as income its proportionate share of the net income of the investee. Dividends received are then considered to be a partial liquidation of the investment.

The equity method can be illustrated for the same example used earlier. Assume as additional data that Company XYZ earns $3 per share in 1974 and $2 per share in 1975.

Equity Method	Earnings Recognized		Ending Balance Sheet Amount
1974	$3	(share of XYZ earnings)	$12 (10+3-1)
1975	$2	(share of XYZ earnings)	$13 (12+2-1)
1976	$(1)	(realized capital loss of 13-12=1)	0
Total	$4		

Under the equity method, the investment is carried on the balance sheet at the original cost plus the investing company's proportionate share of the investee's profits since the date of acquisition minus the dividends received from the investee. The equity method is *required* if the investing company can exercise significant influence over the operating and financial policies of the investee. As a guide, APB Opinion 18 states that it is assumed that a "parent" company can exercise this control if it owns more than 20 per cent of the voting stock. If more than 20 per cent of the stock is owned but the company wants to use the cost method, the burden of proof is on it to show that it does not exercise this control. Owens-Illinois Company (O-I), for example, owns more than 20 per cent of the stock of Owens Corning Fiberglas Company (OCF). However, O-I operates under a Federal Trade Commission order not to exercise any control over the operations of OCF. O-I thus accounts for its investment in OCF under the cost method.

The cost method makes it possible for a parent company to exercise considerable influence over *its* earnings if it has relatively large subsidiaries. It can simply require the subsidiary to pay out dividends or not, depending on the profit desired by the parent company. For this reason, the APB has restricted the use of the cost method to those cases in which the investing company does not have effective control of the operating or financial policies of the investee.

Long-term Majority Investments

If a company owns more than 50 per cent of the stock of another company, it will usually consolidate the subsidiary in its financial statements. A *consolidated* subsidiary is one in which the subsidiary is treated as though it were part of the parent company for financial statement purposes. In short, the legal entities are set aside. The process for making this conversion is called "consolidating the subsidiaries." The resulting statements are called "consolidated financial statements." The process of consolidation is explained later in this chapter. In general, a company must consolidate all subsidiaries that are more than 50 per cent owned. (the parent company owns more than 50 per cent of the voting stock). There can be several exceptions to this rule, however. The principal exception occurs if the subsidiary is in such a different type of business from the parent company that the resulting consolidation could be misleading.[1]

For example, the automobile companies do not consolidate their finance subsidiaries nor does Sears & Roebuck consolidate the Allstate Insurance Company, even though these subsidiaries are 100 per cent owned. Another common exception is foreign subsidiaries in countries experiencing major political or economic problems. If the investment in non-consolidated subsidiaries is material in relation to the financial position of the parent company, the details of the subsidiary's financial position and the results of their operations must be disclosed in the annual report of the parent company.

If a company does not consolidate a subsidiary in which it holds more than 50 per cent of the voting stock, it must generally account for this subsidiary by the equity method. Exceptions to this rule are rare; they include situations in which there is substantial uncertainty regarding the relationship between the parent and the subsidiary. Pepsi-Co., for example, carried its 82 per cent interest in Rheingold under the cost method in 1972 because Pepsi-Co. was trying to divest part of Rheingold and has suspended the brewing operations of Rheingold pending the divestiture.

Accounting for the Acquisition of a Subsidiary—
Purchase vs. Pooling of Interest

When one company acquires substantially all the voting stock of another company, there are two ways of accounting for the acquisition. First, it can be

---

[1] Other exceptions are for such situations as temporary ownership, or if the controlling interest does not rest with the majority owner (e.g., the company is in legal reorganization).

treated as a purchase. Second, it can be treated as a pooling of interests. The method of accounting for an acquisition can have a significant effect on future operating results of the combined entity.

If the purchase method of accounting is used, the assets and liabilities of the acquired company are recorded on the financial statements of the acquiring company at their "fair" value. The difference between the price paid and the fair value of the assets minus the liabilities is termed "goodwill." If the pooling of interest method is used, the assets and the liabilities of the acquired company are recorded on the financial statements of the acquiring company at the acquired company's book value. There is thus no recorded "goodwill."

For example, assume that Company A acquired Company B for $15,000,000 in cash. Company B has the following assets and liabilities:

($000)	Book Value	Fair Value
Cash	$ 490	$ 490
Accounts Receivable	1,760	1,700
Inventories	2,490	3,500
Patents		1,060
Property Assets (net)	5,810	7,000
Total Assets	$10,550	$13,750
Accounts Payable	3,900	3,900
Capital Stock	5,000	
Retained Earnings	1,650	
Total Equities	$10,550	

Using the purchase method, the entry to record the acquisition would be as follows:

Cash	490	
Accounts Receivable	1,700	
Inventories	3,500	
Patents	1,060	
Property Assets	7,000	
Goodwill	5,150	
Accounts Payable		3,900
Cash		15,000

Assume that instead of acquiring the B Company for cash, common stock with a current market value of $15,000,000 was exchanged for all the common stock of the B Company. If certain conditions were met, this would be a pooling of interests and would be recorded on the books of the A Company as follows:

Cash	490	
Accounts Receivable	1,760	
Inventories	2,490	
Property Assets (net)	5,810	
Accounts Payable		3,900
Capital Stock		5,000
Retained Earnings		1,650

The rationale behind the pooling of interests concept is that two businesses have simply combined their resources into a single business and, consequently, no new business entity has been created. The pooling of interest method of accounting leaves the accounts of both firms exactly as they would have been had the two always been combined. Notice that the $15,000,000 market value of the stock that was exchanged does not enter into the transaction.

During the 1950s and 1960s, pooling of interest became a very popular way of recording acquisitions, particularly by conglomerates. The reason was that the assets could usually be brought onto the acquiror's books at considerably less than their fair value. Also, goodwill, which was present in many acquisitions, would not have to be recorded. This had the advantage of understating future costs, relative to the purchase method. In the example cited above, using the purchase method, inventories would be $1,010,000 higher; patents, $1,060,000, property assets, $1,190,000; and goodwill $5,150,000—a total of $8,410,000 in higher costs that would eventually have to be reflected in lower earnings. Also, pooling of interest provided the acquiring company with the potential for showing "instant earnings" by selling off acquired assets that were still shown on the books at unrealistically low values.

Because of the advantages of the pooling of interest method, it became widely used even if there was really no merger or pooling of interests, but simply an acquisition—one company buying another. As a result, in 1970 the APB published Opinion 16. This opinion did several things. First, it defined conditions that must be met before a company could use the pooling of interest method. Second, it made it mandatory to use pooling of interests if these requirements were met. If these conditions were not met, a company could *not* use the pooling of interest method. In other words, the opinion eliminated any option concerning the method that could be used. Third, it set down rules for valuing the assets and liabilities under the purchase method. A companion opinion, No. 17, specified that goodwill must be amortized over a period not to exceed 40 years. Amortization of goodwill is not an allowable deduction for federal income tax purposes, however.

Pooling of Interest. APB Opinion 16 lists twelve conditions that must be met before a business combination can be treated as a pooling of interests. In general, the businesses must be autonomous and independent and the combination must be effected by an exchange of common stock. At least 90 per cent of the stock of the acquired company must be exchanged for the stock of the acquiring company. The other requirements are essentially to insure that the combination is a bona fide merger of two independent companies through a valid exchange of common stock. The interested student can find the complete requirements in paragraphs 45 through 48 of Opinion 16.

Purchase. If an acquisition does not qualify for the pooling of interest method, it must be treated as a purchase. Opinion 16 is quite specific on how a purchase is to be treated. If the purchase is made through an exchange of assets, the purchase price is the fair value of the assets distributed plus the fair value of any liabilities assumed. If the purchase is made by an exchange of stock, the purchase price is the fair value of the stock issued. Because of the difficulty in measuring fair value in some instances, the new carrying value may be determined either by the fair value of the consideration given or the fair value of the property acquired, whichever is more evident.

The assets acquired in a purchase acquisition must be recorded at their fair value. Opinion 16 provides some general rules for estimating fair value. For example, plant and equipment that is to be used should be recorded at replacement cost for similar capacity unless the expected future use of the assets indicates a lower value. If the plant and equipment is to be held for resale, it should be recorded at its net realizable value. Finished goods inventories should be included at net realizable value. Intangible assets that can be identified should be included at their appraised value. An interesting feature of these rules is that both receivables and liabilities are to be recorded at their present value. That is, they are to be adjusted for the time period required before the receivables will be collected or the liabilities will require payment. Paragraph 88 of Opinion 16 provides specific rules for valuing the assets and liabilities of the acquired company. These rules leave no doubt that the intent of the opinion is to approximate as closely as possible the fair value of these assets and liabilities.

Finally, Opinion 17 covers the treatment of goodwill. If the purchase price of the acquired company exceeds the fair value of the assets less the liabilities acquired, the difference *must* be recorded as goodwill. It cannot be written off against paid-in capital or retained earnings. Goodwill must be systematically written off against income, using the straight-line method over the period of estimated benefit but, in no case, longer than 40 years. In case the fair value of the net assets exceeds the purchase price of the acquisition (negative goodwill), the excess must be applied to reduce the carrying value of the property assets. This treatment is based on the convention that assets are not recorded at amounts in excess of cost. Once the carrying value of the property assets is reduced to zero, any negative goodwill can be set up as a deferred credit and taken into income over the period of benefit, but not for longer than 40 years.

Single vs. Separate Legal Entities

If one company acquires 100 per cent ownership of another company, it has the choice of dissolving the corporate entity of the acquired company or not. If it dissolves the legal entity of the subsidiary, the assets and liabilities of the subsidiary are recorded directly on the books of the parent company. If, however, the subsidiary remains a separate legal entity, the acquisition is recorded as an investment on the books of the parent company and the books of the subsidiary company are not changed by the transaction. (As far as the subsidiary is concerned, nothing has changed except the ownership of its stock.) Consequently, with either pooling of interests or purchase, when the acquired company retains its separate legal status, the accounting entries required to reflect the acquisitions are made *outside* the books of *either* company. They are made only in the consolidation working papers. The process of consolidation is described in the next part of the chapter.

Summary

If a company acquires less than 20 per cent of another company, it will usually treat this as an ordinary investment and include it on the financial statements at cost. If a company acquires between 20 per cent and 50 per cent of another company, it will normally use the equity method of accounting for the investment. If a company owns more than 50 per cent of another company, it will usually consolidate the subsidiary in its financial reports, with the exceptions mentioned earlier. If a company acquires 90 per cent or more of another company, the acquisition may be treated as a purchase or a pooling of interests, depending on the conditions of the acquisition. If a company acquires 100 per cent of another company, it may dissolve the subsidiary as a legal entity or it may maintain it as a separate legal entity. The process of consolidation involves bringing together the accounts of a number of legal entities and treating them, for financial reporting purposes, as though they were a single company. The idea is that the companies represent one economic entity. This process is described in the next part of this chapter.

THE PROCESS OF CONSOLIDATION

The techniques used in consolidation depend to some extent on the condition of acquisition. To begin, let us assume that the stock of the subsidiary company was purchased for cash and, consequently, the acquisition was treated as a purchase. Second, let us assume that the parent company uses the cost method of accounting for its investment in its subsidiaries.[2] We will turn now to a description of the process of preparing consolidated statements under these assumptions.

The Consolidated Balance Sheet

The rationale for consolidating financial statements is that it is more meaningful to present the financial information of a group of affiliated companies, under a single top management, as a single economic entity. Consequently, the process of consolidation involves combining the financial statements of such a group of companies as they would appear if they were a single economic and legal entity. The process of preparing a consolidated balance sheet involves four steps:

1. Summing all like accounts of parent and subsidiaries.

2. Eliminating intra-company offsetting accounts.

3. Eliminating intra-company profits from the consolidated assets.

4. Elminating the investment of the parent company against the owners' equity accounts of the subsidiaries.

STEP 1—Summing Accounts. The first step in preparing a consolidated balance sheet is to add all the subsidiary balance sheet accounts to the corresponding accounts of the parent company. Thus, each of the account balances (cash,

---

[2] If financial statements for the parent company alone were to be released to the public, the parent would have to use the equity method of accounting for its investment in the subsidiary. If the only public reports are consolidated ones, it is common for the parent to use the cost method with correction to the equity method being part of the consolidation process.

receivables, inventories, property assets, and so forth) of the subsidiaries and the parent are added together. (Notice that it is important to have a uniform account classification.) This is a straightforward process and the following exhibits show how it is accomplished.

STEP 2—Eliminating Offsetting Balances. The parent company and subsidiaries are separate legal entities. Consequently, they deal with one another as such. They may buy and sell from one another, loan money to one another, or engage in any other financial transactions that normally take place between separate businesses. As a result, one of the companies may have receivables owed by other companies in the consolidation. These, of course, are offset by a corresponding amount of payables in the debtor companies. Or a loan receivable made, for example, by a parent company to a subsidiary will show up as a loan payable on the books of the subsidiary. Since, clearly, an organization cannot owe a debt to itself, these offsetting balances must be eliminated from the consolidated balance sheet. This is generally a simple matter of eliminating assets against liabilities. The usual eliminations are:

Assets		*Liabilities*
Accounts Receivable	against	Accounts Payable
Loans Receivable	against	Loans Payable
Bonds Receivable	against	Bonds Payable
Dividends Receivable	against	Dividends Payable
Interest Receivable	against	Interest Payable

STEP 3—Eliminating of Intra-company Profits. As you will remember from your study of income realization, title to goods must usually be passed before profits can be realized. In sales between legal entities such as a parent and a subsidiary, the profits are rightly taken at the time of sale. If these two legal entities are combined in a single economic unit, however, the intra-company profits that are included in the assets must be eliminated.

The usual case of intra-company profits involves the inventories. Suppose that parent Company P sells 1,000 units of product A to subsidiary Company S. The goods cost P $1 per unit to produce and they are sold to S for $1.50 per unit. At the end of the period S has 400 units left in inventory that cost $600. Of this, $200 represents profits of P. Consequently, the inventories of the consolidated company are overstated by $200, because $400 is the cost to the company. The intra-company profits in inventories are substracted from the consolidated inventory. The offset is to consolidated retained earnings.

Although the elimination of intra-company profits usually involves only inventories, other assets could be affected. For example, one company may sell fixed assets to another company at a profit. This profit must also be eliminated.

STEP 4—Eliminating of Parent Company's Investment. The final, and most complex, step is to eliminate the parent company's investment against the subsidiary's owners' equity. You can think of this step as one that simulates what would happen to the balance sheet if the parent company retired the stock of the subsidiary and took direct control over its assets and liabilities. The investment in the subsidiary would be canceled and the capital stock and retained earnings of the subsidiary would also be canceled. Several examples will demonstrate this process.

Example 1 Company P buys 100 per cent of the common stock of Company S for its book value of $100,000. The latter consists of $60,000 in capital stock and $40,000 in retained earnings.

In this case the investment of $100,000 would be eliminated against S's capital stock of $60,000 and S's retained earnings of $40,000. For example, the balance sheet on the date of acquisition would be combined as follows:

Assets	P	S	Total	Elimination	Consolidated Balance Sheet
Investment in S	$ 100	$	$ 100	$100	$
Other Assets	900	150	1,050		1,050
Total	$1,000	$150	$1,150	$100	$1,050
Equities					
Liabilities	$ 300	$ 50	$ 350		$ 350
Capital Stock P	400		400		400
Capital Stock S		60	60	60	
Retained Earnings	300	40	340	40	300
Total	$1,000	$150	$1,150	$100	$1,050

Notice that this elimination would always be the same in subsequent years. For example, 1 year after acquisition the balance sheets would be combined as follows:

Assets	P	S	Total	Elimination	Consolidated Balance Sheet
Investment in S	$ 100	$	$ 100	$100	$
Other Assets	1,000	200	1,200		1,200
Total	$1,100	$200	$1,300	$100	$1,200
Equities					
Liabilities	$ 350	$ 75	$ 425		$ 425
Capital Stock P	400		400		400
Capital Stock S		60	60	60	
Retained Earnings	350	65	415	40	375
Total	$1,100	$200	$1,300	$100	$1,200

Notice that the increase in retained earnings of the subsidiary since the date of acquisition goes into consolidated retained earnings but the amount of retained earnings at acquisition is eliminated. Thus, all profits earned by the subsidiary before the date of acquisition are eliminated from consolidated retained earnings because these are not earnings of the consolidated company.

Example 2—Goodwill Assume the same situation as in Example 1 except that Company P pays $110,000 for Company S. In this instance, Company P has paid

$10,000 more for Company S than its book value. There could be many reasons for such a purchase, among the most probable are:

1. The tangible assets of Company S are understated because of conservative accounting practices (e.g., accelerated depreciation) or because price levels have changed, or both.

2. There could be intangible assets (e.g., patents) that are not reflected on the books at their fair value.

3. The potential earnings of Company S are above normal.

To the extent that the excess purchase cost is attributed to reasons 1 or 2, the amount of the excess should be assigned to those consolidated assets to which they apply. To the extent that the excess is due to 3, the amount is assigned to goodwill or, a term more commonly used today, "cost of investment in subsidiary in excess of book value." In all the examples given in this chapter, we will assume that any excess of cost over book value is due to above normal potential earnings unless otherwise indicated. This is not meant to imply that this is the usual reason for cost being in excess of book value. This assumption is made merely to keep the examples from being unduly complex.

The consolidated balance sheet at the date of acquisition would be developed as follows:

Assets	P	S	Total	Elimination[a]	Consolidated Balance Sheet
Investment in S	$ 110	$	$ 110	$110	$
Other Assets	890	150	1,040		1,040
Goodwill				(10)	10
Total	$1,000	$150	$1,150	$100	$1,050
Equities					
Liabilities	$ 300	$ 50	$ 350	$	$ 350
Capital Stock P	400		400		400
Capital Stock S		60	60	60	
Retained Earnings	300	40	340	40	300
Total	$1,000	$150	$1,150	$100	$1,050

[a]A figure in parenthesis indicates it is to be added to the consolidated balance instead of subtracted.

The consolidated balance sheet 1 year from acquisition would be as follows:

Assets	P	S	Total	Elimination	Consolidated Balance Sheet
Investment in S	$ 110	$	$ 110	$110	$
Other Assets	990	200	1,190		1,190
Goodwill				(10)	10
Total	$1,100	$200	$1,300	$100	$1,200

Equities					
Liabilities	$ 350	$ 75	$ 425	$	$ 425
Capital Stock P	400		400		400
Capital Stock S		60	60	60	
Retained Earnings	350	65	415	40	375
Total	$1,100	$200	$1,300	$100	$1,200

Example 3—Minority Interest and Goodwill Assume the same situation as in Example 1 except that Company P acquires only 90 per cent of the stock of Company S for $100,000. This means that 10 per cent of the assets and liabilities on the consolidated balance sheet are really owned by someone outside the company. Stated another way, Company P really owns only 90 per cent of the assets and liabilities of Company S. One way to handle this would be to reduce all of S's assets and liabilities by 10 per cent. This would not make much sense, however, because Company P *controls* all the assets and liabilities of S and the consolidated balance sheet reflects control rather than simple ownership. As a result, we show assets and liabilities of S at their full amounts and segregate the portion of owners' equity (capital stock plus retained earnings) held by outsiders into an account called "minority interest." On the consolidated balance sheet, this account is shown after liabilities but before owners' equity. There is some disagreement among accounting theoreticians whether minority interest is a liability or an equity account. We are aware of no significant practical implications of this disagreement. As indicated above, it is usually placed between the two.

The consolidated balance sheet at the date of acquisition is developed as follows:

Assets	*P*	*S*	*Total*	*Elimination*	*Consolidated Balance Sheet*
Investment in S	$ 100	$	$ 100	$100	$
Goodwill				$(10)[a]$	10
Other Assets	900	150	1,050		1,050
Total	$1,000	$150	$1,150	$ 90	$1,060
Equities					
Liabilities	$ 300	$ 50	$ 350	$(6)^c$	$ 350
Minority Interest				$(4)^c$	10
Capital Stock P	400		400	6^c	400
Capital Stock S		60	60	54^b	
Retained Earnings	300	40	340	36^b	300
				4^c	
Total	$1,000	$150	$1,150	$ 90	$1,060

Notes:

[a] P paid $100,000 for 90 per cent of S.s $100,000 book value. Consequently, $10,000 in excess of book value was paid. It is assumed that this was goodwill.

[b] The $54,000 and $36,000 represent 90 per cent of the capital stock and retained earnings, respectively, of S at the date of acquisition.

[c] The $6,000 and the $4,000 are the 10 per cent minority interest in P. These are eliminated from consolidated capital stock and retained earnings and moved to the minority interest account.

The consolidated balance sheet 1 year from the date of acquisition is developed as follows:

Assets	P	S	Total	Elimination	Consolidated Balance Sheet
Investment in S	$ 100	$	$ 100	$100	$
Goodwill				(10)	10.0
Other Assets	1,000	200	1,200		1,200.0
Total	$1,100	$200	$1,300	$ 90	$1,210.0
Equities					
Liabilities	$ 350	$ 75	$ 425	$(6.0)	$ 425.0
Minority Interest				(6.5)	12.5
Capital Stock P	400		400	6	400.0
Capital Stock S		60	60	54	
Retained Earnings	350	65	415	6.5[a]	372.5
				36	
Total	$1,100	$200	$1,300	$ 90	$1,210.0

[a]This is 10 per cent of S's retained earnings.

To summarize, the steps for making the eliminations when there is minority interest are:

1. Make the elimination of the parents' investment against the capital stock and retained earnings of the subsidiary at the date of acquisition. This elimination will equal the majority percentage ownership multiplied by the amount of the subsidiaries' capital stock and retained earnings at the date of acquisition. Record the good will, if any.

2. Eliminate from the subsidiary capital stock the minority percentage multiplied by the amount of subsidiary capital stock. (This will eliminate the remaining balance of the subsidiary's capital stock.) Add this amount to the minority interest.

3. Eliminate from the consolidated retained earnings the minority percentage multiplied by the subsidiary retained earnings at the *balance sheet date*. Add this amount to the minority interest. (The amount left in subsidiary retained earnings should be equal to the majority percentage multiplied by the increase in retained earnings since the date of acquisition.)

The Consolidated Income Statement

In addition to a consolidated balance sheet, a company must also prepare a consolidated income statement. The steps for preparing a consolidated income statement are similar to those for preparing a consolidated balance sheet. These steps are:

1. Add together each of the income statement accounts for the parent company and the subsidiaries.

2. Eliminate the intra-company sales and purchases. Subtract the sales value from the consolidated sales and cost of sales.

3. Eliminate any intra-company profit in inventory.

4. Eliminate expenses of one company that are income to another company within the consolidation (e.g., interest),

5. Provide for minority interest, if any.

These steps can best be demonstrated by an example.

The following are the income statements of the parent company, P, and subsidiary companies S-1 and S-2 (000 omitted).

	P	S-1	S-2	Total
Sales	$1,500	$300	$800	$2,600
Cost of Sales	900	210	450	1,560
Gross Margin	600	90	350	1,040
Sales and Administrative Expense	300	85	200	585
Interest Expense			15	15
Interest (income)	(20)			(20)
Management Fee	(30)	15	15	—
Profit before Taxes	$ 350	$ (10)	$120	$ 460
Income Taxes	175	—	60	235
Profit after Taxes	$ 175	$ (10)	$ 60	$ 225

The relationships between Company P and companies S-1 and S-2 are as follows:
1. P's sales include $30,000 to S-1 and $50,000 to S-2.

2. Profit margins to P on the intra-company sales left in the ending inventories are S-1, $10,000; S-2, $20,000.

3. Of the $15,000 interest expense of S-2, $10,000 was paid to P.

4. P's management fee income of $30,000 was received from S-1 and S-2.

5. P has a 90 per cent interest in S-1 and an 80 per cent interest in S-2. The consolidated income statement is developed as follows:

	Combined Total	Elimination	Consolidated Income Statement
Sales	$2,600	80[a]	$2,520
Cost of Sales	1,560	80[a],(25)[b]	1,505
Gross	1,040		1,015
Sales and Administrative Expense	585		585
Interest Expense	15	10[c]	5
Minority Interest's Share in Net Income		11[d]	11
Interest Income	(20)	10[c]	(10)

Net Profit before Taxes	$ 460	$ 424
Income Taxes	235	235
Net Profit after Taxes	$ 225	$ 189[e]

[a]This eliminates the sales of P to S-1 and S-2.

[b]This adds back to cost of sales the intra-company profit in the inventory:

$$S\text{-}1: \$10,000 \times 90 \text{ per cent} = \$ 9,000$$
$$S\text{-}2: \$20,000 \times 80 \text{ per cent} = \$16,000$$
$$\$25,000$$

[c]This eliminates the interest paid by S-2 to P.

[d]This eliminates the minority interest from the consolidated net income as follows:

$$10 \text{ per cent of the } \$10,000 \text{ S-1 loss } = \$ (1,000)$$
$$20 \text{ per cent of the } \$60,000 \text{ S-2 profit} = 12,000$$
$$\text{Minority Interest in Net Income } = \$ 11,000$$

[e]This can be broken down as follows:

Combined before Eliminations	$225
Less Intra-company Profit in Inventory	(25)
Less Minority Interest	(11)
Consolidated Basis	$189

EXAMPLE OF CONSOLIDATED STATEMENTS

The purpose of this part of the chapter is to provide an example of the entire consolidation process.

The 1975 financial statements of the Parent Company and its 90 per cent-owned subsidiary, the Subsid Company, are presented below.

The Balance Sheet
as of December 31, 1975
($000)

Assets	Parent	Subsid	Combined Totals
Cash	$ 550	$ 120	$ 670
Accounts Receivable	830	250	1,080
Inventories	1,420	800	2,220
Investments	3,410	500	3,910
Loans to Subsid	1,000		1,000
Property Assets (net)	3,550	1,800	5,350
Total	$10,760	$3,470	$14,230

	Parent	Subsid	Total
Equities			
Accounts Payable	$ 310	$ 350	$ 660
Taxes Payable	150	80	230
Dividends Payable	100		100
Interest Payable	320	20	340
Loans Payable to Parent	—	1,000	1,000
Bonds Payable	3,500	—	3,500
Capital Stock	4,700	1,500	6,200
Retained Earnings	1,680	520	2,200
Total	$10,760	$3,470	$14,230

Income Statement
Year Ending December 31, 1975
($000)

	Parent	Subsid	Combined Totals
Sales	$9,500	$2,400	$11,900
Cost of Sales	7,700	1,800	9,500
Gross Margin	$1,800	$ 600	$ 2,400
Selling Expense	690	220	910
Administrative Expense	330	150	480
Interest Expense	180	60	240
Management Fee	(30)	30	—
Interest Income	(60)	—	(60)
Profit before Taxes	$ 690	$ 140	$ 830
Income Taxes	340	60	400
Profit after Taxes	$ 350	$ 80	$ 430

Reconciliation of Retained Earnings
Year Ending December 31, 1975
($000)

	Parent	Subsid	Combined Totals
Retained Earnings, January 1	$1,730	$440	$2,170
Profits after Taxes	350	80	430
Total	$2,080	$520	$2,600
Dividends Paid	400	—	400
Retained Earnings, December 31	$1,680	$520	$2,200

The Balance Sheet

1. Of the receivables on Parent's balance sheet, $300,000 are due from Subsid.

2. Inventories of the Subsid Company include $200,000 of products purchased from the Parent Company. The cost of these products to the Parent Company was $160,000.

3. The investments of $3,410,000 include $1,600,000 paid for 90 per cent of the common stock of the Subsid Company 2 years ago. At the date of purchase, capital stock of the Subsid Company was $1,500,000 and the retained earnings were $200,000.

4. The $20,000 interest payable on the balance sheet of the Subsid Company is owed to the Parent Company.

5. Goodwill is to be written off over 35 years.

The Income Statement

6. Of the sales of the Parent Company, $1,500,000 were to the Subsid Company.

7. Subsid's $60,000 interest expense was paid to Parent.

8. A management fee of $30,000 was paid by Subsid to Parent. The consolidated financial statements are developed as follows:

The Balance Sheet

	Combined Totals	Elimination	Consolidated Balance Sheet
Assets			
Cash	$ 670		$ 670
Receivables	1,080	300[a],20[f]	760
Inventories	2,220	36[b]	2,184
Investments	3,910	1,600[c]	2,310
Loan to Subsid	1,000	1,000[e]	
Goodwill		(70)[c],4[g]	66
Property Assets (net)	5,350		5,350
Total	$14,230	2,890	$11,340
Equities			
Accounts Payable	$ 660	300[a]	$ 360
Taxes Payable	230		230
Dividends Payable	100		100
Interest Payable	340	20[f]	320
Loans Payable	1,000	1,000[e]	
Bonds Payable	3,500		3,500
Minority Interest		(202)[d]	202
Capital Stock	6,200	150[d], 1,350[c]	4,700

Retained Earnings	2,200	52^d, 180^c, 36^b, 4^g	1,928
Total	$14,230	$2,890	$11,340

[a]To eliminate Parent's receivables owned by Subsid.

[b]To eliminate intra-company profit in inventories (90 per cent $\times$ $40,000 = $36,000).

[c]Parent paid $1,600 for 90 per cent of Subsid. At the date of purchase, Subsid had $1,500 in capital stock and $200 in retained earnings. Parent's share was $1,350 and $180, respectively, for a total of $1,530. Since Parent paid $1,600, there was goodwill of $70.

[d]To take the minority interest in the capital stock of Subsid ($150) and retained earnings (10 per cent of $520, or $52) out of owners' equity and record it as minority interest.

[e]To eliminate Parent's loan to Subsid.

[f]To eliminate Subsid's liability to Parent for interest.

[g]To record 2 years amortization of goodwill, based on a 35-year life.

The consolidated income statement is developed as follows:

	Total	Elimination	Consolidated Income Sheet
Sales	$11,900	1,500[a]	$10,400
Cost of Sales	9,500	1,500[a], (36)[b]	8,036
Gross Margin	$ 2,400		$ 2,364
Selling Expense	910		910
Administrative Expense	480		480
Interest Expense	240	60[c]	180
Minority Interest in Net Income		(8)[d]	8
Amortization of Goodwill		(2)	2
Interest Income	(60)	60[c]	
Profit before Taxes	$ 830	(46)	$ 784
Income Taxes	400		400
Profit after Taxes	$ 430		$ 384

[a]To eliminate the sale of the Parent Company to the Subsid.

[b]To eliminate the intra-company profit in the ending inventories.

[c]To eliminate the interest paid by Subsid to Parent.

[d]To record the minority interest in Subsid profits (10 per cent of $80,000).

[e]To record the amortization of goodwill.

The reconciliation of retained earnings is as follows:

	P	S	Combined Totals	Elimination	Consolidation
Retained Earnings, 1/1	$1,730	$440	$2,170	180[a],2[d],44[b]	$1,944
Profits	350	80	430	46[c]	384
Total	$2,080	$520	$2,600		$2,328
Dividends	400	—	400		400
Retained Earnings, 12/31	$1,680	$520	$2,200		$1,928

[a]To eliminate 90 per cent of the Subsid's retained earnings at the date of acquisition.

[b]To eliminate the minority interest in Subsid's retained earnings on January 1.

[c]To adjust to the consolidated profit.

[d]To adjust beginning retained earnings for amortization of goodwill.

The consolidated financial statements would be as follows:

THE PARENT COMPANY
Consolidated Balance Sheet as of December 31, 1975
($000)

Assets

Current Assets		
Cash	$ 670	
Accounts Receivable	760	
Inventories	2,184	$ 3,614
Property Assets (net)		5,350
Other Assets		
Investments	$2,310	
Goodwill	66	2,376
		$11,340

Equities

Current Liabilities		
Accounts Payable	$ 360	
Taxes Payable	230	
Dividends Payable	100	
Interest Payable	320	$ 1,010
Bonds Payable		3,500
Minority Interest in Consolidated Subsidiary		202
Owners' Equity		
Capital Stock	4,700	
Retained Earnings	1,928	6,628
		$11,340

THE PARENT COMPANY
Consolidated Income Statement for Year Ending December 31, 1975
($000)

Sales	$10,400
Cost of Sales	8,036
Gross Margin	$ 2,364
Selling Expense	910
Administrative Expense	480
Interest Expense	180
Amortization of Goodwill	2
Minority Interest in Net Income	8
Income Taxes	400
Net Income	$ 384

Reconciliation of Consolidated Retained Earnings
Year Ending December 31, 1975
($000)

Retained Earnings on January 1	$1,944
Plus Income for Year	384
	$2,328
Less Dividends Paid	400
Retained Earnings on December 31	$1,928

THE EQUITY METHOD vs. CONSOLIDATION

The equity method is sometimes called "one-line consolidation" because it reflects the net balance of all the assets, liabilities, and equity accounts of the subsidiary in one line on the parent's balance sheet and the parent's share of the earnings of the subsidiary in one line (investment income) on the parent's income statement. Consolidation, of course, reflects each balance sheet and income statement item of the subsidiary individually in the published statements. The equity method, in other words, shows the same net effect on earnings and retained earnings as does consolidation. Consolidating a subsidiary versus carrying it on the equity method thus has no effect on net income. Consolidation does differ from the equity method in three important respects.

1. Under consolidation, subsidiary earnings show up as operating earnings whereas under the equity method, they show up as investment income, which often is considered a non-operating item.

2. Under consolidation, the long-term debt of the subsidiary and parent are combined whereas the subsidiary's debt is netted against its assets in the equity method. This can have a substantial impact on reported debt/-equity ratios. Consider the following example:

	P*	S	Consolidated
Assets	$1,000	$500	$1,450
Current Liabilities	$ 100	50	150
Long-term Debt	300	400	700
Owners' Equity	600	50	600
	$1,000	$500	$1,450

*Included in the assets of the parent company is $50 for its 100 per cent investment in the subsidiary, carried under the equity method (Book value of S at acquisition, $35; retained earnings of S *since* acquisition, $15).

The debt/equity ratio of P (with S on the equity method) is 300/900 = 33 per cent whereas the consolidated debt/equity ratio is 700/1,300 = 54 per cent.

3. Under the equity method there is no separate disclosure of the amount of goodwill, if any, involved in the acquisition of the subsidiary.

CONSOLIDATION IF SUBSIDIARY WAS ACQUIRED UNDER POOLING OF INTERESTS

If the pooling of interest method is used to account for an acquisition, the eliminations are different from those described above. The investment, recorded by the acquiring company, is always equal to the net worth of the acquired company. For example, assume that Company A acquired Company B. The balance sheets at the date of acquisition are as follows:

($000)

	Company A	Company B
Assets	$10,000	$2,000
Liabilities	$ 4,000	$1,000
Capital Stock	4,000	500
Retained Earnings	2,000	500
	$10,000	$2,000

Company A acquires Company B by exchanging common stock for all the outstanding Company B stock. The entry on A's books would be:

Investment in Subsidiary	1,000	
Capital Stock		500
Retained Earnings		500

Notice that this entry is the same *regardless* of the market value of the stock being issued.

The consolidated balance sheet would be developed as follows:

Assets	Company A	Company B	Combined Totals	Elimin- ation	Consolidated Balance Sheet
Investment in Subsidiary	$ 1,000	$	$ 1,000	$1,000	$
Other Assets	10,000	2,000	12,000		12,000
Total Assets	$11,000	$2,000	$13,000	$1,000	$12,000
Equities					
Liabilities	$ 4,000	$1,000	$ 5,000		$ 5,000
Capital Stock	4,500	500	5,000	$ 500	4,500
Retained Earnings	2,500	500	3,000	500	2,500
Total Equities	$11,000	$2,000	$13,000	$1,000	$12,000

Notice that when the pooling of interest method is used the retained earnings of the subsidiary at the date of acquisition are *not* eliminated from consolidated retained earnings. The pooling of interest method allows a company to add the retained earnings of the acquired company to its own. This is the only significant difference in consolidation mechanics between purchase and pooling of interests.

SOME MISCELLANEOUS CONSIDERATIONS

The purpose of this part of the chapter is to cover some general topics concerning consolidated statements.

Complexity

We believe that, in order to understand financial statements, it is necessary to understand the process of consolidation. A large proportion of the financial statements that you will read and analyze will be consolidated. The process of consolidation in actual business situations is accomplished as described in the chapter. In many actual business situations, however, the consolidation process can be very much more complex, although the principles are exactly the same. Some of the complexities, for example, result for the following:

1. *Number of subsidiaries.* Some companies have over 200 subsidiaries, both consolidated and non-consolidated. As you can understand, the process of consolidating a great number of subsidiaries, especially if there are complex interrelationships among many of them, can be very complicated.

2. *Acquisitions at different dates.* Sometimes a subsidiary is acquired over a period of time. That is, there are several dates of acquisition.

3. *Inter-ownership.* The possible inter-ownership combinations are nearly infinite. For example, P could hold a 90 per cent interest in S, which could hold 90 per cent in T. T in turn could hold a 10 per cent interest in P.

4. *Methods of payment.* Most of the examples in the text have assumed that the acquisitions were made for cash. There are many other ways in which one company can obtain control of another—e.g., exchanging stock, issuing bonds, giving a note payable, etc.

As a consequence of these complexities, it is usually necessary for the accountant responsible for consolidation to be highly specialized and qualified. For example, most advanced accounting texts devote from five to ten chapters to consolidations and, even these, cover only the most common complexities. It is not necessary, however, for you to be an expert in consolidated financial statements to understand the process of consolidations. It is sufficient that you understand generally how consolidated statements are prepared from the separate statements and to be aware that the consolidated entity is merely an accounting convention.

Analyzing Consolidated Data

Financial analysis of consolidated financial statements should always be done in light of the realization that such statements do not represent one entity in a day-to-day operating sense. In the example on page 270, Parent has a current ratio of $2,800/880 = 3.2$ and Subsid has a current ratio of $1,170/450 = 2.6$. Is the consolidated current ratio some average of these two numbers? Strangely enough, it is 3,614/1,010 = 3.6! To the extent that current ratios represent useful analytic data, what is the significance of the hypothetical consolidated ratio versus the actual ratios for the two separate operating companies? We are not necessarily suggesting that the consolidated statements are less useful than the individual statements for the companies making up the consolidation. What we are suggesting is that the process of consolidation produces numbers that do not represent any actual operating entity. Analysis of consolidated statements must be tempered by the reader's judgment about what such numbers really imply. The accounting profession is firmly committed to the concept of consolidation. Many readers of financial statements do not seem to be aware that consolidation is only an accounting convention and that the resulting data is not *necessarily* appropriate for financial analysis.

Income Taxes

Income taxes, are, of course, a complicated and specialized field and must be left to the expert. It may be useful, however, to have some understanding of the income tax law as it applies to consolidated statements. Subsidiaries, whether consolidated or non-consolidated, are independent legal entities and must pay taxes as separate companies. A company may, however, file a consolidated tax return for the parent company and those subsidiaries that quality for consolidation under the tax law. Although the tax rules are complex, as you might expect, the principal requirement for tax consolidation is that the parent company own 80 per cent of the outstanding stock of the subsidiary. A company has the option of filing a separate return for itself and for each of its subsidiaries or of filing a consolidated return with any of the 80 per cent-owned subsidiaries plus separate returns for the other subsidiaries.

There will generally be a tax advantage to filing a consolidated tax return. First, taxes are not paid on intra-company profits. (In other words, profits on intra-company transactions are eliminated from taxable income.) Second, losses incurred in one subsidiary can be used to offset profits earned by another subsidiary. Third, it is not necessary to pay a tax on dividends paid by a subsidiary to the parent corporation. (Most, if not all, of such dividends are generally not taxable, anyway.) In general, the decision which subsidiaries to consolidate for tax purposes is quite different from the decision as to which subsidiaries to consolidate for accounting purposes.

QUESTIONS

1. What do you think the rationale is behind the APB rule that, if a company owns 20 per cent or more of another company, it is presumed to have control over its operating and financial policies?

2. Explain the difference between the cost method and the equity method of accounting for non-consolidated subsidiaries. Why should the APB require that

the equity method be used if the parent company controls either the operating or financial policies of the subsidiary? Do you agree? Why?

3. What are the arguments for using the pooling of interests method when two businesses combine? One exposure draft of APB Opinion 16 included a size restriction on the pooling of interest. The acquisition had to be at least 25 per cent of the combined company before the pooling of interest method could be used. This restriction was dropped. Why do you think it was dropped? Do you believe that this restriction should have been left in the opinion?

4. Explain how a consolidated balance sheet would differ from an identical one in which the subsidiaries were not consolidated. Assuming that the subsidiaries were more than 50 per cent owned, why would the consolidated balance sheet be more meaningful than the non-consolidated one? In what ways is it perhaps less meaningful?

5. Why should the APB require that goodwill be recorded on the books and systematically amortized? Do you agree? If so, why? If not, how would you handle the excess of purchase price over fair value?

6. Make a list of intangible assets. For each, describe how you would establish their initial carrying value and the length of time to amortize them.

7. What are intra-company profits in inventories? Why should they be eliminated when a consolidated balance sheet is prepared?

8. How does minority interest occur? Where does it appear on a consolidated balance sheet? Is it a liability? If not, how would you classify it?

9. Explain what you would do about minority interests in subsidiaries when preparing a consolidated income statement.

10. Consolidated balance sheets and income statements are also accompanied by a statement of changes in financial position. How would you go about preparing such a statement?

PROBLEMS

Problem 11-1

In each of the situations listed below:

 1. Make the journal entries required by the transaction:
   (a) Using the cost method for accounting for non-consolidated subsidiaries, and
   (b) Using the equity method for accounting for non-consolidated subsidiaries.

 2. Indicate the amount that would appear on the balance sheet for the investment in the non-consolidated subsidiary under each method.

	Situation				
	1	*2*	*3*	*4*	*5*
Purchase Price of Stock	$10,000	$100,000	$500,000	$1,000,000	$2,000,000
Percentage of Total Stock	20%	15%	25%	8%	12%
Date of Purchase	1/1/75	1/1/75	1/1/75	1/1/75	1/1/75
Profits for 1975	1,000	10,000	(50,000)	20,000	—
Dividends During 1975	500	—	20,000	20,000	50,000

Problem 11-2

In each of the following situations, calculate investment income for 1975 and 1976 under each of four accounting methods: cost, lower of cost or market, market, equity:

	Situation			
	1	*2*	*3*	*4*
Bought one share of Acme Co. stock on January 1, 1975	$20	$20	$20	$20
Dividends Received—1975	$ 3	3	3	3
Earnings per Share of Acme Co. for 1975	$ 5	5	5	5
Market price of Acme Stock on December 31, 1975	$26	16	15	20
Dividends Received—1976	3	3	3	3
Acme Earnings per Share—1976	2	2	2	2
Market price of Acme Stock on December 31, 1976	15	16	21	21
Selling Price and Date Sold	15 , on 12/31/76	Still 12/31/76	Still Held	Still Held

Problem 11-3*

The balance sheets of the P Company and the S Company on December 31, 1974 are as follows:

($000)

	P	S
Cash	$1,500	$ 100
Receivables	750	200
Inventories	500	400
Property Assets (net)	3,000	1,000
Total Assets	$5,750	$1,700
Payables	850	700
Capital Stock	4,000	600
Retained Earnings	900	400
	$5,750	$1,700

*Unless otherwise indicated, assume in all the problems that:
1. The purchase method of acquisition was used;
2. The parent company uses the cost method of accounting for its investment in the subsidiary.
3. The fair value of the assets and liabilities acquired is the same as the book value.

On January 1, 1975, the P Company acquired controlling interest in the S Company under different conditions, as described below. For each condition, develop a consolidated balance sheet. (All transactions are for cash.)

Situation 1: P acquired 100 per cent of the stock of S for $1,000.

Situation 2: P acquired 100 per cent of the stock of S for $1,200.

Situation 3: P acquired 100 per cent of the stock of Company S for $900. (It was estimated that the book value of S's fixed assets were $100 in excess of their market value.)

Situation 4: P acquired 90 per cent of the stock of S for $900.

Situation 5: P acquired 90 per cent of the stock of S for $1000.

Problem 11-4

The balance sheets for companies P and S on December 31, 1975, are shown below. Consolidate these statements assuming that the acquisition was made in accordance with situations 1 through 5 in Problem 11-3.

	P	S
Cash	$ 500[a]	$ 100
Receivables	1,000	300
Inventories	700	450
Property Assets (net)	3,500	1,500
Investments	1,000[a]	
	$6,700	$2,350
Payables	800	800
Capital Stock	4,000	600
Retained Earnings	1,900	950
	$6,700	$2,350

[a]This is the balance sheet assuming situations 1 and 5. The cash account will be $100 more and the investment account $100 less for situations 3 and 4. The cash account will be $200 less and the investment account $200 more for situation 2.

Problem 11-5

Listed below are the balance sheets for the Mark Corporation and its subsidiary, the Era Company, as of December 31, 1974.

($000)

	Mark Corp.	Era Co.
Assets		
Cash	$ 1,260	$ 320
Accounts Receivable	8,920	1,690
Inventories	12,460	2,310
Dividends Receivable	250	
Notes Receivable	1,000	
Investments	3,000	
Property Assets (net)	8,410	3,630
	$35,300	$7,950

Equities

Accounts Payable	$ 9,420	$2,360
Dividends Payable		250
Taxes Payable	1,063	530
Notes Payable		1,000
Preferred Stock	5,000	
Common Stock	15,000	2,000
Retained Earnings	4,817	1,810
	$35,300	$7,950

Notes:

1. Of the Mark Corporation's accounts receivable, $1,450 is due from the Era Company.

2. The inventories of the Era Company include products purchased from Mark for $1,250. These products cost the Mark Corporation $950 to produce.

3. The $1,000 notes receivable on Mark's balance sheet is a 5-year note owed by Era.

4. The $250 dividends receivable on Mark's balance sheet is from Era Company's stock.

5. The Mark Corporation purchased 90 per cent of the common stock of the Era Corporation 2 years ago for $3,000. At the date of acquisition, Era's capital stock was on the books at $2,000 and retained earnings equaled $1,000.

Required:

1. Using the equity method, prepare a balance sheet for the Mark Corporation showing the Era Corporation as a non-consolidated subsidiary.

2. Prepare a consolidated balance sheet.

Problem 11-6

Listed below are the balance sheets for the P Company and its three subsidiaries, S, T, and U companies, as of December 31, 1974:

($000)

	P	S	T	U	Total
Cash	$ 450	$ 50	$ 360	$ 580	$1,440
Receivables	1,040	310	400	730	2,480
Inventories	2,930	740	1,050	1,420	6,140
Investments	7,600				7,600
Property Assets (net)	370	1,260	2,700	3,640	7,970
	$12,390	$2,360	$4,510	$6,370	$25,630
Payables	$ 630	$ 120	$ 530	$ 780	$ 2,060
Bank Notes Payable		100	250	300	650
Taxes Payable	140	50	100	120	410
Bonds Payable		1,000	2,000	2,500	5,500
Common Stock	8,000	600	1,000	2,000	11,600
Retained Earnings	3,620	490	630	670	5,410
	$12,390	$2,360	$4,510	$6,370	$25,630

Notes:

1. The investments of $7,600 in P's balance sheet consist of the following:

	S	T	U	Total
(a) Common stock:				
Purchase Price of Stock	$1,000	$1,500	$2,000	$4,500
At Date of Acquistion:				
Capital Stock	600	1,000	2,000	
Retained Earnings	200	300	300	
Percentage of Stock Acquired	90%	80%	70%	
(b) Bonds	$ 500	$1,000	$1,000	$2,500
(c) Other Investments				600
Total Investments				$7,600

2. P's receivables include:
    $20 from S for interest
    $30 from T for dividends
    $15 from U for interest
    $30 from U for dividends

   (Interest and dividends payable are included in payables.)

3. T's accounts receivable contains $70 due from S.

4. P's inventories include the following:

Purchased From	Cost to P	Cost to the Selling Subsidiary
S	$100	75
T	50	35
U	75	65

Required:

1. Prepare a balance sheet for P, with S, T and U included as non-consolidated subsidiaries, using the equity method.

2. Prepare a consolidated balance sheet for P and its three subsidiaries.

3. Which statement do you believe best represents the financial position of P? Why?

Problem 11-7

1. S and T are wholly owned subsidiaries of P. Indicate the eliminations that you would make in the consolidated income statement for the following situations:

(a) Sales of S to P are $50,000 during 1973. P has in it's inventory $10,000 of the goods purchased from S. These goods cost S $7,000 to manufacture.

(b) Sales of P to S were $30,000 during 1973. S had in it's inventory $15,000 of the goods purchased from P. These goods cost P $10,000 to manufacture.

(c) Sales of T to S were $80,000 during 1973. S had in its inventory $10,000 worth of the goods purchased from T. These goods cost T $12,000 to manufacture.

2. How would your answers to 1 differ if S had been 90 per cent owned and T 80 per cent owned?

Problem 11-8

Listed below are the income statements for the Boston Company and its subsidiary, the Area Company, for the year 1974.

($000)

	Boston Company	Area Company
Sales	$95,440	$40,460
Cost of Sales	62,370	27,390
Gross Margin	$33,070	$13,070
Selling Expense	10,940	4,580
Administrative Expense	5,630	3,200
Net Operating Profit	$16,500	$ 5,290
Interest Expense		1,000
Interest Income	600	
Dividend Income	500	
Profit before Taxes	$17,600	$ 4,290
Income Taxes	8,900	2,000
Profit after Taxes	$8,700	$ 2,290

Notes:

1. The Boston Company sold $25,490 worth of goods to the Area Company. Of this amount, $9,840 worth of goods still are in the inventory of the Area Company. These goods cost Boston $7,690 to produce.

2. The $600 interest income for the Boston Company was received from the Area Company.

3. The $500 dividend income from the Boston Company was received from the Area Company.

4. The Boston Company owns 80 per cent of the stock of the Area Company.

Required:

Prepare a consolidated income statement.

Problem 11-9

Listed below are the income statements for the W Company and it's three subsidiaries—thè X Company, the Y Company, and the Z Company. The W Company is a holding company that controls and coordinates the operations of the X, Y, and Z companies.

($000)

	W Company	X Company	Y Company	Z Company	Total
Sales		$71,680	$85,420	$52,690	$209,790
Cost of Sales		30,430	64,370	20,380	115,180
Gross Margin		$41,250	$21,050	$32,310	$ 94,610
Selling Expense	$20,850	10,990	6,950	8,410	47,200
Administrative Expense	10,590	11,500	11,460	12,500	46,050
Net Operating Profit	($31,440)	$18,760	$ 2,640	$11,400	$ 1,360
Interest Expense		5,850	6,990	3,560	16,400
Interest Income	10,000				(10,000)
Dividend Income	6,000				(6,000)
Management Fee	30,000				(30,000)
Net Income (BT)	$14,560	$12,910	($ 4,350)	$ 7,840	$ 30,960
Income Taxes	7,250	5,000	—	3,000	15,250
Net Income (AT)	$ 7,310	$ 7,910	($ 4,350)	$ 4,840	$ 15,710

Notes:

1. The following intra-company sales occurred during the year:

Selling Company	to	Buying Company	of	Amount
X		Y		$10,500
X		Z		14,000
Y		X		5,600
Y		Z		1,400
Z		X		3,900
Z		Y		2,100

2. The following products, sold between companies, were still in inventory on December 31 (there were no intra-company items in inventory on January 1):

Company Holding Inventory	Selling Company	Cost to Purchaser (sales price)	Cost to Seller (mfg. cost)
X	Y	$1,400	$1,010
Y	Z	3,200	2,300
Z	X	4,100	2,900

3. The administrative expenses of companies X, Y, and Z included a management fee of $10,000 each, paid to company W.

4. The interest expenses of companies X, Y, and Z included the following amounts paid to W:

Company	Amount
X	$4,000
Y	4,000
Z	2,000

5. The dividend income of Company W was entirely from companies X, Y and Z, as follows:

Company	Amount
X	$2,000
Y	2,000
Z	2,000

6. Company W owns the following percentages of the capital stock of X, Y, and Z.

Company	Amount
X	80%
Y	70%
Z	60%

Required:

Prepare a consolidated income statement for P and its partially owned subsidiaries X, Y, and Z.

Problem 11-10

The Penn Electronics Company produced various electronic units for both the United States government and for private industrial enterprises.

The company had two fully owned subsidiaries:

1. *The Resistor Corporation* made tubes, resistors, and related parts and sold them to the parent company. This company was organized in 1963 with an authorized capital of 1,000 shares of no par value common stock. The entire amount of this stock was purchased by the parent company for $1,000,000.

2. *The Penn Sales Company* sold all the commercial production of the parent company. This company was also organized in 1963 with an authorized capital of 1,000 shares of no-par value stock. The entire amount of this stock was purchased by the parent company for $2,000,000.

Exhibits 1 through 6 present the 1974 balance sheets and income statements for the three companies.

Required:

Prepare a consolidated balance sheet for the Penn Electronics Company as of December 31, 1974, and a consolidated income statement for the year 1974. (Disregard income taxes.)

Exhibit 1
PENN ELECTRONICS COMPANY
Non-Consolidated Balance Sheet as of December 31, 1974

Assets

	($000)
Cash	$10,000
Receivables[a]	5,000
Inventories[b]	10,000
Loan to Resistor Corporation	500
Property Assets (net of depreciation)	40,000
Investment in Resistor Corporation	1,000
Investment in Penn Sales Company	2,000
Total Assets	$68,500

Equities

Accounts Payable and accruals[c]	$ 7,000
Bonds Payable	10,000
Capital Stock	40,000
Retained Earnings	11,500
Total Equities	$68,500

[a] Includes $500,000 from Penn Sales Company.
[b] Includes $1,000,000 worth of products purchased from the Resistor Corporation; cost to the Resistor Corporation was $750,000. The inventory on January 1 had included $500,000 of Resistor products that had cost Resistor $300,000 to produce.
[c] Includes $400,000 owed to the Resistor Corporation.

EXHIBIT 2

PENN ELECTRONICS COMPANY
Non-consolidated Statement of Income
For Year Ended December 31, 1974

Sales	*(000)*
To United States government	$40,000
To Penn Sales Company	30,000
Total	$70,000
Operating Costs	60,000
Operating Profit	$10,000
Management Fee[a]	1,000
Total	$11,000
Less: Interest on Bonds	600
Profit before Taxes	$10,400

[a] $500,000 from the Resistor Corporation and $500,000 from the Penn Sales Company.

EXHIBIT 3

RESISTOR CORPORATION
Balance Sheet as of December 31, 1974

Assets

	(000)
Cash	$ 100
Accounts Receivable[a]	400
Inventories	400
Property Assets (net of depreciation)	1,500
Bonds of Penn Electronics Company	100
Total Assets	$2,500

Equities

	(000)
Accounts Payable and Accruals	$ 200
Loan from Penn Electronics Company	500
Capital Stock	1,000
Retained Earnings	800
Total Equities	$2,500

[a]Due from the Penn Electronics Company.

EXHIBIT 4

RESISTOR CORPORATION
*Statement of Income
for Year Ending December 31, 1974*

	(000)
Sales to Penn Electronics Company	$3,000
Operating Costs	2,000
Operating Profit	$1,000
Less: Management Fee	$ 500
	$ 500
Plus: Interest on Bonds	6
Income before Taxes	$ 506

EXHIBIT 5

PENN SALES COMPANY
Balance Sheet as of December 31, 1974

Assets

	(000)
Cash	$ 500
Receivables	1,500
Inventories[a]	1,500
Property Assets (net of depreciation)	5,050
Total Assets	$8,550

Equities

	(000)
Accounts Payable[b]	$ 500
Accruals	150
Capital Stock	2,000
Retained Earnings	5,900
Total Equities	$8,550

[a] Includes $100,000 worth of goods purchased from the Penn Electronics Company; the cost to Penn Electronics was $80,000. The $80,000 included $10,000 worth of items purchased from the Resistor Corporation; the cost to the Resistor Corporation was $7,000. The Inventory on January 1 had included $80,000 of Penn Electronics items that had cost the parent $60,000. This $60,000 included $10,000 of Resistor parts that had cost Resistor $8,000.
[b] Due to Penn Electronics Company.

EXHIBIT 6

PENN SALES COMPANY
Statement of Income
For Year Ending December 31, 1974

	(000)
Sales	$40,000
Operating Costs	36,000
Operating Profits	$ 4,000
Less: Management Fee	500
Income before Taxes	$ 3,500

The Quality of Earnings

Quality or Quantity?

*"Things are not what they seem
Skim milk masquerades as cream."*

                    Gilbert & Sullivan

12

In several of the earlier chapters, we described instances in which alternative accounting treatment was acceptable for identical transactions. To the extent that these alternative procedures affect the income statement, identical companies can show different profits or companies with different operating results can show identical profits. If identical companies show different profits, one company's profit is overstated with respect to the other. The company with the lower earnings is using more conservative accounting practices. If the difference is material, we could say that the "quality of earnings" is different betweeen the two companies. Although *lower* earnings for identical transactions do not necessarily mean *higher quality* earnings, there is a general tendency to equate conservatism in this regard with prudence. In this chapter we will not assume that "lower is better" but rather will focus on an overview of how such differences arise. We believe that it is important for the user of financial statements to be aware of these possible differences in the quality of earnings among companies.

The purpose of this chapter is to explain the most important instances of optional accounting procedures and practices that can affect the reported earnings in a given time period.

OPTIONAL PROCEDURES AND PRACTICES

Depreciation

The depreciation of identical assets may differ in the following two ways: (1) the method of depreciation used; (2) the depreciable life assigned to the asset.

Depreciation Methods. A company may use either some form of accelerated depreciation (e.g., declining balance or sum-of-the-year's digits) or it may use straight-line. As we explained in Chapter 9, accelerated methods of depreciation may result in a permanent deferment of income tax payments. By the same reasoning, a company using accelerated depreciation for accounting purposes will show less profits, in total, then a company using straight-line depreciation. If the company using accelerated depreciation does not contract in size, the difference will never be offset. The difference in profitability, therefore, betweeen the two companies is not just in the timing of income. The company using accelerated depreciation will show lower earnings per share, lower owners' equity, and lower property asset net book value than the company using straight-line depreciation.

Depreciable Life. The depreciable life of identical property assets can differ materially, particularly assets that are subject to potential technological obsolescence. Perhaps the best example is the life assigned by manufacturers and leasing companies to leased computers. Depreciable lives for an IBM 360 model vary from the 5 years assigned by IBM to the 10 years assigned by Leasco Data Processing. (It is, of course, possible that different operating strategies for such firms could mean that both estimates are accurate.) Such differences are normally much less for property assets with more predictable lives, although even here, differences do exist.

Inventories

Physically identical inventories purchased for identical prices can carry widely different values on the financial statements for two reasons: (1) the method of accounting for inventory usage; (2) the extent to which reserves for inventory losses have been recorded.

LIFO vs. FIFO or Average. In both chapters 5 and 9, the difference between LIFO and FIFO or average inventory costing systems were described, so there is no necessity to go into these differences in detail in this chapter. To summarize, however, under rising price levels LIFO will result in lower profits and lower inventory values than FIFO or average. As long as the LIFO company does not reduce its level of inventories, this difference will be permanent. Moreover, as the amount of inventory increases and the level of prices increases, the difference in reported earnings between the LIFO and the FIFO company will continue to increase. Again, as with depreciation, the difference is not just one in timing. The company using FIFO will show higher earnings, higher inventory values, and higher owners' equity than an identical company using LIFO.

Inventory Reserves. Some businesses set up reserves for potential inventory losses. These reserves are subtracted from the inventory value and the net amount is shown on the financial statements. The reason for using a reserve is that the manager does not know which specific items of inventory will become obsolete or spoil. If he did, he would write that inventory down directly. (This is identical to the allowance for doubtful accounts situation. Management knows from experience that some accounts will be uncollectible but it does not know which ones.) Also, the extent of the loss often is uncertain. As with property assets, the problem of inventory reserves becomes more acute if high technology inventory is involved. In any event, the amount of such an inventory reserve is subject to a considerable amount of judgment. As a result, identical inventories can be reduced by different amounts by different managements.

Investment Credit

The investment credit may be taken as an increase in the after tax earnings in the year that it is received (the flow through method) or it may be written off over the life of the investment to which it applies (the deferral method). (See Chapter 9.) If the investment credit is consistently deferred, the company will show lower profits than an identical company that flows through the investment credit. Here, again, this will be a permanent difference, not just a matter of timing. The process will reverse itself (i.e., the flow through company will show less profit) only if (1) the investment credit is repealed, or (2) the amount of new investment eligible for the investment credit is reduced. Even then, it would take several years for the process to be completely reversed.

Percentage Completion

A company working on long-term fixed-price construction contracts has the option of recognizing income in each accounting period based on the percentage of the contract that has been completed, or it may wait to recognize the income from the entire contract in the period in which it was completed. (See Chapter 9.) A company using the completed contract method will generally show a lower profit than one using the percentage of completion method as long as its contracts are profitable. Again, this difference is permanent and will never reverse itself completely as long as the company is profitable. The completed contract method can sometimes result in higher profits for a particular year if a high number of jobs are completed in any one period.

Deferred Marketing and Development Costs

Some companies defer part of their marketing or development costs. The rationale for this procedure is, of course, that these expenses benefit future periods and, consequently, should be written off as expenses in the years that the benefits from these costs are reflected in income. If, for example, a company is working on developing a new market, the cost of this should not be written off against current income but should be deferred and charged against the income from the new market.

Until 1975, some companies deferred part of their research and development costs. The FASB has ruled that this is no longer acceptable accounting practice. It is probable that similar restrictions will be placed on other types of deferred costs.

Pension Accounting

Pension accounting represents one of the least appreciated and most misunderstood areas in financial accounting.

The purpose of this section of the chapter is twofold: (1) to try to dispel the notion that pension accounting is so technical that no one but an actuary or a CPA can understand it, and (2) to dispel the myth that pension accounting can be ignored because all companies do it the same way and that way is "right." This myth is quite prevalent today and can have far-reaching consequences in terms of understanding a firm's financial situation.

Pension Plans. As you probably know, a pension is a payment made to a retired employee in recognition of his/her years of employment. Although there are a large number of possible arrangements, the typical agreement calls for a fixed payment to be made each month to the retiree, from date of retirement to date of death, over and above any social security benefits. Although the pension payments to a current employee will not start until after the person retires, the payments are made because of employment services currently being rendered. It is thus considered "good accounting" to record the pension expense *now* in order to match the expense with the services giving rise to it.

It is possible to get a current tax deduction for this pension expense only if a separate legal entity is established to handle pension payments (the pension fund) and if the amount of current expense is paid in cash to the pension fund. Many managements consider it prudent to establish a separate pool of assets to provide for pension payments. The desirability of establishing such a fund is further enhanced by the tax deductibility of payments made to it. For these reasons, most companies with a formal pension plan to set up pension funds as separate legal entities with separate assets.

Because of the time value of money, the long lag between the current cash payment by the company to the fund and the subsequent payments by the fund to the retirees means that the full amount of the subsequent payments does not have to be set aside now. Because of fluctuations in interest rates, however, there is uncertainty about the "present value" amount that should currently be set aside. Furthermore, there are other uncertainties regarding the amount currently required to be set aside. These involve the probability that an employee will live until retirement, the probability that the employee will stay with the company until retirement in order to earn the pension, and the employee's life expectancy after retirement. In short, the amount of pension expense to be recorded currently is an *estimate,* although very sophisticated actuarial techniques are available for making such estimates.

An Overview of Pension Accounting Problems. There are three main problems involved in interpreting a firm's accounting policies in the pension area. First, what shows on corporate balance sheets as pension liability is, in nearly all cases, not a legal liability at all. Its appearance is just a quirk of double-entry bookkeeping. It represents that part of what has been recorded on the books as pension expense that has not been matched by a cash contribution to the pension fund. Specifically, when expense is debited the liability is credited, and when cash is paid to the fund the liability is debited. Often, cash payments do not equal the expense recorded. The resulting credit balance is called "pension liability" even though nearly all pension plans are written such that the pension fund has no legal claim against this "unfunded" expense.

Second, corporate balance sheets do not reflect at all the economic obligation of the corporation to its current and future retirees. The deficit relationship that usually exists between the asset holdings of the pension fund and the actuarially computed expected present value of its liability to present and future pensioners is not considered as a liability of the corporation because no legal claim exists. In an economic sense, however, for a "going concern," the resources to meet future pension payments must come from the corporation to the extent that pension fund assets are insufficient. In terms of an overview of corporate financial commitments, therefore, this economic obligation must be considered.

The third, and probably most important, accounting problem relates to the subjectivity of the pension expense calculation. For the reasons cited above and for others to be cited later, companies have a great deal of latitude in the amount of expense they record for pensions. The range of allowable numbers under GAAP is wide in relation to net earnings for a great many firms. Before considering GAAP for pension expense, however, we believe it will be useful to review our discussion so far by summarizing the cash flows in the pension area.

Pension Cash Flows. To understand the fundamentals of pension accounting procedures and reporting conventions, it is important to keep three distinct entities clearly in mind. Much confusion about terms and about concepts relates to failure to distinguish among these entities. The following chart shows the three entities graphically and indicates the direction in which cash flows in the overall system. The pension fund is usually a separate legal and accounting entity from the corporation. Claims of pensioners typically run to the pension fund and *not* to the corporation.

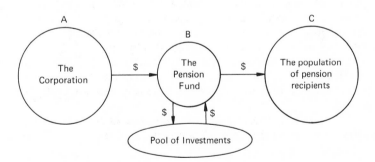

The corporation records pension expense on its books in accordance with management policy under the guidelines set down in Opinion 8 of the Accounting Principles Board. We will return later to the computation of pension expense. The corporation makes cash payments to the pension fund in accordance with policy guidelines set jointly by corporate management and the trustees of the pension plan. Any excess of recorded pension expense over cash contributions to the pension fund shows up as pension liability on the corporation's balance sheet. Correspondingly, an excess of payments over expense would show up as an asset, a prepaid expense. Since no direct or necessary relationship exists between pension expense and payments to the pension fund, as is the case, for example, between rent expense and payments to landlords, it is possible for a pension liability to remain on the books indefinitely.

The pension fund invests the payments it receives from the corporation in ways approved by the plan trustees. It then uses the income from its investments to make pension payments to retired employees. Unexpended income can be reinvested to provide for future pension payments. At any point in time, it is possible for actuaries to compute the expected present value of future pension payments (the so-called expected pension liability). This liability is equivalent to the size of the fund that would have to be available now, assuming no further contributions by the corporation, so that the investment income from the fund and the gradual depletion of the fund itself would exactly cover all expected future payments to present and expected future retirees over their expected lifetimes for employment services already rendered to the corporation, in accordance with the terms of the pension plan. You should re-read the preceding sentence enough times to fully understand it. It is important to emphasize that this calculation applies only to the expected payments for employment services *already* rendered.

A "fully-funded" pension plan is one for which pension fund assets equal or exceed the expected pension liability. The term "funding," as used in this context, refers to the relationship between pension fund assets and the expected present value of future payments to retirees. This is in contrast to a different use of the term "funding" to refer to payments by the corporation to the pension fund. This use of the same term in two ways in particularly confusing because it is possible, and even typical, for a corporation to be "fully funding" its recorded pension expense and yet for the pension fund to be substantially "under funded" in an actuarial sense. We will return later to why and how this is possible.

The expected pension liability (an actuarial concept) must also be distinguished from the accounting pension liability that appears on the corporation's balance sheet. The former is an economic (though usually not legal) liability under the pension plan for future cash payments to retirees whereas the latter is nothing more than a credit balance on the balance sheet. It has nothing to do with the economic obligations under the plan to retirees and is usually also not legally owed to the pension fund.

The table on page 293 summarizes the various flows of funds among the three entities and the nature of their claims against one another.

Pension Expense. The common situation described earlier, in which pension expense (even if fully matched by contributions to the pension fund) does not provide an asset pool for the pension plan equal to the present value of its expected liability, results because pension expense bears no necessary direct relationship to the economic obligation for future pension benefits. Typically, when a pension agreement is initiated, it provides for benefits to be paid for employment services that have already been provided. These benefits were "earned" by the employees over the years before the pension plan went into effect. Yet, the expected liability

A
The Corporation
Accounting Pension Liability

1. The liability is increased by recorded pension expense.
2. The liability is decreased by payments made to the pension fund.

The corporation sets up the pension fund as a separate entity with its own assets, separate from general corporate assets, for the purpose of carrying out the payment agreements to retirees specified in the pension plan.

The calculation of pension expense must follow the guidelines set down in APB 8. The determination of how much cash will be paid to the fund by the corporation is completely a matter of management prerogative with approval by the pension fund trustees (who are often appointed by management).

B
The Pension Fund
Assets Expected Pension Liability

Assets

1. Assets are increased by payments from the corporation.
2. Assets are increased by earnings of the pension fund investments.
3. Assets are decreased by payments to retirees.

The fund typically has no legal claim against the corporation.

Expected Pension Liability

1. The liability is increased by expected pension benefits related to employment services currently rendered by employees.
2. The liability is increased by assumed earnings of the assumed fully funded asset pool.
3. The liability is decreased by payments to retirees.
4. The liability is changed by amendments or modifications to the plan agreement.
5. The liability is changed by changes in actuarial assumptions.

C
The Pensioners

1. The pensioners are entitled to receive payments after retirement in accordance with the provisions of the pension plan, typically based on employment service rendered.
2. They have a legal claim against the pension fund to the extent their benefits have "vested."*
3. Their legal claims are usually limited to the assets of the fund.

*Vesting is explained later in this chapter.

of the plan to the employees does not go into effect until the plan is initiated. At the date a plan is initiated, the newly created expected pension liability must necessarily relate to services already rendered[1] by employees and is thus called the "past service liability." Generally Accepted Accounting Principles as defined in APB 8 do not allow a past service liability to be counted as an expense in the period in which the plan is set up. Opinion 8 does set up a range within which annual pension expense must fall.

The following is a somewhat simplified description of the key aspects of Opinion 8. Some of the technicalities have been ignored. The minimum number for pension expense, the "floor," is "normal cost" plus implicit interest on any unfunded expected pension liability plus 5 per cent of unfunded "vested" benefits. These segments are explained as follows. Normal cost for any accounting period is just another name for the increment to the expected pension liability for employment services rendered during that period. If the assets of the pension fund are not equal to the expected pension liability, the implicit interest problem arises. This problem requires recognition in current expense. Consider a new pension plan that goes into effect on January 1 for which a corporation does not immediately set up any pension fund. There is an expected pension liability as of January 1—called the past service liability—but there are no pension fund assets. The expected liability will grow each year as a result of newly earned retirement benefits—called "normal costs" for that year. If the pension plan is fully funded at the beginning of the year, payment by the company to the fund of the current year's normal cost will keep the plan fully funded at year end as well. If the plan is not fully funded, however, payment by the company to the plan of only normal cost causes the deficit to grow by the amount of the lost income that the pension fund assets would have earned during the year had there been a pension fund. In calculating the expected pension liability at the beginning of a year, investment income is assumed to be available to the fund during the year. If investment income is not available to the pension fund, the excess of the expected liability over the assets of the fund as of December 31 will be greater by the amount of the lost investment income for the year as well as the year's normal cost. Although GAAP does not require that the expected pension liability created when a plan is initiated be picked up as an expense of future periods, it does require that implicit interest on any unfunded part of that liability be charged as an expense to the periods in which this interest is assumed to be earned by the fund.

The "ceiling" under GAAP for allowable pension expense is normal cost plus one-tenth of the past service liability plus implicit interest on any unfunded

---

[1] You should remember that in defining the expected pension liability as of any point in time we stated that it relates only to employment services *already* rendered and not to expected *future* employment services. Assume, for example, that a plan calls for a pension of $10 per month after age 65 for every year of service. Then, for a 40-year-old employee with 15 years of service, the expected pension liability would consider the probability of his staying with the firm until age 65, his expected life span after retirement, and the $150 per month pension he has already earned. It would not, however, consider the extra benefits he will earn in the next 25 years ($250 per month after retirement) if he does in fact stay alive and remain with the company. The expected liability for these benefits will be picked up as increments to the overall expected pension liability each year as the benefits are earned.

expected pension liability. Since most corporations have a stated policy that, in the long run, they will make payments to the pension fund equal to the expense they record on the books, the result of this ceiling limitation is to allow no shorter than a 10-year period for picking up as expense the expected pension liability created immediately on the date the plan was initiated. Taking any portion of this past service liability as a current expense constitutes poor matching of the expense to the period during which the employment services were rendered. For this reason, GAAP does not *require* that any past service liability ever be recognized as pension expense. On the other hand, as long as the period of amortization is not too short, conservative accounting suggests picking up as an expense a portion of the liability for the payments to be made because of services rendered in earlier years.

As long as the pension expense for a firm falls between the floor amount (normal cost + interest on any unfunded expected liability + 5 per cent of unfunded vested benefits) and the ceiling amount (normal cost plus one-tenth the past service cost + implicit interest on any unfunded expected liability), any consistently applied policy for computing pension cost is acceptable under GAAP.

It is quite common for firms not to fund the past service liability because such funding often is not considered necessary to the financial integrity of the pension fund. Many firms never fund all the current expense if that expense *excludes* amortization of past service liability. As long as the fund contains enough money to meet the payments to current retirees, it remains solvent. Just as our federal social security system uses payments by current employees to pay benefits to current retirees and has no pool of assets, a pension plan for an individual firm can usually get by indefinitely if the firm funds only the normal cost each year. If the firm falls on hard times, there may well be no assets available in the fund to pay pensions. However, as long as the firm continues to prosper, setting aside "excess" assets in the pension fund is frequently viewed as unnecessary and as a waste of scarce corporate resources.

"Past" service liability. "prior" service liability. We have already mentioned that the expected pension liability as of the date a pension plan is initiated is called the past service liability. At any subsequent date the expected liability can be broken into two parts—the liability created at the date the plan was initiated and the remainder that relates to events *after* the plan went into effect. The *former part* continues to be called the past service liability. The *full amount* is sometimes called a "prior service liability." Notice that "past" in this context relates to the date of initiation of the plan. At any date subsequent to the inception of the plan, *all* the expected liability relates to prior employment services, but only those rendered before inception are part of the past service liability. It *is* possible for the past service liability to change from year to year if changes in the plan are made retroactive or if the actuarial assumptions underlying the calculation are changed. Otherwise, the past service liability will remain as a fixed number forever.

Vested Benefits. It is possible to dichotomize the expected pension liability in terms of whether or not the benefits have "vested." Vested benefits are those to which an employee is entitled after retirement even if he leaves the company before retirement. Thus, to the extent that benefits vest, a present employee is entitled at retirement to benefits already earned, regardless of his future job history. If payments for benefits already earned are contingent on staying with the company until retirement, the plan is said to be non-vesting. Because of the higher probability that vested benefits will actually have to be paid someday, in contrast to non-vested benefits, GAAP requires expense recognition over a period not longer than 20 years for the vested portion of any unfunded pension liability. This is the third part of the minimum expense limitation referred to earlier. We will turn now to an example of how pension expense is calculated under APB 8.

Pension Expense Calculations—An Illustration. Suppose that as of December 31, 1975, the expected pension liability of the pension fund for Aztec Industries is $10,000,000. Of this amount, $5,000,000 represents past service liability. Of the total, $4,000,000 represents vested benefits. The consulting actuary uses an interest rate of 6 percent in making these calculations. At the same date, the assets of the pension fund totaled $2,000,000. Normal cost for 1975 was estimated by the consulting actuary to be $220,000.

Under these assumptions, the floor and ceiling for pension expense for 1975 would be computed as follows:

Floor Expense	
Normal Cost	$220,000
Imputed interest at 6% on the unfunded expected liability—6% × $8,000,000	$480,000
5% of the unfunded vested liability = 5% × $2,000,000	$100,000
Total	$800,000

Ceiling Expense	
Normal Cost	$220,000
Imputed Interest on the unfunded liability	$480,000
1/10 of the past service liability—1/10 × $5,000,000	$500,000
Total	$1,200,000

If Aztec earned $2,000,000 before taxes and before pension expense in 1975, the range of allowable pension expense is from 40 per cent of base earnings ($800,000) to 60 per cent of base earnings ($1,200,000). Thus, the range of allowable after-tax earnings (with a 50 per cent tax rate) is from $400,000 to $600,000. Aztec's policy on pension expense is to record normal cost, imputed interest on the unfunded liability, and one-fortieth of the unfunded liability—a total of $825,000 for 1975. Since this figure falls between the ceiling and floor amounts, it is acceptable under Opinion 8.

Because of delays in receiving reports from actuaries, many firms use asset and liability data for the pension fund from the prior year in making their calculations of pension expense for the current year. The Bethlehem Steel case at the end of the chapter illustrates this practice.

Pension Disclosure in Financial Reports. Companies are required to disclose in a footnote the magnitude of their pension expense and the size of any unfunded expected pension liability for vested benefits. Companies are not required to disclose their policy on calculating pension expense even though the range of acceptable figures under GAAP can vary widely in industries with extensive pension benefits. The following footnote taken from the 1973 annual report of the Cyclops Corporation is typical of the disclosures usually provided.

Note 8—Pension Plans

Pension costs for all plans were $9,174,000 in 1973, and $7,413,000 in 1972. The increase in pension costs during 1973 is primarily attributable to increased pension benefits effective August 1, 1972 which are included for all of 1973. The actuarially estimated value of vested benefits for all plans as of the date of the last valuation exceeded the total of the pension funds and balance sheet accruals by approximately $34,600,000.

Companies are not required to disclose the size of the expected pension liability for their pension fund, or the size of the pension fund, or the composition of the assets comprising the pension fund. Since such disclosures are not mandatory, most companies do not make them. The extent, if any, to which the vested portion of the expected liability exceeds pension fund assets must be disclosed. Vesting, however, does not really affect the economics of the pension liability calculation. It merely removes one element of uncertainty from the calculation—the uncertainty that an employee will remain on the job until retirement. The vesting/non-vesting distinction is very significant for an individual employee, but it has no particular significance in interpreting the expected pension liability. For this reason the authors see no reason for requiring disclosure of only the vested portion of any unfunded expected pension liability. We believe that the full unfunded liability should be disclosed along with a description of the company's long-run funding plans. Furthermore, we believe that serious questions about the financial integrity of a pension plan arise if the long-run solvency of the pension fund depends on indefinitely continuing prosperity for the company.

On a scale of one to ten, current disclosure practices regarding the pension area are about two or three. Anyone trying to understand the financial situation of a firm operating in an industry characterized by heavy pension benefits, such as steel, rubber, or automobiles, must look far beyond what is publicly available. As a result of the 1974 Pension Reform Act, the FASB will undoubtedly make changes in pension accounting. As of this date, none have yet been made.

Loss From
Discontinued Operations

In some cases, the management of a company will decide to discontinue producing and selling a line of products or to close a division. This decision is often made in anticipation of substantial losses. In many instances, however, a major divestiture takes a period of years to complete. Contractual obligations often require the continuation of at least part of the operations for some time. The disposition of assets also is likely to require some time. As a consequence, the losses resulting from a decision to discontinue operations would normally be reflected in the financial statements over the period of time necessary to complete the discontinuance. These losses could be both from operations and from the sale of the assets of the discontinued operations. In the past, losses from discontinued operations were generally reflected in the income of the period in which the loss was actually incurred. That is, losses from operations would be reflected in the years when the costs of the operations being discontinued exceeded the revenues. The losses from the sale of assets would be reflected in the financial statements of the period in which these assets were sold or otherwise disposed of.

In the past few years, several companies have taken the entire loss from discontinued operations as a loss in the period in which the decision to discontinue these operations was made. For example, assume that a company decides to discontinue the operations of a division. It is estimated that this will result in losses of $3,000,000 over the next 3 years. In the year the decision is made to discontinue the division, the following entries are made.

Extraordinary Loss from Discontinued Operations	3,000,000	
Deferred Income Taxes	1,500,000	
Income Tax Expense		1,500,000
Provision for Discontinuance of Certain Operations		3,000,000

The "provision for discontinuance of certain operations" is shown on the balance sheet as a non-current liability.

In subsequent years the actual losses are written off against the provision for discontinuance of certain operations. In the example cited above, suppose that in the year after the provision was set up, the status of the operation being discontinued was as follows:

Revenues	$ 600,000
Cost	1,000,000
Loss on Sale of Property Assets	500,000

These items would be charged to the "provision" account as follows:

Revenues	$600,000
Provision for Discontinuance of Certain Operations	900,000

Costs		1,000,000
Losses on Sales of Fixed Assets		500,000
Income Tax Expense	450,000	
Deferred Income Taxes		450,000

When the operation is finally discontinued, any amount left in the provision will be closed out on the income statement.

Notice that the use of a procedure such as the one described above simply affects the timing of the recognition of the loss. The process will reverse itself, usually in 2 or 3 years. The writeoff generally appears to be conservative accounting in that losses are taken into the income statement earlier than if there had been no writeoff. However, since the writeoff reverses itself so quickly, it can affect the profit trend. If a company is having a poor year or if new management has just taken over a company, it might look better to take an immediate loss. For example, assume that a company had the following earnings from continuing operations:

1969	$(1,000,000)
1970	1,000,000
1971	2,000,000
1972	3,000,000

In 1969, the company decided to discontinue certain operations, with resulting losses of $5,000,000. The losses were realized in the following periods:

1970	$1,000,000
1971	2,000,000
1972	2,000,000

The profit pattern under the two alternative methods of recognizing these losses would appear as follows:

	Immediate Write Off	Write Off as Incurred
1969	$(6,000,000)	(1,000,000)
1970	1,000,000	—
1971	2,000,000	—
1972	3,000,000	1,000,000

The immediate write off pattern might be interpreted by the uninformed investor as more favorable than writing off the losses as they are incurred, although the two patterns reflect exactly the same sequence of economic events.

Another problem with this type of accounting treatment is that it depends on an explicit management decision. If management did not wish to take an immediate write off, it could defer making a decision (or at least defer communicating this decision) to discontinue an operation. On the other hand, the decision to discontinue an operation may be made at an advantageous time for management, as indicated above. In short, the decision to write off expected losses from operations to be discontinued might not be so conservative as it appears. You might want to review the Allis Chalmers case (10-1) in this regard. Do you believe that the actions of management in that situation can be described as conservative?

Lease Capitalization

Accounting problems can arise if businesses acquire the *use* of assets without acquiring *ownership* of the assets. One common way to acquire the use of an asset without owning it is through a lease. If the lease is short term and the owner of the asset is subject to a potential decline in value from technological obsolescence or casualty loss, the accounting treatment of the transaction is very simple. As each lease payment is made, the accounting entry by the lessee is to debit lease (or rental) expense and credit cash. The asset does not show on the books of the lessee, nor does the liability for the future lease payments. No balance sheet recognition is accorded the transaction because the contract can easily be voided on short notice by either the lessor or the lessee. Each lease payment is charged against income as it is paid, but no assumptions are made about continuing future use of the asset.

In contrast to this situation, many leases are arranged in which the lessee agrees to make payments over a long period of years. Sometimes such long-term leases are arranged directly between a manufacturer of a product and the customer. An example would be a large paper company's leasing a process control computer from the manufacturer, such as Measurex Corporation, the lease being non-cancelable over an 8-year period (see Case 14-3). Sometimes such long-term leases are arranged through financial institutions such as a bank or a leasing company that buys the asset from the manufacturer and then leases it to the ultimate user. In these situations, the lease is, in effect, a financing device. The "third party lessor" fully expects to get back from the lessee a stream of payments that will cover the cost of the leased asset *and* ensure a fair return on the capital that the lessor has invested. Such leases are sometimes termed "full payout" leases or "financing" leases.

Accounting treatment for financing leases involves two aspects: First, the lease obligation is considered to be equivalent (for accounting purposes) to long-term debt and is accounted for by the present value approach outlined in Chapter 7. Second, the "right to use leased property" is considered to be an asset that is amortized over the life of the lease, usually on a straight-line basis. In general, these procedures are referred to as "lease capitalization" accounting. Consider the following example:

A machine that sells for $3,605 and has a useful life of 5 years is purchased by a bank because a manufacturing company has agreed to lease the machine from the bank over the 5-year period. The bank requires a 12 per cent rate of return from the lease. The annual payment is thus set at $1,000 because five annual payments of $1,000 will return to the bank its $3,605 investment plus compound interest at 12 per cent. The following table summarizes the amortization of the principal sum with compound interest:

Year	Ending Principal Balance	Annual Payment	Interest at 12%	Reduction of Principal
0	$3,605	$	$	$
1	3,037	1,000	432	568
2	2,402	1,000	365	635

3	1,690	1,000	288	712
4	893	1,000	203	797
5	0	1,000	107	893
Totals		$5,000	$1,395	$3,605

The asset would be recorded initially at $3,605 and would be reduced by one-fifth or $721, each year.

In summary, the accounting entries for the lessee for this example would be as follows:

At Initiation of the Lease

Dr/ Right To Use Leased Machine	$3,605	
Cr/ Capitalized Lease Obligation		$3,605

Year 1

Dr/ Interest Expense	432	
Capitalized Lease Obligation	568	
Cr/ Cash		1,000
Dr/ Amortization Expense	721	
Cr/ Accumulated Amortization of Right To Use Leased Machine		721

Year 5

Dr/ Interest Expense	107	
Capitalized Lease Obligation	893	
Cr/ Cash		1,000
Dr/ Amortization Expense	721	
Cr. Accumulated Amortization		721

If a lease is clearly just a temporary agreement for the use of property owned by someone else or is clearly a long-term financing arrangement equivalent to an installment purchase, it is clear how to account for the lease. Unfortunately, in practice many leases fall somewhere between these two extremes. If a lease has some of the aspects of a long-term contractual obligation and some of the aspects of a temporary rental agreement, a problem may arise in evaluating the quality of reported earnings. Consider the following table, which shows the difference in reported annual expense for the leased machine described in the preceding example:

Annual Expenses

Year	If the Lease Is Considered To Be a Rental	If the Lease Is Capitalized Interest	+ Amortization	= Total
1	$1,000	$ 432	$ 721	$1,153
2	1,000	365	721	1,086
3	1,000	288	721	1,009
4	1,000	203	721	924
5	1,000	107	721	828
Total	$5,000	$1,395	$3,605	$5,000

If the lease is *not* capitalized, the lease expense is spread evenly over the life of the lease and there is no balance sheet effect at all. If the lease *is* capitalized, the sum of interest expense plus amortization exceeds the level lease payment in the early years and declines fairly steeply over the life of the lease. Also, under lease capitalization there is an increase in reported assets and liabilities over the term of the lease. *Total expense* over the life of the lease is the same in both cases; only the timing of recognition of the expense differs. This timing difference, however, can be significant for firms that make heavy use of leasing.

Given the option, most firms prefer not to capitalize leases. The thrust of GAAP and SEC rules in this area is thus toward defining the conditions under which leases should be capitalized.

In 1964 the Accounting Principles Board issued Opinion 5. In this opinion, the Board stated that leases for which the lessee ends up with a "material equity interest" were in fact conditional installment purchases. In such cases they prescribed that the property and the related lease obligation should be included among the assets and liabilities on the balance sheet. The present value of the lease payments should be capitalized as an asset and then depreciated over the asset's useful life. Compound interest expense would then also be charged on the outstanding lease liability.

Opinion 5 included specific circumstances that would indicate if a lease were really an installment purchase. One such circumstance was the typical "full-payout net-net-net" lease in which the lessee pays all additional charges such as insurance, maintenance, and taxes and the lease payments cover the full value of the asset leased, plus a fair return to the lessor. Very few such leases were actually capitalized in practice during the 10 years following the release of APB 5.

In response to this apparent lack of compliance, the APB issued Opinion No. 31 in June 1973. Rather than forcing companies to capitalize leases, this opinion required footnote disclosure of certain information. Specifically, companies were required to disclose:

1. Total rental expense, reduced by rentals from subleases, with disclosures of such amounts.

2. The minimum rental commitments under all non-cancellable leases for:

   (a). Each of the five succeeding fiscal years;
   (b). Each of the next three 5-year periods, and
   (c). The remainder as a single amount.

3. The basis for calculating rental payments if dependent on factors other than the lapse of time.

4. Existence and terms of renewal or purchase options, escalation clauses, etc.

5. The nature and amount of related guarantees made or obligations assumed.

6. Restrictions on paying dividends, incurring additional debt, further leasing, etc.

7. Any other information necessary to assess the effect of lease commitments.

The SEC was not satisfied with Opinion No. 31, which, in the commission's view, did not provide sufficient disclosure to meet the needs of investors. Subsequent to the issuance of Opinion 31, the SEC issued Accounting Series Release No. 147, which required footnote disclosure to include the following:

1. Total lease rental expense for all years for which income statements are presented, with segregation of contingent rentals and rentals on financing leases.

2. Lease rentals payable for each of the next 5 years, for the next three subsequent 5-year periods, and any subsequent payments due.

3. The capitalized present value of "financing" leases in the aggregate and by major category of assets.

4. The impact on net income if "financing" leases had been capitalized and the related assets has been depreciated on a straight-line basis and interest cost had been accrued on the basis of the outstanding lease liability.

A "financing" lease was defined by the SEC as a lease for which the non-cancelable period covers 75 per cent or more of the economic life of the property or a lease whose terms assure the lessor a full recovery of the fair market value of the property at the inception of the lease plus a reasonable return. The very subjective nature of the decision concerning when a lease is "really" a "financing" device and when it is "really" just a "rental agreement" is one reason why so few leases were capitalized under Opinion 5. It is hard to say when a given lease becomes a purchase. The SEC solved this problem by stating clear-cut operational rules for deciding when to capitalize.

A general discussion of whether leases should or should not be capitalized is not particularly useful since the decision really should hinge on the nature of the specific lease in question. Furthermore, actual lease agreements almost never conform to the illustrations used in accounting textbooks. For purposes of this textbook, we want to stress three points. First, lease capitalization can make a significant difference in the balance sheet and income statement of a company that makes significant use of leasing; second, most leases are not capitalized in practice; and third, the reader of the financial statements of a company with significant non-capitalized leases should be aware of the potential impact of lease capitalization on those financial statements.

Other Alternative Accounting Practices

The alternative acceptable accounting practices described in this part of the chapter are not exhaustive. They are the principal alternatives that are available to almost all types of companies.[2] There are also some alternative accounting practices available to particular types of companies such as the extractive industries or public utilities. For example, in the petroleum industry, most large companies write off the cost of exploration and drilling as they are incurred. Smaller companies, however, tend to capitalize these costs and amortize them in subsequent periods.

[2] An alternative procedure available to international companies is the translation of financial statement values in foreign countries into United States dollars. This is discussed in Chapter 13.

APB OPINION NO. 20

There are two considerations in evaluating the effect of alternative accounting practices on financial statements. The first is to determine the general quality of the earnings—that is, to decide on the degree of conservatism reflected in the earnings figure. The second consideration concerns the change in earnings—that is, determining the extent to which changes in earnings have resulted from changes in operations and the extent to which they have resulted from changes in accounting practices. The purpose of this part of the chapter is to consider the problem of changing from one acceptable accounting practice to another.

Clearly, if companies could change their accounting practice at will, a great deal of profit manipulation would be possible. For example, in years when a higher profit was needed, the company could use the less conservative practices, and vice versa. This, of course, is why the accountant's opinion comments on the *consistency* with which accounting principles have been applied. It would not be logical, however, to prevent companies from ever changing their accounting practices. Conditions change and, as a result, different accounting principles may reflect better the financial situation of a company in different years. APB No. 20 deals with the problem of accounting changes.

Types of Accounting Changes

APB No. 20 classified accounting changes into three types: changes in accounting principles, changes in accounting estimates, and changes in the reporting entity.

A change in *accounting principle* results from "adoption of a generally accepted accounting principle different from the one used previously for reporting purposes." Most of the changes discussed thus far in this chapter are changes in accounting principle: for example, changing from LIFO to FIFO, changing from accelerated depreciation to straight-line, changing from the completed contract method for long-term construction contracts to the percentage completion method, and changing from direct charge of marketing and development expense to deferring part of this expense and amortizing it.

A change in *accounting estimate*, as the name implies, results from a change in opinion concerning the outcome of some uncertain event, including such accounting estimates as "uncollectible receivables, inventory obsolesence, service lives and salvage value of depreciable assets, warranty costs, periods benefited by a deferred cost, and unrecoverable portion of mineral reserves." The board pointed out that it was sometimes not possible to distinguish between a change in an accounting principle and a change in an accounting estimate. For example, a change from deferring marketing costs to writing them off as incurred could come about partly because future benefits from these costs have become more uncertain.

A special change in accounting principles results from a change in the *reporting entity*. A change in the reporting entity is limited mainly to situations involving presentation of consolidated or combined statements in place of individual statements and to the specific set of subsidiaries or companies included in the consolidated or combined statements. This provision covers the restatement of financial statements to include companies acquired under pooling of interest accounting.

APB Opinions with Respect to Accounting Changes

Changes in Accounting Principle. The board made two major rules with respect to changes in accounting principle. First, it concluded that a company should change to an alternative acceptable principle *only if* it could justify the new principle on the basis that it is *preferable*. Second, it provided that, with the exceptions stated below, a company could not make a prior period adjustment because of an accounting change. The exceptions are: (1) a change from LIFO to some other method of inventory pricing; (2) a change in accounting for long-term construction type contracts, and (3) a change from the "full cost" method of accounting in the extractive industries.[3] In addition, prior period adjustments may be made for changes that are required as a result of an APB opinion. (These changes were discussed in Chapter 10.) The opinion also requires that the pro forma effect of these changes should be disclosed on the income statement or on a separate schedule.

Changes in Accounting Estimates. The board concluded that no prior period adjustments should be made for a change in accounting estimates. The impact of changes in estimates should be treated prospectively—that is, it should be spread over the remaining lives of the items in question. Disclosure of the effect of changes in accounting estimates is required if the effect of these changes is material.

Changes in Entity. The board concluded that a prior period adjustment should be made for a change in the reporting entity. That is, the financial statements should be restated for all prior periods presented. The statements should disclose the nature of the change and the reasons for it, as well as the effect of the change on income.

Impact of APB Opinion No. 20 on Accounting Changes

We believe that in most instances a company will be able to justify any single change between two accepted accounting principles. If alternative principles are well accepted and if both methods are widely used, a convincing case can usually be made for a change from one principle to another. We believe that the main impact of APB No. 20 on the quality of earnings, therefore, will be to limit a company to a single change for a given accounting principle. For example, we believe that most companies could justify the use of FIFO inventory or straight-line depreciation if they are currently using LIFO and accelerated depreciation. However, after a change in accounting principle has been made, Opinion No. 20 makes it very difficult to justify changing back at some future period. Conditions will have to change to such an extent that the original justification for adopting, FIFO or straight-line depreciation, for example, no longer apply. Such changes are unlikely. In most instances, it would require a new APB opinion expressing a preference for

---

[3] This subject is beyond the scope of this book.

the alternative accounting principle to justify a change back to a previously used principle.

MANAGEMENT IMPLICATIONS OF QUALITY OF EARNINGS

There can be wide differences in earnings among identical companies because of the use of alternative but generally accepted accounting procedures. Some of these differences are only differences in timing. For many, however, profits, and consequently owners' equity, will probably differ permanently. Furthermore, it does not appear likely that future decisions of the FASB will restrict entirely available alternatives. One of the problems is that if a particular accounting practice can be justified, it is difficult to prohibit a more conservative approach. For example, accelerated depreciation can be theoretically justified as an acceptable accounting practice. However, it would be difficult for any rule-making body to prescribe that everyone, or nearly everyone, should accelerate depreciation. It is even more complicated to get uniformity on accounting estimates. Consequently, we believe that the users of financial statements will have to accept the fact that different accounting treatments will be used for identical situations.

In analyzing financial statements, we find it helpful to consider explicitly the quality of earnings. In most financial statements, there is a great deal of information (mostly in footnotes) that describe the accounting principles and estimates that have been used and, in many instances, the financial impact of these principles and estimates over alternative procedures. If a set of financial statements appear to be prepared on the basis of accounting principles and practices that are consistently non-conservative (that is, the less conservative alternative practices have generally been followed), we find it useful to restate the profit, to the extent that we can, on the basis of conservative practices. (Sometimes this can be a real eye-opener.) If a company's profits are changed to losses because of the application of more conservative principles, it does not mean that the published profits are incorrect. It does mean, however, that they are overstated in relation to other similar companies that use more conservative accounting.

The opposite is also true. If a company uses consistently conservative practices, it might be well to restate the income on a less conservative basis to see if your evaluation of the company's performance will change.

QUESTIONS

1. State all the arguments that you can think of in favor of keeping the present alternative accounting treatment of identical transactions.

2. State all the arguments that you can think of for limiting the alternative accounting treatment of identical transactions.

3. Assume that a decision has been made to limit the alternative accounting treatment of identical transactions. For each of the optional procedures and practices described in this chapter, what action would you recommend be taken?

4. Why do you think Congress prevented the accounting profession from prohibiting the flow through method of treating the investment credit?

5. Explain the difference between a funded and an unfunded pension plan. Explain how life expectancy and interest rates can affect the cost of a pension plan.

6. Describe some lease arrangements that are neither clearly financing devices nor rental agreements.

7. What is the rationale for writing off immediately expected future losses from discontinuing a product line? Under what conditions would writing off such losses *not* be considered to be conservative accounting?

8. Explain the difference between a change in accounting principle and a change in accounting estimate. Give examples of changes in which it might not be clear whether it was a change in principle or a change in estimate.

9. Explain why APB No. 20 may not have much effect on a company's making an initial change in accounting principle but would make it difficult to change back.

10. How would you go about evaluating the quality of earnings reflected in the financial statement of a company?

11. What do you think the FAPB should do, if anything, to make the quality of earnings more consistent among companies?

PROBLEMS*

Problem 12-1

The A Company was considering a change in both accounting principle and accounting estimate in depreciating its machinery and equipment acquired after January 1, 1973. Currently, the company uses a 10-year life and straight-line depreciation. It is considering changing to an 8-year life and sum-of-the-year's digits depreciation. (This is the basis for the company's tax depreciation.) The expected acquisitions of machinery and equipment over the next 5 years are as follows:

1973	$1,600,000
1974	2,400,000
1975	800,000
1976	1,200,000
1977	1,600,000

(Assume that the acquisitions are made at the beginning of each year.)

Required:

1. Calculate the difference between the present and the proposed methods on the income for each year.

*If tax calculations are required for problems in this chapter, assume a tax rate of 50 per cent.

2. Calculate the difference between the present and the proposed methods on any balance sheet accounts as of December 31, 1977.

Problem 12-2

The B Company is considering making a change from LIFO to FIFO. For internal accounting purposes, the inventory is maintained on a FIFO basis. A "reserve account" is maintained that reflects the difference between the inventory valued on a FIFO basis are the inventory valued on a LIFO basis. When published financial statements or tax returns are prepared, the inventory balances are reduced by the amount of the LIFO reserve. Balances in the inventory and the LIFO reserve and certain other accounts were as follows:

	December 31, 1972	December 31, 1973
Inventory on FIFO basis	$ 5,643,980	$8,368,490
LIFO Reserve	1,525,000	2,360,000
Inventories at LIFO	$ 4,118,980	$6,008,490
Retained Earnings	18,921,650	
Earnings after tax for 1973 using LIFO		6,439,820
Dividends Paid during 1973		3,000,000

The company decides to change to FIFO for accounting statement (and consequently, tax) purposes.

Required:

1. Show the reconciliation of retained earnings for 1973.

2. What balance sheet accounts will be affected by this change and by how much will they be changed as of December 31, 1973?

Problem 12-3

The AB Company uses the LIFO method of inventory valuation. During 1973, the company decided to adopt the FIFO method. The change was approved by the Internal Revenue Service. Following are certain account balances of the AB Company:

($000)

	On January 1, 1973	On December 31, 1973
Inventories at FIFO	$23,680	$29,460
Inventories at LIFO	16,388	20,190
Retained Earnings	54,670	
Earnings after Tax for 1973 Using LIFO		15,640
Dividends Paid during 1973		8,000

Required:

1. Show the reconciliation of retained earnings for 1973.

2. What balance sheet accounts will be affected by this change and by how much will they be changed as of December 31, 1973?

Problem 12-4

The C Company is a construction firm working under long-term fixed price contracts. The following contracts were uncompleted as of December 31, 1972 and December 31, 1973:

Uncompleted Contracts on December 31, 1972

Contract Number	101	102	103
Price	$465,000	$520,000	$496,000
Amount Spent to Date	320,000	220,000	100,000
Expected Cost to Complete	100,000	250,000	350,000

Uncompleted Contracts on December 31, 1973

Contract Number	103	104	105
Price	$496,000	$848,000	$1,563,000
Amount Spent to Date	300,000	400,000	500,000
Expected Cost to Complete	140,000	400,000	900,000

The following are the balances in certain accounts as of the dates indicated:

Retained Earnings on 12/31/72	$3,496,000
Before-tax Profits during 1973	105,000
Dividends Paid during 1973	30,000

The company has been using the completed contract method of accounting for its long-range construction contracts. In 1973 the Company decided to change to the percentage completion method for accounting purposes.

Required:

1. Prepare a retained earnings reconiliation for 1973 reflecting the change to the percentage completion method.

2. How will the balance sheet accounts as of December 31, 1973 differ from what they would have been had the company continued to use the completed contract method of accounting?

Problem 12-5

The BC Company is a construction firm working under long-term fixed-type construction contracts. Uncompleted contracts were as follows:

Uncompleted Contracts on December 31, 1972

($000)

Contract Number	6461	6462	6463	6464
Price	$2,500	$1,800	$4,000	$10,000
Amount Spent to Date	1,500	900	1,000	2,000
Expected Cost to Complete	400	500	3,000	7,000

Uncompleted Contracts on December 31, 1973
($000)

Contract Number	6463	6464	6465	6466
Price	$4,000	$10,000	$5,000	$6,000
Amount Spent to Date	3,000	5,000	2,000	1,200
Expected Cost to Complete	800	4,500	2,000	4,300

The following are the balances of certain accounts as of the date indicated ($000):

Retained Earnings on 12/31/72	$20,468
Before-tax Profits for 1973 on a	
Completed Contract Basis	1,000
Dividends Paid during 1973	2,000

The company has been using the completed contract method of accounting for both tax and accounting purposes. In 1973, the company decided to adopt the percentage completion method for accounting purposes.

Required:

1. Prepare a retained earnings reconciliation for 1973 reflecting the change to the percentage completion method.

2. How will the balance sheet accounts as of December 31, 1973, be different from what they would have been had the company continued to use the completed contract method?

Problem 12-6

Azure, Inc., had the following earnings before taxes and market development costs for the years between 1966 and 1973.

Year	Market Development Costs ($000)	Earnings before Income Taxes and Research and Development Costs ($000)
1966	$ 600	$1,462
1967	700	1,944
1968	800	2,324
1969	1,000	2,400
1970	900	960
1971	900	1,320
1972	1,200	1,640
1973	1,200	1,930

Until 1969, the company wrote off market development costs as incurred. Beginning with January 1, 1970, the company decided to defer one-half of its market development costs. These costs were to be deferred for 2 years and then written off over a subsequent 5-year period.

Required:

Calculate Azure's profits after taxes for 1966 through 1973:

1. Assuming that the policy of writing off market development costs as they were incurred had been maintained.

2. Under the new policy.

3. What balance sheet accounts will be different under 2 than under 1 on December 31, 1973, and by how much will they differ?

Problem 12-7

The Cobalt Corporation's after-tax income from continuing operation for the years 1969 through 1973 was as follows:

Year	After-tax Income from Continuing Operations ($000)
1969	$10,860
1970	9,940
1971	11,200
1972	10,420
1973	10,600

In 1969, the company decided to discontinue certain operations. The loss from the discontinued operation was estimated to be $20,000,000 before taxes, spread over the next 5 years. The company decided to take the entire loss as an extraordinary item in 1969. Subsequently, the losses from these discontinued operations turned out to be as follows:

Year	Revenue from Discontinued Operations ($000)	Cost Attributable to Discontinued Operations ($000)	Loss from Sale of Property Assets of Discontinued Operations ($000)
1969	$1,470	$2,930	$ 400
1970	760	3,300	1,960
1971	320	2,850	2,690
1972	100	1,950	2,990
1973	—	300	3,500

By December 31, 1973, the discontinued operations were entirely liquidated and the reserve account was closed out.

Required:

1. For each year, make the general journal entries that affect the reserve for discontinued operations account and the related tax transactions.

2. Calculate the profit after taxes for the years 1969 through 1973:

(a) Assuming the reserve for discontinued operations had been used;

(b) Assuming that the losses were written off as incurred.

Problem 12-8

The before-tax profits for Lavender Scents, Limited, from continuing operations and before market development costs are as follows:

	($000)
1970	165,420
1971	180,390
1972	170,150
1973	168,400

In 1970, the company decided to close down a major division. The before-tax financial impact of taking this action was as follows:

	From Discontinued Operations		
		($000)	Loss on Sale
	Revenues	Costs	of Assets
1970	$50,000	$100,000	$50,000
1971	30,000	150,000	70,000
1972	20,000	75,000	90,000
1973	—	50,000	20,000

Expenditures for market development were as follows:

	($000)
1970	50,000
1971	60,000
1972	70,000
1973	80,000

Required:

1. Calculate the after-tax profits for Lavendar Scents Limited:

   (a) Assuming that the loss from the discontinued operations was written off as it was incurred and that the market development costs were expensed as incurred.

   (b) Assuming that the entire loss from the discontinued operations was taken in 1970 and that, beginning in 1970, one-half of the market development expenditures was deferred and written off over a 5-year period beginning the year after the expenditure was made.

2. How will the balance sheet account differ on December 31, 1973, between the two methods?

Problem 12-9

Inca Ink, Inc., adopted a formal pension plan for its employees on January 1, 1975. At that time, the consulting actuary estimated the expected pension liability to be $5,000,000, using an interest rate of 6 per cent. The pension plan was non-vesting. The plan was approved by the IRS and Inca started the pension fund off with a contribution of $500,000. During 1975, the fund earned $50,000 on its investments and paid out $75,000 to retirees covered under the plan. Normal cost for 1975 was estimated by the actuary to be $100,000. Inca has adopted a policy of recording pension expense equal to normal cost plus one-fifteenth of the unfunded past service liability (as of year's end). The company plans to make an annual payment to the pension fund equal to the expense recorded for that year. The initial contribution to the fund is to be considered part of the company's payments under this plan.

Required:

1. Calculate pension expense for Inca Ink, Inc., for 1975 under the stated policy. Is this amount allowable under GAAP?

2. Prepare the pension-related journal entries for Inca for 1975.

3. What are the total assets of the pension fund at year's-end? What is the expected pension liability at year's end?

4. Draft the pension footnote for the annual report of Inca Ink, Inc., for 1975.

Problem 12-10

The balance sheet and the income statement for the Codmium Corp. for 1973 are as follows:

CODMIUM CORP.
Balance Sheet as of December 31, 1973
($000)

Assets

Cash	$ 436
Receivables	828
Inventories	1,720
Prepaid Expenses	30
Land	560
Plant and Equipment	3,940
Allowance for Depreciation	(1,360)
Deferred Research and Development	1,150
Total Assets	$7,304

Equities

Accounts Payable	$ 820
Accrued Expenses Payable	80
Deferred Income Taxes	800
Bonds Payable	2,320
Common Stock	2,000
Retained Earnings	1,284
Total Equities	$7,304

CODMIUM CORP.
Income Statement for Year Ending December 31, 1973
($000)

Sales		$4,950
Cost of Sales		
Beginning Inventory	$1,205	
Cost of Production	3,665	
Goods Available for Sale	$4,870	
Less Ending Inventory	1,720	
Cost of Sales		3,150
Gross Margin		$1,800
Research and Development Expense		350
Selling and Administrative Expenses		500
Profit before Taxes		950
Taxes		415
Net Income		$ 535

In preparing the financial statements, the following accounting practices were used:

1. Inventories were stated at FIFO. If they had been stated at LIFO, the value of the beginning inventories would have been $889,000; the value of the ending inventories would have been $1,270,000.

2. The plant and equipment was depreciated on a straight-line basis. If declining balance depreciation had been used, the depreciation expense for 1973 would have been $230,000 more. The balance in the accumulated depreciation account on December 31, 1973, would have been $450,000 greater. Accelerated depreciation is used for tax purposes.

3. The research expense for 1973 represents one-half of the actual expenditure on research during the year. The difference was debited to the deferred research and development expense account.

4. During the year, investment credits of $60,000 were earned. The flow through method was used. No investment credit had been earned before 1973.

5. Pension costs (included in administrative expenses) make no provision for past service costs. The estimated liability for past service costs on January 1, 1973, was $1,000,000.

Required:

1. Restate Codmium Corp.'s 1973 financial statements on the following basis:

   (a) The LIFO inventory method had been used.

   (b) Declining balance depreciation was used for books as well as for taxes.

   (c) Research expense was written off as incurred.

   (d) The deferred method of accounting for investment credit was used (assume a 10-year life and that the assets on which the investment credit was taken were acquired at the middle of the year).

(e) Past service pension costs were written off over a 10-year period, beginning in 1973.

2. Calculate the following ratios on both the original and revised statements:

(a) Current ratio.

(b) Debt/equity ratio.

(c) Return on owners' equity.

Problem 12-11

The balance sheet and the income statement for Love Bug Imports are as follows:

LOVE BUG IMPORTS
Balance Sheet as of December 31, 1973
($000)

Assets

Cash	$ 872
Receivables	1,656
Inventories	3,800
Prepaid Expenses	60
Land	1,020
Plant and Equipment	7,880
Deferred Investment Credit	(400)
Allowance for Depreciation	(3,250)
Total Assets	$11,638

Equities

Accounts Payable	$2,760
Account Expenses Payable	160
Bonds Payable	3,000
Common Stock	4,000
Retained Earnings	1,718
Total Equities	$11,638

LOVE BUG IMPORTS
Income Statement for Year Ending December 31, 1973

Sales		$10,588
Cost of Sales:		
Beginning Inventory	$ 2,640	
Cost of Production	8,470	
Goods Available for Sale	$11,110	
Ending Inventory	3,800	
Cost of Sales		7,310

Gross Margin	$ 3,278
Research and Development Expense	514
Selling and Administrative Expense	1,600
Profit before Taxes	1,164
Taxes	562[a]
Profit after Taxes	$ 602

[a]This is the actual tax liability of $1,582 minus $20 for the investment credit.

In preparing these accounting statements, the following accounting practices were used:

1. Inventories were stated at LIFO. The FIFO value of these inventories was as follows: beginning inventory, $3,640; ending inventories, $5,200.

2. The plant and equipment was depreciated on a declining balance basis. Had straight-line depreciation been used, the depreciation expense for 1973 would have been $105,000 less and the allowance for depreciation on December 31, 1973 would have been $950,000 less.

3. Research and development costs were written off as incurred.

4. An investment credit of $100,000 was earned in 1973. It was the policy of the company to defer the investment credit and write it off over the life of the asset for which the credit was given. In 1973, income tax expense was reduced by $20,000 by writing off deferred investment credits.

5. Pension costs (in administrative expenses) included a $200,000 payment into a pension fund to cover one-tenth of the company's past service liability.

Required:

1. Restate Love Bug's 1973 financial statements on the following basis:

   (a) The FIFO method of inventory valuation had always been used. (Be sure to take into account the difference in tax payments that this would require. Assume that additional tax liabilities for prior years were paid in cash.)

   (b) Straight-line depreciation had been always used, for book purposes only.

   (c) Beginning in 1973, one-half of the research and development expense was deferred to future periods, for book purposes only.

   (d) The flow through method had always been used for the investment credit.

   (e) In 1973, the company stopped funding and accruing the past service liability cost.

   The company had no deferred taxes because its tax returns and its accounting statements were consistent. In making the above changes, be sure to account for the deferred taxes that would have resulted.

2. Calculate the following ratios for both the original and revised statements:

1. Current ratio.
2. Debt/equity ratio.
3. Return on owners' equity.

Problem 12-12

On January 1, 1974, Zebra, Inc., acquired the use of an industrial milling machine under a long-term lease from the manufacturer of the machine. The lease called for annual payments of $5,000 for 10 years and was non-cancelable. The life of the machine was estimated to be between 8 and 12 years.

Required:

1. What expense would show in 1974 and 1975 on the books of Zebra, Inc., for the use of this machine if the lease were not capitalized?

2. What expense would show in 1974 and 1975 if the lease were capitalized? (What interest rate did you choose and why?)

3. Prepare the journal entries for 1974 and 1975 under the assumption that the lease is to be capitalized.

Adjusting, Converting, and Translating Financial Statements

Accounting and Economic Planning

Reporter: Senator, what do you think of inflation?

Senator: I'm against it.

Reporter: What do you think of deflation?

Senator: I'm against that too.

Reporter: Senator, what are you for?

Senator: Flation.

13

In this chapter we shall consider three different though similar topics: fair value accounting, price level accounting, and foreign exchange conversions. All three topics involve techniques for restating a set of financial statements. In fair value accounting, the financial statements are restated from historical values to some form of current value. In price level, or "inflation," accounting, the statements are restated to reflect the current purchasing power of the dollars invested. In foreign exchange conversions, financial statements are restated from one currency into another.

FAIR VALUE ACCOUNTING

Inflation occurs when the purchasing power of the monetary unit of a country decreases over time. That is to say, identical goods will cost more today than they did during some past period. We say that price levels are rising. The United States has been experiencing more or less constant inflation since 1939.

During periods of inflation, the practice of recording assets at their original cost means that the typical company will have assets on its books that are recorded at different price levels. Thus, two identical assets could have different accounted book values if they were acquired at different dates. In particular, the book value of assets purchased in earlier years may be materially understated in terms of their present replacement costs. This situation, of course, results in some marked inconsistencies in the financial statements.

Balance sheet values also may be unrealistic because of developments other than changes in price levels. The practice of writing off many costs, such as marketing and product development, in the period in which they are incurred can result in a substantial understatement of a company's assets. Also, the value of an efficient organization and many other intangibles are rarely reflected on the balance sheet directly. On the other hand, technological developments can make the replacement value of an asset much less than its original cost minus accumulated depreciation. For example, pocket calculators that sell for $50 in 1974 sold for $100 in 1972 and for $150 in 1971.

The practice of showing assets at their original cost on the balance sheet and writing off these costs over the useful life on the income statement has come under considerable criticism from persons both inside and outside the accounting profession. As a result, there has been a movement in the accounting profession to discard the historical cost principle in favor of some form of "fair value" accounting. The purpose of this part of the chapter is to describe the major approaches to fair value accounting.

Differing Approaches to Fair Value

One of the principal reasons why the accounting profession has traditionally used historical cost is the difficulty in estimating fair value or even agreeing on a method for estimating it. Consequently, an understanding of the methods available for estimating fair value is vital to an understanding of the fair value problem.

Replacement Value. The conceptual support for stating assets and liabilities at replacement value derives from the economic concept of "value in use." An item is worth to a company what the company would have to forgo in economic resources to replace the item if it did not already have it.

Historical Cost Adjusted for Specific Price Level Changes. One method of estimating replacement value is to adjust the historical cost figures for the changes in price levels of specific assets that have occurred since the dates of acquisition. This is done by means of indices that measure the changes in price levels for specific items over the years. One of the most comprehensive of such indices for buildings is the construction price index prepared by the Office of Business Economics of the U.S. Department of Labor.

One advantage of using a price level index is that it is *objective.* The independent accountant can check the original cost of the assets and the date of purchase. He can also ascertain whether the index has been applied correctly. Thus, he can attest to the accuracy of the figures. A second advantage in using a specified price index is that price level adjustments will be *consistent* among companies. There are, however, several disadvantages.

First, specific price level indices do not exist for many kinds of assets. For these assets replacement value must be estimated in other ways. Second, many assets would not actually be replaced with an identical asset if the opportunity arose. Consequently, to the extent that technological advances had occurred, historical cost adjusted for price level changes would overstate the replacement value. Third, this technique can be used only for tangible assets. Intangible values would still not be reflected on the accounting statements.

Economic Value. The economic value of an asset is the present value of all future cash flows that will be created by that asset. Economic value is a theoretically appealing technique for estimating fair value, because it reflects the underlying rationale of how much any asset should be worth to the holder. In fact, this is precisely the basis on which an investor or potential investor, implicitly or explicitly, makes a decision with respect to the value of a share of stock. Unfortunately, the problems of estimating future cash flows and deciding on a discount rate make this approach to valuation impractical in almost all cases.

Market Value. Market value, as the name implies, is the price at which the asset could be sold. The conceptual support for accounting statements based on market values derives from the idea that market value represents the best measure of a firm's command over economic goods and services at any point in time. The cost of an asset was, of course, its market value on the day that it was purchased. Market value is a reasonable means for measuring current value where a market exists—for example, for marketable securities, inventories, or land. For many assets, however, there may not be a market. Polaroid, for example, might not be able to sell the equipment that it uses to produce its cameras because Polaroid holds an exclusive patent on the right to manufacture the cameras. This does not mean, however, that this equipment is worthless to Polaroid.

Furthermore, many people question the idea of valuing at current selling prices assets that management intends to use, not sell. These people prefer an approach based on "value in use," not "value in exchange." The market value proponents counter by arguing that the best measure of current wealth is current command over current goods and services. The market value approach is often called "exit value" accounting in contrast to the replacement cost approach, which is called "entry value" accounting.

Stock Market Value. One method for obtaining the value of an entire corporation is to multiply the number of outstanding shares by the market value per share. In theory, this should be the value that the market places on the company, including both its tangible and intangible assets. There are several problems with this technique. One is that the market price of most stocks is based on trading a relatively small proportion of the total number of shares outstanding. The price may not apply to large blocks of the stock or to the total shares outstanding. A second problem is that this information would not be of much help to the stockholder or potential stockholder, since he can obtain such information himself. Third, there may be some question of circular reasoning. One of the objectives of financial statements is to help the investor make decisions with respect to the acquisition or divestiture of stock. Can you, then, use the market value of these stocks to place a value on the company?

Summary. As you can see from this very brief overview, none of the approaches satisfies everyone. Specific price level adjustments can be calculated objectively but there are considerable questions about what some of the results mean. On the other hand, direct estimates of replacement costs, which would give some approximation of current values, can be quite subjective. Market prices represent a satisfactory estimate of fair value in certain instances. In other cases, however, there may be no market prices available, or, as in the case of special purpose equipment, the market price may not be a measure of fair value. Clearly, the difficulty in estimating fair value has been one of the major reasons for the accounting profession's adherence to the cost principle.

Fair Value Reporting

The proposals for providing the financial statement reader with fair value information can be divided into the following:

1. The use of additional parenthetical and footnote information on the fair value of certain financial statement items.

2. The use of supplementary fair value financial statements.

3. The replacement of the traditional financial statements with fair value financial statements.

Parenthetical and Footnote Information. The position of many accountants who favor traditional financial reporting techniques is that it is sufficient to provide fair value information in parenthetical form or in footnotes. For example, if LIFO inventory values are used, the current market value of the inventory could also be indicated. The market value of marketable securities, land, and other assets for which a market value exists could be shown in footnotes. Some accountants also favor showing the replacement value of fixed assets and the current amount of depreciation based on this value. All of this supplementary information would be in the form of parenthetical disclosures or footnotes. For example, marketable securities might be shown as follows:

Marketable Securities at Cost
(market value $1,500,000) $1,000,000

The financial statements would be prepared and published in the usual manner and both the balance sheet and the income statement would be based on original cost.

Supplementary Statements. Some people prefer showing more than one set of financial statements, with each set prepared using a different approach to valuation. In general, such proposals involve maintaining historical statements but showing statements based on other valuation schemes as supplementary data.

Complete Elimination of Historical Financial Statements. Many accounting theorists favor the complete elimination of financial statements based on historical costs. Some of the principal reasons for this position are:

1. Historical costs are of little or no use to either the manager or the investor.

2. Managers and investors need current instead of historical values. If the accountant will not provide these values, managers and investors must make their own estimates. It is doubtful if individual estimates will be as useful as those prepared by the accountant.

3. The accountant uses historical cost only because it is objective and thus provides him with some protection against claims that statements are too subjective.

In short, the proponents of fair value believe that historical costs are useless and that current values will be estimated anyway because managers and investors need current values for making decisions. It appears inappropriate to them to prepare *useless* information just because the *useful* information is more subjective. One accountant has said that "It is better to be vaguely right than precisely wrong."

Probable Future Developments. The principal problem with eliminating historical cost statements is that there is little agreement on any one alternative method for preparing fair value statements. Consequently, it appears to us that the businessman will probably have to continue to live with financial statements based generally on historical costs. We see, however, three changes that will make the traditional financial statements more useful:

1. There will be departures from historical costs in specific cases wherein the fair value can be accurately and objectively determined. This has, in fact, already occurred in a few instances. For example, the LIFO inventory method is a step toward current values on the income statement. We expect departures from historical costs to become more frequent.

2. Footnotes to the financial statements that provide current value information will become more frequent and more complete. We also anticipate that certain types of footnotes, providing current value information, will be required (as contrasted to the present practice of making current value information entirely voluntary).

3. More companies will provide supplementary statements providing current value data.

GENERAL PRICE LEVEL ACCOUNTING

APB Statement No. 3, *Financial Statements Restated for General Price Level Changes,* contains the recommendation that companies present supplemental financial statements adjusted for the effects of general price level changes. (Since APB Statements are not opinions and, therefore, are not binding on management or the public accounting profession, price level financial statements are not required and, in fact, are being prepared by only a very few companies.)

APB Statement No. 3 states: *"The same accounting principles used in preparing historical dollar financial statements should be used in preparing general price level financial statements except that changes in the purchasing power of the dollar are recognized in general price level financial statements.* General price level statements are an extension of and not a departure from the historical cost basis of accounting." The idea is to reflect the current purchasing power of the original cost dollars represented in financial statements.

APB Statement No. 3 includes instructions for preparing price level adjusted statements. In general, price level adjusted statements are prepared using the same principles that were used in the preparation of the historical statements except that the accounts are adjusted for the appropriate change in the level of "general" prices since the dates of acquisition. Statement 3 recommends that all accounts be classified as monetary or non-monetary. Monetary accounts are assets and liabilities for which the amounts are fixed, by contract or otherwise, in terms of specific dollar amounts regardless of changes in prices or price levels. Examples of monetary accounts are cash, accounts and notes receivable, accounts and notes payable, and bonds. All other accounts are called non-monetary and are adjusted for changes in price levels. Examples of non-monetary accounts are inventories, property assets, and investments in common stock.

APB Statement No. 3 recommends using the Gross National Product Price Deflator as the index for measuring price level changes. The Bureau of Labor Statistics Consumer Price Index may also be used if it does not deviate significantly from the GNP Price Deflator. An example of the recommended methods for adjusting financial statements for price level changes is provided in the next part of the chapter.

Example of Financial Statements
Restated for General Price Level Changes

In this part of the chapter we shall describe the technique recommended in APB Statement No. 3 for restating historical financial statements for general price level changes.

THE ABC COMPANY
Balance Sheet
($000)

| | As of December 31 | |
	1971	1972
Cash	$ 110	$ 150
Accounts Receivable	290	360
Inventories	1,400	1,200
Property Assets	2,600	3,000
Accumulated Depreciation	(890)	(1,190)
Total Assets	$3,510	$3,520
Accounts Payable	$ 400	$ 500
Taxes Payable	200	150
Mortgage Payable	1,000	1,000
Capital Stock	1,000	1,000
Retained Earnings	910	870
Total Equities	$3,510	$3,520

THE ABC COMPANY
Income Statement for Year Ending December 31, 1972

Sales		$1,900
Cost of Sales		
Beginning Inventory	$1,400	
Depreciation	300	
Other Costs	700	
	2,400	
Ending Inventory	1,200	
Cost of Sales		1,200
Gross Margin		700
Selling and Administrative Expense		500

Profit before Taxes	200
Income Taxes	100
Net Income	100
Retained Earnings, 12/31/71	910
Dividends Paid	(140)
Retained Earnings, 12/31/72	$ 870

Supplementary Data

1. The inventories, stated at cost, were acquired evenly throughout the year and are, on average, 6 months old.

2. Fixed assets were acquired as follows:

January 1, 1968	$1,600
January 1, 1969	500
January 1, 1970	500
January 1, 1972	400

3. Depreciation for all fixed assets was accumulated by the straight-line method on a 10-year life.

4. The capital stock was issued on January 1, 1968.

5. Assume that the price level deflator is as follows:

	Price Level Deflator	Conversion Factors (fourth quarter 1972=100)
Fourth quarter 1967	120	1.23
Fourth quarter 1968	122	1.21
Fourth quarter 1969	125	1.18
Fourth quarter 1970	130	1.14
Fourth quarter 1971	140	1.06
First quarter 1972	145	1.02
Second quarter 1972	146	1.01
Third quarter 1972	147	1.01
Fourth quarter 1972	148	1.00
Average 1972	146.5	1.01

In the Gross National Product Implicit Price Deflator the 1958 price level is equal to 100. In order to convert this index into a series of factors that can be used to express current price levels, divide each of the applicable factors into the current factor. In the example, we wish to convert our accounting data into 1972 price levels. Therefore, we make the fourth quarter of 1972 equal to 100. Prior quarters are expressed as a percentage of the fourth quarter of 1972 by dividing each index number into 1.48.

6. Sales and costs were incurred evenly throughout the year.

The procedure for making price level adjustments is as follows:

1. Adjust the 1971 balance sheet to 1972 price levels:

    (a) All monetary assets and liabilities are converted to fourth quarter 1972 monetary values by multiplying them by 1.06. (Monetary assets and liabilities are those whose amounts are fixed by contract or otherwise, in terms of number of dollars.)

	December 31, 1971	Adjusted to December 31, 1972, Price Levels
Cash	$ 110	$ 117
Accounts Receivable	290	307
Accounts Payable	400	424
Taxes Payable	200	212
Mortgage Payable	1,000	1,060

    (b) Convert 1971 inventories by multiplying their cost by 1.10 (the average of the 1970 conversion factor and the 1971 conversion factor): $1,400 \times 1.10 = 1,540$.

    (c) Convert property assets by multiplying the original cost by the appropriate conversion factor.

Date Acquired	Historical Cost	Conversion Factor	Adjusted Amount
1/1/68	$1,600	1.23	$1,968
1/1/69	500	1.21	605
1/1/70	500	1.18	590
Total	$2,600		$3,163

    (d) Convert accumulated depreciation to 1972 price levels

Date Asset Acquired	Accumulated Depreciation as of 12/31/71	Conversion Factor	Adjusted Amount
1/1/68	$640	1.23	$ 787
1/1/69	150	1.21	182
1/1/70	100	1.18	118
Total	$890		$1,087

    (e) Convert the capital stock by multiyplying the original issue price by 1.23

$$1,000 \times 1.23 = 1,230$$

    (f) Retained earnings is the exact balancing figure needed to equate total assets and total equities.

2. Convert the 1972 balance sheet to *current* 1972 price levels.

(a) All monetary items are *already* at 1972 price levels and, consequently, need no adjustment.

(b) Convert the inventories to 1972 price levels by multiplying the historical amounts by 1.01, reflecting the 6-month average age.

$$1,200 \times 1.01 = 1,212$$

(c) Convert the fixed assets to 1972 price levels by adjusting the acquisitions made during 1972 and adding this total to the 1971 balance

$$400 \times 1.06 = 424$$
$$424 + 3,163 = 3,587$$

(d) Convert accumulated depreciation to 1972 price levels.

Date Acquired	Accumulated Depreciation as of 12/31/72	Conversion Factor	Adjusted Amount
1/1/68	$ 800	1.23	$ 984
1/1/69	200	1.21	242
1/1/70	150	1.18	177
1/1/72	40	1.06	42
Total	$1,190		$1,445

(e) Capital stock remains at the adjusted 1971 balance sheet amount.

(f) Retained earnings will again be the balancing figure.

The adjusted balance sheet will be as follows:

THE ABC COMPANY
Balance Sheet Adjusted to 1972 Price Levels

	As of December 31	
Assets	*1971*	*1972*
Cash	$ 117	$ 150
Accounts Receivable	307	360
Inventories	1,540	1,212
Property Assets	3,163	3,587
Accumulated Depreciation	(1,087)	(1,445)
Total Assets	$4,040	$3,864
Equities		
Accounts Payable	$ 424	$ 500
Taxes Payable	212	150
Mortgage Payable	1,060	1,000
Capital Stock	1,230	1,230
Retained Earnings	1,114	984
Total Equities	$4,040	$3,864

3. Convert the income statement to 1972 price levels.

    (a) Multiplying sales and out-of-pocket costs by 1.01

	Historical Amount	Adjusted Amount
Sales	1,900	1,919
Other Costs	700	707
Selling and Administrative Expense	500	505
Income Taxes	100	101

    (b) The beginning and ending inventories are taken from the adjusted balance sheet.

    (c) The depreciation is equal to the change in beginning and ending accumulated depreciation after adjustment for price level changes: $358.

    (d) Convert the dividends into 1972 price levels by multiplying by 1.01. (It is assumed that dividends were paid quarterly)

$$140 \times 1.01 = 141$$

    (e) Calculate the monetary gain or loss from changes in the price levels. (This should be included as a separate item on the income statement.) Calculate the total monetary items on an historical basis and the total on an adjusted basis. The difference is the gain or loss from price level changes.

	Historical	Adjusted to 1972 Price Levels
Monetary Items on January 1:		
Cash	$ 110	$ 117
Accounts Receivable	290	307
Accounts Payable	(400)	(424)
Taxes Payable	(200)	(212)
Mortgage Payable	(1,000)	(1,060)
Net Monetary Items	(1,200)	(1,272)
Add Monetary Receipts during 1972:		
Sales	1,900	1,919
Subtract Monetary Payments:		
Other Costs	(700)	(707)
Selling and Administrative Expense	(500)	(505)
Income Taxes	(100)	(101)
Dividends	(140)	(141)
Purchase of Equipment	(400)	(424)
Monetary Items 12/31/72	(1,140)	(1,231)

Cash	150
Accounts Receivable	360
Accounts Payable	(500)
Taxes Payable	(150)
Mortgage Payable	(1,000)
	(1,140)

The difference between the historical monetary items and the adjusted amount ($1231 − $1140 = $91) is the monetary gain from changes in price levels. It represents the impact on the financial statements of holding more monetary liabilities than monetary assets during a period of rising price levels.

We are now ready to prepare an income statement and a reconciliation of retained earnings.

THE ABC COMPANY
Income Statement for Year Ending December 31, 1972,
Adjusted to 1972 Price Levels

Sales		$1,919
Cost of Sales		
Beginning Inventory	1,540	
Depreciation	358	
Other Costs	707	
	2,605	
Less Ending Inventory	1,212	
Cost of Sales		1,393
Gross Margin		526
Selling and Administrative Expense		505
Net Operating Profit		21
Gain from Price Level Changes		91
Profit before Taxes		112
Taxes		101
Profit after Taxes		11
Retained Earnings, January 1		1,114
Dividend		(141)
Retained Earnings, December 31		$ 984

This example of price level adjustments has been considerably simplified. Students interested in more complex examples should study Appendix C of APB Statement No. 3. In conclusion, however, we should note that price level adjustment can either increase, decrease, or fail to change the reported profits of a firm, depending on the firm's investment and financing policies. The cases and problems at the end of the chapter illustrate this point further.

FOREIGN EXCHANGE CONVERSIONS

Whenever a company has a foreign subsidiary[1] that it wants to consolidate for reporting purposes, it is necessary to convert the account balances of this subsidiary from the foreign currency into U.S. dollars[2] because subsidiary accounts are always maintained in the currency of the country in which the subsidiary is operating. The conversion (or "translation" as it is sometimes called) must be made each time consolidated financial statements are prepared. The process of conversion is somewhat similar to that for making price level adjustments. Consequently, we have considered the process of foreign currency conversion in the same chapter with price level adjustments. You should note, however, two major differences. First, unlike price level conversions, which are voluntary, foreign currency conversions must be made before consolidated statements can be prepared. Second, these conversions affect the basic financial statements; thus, the method used can affect the reported earnings of the company.

Corporate Relationships

The same type of relationships exist between a parent company and its foreign subsidiaries as between a parent company and its domestic subsidiaries. That is, if the subsidiary is less than 20 per cent owned, the investment is usually maintained on the balance sheet at its original cost in dollars, and any dividends received are treated as income in dollars in the period in which they are received. As a consequence, there are no problems of foreign exchange conversion in this situation. If the subsidiary is 20 per cent to 50 per cent owned, however, the parent company must generally maintain the investment at original cost plus its share of the subsidiary's earnings minus the dividends received (i.e., the equity method). The earnings are usually converted into dollars at the average exchange rate that existed during the period. Dividends are converted at the exchange rate on the date of receipt. If the subsidiary is more than 50% owned, it will usually be necessary to include it as part of the consolidated financial statements. In this case, all the foreign accounting balances must be converted to U.S. dollars. This conversion can be made in a number of ways. In this part of the chapter, we will consider the methods for converting the account balances of foreign subsidiaries into U.S. dollars so that the subsidiary statements can be consolidated into the financial statements of the parent American company.

Exchange Rates

An exchange rate is the relationship between two currencies. In the cases we will discuss, it is the relationship between the dollar and some other foreign currency. For example, the exchange rates on November 26, 1974, for the following foreign currencies were:

---

[1] Throughout this chapter we will assume that the foreign operation is a subsidiary because this is the most common corporate relationship. The same principles, however, apply to other corporate relationships such as joint ventures.

[2] Throughout this chapter we will be concerned with converting foreign currencies into U.S. dollars. Exactly the same process applies to converting any currency into any other currency.

Exchange Rates for Various Foreign Currencies
on November 26, 1974

Country	Monetary Unit	Value of Foreign Monetary Unit in U.S. Dollars	Number of Foreign Monetary Units Equal to One U.S. Dollar
Argentina	Peso	$ .1020	9.8
Australia	Dollar	1.3220	.75
Brazil	Cruzeiro	.1400	7.14
Britain	Pound	2.3240	.43
France	Franc	.2158	4.63
Japan	Yen	.003331	297.67
Switzerland	Franc	.3720	2.69
West Germany	Mark	.4052	2.47

This schedule indicates that on that date a dollar was worth 2.7 Swiss francs, 4.6 French francs, 2.4 West German marks, and so forth. This means that banks in foreign countries would accept United States dollars at these rates and, conversely, they would convert dollars into foreign currencies at these rates. Under the world monetary system currently in operation, the rate of exchange of the dollar with other currencies can vary significantly over the course of a year. Also, these changes in rates can be different for different currencies. For example, during a given year, the value of the dollar could increase relative to the British pound and decrease relative to the West German mark. At one time, the rate of exchange of the currencies of most developed countries was fixed within small limits because the value of each currency was based on a specific amount of gold. Consequently, significant changes in exchange rates were generally confined to third world currencies and an occasional revaluation by one of the developed countries (for example, the devaluation of the British pound in 1967 and the French franc in 1969). At present, currencies are no longer based on gold. As a result, their values fluctuate with supply and demand. Also, speculative activities can affect exchange rates in somewhat the same way that stock prices fluctuate with buyer and seller expectations. This situation makes the conversion problem now considerably more important to the accountant than has been true in the past.

Methods of Translation

In this part of the chapter, we will describe the commonly used methods for converting the financial statements of foreign subsidiaries into U.S. dollars for inclusion in the consolidated financial statements of the parent company.

The Current/Non-current Method. Under the current/non-current method, the current assets and current liabilities of the foreign subsidiary are translated into dollars at the exchange rate that existed on the balance sheet date. Non-current assets and liabilities are translated into dollars at the rate that existed on the date that the asset was acquired or the liability incurred.

The rationale behind this method is that current assets and current liabilities are essentially equivalent to foreign currency, and, consequently, are treated in the same way as foreign monetary balances. Property assets, however, are translated at the historical exchange rates because the dollar value of these assets would not be expected to fluctuate with changes in the exchange rate of the foreign currency. For example, assume that a company imports machinery into a plant in Brazil when the exchange rate is 5 cruzeiros for each dollar. Thus, machinery would be recorded in cruzeiros on the books of the Brazilian subsidiary at five times the dollars cost. If the exchange value of the cruzeiro subsequently dropped to 10 for each dollar, you could expect the value of the imported machinery to double in terms of cruzeiros. By translating the fixed asset accounts at the historical rate, the original relationship is maintained. Expressed in another way, fixed assets are reflected on the consolidated balance sheet at their original cost by using the exchange rate in effect at the date of acquisition.

The rationale for translating non-current liabilities at the historical exchange rate, however, is not so clear as it is with property assets. Since non-current liabilities need not be paid until some time in the future, minor and temporary changes in exchange rates can logically be ignored. If, however, the change in the exchange rate is significant and likely to be permanent, it appears to us that this situation should be reflected on the statements of the parent company by translating these liabilities at current rates. In APB Number 6 the Accounting Principles Board recognized this situation and stated that: "The Board is of the opinion that translation of long-term receivables and long-term liabilities at current exchange rates is appropriate in many circumstances."

Also, a problem of inventory valuation sometimes occurs when the current/non-current method of conversion is used. If the inventory is valued at net realizable value, it is appropriate to translate this value at the current exchange rate. If, however, the inventory is valued at cost, the current exchange rate may not be appropriate. If the exchange rate has changed since the date of acquisition, a corresponding change in the value of the inventory, as expressed in the foreign currency, could be expected. Consequently, many accountants believe that under an historical cost approach it is more appropriate to translate inventories at the historical exchange rate in the same way that fixed assets are translated.

The income statement accounts are translated at the average exchange rates in existence during the period, except for those items that are related to balance sheet accounts (principally depreciation), which are translated at historical exchange rates.

Example of Exchange Translation.

THE XYZ SUBSIDIARY
GENEVA, SWITZERLAND

Balance Sheet
December 31, 1972
(In thousands of Swiss francs)

Assets

	S.F.
Cash	1,050
Accounts Receivable	2,490
Inventories	5,880

Property Assets	9,340	
Less Accumulated Depreciation	(5,220)	4,120
Non-current Account Receivable		1,000
Total Assets		14,540

Equities

Accounts Payable	2,490
Taxes Payable	540
Long-Term Notes Payable	3,000
Capital Stock	5,000
Retained Earnings	3,510
Total Equities	14,540

The following assumptions are made with respect to exchange rates:

December 31, 1972: $1 = 3 S.F.
Average during 1972: $1 = 3.5 S.F.
At date of acquisition of fixed assets: $1 = 5 S.F.
At date when long-term debt was incurred: $1 = 5 S.F.
At date of acquisition of the non-current accounts
receivable: $1 = 4 S.F.

The translation of the Balance Sheet of the XYZ Company as of December 31, 1972, would be as follows:

Assets	Amount in S.F.	Conversion Rate	Amount in U.S. $
Cash	1,050	3	350
Accounts Receivable	2,490	3	830
Inventories	5,880	3	1,960
Fixed Assets	9,340	5	1,868
Less Accumulated Depreciation	(5,220)	5	(1,044)
Non-current Accounts Receivable	1,000	4	250
Total Assets	14,540		4,214

	Amount in S.F.	Conversion Rate	Amount in U.S. $
Equities			
Accounts Payable	2,490	3	830
Taxes Payable	540	3	180
Notes Payable			
(long term)	3,000	5	600
Capital Stock	5,000 ⎱		
Retained Earnings	3,510 ⎰		2,604[a]
Total Equities	14,540		4,214

[a]This is the balancing amount.

It should be noted that after the subsidiary statements are translated into dollars, it will be necessary to prepare consolidating entries similar to those described in Chapter 11.

The Monetary/Non-monetary Method. The monetary/non-monetary method of foreign exchange translation is as follows: All monetary assets and liabilities are translated at the current exchange rates. (Monetary assets and liabilities for purpose of foreign exchange conversion are defined the same way as monetary assets and liabilities for price level adjustment purposes: cash, accounts and notes receivable, acounts and notes payable, and so forth.) Non-monetary assets and liabilities are translated at the rates that existed at the time of acquisition or when incurred. Income statement items are translated at average rates for the year, except for those related to assets and liabilities that have been converted at the historical rates. As with the current/non-current method, such items will also be translated at the historical rates. The application of the monetary/non-monetary method to the preceding example is as follows:

Assets	Amount in S.F.	Conversion Rate	Amount in U.S. $
Cash	1,050	3	350
Accounts Receivable	2,490	3	830
Inventories	5,880	3.5	1,680
Fixed Assets	9,340	5	1,868
Accumulated Depreciation	(5,220)	5	(1,044)
Non-current Accounts Receivable	1,000	3	333
Total Assets	14,540		4,017
Equities			
Accounts Payable	2,490	3	830
Taxes Payable	540	3	180
Notes Payable (long term)	3,000	3	1,000
Capital Stock	5,000		
Retained Earnings	3,510		2,007
Total Equities	14,540		4,017

It is assumed that 3.5 is the average historical rate at which the inventories were acquired. Notice the substantial difference between the translated owners' equity accounts under these two methods.

Current Rate Method. The current rate method, as the name implies, involves the translation of all assets and liabilities at current rates. This method is favored in the United Kingdom but is seldom used in the United States. The current rate method, as applied to the preceding example, is as follows:

Assets	Amount in S.F.	Conversion Rate	Amount in U.S. $
Cash	1,050	3	350
Accounts Receivable	2,490	3	830

Inventories	5,880	3	1,960
Fixed Assets	9,340	3	3,113
Less: Accumulated Depreciation	(5,220)	3	(1,740)
Non-current Accounts			
Receivable	1,000	3	333
Total Assets	14,540		4,846

Equities	Amount in S.F.	Conversion Rate	Amount in U.S. $
Accounts Payable	2,490	3	830
Taxes Payable	540	3	180
Notes Payable	3,000	3	1,000
Capital Stock	5,000		
Retained Earnings	3,510		2,836
Total Equities	14,540		4,846

Again, notice that this method results in significantly different owners' equity balances. The choice of a method clearly can have an important impact on reported earnings.

Other Methods. There are several other conversion methods that involve combinations of the above methods. Also, although almost all conversions are made at the published exchange rates, a "constructed" rate, based on the relative rates of inflation between the two countries involved, has been recommended.[3]

The following table illustrates the main differences among the three principally used translation methods:

Balance Sheet Items	Current/ Non-current	Exchange Rates Used in Translation Monetary/ Non-monetary	Current
Monetary Assets	current/historical	current	current
Non-monetary Current Assets (principally inventory)	current	historical	current
Current Liabilities	current	current	current
Long-term Non-monetary Assets	historical	historical	current
Long-term Monetary Assets	historical	current	current
Long-term Liabilities	historical	current	current

Exchange Gains and Losses. In translating the income statement from the foreign currency to U.S. dollars, exchange gains or losses will occur if the exchange rates used to translate the preceding year's balance sheet and income statement are

[3] See Research Report Number 36 by the National Association of Accountants and "Inflation and Foreign Investments" by S.R. Sapienza, *Financial Executive*, April 1963.

different from the current year's exchange rates. To illustrate, assume that in the preceding example, the balance sheet as of December 31, 1973, and the income statement for the year 1973 were as follows:

THE XYZ SUBSIDIARY
GENEVA, SWITZERLAND

Balance Sheet as of December 31, 1973
(In thousands of Swiss francs)

Assets

Cash	1,100
Accounts Receivable	2,700
Inventories	6,500
Property Assets	9,340
Accumulated Depreciation	(5,920)
Non-current Accounts Receivable	1,000
Total Assets	14,720

Equities

Accounts Payable	2,000
Taxes Payable	500
Long-term Notes Payable	3,000
Capital Stock	5,000
Retained Earnings	4,220
Total Equities	14,720

THE XYZ SUBSIDIARY
GENEVA, SWITZERLAND

Income Statement for the Year Ending December 31, 1973
(In thousands of Swiss francs)

Sales		15,680
Cost of Sales		
Beginning Inventory	5,880	
Depreciation	700	
Other Costs	10,000	
	16,580	
Ending Inventory	6,500	
Cost of Sales		10,080
Gross Margin		5,600
Selling and Administrative Expense		3,300
Profit before Taxes		2,300
Taxes		1,100
Net Income		1,200
Owners' Equity, January 1		8,510
Dividends		(490)
Owners' Equity, December 31		9,220

The conversion assumptions are as follows:

1. The exchange rate on December 31, 1973, was 2 S.F. to the U.S. dollar.
2. The average exchange rate for 1973 was 2.5 S.F. to the U.S. dollar.
3. The monetary/non-monetary method of conversion is used.
4. Other assumptions are the same as in the preceding example.

The balance sheet as of December 31, 1973, would be as follows:

Assets	Amount in S.F.	Conversion Rate	Amount in U.S.
Cash	1,100	2	550
Accounts Receivable	2,700	2	1,350
Inventories	6,500	2.5	2,600
Property Assets	9,340	5	1,868
Accumulated Depreciation	(5,920)	5	(1,184)
Non-current Accounts Receivable	1,000	2	500
Total Assets	14,720		5,684
Equities			
Accounts Payable	2,000	2	1,000
Taxes Payable	500	2	250
Long-term Notes Payable	3,000	2	1,500
Capital Stock	5,000 }		2,934[a]
Retained Earnings	4,220 }		
Total Equity	14,720		5,684

[a]The balancing figure.

The income statement for 1973 would be as follows:

	Amount in S.F.	Conversion Rate	Amount in U.S. $
Sales	15,680	2.5	6,272
Cost of Sales			
Beginning Inventory	5,880	3.5	1,680
Depreciation	700	5.0	140
Other Costs	10,000	2.5	4,000
	16,580		5,820
Ending Inventory	6,500	2.5	2,600
Cost of Sales	10,080		3,220
Gross Margin	5,600		3,052
Selling and Administrative Expense	3,300	2.5	1,320

Operating Profit	2,300		1,732
Exchange Gain (loss)	–		(169)[a]
Profit before Taxes	2,300		1,563
Taxes	1,100	2.5	440
Profit after Taxes	1,200		1,123
Owners' Equity, January 1	8,510		2,007
Dividends	(490)	2.5	(196)
Owners' Equity, December 31	9,220		2,934

[a]This is the amount that must be added or subtracted from the net income in order to make the January 1 owners' equity plus the income earned in 1973 minus the dividends paid during 1973 equal to the December 31 owners' equity.

Accounting Treatment of Exchange Gains and Losses. APB No. 30 specifically provides that exchange gains or losses must not be treated as an extraordinary item. Consequently, if they appear on the income statement they must be treated as ordinary income or expense. Some companies take all such gains and losses into income when they occur. Other companies defer the gains and losses and spread them over a period of years. Still other companies defer gains and spread them but charge off losses as incurred. There is no uniformity of practice in this area. A few companies even defer just the losses.

Management Implications

In the early 1970s, a significant change in international monetary policy went into effect. Currencies, instead of being fixed in relationship to each other, were allowed to "float." This is, the exchange rate was allowed to be determined day by day in terms of supply and demand conditions. This has resulted in wide changes in exchange rates in relatively short periods of time. Furthermore, this new policy resulted in the devaluation of the U.S. dollar in relation to most European currencies. The net effect has been that the choice of a method of currency conversion now has a significantly greater impact on the resulting financial statements than was previously the case. At the present time, there is considerable latitude in the method of conversion acceptable under generally accepted accounting principles as well as in the treatment of exchange gains and losses. The APB did not publish an opinion on currency conversions and thus current practices are quite varied. Consequently, the method of foreign exchange conversion can be added to the list of practices that are subject to flexible accounting rules. Because of its increasing importance, however, it appears likely that the FASB will issue an opinion on foreign exchange conversion in the near future. The FASB Standard No. 1 established new requirements for disclosing foreign exchange practices.

QUESTIONS

1. How would you explain to someone who had never studied accounting the rationale for including assets at their original cost on the balance sheet?

2. Explain why a method that uses a price level index to adjust historical cost is considered objective? Would all competent accountants end up with the same figures for a specific company? In what areas might differences of opinion exist?

3. How would you calculate the economic value of a given asset or group of assets? Why is this method generally considered of academic interest only?

4. Explain the difference between replacement cost and reproduction cost. Which would be more useful for balance sheet purposes?

5. Name some types of assets for which market values could readily be estimated? Name some assets for which market values might be difficult or impossible to estimate?

6. In what ways are the process of converting the financial statements of foreign subsidiaries into U.S. dollars similar to the process of converting domestic financial statements into current dollars? In what ways are the processes different?

7. What is an exchange rate? How is it determined? Why do exchange rates fluctuate?

8. Explain how the choice of method for converting the financial statements of foreign subsidiaries can effect a company's reported earnings.

9. Compare the current/non-current method, the monetary/non-monetary method, and the current method of converting foreign financial statements. What are the advantages and disadvantages of each? Which would you support?

10. How has the use of "floating" exchange rates affected the preparation of financial statements?

PROBLEMS

Problem 13-1

The balance sheet for the Union Company on December 31, 1971, was as follows:

THE UNION COMPANY
Balance Sheet, December 31, 1971
($000)

Assets	
Cash	$ 1,000
Accounts Receivable	2,000
Inventories	5,000
Property Assets	10,000
Accumulated Depreciation	(4,600)
Total Assets	$13,400

Equities

Accounts Payable	$ 3,000
Taxes Payable	1,000
Notes Payable	4,000
Capital Stock	4,000
Retained Earnings	1,400
Total Equities	$13,400

Supplementary Data:

1. Inventories, stated at cost, were acquired evenly throughout the year, and are, on average, 6 months old.

2. Property assets were acquired as follows:

January 1, 1966	$ 5,000
January 1, 1968	3,000
January 1, 1970	2,000
Total	$10,000

3. Depreciation on all fixed assets was accumulated by the straight-line method on a 10-year life.

4. The capital stock was issued on January 1, 1966.

5. The price deflation conversion rates, with the fourth quarter of 1971 equal to 100 per cent, is as follows:

Fourth quarter 1965	1.16
Fourth quarter 1966	1.14
Fourth quarter 1967	1.12
Fourth quarter 1968	1.10
Fourth quarter 1969	1.08
Fourth quarter 1970	1.05
Fourth quarter 1971	1.00
Average 1971	1.02

Required:

Restate the 1971 balance sheet at the 1971 price levels in accordance with the rules recommended in APB Statement 3.

Problem 13-2

The financial data for the Union Company for 1972 is as follows:

Balance sheet as of December 31, 1972

Assets	*($000)*
Cash	$ 1,100
Accounts Receivable	2,600
Inventories	4,800
Property Assets	12,000
Accumulated Depreciation	(5,800)
Total Assets	$14,700

Equities

Accounts Payable	$ 3,000
Taxes Payable	1,500
Notes Payable	4,000
Capital Stock	4,000
Retained Earnings	2,200
Total Equities	$14,700

Income statement for Year Ending December 31, 1972

		($000)
Sales		$8,000
Cost of Sales		
Beginning Inventory	$5,000	
Depreciation	1,200	
Other Costs	3,000	
	9,200	
Ending Inventories	4,800	
Cost of Sales		4,400
Gross Margin		3,600
Selling and Administrative Expense		1,000
Profit before Taxes		2,600
Taxes		1,400
Net Income		1,200
Retained Earnings, January 1		1,400
Dividends		(400)
Retained Earnings, December 31		$2,200

1. Inventories were acquired evenly throughout the year, with an average age of 6 months.

2. Property assets of $2,000 were acquired on January 1, 1972.

3. The price deflator conversion rates, with the fourth quarter of 1972 equal to 100 per cent, is as follows:

Fourth quarter 1965		1.22
Fourth quarter 1966		1.20
Fourth quarter 1967		1.18
Fourth quarter 1968		1.15
Fourth quarter 1969		1.13
Fourth quarter 1970		1.10
Fourth quarter 1971		1.06
Average	1971	1.08
Fourth quarter 1972		1.00
Average	1972	1.03

Required:

Prepare the following statements adjusted to 1972 price levels:

1. Comparative 1971 and 1972 balance sheets.

2. Income statement and reconciliation of retained earnings for 1972.

Problem 13-3

The financial data for the Union Company for 1973 is as follows:

Balance Sheet as of December 31, 1973

Assets	($000)
Cash	$ 1,000
Accounts Receivable	1,700
Inventories	6,000
Marketable Securities	1,000
Property Assets	14,200
Accumulated Depreciation	(6,320)
Total Assets	$17,580
Equities	
Accounts Payable	$ 5,700
Taxes Payable	1,000
Notes Payable	4,000
Capital Stock	5,000
Retained Earnings	1,880
Total Equities	$17,580

Income Statement for Year Ending December 31, 1973

		($000)
Sales		$ 9,000
Cost of Sales		
Beginning Inventory	$ 4,800	
Depreciation	1,600	
Other Costs	5,000	
	11,400	
Ending Inventory	6,000	
Cost of Sales		5,400
Gross Margin		3,600
Selling and Administrative Expense		1,200
Net Income before Taxes		2,400
Taxes		1,500
Net Income		900
Retained Earnings, January 1		2,200
Dividends		(1,220)
Retained Earnings December 31		$ 1,880

1. Inventories were acquired evenly throughout the year, with an average age of 6 months.

2. Property assets were purchased on January 1, 1973, for $4,000. Property assets, purchased on January 1, 1968, for $1,800, were sold on December 31, 1973, for $720.

3. The marketable securities were purchases on July 1, 1973.

4. New capital stock was issued on January 1, 1973, for $1,000 cash.

5. The price deflator conversion rates, with the fourth quarter of 1973 equal to 100 per cent, is as follows:

Fourth quarter 1965	1.30
Fourth quarter 1966	1.28
Fourth quarter 1967	1.26
Fourth quarter 1968	1.23
Fourth quarter 1969	1.21
Fourth quarter 1970	1.18
Fourth quarter 1971	1.14
Fourth quarter 1972	1.08
Average 1972	1.11
Second quarter 1973	1.04
Fourth quarter 1973	1.00
Average 1973	1.04

Required:

Prepare the following statments adjusted to 1973 price levels:

1. Comparative 1972 and 1973 balance sheets.

2. Income statement and reconciliation of retained earnings for 1973.

Problem 13-4

The XYZ Company disposed of marketable securities during 1968 as follows:

	Date of Acquisition	Date of Disposition	Cost	Selling Price
Security A	1/1/65	4/1/68	$10,000	$15,000
Security B	12/31/67	7/1/68	20,000	15,000
Security C	7/1/67	10/1/68	30,000	25,000
Security D	10/1/66	12/31/68	15,000	20,000
Security E	12/31/67	12/31/68	18,000	20,000

The Gross National Product Implicit Price Deflator for the periods involved is as follows:

Year	Quarter	Deflator	Year	Quarter	Deflator
1964	4	109.6	1968	1	120.0
1966	3	114.4	1968	2	121.2
1967	2	116.6	1968	3	122.3
1967	4	118.9	1968	4	123.5

Required:

Calculate the gain or loss on the sale of each security:

1. On the basis of historical data.

2. On the basis of data adjusted to the price level at the date of disposition.

Problem 13-5

Described below are three situations involving the acquisition and subsequent disposition of a property asset.

Original Cost	$100,000	$150,000	$200,000
Date of Acquisition	1/1/64	1/1/65	1/1/66
Depreciation Method	Straight-line	Straight-line	Straight-line
Estimated Life	5 years	5 years	4 years
Amount Received on Disposition	0	$20,000	$50,000
Date of Disposition	12/31/68	12/31/68	12/31/68

The Gross National Product Implicit Price Deflator for the period involved was as follows:

Year	Quarter	Deflator
1963	4	107.8
1964	4	109.6
1965	4	111.6
1966	4	115.3
1967	4	118.9
1968	4	123.5

Required:

Calculate the amount of gain or loss in each of the above situations:

1. Based on historical data.

2. After making the appropriate adjustments to the December 31, 1968, price levels.

Problem 13-6

The balance sheet for the Gnome Company of Switzerland, a wholly owned subsidiary of the Elf Corporation of the United States, was as follows:

THE GNOME COMPANY

Balance Sheet for the Year Ending December 31, 1972
(In thousands of Swiss francs)

Assets	*S.F.*
Cash	10,000
Accounts Receivable	20,000
Notes Receivable (short term)	20,000
Inventories (at cost)	50,000

Notes Receivable (long term)	100,000
Property Assets	500,000
Accumulated Depreciation	(200,000)
Total Assets	500,000

Equities	
Accounts Payable	40,000
Notes Payable (short term)	40,000
Notes Payable (long term)	200,000
Capital Stock	150,000
Retained Earnings	70,000
Total Equities	500,000

The exchange rates are as follows:

1. On December 31, 1972, $1 = 3 Swiss francs

2. When the long-term notes payable and receivable were incurred, $1 = 4 Swiss francs

3. When the property assets were purchased, $1 = 5 Swiss francs

4. The inventories were purchased when, on average, $1 = 3.5 Swiss francs.

Required:

Convert the balance sheet of the Gnome Company to U.S. dollars using the current/non-current method.

Problem 13-7

Required:

Convert the balance sheet in Problem 13-6 to U.S. dollars using the monetary/non-monetary method.

Problem 13-8

Required:

Convert the balance sheet in Problem 13-6 to U.S. dollars using the current method.

Problem 13-9

The financial statements for the Gnome Company for 1973 were as follows:

GNOME COMPANY
Balance Sheet as of December 31, 1973
(In thousands of Swiss francs)

Assets	*S.F.*
Cash	15,000
Accounts Receivable	25,000
Notes Receivable (short term)	20,000
Inventories (at cost)	55,000

Notes Receivable (long term)	100,000
Property Assets	500,000
Accumulated Depreciation	(250,000)
Total Assets	465,000

Equities	
Accounts Payable	15,000
Notes Payable (long term)	200,000
Capital Stock	150,000
Retained Earnings	100,000
Total Equities	465,000

GNOME COMPANY
Income Statement for Year Ending December 31, 1973

		S.F.
Sales		500,000
Cost of Sales		
Beginning Inventories	50,000	
Depreciation	50,000	
Other Costs	305,000	
	405,000	
Ending Inventory	55,000	
Cost of Sales		350,000
Gross Margin		150,000
Selling and Administrative Expense		50,000
Profit before Taxes		100,000
Taxes		50,000
Net Income		50,000
Owners' Equity, January 1		220,000
Dividends		(20,000)
Owners' Equity, December 31		250,000

1. Assume that on December 31, 1973, $1 = 2 Swiss francs.

2. The average exchange rate during the year was $1 = 2.5 Swiss francs.
   (See Problem 13-6 for other exchange rates.)

Required:

Convert the balance sheet and the income statement to U.S. dollars using the current/non-current method.

Problem 13-10

Required:

Convert the balance sheet and the income statement in Problem 13-9 into U.S. dollars using the monetary/non-monetary method. (Note: inventories are at cost and were purchased evenly throughout the year.)

Review Cases

14

Case 1-1

Smoky Valley Cafe[1]

On August 12, 1946, three people, who had previously been employed to wait on tables in one of the cafes in Baxter, Oregon, formed a partnership. The eldest of the three was Mrs. Bevan, a middle-aged widow. The other two were Mr. and Mrs. Elmer Maywood. The partnership lasted for slightly more than 4 months, and in connection with its dissolution the preparation of a balance sheet became necessary.

Each of the partners contributed $2,000 cash, a total of $6,000. On August 12, the partnership purchased the Smoky Valley Cafe for $16,000. The purchase price included land valued at $2,500, improvements to land at $2,000, buildings at $10,500, and cafe equipment at $1,000. The partnership made a down payment of $4,500 (from its $6,000 cash) and signed a mortgage for the balance of the $16,000. The doors of the cafe were opened for business shortly after August 12.

One of the things that made this particular piece of property attractive to them was the fact that the building contained suitable living accommodations. One of these rooms was occupied by Mrs. Bevan, another by the Maywoods.

The Maywoods and Mrs. Bevan agreed on a division of duties and responsibilities which would allow them to keep the cafe open 24 hours a day. They agreed that Mrs. Bevan would operate the kitchen, Mrs. Maywood would have charge of the dining room, and that Mr. Maywood would attend the bar. Mrs. Bevan agreed to keep the accounting records. She was willing to perform this task because she was vitally interested in making the business a success. She had invested the proceeds from the sale of her modest home and from her husband's insurance policy in the venture. If it failed, the major part of her financial resources would be lost.

A beer license was granted by the state authorities. On August 15, the partnership sent a check for $35 to the distributor who supplied beer. This $35

[1] Based on a case argued before the Supreme Court of the State of Oregon, March 28, 1950. See 216 P.2d 1005.

Case material of the Harvard Graduate School of Business Administration is prepared as a basis for class discussion. Cases are not designed to present illustrations of either effective or ineffective handling of administrative problems.

constituted a deposit on bottles and kegs necessary for the operation of the bar and would be returned to the Smoky Valley Cafe after all bottles and kegs had been returned to the beer distributor.

The Smoky Valley Cafe was located on a major highway, and a great deal of business was obtained from truck drivers. One of these truck driver patrons, Fred Mead, became a frequent customer. He soon gained the friendship of Mrs. Maywood.

In October, the partners decided that to continue to offer their patrons quality food, they would have to add to their equipment. This new equipment cost $415.95, and because the supplier of the equipment was unimpressed with the firm's credit rating, the equipment was paid for in cash.

The month of November did not improve the cash position of the business. In fact, the cash balance became so low that Mrs. Bevan contributed additional cash in the amount of $400.00 to the business. She had hopes, however, that the future would prove to be more profitable.

On the night of December 12, Fred Mead stopped in the cafe to see Mrs. Maywood. Shortly after he left, Mrs. Maywood retired to her room. A few hours later, Mr. Maywood came in and asked for her, and after a brief search discovered that she had departed through a window. Her absence led him to the conclusion that she had departed with Fred Mead, and he thereupon set out in pursuit of the pair.

On December 16, Mrs. Bevan decided that the partnership was dissolved because she had not heard any word from either of the Maywoods. (The courts subsequently affirmed that the partnership was dissolved as of December 16, 1946.) Although she had no intention of ceasing operations, she realized that an accounting would have to be made as of December 16. She called in Mr. Bailey, a local accountant, for this purpose.

Mrs. Bevan told Mr. Bailey that they had been able to pay $700 on the mortgage while the partnership was operating. Cash on hand amounted to $65.35, but the bank balance was only $9.78. Mr. Bailey found bills owed by the cafe totaling $92.01. Mrs. Bevan said that her best estimate was that there was $100 worth of food on hand.

Mr. Bailey estimated that a reasonable allowance for depreciation on the fixed assets was as follows:

Asset	Depreciation Allowance
Land Improvements	$ 44.45
Buildings	233.45
Cafe Equipment	44.19
	$322.09

QUESTIONS

1. Draw up a balance sheet for the Smoky Valley Cafe as of August 12, 1946, taking into account the events described in the first two paragraphs of the case.

2. Draw up a balance sheet as of December 16, 1946.

3. What were the equities of the Maywoods and Mrs. Bevan, respectively? (In partnership law, the partners share equally in profits and losses unless there is a specific provision to the contrary. Each partner in the Smoky Valley Cafe, therefore, would have an equity in one-third of the profits, or his equity would be decreased by one-third of the losses.)

4. Do you suppose that the partners received these amounts? Why?

Case 1-2

John Bartlett[1]

John Bartlett was the inventor of a hose-clamp for automobile hose connections. Having confidence in its commercial value, but possessing no excess funds of his own, he sought among his friends and acquaintances for the necessary capital to put the hose-clamp on the market. The proposition which he placed before possible associates was that a corporation, Bartlett Manufacturing Company, should be formed with capital stock of $25,000 par value.

The project looked attractive to a number of the individuals to whom the inventor presented it, but the most promising among them—a retired manufacturer—said he would be unwilling to invest his capital without knowing what uses were intended for the cash to be received from the proposed sale of stock. He suggested that the inventor determine the probable costs of experimentation and of special machinery and prepare for him a statement of the estimated assets and liabilities of the proposed company when ready to begin actual operation. He also asked for a statement of the estimated transactions for the first year of operations, to be based on studies the inventor had made of probable markets and costs of labor and materials. This information Mr. Bartlett consented to supply to the best of his ability.

After consulting the engineer who had aided him in constructing his patent models, Mr. Bartlett drew up the following list of data relating to the transactions of the proposed corporation during its period of organization and development:

1. The retired manufacturer would pay the corporation $10,000 cash for which he would receive stock with a par value of $10,000. The remaining stock (par value, $15,000) would be given to Mr. Bartlett in exchange for the patent on the hose-clamp.

2. Probable cost of incorporation and organization, including estimated officers' salaries during developmental period, $825.

3. Probable cost of developing special machinery, $5,000. This sum includes the cost of expert services; materials, rent of a small shop; and the cost of power, light, and miscellaneous expenditures.

4. Probable cost of raw materials, $500, of which $300 is to be used in experimental production.

On the basis of the above information, Mr. Bartlett prepared the estimated balance sheet shown in Exhibit 1.

EXHIBIT 1
BARTLETT MANUFACTURING COMPANY
Estimated Balance Sheet
as of Date Company Begins Operations

Assets		Equities	
Cash	$ 3,675	Stockholders' equity	$25,000
Inventory	200		
Machinery	5,000		
Organization costs	825		
Experimental costs	300		
Patent	15,000		
Total Assets	$25,000	Total Equities	$25,000

Mr. Bartlett then set down the following estimates as a beginning step in furnishing the rest of the information desired:

1. Expected sales, all to be received in cash by the end of the first year of operation, $28,000.

2. Expected additional purchases of raw materials and supplies during the course of this operating year, all paid for in cash by end of year, $9,000.

3. Expected borrowing from the bank during year but loans to be repaid before close of year, $2,000. Interest on these loans, $50.

4. Expected payroll and other cash expenses and manufacturing costs for the operating year; $11,000 of manufacturing costs plus $3,000 for selling and administrative expenses, a total of $14,000.

5. New machinery and equipment to be purchased for cash, $1,000.

6. Expected inventory of raw materials and supplies at close of period, at cost, $1,800.

7. No inventory of unsold hose-clamps expected as of the end of the period. All products to be manufacturered on the basis of firm orders received; none to be produced for inventory.

8. All experimental and organization costs, previously capitalized, to be charged against income of the operating year.

9. Estimated depreciation of machinery, $600.

10. Dividends paid in cash, $3,000.

It should be noted that the transactions summarized above would not necessarily take place in the sequence indicated. In practice, a considerable number of separate events, or transactions, would occur throughout the year, and many of them were dependent on one another. For example, operations were begun with an initial cash balance and inventory of raw materials, products were manufactured, and sales of these products provided funds for financing subsequent operations. Then, in turn, sales of the product subsequently manufactured yielded more funds.

QUESTIONS

1. Trace the effect on the balance sheet of each of the projected events appearing in Mr. Bartlett's list. Thus, Item 1, taken alone, would mean that cash would be increased by $28,000 and that (subject to reductions for various costs covered in later items) stockholders' equity would be increased by $28,000. Notice that in this question you are asked to consider all items in terms of their effect on the balance sheet.

Case 1-3

Desa Industries, Inc.

The balance sheet of Desa Industries, Inc., as of September 1, 1973, and August 31, 1972, follows. What conclusions about this company can you draw from these data?

DESA INDUSTRIES, INC.
Consolidated Balance Sheet
September 1, 1973 and August 31, 1972

ASSETS	1973	1972
Current assets:		
Cash	$ 1,185,481	$ 1,277,770
Accounts and notes receivable, less allowance for doubtful accounts of $256,982 in 1973 and $341,675 in 1972 (Note 3)	9,191,730	7,388,917
Inventories (Note 3):		
Finished goods	2,062,911	2,557,363
Work in process	4,717,586	3,930,712
Raw materials	5,162,490	4,345,284
	11,942,987	10,833,359
Prepaid expenses	131,679	89,023
Total current assets	22,451,877	19,589,069
Property, plant and equipment, at cost (Note 3):		
Land	261,448	261,088
Buildings	2,475,868	2,402,537
Machinery and equipment	3,925,345	3,531,168
	6,662,661	6,194,793
Accumulated depreciation	(2,960,539)	(2,502,867)
Net property, plant and equipment	3,702,122	3,691,926
Other assets	52,232	88,197
	$26,206,231	$23,369,192

LIABILITIES AND STOCKHOLDERS' EQUITY	1973	1972
Current liabilities:		
Accounts payable	$ 5,670,024	$ 3,528,903
Accrued liabilities	1,632,306	1,481,723
Income taxes (Note 4):		
Current	343,000	62,000
Deferred	712,000	245,000
Current portion of long-term debt	710,681	1,333,237
Total current liabilities	9,068,011	6,650,863
Notes payable under a Revolving Credit Agreement (Note 3)	11,000,000	11,000,000
Other long-term debt (Note 3)	842,410	1,552,995
Deferred income taxes (Note 4)	172,000	126,000
Stockholders' equity (Notes 3 and 5):		
5% non-cumulative, convertible preferred stock, $100 par value; 50,000 shares authorized, 26,307 shares issued and outstanding	2,630,700	2,630,700
Common stock, $1 par value; 2,000,000 shares authorized, 407,269 shares in 1973 and 405,519 shares in 1972 issued and outstanding	407,269	405,519
Additional paid-in capital	60,074	49,824
Retained earnings	2,025,767	953,291
Total stockholders' equity	5,123,810	4,039,334
	$26,206,231	$23,369,192

Case 2-1

John Bartlett

See the John Bartlett case (Case 1-2) on page 351.

Required:

1. Prepare an income statement covering the first year of planned operations and a balance sheet as of the end of that year.

2. *Assume* that the retired manufacturer received capital stock with a par value of $8,000 for the $10,000 cash he paid to the corporation, with John Bartlett still receiving stock with a par value of $15,000 in exchange for his patent. Under these circumstances, how would the balance sheet in Exhibit 1 appear?

3. *Assume* that the management is interested in what the results would be if no products were sold during the first year, even though production continued at the level indicated in the original plans. The following changes would be made in the ten items listed above: Items 1, 6, 7, and 10 are to be disregarded. Instead of Item 3, assume that a loan of $29,000 is obtained, that the loan is not repaid, but that interest thereon of $1,050 is paid during the year. Prepare an income statement for the year and a balance sheet as of the end of the year. Contrast these financial statements with those prepared in Question 2.

Case 2-2

Free-Breeze Motel

For many years Mr. Charles Dalphson, a salesman for a large manufacturer of industrial chemicals, had taken his vacation at a beach a few miles outside of Tampa, Florida. For the past 4 years, Mr. Dalphson had stayed at the Free-Breeze Motel. During this time he had become quite friendly with the owner of the motel, Mr. Frederick Palmer.

While Mr. Dalphson was on his vacation in February 1976, Mr. Palmer indicated that he was going to sell the motel and retire. (He was now 67.) He suggested, partly in jest, that Mr. Dalphson buy it. Mr. Dalphson, who was then 55, became immediately interested. It had been his plan for several years to retire eventually to Florida. The idea of retiring early and running a motel appealed to him; he was a bachelor and had managed to save $60,000. He asked Mr. Palmer for particulars on the proposition, indicating that he might be interested in buying.

The Free-Breeze Motel was located on one-and-one-half acres of land about three blocks from the beach and one block from a main highway. It was of cinder-block construction and consisted of seven single units (bedroom and bath) and seven housekeeping units (bedroom, living room, kitchenette, and bath), and a proprietor's apartment (two bedrooms, living room, kitchen, and bath).

Mr. Palmer had purchased the motel new in 1960 for $80,000. Since then, he and his wife had run the motel without outside help. Mr. Palmer kept no formal accounting records; he had a local accountant come in once a year and prepare his income tax return based on his canceled checks, receipted bills, and occupancy records. When the accountant filed the tax return, he also gave Mr. Palmer a statement of his annual profit. Exhibit 1 is a summary of the 1974 and 1975 statements.

Mr. Palmer told Mr. Dalphson that he was asking $155,000 for the motel. Mr. Palmer stated that he believed that he had a successful business. He pointed to the fact that his profits for the past two years had averaged about $36,400. At a price of $155,000, anyone buying his motel would be earning 20 per cent on his investment. He estimated that the land and building were worth $120,000 and that the furniture was worth $15,000. He stated that the additional $20,000 that he was asking was "goodwill." This goodwill consisted of repeat customers (such as Mr. Dalphson), and he believed that the high rate of return on his investment was the evidence that this goodwill actually existed. As further evidence, Mr. Palmer stated

EXHIBIT 1
FREE-BREEZE MOTEL
Summary of Operations

	1974	1975
Revenue	$51,071	$54,040
Expenses:		
Depreciation—Building[a]	$ 3,000	$ 3,000
Depreciation—Furniture[b]	1,000	1,000
Laundry	1,980	2,052
Heat, light, and power	2,863	2,932
Advertising, printing, and stationery	1,850	1,865
Repairs and maintenance	2,050	1,977
Real estate and property taxes	1,689	1,689
Other expenses (telephone, supplies, etc.)	1,639	1,725
Total	$16,071	$16,240
Profit	$35,000	$37,800

[a]$60,000 (cost of building) ÷ 20 (estimated life) = $3,000.
[b]$10,000 (cost of furniture) ÷ 10 (estimated life) = $1,000.
Note: The expenses in the exhibit apply to the entire motel, including the owner's apartment.

that average occupancy had been about 65 per cent in 1974 and 70 per cent in 1975.

Mr. Dalphson said that he would think about the proposal. He had the property appraised and established to his own satisfaction that $135,000 was a reasonable price for the land, building, and furniture. The appraiser estimated the land was worth $25,000, the building was worth $95,000, and the furniture, $15,000. The appraiser believed that a reasonable life would be 20 years for the building and 5 years for the furniture. Mr. Dalphson wondered, however, about the existence of the goodwill and whether the business was worth the extra $20,000 that was being asked. He believed that 20 per cent was a satisfactory return, but he felt unsure about how goodwill should be calculated.

He also talked to a local banker who told him that he felt fairly certain that he would be able to obtain a 20-year mortgage for $110,000 on the property. Interest would be 7 per cent per year.

QUESTIONS

1. What do you think Mr. Dalphson's return on his investment would be if he purchased the motel for $155,000?

2. Do you think $155,000 is a fair price for the motel? If not, what do you think a fair price would be?

Case 2-3

Oliver Optics Company[1]

When John Oliver graduated from technical school he started making plans for a small business to grind special lenses and to make certain high-quality optical items for the scientific and military markets. At the time there was keen demand for a high-quality product and Oliver thought he could build a substantial business by stressing this quality element. He started his business January 1 and after a year of some very disturbing and revealing difficulties in meeting customers' higher standards, Oliver thought he had things going well. By working hard and personally satisfying all complaints, he knew he had created much goodwill for his firm.

Oliver began his business with $5,000 of savings, including some money he had inherited. On March 31, he borrowed $2,000 on a 1-year note (4 per cent) from his uncle, who had intimated he would renew the note every year so long as Oliver needed the money. He had had large bills for materials, but had been able to keep from falling too far behind in his payments. Except for the accounts indicated below as unpaid, all bills had been paid in cash, including the interest on the note. On April 1, he had paid in advance the first 12 months' interest on the loan.

Mr. Oliver purchased some standard equipment at the first of the year "on time," agreeing to make a partial payment of $1,000 and to pay $250 every 3 months for 4 years. Since the payments were scheduled to start at once and since he had agreed to pay $60 interest every 6 months in advance, his initial payment was $1,310. A year having passed, the fifth payment of $250 would now have to be met, plus $60 interest. Previous installments had been paid in cash.

When the equipment was bought, the company insisted on Oliver's taking out 4 years' insurance, which had cost a total of $200. The equipment presumably would be useful for at least 10 years, though Oliver contemplated that if all went according to his plans, he would have to get rid of the equipment in 5 years and buy some with a greater operating capacity. He estimated that the equipment could probably be sold for $1,000 at that time.

[1] Case material of the Harvard Graduate School of Business Administration is prepared as a basis for class discussion. Cases are not designed to present illustrations of either effective or ineffective handling of administrative problems.

By the end of the first year Oliver had three people working for him. One was a young lady who took care of his office work as well as spending about one-third of her time packing the delicate products as they were completed in the shop. The other two workers, hired on about the third month, spent all of their time in the shop. About 20 per cent of Mr. Oliver's time was spent in office work and on selling trips, but the rest of the time he was to be found in the shop working with the other men.

At the end of the year, Oliver's records included the following:

Salaries Paid (through December 31)
Miss Schultz	$1,200
John Bardell	3,200
Peter Nutchell	3,500
John Oliver	6,000
Rent	2,000
Unpaid Bills from Suppliers[a]	5,130
Paid Bills from Suppliers (Includes the initial payment and all subsequent interest and principal payments on the equipment loan)	12,120
Uncollected Accounts	
U.S. Government	5,150
Universities Scientific Supply Co.	4,130
Payment Due Oliver for Subcontract Work, Completed and shipped, December 17—Pegasus Aircraft Co.	970
Spent on Office Supplies	250
Inventory on Hand, at Estimated Cost	3,200
Office Supplies	50
Various Administrative and Selling Expenses (inc. travel, advertising, and interest on uncle's loan)	2,730
Electricity, etc.	430
Cash on Hand[b]	730

[a]Does not include the balance due for the equipment referred to in the third paragraph on page 359.
[b]Does not include a check for $2,030 from Universities Scientific Supply Co., believed to be in the mail as their regular settlement of accounts as of the close of the preceding month. December billings to Universities Scientific Supply Co. were $2,100.

Most of Oliver's sales were to two buyers, the U.S. government and the Universities Scientific Supply Company. Oliver had sold some $310 worth of goods to one buyer earlier in the year when business was slow, and when the man became bankrupt with no assets whatever and without having paid his bill, Oliver promised himself, "Never again." Other firms, he was told, protected themselves against such losses by use of a charge of 1 per cent of year-ending accounts receivable as an allowance for bad debts.

In October, the Pegasus Aircraft Company had asked Oliver to do some work for them, altering special equipment that they sent on to Oliver's shop. The first lot had been completed before the year's end, but the payment for the work, $970, had not been received. A second shipment, apparently valued at $3,000, had just come in (afternoon of December 31) from the Pegasus plant, but the alteration work (which would come to about $1,000) had not yet been started. Mr. Oliver ascertained that the $3,000 value of this incoming material had not been included in the totals for inventory listed above.

Of the inventory, $800 consisted of 200 special items that had been made for a government order, but had not as yet been shipped. Frankly, Mr. Oliver had wanted the situation to settle a little before making delivery, for a previous shipment of the same size (one-half the original order) had not met the specifications of the government inspectors and 20 per cent of the shipment was being returned as unsatisfactory. Fortunately the items carried a 30 percent markup over Oliver's cost, so he was not too badly off. Still, Oliver was disturbed about the matter because he thought his inspection standards when the first batch had been made had been no different from those in force at any other time, and besides he was advertising high-quality products. He certainly had no idea why the 20 per cent had been rejected. He intended to file an appeal to try to collect the full amount that he had billed the government (included in the $5,150 in the year's-end listing given above), particularly since the rejected items could not be reworked and were not worth much to any other possible buyer.

QUESTION

1. Work out Mr. Oliver's operating statement for the year and his ending balance sheet. You should show clearly how any figure not taken directly from the text has been determined.

Case 2-4

DESA Industries, Inc.

Following is a comparative income statement for the DESA Company. (The balance sheet was provided in Case 1-3 on page 354.) What new conclusions about the DESA Industries can you draw?

DESA INDUSTRIES, INC.
Consolidated Statement of Income
Years ended September 1, 1973 and August 31, 1972

	1973	1972
Net sales	$41,850,173	$35,614,182
Costs and expenses:		
Cost of sales and operating expenses	32,733,814	27,538,190
Selling, general and administrative expenses	5,857,832	5,768,478
Operating income	3,258,527	2,307,514
Miscellaneous income-net	139,271	122,299
Interest expense	(1,130,379)	(949,803)
Income from continuing operations before income taxes and extraordinary items	2,267,419	1,480,010
Provision for income taxes (Note 4)	1,066,000	649,000
Income from continuing operations	1,201,419	831,010
Loss from discontinued operations (Note 2)	(21,884)	(80,000)
Income before extraordinary items	1,179,535	751,010
Extraordinary items (Note 2)	(107,059)	(44,349)
Net income	$ 1,072,476	$ 706,661
Earnings per common and common equivalent share:		
Income from continuing operations	$2.24	$1.55
Income before extraordinary items	2.20	1.40
Net income	2.00	1.32

Case 3-1

Macke Vending Corporation

Following is the annual report of the Macke Vending Corporation. Is the president's statement on the first page that "we have generated sufficient funds from our ordinary operations to finance, in effect, this very substantial expansion" correct? What other conversions do you draw from this report?

**EXCERPT FROM ANNUAL REPORT
FOR THE YEAR ENDED SEPTEMBER 30, 1962**

President's Message

*To Our Shareholders...*This annual Report for 1962, which I am pleased to send to each of you, contains the record of Macke's most successful year. In every measurable aspect of our business—sales, net income, cash flow, shareholders' equity, number of machines—unprecedented increases were achieved over the previous year.

Sales and other operating revenues reached a new high of $33.8 million compared to $20.5 million in the earlier year—an increase of more than 65 per cent. Net income after taxes rose to $863,000, equal to $1.04 *per share*, compared to $387,000, equal to 58¢ *per share* in 1961—an increase, on a *per share* basis, of almost 80 per cent.

GROWTH HIGHLIGHTS AT A GLANCE
Years Ended September 30

	1962	*1961*	*Increase*
Gross Revenue	$33,858,522	$20,450,934	66%
Net Income	$ 863,241	$ 387,355	123%
Per Share			
Net Income	$1.04	$.58	79%
Depreciation &			
Amortization	2.34	1.82	29%
Cash Flow	3.38	2.40	41%

Shareholder's Equity	10.64	8.23	29%
Number of Vending Machines	30,569	24,342	26%

Depreciation and amortization write-offs for the year totalled $1,946,000, which when added to net income, provided an aggregate *cash flow* of $2,809,000, equal to $3.38 *per share* compared to $2.40 *per share* in 1961. Since our purchases of new vending and other depreciable capital equipment in 1962 amounted to approximately $2.4 million, it will be noted that we have been able to generate sufficient funds from our ordinary operations to finance, in effect, this very substantial expension of our principal capital assets. These figures highlight the importance of *cash flow* to our business.

Shareholders' equity, which stood at $8.23 *per share* a year ago, has grown to $10.64 on the books of the company as of September 30, 1962, despite an increase in outstanding stock of 98,000 shares over the 12-month period.

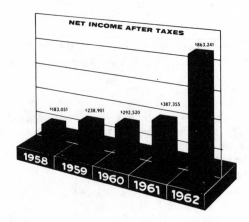

On September 30, 1962, we had in operation more than 30,500 vending machines. located in eight middle-Atlantic states and the District of Columbia. A year earlier the number of machines was 24.340. Since the close of our fiscal period we have entered two new markets—Atlanta, Georgia, and Jacksonville, Florida—raising to ten the number of states in which we now operate.

As forecasted in our previous Annual Report, 1962 was the year in which we began to realize in a tangible way the benefits accruing from the extensive acquisition and modernization programs which were undertaken during the 1960-1961 period. More efficient procedures, both operational and administrative, tighter cost controls, and, most important, more highly trained and skillful people—these were the essential ingredients which combined to produce our most successful year.

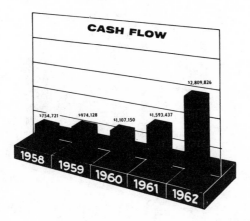

Over the past 5 years Macke's growth has been impressive. Sales have tripled and net income has increased more than four-fold between 1958 and 1962. At the same time profit margins, as a percentage to sales, have increased from 1.8 to 2.4 *per cent*. Shareholders' equity *per share* has quadrupled over the five-year span.

So much for the past 5 years. What are our prospects for 1963 and the next 5 years? Vigorous sales programs now underway throughout our entire territory give support to my projection that we can continue an *internal* annual growth rate of better than 15 per cent. At the present sales rate, this forecasts gross revenues in 1963 of well over $40 million. It is also my opinion that we can maintain or increase present profit margins as the "product mix" of our business moves increasingly in the direction of food and refreshment vending.

Sales of cigarettes, although showing a modest dollar increase in 1962, account today for approximately 50 per cent of total revenues. It appears that this percentage, once much larger, will continue to diminish as a more rapid growth takes place in the refreshment and food aspects of our business.

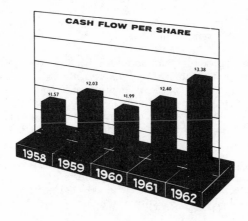

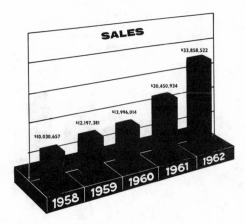

Increasingly during 1963 our Food Systems Division will be developing various *combinations* of automated and over-the-counter food services. Custom-designed facilities will be constructed to take advantage of important technological advancements in vending equipment and in food processing and packaging. One such development, for example, is likely to be further refinement of devices for applying micro-wave (instant) heating to frozen products. This, and similar developments, will open a yet-to-be explored dimension of modern automatic merchandising.

Additionally, the basic economic factors which have encouraged vending's growth over the past several years remain very much in evidence. The vending machine still appears to be the best answer for holding down costs in industrial and institutional situations where tasty, wholesome food must be served inexpensively and rapidly, and in many instances, around-the-clock.

Macke Vending has been a leading company in developing the methods and logistics to provide this kind of automated feeding to industry. Macke automatic cafeterias or the smaller *AutoMacs* are now being installed at the rate of two each week in such diverse places as universities, hospitals, government buildings, bus terminals, factories, laboratories, television studios, and similar outlets. This trend is bound to continue in view of the inherent advantages of the vending method.

In 1963 we expect to spend about $2.7 million for new vending and other income-producing equipment and about $300,000 for the improvement and expansion of certain operational facilities to support this rapid sales growth. It is anticipated that the principal funds for the financing of this capital-outlay program will be generated from the normal cash flow referred to earlier in this Report. It is not anticipated that additional equity capital will be required.

As I have often noted, in these Annual Reports and elsewhere, our company's progress will stem from the devoted efforts of the men and women who belong to the Macke *family* and who are pledged to the tradition of Macke service. Together, they constitute the indispensable *human* factor in this *automated* business. I am pleased to have this renewed occasion to express my appreciation for their skills and loyalties to our firm.

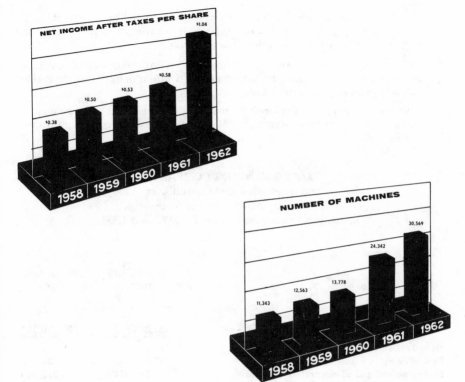

To each of the shareholders I extend, on behalf of my fellow officers, our appreciation for your support and confidence.

Sincerely,

President

Reprinted from article appearing in "INPLANT FOOD MANAGEMENT," October, 1962.

LOOKING TO THE FUTURE

President Goldman sums up Macke's outlook as follows:

"There are some basic economic and social trends which will sustain, in our opinion, a continued growth in automatic food service.

"One is the decentralization and suburbanization of industry. Many large plants are now far removed from business centers and also from eating establishments.

"Another is the definite trend toward the shorter work day. Many workers prefer a 20 minute rather than the old 45 minute or 1 hour lunch period.

"A third factor of significance to automatic merchandising is the changing pattern of eating habits. There is a definite trend toward 'snack-type' eating as well as growing standardization in taste preference.

"Finally, rising costs of selling low-priced food items makes vending machines an attractive alternative for businesses and institutions obliged to furnish their employees an implant food service.

"We are continuing to explore new products, new methods and new markets in automatic vending to insure that Macke maintains its favorable position in the industry."

MACKE VENDING COMPANY
and its wholly-owned subsidiaries
Consolidated Statement of Income
For the years ended September 30, 1962 and 1961

	September 30 1962	September 30 1961
Sales and other operating income, less state and local cigarette taxes	$33,858,522	$20,450,934
Cost and expenses:		
Cost of Sales	22,975,670	14,131,811
Selling, general and administrative expenses	7,549,031	4,372,242
Depreciation and amortization (note 1)	1,946,585	1,206,082
Total	32,471,286	19,710,135
Income from operations	1,387,236	740,799
Other income	137,098	57,930
Net profit before income taxes	1,524,334	798,729
Provision for income taxes (note 2)	661,093	411,374
Net income to retained earnings	$ 863,241	$ 387,355
Earnings *per share* (based on average number of shares outstanding: current year 831,013, prior year 663,240)	$1.04	58c
Cash flow (net income plus depreciation and amoritization) *per share*	$3.38	$2.40

Consolidated Statement of Retained Earnings
For the years ended September 30, 1962 and 1961

Balance at beginning of year	$ 1,372,001	$ 1,136,765
Add: Net income for the year	863,241	387,355
Total	2,235,242	1,524,120

Deduct: Dividends paid on common stock
(note 1):

Class A—45¢ *per share*	200,489	103,853
Class B—10¢ *per share*	43,439	48,266
Balance at end of year	243,928	152,119
See notes to financial statements	$ 1,991,314	$ 1,372,001

ACCOUNTANT'S OPINION

We have examined the consolidated balance sheet of Macke Vending Company and its wholly owned subsidiaries as of September 30, 1962 and the related statements of consolidated income and retained earnings for the year then ended. We were furnished with the financial statements of certain subsidiaries certified by their respective independent public accountants.

Our examination was made in accordance with generally accepted auditing standards, and accordingly included such tests of the accounting records and such other auditing procedures as we considered necessary in the circumstances.

In our opinion, based upon our examination and upon the reports of the other independent accountants, the accompanying statements present fairly the consolidated financial position of Macke Vending Company and its wholly-owned subsidiaries at September 30, 1962 and the consolidated results of their operations for the year then ended, in conformity with generally accepted accounting principles applied on a basis consistent with that of the preceding year, except for the changes, which we approve, set forth in note 1 to the financial statements.

OSCAR J. BERNSTEIN & COMPANY
Certified Public Accountants

MACKE VENDING COMPANY
Consolidated Balance Sheet

Assets	September 30, 1962	September 30, 1961
Current Assets		
Cash	$ 1,264,608	$ 792,957
Temporary investments—U.S. Bills, amortized value	99,535	
Accounts and notes receivable	763,602	546,965
Inventories—at average cost—first in—first out	1,938,846	1,516,860
Prepaid expenses	665,993	493,783
Total current assets	4,732,584	3,350,565
Investments—At Cost	13,329	2,668
Subscriptions Receivable—Common stock, class A	34,422	67,914
Property, Plant and Equipment—At Cost (note 1)		
Vending Equipment	12,985,639	9,423,855
Real estate	1,585,597	1,253,050
Machinery and equipment	566,804	423,782
Delivery equipment	1,067,262	737,392
Improvements to leased properties	86,947	58,843
Total	16,292,249	11,896,922
Less: Accumulated depreciation and amortization	7,963,366	5,658,675
Net property, plant and equipment	8,328,883	6,238,247
Deferred Charges and Other Prepaid Expenses	1,017,344	828,433

Other Assets
Excess of cost of capital stock of subsidiaries over

net asset value at acquisition	3,813,748	2,111,306
Goodwill and miscellaneous	191,800	117,493
Total other assets	4,005,548	2,228,799
Totals	$18,132,110	$12,716,626

NOTES TO FINANCIAL STATEMENTS

1. The Company and its subsidiaries changed the depreciable life of vending equipment acquired during the year to an eight year for new and a forty-seven month life for used equipment. In addition, the cost of qualified equipment, vending and other, acquired since January 1, 1962, has been reduced by $132,395, representing the new investment credit allowable under the federal income tax law. Depreciation has been computed on the reduced book cost of such assets. The net effect of these changes was to decrease reported depreciation by $99,000 from $2,045,585 to $1,946,585; to increase net profit after taxes approximately $55,000; to decrease cash flow by 5¢ per share from $3.43 to $3.38.

2. Heretofore the Company and two subsidiaries have used straight line depreciation on their books and accelerated depreciation for tax purposes. During the year other subsidiaries adopted this same method of reporting depreciation. Provision for deferred income taxes on the additional accelerated depreciation for tax purposes has been deducted from book income, amounting to $112,463 deferred income taxes for the current year and $45,353 for the prior year.

3. In connection with the issuance of $1,550,000 5% notes due 1977, the Company granted the noteholders warrants to acquire 30,000 shares of Class A common stock which may be exercised at $28 per share during the first ten years and at $32 per share during the eleventh through fifteenth years.

4. The Board of Directors has authorized the issue of 19,991 shares of Class A common stock in connection with acquisitions subsequent to September 30, 1962. In addition the Company issued, in December 1962, 3,000 additional shares to the former shareholders of a previously acquired subsidiary in compliance with terms of the original agreement.

September 30, 1962 and 1961

Liabilities	*September 30, 1962*	*September 30, 1961*
Current Liabilities		
Notes and current maturities of long term debt	$ 1,820,595	$ 2,285,156
Accounts payable	1,305,069	1,120,114
Accrued income taxes, profit-sharing and other expenses	1,173,449	883,663
Other current liabilities	2,231	2,619
Total current liabilities	4,301,344	4,290,552
Long Term Debt (excluding current maturities included above) (note 3)	4,552,619	2,133,043
Reserve for Deferred Income Taxes (note 2)	159,784	46,852
Commitments and Contingent liabilities (note 4)		
SHAREHOLDERS' EQUITY		
Capital Stock. (note 5)		
Common stock, class A, par value $1.00 each; authorized 1,500,000 shares 1962 and 1,000,000 shares 1961, outstanding 470,563 shares 1962 and 324,206 shares 1961	470,563	324,206

	1962	1961
Common stock, class A, subscribed 4,350 shares 1962 and 8,225 shares 1961	4,350	8,225
Common stock, class B, par value $1.00 each; authorized 500,000 shares, outstanding 386,126 shares 1962 and 434,393 shares 1961	386,126	434,393
Total capital stock	861,039	766,824
Surplus:		
Capital in excess of par value (note 6)	6,238,333	4,079,677
Other capital surplus	29,752	29,752
Retained earnings	1,991,314	1,372,001
Total surplus	8,259,399	5,481,430
Total capital stock and surplus	9,120,438	6,248,254
Less: Capital stock, class A owned by subsidiary—100 shares	2.075	2,075
Total shareholders' equity	9,118,363	6,246,179
Totals	$18,132,110	$12,716,626

The Company and its subsidiaries may have a liability to repay, as additional federal income tax, such portion of the $92,816 investment credit applied to reduce federal income tax liability as may result from the premature disposition of certain qualified assets.

5. The Company has two classes of stock, each having the same voting rights. With respect to dividends the Class B shares are subject to the following restriction as set forth in the Certificate of Incorporation, as amended:

Cash dividends shall not be declared in any calendar year in Class B shares unless and until cash dividends in the amount of 35¢ per share have been declared in such year on Class A shares; provided however, that such dividend rights of Class A shares shall not be cumulative. After cash dividends in the amount of 35¢ per share have been declared in any calendar year on Class A shares, any additional cash dividends declared in such year shall be declared equally on all shares of Common Stock regardless of class.

The foregoing restriction on dividends shall terminate as to 10% of the presently outstanding Class B shares on December 31, 1960 and as to an additional 10% on each succeeding December 31st, so that all such restrictions will terminate by December 31, 1969.

During the year 48,267 shares of Class B common stock were exchanged for Class A shares.

In addition to the shares specified in notes 3 and 4, the following Class A shares are reserved:

386,126 for future exchange of Class B shares.

4,350 for issue to employees upon payment of their stock subscriptions.

40,000 for issue to employees under a stock option plan, approved by the shareholders on February 20, 1962. At September 30, 1962 the Company had granted options totalling 21,500 shares.

6. The increase of $2,158,656 in Capital in excess of par value during the year represents the net excess of issue price over par value of 94,215 shares of Class A common stock issued in connection with the acquisitions of subsidiaries and/or businesses.

Case 3-2

DESA Industries, Inc.

Reproduced below is the statement of changes in position for DESA Industries. What additional information does this provide to you? What conclusion can you now draw about DESA Industries from all three financial statements.

DESA INDUSTRIES, INC.
Consolidated Statement of Changes in Financial Position
Years ended September 1, 1973 and August 31, 1972

	1973	*1972*
Sources of funds:		
Current operations:		
Income before extraordinary items	$1,179,535	$ 751,010
Add (deduct) items not affecting working capital:		
Depreciation and amortization:		
Plant and equipment	504,371	472,797
Deferred debt issuance expenses and other	35,965	40,116
Deferred income taxes	46,000	117,000
Working capital provided from operations	1,765,871	1,380,923
Extraordinary items (Note 2):		
Loss on discontinued operations less income tax benefit	(14,742)	(156,000)
Loss on write-off of costs incurred in proposed public offering less income tax benefit	(92,317)	—
Proceeds, less income taxes, on sale of Canadian land and building	—	290,113
	(107,059)	134,113
Book value of plant and equipment at times of disposition	9,548	26,659
Increase in long-term debt	—	90,839
Proceeds on exercise of stock options on 1,750 shares, $1 par value	12,000	—
	1,680,360	1,632,534

Application of funds:

Additions to property, plant and equipment	524,115	481,987
Reductions in long-term portion of long-term debt	710,585	1,334,827
	1,234,700	1,816,814
Increase (decrease) in working capital	$ 445,660	$ (184,280)

Case 3-3

Prepare an analysis of Dan River, Inc., from the financial statements included in Problem 3-7, together with your statement of changes in financial position.

Case 3-4

Prepare an analysis of Hercules, Inc., from the financial statements included in Problem 3-8, together with your statement of changes in financial position.

Case 5-1

F. J. Sullivan Insurance Agency

Mr. Frederick J. Sullivan operated an insurance agency in Monson, Massachusetts, a town of about 5,000 inhabitants. Mr. Sullivan, an independent agent representing several fire and casualty companies, sold principally fire and automotive insurance to businessmen and residents of Monson and surrounding towns. The agency was a small one, employing, in addition to Mr. Sullivan, only a part-time secretary.

The business had grown steadily since its founding in 1948 and so had outstanding accounts receivable. Exhibit 1 indicates gross premiums and accounts receivable for the past 5 years. Exhibit 2 shows the accounts receivable as of December 31, 1974 and 1975, broken down by the age of the account.

The balance in the allowance for doubtful accounts on December 31, 1974, was $120.

Required:

1. Make the appropriate adjusting entry to the allowance for doubtful accounts for December 31, 1974. (Mr. Sullivan uses the following rates to calculate his allowance for doubtful accounts: 1 month or less, 1 per cent; 2 to 6 months, 10 per cent; 6 months to a year, 25 per cent; over 1 year, 50 per cent.)

2. On February 15, 1975, Mr. Sullivan discovered that one of his customers had left town without a forwarding address. This customer owed $325. What entry, if any, would you make?

3. In March of 1975, Mr. Sullivan turned over $2,430 in delinquent accounts to his lawyer for collection. By April, the lawyer had collected $1,575. The remainder, the lawyer believed, could not be collected. What entries would you make to reflect these transactions?

4. In July, a customer owing $250 was adjudged a bankrupt. It was expected that he would pay his creditors $.10 on the dollar.

5. In September, the customer who had left town in February returned. He had no money, however, and made no indication that he would pay.

6. In October, a customer owing $150 who had been written off as a bad debt in April, paid $50 on his account. He promised to pay the remaining amount within the next few months.

7. No other entries to the allowance for doubtful accounts were made during the remainder of the year. Exhibit 2 shows the balance of the accounts receivable, by age group, as of December 31, 1975. Make the appropriate adjusting entry to the allowance for doubtful accounts for December 31, 1975.

EXHIBIT 1
Gross Premiums and Accounts Receivable

	Gross Premiums	Accounts Receivable as of 12/31
1970	$25,948	$ 4,325
1971	30,262	6,544
1972	38,356	8,613
1973	40,633	9,821
1974	45,431	10,972
1975	50,325	12,464

EXHIBIT 2
Accounts Receivable

	December 31 1974	1975
1 month	$ 2,150	$ 3,410
2 to 3 months	4,972	5,982
3 to 6 months	1,640	840
6 months to 1 year	1,035	1,462
1 to 2 years	893	630
Over 2 years	282	140
Total	$10,972	$12,464

Case 5-2

MacDonald's Farm[1]

Dennis Grey, an assistant vice president dealing with consumer credit at a large New York bank, was opening his mail in his office high above the street at No. 23 Wall. Among the letters was notification from a lawyer that the estate of his recently deceased uncle, Jeremiah MacDonald, had been settled, leaving Dennis as the owner of a 2,000 acre wheat farm in east central Iowa. Included in the letter were data on revenues and expenses for the past year and other information that might constitute the basis for a balance sheet.

Dennis had taken a course in agribusiness at a leading eastern business school and, despite the distance between New York and Iowa, he was interested in retaining ownership of the farm if he could determine its profitability. During the last 10 years of his life, Jeremiah MacDonald had hired professional managers to run his farm while he remained in semi-retirement in Florida.

Keeping the farm as an investment was particularly interesting to Dennis for the following reasons:

1. Recent grain deals with communist countries had increased present farm commodity prices substantially; many experts believed these prices would remain high for the next several years.

2. Although the number of small farms had decreased markedly in the last 20 years, large farms such as MacDonald's, using mechanization and new hybrid seed varieties, could be extremely profitable.

3. The value of good farm land in Iowa was appreciating at about 10 per cent to 15 per cent a year. Also, a proposed interstate highway would border on 100 acres of the farm. Such highways, if actually built, usually increase the value of frontage property by several times.

.[1]This case was written by Jonathan Brown, Research Assistant, under the supervision of Assistant Professor John K. Shank, as the basis for class discussion rather than to illustrate either effective or ineffective handling of an administrative situation.

Looking over the data on revenues and expenses, Dennis discovered that there was no number for total revenues for the year or for the beginning or ending inventory. The lawyer's letter explained that there was some doubt in his mind about when revenue for the farm should be recognized and about the appropriate way to value the grain inventory. There are at least three alternative stages in the wheat growing cycle at which revenue could be counted.

First, the *production method* could be used. Since wheat has a daily valuation on the Chicago Commodity Exchange, any unsold inventory as of December 31 could be valued at market price very objectively. In this way, revenue can be counted for all wheat produced in a given year, regardless of whether it is sold or not. A decision not to sell this wheat before December 31 is based on speculation about future wheat price increases.

Second, the *sale method* could be used. This would recognize revenue when the grain is purchased from the farm by the grain elevator operator in the neighboring town. In this instance, the owner of the grain elevator had just sold control to a Kansas City company with no previous experience in running such a facility. The manager of the MacDonald Farm had expressed some concern about selling to an unknown operator.

Third, the *collection method* could be used. Under this approach revenue is counted when the cash is actually received by the farm from the grain elevator operator. Full collection often took several months because a grain elevator operator might keep wheat for a considerable time in the hope that prices would rise so he could sell at a greater profit. Under the present arrangement, the farm is paid 75 per cent of the price of its wheat when the wheat is delivered to the elevator and 25 per cent over several months as the elevator operator sells the wheat.

The following data for 1972 were sent by the lawyer.

INVENTORY:

Beginning Inventory	0 bushels
1972 Wheat Production	210,000 bushels
Sold to Grain Elevator	180,000 bushels
Ending Inventory	30,000 bushels

PRICES:

The average price per bushel for wheat sold to the grain elevator operator in 1972 was $2.20. The price per bushel at the time of the wheat harvest was $2.10. The closing price per bushel on December 31, 1972, was $2.28.

ACCOUNTS RECEIVABLE:

At year end, the proceeds from 20,000 bushels had not yet been received from the elevator operator. The average sales price of this wheat had been $2.22 per bushel. There were no uncollected proceeds as of December 31, 1971.

CASH:

The farm has a checking account balance of $5,800 and a savings account totaling $15,000.

LAND:

The original cost of the land was $250,000. It was appraised for estate tax purposes at $700 per acre.

BUILDINGS AND MACHINERY:

Buildings and machinery with an original cost of $275,000 and accumulated depreciation of $200,000 are employed on the farm. The equipment was appraised at book value.

CURRENT LIABILITIES:

The farm has notes payable and accounts payable totaling $22,000.

OWNERS' EQUITY:

Common stock has a par value of $5,000 plus additional paid-in capital of $300,000. There was no record of retained earnings although it was known that Jeremiah MacDonald withdraw most of the earnings in the last few years in order to continue the life style to which he had become accustomed in Florida.

1972 Expenses for the MacDonald Farm

1. Variable costs per bushel (assuming a yield per acre of 100 bushels, which was the average over the past 5 years):

Seed	$.035
Fertilizer and Chemicals	$.210
Machinery Costs, Fuel, and Repairs	$.065
Part-time Labor and Other Costs	$.025
Variable Cost per Bushel	$.335

2. Annual costs not related to the volume of production:

Salaries and Wages	$ 45,000
Insurance	$ 4,000
Taxes[a]	$ 15,000
Depreciation	$ 19,000
Other Expenses	$ 30,000
Total	$113,000

[a]This figure excludes income taxes since the corporation was taxed as a sole proprietorship.

QUESTIONS

1. Compute the 1972 income statement and related ending balance sheet for the MacDonald Farm, recognizing revenue by the:

(a) production method
(b) sales method
(c) collection method

2. Assume that the new interstate highway was approved and Mr. Grey received on December 31 a bona fide offer of $300,000 for the 100 acres fronting on the road. How would you account in the 1972 financial statements for the economic gain represented by this unrealized appreciation in land values?

Case 5-3

Goldfinger, Incorporated[1]

ALTERNATIVE REALIZATION CRITERIA

Early in 1970 Goldfinger, Incorporated, was formed to acquire and operate a Nevada mining property, using newly developed extraction methods capable of processing profitably low-grade ores containing small quantities of gold.

Operations began promptly in 1970. Engineers' reports based on extensive geological surveys indicated that 1.6 million ounces of gold would be recovered over the life of the mining properties. The mining properties were located in an arid mountainous area and would have no residual value after the gold deposits were exhausted. The existing equipment and property improvements were expected to be used during the period of production and would be abandoned thereafter. All production and operating expenses were paid during the year. Goldfinger's cash receipts and disbursements for the year are summarized in Exhibit 1.

The Gold Reserve Act of January 1934 defined the United States dollar as 15 and 5/21 grains of gold 9/10 fine. Since there are 480 grains of pure gold to the ounce, the mint price for 9/10 fine gold became $35. Since the adoption of the gold bullion standard, it is illegal for the ordinary citizen to have in his possession more than a nominal amount of gold. The United States Treasury stands ready to buy gold from miners or importers at the $35 mint price, and to sell to industrial users, dentists, foreign governments, or central banks at the same price. Thus, gold is readily marketable at the fixed price of $35 and this price is subject to change only by the federal government.

Goldfinger's production records for 1970 show the following information:

Sold, Delivered, and Proceeds Collected	30,000 ounces
	(9/10 fine)

[1] This case was prepared by F. Robert Madera, Research Assistant, under the direction of David F. Hawkins, Assistant Professor of Business Administration. Case material of the Harvard Graduate School of Business Administration is prepared as a basis for class discussion. Cases are not designed to present illustrations of either effective or ineffective handling of administrative problems.

Sold and Delivered but Proceeds Not Collected	20,000
Produced but Not Sold or Delivered	40,000
Total Production	90,000 ounces
	(9/10 fine)

QUESTIONS

1. Prepare a balance sheet at December 31, 1970, and an income statement for the year based on each of the following:

   (a) Revenues are recognized on the receipt of cash.

   (b) Revenues are recognized at time of sale and delivery.

   (c) Revenues are recognized on the basis of production.

   (Ignore any income tax considerations.)

2. Evaluate the three sets of statements that you prepared in terms of the criteria of:

   (a) usefulness

   (b) feasibility

   (c) conformity to accepted definitions of income

EXHIBIT 1

GOLDFINGER, INCORPORATED

Schedule of Cash Receipts and Disbursements
For the Year 1970

Cash Receipts:		
Sales of Capital Stock at Par Value		$10,000,000
Collections from Sales (30,000 ounces at $35 per ounce)		1,050,000
		$11,050,000
Cash Disbursements:		
Cost of Mining Properties	$8,000,000	
(including all mineral rights, engineers' surveys, roads, mine shafts, and equipment)		
Production Costs	2,250,000	
Delivery Expenses	25,000	
Administrative Expenses	150,000	
Total Disbursements		$10,425,000
Cash on Hand—Balance on December 31, 1970		$ 625,000

Case 5-4

Great Southwest Corporation (C)[1]

On June 30, 1969, Great Southwest Corporation (GSC) sold its amusement park in Dallas, called Six Flags Over Texas, to a group of private investors. The purchase price was $40 million. The terms were $1.5 million down and the balance over 35 years with interest at 6 1/2 per cent. The note receivable of $38.5 million was to be paid off in 35 annual payments of $2.8 million. (The present value of 35 annual payments of $2.8 million discounted at 6 1/2 per cent interest is $38.5 million.) The note was secured only by the amusement park. GSC signed an agreement with the new owners whereby GSC would continue to operate the park for an annual management fee.

The amusement park had been carried on the books of GSC at a gross cost of $14.2 million, offset partially by accumulated depreciation of $4.8 million. GSC paid a 5 per cent commission ($2 million) to a real estate firm for finding a buyer for the park. You may assume that any gain on the sale would be taxed to GSC at the rate of 25 per cent, which then applied to "capital gains."

The new owners allocated the $40 million purchase price as follows:

Land	$ 5 million
Buildings and Equipment	25 million
Non-competition Agreement With GSC for 10 Years	8 million
License to Use the "Six Flags Over Texas" Name—Unlimited Life	2 million
Total	$40 million

[1] This case was prepared by Associate Professor John K. Shank as the basis for class discussion rather than to illustrate either effective or ineffective handling of an administrative situation.

QUESTIONS

1. Should GSC recognize the full profit on the sale of this amusement park in 1969? What factors would you consider in deciding when to recognize the gain?

2. Assuming that the gain was to be recognized in 1969, how would you compute the gain? What is the amount of the gain, after taxes?

3. How would your answer to Question 2 change if the sale had taken place in 1972 (after adoption of the imputed interest accounting principle)? You may use an interest rate of 9 per cent for purposes of this question.

4. Should the accounting treatment by the new owners regarding the "non-competition agreement" influence the way the sale transaction is recorded by GSC?

Case 5-5

Chrysler Corporation[1]

The following paragraph is taken from the president's letter in the 1970 Annual Report of Chrysler Corporation:

> Net earnings for 1969 are restated to reflect a retroactive change in the company's method of valuing inventories, from a LIFO (last-in, first-out) to a FIFO (first-in, first-out) cost basis, as explained in the notes to financial statements. The LIFO method reduces inventory values and earnings in periods of rising costs. The rate of inflation in costs in 1970 and for the projected short term future is so high that significant understatements of inventory values and earnings result. The use of the LIFO method in 1970 would have reduced inventory amounts at December 31, 1970 by approximately $150 million and did reduce inventory amounts reported at December 31, 1969 by approximately $110 million. Also, the use of the LIFO method in 1970 would have increased the loss for the year by approximately $20.0 million, and its use in 1969 reduced the earnings as reported for that year by $10.2 million. The other three U.S. automobile manufacturers have consistently used the FIFO method. Therefore the reported loss for 1970 and the restated profit for 1969 are on a comparable basis as to inventory valuation with the other three companies. Prior years' earnings have been restated to make them comparable.

The footnotes that year included the following further explanation of this accounting change and its impact on the financial statements.

Inventories—Accounting Change

> Inventories are stated at the lower of cost or market. For the period January 1, 1957 through December 31, 1969 the last-in, first-out (LIFO) method of inventory valuation had been used for approximately 60% of the consolidated

---

[1] This case was prepared by Associate Professor John K. Shank as the basis for class discussion rather than to illustrate the effective or ineffective handling of an administrative situation.

inventory. The cost of the remaining 40% of inventories was determined using the first-in, first-out (FIFO) or average cost methods. Effective January 1, 1970 the FIFO method of inventory valuation has been adopted for inventories previously valued using the LIFO method. This results in a more uniform valuation method throughout the Corporation and its consolidated subsidiaries and makes the financial statements with respect to inventory valuation comparable with those of the other United States automobile manufacturers. As a result of adopting FIFO in 1970, the net loss reported is less than it would have been on a LIFO basis by approximately $20.0 million, or $0.40 a share. Inventory amounts at December 31, 1969 and 1970 are stated higher by approximately $110.0 million and $150.0 million, respectively, than they would have been had the LIFO method been continued.

The Corporation has retroactively adjusted financial statements of prior years for this change. Accordingly, the 1969 financial statements have been restated resulting in an increase in Net Earnings of $10.2 million, and Net Earnings Retained for Use in the Business at December 31, 1969 and 1968 have been increased by $53.5 million and $43.3 million, respectively.

For United States income tax purposes the adjustment to inventory amounts will be taken into taxable income ratably over 20 years commencing January 1, 1971.

The comparative income statement from the 1970 Annual Report is reproduced as Exhibit 1.

EXHIBIT 1
CHRYSLER CORPORATION AND CONSOLIDATED SUBSIDIARIES
Consolidated Statement of Net Earnings

Year Ended December 31	1970	1969*
Net sales	$6,999,675,655	$7,052,184,678
Equity in net earnings (loss) of	(6,210,013)	(6,286,309)
unconsolidated subsidiaries	(19,962,022)	23,261,424
Other income and deductions	6,973,503,620	7,069,159,793
Cost of products sold, other than items below ...	6,103,250,974	5,966,732,377
Depreciation of plant and equipment	176,758,139	170,305,745
Amortization of special tools	172,568,348	167,194,002
Selling and administrative expenses	386,041,866	431,706,851
Pension and retirement plans	121,406,136	114,577,630
Interest on long-term debt	46,998,713	31,702,530
Taxes on income (credit)	(21,400,000)	91,700,000
	6,985,624,176	6,973,919,135
Net Earnings (Loss) Including Minority Interest	(12,120,556)	95,240,658
Minority interest in net loss of		
consolidated subsidiaries	4,517,536	3,730,564

*Restated to reflect the change made in 1970 in accounting for inventories and to conform to 1970 classifications. The 1969 net earnings and net earnings a share, as previously reported, were $88.8 million and $1.87 respectively, See Inventories—Accounting Change note.

Net Earnings (Loss)	$(7,603,020)	$ 98,971,222

Average number of shares of Common Stock outstanding during the year	48,693,200	47,390,561
Net earnings (loss) a share	$(0.16)	$2.09

QUESTIONS

1. What reasons can you give for Chrysler to switch from LIFO to FIFO?

2. What arguments can be advanced against the switch?

3. Do you agree with management's actions in this matter?

4. How much will it cost Chrysler to switch from LIFO through 1970?

Case 6-1

Macadoo Corporation (A)

The Macadoo Corporation was a major producer of machine tools, located in a large midwestern city.

During 1954, the federal income tax law was changed to allow the use of certain accelerated methods of depreciation on fixed assets acquired after December 31, 1953. The controller of the Macadoo Corporation, Mr. MacKensie, was interested in changing to the declining balance method of depreciation for tax purposes. Because of the accounting system employed at Macadoo, it would have been inconvenient to have the tax treatment of fixed assets differ from the accounting treatment. Mr. MacKensie, therefore, recommended to Mr. Randall, the president, that the corporation adopt the declining balance method of depreciation, for both tax and corporate accounting, for all fixed assets acquired after January 1, 1954. Mr. Randall was generally agreeable to the proposed change. Before making a final decision, however, he wanted to know what effect the change would have on the amount of cash the corporation would receive and the profit it would earn during the next years.

The company planned to undertake a major expansion during the next 5 years. Expenditures were planned as follows:

Year	Land	Buildings	Machinery and Equipment
1954	$20,000	$200,000	$1,000,000
1955	50,000	800,000	3,000,000
1958	10,000	800,000	1,500,000

In addition, it was expected that replacement of present machinery would require an annual expenditure of $1 million. None of the assets acquired after January 1, 1954, were expected to be retired before December 31, 1958.

The corporation employed the straight-line method of depreciation. Buildings were depreciated at the rate of 5 per cent a year and machinery and equipment at 10 per cent. Tax rates were expected to be 50 per cent of profits, and the corporation was expected to earn a profit during each of the next 5 years.

A profit sharing bonus of 1 per cent of net income before taxes was paid each year to the executives of the corporation.

Required:

Calculate, for the years 1954 through 1958, the effect on cash and profits of adopting declining balance depreciation at double the straight-line rate (for both tax and accounting purposes) rather than maintaining a straight-line method of depreciation. Assume all assets were acquired on January 1 of the year indicated. Make only one calculation for each year, based on the net book value at the beginning of the year. In other words, ignore the monthly decline in net book value. (Work all calculations to the nearest thousand dollars.)

Case 6-2

Macadoo Corporation (B)

The Macadoo Corporation decided to adopt the declining balance method of depreciation on assets acquired after December 31, 1953. (Assets acquired before this time were to continue to be depreciated by the straight-line method.) The acquisitions for 1954 and 1955 were the same as was indicated in the (A) case.

The retirements during these years were as follows:

Year	Gross Book Value	Accumulated Depreciation	Sales or Salvage Price
1954			
Machinery and Equipment	$603,000	$595,000	$ 25,000
1955			
Land	50,000		
Building	145,000	100,000 ⎫	
Machinery and Equipment	500,000	460,000 ⎭	125,000

The balance in the fixed asset accounts as of December 31, 1953, were:

	Gross Book Value	Accumulated Depreciation
Land	$ 1,163,000	
Building	6,578,000	$ 3,478,000
Machinery and Equipment	30,482,000	18,936,000

Required:

Make the necessary journal entries to record for each year:

1. The acquisition of new assets.

2. The retirement or sale of old assets.

3. The additions to accumulated depreciation.

Notes: (1) Assume that all assets were sold or retired as of January 1 of the year indicated.

(2) All assets sold or retired were acquired prior to January 1, 1954.

(3) Make all calculations to the nearest thousand dollars.

Case 6-3

Monson Knitters Corporation

The Monson Knitters Corporation was a small knitting firm located in the town of Monson, Massachusetts. During 1975, Monson Knitters moved out of the plant that they had occupied for 20 years into a new plant located in Palmer, Massachusetts, a nearby town. In connection with this move, the events listed below took place. Prepare the journal entries that you believe would be appropriate to record each of these events.

1. The plant in Monson was sold for $50,000 cash. The plant was recorded on the books as follows: land $10,000; building, $90,000; accumulated depreciation—building, $60,000.

2. Equipment was sold for $50,000. This equipment was recorded on the books as follows: equipment, $80,000; accumulated depreciation—equipment, $45,000. The purchaser of the equipment gave the Monson Knitters a $50,000 noninterest-bearing note. This note was to be paid in five equal annual installments beginning 1 year from the date of purchase. The interest rate on a note of comparable risk was 8 per cent at the time of the sale.

3. New equipment with a list price of $100,000 was purchased. Old equipment that had cost $40,000 and had an accumulated depreciation of $20,000 was given as a trade in. The trade in allowance was $15,000. The difference was paid in cash. It was estimated that the old equipment could have been sold for cash on the open market for $10,000.

4. The town of Palmer gave the Monson Knitters a four-acre piece of land containing an old wooden building, on the condition that a new knitting mill be built on it. The land had an assessed valuation of $30,000. A similar piece of land, without a building, had been sold 2 months ago for $60,000.

5. Monson Knitters demolished the building, graded the land, installed sewers, and landscaped the land. The cost of demolishing the building was $7,000. The cost of sewers and landscaping was $5,000. The cost of grading the land was $3,000.

6. The Palmer Development Company built a new knitting mill on the land in Palmer. This building was sold to the Monson Knitters for $80,000. Monson Knitters gave the Palmer Development Company a note for this amount. This note, which carried an interest rate of 4 per cent, was to be paid in eight equal installments, beginning 1 year from the date of the note. At the time the purchase price was negotiated, a note with comparable risk would pay 8 per cent interest.

7. The cost of moving the equipment and installing it in the new plant was $44,000.

8. At the time of the move, Monson Knitters took the opportunity to do extensive maintenance. On one machine the company spent $10,000. The speed of the machine was increased 25 per cent. It was estimated that the cost of repairs would have been only $7,500 if the capabilities of the machine had not been increased.

9. In moving the equipment, one piece of equipment was accidentally dropped. Although the damage was repaired for $500, it was estimated that the equipment would last only 3 years more. The machine was purchased 5 years ago for $5,000. At that time, its estimated life was 10 years.

Case 6 - 4

Control Data Corporation (D)[1]

In the Spring of 1965, the management of Control Data Corporation was considering a revision in the company's depreciation policies for computers that it manufactured and rented to customers. The company defined its principal product as computer "systems," one or more electronic data processing machines plus related peripheral equipment and coded operating instructions that were combined from a set of basic components in such a way as to satisfy the computational requirements of the customer. Such systems were offered for outright sale, or the customer could elect to lease the system from the company for a monthly rental fee.

Rental of data processing equipment was a well-established industrial practice. The acknowledged industry leader, International Business Machines Corporation (IBM), had originally offered its punched-card and electro-mechanical calculating equipment only on a rental basis. During the early 1950s, antitrust action by the federal government forced IBM to also establish selling prices for its products. The industry, however, had long been characterized by rapid technological change, a trend that was accelerated by the development of the electronic computer. Thus, many customers continued to prefer the flexibility of renting such equipment; when new and better machines became available the rental customer could return his old equipment to the manufacturer without penalty and replace it with the latest model, perhaps from a different manufacturer.

Control Data Corporation (CDC), organized in July 1957, had originally concentrated on the design of very large-scale electronic computers developed under contract for the federal government. During the early years, most of its systems were sold outright. CDC was a successful company almost from the start (see Exhibit 1) and grew at a rapid rate as it developed new models to serve industrial and commercial customers. A listing of the company's principal product lines, as of mid-1965, is shown in the table on next page.

[1] This case was made possible by the cooperation of Control Data Corporation. It was prepared by Professor Richard F. Vancil as the basis for class discussion rather than to illustrate either effective or ineffective handling of an administrative situation.

Main Memory Characteristics

Series Designation	Model Number	Date of First Delivery	Memory Cycle Time (Millionths of a second)	Maximum Character Storage
	160	May 1960	6.4	8,192
Under 2000	160-A	July 1961	6.4	65,536
	1604	Jan. 1960	6.4	262,144
	3100	Jan. 1965	1.75	131,072
lower 3000	3200	May 1964	1.75	131,072
	3400	Nov. 1964	1.5	262,144
Upper 3000	3600	June 1963	1.5	2,097,152
	6600	Sept. 1964	1.0	1,310,720
	8090	July 1964	6.4	65,536

The model numbers refer to the computer system. The system includes a central processing unit (main frame); main memory; a variety of peripheral equipment, such as printers, readers, and auxiliary storage devices; and sets of instructions (software) to direct the system in its solution of a problem. Application programs are developed for the solution of particular problems or the accomplishment of specific data processing tasks.

Beginning in 1960, the company adopted the traditional practice of offering to rent its computer systems to customers. For the fiscal year ended June 30, 1964, CDC reported that 40 per cent of the systems installed during that year were on a rental basis. As may be seen in Exhibit 2, rental and service income for that year was only 21 per cent of total revenue, because the first year's rental income was only a fraction of the revenue that was recognized if the system were sold. A condensed balance sheet as of June 30, 1964, is shown in Exhibit 3.

Company officials expected that the trend toward renting would continue and believed that the depreciation policy adopted in 1960 ought to be reviewed to make sure that it was still appropriate under the changing circumstances. An accurate determination of annual profit was regarded as particularly critical by CDC officials; the common stock of the company had been listed on the New York Stock Exchange in March 1963 and had traded as high as $75 per share[2] that year. In early 1965, the stock was trading in the mid-$50s.

Depreciation Policy. For computer systems rented to its customers, CDC followed the practice of depreciating the cost of the equipment over 4 years using a modified double-declining balance method. The equipment was assumed to have no salvage value at the end of 4 years. Thus, in the first 12 months on rental, 50 per cent of the cost of the equipment was charged as depreciation expense (double the

---

[2] Adjusted to reflect the three-for-one stock split in September 1961 and the three-for-two split in September 1964.

25 per cent rate that would result from straight-line depreciation). One-twelfth of this amount was recorded for each month of the taxable year after the equipment was first accepted by a customer. In the second 12 months, 50 per cent of the unrecovered cost (25 per cent of the original cost) was taken as depreciation. For the third and fourth years, the company then switched to straight-line depreciation; one-eighth of the original cost was written off each year. Idle equipment, returned by the original customer and not yet sold or rented to another customer, continued to be depreciated even though it produced no revenue. Salvage value was ignored because of the uncertainty concerning the economically useful life of the equipment in the face of rapid technological change. The company's depreciation policy was used for calculating taxable income and was also used in determining income reported to stockholders.

Prices and Gross Margin. Sales and rental prices in the industry were determined by competitive interplay among the major computer manufacturers. Many well-known companies shared a part of the electronic data processing industry. The market shares, based on the selling value of installed equipment, were estimated by one firm of security analysts in a report made available to the investing public in January 1965 as follows:

	%
International Business Machines	72.0
Sperry Rand	8.7
Control Data	4.5
Radio Corp. of America	2.9
Honeywell	2.5
Burroughs	2.4
National Cash Register	2.2
General Electric	2.1
All Others	2.7
	100.0%

The price for a CDC system was the sum of the list prices for the various pieces of equipment required, and the list prices were revised from time to time. A major price reduction was announced by the company in 1964. The table below illustrates the impact of that change for three of the most popular CDC systems.

	Price of Average Installation		Rental per Month	
Model	Before July 1 1964	After July 1 1964	Before July 1 1964	After July 1 1964
3200	$ 700,000	$ 500,000	$ 15,000	$ 12,000
3600	$2,400,000	$2,300,000	$ 60,000	$ 41,000
6600	$7,900,000	$6,900,000	$197,000	$116,000

Despite these price reductions, Mr. William C. Norris, president of CDC, was able to report at the seventh annual stockholders' meeting in September 1964, that,

"Today the rate of gross profit on our computer systems is greater than any time in the history of Control Data . . . even though we are also at the same time offering more computing per dollar to our customers through reduced selling prices. These reductions in selling prices have come about because of a number of reasons, the principal one being the reduction in manufacturing costs, particularly in the cost of components."

The cost of components was an important factor in CDC's profitability. Management believed that the company's primary competitive advantage lay in its ability to design the most advanced computer systems. Major emphasis was also placed on the distribution function, particularly systems engineering, to tailor a system composed of CDC equipment to meet the user's need. The company prepared specifications for each piece of equipment and contracted for the production of various components with other manufacturers. CDC's production operation in 1965 was primarily one of assembling components into completed units. Purchased materials and components accounted for about 90 per cent of the manufacturing costs.

The Controller's Opinion. Mr. B. R. Eng, controller of CDC, was one member of management who believed that a change in depreciation policy was necessary, despite the difficulties that might arise in explaining such a change to the investment community. Expressing his view on the situation in mid-1965, Mr. Eng said, "When a company makes a change in accounting practices it means that either the practices it *was* using were wrong, or *conditions* have changed and the former practices are no longer correct and must be changed. It is the latter situation in which we find ourselves. There was nothing wrong with the accounting practices we have been following, but conditions have changed.

"It all stems from an unavoidable conflict in the application of accounting principles—the conflict between the principle of conservatism and the principle of the proper matching of costs against related revenues. Conservatism demands that you not anticipate income but that you do anticipate all losses; thus, it encourages charging off costs as incurred if there is any doubt about recovering those costs in the future. But the proper matching of costs against revenues demands that costs and expenses not be charged off as incurred, but that they be deferred and applied against the revenues to which such costs and expenses relate.

"The fundamental objective is the proper determination of income. If you're too conservative, you understate current income and overstate future income, which is wrong. If you are not conservative enough, you overstate current income and understate future income, which is also wrong. So the application of the principle of conservatism must, of necessity, be a matter of judgment. Of course, the greater the risk, the greater the degree of conservatism to be applied.

"The computer business is a fast moving, highly competitive business. When Control Data Corporation started its operations 8 years ago the risk was tremendous. But we have learned a great deal in the past 8 years, and we've gained a lot more confidence. The risks that Control Data faced in its formative years demanded ultra-conservative accounting practices.

"But an even more significant change has occurred that has demanded the more realistic application of the principles of conservatism and the matching of costs against related revenues. I'm referring to the significant increase in our lease business. Approximately 55 per cent of the orders booked by the company in fiscal year 1965 were lease orders, compared with 40 per cent in fiscal year 1964, and this upward trend appears to be continuing.

"This problem is not unique with Control Data. Many other companies are encountering the same problem and are doing something about it. One of those companies depreciates its leased equipment over a 5-year period, another uses 6 years, and the third uses 5-8 years for its various classes of leased equipment."

ASSIGNMENT

1. Evaluate alternative depreciation policies for CDC's leased equipment. Which combination of depreciable life and depreciation method do you believe would provide the best matching of equipment cost against rental income? It may be assumed that, on the average, the total manufacturing cost of a piece of CDC equipment was approximately 50 per cent of the listed selling price for commercial and industrial customers.

2. Should CDC change its depreciation policy? If so, what policy should be adopted? How should this change be explained to stockholders?

EXHIBIT 1
CONTROL DATA CORPORATION
Seven-Year Financial Summary[a]
(In thousands except for per share data)

	1958	1959	1960	1961	1962	1963	1964[b]
Profit and Loss Data							
Net Sales	$ 625	$4,588	$9,442	$18,062	$32,128	$44,861	$105,452
Rentals and Service Income	—	—	222	1,721	8,905	18,249	25,618
Total Revenues	$ 625	$4,588	$9,665	$19,783	$41,034	$63,111	$131,071
Research and Development Expenditures—							
Company Sponsored	50	16	355	1,707	2,615	5,129	12,323
Earnings before Income Taxes	(114)	418	1,306	2,197	3,532	8,004	15,215
Net Earnings after Income Taxes	(114)	283	551	842	1,542	3,064	6,018
Earnings Per Share of Common Stock after Preferred Stock Dividends[c]	(.04)	.07	.12	.16	.26	.50	.84
Depreciation of Property, Plant, and Equipment	31	53	235	1,377	5,181	8,852	13,614
Balance Sheet Data							
Current Assets	$ 857	$2,092	$6,037	$14,336	$26,536	$47,326	$102,926
Current Liabilities	473	470	3,526	8,884	16,760	22,149	38,452
Net Working Capital	384	1,621	2,510	5,451	9,775	25,177	64,474
Current Ratio	1.8	4.4	1.7	1.6	1.6	2.1	2.7
Net Property, Plant, and Equipment	295	251	1,809	4,586	12,959	21,382	33,105
Long-term Debt	100	75	33	71	35	19,535	38,470
Stockholders' Equity	650	1,828	4,318	9,793	23,390	29,468	61,252
Other Information							
Thousands of Shares of Common Stock Outstanding[c]	2,992	3,531	4,358	5,040	5,796	6,065	7,208
Total Building Occupancy (thousands of sq. ft.)	32	75	110	238	455	735	1,465
Expenditures for Property, Plant, and Equipment	$ 326	$ 26	$1,643	$ 4,161	13,756	$18,363	$ 29,754

[a] As reported in annual reports pertaining to the respective periods except for 1964, which has been adjusted to reflect retroactively acquisitions since June 30, 1964 accounted for as poolings of interests.

[b] Operating results for 1964 as reported for that year were:

Net Sales	$ 95,820,961
Rentals and Service Income	25,618,729
Total Revenues	$121,439,690
Net Earnings	$ 6,072,921
Earnings per Share of Common stock	$0.88

[c] Adjusted for three for one stock split in September 1961 and three for two stock split in September 1964.

Source: Annual Report for 1965.

EXHIBIT 2
CONTROL DATA CORPORATION (D)

Consolidated Statement of Earnings
Years Ended June 30, 1964 and 1963
(Amounts in thousands)

	1964	*1963*
Net Sales	$ 95,820	$47,845
Rentals and Service Income	25,618	18,302
	121,439	66,147
Cost of Sales, Rentals, and Service	70,117	42,690
Gross Profit	51,322	23,456
Selling, Administrative and General Expenses	22,499	9,502
Research and Development Expenses	12,123	5,625
	34,623	15,128
Operating Profit	16,698	8,328
Other income	219	138
	16,918	8,466
Interest and Other Deductions	1,795	962
Earnings Before Taxes	15,122	7,503
Federal, State, and Foreign Income Taxes (est.)	9,050	4,830
Net Earnings	$ 6,072	$ 2,672
Net Earnings per Share of Common Stock (after preferred stock dividends)[a]	$ 1.32	$ 0.64
Depreciation and Amortization of Fixed and Intangible Assets Included in Costs and Expenses	$ 13,513	$ 8,991

[a]Net earnings per share of common stock have been calculated to include the shares issued in the several pooling of interest acquisitions and to reflect retroactively to September 1, 1962, the conversion since June 20, 1963, of the 4 1/4% convertible subordinated debentures.

Source: Annual Report for 1964.

EXHIBIT 3
CONTROL DATA CORPORATION (D)

Condensed Consolidated Balance Sheet
As of June 30, 1964 and 1963
(Amounts in thousands)

ASSETS

Current Assets	1964	1963
Cash	$ 4,426	$ 2,068
Receivables	45,969	22,692
Inventories	47,675	24,129
Prepaid Expenses and Deposits	882	89
Total Current Assets	98,953	48,979
Investments and Other Assets	1,023	2,590
Property, Plant, and Equipment at Cost		
Land	728	403
Buildings and Improvements	6,373	2,696
Machinery, Equipment, and Rental Machines	47,574	33,666
Construction in Progress (approximate cost to complete, $1,900,000)	648	283
	55,323	37,050
Less Allowance for Depreciation and Amortization	23,548	15,157
Net Property and Plant Equipment	31,775	21,893
Deferred Charges	1,301	307
Total Assets	$133,054	$73,770

LIABILITIES

Current Liabilities		
Notes Payable to Banks	$ 3,200	$10,368
Current Maturities of Long-term Debt	1,355	1,010
Customer Advances	6,241	—
Accounts Payable	8,258	5,340
Accrued Taxes	13,179	5,138
Other Accrued Liabilities	3,626	1,222
Total Current Liabilities	35,861	23,080
Long-term Debt, Less Current Maturities		
Equipment Purchase Contract Due in Monthly Installments to March 15, 1966	2,210	4,535
3 3/4% Convertible Subordinated Debentures, due February 1, 1989	35,000	—
4 1/4% Convertible Subordinated Debentures, due September 1, 1977	—	15,000
Other Mortgages and Notes	98	10
Total Long-term Debt	37,309	19,545

Reserve for Product and Service Warranties	172	186
Minority Interest in Foreign Subsidiary	92	–
Stockholders' Equity:		
Cumulative Preferred Stock of $25 Par Value per Share		
6% series issued and outstanding—1963, 13,000 shares	–	325
Common Stock of $.50 Par Value per Share		
Issued and Outstanding—1964, 4,619,939 shares;		
1963, 4,100,526 shares	2,309	2,050
Additional Paid-in Capital	46,259	23,584
Retained Earnings	12,381	6,330
	60,951	32,290
Deduct Cost of 35,000 Shares of Control Data Corp.		
Common Stock Held by Subsidiary	1,332	1,332
Total Stockholders' Equity	59,618	30,958
Total Liabilities and Equity	$133,054	$73,770

Source: Annual Report for 1964.

Case 7-1

Piqua Products[1]

On December 31, 1969, Piqua Products issued 10-year bonds having a maturity value of $5,000,000. The bonds were issued at a price to yield 9 per cent, although they carried only an 8 per cent coupon.

The Piqua bonds required semi-annual interest payments and they were redeemable between June 30, 1975, and June 30, 1978, at 104; thereafter until maturity they were redeemable at 102. They were also convertible into Piqua's $10 par value common stock according to the following schedule:

Before June 30, 1975:	Fifty shares of common per $1,000 face value of bonds.
July 1, 1975 to June 30, 1978:	Forty shares of common per $1,000 face value of bonds.
After June 30, 1978:	Thirty shares of common per $1,000 face value of bonds.

The following transactions occurred in connection with the bonds:

December 31, 1974:	Bonds having a face value of $1,000,000 were converted into common stock.
December 31, 1975:	Bonds having a face value of $1,000,000 were reacquired by Piqua on the open market at a price of 90. The reacquired bonds were canceled immediately.

QUESTIONS

1. Determine the amount of the proceeds from the bond issue. How would the bonds be carried on the balance sheet on December 31, 1969?

[1] This case was prepared as the basis for class discussion rather than to illustrate either the effective or ineffective handling of an administrative situation.

2. Determine the amount of interest expense to be deducted in arriving at net income for the year ended December 31, 1970.

3. Show the entries to record the conversion of the bonds in 1974.

4. Show the entries to record the retirement of the bonds in 1975.

Case 7-2

United Brands[1]

Late in 1968, United Fruit Company issued over $250 million of 5 1/2% convertible subordinated debentures, due 1994, in connection with the acquisition of AMK Corporation. The debentures were convertible into United Brands' (the merged entity) common at one share for each $55 face value of debentures. The stock of United Brands did not do well subsequently and the debentures were selling at 64 in early 1973, having dipped earlier into the 50's.

In January 1973, the company, pursuant to a plan of recapitalization and a pledge to offer debenture holders a package with a more attractive market value than the convertible issue, announced that it would offer new debentures and cash for the old debentures. Details of the exchange were forthcoming the following month. If more than $20 million face value of the old debentures were tendered, the company obligated itself to acquire any amount offered up to $80 million. The exchange offer of $10 cash and $60 principal amount of a new 9 1/8% subordinated debenture, due 1998, in exchange for each $100 principal amount of the 5 1/2% issue was to remain open for approximately 3 weeks.

In March 1973, at the termination of the exchange offer, $125,000,000 principal amount of the 5 1/2% debentures had been exchanged, reducing outstanding debt by approximately $50,000,000 and reducing potential dilution of common stock from debt conversion by approximately 50 per cent.

QUESTIONS

1. Summarize what someone who accepted the exchange offer gave up and what he/she received.

2. How large is the gain or loss that United Brands will realize on the exchange?

3. How will United Brands account for the transaction?

[1] This case was prepared by Laird H. Simons, III, Research Assistant, under the supervision of Associate Professor John K. Shank, as the basis for class discussion rather than to illustrate the effective or ineffective handling of an administrative situation.

407

4. What was the effective dollar cost to United Brands over the period 1968-1972 for the use of the $125,000,000 in tendered debentures? Do the financial statements fairly reflect this cost?

EXHIBIT 1

UNITED BRANDS
Consolidated Balance Sheet
(In thousands)

Assets	December 31 1972	1971
Current Assets:		
Cash	$ 18,894	$ 21,514
Marketable Securities, at Cost which		
Approximates Market	64,225	49,082
Receivables—Less Allowance for		
Doubtful Accounts of $3,561		
(1971-$2,723)	119,847	92,289
Inventories	94,412	83,696
Growing Crops	29,678	31,885
Materials and Supplies	25,331	28,441
Prepaid Expenses	10,997	11,593
Total Current Assets	363,384	318,500
Investments at Long-term Receivables (Note 3)	67,417	44,324
Deferred Charges	11,197	12,736
Property, Plant, and Equipment—net (Note 4)	331,018	334,530
Trademarks and Leaseholds (Note 5)	50,249	49,882
Excess of Cost Over Fair Value of Net Assets		
,Acquired (Note 5)	279,069	285,255
Assets Held for Disposal, at Estimated		
Realizable Value (Note 11)	15,505	24,000
	$1,117,839	$1,069,227

Liabilities and Shareholders' Equity	December 31 1972	1971
Current Liabilities		
Notes and Loans Payable to Banks	$ 43,419	$ 28,933
Accounts Payable and Accrued Liabilities	87,692	92,806
Long-term Debt due within 1-Year	14,719	7,656
U.S. and Foreign Income Taxes (Note 10)	22,820	19,874
Deferred U.S. and Foreign Income Taxes (Note 10)	10,882	11,436
Total Current Liabilities	179,532	160,705
Long-term Debt (Note 6)	402,487	380,280
Accrued Severance and Other Social Benefits (Note 7)	34,596	37,095
Other Liabilities and Deferred Credits	7,689	13,158
Total Liabilities	624,304	591,238

Shareholders' Equity (Notes 6, 8, and 9)

$3.00 Cumulative Convertible Preferred Stock	2,738	2,769
$1.20 Cumulative Convertible Preference Stock	29,610	29,610
$3.20 Cumulative Convertible Preference Stock	7,452	7,452
Capital Stock, $1 Par Value	10,773	10,781
Warrants and Options to purchase Capital Stock (Notes 8 and 9)	366,322	366,303
Capital Surplus	76,740	61,074
Income Retained in the Business (Note 6)	493,535	477,989
Total Shareholders' Equity	$1,117,839	$1,069,227

Note 6–LONG-TERM DEBT

	1972	1971
	(in thousands)	

Long-term debt comprises the following:

5 1/2% subordinated debentures, due 1994, redeemable at approximately 5 per cent above par in 1973 and at slightly lesser amounts thereafter, convertible into capital stock at $55.00 a share, with sinking fund redemptions commencing in 1980 at annual rates of 4 per cent (1980–1984), 7 per cent (1985-1989) and 9 per cent (1990-1993) of the principal amount outstanding on January 31, 1980, less unamortized debt discount of $7,032,000 in 1972, $7,560,000 in 1971.	$242,548	$247,020
6 1/2% subordinated debentures, due 1988, redeemable at approximately 5 per cent above par in 1973 and slightly lesser amounts thereafter with required sinking fund redemptions of $1,200,000 in each of the years 1975-1978, $1,800,000 in each of the years 1979-1983 and $2,400,000 in each of the years 1984-1987, less unamortized debt discount of $4,570,000 in 1972, $5,009,000 in 1971.	25,395	24,956
Eurodollar loans payable to banks at interest rates generally 3/4 of 1 per cent over the London interbank rate, $30,000,000 matures in 1975 and the balance matures 1973-1980.	80,134	62,500
6 7/8% subordinated notes due in annual installments of approximately $1,761,000 from 1973-1979.	12,324	14,085
Other loans, notes, and debentures and other liabilities payable to banks and others with interest rates from 4 1/2 per cent to 9 per cent including $10,000,000 with interest to 1/2 per cent over prime rate, maturing from 1973 to 1997.	47,805	39,375
Less current maturities	(14,719)	(7,656)
	$402,487	$380,280

Case 7-3

The Southland Corporation[1]

In March of 1972, The Southland Corporation decided to force the conversion of its 5 1/2% convertible subordinated debentures that were carried in the 1971 financials at $39.4 million. Conversion was induced by announcing that the company would be redeeming all outstanding convertible debentures 1 month hence by paying the necessary call premium of 5 per cent above par value. During the month all debenture holders would have the option of converting their holdings at a rate of 4.202 shares of common stock per $100 face value of debentures. The OTC bid price for the common stock stood at $36.80 at that time.

QUESTIONS

1. Why had the debenture holders not converted earlier?

2. Make sure you fully understand how the company has accounted for this conversion.

3. Assuming the debentures were issued in January 1969, what was the total dollar cost paid by Southland for the use of these funds from 1969-1972? *Be careful because this is a loaded question.*

4. To what extent does GAAP reflect "fair" accounting for the cost of convertible debt?

---

[1] This case was prepared by Laird H. Simons, III, Research Assistant, under the supervision of Associate Professor John K. Shank, as the basis for class discussion rather than to illustrate either the effective or ineffective handling of an administrative situation.

EXHIBIT 2

SOUTHLAND CORPORATION
Consolidated Balance Sheet

	December 31, 1972	December 31, 1971
Current Assets:		
Cash	$ 33,120,375	$ 38,563,851
Cash investments	26,193,151	–
Accounts and notes receivable (Note 3)	46,024,739	39,366,520
Inventories at the lower of cost or market	53,747,359	49,076,601
Deposits and prepaid expense	8,099,136	8,649,379
Investment in property (Note 4)	35,598,687	25,561,540
Total Current Assets	202,783,447	161,217,891
Investments in Affiliates (Note 2)	19,568,903	8,371,942
Other Assets	1,729,878	1,200,133
Property, Plant and Equipment (Note 5)	165,270,306	155,688,095
Liabilities and Shareholders' Equity	$389,352,534	$326,478,061

	December 31, 1972	December 31, 1971
Current Liabilities:		
Long-term debt due within one year	$ 6,757,630	$ 6,718,133
Accounts payable and accrued expense	86,313,975	67,302,432
Income taxes	1,800,241	3,508,187
Total Current liabilities	94,871,846	77,528,752
Deferred Credits (Note 7)	15,620,385	14,437,289
Reserves for Self Insurance	2,615,183	2,187,878
Long-Term Debt, due after one year (Note 6)	82,042,893	95,191,759
Contingencies and Commitments (Note 9)		
Shareholders' Equity (Notes 6 and 8):		
Common stock, $.01 par value, authorized 40,000,000 shares, issued and outstanding 15,917,385 and 13,685,704 shares	159,174	136,857
Additional paid-in capital	153,464,415	99,149,745
Earnings retained in the business	40,578,638	37,845,781
	194,202,227	137,132,383
	$389,352,534	$326,478,061

EXHIBIT 3

THE SOUTHLAND CORPORATION AND SUBSIDIARIES
Statement of Consolidated Shareholders' Equity

Year ended December 31

	1972	1971
Common Stock:		
The Southland Corporation	$ 136,857	$ 81,162
Shares issued in poolings	—	5,325
Balance January 1, restated for poolings	136,857	86,487
Exercise of stock options	671	750
3% Stock dividend	4,592	3,939
Conversion of notes and debentures	17,054	4,769
Purchase acquisition	—	142
Stock split—3-for-2	—	40,770
Balance December 31	159,174	136,857
Additional Paid-in Capital:		
The Southland Corporation	99,149,745	78,381,952
Pooled companies	—	289,266
Balance January 1, restated for poolings	99,149,745	78,671,218
Exercise of stock options	786,363	1,077,480
3% Stock dividend	14,001,161	11,840,486
Conversion of notes and debentures	39,527,146	7,183,224
Purchase acquisition	—	418,107
Stock split—3-for-2	—	(40,770)
Balance December 31	153,464,415	99,149,745
Earnings Retained in the Business:		
The Southland Corporation	37,845,781	30,576,349
Pooled companies	—	3,950,978
Balance January 1, restated for poolings	37,845,781	34,527,327
Net earnings for the year	20,365,987	17,796,595
Less:	58,211,768	52,323,922
Cash dividends	3,491,311	2,423,341
Cash paid in lieu of fractional shares	136,066	210,374
3% Stock dividend	14,005,753	11,844,426
	17,633,130	14,478,141
Balance December 31	40,578,638	37,845,781
Total Shareholders' Equity (Notes 6 and 8)	$194,202,227	$137,132,383

EXHIBIT 4

THE SOUTHLAND CORPORATION AND SUBSIDIARIES
Statement of Consolidated Changes in Financial Position

Year ended December 31

	1972	1971
Source of Funds:		
From operations:		
Net earnings before extraordinary item	$ 20,365,987	$ 17,299,759
Depreciation	17,862,325	16,246,787
Deferred income taxes and other credits	1,183,096	1,214,478
Funds provided by operations	39,411,408	34,761,024
Extraordinary item	—	496,836
5% Convertible subordinated debentures	30,000,000	—
Long-term debt	7,782,559	11,398,085
Conversion of notes and debentures	39,544,200	7,187,993
Exercise of stock options	787,034	1,078,230
Value of shares issued in purchase acquisition	—	418,249
Increase in accounts payable, accruals and income tax	17,303,597	2,576,062
Property retirements and sales	4,619,882	3,676,514
Decrease in cash and cash investments	—	7,144,275
Other	977,548	—
	$140,426,228	$ 68,737,268
Application of Funds:		
Payment of long-term debt	$ 11,347,728	$ 6,954,314
Conversion of notes and debentures	39,544,200	7,187,993
Cash dividends	3,491,311	2,423,341
Cash paid in lieu of fractional shares	136,066	210,374
Investments in affiliates	11,196,961	8,273,942
Property, plant and equipment .:..............	32,064,418	31,494,017
Increase in cash and cash investments	20,749,675	—
Increase in accounts and notes receivable	6,658,219	2,900,307
Increase in inventories	4,670,758	3,729,842
Increase in investment in property	10,037,147	4,605,838
Net assets of business purchased	—	418,249
Other	529,745	539,051
	$140,426,228	$ 68,737,268

EXHIBIT 5

1972 ANNUAL REPORT

NOTE 6—LONG-TERM DEBT:
At December 31, 1972, long-term debt and amounts due within one year were as follows:

	Amount outstanding	Current portion	Balance Included in long-term debt
5¾% Promissory notes due 1976	$10,312,500	$ 3,437,500	$ 6,875,000
4%—9% Real estate and equipment notes (Mature 1973 to 1995)	37,938,023	3,320,130	34,617,893
5% Convertible subordinated notes due 1984 .	6,000,000	—	6,000,000
5¾% Convertible subordinated notes due 1987	4,550,000	—	4,550,000
5% Convertible subordinated debentures due 1987	30,000,000	—	30,000,000
	$88,800,523	$ 6,757,630	$82,042,893

The 5% and 5¾% convertible notes and the 5% convertible debentures may, at the option of the holders, be converted at any time into common stock of the Company at the ratios, respectively, 85.55, 69.78, and 23.94 shares of stock for each $1,000 of principal. As to the notes, these ratios decrease to 75.29 and 66.33 shares on January 1, 1975 and December 1, 1977, respectively. At December 31, 1972, there were 1,548,999 shares of common stock reserved for the conversion of the notes and debentures. Principal payments on the notes are due annually beginning in 1975 and 1978 respectively, in amounts equal to 10% of the aggregate principal amount outstanding one year prior to the date of the first required payment.

Under a revolving credit facility with certain banks the Company may borrow, repay and reborrow up to $32,000,000 at an interest rate equal to ¼% above the prime rate. On or before July 2, 1973, the banks have agreed to make a term loan to Southland in an amount up to $32,000,000. No amounts were borrowed under this facility at December 31, 1972, nor does the Company anticipate any borrowings thereunder to the date it terminates on July 2, 1973. At December 31, 1972, the aggregate amount of long-term debt maturities is as follows for the years ended December 31: 1973—$6,757,630; 1974—$6,513,087; 1975—$6,809,419; 1976—$3,260,273; 1977—$3,278,497.

The agreements under which the promissory notes and the convertible notes were issued place certain restrictions on the payment of cash dividends. Under the most restrictive of these provisions, retained earnings totaling $38,400,000 at December 31, 1972, were not so restricted.

Other provisions of the agreements include requirements as to maintenance of working capital and net worth. The Company has complied with these requirements.

Case 8-1

Fairmuir Instrument Corporation[1]

Fairmuir Instrument Corporation sold a line of high-temperature measuring instruments (pyrometers). The principal users of the equipment were steel mills and various metal extraction companies, and Fairmuir's small sales force had concentrated almost exclusively on establishing good relations with these customers. Occasional inquiries and orders came from other sources, such as scientific laboratories, but the company had never actively solicited these markets.

The device in its present form had been developed and put into production in the early 1950s. Essentially it utilized principles that had been known for almost a hundred years, but until recently the accuracy attainable had fallen short of the requirements of modern industry. The company had introduced no new products until the last quarter of 1964. Effectively, the company had not faced any serious competition in its market area until 1960 and had maintained a stable sales level of around $3 million until that time.

During 1960 a competing product had been introduced to the market. Operating on completely different principles, this device performed substantially the same job as Fairmuir's product and gave similar levels of accuracy. The only major differences were in its useful life (5 years) and its purchase price, each of which were about half of those of the Fairmuir product. The lower purchase price was a telling sales advantage and Fairmuir's sales had suffered accordingly. Exhibit 1 gives some of the financial data of Fairmuir Instrument Corporation from 1960 through 1964.

By 1961 the management of Fairmuir realized that without a new product to bolster its faltering sales volume, the company was facing a serious predicament. They, therefore, began a search for an additional product that would be suited to the competences of the company. In 1962 they approached an inventor, who held patents for just such a product, with a view to buying the patents. After some

[1] Case material of the Harvard Graduate School of Business Administration is prepared as a basis for class discussion. Cases are not designed to present illustrations of either effective or ineffective handling of administrative problems.

EXHIBIT 1

FAIRMUIR INSTRUMENT CORPORATION

Financial Data as of December 31
(Dollar figures in thousands)

| | Audited Results | | | Unaudited |
	1960	*1961*	*1962*	*1963*	*1964*
Inventories Related to					
Pyrometers	791	806	909	805	627
Working Capital	933	1,021	1,165	1,155	819
Net Assets	1,889	1,965	1,995	1,926	1,549
Net Sales of Pyrometers	2,881	2,475	2,025	996	583
Other Sales (Net)	—	—	—	—	115
Net Income (loss)	108	77	67	(91)	(376)

negotiation a mutually satisfactory price was reached, and, as part of the agreement, the inventor agreed to join the company and lead the additional development work that was required before a commercial product was ready for marketing.

On top of the cost of the patents and the development expenses, the company was faced with substantial start-up costs and investment in inventories. The company's financial resources, already adversely affected by the lagging sales of pyrometers, were inadequate without an injection of fresh capital. The company's capital stock was closely held by members of top management and a few of their friends and family members. None of these people was willing to contribute any further capital.

Management believed that the recent poor operating results made it unwise to seek fresh equity capital at that time and they, therefore, decided that a bank loan was the only feasible recourse. It did not prove an easy matter to find a bank willing to make the required loan, but eventually the capital was obtained from a bank. In extending the loan the bank imposed several restrictions upon the management of Fairmuir, one of these being that a minimum working capital level of $800,000 should be maintained. By the end of 1964, with the sales of pyrometers still falling and the new product only just introduced to the market, the company was close to defaulting on the requirements of the working capital covenant.

In the 1964 audit, the public accountant was satisfied with all the accounts except for the valuation of the inventories related to pyrometers. Most of this inventory was in good condition, and had been carefully handled and stored. A few items of purchased parts had become obsolete and management had written them down. This represented an insignificant adjustment, however, and the bulk of the inventory was still reported on the company's books at cost. The auditor was not concerned about the physical condition of the inventory, but he had serious reservations as to the marketability of the product, and therefore the realization of the investment through profitable sales. In approaching management on this matter the auditor was aware that a large adjustment would throw the company into default on its loan convenant concerning working capital.

The auditor, Mr. Bill Adams, arranged a meeting with the president of Fairmuir Instrument Corporation, Mr. Tom Fairmuir, in order to discuss the 1964 financial statements. Part of the meeting is recorded below.

Mr. Adams: Everything seems to be in fine order except for your valuation of inventories relating to pyrometers, Tom. Now we discussed this matter briefly a few days ago and you expressed the opinion that there would be no material loss of value in the inventories and that you would in fact be able to sell it all in the normal course of business. Since then I have examined your record of sales orders, and at present you have only $58,000 worth of open orders on your books, compared with $65,000 worth at the beginning of the year. Your billings by quarters for the past year were fairly stable: $149,000 first quarter, $136,000 second quarter, $141,000 third quarter and $157,000 in the final quarter.

I have also read several articles in trade publications, such as this one in *Steel Monthly*, which seem to indicate that your type of pyrometer is at a technical as well as an economic (in terms of purchase price) disadvantage.

Frankly, it appears to me that you are going to be left with a lot of inventory that will have to be marked down very significantly to sell it.

Mr. Fairmuir: Now hold it, Bill, things are not so bleak as that. In fact, we have plans for our pyrometers that will return the sales volume to its previous level, or close to it. Look at these letters, Bill. These are inquiries concerning substantial orders, and we have been receiving such inquiries at a greatly increased rate recently. If this continues, and I have no doubt that it will, and even half of them become firm orders, we shall be selling pyrometers in 1965 at twice the 1964 level.

You know we hired a new sales manager this year? Well, he has reorganized our sales force and is beginning to get results. At the same time we have gone over our production process and reduced the manufacturing cost of our lines by some 10 per cent. No doubt you noticed that our cost of goods figures, which have been stable at about 60% of selling price for several years, were lower for the past 2 or 3 months. We expect to improve on that further in 1965. Of course, this gives us some price flexibility when we are faced with a competitive situation. So you see, I have good reason to predict better results in the future.

Mr. Adams: What exactly has the new sales manager done?

Mr. Fairmuir: He reorganized the sales territories and reassigned the salesmen so that we should get greater market penetration. He released a couple of the men who have clearly not been pulling their weight and hired a couple of bright young men to replace them. The main thing is that he has done wonders for the morale of the sales force.

In addition, he has identified new markets and is helping the men to break into these markets.

Mr. Adams: Why don't we look at the prospects market by market, Tom? You had sales of only $62,000 to steel mills in 1964. It seems as if the steel mills market is almost defunct, wouldn't you agree?

Mr. Fairmuir: It has certainly declined. However, some of our men have built up a good relationship with their customers in the steel industry and we expect this to produce a certain loyalty. We should keep a small part of the business, say, billings of about $50,000 a year.

Then in the other metal extraction industries we know that our product has some distinct competitive advantages, such as its ruggedness and lower maintenance costs. With the new emphasis on selling we expect that our customers will be well aware of these advantages, and the downward sales trend should be reversed this year. On this basis we expect 1965's sales to this market to be at least $400,000 and to increase further in the future.

Mr. Adams: But look, Tom, that means an increase over this year's sales, bucking a strong downward trend. I can't base my opinion on your optimism, you know.

Mr. Fairmuir: Well, look at this market, which we think has great potential—scientific laboratories. We are going to place advertisements in some of the engineering journals and pay direct sales calls to many of the labs in our market areas, those that do a lot of high-temperature work. We anticipate a yearly volume of $200,000 to $300,000 in this market.

And, finally, we have set up a contact with a representative in Washington to handle our line in government sales. He has already got some orders for us and he seems certain that we can build up a stable volume of some $300,000 a year. Several government agencies are testing our product at the moment, including the Atomic Energy Commission. If we get our equipment specified for installation into government nuclear plants, we shall have a large continuing market.

Mr. Adams: So you expect sales of about $1 million this year, twice 1964's sales?

Mr. Fairmuir: No, not right away. But we are confident of substantially reversing the trend of recent years and eventually, say in 2 years or so, building our sales up to at least $1.5 million for pyrometers. For 1965 we predict sales of about $800,000.

Mr. Adams: Well, look at this from my point of view. I have a professional responsibility to give an opinion on your company's financial statements and I cannot base my opinion on your predictions. I have to go on historic facts and reasonable expectations. The historic facts are that sales of pyrometers have been falling and you have only a small volume of open orders on your books.

You have a substantial inventory, the value of which can only be realized through the sale of pyrometers. Any other representation of these facts would mislead the reader of the statements.

Mr. Fairmuir: I agree with you on that, and in my opinion, we *will* realize the value of our inventory through normal sales. I could not contemplate a write down in the value of the inventory. For one thing, it would not be right to do so since it would be misleading in valuing our assets. And for another, it could easily lead to a difficult situation with the bank and, at worst, lead to liquidation of the company. True, we have experienced a few bad years. But we are fighting back and I am confident we shall save our pyrometer line. And also our new line will start to contribute to profits this coming year.

The discussion continued for some time and became fairly heated. Finally, Mr. Adams terminated the discussion in order to consider the question further. He arranged a meeting with Mr. Fairmuir for 3 days later, at which time the two men agreed they would come to a decision whether or not the value of the inventory should be written down. Mr. Adams was concerned about what opinion he should issue on Fairmuir's financial statements of 1964.

QUESTIONS

1. What further steps should Mr. Adams take in preparing for the coming meeting with Mr. Fairmuir?

2. Putting yourself in Mr. Fairmuir's position, what steps would you take in preparing for the meeting? If Mr. Adams insists that the value of the inventory be written down, what would you do?

3. Do you think that the value of the inventory should be written down? If so, how should the adjustment be made?

4. If it were not written down, how would you, as auditor, phrase your opinion?

Case 8-2

Allegheny Beverage Corporation (A)[1]

In early April 1972, the shareholders of the Allegheny Beverage Corporation, a Baltimore, Maryland, soft-drink distributor, were informed in a news release issued by the company that earnings from operations totaled $1.05 per share for 1971, approximately a 300 per cent increase in earnings over 1970.

In the calendar year 1971, Allegheny Beverage Corporation established record sales of $73,441,000, an increase of 41 per cent above the preceding year's sales of $52,036,000. Net income rose to $3,276,000 in 1971 from $1,121,000 in calendar year 1970. Total assets of the corporation rose from $49,481,000 to $75,269,000 during 1971.

VALU VEND—ACCOUNTING FOR SALES

The Annual Report reported in Footnote 2:

Valu Vend, Inc., (a wholly owned subsidiary) was formed in December 1970 to sell vending machines and the products to be vended through such machines. Valu Vend has adopted the policy of recognizing revenue from the sale of vending machines and related costs and expenses at the time a machine is sold. The machines are sold under conditional sales contracts with payments due over a 4-year period. If income on these sales had been deferred until collected, primary earnings per share for 1971 would have been $.62.

Installment notes receivable under conditional sales contracts aggregated $19,150,000 after allowance for doubtful accounts of $505,000 at December 31, 1971. Finance charges to customers included in such receivables aggregated $3,875,000 at December 31, 1971, and are reflected as a deferred item. Such charges will be taken into earnings as installment payments are received. . . .

---

[1] This case was prepared by Donald E. Bryant, Research Associate, under the supervision of Professor David F. Hawkins and Lecturer Mary Wehle, as a basis for class discussion rather than to illustrate either effective or ineffective handling of an administrative situation.

In the "Valu Vend Operations" section of their Form 10-K annual report to the SEC, these sales were described:

> Valu Vend sells its machines under conditional sales contracts. Under these contracts, a purchaser is required to make a $50 down payment and to pay the balance in equal monthly installments over a 48-month period after purchase. Under moratorium plans, the first of such monthly payments may begin 120 days or 210 days after the date of purchase, but all payments are completed within 48 months after purchase.
>
> The machines are sold to distributors and through the distributors to other purchasers, who may have their own locations for the machines. Each distributor appointee is required to warehouse and distribute beverages in his marketing territory and to establish sales and maintenance organizations.

OTHER ACCOUNTING POLICIES

Other accounting policies outlined in the footnotes included an election to capitalize certain start-up costs incurred during the initial production period of a new bottling plant amounting to $375,000 and to capitalize start-up and test market costs amounting to $3,531,000. The unamortized portion of such costs at December 31, 1971, was $3,409,000. The company used straight-line depreciation for book purposes.

CHANGE OF AUDITORS

Two weeks after the news release, on April 20, 1971, the shareholders received a copy of the official annual report. Included in the chairman of the board's letter to the shareholders were these comments:

> *CHANGE OF AUDITORS.*
>
> At the late date of March 27, 1972, the Company found it necessary to replace its auditor, Alexander Grant & Company, with a new auditor, Benjamin Botwinick & Co.
>
> Prior to the time its audit begins, the company receives a letter from the certified public accounting firm stating what information will be needed, how long they estimate the audit to take, and what fee will be charged for the audit. For the 1971 audit, Alexander Grant estimated a fee not to be in excess of the staggering amount of $150,000, and a completion date of February 23, 1972. Our internal accounting staff had been working closely with Alexander Grant throughout the year and had determined to adopt the accrual method of accounting, which is the method used in our industry. This is the basis on which our 6 months earnings, our 9 months earnings, and our preliminary year-end earnings were reported. On March 2nd, 1 week after the audit was scheduled to have been completed, we were informed by the Baltimore office of Grant that their position had been reversed by their Chicago office, and that we must defer earnings from our Valu Vend subsidiary. During a long discussion, we were requested to provide supporting information from similar companies. This was done and our accounting

method was substantiated. Also, at that same meeting, we were told that if we chose to terminate Grant because of their change of position, certification would be given for all divisions except Valu Vend.

After much additional research and many meetings, on March 18, 1972, the Baltimore Grant office once again was prepared to return to the accrual method of accounting with substantially the same figures we had reported preliminarily. A meeting was held at the Grant main offices in Chicago on March 21st, and we were informed that they would not accept our accrual accounting and proposed a hybrid approach that was unacceptable to us. We had no choice but to recommend to our board that Grant be terminated.

We agreed to pay the remaining fees for the audit to date, which should have been approximately $30,000, and Grant agreed to cooperate with a new auditor in the changeover, make available their work papers for review, and to certify the divisions other than Valu Vend as promised by the Baltimore office. Two days later, we were told that if we didn't pay them $77,000 ($100,000 had been paid to date), that we would not be able to have access to their work papers, and were furthermore told that there would be no certification whatsoever. We had no choice but to submit to this pressure in order to finish the audit.

We are reviewing this entire matter because substantial amounts of time and money were expended on an audit that was never completed. The attitude of the courts and other authorities has been to protect all accountants and lawyers to the detriment of the company and its shareholders. We think that it is important for our shareholders to be aware of situations such as this, because they happen too often not to be brought to the public eye.

NET EARNINGS.

Earnings from operations totaled $1.05 per share. We had two extra-ordinary items causing a reduction in total earnings of 13¢ per share. Approximately 5¢ was due to the sale of all remaining airplanes in our leasing company, which has now discontinued operations. The remaining 8¢ was due to a guarantee issued 3 years ago, which after much litigation, the company was called on to meet. This call actually occurred in 1972 but a reserve was established for the expense in 1971. We are pleased with our net of 92¢ per share, which is approximately a 300 per cent increase in earnings over 1970.

A reporter from the *Wall Street Journal* asked why the change in auditors hadn't been discussed in the company's earlier news release. Morton M. Lapidus, chairman of Allegheny Beverage Company, is reported to have said:

There was no reason to tell the general public. It had already been reported to the Securities and Exchange Commission.

Another *Wall Street Journal* article reports Mr. Lapidus as saying "the Company plans to sell 400,000 machines during the next 4 to 5 years." This projection provides some perspective on the future materiality of these adjustments. As reported in their SEC Form 10-K, total 1971 sales were only 16,132 machines.

QUESTIONS

1. What is the accounting issue in this case? How shall it be resolved?

2. What should the author have done about the deferred start-up and marketing costs?

3. What do you think the impact of requiring both the company and the auditor to file a K.8 statement when a firm changes its auditors?

Case 8-3

Reichman Pinball Machines, Inc. (A)[1]

Early in February of 1973, Bill Lamprechter, a partner in the New York office of the "big eight" accounting firm of Kincaide, Cramer and McKee, sat back to reflect for a moment on a problem that had arisen in one of the audits for which he was responsible. The problem resulted from financial transactions between Reichman Pinball Machines, Inc., and Ridge Lending Corporation, a finance company that lent money to Reichman and other companies in the pinball machine business. Lamprecther asked Martha Hardcastle, the senior on the Reichman job, and Ted Hellman, the newly assigned manager on the job, to come into his office to review the problem and arrive at a final decision on the firm's position regarding the matter.

Lamprechter: We've dragged out this audit for long enough. I'd certainly like to get it cleared up as quickly as possible because we're spending entirely too much of our time on a client that hasn't even paid for last year's audit. Martha, could you fill Ted in a little on the history of the account—maybe we can find a solution to our problems.

Hardcastle: I've been following the Ridge situation rather closely since 1969, but it's been going on since 1966 when we first picked up the Reichman audit. The key to the problem is Arnold Ross, who is president, chairman of the board, and the major stockholder and supervisor of the day-to-day operations of Ridge. Ridge is even operated from an office on Reichman's premises. The way I see the situation, Reichman issues negotiable notes to Ridge, which endorses them and uses them as collateral for drawing on two lines of credit of $1 million each at the Exchange National Bank and the Nazarian National Bank. Ridge then transfers to Reichman the discounted amount of the notes, giving rise to the "Ridge payable" on Reichman's balance sheet. There is also a parallel and continuous series of loans by Reichman to Ridge, leading to the

---

[1] This case was prepared by Laird H. Simons, III, under the supervision of Associate Professor John K. Shank, as the basis for class discussion rather than to illustrate either effective or ineffective handling of an administrative situation.

"Ridge receivable" account on Reichman's books. Most of these loans arise from Ross's custom of using Reichman and Ridge as sources of cash to cover his stock market endeavors. As soon as Ridge receives money from Reichman, Ross withdraws it for his own uses, leaving an account receivable from Ross on Ridge's books. As long as these borrowings and repayments substantially matched and the size was small, we did not feel it significant enough to press Ross for detail. Lately, however, it seems to be getting out of hand.

Lamprechter: That's certainly true! Reichman's cash payments to Ridge of $1,186,000 in 1969 apparently served no other purpose than to provide Ridge with cash, but by year's end the receivable stood at 0. The following year we noticed that the payments were becoming more frequent, were in round amounts, and were unaccompanied by written explanations. In fiscal 1970 the receivable ranged from $695,000 at the beginning of the year to $398,000 at year end, with a high during the year of $1,583,000 in April. The balance in the receivable account seemed, in some sense, seasonal, rising after the end of one fiscal year and falling prior to the end of the next. This sort of "window dressing" raised questions about the fairness of the year-end statements. Last year the amount got as high as $2 million so I telephoned Ross to discuss the situation. This "memo to the file" of mine summarizes our conversation. (Lamprechter distributes copies of the following memo)

Telephone Conversation with Arnold Ross January 10, 1972

Lamprechter: I've been going over this year's audit (1971) and everything seems to be in order. I'm a little worried though about the Ridge receivable account—it's more than double what it was last year.

Ross: Just because the amount is large doesn't mean there's a problem, does it? From what you've told me in the past, our treatment of the matter is well within the bounds of generally accepted accounting principles. I see no reason to make an issue of this item.

Lamprechter: Technically, you're probably right. Martha has confirmed the balance in writing and reconciled it to the amount appearing on Reichman's books. The computation of accrued interest was checked, Reichman's vouchers supporting disbursements to Ridge were examined, and the canceled checks representing the advances to Ridge were also examined, noting that they were received by Ridge and endorsed for deposit to Ridge's account at the Exchange National Bank.

At a minimum, we'll have to mention your position with the two companies on Reichman's financial statements. We won't comment in detail on the receivable, though, since we are only auditing Reichman, not Ridge. If this Ridge receivable account is as large next year as it is now, however, we'll have to take a look at Ridge's books as well.

Ross: I guess I can live with that, but I don't like the implication that there is anything wrong with this account.

Hellman: Well, what has happened to the Ridge receivable since then?

Hardcastle: Just before the end of the fiscal year, I talked with the assistant comptroller at Reichman. The receivable was slightly higher then and other problems had arisen. At that time I put this memo into our work paper file (Hardcastle distributes copies of the following memo).

Conversation with Dick Hartman–September 15, 1972

Hardcastle: In working on this year's audit, we'll need more information on the Ridge receivable. What's it up to now?

Hartman: As of July 31, it was up to $3.6 million and I haven't posted any transactions since then. That's not the big problem, though. For several months, we've been operating a check float in excess of $500,000 a day–cash is really tighter than ever. I've been spending most of the summer just trying to juggle cash!

Hardcastle: Why does Ridge need so much money?

Hartman: Ross needed it to maintain his margin accounts on the Goren, Inc., stock and bonds and the Reichman stock he owns.

Hardcastle: I see. This could create some interesting reporting problem.

Hardcastle: That was only the beginning. The October cash audit showed just how critical the shortage of funds had become. The $300,000 cash balance on September 30, resulted only from 30-day bank loans of $1.5 million. The Ridge receivable was still up around $3.5 million and the Ridge payable was $1 million, half of which is due within the coming year. I have copies here of the draft statements for 1972 (see Exhibit 2).

Lamprechter: We don't have any choice, do we? We'll have to look at Ridge's books. The receivable is completely out of line.

Hellman: I agree. From what the figures show and what you've told me, it looks like Reichman is in a very shaky financial position.

Hardcastle: You're right, of course; a full examination would be in order. But the Ridge financial statements just aren't available because their audit isn't completed. We've got to finish our audit right away–we're already a month late.

Hellman: Can't we protect ourselves with a "subject to" opinion and full disclosure in the footnotes? That would eliminate the need to look at Ridge's books and would still be in line with generally accepted accounting principles. We've established a pattern of disclosing the advances to Ridge on the balance sheet and Ridge's relationship to Ross. This extra step should get us off the hook with GAAP and with the client.

Lamprechter: Yes, I think the three of us could readily agree on this, but I doubt if Ross will go for it. He knows as well as we do that a "subject to" opinion is a real red flag. Breaking our pattern of disclosure on this issue clearly suggests we think something is wrong.

That afternoon, Lamprechter contacted Ross:

Lamprechter: There seem to be a few problems with this year's audit, Arnold, which I would like to clear up as quickly as possible.

Ross: Yes, I've looked over your preliminary audit and, to say the least, I'm very displeased. What we presented to you as a $109,000 profit has suddenly become a $900,000 loss. From the looks of things, you're trying to ruin Reichman. What happened?

Lamprechter: That's not really what I called to discuss, but we might as well go over it since you mentioned it. You deferred R & D expenses this year that, as far as we can determine, should be written off since there is no solid indication of future worth. There was also a lot of obsolete inventory that had to be written off.

Ross: What are you trying to do to us? Perhaps we should get new accountants. Our ideas are miles apart!

Lamprechter: I'm sorry, Arnold, but there really is no choice for us on these matters. It's always your prerogative to fire us, but if you were to start over with new accountants at this late date, there is no way the audit could be completed before summer. Since we're already flirting with violations of the S.E.C.'s 10K deadline, I think you'll have to go along with us for this year.

Ross: What the devil did you call for anyway? I hope you're not going to bother me about the Ridge receivable again! I thought we had that problem all straightened out last year—you haven't changed your mind, have you? Besides, if you back out now I guarantee that we'll sue for failure to get our reports out on time.

Lamprechter: Remember last year when I warned you that if the receivables were as large again this year we'd have to look at Ridge's books?

Ross: If Ridge's audit were completed, I'd happily make the statements available, but it's going to be a while. Isn't there some way we can clear up the problem? Ridge is solvent, but we're just not in a position right now to repay the $3.5 million debt to Reichman.

Lamprechter: Why not?

Ross: It's a personal matter. I've borrowed approximately the same amount from Ridge, which I'm temporarily unable to repay. Perhaps we can work out some arrangement. I can personally secure this indebtedness with my equity in stocks, bonds, and other securities. I'll even put mortgage on my home and personal assets if necessary as additional collateral, but I just can't come up with the cash now. What do you say?

Lamprechter: Would you go along with a footnote to the financial statements saying that the amount in the Ridge receivable is uncollectible since Ridge has loaned approximately the same amount to you, but that you have pledged as security for the repayment of the obligation, securities in Reichman and other companies totaling approximately the same amount.

Ross: Not on your life. You're trying to make me look like a crook. You know as well as I do that generally accepted accounting standards don't require that kind of disclosure as long as the value of the receivables is assured.

Lamprechter: We'll have to see what we can do. We all want to finish up this audit as soon as possible.

The next day, Lamprechter, Hellman, and Hardcastle met once again:

Lamprechter: Ross is hopping mad. He'd like to find a new set of auditors but, for this year, that's unrealistic. Nevertheless, if we miss the 10K deadline and the S.E.C. goes after him for tardiness, we could well get sued. More to the point—Ross is a wealthy, solid citizen who has paid us substantial fees in the past and continues to use us for tax work, as well as year-end and special audit work. He's not about to go under. He may be "slow-paying" this year but the problems with this year's audit have pushed the bills way up. He's in a cash bind but has always paid on time until the last 15 months. If we walk away now we'll have a tough time collecting the $63,000 in outstanding bills, and will have lost $50,000 a year in billings. I hope we can find a compromise position within generally accepted accounting principles that will satsify him.

Hellman: I don't like it. We're asking for trouble if we permit personal loans of this size to go unchallenged. This company is on the verge of serious trouble.

Lamprechter: You may be right Ted, but if we indicate that the loans are collateralized, doesn't that mean that we look not to Ross or Ridge but to the value of the collateral as the ultimate backing for Reichman's receivable?

Hardcastle: Even if that's true, don't we take a risk that the collateral, most of which would be Reichman and Goren securities, will fail to cover the receivable once this annual report showing a loss is made public. If we use this collateral we'd better disclose fully, in the footnotes what types of securities we're talking about—stock, letter stock, or bonds—from what companies they arise, and what liens or other encumbrances are outstanding against them.

Lamprechter: Ross will never go for that. He knows generally accepted accounting principles don't require it. All we are required to do is verify that the market value of the securities at date of certification is sufficient to make the receivable collectible. I don't see how we can insist that he disclose more. What right do we have to hold a client to a higher standard than the accounting profession requires? We've already forced him to show a big loss for this year when he thought it should be a profit. That should be sufficient to alert the stockholders that the situation requires careful review on their part.

Hellman: I hope you're not letting your desire to keep a client unduly influence your judgment, Bill.

Lamprechter: So do I, Ted.

QUESTIONS

1. What are the options open to Bill Lamprechter?

2. What would you do in his situation?

EXHIBIT 1
REICHMAN PINBALL MACHINES, INC.
Consolidated Balance Sheet
September 30, 1971

Assets

Current Assets:

Cash		$ 1,500,000
Accounts and notes receivable:		
Trade (Note 2)		$ 7,900,000
Ridge Lending Corp., affiliate		850,000
Others including $671,460 from sales of		
pinball machines in operating locations and other		
capital assets		1,000,000
		9,750,000
Less Allowance for doubtful accounts	130,000	9,620,000
Inventories, at lower of cost (average or first-in,		
first-out) or market		3,800,000
Advance commissions		150,000
Prepaid expenses		680,000
Total current assets		15,750,000
Mortgage receivable (noninterest-bearing, due 12/1/74)		200,000
Investment, at cost		500,000
Noncurrent accounts and notes receivable, including $802,166		
from sales of pinball machines in operating locations and		
other capital assets		2,350,000
Property, plant and equipment (Note 2):		
Pinball machines	3,400,000	
Other, principally buildings, machinery & equipment	2,800,000	
	6,200,000	
Less Reserve for depreciation	1,500,000	
	4,700,000	
Land	100,000	4,800,000
Property held for sale,		100,000
Excess of cost of companies or operating properties		
acquired over related net assets, less amortization		1,900,000
Patents, at cost less amortization		1,500,000
Deferred charges and other assets:		
Research and development	1,500,000	
Advance commissions	400,000	
Other	1,250,000	2,150,000
		$29,250,000

Liabilities

Current Liabilities:

Notes and loans payable (Note 3)		$ 5,000,000
Long-term debt, portion due within one year (Note 4):		
Ridge Lending Corp., affiliate	$ 500,000	
Other	3,000,000	3,500,000
Accounts payable		3,000,000
Accrued expenses and taxes:		
Federal Income Tax	700,000	
Other	800,000	1,500,000
Total current liabilities		13,000,000
Long-term debt (Note 4):		
Ridge Lending Corp., affiliate	300,000	
Other	3,200,000	3,500,000
Liabilities paid from proceeds of debenture issue (Note 5):		3,500,000
Deferred federal income tax		100,000
Deferred income		150,000
Contingent liabilities (Note 6)		
CAPITAL		
Common stock, par value $.10 a share; 4,750,000 shares authorized, 4,000,000 shares issued and outstanding	400,000	
Capital surplus, as annexed	7,200,000	
Retained earnings, as annexed (Note 6)	1,400,000	9,000,000
		$29,250,000

REICHMAN PINBALL MACHINES, INC.

Consolidated Statement of Income and Retained Earnings
For the Year Ended September 30, 1971

Sales and operating income	$29,200,000
Cost of sales	21,200,000
	8,000,000
Selling and administrative expenses	6,300,000
	$ 1,700,000
Depreciation and amortization	750,000

Other income, including net profits of $2,027,802 from sales of pinball machines in operating locations and other capital assets	$ 2,000,000	
Other deductions, principally interest	1,000,000	1,000,000
Income before provision for federal income tax		$ 1,950,000
Provision for federal income tax		700,000
Net income		1,250,000
Retained earnings, September 30, 1970	2,750,000	
Deficit, Pyramid Pinball Co., Inc., September 30, 1970	500,000	
	2,250,000	
Less, adjustments in connection with pooling of interests	250,000	2,000,000
Retained earnings, September 30, 1970, as adjusted		3,250,000
Deduct, amount based on market quotation for 252,698 shares of common stock issued as a 15% stock dividend		1,850,000
Retained earnings, September 30, 1971 (Note 5)		$ 1,400,000

Consolidated Statement of Capital Surplus
For the Year Ended September 30, 1971

Balance, September 30, 1970	$ 3,600,000
Excess of capital stock account of Pyramid Pinball Co. Inc. over par value of 147,079 shares of the Company's common stock issued in connection with pooling of interests	200,000
Balance, September 30, 1970 as adjusted	3,800,000
Excess of market over par value of shares of common stock issued or to be issued 252,698 shares issued as a 15% stock dividend, less expenses of issue, etc.	1,875,000
87,418 shares issued in exchange for capital stock of two companies and capital stock and debentures of another company	1,525,000
Balance, September 30, 1971	$ 7,200,000

Notes to Consolidated Financial Statements—1971

[1] Accounts and notes receivable in the approximate amount of $4,880,000 are pledged as collateral for notes and loans payable.

[2] Property, plant and equipment, with minor exceptions, is recorded at cost. Pinball machines include equipment that in effect is pledged as collateral security for certain notes payable, and equipment subject to chattel mortgages as collateral for unpaid purchase prices. Other properties are subject to mortgages payable. The aggregate recorded amount of property subject to such liens is approximately $2,800,000 and the aggregate of unpaid notes and mortgages is approximately $2,200,000.

[3] Approximately $4,200,000 of the notes and loans payable is secured by collateral.

[4] Long-term debt includes approximately $1,866,000, $1,317,000, $124,000, and $124,000 payable in the fiscal years ending September 30, 1973, through 1976, respectively, and $101,000 payable thereafter.

Interest is payable at 6 per cent per year discounted in advance on loans from Ridge Lending Corp. (an affiliate, of which company Mr. Arnold Ross is an officer, director, and stockholder). Interest on other long-term debt, including the portion due within 1 year, is payable currently at 6 per cent a year on $2,595,000, at approximately 12 per cent a year on $997,000 and at various other rates on $589,000; interest is discounted or paid in advance, principally at 6 per cent a year, on $1,949,000; approximately $150,000 is noninterest-bearing. Approximately $4,033,000 of these amounts was secured by collateral.

[5] In December 1971 the company sold $5,052,700 of 6 per cent convertible subordinated debentures due September 1, 1986. The debentures are (a) convertible into the company's common stock from June 1972 through August 1986 at $8 1/3 per share, subject to adjustment under certain conditions, (b) subordinated to all "senior indebtedness" of the company, as defined in the indenture, and (c) redeemable at any time at the option of the company as a whole or in part at prices ranging from 106 per cent of principal amount in 1972 to par in 1975.

The indenture provides, among other things, that the company will make payments to a purchase or sinking fund on December 1 of each of the years 1972 through 1985 in the annual amount of $333,000 reduced by the amount of debentures converted into common stock and by the amount of debentures redeemed or purchased by the company. The indenture places certain restrictions on declaration of dividends (other than stock dividends) and on the purchase or redemption by the company of its capital stock. None of the September 30, 1971, balance of retained earnings is available for dividends or stock acquisitions.

A portion of the proceeds of the sale of the convertible debentures was used to pay notes payable in the amount of $3,250,000. These notes are therefore shown in the consolidated balance sheet as non-current liabilities.

[6] At September 30, 1971, the company and its subsidiaries were contingently liable in the approximate amount of $13,000,000 in connection with notes discounted or guaranteed.

In accordance with the terms of the agreement dated December 30, 1970, whereby the company acquired all the properties and assets of certain subsidiaries of Goren, Inc., called the "Apco Group," and assumed substantially all liabilities of such subsidiaries, 20 per cent of the capital shares of a subsidiary is pledged as collateral for certain obligations owing by Goren, Inc., amounting to $300,000 at September 30, 1971. The remaining 80 per cent of the stock of this subsidiary is pledged as collateral for notes payable by the company to Goren, Inc., under the terms of the December 30, 1970, agreement. The aggregate balance of such notes at September 30, 1971, was $2,600,000 of which $800,000 was paid in December 1971 from the proceeds of the sale of convertible debentures. (See Note 6.)

In January 1971 stockholders of Goren, Inc., instituted a derivative action to cancel and rescind the sale of the "Apco Group" to the company. The company is named in the action as a party defendant. It is the belief of counsel that there is no merit to this action.

An annual rental of $107,125 is payable for a period of 25 years from November 1, 1967, on property leased by the company at Westbury, New York. Under renewal options such annual rental is reduced to $53,562. The company has a contingent liability of approximately $469,000 at September 30, 1971, as guarantor of a first mortgage on such property. Annual rentals of approximately $81,000 are payable on other leases expiring after 3 years from September 30, 1971.

[7] There is an appeal pending against the company for a breach of contract, and an action pending arising out of a counterclaim asserted in an action brought by the company. It is the

belief of management and of counsel that the appeal and counterclaim are without merit or substance and that there should be no recovery thereon.

In December 1971 the company and two of its officers and directors were indicted on three counts alleging violation of the Taft-Hartley Act. In the opinion of counsel, the charges are without merit.

The company has agreed to repurchase certain pinball equipment, sold to a leasing corporation by subsidiaries, in the event the operators of the equipment default under their rental agreements with such corporation. At September 30, 1971, the exposure of the company amounted to approximately $2,000,000.

Accountants' Opinion

To the Board of Directors
Reichman Pinball Machines, Inc.:

We have examined the consolidated balance sheet of Reichman Pinball Machines, Inc., and its subsidiaries as of September 30, 1971, and the related consolidated statements of income and retained earnings and of capital surplus for the year then ended. Our examination was made in accordance with generally accepted auditing standards, and accordingly included such tests of the accounting records and such other auditing procedures as we considered necessary in the circumstances.

In our opinion, the accompanying consolidated financial statements present fairly the consolidated financial position of Reichman Pinball Machines, Inc. and its subsidiaries at September 30, 1971, and the consolidated results of their operations for the year then ended, in conformity with generally accepted accounting principles applied on a basis consistent with that of the preceding year.

Kincaide, Cramer and McKee

New York, February 1, 1972.

EXHIBIT 2
DRAFT FINANCIAL STATEMENTS
REICHMAN PINBALL MACHINES, Inc.
Consolidated Balance Sheet
September 30, 1972

Assets

Current Assets:

Cash		$ 300,000
Accounts and notes receivable:		
Trade	$6,200,000	
Other	700,000	
	6,900,000	
Less allowance for doubtful accounts	150,000	

	6,750,000	
Ridge Lending Corporation	3,500,000	10,250,000
Inventories at lower of cost (average or first-in, first-out) or market		5,250,000
Amounts receivable from purchasers of assets sold subsequent to September 30, 1972		3,300,000
Prepaid Expenses		1,000,000
Total current assets		20,100,000
Mortgage receivable (noninterest-bearing, due December 1, 1974)		200,000
Noncurrent accounts and notes receivable:		
Amounts receivable from purchase of assets sold subsequent to September 30, 1972	1,400,000	
Other	650,000	2,050,000
Property, Plant and Equipment:		
Pinball machines	2,900,000	
Other, principally machinery and equipment	2,900,000	
	5,800,000	
Less accumulated depreciation	1,350,000	
	4,450,000	
Land	50,000	
		4,500,000
Assets held for sale, at estimated net realizable value		1,600,000
Excess of cost of companies or operating properties acquired over related net assets		1,200,000
Patents, at cost less amortization		1,500,000
Deferred charges and other assets		1,500,000
		$32,650,000

Liabilities

Current Liabilities:

Notes and loans payable	$ 7,800,000
Long-term debt, portion due within one year	8,200,000
Accounts payable	2,300,000
Accrued expenses and taxes	700,000
Total current liabilities	19,000,000

Long-term debt

6% convertible subordinated debentures	$ 4,700,000	
Ridge Lending Corp., affiliate	500,000	
Other	2,700,000	7,900,000
Deferred federal income tax		100,000
Deferred income		450,000

CAPITAL

Common stock, par value $.10 a share; 4,750,000 shares authorized, 4,080,701 shares issued and outstanding	400,000	
Capital surplus	7,200,000	
Retained deficit	(2,400,000)	
		5,200,000
		$32,650,000

REICHMAN PINBALL MACHINES, INC.

Consoldiated Statement of Income (loss) and Retained Earnings
For the Year Ended September 30, 1972

Sales and Operating Income	$23,000,000
Cost of Sales	15,300,000
	7,700,000
Selling and Administrative Expenses	6,800,000
	900,000
Depreciation and Amortization	800,000
	100,000
Other Income, Principally Interest	300,000
	400,000
Interest Expense	1,600,000
Income (loss) before Provision (credit) for Federal Income Tax and Extraordinary Items	(1,200,000)
Provision (credit) for Federal Income Tax	(300,000)
Net Income (loss) before Extraordinary Items	(900,000)

Extraordinary Items:

Write offs as of October 1, 1971:

| Deferred Research and Development Expenses | $1,500,000 | |
| Deferred Expenses Related to Development of In-plant Recreation Program | 500,000 | |

Write Down to Estimated Net Realizable Value as of September 30, 1972:

Assets Sold Subsequent to September 30, 1972 and assets for sale	800,000 600,000	
Excess of Cost of Companies or Operating Properties Acquired over Related Net Assets Less Federal Income Tax Adjustments	3,400,000 500,000	2,900,000
Net Income (Loss)		(3,800,000)
Retained Earnings—September 30, 1971		1,400,000
Retained Earnings (deficit)—September 30, 1972		$(2,400,000)

Case 9-1

Golden Stores, Inc.[1]

Golden Stores, Inc., operated a chain of department and mail-order stores in the western United States. The chain had experienced a large expansion in recent years, through the opening of new stores and the continuing increase in the region's retail sales. Golden Stores' financial condition was sound (see exhibits 1 and 2). The past few years, however, had seen the growing use of liberal credit terms as a sales tool. By 1974, the company's credit sales had reached 50 per cent of its total sales. This trend, although not new, had important implications from the point of view of the company's finances and accounting.

As indicated in Exhibit 2, Golden Stores' credit sales increased from 41 per cent of $165 million in 1970 to 50 per cent of $202 million in 1974, or from $68 million to $101 million. Thus, substantially all the sales increase in the past 5 years had been additional credit sales. The company was very much aware of this trend; in fact, Golden Stores had been stressing its credit facilities in order to gain new sales and planned to continue this emphasis in the future.

Mr. James Voss, the treasurer of Golden Stores, Inc., was cognizant of the effect that the company's expanding credit volume had on its financial needs. He pointed out that the company's receivables averaged about 8 months' credit sales and that the period was increasing annually. Obviously, this growth in receivables created a major financing need for the company.

Two "long-term" credit plans were offered by Golden Stores to its customers. Almost all credit customers used one of these two plans. The volume of monthly account sales was very small, as customers usually preferred either to pay cash at the time of the sale or to finance their purchases over a period of several months.

The more popular plan was based on a regular installment agreement on some specific purchases. Customers would make a down payment on the articles they selected and pay off the balance plus a finance charge over an agreed period of

[1] Case material of the Harvard Graduate School of Business Administration is prepared as a basis for class discussion, and is not designed to illustrate either effective or ineffective handling of administrative problems.

EXHIBIT 1

GOLDEN STORES, INC.
Consolidated Balance Sheet
December 31, 1974
(All amounts in thousands)

Current Assets

Cash and U.S. Treasury Bills		$ 10,755
Accounts Receivable		
(less $5,900 reserve[a])		68,540
Inventories, at Lower of Cost and Market		35,278
Prepayments		1,434
Total Current Assets		$116,007
Investments, at or below Cost		10,671
Property, Plant, and Equipment at Cost	$28,278	
Less: depreciation	12,474	
Net		15,804
Debenture Discount		169
Total Assets		$142,651

Current Liabilities		
Accounts Payable		$ 5,118
Accrued Expenses		4,638
Federal Income Taxes		7,355
Other Taxes Payable		3,694
Short-term Notes Payable		30,217
Total Current Liabilities		$ 51,022
5% Debentures, due 1996		17,500
Stockholders' Equity		
Capital Stock—$1.00 Par Value	$11,250	
Paid in Surplus	3,420	
Retained Earnings	59,459	
Total Stockholders' Equity		74,129
		$142,651

[a]Comprising deferred finance charges on installment accounts and a provision for bad and doubtful debts (see bottom of Exhibit 3).

EXHIBIT 2

GOLDEN STORES, INC.

Comparative Income Statement Data, 1970 to 1974
($'000,000)

	1974	1975	1972	1971	1970
Net Sales	$202	$186	$180	$178	$165
Net Income before Taxes	20.2	16.9	16.7	17.2	16.7
Year-end Receivables (net)	68.5	58.7	54.0	50.4	44.4
(see Exhibit 3)					
(Percentages)					
Realized Gross Margin[a]	36.0%	35.3%	35.4%	35.8%	36.0%
Credit Sales/Total Sales	50	47	46	44	41
Installment Plan	37	38	39	38	37
Revolving Credit	13	9	7	6	4

[a]Gross margin (sales, less cost of goods sold) expressed as a percentage of net sales.

time.[2] Most of the sales under this plan were so-called "big ticket" items, such as household appliances and furniture, wherein a single purchase represented a large dollar amount.

In recent years, however, Golden Stores had also offered customers with proven creditworthiness the opportunity to finance their purchases of less expensive items, particularly clothing, under a revolving credit plan. Under this plan, approved customers were permitted a monthly maximum purchase on credit. At the same time, they made a monthly payment in reduction of the unpaid balance of their account, the payment being calculated as one-twelfth of the total balance. In this way, 1 year's credit was allowed, and customers could re-utilize the credit granted to them as they paid off their account. Under this plan, a monthly finance charge of 1 per cent of the month's average credit balance was assessed.

ACCOUNTING IMPLICATIONS

The accounting policies that Golden Stores applied to credit sales had been determined when these sales were only a small proportion of the company's total volume. Normal accrual accounting was used; i.e., the sale was shown as revenue when the sale was made, and the profit on the sale was recognized in full at that time. Finance charges on the credit sales were taken into income on a time basis, according to the monthly balances on accounts receivable. The "prepaid" finance charge on installment plan sales was deferred and shown on the balance sheet as a reserve deducted from accounts receivable. Because revolving credit charges were assessed monthly, there was no need for deferral of these finance charges.

[2] The "add-on" for finance charges was 12 1/2 per cent on a year's contract; i.e., 8 1/3 per cent of the face value of the average account, on the basis of the 8-month average for accounts receivable. Thus, the finance charges represented about 7.7 per cent (.083/1.083) of the amount of outstanding installment receivables.

During 1975, as the trend of rising credit sales volume continued, it became apparent to the company's management that their present policies, in effect, produced two possibly unfortunate results. First, immediate recognition of the profit on credit sales meant that the income taxes also had to be provided for and paid, often before a major part of the sales price had been collected in cash. Second, this immediate profit recognition meant that the company's financial statements indicated a source of funds from profits that was, in part, counterbalanced by an application of funds to increased investment in accounts receivable. Both of these phenomena tended to make management's task more difficult: the first because of the cash drain, and the second because of the misleading source of funds that was being indicated.

CHANGE FOR TAX PURPOSES

During 1974 Golden Stores' tax adviser pointed out to the company's management that it could defer paying income taxes on the profit from its installment sales until the actual cash was received. The Internal Revenue Service permitted retailers such as Golden Stores to prorate the gross profit on such sales over the period in which payment was received (Regulation #1.435-1). This had the effect of deferring the gross profit on those sales represented by outstanding accounts receivable. This accounting method was known as the "installment method" and was regarded by the IRS as a remedy to the inequity that arises if income tax is assessed on income not yet actually received in cash.

EXHIBIT 3

GOLDEN STORES, INC.
Accounts Receivable Data, 1970 to 1974 (December 31)
($'000,000)

	1974	*1973*	*1972*	*1971*	*1970*
Installment Accounts	$59.2	$54.7	$51.2	$48.0	$42.6
Revolving Charge Accounts	12.8	6.6	4.8	4.0	2.5
Miscellaneous Accounts	2.4	2.9	3.0	3.1	3.6
	$74.4	$64.2	$59.0	$55.1	$48.7
Less: Reserve[a]	5.9	5.5	5.0	4.7	4.3
Net Total	$68.5	$58.7	$54.0	$50.4	$44.4

[a]See note to balance sheet. The reserve is comprised of:
1. Deferred Finance Charges on Installment Accounts, and
2. Provision for Bad and Doubtful Accounts.

($'000,000)

	1974	*1973*	*1972*	*1971*	*1970*
Deferred Finance Charges on Installment Accounts[b]	4.56	4.21	3.94	3.70	3.28

Provision for Bad and					
Doubtful Accounts	1.34	1.29	1.06	1.00	1.02
Total Reserve	5.90	5.50	5.00	4.70	4.30

[b]7.7% as per footnote 2 on page 00.

To illustrate the installment method, suppose that Golden Stores had used the method in calculating their 1974 income tax. From the $59.2 million installment accounts receivable (Exhibit 3) would first be deducted the amount representing the finance charge add-ons, 7.7 per cent, $4.6 million. To this net receivables amount, $54.6 million, would be applied the 1974 gross margin percentage, 36 per cent (Exhibit 2), yielding $19.7 million deferred gross margin. Because the average installment account receivable is paid within about 8 months, for simplicity it can be assumed that this $54.6 million in receivables will be collected in 1975. Thus, in 1975. Golden Stores would have to pay taxes on the $19.7 million gross margin deferred from 1974. However, the company would have a new dererral in 1975 arising from the new receivables accumulated during that year.

One complication of the installment method of accounting for tax purposes was the possibility of double taxation in the year following the changeover to the new method. This double taxation arose because, prior to the changeover, income taxes had already been paid on total profits as determined by accrual accounting, regardless of whether the total sales providing these profits had been collected in cash. In the changeover year, the gross profit from the uncollected sales of the preceding year, already taxed in that year, would be taxed a second time when the cash was received. The only way this double taxation could be avoided was for the retailer to convert all of his receivables to cash at the end of the year before the change to the installment method. Golden Stores' tax adviser explained that this could be accomplished by selling the year-end installment sales receivables to a "factor," who would give the company cash (less the factor's service charge) for the receivables and would then collect the receivables himself.

The installment method of tax calculation appeared attractive to Golden Stores' management, because the tax deferral would improve the company's cash flow. They inquired of their tax adviser whether the same method could be used on their revolving credit sales, but were told that the IRS was awaiting a judgment from a superior court before agreeing to extend the method to revolving credit plans. Nevertheless, management decided to apply the method to their installment receivables beginning January 1, 1975.

QUESTIONS

1. If Golden Stores had adopted the installment method on January 1, 1970, by what amount would their cash flow have been improved in the years 1970-1974. (Assume a 50 per cent tax rate, ignore the provision for doubtful accounts.)

2. Should Mr. Voss also adopt the installment basis of accounting for reporting to Golden Stores' stockholders? What factors should he consider in his analysis? Should all retail businesses use the installment method of recognizing gross profit?

Case 9-2

Charles Crowne Company[1]

At a meeting on January 16, 1974, of the three officers of the Charles Crowne Company, a general construction firm located in a large midwestern city, Mr. John Crowne, vice president and treasurer, raised a question concerning the method the company was using in recording profits on its construction contracts. He remarked that during a recent conversation he had been told by the treasurer and office manager of a building supply firm that a construction company could report its profits either on a percentage of completion or on a completed contract basis and that the choice of method could have a material effect on a company's net income and financial statements. John Crowne's statement puzzled the other two officers, who asked for a detailed explanation of the alternatives. In reply, John Crowne stated that he could not explain the percentage method or its significance since time pressure had prevented him from questioning his friend about the methods. He added that he was certain that the company was presently following the job completion method of recording profit or loss on contracts only at the completion of the contracts.

John noted that the company's financial statements were furnished to architects and bonding companies that used them as a means of appraising a contractor's ability to perform a contract he was bidding on. In view of the way in which the statements were used, all officers agreed they should be aware of the available alternatives since the use of a different method might influence the company's success in obtaining contracts from architects and gaining coverage from bonding companies.

Another factor mentioned was the future prosperity of the Charles Crowne Company and the construction industry in general. Although over the long run the officers expected to expand the volume of company business, the prospects for 1974 did not appear too favorable. As a final consideration, John Crowne noted

[1] Case material of the Harvard Graduate School of Business Administration is prepared as a basis for class discussion. Cases are not designed to present illustrations of either correct or incorrect handling of administrative problems.

that the company would soon have to furnish financial statements with its request to the Second National Bank for financial assistance for a proposed office and storage building that would be constructed in the spring of 1974. John wondered whether the company's bank credit standing would be influenced by a change in accounting methods.

At the conclusion of the meeting, John Crowne agreed to question his friend about the available alternatives in detail, to review their application to the Charles Crowne Company, and then to submit his recommendation to the other two officers.

COMPANY BACKGROUND

In 1936, Mr. Charles Crowne founded his own masonry contracting firm as a single proprietorship employing a crew of five men. Although the firm grew slowly up to 1961, Mr. Crowne had restricted the company's operations to the masonry business. In 1961 Mr. Crowne's son, John, joined the firm after obtaining a degree in architectural engineering. Shortly thereafter, the company started a gradual move into the general construction field. By 1966, the firm was engaged almost entirely as a general contractor, devoting its major effort to institutional projects such as garages, churches, and fire stations.

In bidding on projects as a general contractor, the Charles Crowne Company usually compiled estimates of the cost to construct a project, adding to these costs a percentage for overhead and profit. A large part of the estimates would be based on the bids of subcontractors for special portions of a job. The general contractor would then compile the total estimate for the project and submit a bid. If the contract was obtained, the contractor would then award subcontracts to those subcontractors who had submitted the lowest bid for portions of the project. The contracts received were almost always of a fixed-price nature.

On January 1, 1973, the company was incorporated with Mr. Charles Crowne, president, holding 60 per cent of the common stock; John Crowne, vice president and treasurer, holding 30 per cent; and Larry Shane, who was not related to the Crownes, owning 10 per cent and holding the position of secretary and office manager.

Although the company acted as general contractor on all projects in which it was engaged, it continued to perform all masonry work on its contracts. In addition, the company employed a force of carpenters on company jobs to handle all rough carpentry work and also to assist in supervision of company-employed laborers and the subcontractors. Most work on company projects was performed by subcontractors.

Mr. Charles Crowne frequently acted as the general superintendent on the most important company jobs while John Crowne traveled between all other job sites carrying out general supervision and checking on work progress and performance. Mr. Shane handled all office work, including the compilation of estimates and proposals for new contracts. Each evening the officers met to discuss the status of jobs and future plans of the company.

RESULTS OF 1973

Because of the high volume of institutional construction activity, 1973 was a record year for the Charles Crowne Company. Sales value of contracts completed in 1973, according to preliminary figures, was $1,143,303.06, as compared with the previous high in 1969 of $819,348.76. Net profit before taxes and officers' compensation in 1973 was estimated at $106,113.74 whereas $62,809.12 had been earned in 1972 (see Exhibits 1, 2, 3, 4).

EXHIBIT 1

CHARLES CROWNE COMPANY
Income Statement
For Year Ended December 31, 1973

Sales Value of Completed Contracts		$1,143,303.06
Cost of Contracts Completed		1,026,112.10
Gross Income from Contracts		$ 117,190.96
Add: Discounts Earned		10,832.66
		$ 128,023.62
Less:		
General and Administrative Expense	$21,909.88	
Officers' Compensation	69,140.00	91,049.88
Net Income before Tax		$ 36,973.74
Federal Taxes		13,893.22
Net Income		$ 23,080.52

EXHIBIT 2
CHARLES CROWNE COMPANY
Sales and Income, 1967-1972

	Sales Value of Contracts Completed	Gross Income from Contracts (including discounts earned)	Profit before[a] Officers' Compensation and Tax
1972	$661,384.74	$87,565.50	$62,809.12
1971	340,381.42	38,199.54	24,589.42
1970	581,220.50	49,487.42	32,562.96[b]
1969	819,348.76	77,423.84	59,475.38
1968	548,424.04	77,799.12	61,713.66
1967	481,302.00	63,071.82	52,816.34

[a]During the years 1967-1972 the company was operated as a partnership.

[b]In 1970 the company suffered a loss of $6,921.26 on a contract having a value of $63,628. This was the largest loss incurred in recent years.

EXHIBIT 3

CHARLES CROWNE COMPANY
Contracts Completed in 1973

Contracts	Costs	Profit
$ 9,061.10	$ 7,390.38	$ 1,670.72
6,970.00	6,566.60	403.40
82,493.66	72,055.38	10,438.28
23,652.00	24,136.52	(484.52)
6,114.00	4,838.70	1,275.30
23,569.00	22,141.30	1,427.70
147,164.00	141,677.58	5,486.42
45,823.84	41,250.24	4,573.60
58,011.66	53,530.28	4,481.38
362,522.40	320,875.78	41,646.62
33,600.00	32,705.52	894.48
43,702.00	37,265.74	6,436.26
27,731.08	25,872.30	1,858.78
3,801.30	3,110.62	690.68
90,199.76	78,103.42	12,096.34
55,314.00	47,195.98	8,118.02
14,070.00	13,556.50	513.50
37,598.00	29,630.64	7,967.36
30,206.06	28,995.40	1,210.66
41,699.20	35,213.22	6,485.98
$1,143,303.06	$1,026,112.10	$117,190.96

The status report of contracts in process (see Exhibit 5) as of December 31, 1973, showed that three contracts having a total value of $464,464 were in various stages of completion. A total cost of $190,816.52 had been incurred to date on these contracts. Of the three contracts the company had in process at the close of the calendar year, two were for fire stations and one for a municipal garage. All contracts had been started after August 1973 and were estimated to be completed in the spring or early summer of 1974. No revenue or costs on these contracts had been recorded in the income statement for 1973.

OUTLOOK FOR 1974

The officers of the company felt that the construction outlook for their area was not too bright. Overall construction activity seemed likely to be high, but the officers believed that profit margins would fall. Increasing competition in the field of institutional construction was expected because a downturn in residential building was forcing residential contractors into the institutional field. As a result, the company had lowered its provision for general overhead and profit in recent bids for new contracts to approximately 10 per cent of the contract sales value. In the past, it had been company practice to include a profit of 10 per cent, plus a

EXHIBIT 4

CHARLES CROWNE COMPANY
Balance Sheet as of December 31, 1973

Assets

Current Assets

Cash in Bank	$ 74,317.34
Cash on Hand	100.00
Accounts Receivable—Contracts	84,559.22
Accounts Receivable—Other	12,342.18
Raw Materials Inventory	49,372.86
Work in Process	(7,183.48)
Deposit Accounts	2,341.86
Notes Receivable	11,918.78
	$227,768.76

Property Assets

Trucks, Tools, and Equipment	$12,922.98	
Office Furniture	2,090.66	
Less: Accumulated Depreciation		10,832.32
Total Assets		$238,601.08

Liabilities

Current Liabilities

Accounts Payable—Trade	$ 75,426.66
Accounts Payable—Miscellaneous	3,503.24
Accrued Taxes	12,531.66
Accrued Insurance	2,079.00
Accrued Management Compensation	21,980.00
	$115,520.56

Stockholders

Stock	$100,000.00	
Retained income	23,080.52	
		123,080.52
Total Liabilities and Equity		$238,601.08

EXHIBIT 5

CHARLES CROWNE COMPANY

Status Report of Contracts

Project	Amount of Contract	Gross Billing 12/31/73	Retainage 10%	Net Billings Rendered 12/31/73	Net Billings Collected 12/31/73	Costs to 12/31/73	Cost Estimated to Complete
#220 Fire Station	$232,294.00	$116,970.00	$11,697.00	$105,273.00	$ 65,446.66	$102,751.50	$106,230
#221 Municipal Garage	110,220.00	90,780.00	9,078.00	81,702.00	47,602.00	76,578.18	9,040
#224 Fire Station	121,950.00	12,250.00	1,250.00	11,025.00	392.12	11,486.84	100,250
	$464,464.00	$220,000.00	$22,000.00	$198,000.00	$113,440.78	$190,816.52	$215,520

provision for general and administrative overhead of 5 per cent in its proposals. Although the officers realized that it was possible that the company might register losses on one or more contracts as a result of bidding at a lower figure than normal, they felt that the losses, if incurred, would be small, and hoped that, in the aggregate, volume would tend to wash out any individual loss and give the company a fair profit. Company records showed that where losses had been incurred on contracts in the past, they had never exceeded 11 per cent of the contract value.

Company officers expected to submit bids in 1974 on projects that were similar in nature to projects in progress or recently completed. As of January 8, 1974, the company had no backlog of contracts on which it had not started work. Activity in the granting of contracts was usually low in January and February but customarily picked up in March.

It was not the present intention of company officers to try to obtain contracts for projects having an individual value in excess of $400,000. There were several reasons for this policy. First was the fact that officers desired to spread risk among a number of contracts. Second was a consideration of keeping the company name before the architects in the area. Architects generally acted as agents for project owners and were usually responsible for examining the reliability of contractors who were bidding on a project. Contractors who were unknown or not considered reliable usually had their bids eliminated from further consideration. The officers of the company recalled that it had taken several years to acquaint architects in their area with the company name and its ability to perform a job. If they committed the company to one or two large long-term contracts, the officers believed they would effectively remove the name of the company from the sight of architects for a considerable period of time. They were unwilling to do this since they felt that they would have difficulty in reestablishing the company with architects when the long-term contracts were completed.

A third reason for not seeking contracts over $400,000 concerned the very important role of the bonding companies. Charles Crowne Company, like every contractor, was usually required to post certain bonds with the architect (or the project owner) which guaranteed that the company would complete the contract according to specifications. Frequently, a clause was included in contracts which specified that the contractor would pay a penalty if the project was not completed by a given date. Nonfulfillment of the stated provisions could result in the forfeiture of the bond and a consequent payment by the bonding company in the stipulated amount of the coverage to the architect and project owner. In order to prevent contractors from overextending themselves, the bonding companies imposed a maximum limit on the contracts that any contractor could have outstanding at any one time. The bonding companies would not provide a bond on a contract if as a result of taking on this contract the total sales value of outstanding contracts exceeded ten times the contractor's net worth. Thus, with the Charles Crowne Company's net worth as of December 31, 1973, of $123,080.52, total contracts of $1,230,800 could be handled at the present time. Therefore, by taking on contracts having a value over $400,000, the officers believed the company would be restricted in satisfying the first and second considerations outlined above. Even if the ratio should be suddenly increased, thereby allowing the company to expand its work, there would be further problems in obtaining a capable work force and acquiring the necessary equipment.

ACCOUNTING PROCESS

Recording of Costs. The company's accounting system was not complex and was capable of being handled on a part-time basis by an outside accountant. This accountant worked two nights a week at the company offices updating the cost and general ledgers, the general journal, and handling other necessary accounting work. The accountant's main job was to keep accurate records of the costs incurred for each job or contract. Separate subledgers for each contract were kept to facilitate this work.

As job costs were incurred by the company, they were posted or charged to the appropriate job or contract ledger after being recorded in the general journal. A voucher was also made out recording the supplier's or subcontractor's name and address along with the amount payable and filed as a liability. Charges for company-employed labor were recorded at the job site and forwarded back to the office. The recording specified for each man the hours worked, his rate, and the nature of the work performed. These recordings, along with being posted to the appropriate jobs, were also used as the basis for computing payrolls. The total of the balances in the job ledger accounts was the company's "work in process."

The job cost accounts tended to be similar for each job. Separate subaccounts were maintained for each subcontract. For instance, on Job #220, a fire station under construction, there were over twenty subcontracts for various portions of the total job.

Separate job subaccounts were also established for major categories of direct costs incurred by the company. For example, separate job accounts were kept for company masonry labor and carpentry labor and for company-purchased masonry and carpeting materials. Separate project accounts were also provided when unusual portions of a contract were to be completed by the company. For instance, in completing Job #220, the company was to install the slide poles to be used in the fire station, and also erect a flag pole. Costs incurred for these purposes would be charged to special slide pole and flag pole accounts. In addition, job accounts were established for the supervisory costs of each job and for the cost of performance bond insurance.

Finally, a separate account called "general conditions" was also established for each job. It was used for all job costs not charged to other accounts. The account contained such items as the cost of the construction shack, telephone and other utilities, general office supplies, wages of timekeeper and watchman (if necessary), and the wages of laborers that could not be easily separated into other accounts. This account did not include any of the company's general and administrative expenses that were not allocated to the jobs.

Billing. On contracts in process the Charles Crowne Company usually submitted a monthly "application for payment" to the architect who represented the project owner. Exhibit 6 shows the detail provided on the application. The items with an asterisk beside them are for company portions of the job while the remainder are for subcontracted sections of the job.

Several steps were involved in determing the amount billed by the contractor. First, an officer of the company estimated the physical percentage of completion of each major portion of the contract. Thus, in the case of the masonry item on

FA
102R

AIA
FORM
702

Exhibit 6

FIELD COPY　　　　　　　　　　　　CONTRACTOR'S APPLICATION NO. Four (4)

ARCHITECT'S JOB No. 56133　　　　　　　　　PERIOD FROM Dec. 1　　TO Dec. 31

TO City of Burriston　　　　　　　　　　　　　　　　OWNER. APPLICATION IS MADE FOR

PAYMENT, AS SHOWN BELOW, IN CONNECTION WITH THE Architectural WORK

FOR YOUR Fire Station PROJECT

	DESCRIPTION OF WORK	CONTRACT AMOUNT	THIS APPLICATION		COMPLETED		BALANCE TO FINISH
			LABOR	MATERIALS	%	TO DATE	
*	Performance Bond	2,400				2,400	
	Site Work	3,500				3,150	350
*	Masonry	51,200	6,120		90	46,080	5,120
	Concrete Work	16,140				8,910	7,230
	Precase Concrete Panels	25,520	18,520		72.5	18,520	7,000
	Aluminum Sash	8,030					8,030
	Sash Erection	1,700					1,700
	Structural Steel	24,580				19,600	4,980
	Glass & Glazing	5,240					5,240
*	Carpentry	8,974					8,974
	Finish Hardware	3,080					3,080
	Modern Fold Door	740					740
	Roofing & Sheet Metal	6,600					6,600
	Overhead Doors	21,560					21,560
	Hollow Metal Work	6,640				2,000	4,640
	Reailient Floor & Base	3,390					3,390
	Hard Tile	1,540					1,540
	Acquistical Work	3,300					3,300
*	Chalkboard & Tackboards	500					500
*	Caulking & Weatherstrips	1,020					1,020
*	Aluminum Sign Allowance	600					600
*	Plaque Allowance	400					400
	Exterior Louvers	730				730	–
*	Slide Poles	9,020		8,020	89	8,020	1,000
	Asphalt Paving	5,620				2,810	2,810
*	Flag Pole	1,020		750	73.5	750	270
	Plastering	4,710					4,710
	Painting	3,190					3,190
	Toilet Partitions	620					620
*	General Conditions	6,400	1,000		62.5	4,000	2,400
	Curtain Wall Panels	4,330					4,330
	TOTAL	232,294	25,640	8,770	50	116,970	115,324

THIS IS TO CERTIFY THAT THE WORK AS LISTED ABOVE HAS BEEN COMPLETED IN ACCORDANCE WITH THE CONTRACT DOCUMENTS, THAT ALL LAWFUL CHARGES FOR LABOR, MATERIALS, ETC., COVERED BY PREVIOUS CERTIFICATES FOR PAYMENT HAVE BEEN PAID AND THAT A PAYMENT IS NOW DUE IN THE AMOUNT OF

Thirty Four Thousand, Four Hundred, and 10 00/100 DOLLARS ($ 34,410.00

FROM WHICH RETAINAGE OF 10 % AS SET OUT IN THE CONTRACT DOCUMENTS SHALL BE DEDUCTED $ 3,441.00

Net Billing　　$ 30,969.00

Charles Crowne Company CONTRACTORS

DATE 1/3 19 74　　　　PER Larry Shane

Exhibit 6, it was estimated that masonry work was 90 per cent complete at the end of the month. Since masonry had been estimated at 78 per cent of completion at the close of the prior month, then 12 per cent of the $51,200 value attached to masonry, or $6,120, was deemed to be the gross amount that should be billed for the current month. Noteworthy is the fact that costs incurred to date as a percentage of total estimated costs did not determine the percentage of completion.

Thus, the gross billing of $6,120 for the current month could be either equal to, less than, or greater than the actual costs incurred in the month plus the allowances for profit and overhead that were predicted in bidding the job.

As in the case of masonry, a similar estimating procedure was followed on the other items of the job. The items were then summed to obtain the gross billing for the current month. From this total gross billing an amount called "retainage," agreed to in the contract as 10 per cent of the gross billing, was deducted to obtain the net billing due the contractor. The application was then forwarded to the architect who had the job of verifying the percentage of physical completion claimed by the contractor. If the architect considered the percentage billed as valid, he certified the application and requested on a separate form that the project owner forward the net billing to the contractor. The contractor usually received his progress payment within 15 days after the date of billing.

Recording of Income. As mentioned above, the company used the completed contract method in recording income from contracts. Under this system the profit or loss on a contract was not booked until the contract was completed and accepted by the project owner.

The company recorded the billings, net of retainage, with an entry such as the following one for Job #220 in December:

> dr. Accounts Receivable–Contracts (Job #220) $30,969.00
>
> cr. Work in Process (Job #220) $30,969.00

Using this method the work in process account for Job #220 had a credit balance in it as of December 31, 1973, which represented billings (net of retainage) in excess of costs.

At the final billing of a contract, the company billed the owner for all retainage, using the same entry as above, and thus crediting the retainage to the work-in-process account. When the contract was complete, the credit balance in the work-in-process account was the profit on the contract. This amount was then closed out to a profit and loss account.

QUESTIONS

1. Determine the effect on net income for 1973 of the three incomplete projects (Exhibit 5) if the percentage of completion method of revenue recognition is adopted by Charles Crowne Company for financial statement (but not income tax) purposes. Consider each of the following methods of estimating degree of completion:

   (a). Percentage of cost incurred to total estimated cost.

   (b). Independent estimate of degree of completion as used by Charles Crowne Company for billing purposes. (It may be assumed that billings have been brought up to date as of December 31, 1973.)

2. How would the adoption of a percentage of completion method be reflected on the Charles Crowne Company balance sheet as of December 31, 1973?

3. Assume that during January 1974, additional costs of $17,248.50 were incurred on project #220. Difficulties were encountered during the month, and on January 31, 1974, it is estimated that the cost to complete the project will amount to $100,000. As of January 31, 1974, gross billings on project #220 total $125,000. Using the two percentage of completion methods, determine the effect of project #220 on net income for January.

4. What should John Crowne's recommendations be?

Case 9-3

Trans Union Corporation[1]

The following excerpt is taken from the president's Letter in the 1972 Trans Union Corporation annual report:

> ...your management has become quite concerned about the serious understatement of our reported earnings that is caused by the way in which we are required to handle our "deferred taxes." The deferred tax account arises primarily because, in order to encourage the construction of all types of rail cars, we are permitted to depreciate our tank cars much more rapidly for tax purposes than they actually wear out. While the accounting for deferred taxes is somewhat complicated, the understatement of earnings can be readily grasped by referring to page 10 where we compute our net income for the year 1972.
>
> On page 10 we have set out the gross revenues for 1972 and have then deducted the related expenses. All of the expenses which we have deducted on this page have already been paid or will be paid in early 1973. The one exception to this statement is deferred taxes, which we have deducted in the amount of approximately $13.4 million. Unlike the other expenses, *this $13.4 million will not be paid for an average of approximately 18 years*! During the 18-year period we are not required to pay any interest on this amount, but we are still required to deduct it today just as though it had already been paid.
>
> It is common knowledge that a dollar due in 18 years is not worth a dollar today. Who would pay one dollar today for just the right to receive one dollar 18 years from now? The same principle applies to expenses. An obligation to pay $13.4 million in 1990 does not require us to set aside $13.4 million today. If we were to set aside only half that amount today and were to earn 4% interest on it, it would total $13.4 million in 1990.

[1]This case was prepared by Guillermo J. Fernandez, Research Assistant, under the supervision of Associate Professor John K. Shank, as the basis for class discussion rather than to illustrate either the effective or ineffective handling of an administrative situation.

In other words, when a liability is due at some time in the future, simple logic says we should discount the amount to determine what the real liability is today. If that were done in our case, we would deduct substantially les than $13.4 million in determining our 1972 income, and our earnings per share would be materially higher.

Our statement that we will pay the deferred taxes 18 years from now is quite conservative. There are well known authorities who argue cogently that the $13.4 million will really never be paid unless the Company were to liquidate its tank car fleet and go out of business, and very likely not even then. These authorities include one of the very top auditing firms and the head of one of the most prestigious graduate schools of business in the country.

We have been forced to account for our deferred taxes by ignoring the 18 year delay in payment, because the Accounting Principles Board (APB) has so ruled. It is interesting to note that at one time the APB created a subcommittee of its own members to study the problem of deferred taxes. In 1966 that committee expressed a preference for discounting, but the APB overruled them. The APB prohibited discounting until a further research study could be made, but they have actually done nothing on the subject in the six years since that time.

It is also pertinent to point out that the handling of deferred taxes required by the APB is directly contrary to the handling they require for pension liabilities. If an employee works for us in 1972 and thereby acquires the right to receive a pension of $1,000 in the year 1990, the APB will not permit us to deduct $1,000 in 1972 but will permit a deduction of only the discounted amount of such future payment. This is directly opposite to the treatment they require for deferred taxes, and the reason for this inconsistency has never been explained by the APB.

The APB is being replaced by a new body known as the Financial Accounting Standards Board. It is only now being formed, but when it is functioning we would hope that it would address itself to this problem. In the meantime we wanted you to understand the situation in order to properly appraise the quality of our earnings.

President

The full financial statements and footnotes for 1972, along with the auditors' opinion, are reproduced as Exhibit 1.

The casewriter discussed the deferred tax issue with Mr. Donald B. Romans, a graduate of a well-known eastern business school, who is vice president-finance for Trans Union.

WALL STREET REACTION TO TRANS UNION'S ACTIONS

Mr. Romans stated that the "market" seemed to be totally insensitive to the qualitative issues raised by the president in the annual report. Trans Union is listed

EXHIBIT 1

TRANS UNION CORPORATION

Auditors' Report

To the Stockholders of Trans Union Corporation:

We have examined the consolidated balance sheet of Trans Union Corporation (a Delaware corporation) and subsidiaries as of December 31, 1972, and December 31, 1971, and the related consolidated statements of income, retained earnings, additional capital, and source and use of funds for the five years ended December 31, 1972. Our examination was made in accordance with generally accepted auditing standards, and accordingly included such tests of the accounting records and such other auditing procedures as we considered necessary in the circumstances.

In our opinion, the accompanying consolidated balance sheet and consolidated statements of income, retained earnings, additional capital, and source and use of funds present fairly the financial position of Trans Union Corporation and subsidiaries as of December 31, 1972, and December 31, 1971, and the results of their operations and the source and use of funds for the five years ended December 31, 1972, in conformity with generally accepted accounting principles consistently applied during the periods.

Chicago, Illinois,
January 22, 1973.

TRANS UNION CORPORATION AND SUBSIDIARIES
Consolidated Statement of Income
For the Year Ended December 31
(Dollars in thousands)

	1972
Revenues:	
Net Sales	$135,387
Services	153,931
Net Income from Finance Lease Business	1,223
Net Income from 50% Owned Companies	1,202
Interest Income	1,642
Royalties and Other	1,573
Amortization of Investment Tax Credit	462
	$295,420

Costs and Expenses:

Cost of Sales	$102,123
Cost of Services	81,492
Selling, General and Administrative Expenses	46,747
Interest Expense	19,693
Minority Interest in Ecodyne Corporation	335
	$250,390

Net Income Before Income Taxes	$ 45,030

Provision for Income Taxes:

Current	$ 4,750
Deferred	13,440
Investment Tax Credit (Deferred)	890
	$ 19,080

Net Income Before Extraordinary Items	$ 25,950
Extraordinary Items, Net of Income Taxes	—
Net Income (Including Extraordinary Items)	$ 25,950

Per Share of Common Stock—

Net Income Before Extraordinary Items	$2.61
Extraordinary Items	—
Net Income (Including Extraordinary Items)	$2.61

1971	*1970*	*1969*	*1968*
$110,324	$109,053	$109,532	$ 92,564
145,936	134,404	120,832	115,924
570	132	—	—
1,483	787	688	(287)
1,992	1,427	850	467
1,585	877	695	737
432	388	302	211
$262,322	$247,068	$232,899	$209,616
$ 83,433	$ 80,676	$ 83,132	$ 71,175
79,282	68,422	61,954	61,318
40,965	40,997	37,492	28,777
18,026	17,372	15,067	10,868
—	—	—	—
$221,706	$207,467	$197,645	$172,138
$ 40,616	$ 39,601	$ 35,254	$ 37,478
$ 2,418	$ 2,315	$ 2,737	$ 6,086
13,980	13,440	10,850	9,920
1,172	1,995	1,973	1,834
$ 17,570	$ 17,750	$ 15,560	$ 17,840

$ 23,046	$ 21,851	$ 19,694	$ 19,638
6,060	1,890	1,625	–
$ 29,106	$ 23,741	$ 21,319	$ 19,638
$2.32	$2.20	$1.98	$1.97
.61	.19	.16	–
$2.93	$2.39	$2.14	$1.97

on both the New York and London Stock Exchanges.

Mr. Romans further stated that security analysts in their research reports regarding Trans Union agree with the company's viewpoint and philosophy but that this agreement, in his opinion, has not been reflected in the company's price earnings ratio or its stock price. Some research reports have mentioned that the deferred income tax charges in the income statement appear "excessive," but in no instance have the analysts actually adjusted the reported earnings per share accordingly.

DEFERRED TAXES: DEBT? EQUITY? NEITHER?

Mr. Romans expressed the view that analysts for the bond rating agencies, such as Moodys, routinely treat deferred income taxes as equity capital in computing debt/equity ratios and coverage of fixed charges in their evaluation procedures. He went on to recount the following incident. While having lunch with three bankers, he requested that each independently compute the company's debt/equity ratio. Three different numbers were produced! Deferred income taxes were considered by one of the bankers to be equivalent to debt, by one of the bankers to be equivalent to equity, and by one of the bankers to be properly disregarded altogether in making the computation. The latter approach, Mr. Romans added, is most common among debtors and analysts. He feels that most of them seem either to disregard the balance sheet's deferred income taxes account entirely or to adopt the more conservative approach and consider it as debt, despite the fact that the company and its auditors are very careful not to label the item as a liability.

MANAGEMENT v. THE ACCOUNTING PROFESSION

Mr. Romans expressed the opinion that the "market" will never adopt an earnings measurement scheme different from that required in the annual report by the accountants, no matter how strongly management objects. He went on, "It appears that security analysts and investors give more credence to earnings per share as computed by the certified public accountants than to the economic realities of discounted cash flows. Stockholders, bankers, and analysts acknowledge the facts as we presented them, but they hesitate in applying this to the valuation process for our common stock.

"In essence," Mr. Romans concluded, "management is at the mercy of the accountants in terms of the quality of the earnings as perceived by the investment community."

QUESTIONS

1. Estimate the impact on the 1972 and 1971 financial statements if deferred taxes were discounted as proposed by Mr. Van Gorkom.

2. In your opinion, should deferred taxes be discounted?

3. Consider carefully the strategy adopted by Trans Union in this matter. What options are open to them? Why did they select the approach they did? What can they gain? What can they lose? If you were Mr. Van Gorkom, what would you do in the 1973 annual report?

TRANS UNION CORPORATION AND SUBSIDIARIES

Consolidated Balance Sheet

December 31

(Dollars in Thousands)

ASSETS

	1972	1971	1972	1971
Cash			$ 23,181	$ 18,381
Accounts Receivable, including $56,675,000 and $51,812,000, respectively, due within one year			63,393	59,716
Inventories (lower of cost or market):				
Materials and Supplies	$ 20,638	$ 20,728		
Finished and In Process	23,593	16,912	44,231	37,640
Prepaid Expenses and Deferred Charges			12,809	11,833
Investments:				
Land Held for Resale, at cost	$ 34,276	$ 31,225		
Finance Lease Subsidiaries	13,307	8,942		
Goodwill of Acquired Businesses	14,650	12,565		
7% Debentures due in 1974	8,500	8,500		
Other	12,647	6,592	83,380	67,824
Tank Car Lease Fleet (minimum future rentals under existing leases at December 31, 1972 total $287,981,000, of which $68,414,000, is due within one year):				
Cost	$578,846	$567,435		
Accumulated Depreciation	(175,514)	(173,156)	403,322	394,279
Ocean Vessel Fleet (minimum future receipts under existing contracts at December 31, 1972 total $106,185,000, of which $28,121,000, is due within one year):				
Cost	$104,370	$ 78,351		
Accumulated Depreciation	(28,084)	(25,447)	76,286	52,904

	1972	1971
Fixed Assets, at cost:		
Land	$ 3,686	$ 2,755
Building and Leasehold improvements	37,608	35,555
Equipment	53,796	47,570
Accumulated Depreciation	(33,619)	(30,026)
	61,471	55,854
	$768,083	$698,431

(Dollars in thousands)

LIABILITIES, DEFERRED ITEMS AND STOCKHOLDERS' EQUITY

	1972	1971
Accounts Payable	$ 26,842	$ 18,071
Accrued Expenses	29,830	28,095
Federal Income Taxes Payable	4,720	5,820
Borrowed Debt:		
Due within one year	$ 79,191	$ 53,776
Due from one to five years	119,068	115,586
Due after five years	157,349	167,901
	355,608	337,263
Total Liabilities	$417,000	$389,249
Minority Interest In Ecodyne Corporation	6,073	—
Deferred Items:		
Federal Income Taxes	$132,530	$119,090
Investment Tax Credit	10,550	10,100
	143,080	129,190
Stockholders' Equity:		
Preferred Stock	$ —	$ —
Common Stock	10,577	10,526
Additional Capital	68,788	59,194
Retained Earnings	129,006	115,983
Less Reacquired Common Stock, at Cost	(6,441)	(5,711)
	201,930	179,992
	$768,083	$698,431

Case 9-4

Southern Railway Company[1]

The following excerpt is taken from the president's letter in the 1972 annual report of the Southern Railway Company (Southern):

> ... Southern Railway's net consolidated income after all taxes was $85,335,000 in 1972, up 17.4 per cent from the $72,715,000 earned in 1971. This represents earnings per common share of $5.74 in 1972 compared with $4.87 in the preceding year. Both net income and per-share earnings are stated on the basis that Southern is required to use in reporting to the Interstate Commerce Commission.
>
> If these earnings were stated on the basis of generally accepted accounting principles as used by most industrial companies (which do not take into account the effect of faster write off of assets for tax purposes), the earnings would be $3.94 per share in 1972 and $3.45 per share in 1971. In both comparisons of per-share earnings, the 1971 figures have been restated to reflect the two for one split of Southern's stock that became effective on June 5, 1972. An explanation of Southern's accounting policies is included with the notes of financial statements in this report. ...

The footnote relating to income taxes to which the president refers is Note 3, which is reproduced as Exhibit 2 of this case. The 1972 income statement and balance sheet and the auditors' opinion are reproduced as Exhibit 1.

The company's policy of *not* using interperiod income tax allocation as required by the Accounting Principles Board results in an "except for" opinion by Price, Waterhouse. Such an opinion is usually grounds for suspension of trading by the SEC and delisting by the New York Stock Exchange. This case reviews the viewpoints of the various parties involved in this situation.

---

[1] This case was prepared by Guillermo J. Fernandez, Research Assistant, under the supervision of Associate Professor John K. Shank, as the basis for class discussion rather than to illustrate effective or ineffective handling of an administrative situation.

EXHIBIT 1

SOUTHERN RAILWAY COMPANY & CONSOLIDATED SUBSIDIARIES
Statement of Income Years 1972 and 1971
(Thousands of dollars)

	1972	1971
Railway operating revenues:	$698,635	$620,712
Freight	3,311	3,379
Passenger	4,777	6,315
Mail	17,075	16,999
Other	723,798	647,405
Other income:		
Recovery under service interruption policy	—	10,590
All other	14,165	12,454
Total income	737,963	670,449
Railway operating expenses:		
Maintenance of way and structures	119,681	113,197
Maintenance of equipment	127,673	116,281
Transportation	213,616	189,088
Other	48,165	44,734
	509,135	463,300
Taxes other than federal income	51,114	45,307
Freight car time/mileage (received)	(4,226)	(4,280)
Other equipment rent expense	30,754	26,974
Joint facility rent expense	931	862
Miscellaneous deductions from income	7,303	7,134
Fixed charges, principally interest	42,464	38,733
Total expenses	637,475	578,030
Income before federal income taxes	100,488	92,419
Less: Federal income taxes—Note 3	15,153	19,704
Net Consolidated Income for the Year	$ 85,335	$ 72,715
Per average share of common stock outstanding:		
In accordance with ICC accounting regulations	$5.74	$4.87
In accordance with generally accepted accounting principles (GAAP)—Note 3	$3.94	$3.45

SOUTHERN RAILWAY COMPANY & CONSOLIDATED SUBSIDIARIES
Balance Sheet
December 31, Years 1972 and 1971
(Thousands of dollars)

ASSETS	1972	197:
Current assets:		
Cash and short-term investments	$ 123,843	$ 101,95(
Accounts receivable	74,942	67,85;
Materials, supplies and other	22,675	20,95(
	221,460	190,76:
Investments in and advances to affiliates—Note 1	11,021	11,81:
Other assets	27,939	14,817
Properties—Note 4	1,470,319	1,425,376
	$1,730,739	$1,642,76!

LIABILITIES AND SHAREHOLDERS' EQUITY		
Current liabilities:		
Accounts payable and accrued expenses	$ 130,459	$ 127,228
Federal income taxes—Note 3	9,581	5,110
Current maturities of long-term debt—Note 5	48,562	45,767
	188,602	178,105
Long-term debt—Note 5	584,156	553,565
Reserve for federal income taxes—Note 3	30,692	35,522
Reserves and other liabilities—Note 4	19,158	23,634
Total liabilities	822,608	790,826
Shareholders' equity:		
Preferred stock—Note 6	58,694	58,694
Common stock—Note 6	143,545	143,545
Capital surplus	13,352	13,352
Income retained in the business	692,540	636,352
Total shareholders' equity	908,131	851,943
	$1,730,739	$1,642,769

Opinion of Independent Accountants

Board of Directors and Shareholders
Southern Railway Company

We have examined the consolidated balance sheets of Southern Railway Company and subsidiaries as of December 31, 1972 and December 31, 1971 and the related statements of consolidated income, income retained in the business, and changes in financial position (pages 24 through 30) for the years then ended. Our examinations were made in accordance with generally accepted auditing standards and accordingly included such tests of the accounting records and such other auditing procedures as we considered necessary in the circumstances.

As explained in Note 3, the accompanying financial statements vary from generally accepted accounting principles in that they do not include provisions for deferred income taxes.

In our opinion, except for the matter outlined in the preceding paragraph, the consolidated financial statements referred to above present fairly the financial position of Southern Railway Company and subsidiaries at December 31, 1972 and December 31, 1971, the results of their operations and the changes in their financial position for the years then ended, in conformity with generally accepted accounting principles consistently applied.

Washington, D. C.
January 23, 1973

Note 3—Federal Income Taxes

Federal income tax expense provided in the statement of income represents the tax it is anticipated will ultimately be paid for each of the years reported upon. Because we use more accelerated depreciation methods and shorter lives incomputing the depreciation for determining taxable income than is used in determing book income, as more fully described later, taxes provided are substantially less than would be required if income taxes were computed on book income. This recognition of the decrease in taxes in computing net income is in accordance with ICC accounting requirements.

Generally accepted accounting principles (GAAP) do not provide for recognition of such tax reduction on the theory that eventually there will be little or no depreciation available for computing taxable income even though the assets involved are still in use.

Thus, under GAAP, it is assumed that the tax benefit received this year is only a temporary deferral and that it ultimately will have to be paid back. However, as a result of the continued need for more and higher capacity equipment at ever-increasing prices, we think it is more realistic to take the ICC position that there is no "deferred" tax liability but in fact such deferral is permanent.

In order to provide data about our Company on the basis consistent with other industries which are not subject to ICC accounting regulations, the following table sets forth our income for the years 1972 and 1971 on the basis of generally accepted accounting principles:

	1972	1971
	(Thousands of Dollars)	
Net income as reported	$85,335	$72,715
Provision for deferred income taxes	25,886	20,312
Net income on a generally accepted accounting principles basis	$59,449	$52,403
Per Common Share	$3.94	$3.45

On a cumulative basis, such deferred taxes which have not been recorded on the books amount to $180 million and $154 million at December 31, 1972 and 1971, respectively. . . .

THE SECURITIES AND EXCHANGE COMMISSION

The SEC requires that companies whose stock is publicly traded cannot receive an "except for" opinion on their financial statements. The statements must conform to GAAP.

The commission, however, did not take issue with Southern's 1972 annual report because of its Rule 13b-1a, which reads as follows: "If a person's (corporation's) methods of accounting are prescribed under any law of the United States or any rules and regulations thereunder, the requirements imposed by such law or rules and regulation shall supersede the requirements prescribed by the rules and regulations of the commission with respect to the same subject matters, insofar as the latter are inconsistent with the former."

The Interstate Commerce Commission, which prescribes railroad accounting practices, does not permit tax allocation. The SEC does not want to get involved in a dispute with another governmental agency and thus accepts Southern's financial statements as filed with the ICC, even though these statements violate GAAP.

The SEC states that it is in full agreement with the generally accepted accounting principle that requires interperiod tax allocation (based on the matching of revenue and expense concept). Furthermore, the commission disagrees with Southern's contention that there will be a continually increasing investment in plant and equipment that will relieve them of any reversal of the hypothetical deferred income tax liability. The commission believes that there can be no certainty that this will be the case.

THE INTERSTATE COMMERCE COMMISSION

The Interstate Commerce Commission does not allow deferred income taxes (i.e., interperiod tax allocation) in railroad accounting since it does not believe that rail freight rates should be based on income numbers that show a deduction for an expense that will involve no cash outlay. However, for published statements of publicly held railroads, the ICC permits carriers to use the deferral method as long as there is footnote disclosure of the variances between ICC accounting rules and GAAP. Nearly all other publicly owned railroads follow this approach. Southern, however, uses the ICC accounting (which it believes is better) and resorts to footnote disclosure to show the impact of the failure to use tax allocation.

THE NEW YORK STOCK EXCHANGE

Under Rule 499 of the NYSE, securities admitted to the list may be suspended from trading or removed from the list at any time. The criteria for delisting include many factors, among which is the failure of a company to make timely, adequate, and accurate disclosures of information to its shareholders and the investing public or to observe good accounting practices in reporting earnings and financial position.

However, the NYSE, like the SEC, will waive its rules if the listed issue is subject to contrary accounting rules prescribed by a regulatory agency, such as the ICC, and is following the required disclosures.

THE ACCOUNTING FIRM

Price Waterhouse & Co., the certified public accountants for Southern Railway, declined to make any direct comments on their issuance of a qualified opinion due to the confidentiality of the client relationship. However, they did make the following general comments on the financial reporting for ICC regulated companies.

"The Accounting Principles Board in an addendum to Opinion #2 acknowledged that regulatory agencies sometimes impose accounting methods which are at variance with Generally Accepted Accounting Principles. However, except for regulations involving the rate-making process, an independent accountant should deal with any such variances in his report in the same manner as if his client were in a non-regulated business. Railroads are generally not considered 'regulated' for purposes of the addendum, and it is common to see qualification or exceptions in auditors' reports on railroads for failure to comply with Accounting Principles Board Opinion #11 on interperiod tax allocation."

THE FINANCIAL COMMUNITY

A leading railroad analyst on Wall Street was asked what effect, if any, Southern's treatment of deferred taxes and the resultant "except for" opinion had on the investment community's evaluation of the company's stock and its view on the "quality" of the firm's earnings.

Not surprisingly, he said that this variance from generally accepted accounting principles had not changed the investment community's evaluation of Southern's stock or the perception of the quality of its earnings.

QUESTIONS

1. Comment on the accounting policy of Southern Railway regarding deferred taxes. Would you recommend a different policy to management?

2. Do you approve of the actions of the SEC and the NYSE in accepting these financial statements?

3. What is the significance, if any, of "Wall Street's" apparent lack of concern over the "except for" opinion accorded Southern by Price Waterhouse?

4. What similarities and differences regarding accounting for deferred taxes are highlighted by a comparison of the Trans Union and Southern Railway cases?

Case 9-5

Worldwide Trade Corporation[1]

On February 18, 1975, Mr. William Girod, chairman of the board of the Worldwide Trade Corporation, was examining the annual report in preparation for the forthcoming annual stockholders' meeting.

Mr. Girod knew that each year an increasing number of shareholders were examining the annual statements with increased expertise. In particular, he was aware that at the prior year's shareholders' meeting there had been some questions regarding the corporate income taxes paid by Worldwide, which he had not been able to answer satisfactorily. Furthermore, the Securities and Exchange Commission had recently adopted revised disclosure requirements for income tax expense. Therefore, despite the fact that the company's fiscal year reporting did not require it to comply with the new ruling this period, Mr. Girod suspected that there would be extensive inquiries made on this subject at the coming meeting. He proceeded to contact Mr. William Fifer, Worldwide's treasurer and vice president of finance, in order to have the necessary information prepared.

THE COMPANY

Worldwide could be classified as a mini-conglomerate, with consolidated sales of $35 million and net income before taxes of $4.2 million for the 1974 fiscal year.

The company's main subsidiary, Worldwide Oil Corporation, had originated with the Girod family's ownership of oil wells in Texas in the late 1930s. Worldwide Oil Corporation emerged from World War II in a very strong financial position as a fully integrated producer and refiner. Expansion into Latin America and Europe was actively pursued, and by the end of the 1950s crude production, refining, and marketing had been established in several countries. In addition, a shipping

---

[1] This case was prepared by Guillermo J. Fernandez, Research Assistant, under the supervision of Associate Professor John K. Shank, as the basis for class discussion rather than to illustrate effective or ineffective handling of an administrative situation.

company, Panamanian Worldwide Tankers Corporation, had been acquired in 1966. It was chartered in Panama and operated from Panama City.

In 1958 a diversification move was made with the purchase of Worldwide Home Appliance Corporation, which was a full-line producer of home appliances with subsidiaries in the United States and in Europe. The present crude oil shortages had delayed further expansion in the petrochemicals field.

INCOME TAXES

Mr. Fifer proceeded to analyze the 1973 consolidated income tax expense in order to arrive at its composition and determine the variance with the current corporate tax rate of 48 per cent. In addition, he had to reconcile the difference between the tax provision and the actual tax payable that gave rise to deferred income taxes.

His examination of the consolidated income statements and related supporting schedules disclosed the following:

1. Permanent Income Differences

   (a) Income included on the books that was excluded for tax purposes.

   $500,000 insurance proceeds received on the policy held by Worldwide on the life of the late Mr. Crow, former president of international operations, deceased in August 1973.

   $55,000 interest income on Westchester County Sewage Authority Bonds.

   $24,000, which represents 85 per cent of the dividend income received from domestic corporations. These investments represent less than 20 per cent of the equity of such corporations and, therefore, are recorded using the cost method of accounting for investments.

   $488,000, which represents 50 per cent of the earnings of Worldwide's Domestic International Sales Corporation, a wholly owned corporation. Earnings of international sales subsidiaries of domestic corporations are taxed only when distributed. However, 50 per cent of the earnings are considered as taxable dividends to the shareholders even if actual payment is not made. The remainder is taxed on actual distribution. Worldwide, however, does not expect to ever make such distribution and, therefore, no deferred tax is provided.

   $216,000 net income of Panama-Worldwide Tankers Corporation. This income is tax exempt since it is derived from and permanently reinvested in a country with very liberal tax provisions for foreign corporations.

   (b) Taxable income that is not considered to be income for financial reporting purposes.

   $330,000 proceeds of stock purchase warrants that expired in August 1973 and were not exercised. This amount was originally credited to additional paid-in capital for accounting purposes, but it is considered as current income for tax purposes.

2. Timing Income Differences

   (a) Income recognized earlier for accounting purposes rather than for tax purposes.

   $236,000 excess of accrued sales revenue on installment sales over the amounts collected by Worldwide Home Appliance Corporation. Accrual accounting is used for stockholders' statements whereas installment accounting is used for tax purposes. This amount represents the excess of recognized accrual income over the taxable installment income.

   $122,000 net income of Worldwide Oil Corporation-Chilean branch that cannot be repatriated due to that country's present currency restrictions. U.S. taxes on blocked foreign income are deferred until restrictions disappear or actual repatriation is made.

   $959,000, which is Worldwide's share of the net income of Home Appliance-France, Inc., a foreign corporation 45 per cent owned by Worldwide's wholly owned U.S. subsidiary. Such income is non-taxable to Worldwide since its is not derived out of transactions with related companies and it is taxed only when repatriated as dividends. Dividends of $273,000 were received in 1973. These will be included in taxable income (no dividend exclusion is allowed) whereas for accounting purposes the amount was recorded as a reduction of the investment account according to the equity method of accounting for intercorporate investments.

   (b) Income recognized earlier for tax purposes rather than for financial reporting purposes.

   $250,000 service contract fees of the home appliance subsidiary collected in 1973 that are recognized as collected for tax purposes but are amortized over the warranty period for book purposes. This amount represents the excess of collections in 1973 over the amount amortized for financial reporting purposes.

3. Permanent Expense Differences

   (a) Expenses included in the books that are not deductible for tax purposes.

   $87,000 of life insurance premiums paid on policies for key executives for which Worldwide is the beneficiary. Both premiums and ultimate proceeds of life insurance policies for which the company is the beneficiary are excluded in income tax calculations.

   $98,000 amortization of goodwill not allowed for tax purposes.

   (b) Expenses deductible for tax purposes that are not shown in the financial statements.

   $30,000 excess statutory depletion over the cost-based depletion recorded as expense on the books.

$5,000 capital appreciation on 100 shares of stock donated to Harvard University. The original cost of the stock was $10,000 and the fair market value at the time of the donation was $15,000. The tax laws allow a deduction for the full market value, limited to a maximum of 30 per cent of adjusted gross income. The donation was expensed at cost for book purposes.

4. Timing Differences for Expenses

   (a) Expenses recognized earlier for tax purposes rather than for book purposes.

   $233,000 excess of accelerated depreciation over straight-line.

   $157,000 excess of capitalized research and development expenses over the amount amortized for reporting purposes. Worldwide capitalizes research and development expenses on the books but expenses such items as incurred for tax purposes.

   (b) Expenses recognized later for tax purposes rather than for book purposes.

   $43,000 excess book deduction for warranty expense. The reserve method of accounting for an expected warranty liability is not allowed for tax purposes. Worldwide's home appliance subsidiary has provided $69,000 of warranty expense on its books; $26,000 was the actual cash outlay for the period.

5. Investment Tax Credit, Foreign Tax Credit, and Tax on Capital Gains

   (a) The tax law provides a 7 per cent credit for new qualified property against the taxes payable, subject to a maximum limitation. Worldwide had qualified investments totaling $570,000 for a $40,000 tax credit (well under the limitation). Worldwide uses the flow through method to account for this credit.

   (b) Worldwide could also claim as a credit against the U.S. corporate taxes the foreign taxes paid on subsidiaries' income, subject to several limitations:

   — $690,000 in income taxes or 55 per cent of its pretax earnings was paid by Worldwide Oil Corporation-Brazilian branch. However, only $450,000 of this could be credited to U.S. income taxes due to the limitation placed by the U.S. government on foreign taxes paid on mineral income earned/by subsidiaries of U.S. corporations.

   — $12,000 in income taxes or 3 per cent of its pre-tax earnings was paid by Worldwide Home Appliance-Swiss branch.

   — $281,000 in income taxes deemed as paid by Worldwide on its portion of the earnings of Home Appliance-France Corporation through the dividends received. Taxes were paid to the French government at a rate of 50 per cent of Worldwide's share of the earnings, plus an additional withholding of 5 per cent. The total foreign income tax credits were within the limitations set by the U.S. government.

    (c) $96,000 capital gains tax on a $319,000 net long-term capital gain arising from the sale of 15 per cent interest in Safeguard Warehouse Corp. The tax was the lowest under the two alternatives allowed by the law. The capital gain was included in the net income before taxes.

With this information Mr. Fifer proceeded to prepare the necessary reconciliations.

Required:

1. Compute the income tax provision for financial reporting purposes for 1973.

2. Prepare a reconciliation between this tax provision and a number equal to 48 per cent of pre-tax earnings.

3. How much income tax will Worldwide actually pay to the U.S. government in 1973?

4. Prepare the journal entry to record income tax expenses for 1973.

5. Prepare a reconciliation between the tax actually due and the tax provision on the income statement.

6. Calculate the effective tax rate for Worldwide.

Case 10-1

Allis - Chalmers Manufacturing Company[1]

In 1969, Allis-Chalmers (A-C) was a worldwide manufacturer and distributor of a diversified line of industrial equipment. The company was a major producer of farm equipment, construction machinery, electric power generation and transmission equipment, pumps, material handling machinery, and process equipment and systems. A summary of sales and earnings for the fifteen years 1953-1967 is presented in Exhibit 1.

In 1962 and 1964, A-C recorded substantial extraordinary write offs, both related to electrical equipment. In 1960, the federal government filed antitrust suits against a group of electrical equipment manufacturers, charging a conspiracy to fix prices on such equipment. The three largest defendants were General Electric, Westinghouse, and A-C. In 1962, A-C announced its "withdrawal from the steam turbine-generator and related condenser businesses," stating in its annual report that "these operations were unprofitable and showed no possibility of satisfactory recovery. Customers were advised that we would complete our backlog during the next 2½ years and remain in the business of servicing the equipment they already own." In the same year, the company closed one transformer plant that had "become uneconomical due to low volume and high costs," consolidating its production into two other plants. "The present and anticipated cost of these two programs has been charged directly to Company Retained Earnings as a single extraordinary, nonrecurring item." The amount was $20.9 million, net of taxes. In a footnote to the statements the amount was detailed as follows:

Cost and Expenses Incurred during the Year for Separation Payments and Other Closing Costs	$ 495,000
Possible Loss on Disposals and Abandonments of Certain Facilities	3,545,000
Costs and Expenses Related to Discontinued Operations	16,810,000
	$20,850,000

---

[1]Data for this case were taken from published material. It is intended for class discussion rather than to illustrate either effective or ineffective handling of an administrative situation.

EXHIBIT 1

ALLIS-CHALMERS MANUFACTURING COMPANY

Financial Summary, 1953-1967

(Amounts in thousands, except per share data)

Year	Sales	Earnings[a]	Extraordinary Charges Net of Tax[b]	Net Income (loss)[b]	Earnings[a]	Per Share Net Income (loss)[b]	Dividends
1967	$821,764	$ 5,001	—	5,001	$ .41	$ .41	$1.00
1966	857,215	26,154	—	26,154	2.67	2.67	.81
1965	714,408	22,109		22,109	2.33	2.33	.56
1964	629,067	12,739	21,060	(8,321)	1.38	(.97)	.50
1963	543,941	6,870	—	6,870	.73	.73	.50
1962	516,093	6,478	16,466	(9,988)	.67	(1.14)	.75
1961	502,243	6,384	—	6,384	.66	.66	1.25
1960	530,019	10,999	—	10,999	1.17	1.17	1.50
1959	539,640	23,091	—	23,091	2.58	2.58	1.25
1958	531,972	19,839			2.36		1.25
1957	534,146	17,909			2.12		2.00
1956	547,439	20,393			2.43		2.00
1955	535,069	24,805			3.03		2.00
1954	492,948	26,130			3.60		2.00
1953	514,474	21,943			3.29		2.00

[a]As reported in the 10-year financial summary included in annual reports for 1967 and earlier. The 1968 annual report presented these data for the years 1959-1968 under the caption "Income (Loss) Before Extraordinary Charges."

[b]As reported in the 10-year financial summary included in the 1968 annual reports.

None of these problems had been mentioned by management or by the auditors in earlier published reports.

In 1964, the annual report stated, "Substantial progress was made in 1964 in resolving the antitrust claims of utility customers through voluntary price adjustments. . . .The settlements made to date plus a provision considered sufficient to dispose of the balance of the cases and cover related expenses aggregate $22.4 million, net of taxes. Since these costs relate to operations of prior years, a charge for this amount was made to Retained Earnings at the year-end and the proper liabilities and reserves were established in the account." This problem had been anticipated by the president in his letter to the stockholders included in the 1962 annual report. The auditors had also "qualified" their opinion in 1962 with respect to the ultimate disposition of their claims.

During the last quarter of 1968, as a result of a major change in management, an extensive study of the company's operations, products, and market was conducted. The study resulted in changes in the company's philosophy and policies whose implementation was expected to result in substantial cost and losses for:

1. Parts replacement, warranty costs, repossession losses, and price allowances.

2. Relocation and discontinuance of facilities and products.

Provisions were recorded in the last quarter totaling $68,750,000 for these anticipated costs and losses as shown in the annual report (Footnote 3 to the financial statements); $40,250,000 of this amount was charged to regular operations, and the remaining $28,500,000 was classified as an extraordinary charge. In contrast to prior years, however, this extraordinary charge was included in computation of net loss for the year.

QUESTIONS

1. Do the 1968 financial statements "fairly present" Allis-Chalmers' financial position at 12/31/68? Do they "fairly present" earnings for the year 1968?

2. Do you agree with the treatment of the estimated future income tax benefits?

3., With respect to the 1968 earnings statement, what were the operating earnings (loss?) for 1968 for those businesses that A-C is planning to continue to operate?

4. Do you agree with the treatment of the special reserves?

5. Does the auditor's opinion on the '68 financial statements give you the assurances you want as a reader of the statements? If not, what might Price Waterhouse have said or done differently?

6. Do the 1968 financial statements indicate that the statements issued in 1966 and 1967 did not really "fairly present" financial position at that time? In other words, did all the problems arise in 1968?

7. Is the treatment of special items in 1962, 1964, and 1968 consistent with the provisions of the current accounting ground rules in 1974?

EXHIBIT 2
ALLIS-CHALMERS MANUFACTURING COMPANY

Anomalies and Paradoxes

A Bit of Rouge for Allis-Chalmers

The accounting that appears in annual reports sometimes serves a cosmetic purpose—it is there not so much to inform stockholders as to help management keep them happy, or at least quiet, by touching up blemishes and brightening beauty spots. When a company is not doing well, and at the same time is trying to fend off an unwanted merger, the cosmeticians of accountancy can sometimes perform wonders—even when they are limited to shades of red. Quite a number of companies in this year's directory used bookkeeping devices of various kinds to brighten their results. But Allis-Chalmers Manufacturing outdid them all at the rouge pot.

As 1968 ended, long-suffering Allis-Chalmers, No. 130 among the 500, found itself with some conflicting needs and desires. It presumably wanted to put the best possible face on 1968 results in order to maintain stockholder support in a bitter battle against a take-over by White Consolidated Industries, No. 143. But the new president of Allis-Chalmers, David C. Scott, who took office September 1, wanted to write off at once the tremendous charges associated with past mistakes and thereby turn the company around. To do that, he had to slap stockholders with some very bad news just when White Consolidated's onslaught was hotting up.

Allis-Chalmers resolved this conflict with some intricate accounting that let it accept Scott's write-off while minimizing the bad news that had to be reported to stockholders. The published results were still pretty dismal: on sales of $767,313,100, the company reported a loss of $54,589,720. That was, however, a whole lot better than the $121,588,931 that the company *actually* lost last year.

Taking credit for a loss

To understand how an actual loss of $122 million can become a reported loss of $55 million requires some comprehension of tax accounting. It is well known, of course, that a corporate dollar earned is roughly 50 cents lost to the tax collector. The converse is also true, i.e., *a dollar lost is 50 cents earned.* Allis-Chalmers simply claimed a credit on its profit-and-loss statement for the taxes that it saved by achieving a loss. The company said, in effect: "If Uncle Sam deserves his slice of the profits, he also deserves his slice of the losses. We cannot be said to have lost $122 million when we thereby hung on to something over $60 million in taxes that we otherwise would have had to pay."

This logic is applicable to stockholder reports, but not to a company's tax returns. The tax carry-forward created by a loss can be used only in years succeeding the one in which the loss occurred. For this reason alone, then, Allis-Chalmers' tax return for 1968 can bear only a passing resemblance to its stockholder report. In addition, not all of that $122 million represented operating losses. The figure included $69 million that Scott charged off in 1968 in the form of special reserves for costs that he expected to incur later; i.e., the company provided for losses that had not yet occurred and that can't be claimed on the tax form until they do occur.

The shakiest aspect of tax-benefit accounting arises from the fact that tax credits are worth nothing until there are profits to apply them to. By using credits to cut the same losses that created the credits, a company's accountants must flout an ancient accounting adage: provide for all losses but *anticipate no profits*. To be sure, not all the $60-odd million of tax credits that Allis-Chalmers used were anticipatory. Some $14 million represented a carryback against taxes that were paid on earnings for 1965, 1966, and 1967. No problem there: the past profits were already available to ensure a tax refund. Nor is there a problem with some other substantial credits that Allis-Chalmers made available to itself by various accounting changes and tax adjustments. But included in the total tax credits used to cut down the 1968 loss that the company reported was around $43 million in "estimated future income tax benefits." In fact, Allis-Chalmers will not get the benefit of any such amount until it comes up with some $86 million in pre-tax profits.

What auditors can't audit

Allis-Chalmers argues that it had no real choice about these prospective tax benefits. In his brief tenure, Scott has lopped 3,300 non-production employees off the payroll, with more to go, thereby assuring savings of perhaps $40 million. Since all the company's projections are for continued high sales, Scott's drastic cost cutting seems certain to show up in profits on the bottom line. With profits thus "assured," Allis-Chalmers felt that it would have been misleading *not* to use the tax credits to reduce its reported loss.

Still, for a company that has just lost $122 million in a single year to assume future income of $86 million might appear a bit presumptuous. And, indeed, Allis-Chalmers' insistence on counting so many unhatched chickens while its incubator was out of order seemed to make its auditors rather nervous. Price Waterhouse's certificate in the Allis-Chalmers annual report was half again as long as the usual auditors' statement, and carried less conviction. There was, of course, the conventional observation that the auditors' examination was made "in accordance with generally accepted auditing standards." But Price Waterhouse commented that Allis-Chalmers' substantial amounts of "reserves and anticipated tax benefits reflect the best current judgment of the Company's management," and that this judgment was beyond the auditors' ability to audit.

Reserved as Price Waterhouse's statement was, it apparently satisfied both the Securities and Exchange Commission and the New York Stock Exchange. Neither has raised any objection to Allis-Chalmers' report to its stockholders. One N.Y.S.E. official says that, in general, a company "hates to have a qualified auditors' opinion," but such a statement does not affect the listing of the company's stock. He adds: "When the unknowns are substantial, we have to assume that any national firm of certified public accountants is using its best professional judgment." That is, of course, precisely the assumption that an ordinary stockholder must make about any company and its auditors.

As it happens, President Scott has been making good on his promise of earnings for Allis-Chalmers. The company had pre-tax profits of $11,700,000 in the first quarter of 1969. Because the tax effect of 1968 losses was applied to 1968 results, however, the company must now deduct taxes from any earnings that it reports to stockholders. The net it can report on that profitable first quarter is only $5,100,000. Explains an Allis-Chalmers accountant: "Since we took our cake in 1968, we have to take taxes out of our 1969 profits."

Reprinted from the May 19, 1969 issue of *Fortune* Magazine by special permission; © 1969 Time Inc.

ALLIS-CHALMERS MANUFACTURING COMPANY
AND CONSOLIDATED SUBSIDIARIES
Statement of Financial Condition
December 31

ASSETS	1968	1967
Current Assets		
Cash	$ 23,483,905	$ 32,778,384
Receivables—less reserves of $16,171,800 and		
$12,990,000, respectively	126,836,883	125,835,967
Inventories—at lower of approximate cost		
(10% valued at LIFO) or market, less progress payments of		
$14,286,644 and $13,816,887, respectively	234,115,066	231,107,182
Income tax refunds and future income tax benefits (Note 3)	35,619,025	21,590,000
Other current assets	3,997,779	4,496,240
Total Current Assets	424,052,658	415,807,773
Estimated Future Income Tax Benefits (Note 3)	42,972,400	—
Investments and Other Assets		
Investment in finance subsidiaries—		
at equity in net assets	53,498,936	46,594,803
Investment in other subsidiaries—		
at cost, less reserves (Note 1)	18,524,117	23,748,137
Intangible assets arising from acquisition (Note 2)	7,389,935	7,389,935
Other investments, assets and deferred charges (Note 5)	6,366,775	5,244,786
	85,779,763	82,977,661
Plants and Equipment at cost		
Land and buildings	110,168,287	103,163,467
Machinery and equipment	190,005,484	180,635,390
Tools and fixtures	32,212,797	29,925,202
Furniture and fixtures	7,136,070	6,391,647
	339,522,638	320,115,706
Accumulated depreciation and amortization (Note 6)	186,714,838	178,989,166
	152,807,800	141,126,540
	$705,612,621	$639,911,974

LIABILITIES AND EQUITY

Current Liabilities

Notes payable and current maturities of long-term debt	$106,382,295	$50,797,500
Accounts payable and payrolls	68,970,051	69,978,681
Federal, state and Canadian income taxes	883,458	4,072,998
Reserves for completion of contracts and product corrections and current portion of special reserves	69,486,985	12,611,115
Other current liabilities	20,606,507	19,237,153
Total Current Liabilities	$266,329,296	$156,697,447

Special Reserves (Note 3)

Estimated costs of parts replacement, warranty costs, repossession losses and price allowances	40,260,106	–
Estimated costs and losses associated with relocation and discontinuance of facilities and products	28,494,304	–
	68,754,410	
Less amount included in current liabilities	48,000,000	–
	20,754,410	–

Long-Term Debt (Note 4)

Notes payable	66,000,000	69,000,000
Sinking fund debentures	45,000,000	45,000,000
Other long-term debt	3,361,924	4,228,487
	$114,361,924	$118,228,487

Deferred Income Taxes	–	1,449,260

Share Owners' Equity (Notes 5 and 9)

Preferred stock, $100 par value, 500,000 shares authorized, 134,594 shares, 4.20% cumulative convertible series outstanding in 1967	–	13,459,400
Common stock, $10 par value, 12,500,000 shares authorized, 10,410,292 and 9,881,481 shares outstanding after deducting 42,869 and 82,869 shares held in treasury, respectively ...	104,102,920	98,814,810
Capital in excess of par value of capital stock	122,548,752	113,198,182
Earnings retained	77,515,319	138,064,388
Total Share Owners' Equity	304,166,991	363,536,780
	$705,612,621	$639,911,974

ALLIS-CHALMERS MANUFACTURING COMPANY AND CONSOLIDATED SUBSIDIARIES
Statement of Income (Loss) and Earnings Retained
For the Year Ended December 31

Income (Loss)	1968	1967
Sales and Other Income		
Sales	$767,313,100	$821,764,535
Discounts, interest earned and other income	11,152,147	6,428,597
Income of finance subsidiaries	9,901,233	6,893,641
	788,366,480	835,086,773

Costs and Expenses

Materials, plant payrolls and services (Note 3)	703,041,018	689,225,155
Depreciation (Note 6)	16,024,167	18,713,666
Selling, general and administrative expense (Note 3)	131,352,862	100,216,572
Discount and interest on receivables sold		
to finance subsidiaries	21,662,133	11,158,812
Other interest expense	9,380,927	9,590,531
	881,461,107	828,904,736
Income (Loss) before income taxes and		
extraordinary charges	(93,094,627)	6,182,037
Federal, state and Canadian income taxes (Notes 3 and 6) .	51,942,000	(1,180,200)
Income (Loss) before extraordinary charges	(41,152,627)	5,001,837
Extraordinary charges—net of income taxes of		
$15,057,211 (Note 3)	(13,437,093)	—
Net Income (Loss) for the Year	$(54,589,720)	$ 5,001,837

Per average share of common stock—

Income (Loss) before extraordinary charges	*($3.96)*	*$.41*
Extraordinary charges, net of income taxes	*1.30)*	
Net Income (Loss) for the Year	*$(5.26)*	*$.41*

Earnings Retained and Used in the Business

Earnings Retained—Beginning of Year	$138,064,388	$143,681,336
Henry Manufacturing Company (Note 5)	493,260	—
Net Income (Loss) for the Year	(54,589,720)	5,001,837
	83,967,928	148,683,173

Dividends Paid

Preferred stock—4.20% series	—	1,099,664
Common stock (per share: 1968—$.62½; 1967—$1.00) . . .	6,452,609	9,519,121
	6,452,609	10,618,785
Earnings Retained—End of Year	$ 77,515,319	$138,064,388

1967 has been restated to conform with current year's account classifications

NOTES TO CONSOLIDATED FINANCIAL STATEMENTS

NOTE 1—BASIS OF CONSOLIDATION / All domestic and Canadian subsidiaries, except finance subsidiaries and a marketing subsidiary, are included in the consolidated financial statements. The Company's investment in and advances to the unconsolidated foreign subsidiaries of $10,134,184, less reserve of $3,855,067, and the investment in and advances to the unconsolidated marketing subsidiary of $19,550,000, less reserve of $7,305,000, were approximately equal to the net assets of the respective subsidiaries at December 31, 1968. In addition, Allis-Chalmers International Finance Corporation, an unconsolidated finance subsidiary, has investments in and advances to unconsolidated foreign subsidiaries of $9,260,160 at December 31, 1968. (See page 19 for finance subsidiaries financial statements.)

NOTE 2—INTANGIBLE ASSETS ARISING FROM ACQUISITION / The excess of the purchase price over the value assigned to the assets acquired from Simplicity Manufacturing Company in October 1965 is not being amortized at present due to a suit brought by the Department of Justice contesting the acquisition. (See Note 8 to the financial statements.)

Management believes that the asset is not diminishing in value and that the suit is without merit and will be successfully defended.

NOTE 3—SPECIAL RESERVES AND INCOME TAXES / During the last quarter of 1968 a major change took place in the Company's management. The new management made an extensive study of the Company's operations, products and markets. This study resulted in changes in Company philosophy and policies relating to organization, products and production facilities, marketing and relations with dealers and customers. The Company has estimated that implementation of these policy changes will result in substantial costs and losses for (a) parts replacement, warranty costs, repossession losses and price allowances and (b) relocation and discontinuance of facilities and products. Provisions were recorded in the last quarter of 1968 to establish special reserves totaling $68,754,410 for these anticipated costs and losses. Of this amount, $28,494,304 ($13,437,093 net of taxes), associated with relocation and discontinuance of products and facilities; is shown as an extraordinary charge in the consolidated statement of income (loss). The remaining provisions, totaling $40,260,106, were charged to sales ($5,627,178), materials, plant payroll and services ($28,190,928) and selling, general and administrative expenses ($6,442,000).

Although the costs and losses to be charged to the special reserves cannot be finally determined at the present time, management believes, based on the Company's extensive studies and evaluations which were reviewed in depth by the independent auditors, that the provisions recorded in 1968 represent a fair and reasonable determination of the amounts required.

The net loss for the year has been determined after giving recognition to income taxes recoverable ($14,345,721) from carryback to prior years of operating losses and to estimated future tax benefits ($50,900,000) of unused losses, including $6,836,276 relating to an accounting change described in Note 6 to the financial statements. The amounts recoverable from carryback to prior years are included in current assets in the consolidated balance sheet together with 1968 tax refunds receivable of $3,970,000 and estimated future income tax benefits of $17,303,304 relating primarily to normal book-tax timing differences applicable to amounts included in current assets and liabilities. The realization of estimated future income tax benefits which total $60,275,704 is dependent upon the Company's ability to generate future taxable income. This amount is included in the financial statements because, in the opinion of management, the realization of such tax benefits is assured beyond any reasonable doubt.

The Company has unrecorded investment tax credit carryforwards of $6,098,722, applicable to the years 1962 through 1968, which may be used to reduce income taxes payable in future years.

NOTE 4—LONG-TERM DEBT / Notes payable at December 31, 1968, consisted of $55,000,000 3-5/8% notes and $11,000,000 3 7/8% notes, all payable to insurance companies, due $3,000,000 annually, maturing in 1982. The sinking fund debentures of $45,000,000, due in 1990, bear interest at 4.85%. The debentures are entitled to a mandatory sinking fund commencing in 1971 sufficient to retire 76% of the debentures prior to maturity ($1,800,000 per year). Other long-term debt consists of (a) capitalized lease obligations of $2,200,000, (b) antitrust claim settlements of $904,479, and (c) mortgage notes payable by a subsidiary company of $257,445.

NOTE 5—SHARE OWNERS' EQUITY AND DIVIDEND RESTRICTIONS / During 1968, the remaining 134,594 shares of the 4.20% convertible preferred stock were converted into 442,621 shares of common stock or were redeemed, 46,190 shares of common stock were issued to acquire the net assets of Henry Manufacturing Company and 40,000 shares of common stock held in the treasury were sold. These transactions are summarized as follows:

	Common Stock	Capital in Excess of Par Value
Balance at beginning of year	$ 98,814,810	$113,198,182
Conversion of preferred stock	4,426,210	8,850,681

Acquisition of Henry Manufacturing Company	461,900	(135,111)
Sale of treasury shares	400,000	635,000
Balance at end of year	$104,102,920	$122,548,752

The acquisition of Henry was a pooling of interests and their accounts have been included in the consolidated financial statements for 1968. The consolidated financial statments for 1967 were not restated because of the relative immateriality of the amounts involved.

Other non-current assets include a note receivable from the president of the Company of $1,035,000, relating to the sale of treasury stock, which is payable on March 4, 1974, with interest at a rate of 5%. The note is secured by a pledge and assignment of the common stock.

Agreements relating to debentures and notes payable and the certificate of incorporation contain certain restrictions relating to the declaration of cash dividends. Under these restrictions the entire amount of earnings retained at December 31, 1968, was not available for the future declaration of cash dividends on the common stock. The required increase in equity before any such amounts become available for dividends was approximately $29,000,000 at December 31, 1968. The issuance and sale of capital stock described in Note 9 to the financial statements will have the effect of making available earnings retained for declaration of cash dividends of approximately $6,000,000, subject to earnings of the Company subsequent to 1968.

NOTE 6—ACCOUNTING CHANGES / The Company has adopted, for financial reporting purposes, the straight-line method of computing depreciation for substantially all plants and equipment. These fixed assets were previously depreciated on an accelerated basis. This change, effective Janaury 1, 1968, reduced depreciation expense by $4,505,109 and decreased the net loss by $2,126,411, equal to $.21 per common share.

In 1968, the Company extended the application of tax allocation accounting procedures to certain reserve accounts to comply fully with new tax accounting requirements effective this year. The extension of these procedures decreased the net loss by $6,836,276, equal to $.66 per common share.

NOTE 7—PENSION PLANS / The Company and its consolidated subsidiaries have several noncontributory retirement and pension plans covering substantially all of their employes. The total pension expense charged to income was $20,866,000 in 1968 and $17,230,000 in 1967; these amounts include amortization of prior service cost of the principal hourly plans over a 30-year period. The Company's policy is to fund pension cost accrued. The actuarially computed value of vested benefits for all plans exceeded the total of the pension funds and balance sheet accruals by approximately $79,000,000 at the 1968 plan valuation dates.

NOTE 8—COMMITMENTS AND CONTINGENCIES / Litigation in which the Company is involved is summarized below:

(a) An action started in the U.S. District Court of the District of Delaware by the Company against White Consolidated Industries, Inc. in December 1968, under Section 7 of the Clayton Act, to enjoin White from, among other things, attempting to obtain control over the Company through the acquisition by White of 3,248,000 shares of the Company's common stock from Gulf & Western Industries, Inc. and to compel divestiture of this holding on terms that would not be injurious to the Company. Denial of a motion by the Company for a preliminary injunction enjoining White from acquiring additional stock and attempting to obtain control pending the outcome of the suit has been appealed to the U.S. Court of Appeals.

(b) An action started by the Company against Gulf & Western Industries, Inc. in January 1969, under Section 16(b) of the Securities and Exchange Act of 1934, to recover "short-swing profits" realized by Gulf & Western from its sale of 3,248,000 shares of the Company's common stock to White Consolidated Industries, Inc. Gulf & Western has filed a cross complaint seeking exemption from the provision of such Act on the ground that it was obliged to sell such stock under duress.

(c) An action started by the Department of Justice against the Company in 1965, under Section 7 of the Clayton Act, to obtain injunctive relief and an order of divestiture arising out of the

Company's acquisition of the assets of Simplicity Manufacturing Company. Trial of this action was closed in November 1968, and briefs and proposed findings are to be filed by September 1969.

(d) An action brought against the Company by White Consolidated Industries, Inc. in February 1969, to obtain rescission of an acquisition agreement between the Company and Standard Steel Corporation, damages and injunctive relief to prohibit the Company from taking any steps, by acquisition or otherwise, which would have the effect of unreasonably diluting the voting equity of White in the Company. Action is pending the filing of pleadings or motions by the Company. There are various other lawsuits pending against the Company, arising in the normal course of business. Management believes, based on the opinion of legal counsel, that disposition of these actions will not have a significant adverse effect on the Company's financial position.

The Company has guaranteed payment of the $15,000,000 of 6-5/8% notes payable of its wholly-owned subsidiary, Allis-Chalmers International Finance Corporation and of approximately $7,000,000 of short-term bank borrowings of foreign subsidiaries.

Under certain circumstances, the Company is obligated to repurchase delinquent financing paper sold to its finance subsidiaries. The repurchase price is generally the net carrying value of the paper at time of repurchase, or if there is no recourse to a solvent dealer, the estimated market value of the machinery.

Annual rental commitments under long-term leases, which expire at various periods through 1991, amounted to approximately $700,000 at December 31, 1968.

NOTE 9—EVENTS SUBSEQUENT TO DECEMBER 31, 1968 / See Note 8 to the financial statements for comments on litigation developments in 1969.

On January 13, 1969, the Company issued 280,000 shares of its common stock in exchange for the net assets of Standard Steel Corporation in a transaction which will be accounted for as a pooling of interests. The accounts of Standard Steel for 1968 are not material in relation to the consolidated accounts. Standard's sales for the year ended December 31, 1968, amounted to $12,000,000.

On March 3, 1969, the Company sold to private investors 450,000 shares of 4% $100 par value cumulative convertible preferred stock. The net proceeds to the Company were $45,000,000, less expenses. Each share of the preferred stock is convertible into four shares of common stock and is entitled to the same number of votes as the common stock into which it is convertible. The preferred stock is redeemable at $104 per share. In connection with the sale of the preferred stock is redeemable at $104 per share. In connection with the sale of the preferred stock, the Company returned to authorized but unissued stock 33,161 shares of treasury common stock, and reserved 1,800,000 of authorized but unissued shares of common stock for issuance upon conversion of the 450,000 shares of preferred stock.

REPORT OF INDEPENDENT ACCOUNTS

To the Board of Directors of
Allis-Chalmers Manufacturing Company

We have examined the consolidated statement of financial condition of Allis-Chalmers Manufacturing Company as of December 31, 1968 and the related statement of consolidated income (loss) and earnings retained for the year. Our examination was made in accordance with generally accepted auditing standards and accordingly included such tests of the accounting records and such other auditing procedures as we considered necessary in the circumstances.

As explained in Note 3 to the financial statements, in the last quarter of 1968 the Company recorded substantial amounts associated with (a) reserves for anticipated costs and losses, and (b) estimated income tax benefits expected to be realized in the future. Although these reserves and anticipated tax benefits reflect the best current judgment of the Company's management, we cannot determine at this time the amounts of costs and losses which ultimately will be charged against the reserves, and the amounts of future tax benefits which ultimately will be realized.

In our opinion, subject to the effect of any adjustments which may result from ultimate determination of the matters referred to in the preceding paragraph, the accompanying consolidated financial statements examined by us present fairly the financial position of Allis-Chalmers Manufacturing Company and its subsidiaries at December 31, 1968 and the results of their operations for the year, in conformity with generally accepted accounting principles applied on a basis consistent with that of the preceding year, except for the changes in accounting for depreciation and income taxes as explained in Note 6 to the financial statements.

Milwaukee, Wisconsin
March 26, 1969   PRICE WATERHOUSE & CO.

Case 10-2

Atlantic Richfield Company[1]

Following is the income statement for Atlantic Richfield from the 1972 annual report. The extraordinary charge of $3,045,000 is explained in Footnote 12, which is also reproduced here.

ATLANTIC RICHFIELD
Consolidated Statement of Income and Retained Earnings
Years 1972 and 1971

	1972	*1971*
Revenues:		
Sales and other operating revenues		
(including excise taxes)	$3,831,255,000	$3,658,437,000
Earnings of affiliated companies accounted for on the		
equity method	7,674,000	6,949,000
Interest and other revenues	60,504,000	57,591,000
	3,899,433,000	3,722,977,000
Expenses:		
Costs and operating expenses	2,325,076,000	2,130,604,000
Selling, delivery, general and administrative expenses	326,414,000	351,234,000
Taxes other than income taxes (note 10)	628,633,000	630,322,000
Depreciation, depletion, amortization and retirements	242,926,000	227,296,000
Interest	62,275,000	61,045,000
	3,585,324,000	3,400,501,000
Income before income taxes and extraordinary item	314,109,000	322,476,000
Provision for taxes on income (note 11)	121,593,000	111,943,000
Income Before Extraordinary Item	192,516,000	210,533,000

[1] This case was prepared from published sources as the basis for class discussion rather than to illustrate either the effective or ineffective handling of an administrative situation.

Extraordinary item (note 12)	3,045,000	(11,831,000)
Net Income	$195,561,000	$198,702,000
Earned Per Share (note 8)		
Income before extraordinary item	$3.40	$3.73
Extraordinary item	.06	(.21)
Net Income	$3.46	$3.52
Net Income Retained For Use In The Business:		
Balance January 1	$1,905,300,000	$1,837,749,000
Net income	195,561,000	198,702,000
Cash dividends:		
Preferred	(39,917,000)	(40,210,000)
Common (per share, 1972—$2.00; 1971—$2.00)	(91,937,000)	(90,941,000)
Balance December 31	$1,969,007,000	$1,905,300,000

12. Extraordinary Item

The 1972 extraordinary credit of $3,045,000, after tax, reflects the gain from divestiture under a court decree of August 1970 of certain former Sinclair marketing, refining, and related producing properties to Pasco, Inc., after offsetting extraordinary charges associated with a related program for restructuring and rebalancing facilities, relocating administrative activities, and the provision for write down to realizable values reflecting planned modifications of agricultural chemical operations.

The key elements of the restructuring and rebalancing program were dismantling and write off of portions of certain refineries, principally Philadelphia, reflecting the impact of the divestiture to Pasco, Inc., as well as the curtailment of certain marketing operations, withdrawal from marketing in certain southern states extending as far west as Arizona. The consolidation and relocation of administrative activities included the transfer of corporate headquarters to Los Angeles, consolidation of the administrative centers in Chicago and Philadelphia into one unit located in Philadelphia, and the centralization of the responsibilities for the refining and marketing functions in Los Angeles.

The effect of these items was as follows:

(Thousands of dollars)

	Credit (charge)	Income Taxes	Extra-ordinary Item
Divestiture under Court Decree	$89,391	$(24,100)	$65,291
Refining and Marketing Restructuring and Re-balancing	(33,434)	7,800	(25,634)
Consolidation and Relocation of Offices (including $10,116 after tax for relocation of executive offices to Los Angeles)	(29,412)	7,000	(22,412)

Agricultural Chemical assets—
  Provision for Write down to

Realizable Values	(18,500)	4,300	(14,200)
	$ 8,045	$ (5,000)	$ 3,045

Investment tax credits reflected in the above income taxes were $600,000.

The 1972 results of operations of the properties divested to Pasco, Inc., are included in the consolidated financial statements and operating statistics in the following amounts: crude oil production approximately 18,900 b/d; natural gas production approximately 48,400 b/d, while product sales amounted to approximately $14,700,000 (including excise taxes). The consolidated financial statements and operation statistics have not been restated to segregate these operations since this divestiture resulted in cash proceeds of approximately $156,900,000, and after considering interest on such funds the effect on earnings is not material.

The 1971 extraordinary charge of $11,831,000 (net of applicable income tax benefit of $5,300,000) reflects the company's withdrawal from nuclear fuel operations.

QUESTIONS

1. How would the items treated by Atlantic Richfield as extraordinary in 1971 and 1972 be treated under APB 30?

2. Why do you think Atlantic Richfield nets these items against one another and uses the singular form in the income statement?

Case 10 - 3

Vincent Industries[1]

Vincent Industries was located in Atlanta, Georgia. Its stock was traded in the local over-the-counter market. Trading seldom reached a thousand shares per day. Certain data related to the company's earnings, capital structure, and security prices are presented below.

Market price of common stock. The market price of the common stock was as follows:

	1974	1973	1972
Average Price:			
First Quarter	50	45	40
Second Quarter	60	52	41
Third Quarter	70	50	40
Fourth Quarter	70	50	45
December 31 closing price	72	51	44

Cash Dividends. Cash dividends of $0.125 per common share were declared and paid for each quarter of 1972 and 1973. Cash dividends of $0.25 per common share were declared and paid for each quarter of 1974.

Convertible Debentures. Six per cent convertible debentures with a principal amount of $10,000,000, due 1992, were sold for cash at a price of 100 in the last quarter of 1972. Each $100 debenture was convertible into two shares of common stock. No debentures were converted during 1972 or 1973. The entire issue was converted at the beginning of the third quarter of 1974 because the issue was called by the company. At the date of issue, the bank prime rate was 9 per cent.

Convertible Preferred Stock. A total of 600,000 shares of convertible preferred stock were issued for assets in a purchase transaction at the beginning of the second quarter of 1973. The annual dividend on each share of this convertible preferred

[1] This case is adpated from Exhibit B of Appendix C of APB Opinion 15. It is intended as the basis for class discussion rather than to illustrate either the effective or ineffective handling of an administrative situation.

Copyright © 1974 by the President and Fellows of Harvard College.

stock was $0.20. Each share was convertible into one share of common stock. This convertible stock had a market value of $53 at the time of issuance and the bank prime rate was 10 per cent.

Holders of 500,000 shares of this convertible preferred stock converted their preferred stock into common stock during 1974. (Assume even conversion throughout the year.)

Warrants. Warrants to buy 500,000 shares of common stock at $60 per share for a period of 5 years were issued along with the convertible preferred stock mentioned above. No warrants have been exercised.

Common Stock. The number of shares of common stock oustanding were as follows:

	1974	1973
Beginning of Year	3,300,000	3,300,000
Conversion of Preferred Stock	500,000	—
Conversion of Debentures	200,000	—
End of Year	4,000,000	3,300,000

Net Income. The 1973 and 1974 net income before dividends on preferred stock was (thousands):

1973: Net Income	$10,300
1974: Income before Extraordinary Item	12,900
Net Income	13,800

You may assume a 50 per cent tax rate.

QUESTION

1. Compute the company's primary and fully diluted earnings per share for 1974 and 1973.

Case 10 - 4

Total Electronics Corporation (A)[1]

Total Electronics Corporation (TEC) is a vertically integrated manufacturer and distributor of complex electronics equipment for both military and civilian markets. Founded and incorporated in California in 1964, the firm has grown primarily through a combination of intensive new product development and the acquisition of other high technology firms. Such mergers have often been accomplished with cash payments, but several larger acquisitions involved instead the use of convertible securities.

TEC made its first public offering in early 1966 and its stock was subsequently afforded a price-earnings ratio high enough to facilitate the use of equity-based instruments for acquisitions. Yet, by the end of 1970, TEC's stock had fallen substantially in price and an antitrust consent decree in that year prevented the firm from making any further major acquisitions. Thus, in the period 1970-1973, TEC's management concentrated on internal growth within the constraints of the firm's complex capital structure.

Exhibit 1 presents data on outstanding issues of TEC securities.

Exhibit 2 provides information on TEC's performance in fiscal year 1973.

QUESTION

1. Based on the information in the case, calculate TEC's primary and fully diluted earnings per share for the 1973 fiscal year. Assume that APB Opinion No. 15 applies to all outstanding securities. You may also assume a 50 per cent tax rate.

[1] This case was prepared by Steven E. Levy, Research Assistant, under the supervision of Associate Professor John K. Shank, as the basis for class discussion rather than to illustrate either the effective or ineffective handling of an administrative situation.

EXHIBIT 1

TOTAL ELECTRONICS CORPORATION
Outstanding Securities Issues
December 31, 1973

(1) Issue	(2) Issue Date	(3) Amount	(4) Issue Price	(5) Coupon Rate/Stated Dividend Rate	(6) Conversion Rate	(7) Prime Rate at Time of Issue	(8) Maturity/Expiration
I. Convertible Debentures	12/67	$15,000,000	$1000/bond	3.75%	Each bond convertible into 12 shares of common	6.00%	1987
II. Convertible Preferred Stock Series A	3/68	$12,000,000	$ 100/share	$5.00	Each share convertible into 2.75 shares of common	6.00%	—
III. Convertible Preferred Stock Series B	10/68	$25,000,000	$ 100/share	$6.50	Each share convertible into .3 shares of common	6.25%	—
IV. Convertible Debentures	1/70	$20,000,000	$987.50/bond	6%	Each bond convertible into 50 shares of common	8.50%	1985
V. Convertible Preferred Stock Series C	4/70	$10,000,000	$ 100/share	$5.25	Each share convertible into 4 shares of common	8.00%	—
VI. Common Stock Purchase Warrants	9/68	5 million warrants	—	—	Each warrant convertible into 1 share of common at exercise price of $60	6.50%	1988
VII. Common Stock Purchase Warrants	2/66	200,000 warrants	—	—	Each warrant convertible into 1 share of common at exercise price of $10	5.00%	1982

EXHIBIT 2

TOTAL ELECTRONICS CORPORATION
TEC Data
Fiscal Year 1973

A. Profit before Tax	$20,400,000	
Tax	10,200,000	
Net Income after Tax	10,200,000	
Preferred Dividends	2,750,000	
Net Income to Common Stock	$ 7,450,000	

B. Common Share Outstanding (12/31/72): 3,200,000 shares
Common Stock Offering (3/31/73): 120,000 shares
Common Shares Outstanding (12/31/73): 3,320,000 shares

C. Price/Share (1/1/73): $32.75
Average Price/Share for Fiscal Year 1973: $28.00
Price/Share (12/31/73): $26.25

Case 10-5

Bunker-Ramo Corporation[1]

The following letter was mailed to all shareholders of Bunker-Ramo Corporation in early 1971:

March 29, 1971

Dear Shareowner:

The Annual Report recently mailed to you reported that net income for 1970 of $9,141,013 was equivalent to 39¢ per share. The 39¢ per share figure was determined by dividing 23,575,685 shares (which include preferred stock assumed to be converted into 5,435,499 shares of common stock) into net income for the year of $9,141,013. The same procedure was correctly used in 1969.

A technical accounting rule called to our attention by our auditors, Haskins & Sells, after the mailing of our Annual Report states that if the assumed conversion of preferred stock results in increasing earnings per share, conversion should not be assumed. Since this rule applies to 1970, net income per share should have been determined by dividing the weighted average outstanding shares of common stock plus applicable options and warrants amounting to 18,140,236 shares into net income for the year of $9,141,013 less dividends paid of $2,697,075 to preferred shareholders. This would have resulted in 36¢ per share with no change in the net income of $9,141,013.

Sincerely,

George S. Trimble
President

[1] This material was prepared from published sources as the basis for class discussion rather than to illustrate either the effective or ineffective handling of an administrative situation.

QUESTIONS

1. What is the *preferred* dividend expressed per *common* share for the shares into which the preferred is convertible?

2. In 1969, Bunker-Ramo reported eps of $.53. In that year, was the convertible preferred stock dilutive or anti-dilutive?

3. Is the convertible preferred dilutive or anti-dilutive in 1970?

4. If eps before considering the convertible preferred had been $.49 in 1970, how would the convertible preferred have been treated for purposes of computing eps?

Case 11-1

Gulf & Western Industries, Inc. (A)[1]

The following quote is taken from the fiscal year 1969 mid-year report of G & W:

> In utilizing G & W's assets in a manner to best serve its shareholders, management from time to time has invested in marketable securities and realized profits from such activities. On January 31, 1969, the marketable securities portfolio, at cost, and receivable from sale of marketable securities, amounted to $276 million. While management cannot assure that there will continue to be gains from its investment activities, it intends, when the opportunity is presented, to attempt to enhance our shareholders' value through prudent and timely investments in marketable securities.

In *Accounting Research Bulletin Number 43*, the AICPA adopted the following position:

> Marketable securities represent the investment of cash available for current operations. . . . Marketable securities specifically excluded investments made for the purpose of control, affiliation, or other continuing business advantage. . . . It is important that the cost of temporary investments be supplemented by information which reveals their market value at the balance sheet date. . . . Only in the case of certain investment companies whose business is trading in securities is it generally accepted to take unrealized appreciation of securities into the accounts.

During 1968 G & W had acquired 505,000 shares of Sinclair Common Stock in the open market for cash at prices ranging upward from $72 a share. Pursuant to exchange offers in November and December 1968, G & W acquired an additional 186,000 shares of Sinclair Common. On January 8, 1969, G & W granted to Atlantic Richfield Refining an option to purchase 618,360 shares of Sinclair between August 1, 1969, and September 3, 1969, at a price of $130 per share. At

[1] Data for this case were taken from published material. It is intended for class discussion rather than to illustrate either effective or ineffective handling of an administrative situation.

that time, Sinclair was selling publicly for $116 per share. On the same date, Atlantic issued to G & W a warrant, exercisable between January 1, 1971, and December 31, 1976, to purchase 618,360 shares of Atlantic Common for $125 a share. Atlantic was selling publicly at that time for $108 per share. On March 4, 1969, Sinclair merged with Atlantic and each share of Sinclair held by G & W (including 177,400 additional shares purchased in the open market during 1969) was exchanged for .6 shares of Atlantic Common and one share of Atlantic's 2.80 cumulative convertible preference stock.

On August 28 the following announcement appeared in *Moody's Industrials News:*

> Gulf and Western announced yesterday that it had sold on the New York Stock Exchange approximately 371,000 shares of Atlantic-Richfield Common at $110.75 a share and approximately 618,000 shares of Atlantic's $2.80 Preferred at $70.75 a share. The proceeds were approximately $84,500,000. Lehman Brothers acted as brokers for the sale, placing the shares with institutional buyers. . . . In consideration for Atlantic cancelling its option to buy the shares for approximately $80.5 million, G & W agreed to pay Atlantic approximately $2,000,000. . . . Gulf & Western still holds a considerable block of Atlantic-Richfield.

Gulf & Western's fiscal year ended on July 31, 1969. Its annual report was to be released in October 1969.

QUESTIONS

1. Assuming that G & W's cost for the Sinclair stock averaged $90 a share and that zero value was assigned to the warrant received on January 8, 1969, what was the gain on the shares sold on August 27, 1969? What was the unrealized gain on the shares still held by G & W?

2. Should the gain on the Atlantic stock sold in August 1969 be recognized in G & W's earnings statement for the year ended July 31, 1969, or in the next fiscal year? When should the unrealized gain on the remaining Atlantic shares be recognized? Do you believe that G & W should carry marketable securities at cost or at market on its balance sheet?

Case 11-2

Owens-Illinois Glass Company[1]

Owens-Illinois is the largest domestic manufacturer of bottles and other types of glass containers used by the food, drug, milk, liquor, beverage, and brewing industries. The company also makes plastic containers, metal and plastic closures, container board, corrugated and solid fiber shipping boxes, glass television bulbs and other electronic products, scientific laboratory glassware, glass tubing and rod and products made from tubing, glass tumblers, stemware, tableware, and various plastic noncontainer products.

For a number of years Owens-Illinois maintained a significant investment in certain common shares that were listed on the New York Stock Exchange and that were reported by Owens-Illinois among its current assets as "listed securities, at cost." A 10-year statistical review contained in the Owens-Illinois 1962 annual report showed that this investment had grown from a cost of $12.8 million in 1953 to a cost of $20.8 million in 1962. During 1962, the dividend income on these listed securities amounted to $3,261,898, which, after applicable taxes, amounted to $0.41 per Owens-Illinois common share. Referring to the investments in common stocks, the 1962 annual report stated:

> Our policy relating to these investments is re-examined periodically and the means and extent of any disposition will be governed by capital needs of the company and general economic conditions.

In addition to the "listed securities," certain investments in uncontrolled domestic and foreign affiliates were reported in the consolidated balance sheet as

[1] This case was prepared by Robert T. Sprouse, Lecturer on Business Administration, on the basis of the company's published annual reports. Case material of the Harvard Graduate School of Business Administration is prepared as a basis for class discussion. Cases are not designed to present illustrations of either effective or ineffective handling of administrative problems.

Note: Section 243 of the Internal Revenue Code of 1954 provides that in the case of a corporation, an amount equal to 85% of dividends received from taxable domestic corporations may be deducted in arriving at taxable income.

EXHIBIT 1

OWENS-ILLINOIS GLASS COMPANY
Listed Securities

	1962	1961	1960	1959	1958
Owens-Corning Fiberglas Corp.					
Number of Common Shares Held as Current Asset	1,245,520	1,235,860	1,235,860	1,235,859	1,235,859
Cost	$ 1,447,571	$ 1,437,508	$ 1,437,508	$ 1,437,507	$ 1,437,507
Market Value	71,150,330	104,739,135	121,114,280	110,300,416	78,477,047
Monsanto Chemical Company					
Number of Common Shares Held	358,826	351,790	344,892	338,130	331,500
Cost	$ 10,298,438	$ 10,298,428	$ 10,298,420	$ 10,298,437	$ 10,298,437
Market Value	17,672,180	18,512,949	15,994,366	18,776,215	13,052,812
Continental Can Co., Inc.					
Number of Common Shares Held	334,813	334,813	334,813	334,813	319,500
Cost	$ 8,291,513	$ 8,291,513	$ 8,291,513	$ 8,291,513	$ 7,855,362
Market Value	15,108,437	16,154,727	11,760,307	15,610,656	18,491,062
Container Corp. of America					
Number of Common Shares Held	120,000	140,000	160,000	180,000	200,000
Cost	411,692	419,097	426,501	433,906	441,310
Market Value	2,940,000	3,692,500	3,780,000	5,085,000	5,800,000
Pennsylvania Glass Sand Corp.					
Number of Common Shares Held	74,428	74,428	74,428	74,428	37,214
Cost	$ 328,200	$ 328,200	$ 328,200	$ 328,200	$ 328,200
Market Value	2,251,447	2,437,517	2,604,980	2,595,677	2,325,875
Subtotal					
Cost	$ 20,777,414	$ 20,774,746	$ 20,782,566	$ 20,789,566	$ 20,360,816
Quoted Market Value	109,122,394	145,536,828	155,253,933	152,357,964	118,146,796

Owens-Corning Fiberglas Corp.

Number of Common Shares Reserved for Exchange
of Preferred Shares (included in other security
investments)

	854,407	864,067	864,088	864,141	864,141
Cost	$ 881,862	$ 891,925	$ 891,945	$ 891,997	$ 891,997
Market Value	48,808,000	73,229,678	84,680,624	77,124,584	54,872,953
Total					
Cost	$ 21,659,726	$ 21,666,671	$ 21,674,087	$ 21,681,563	$ 21,252,813
Quoted market value	157,930,394	218,766,506	239,934,557	229,482,548	173,019,749

In the annual reports, the cost and quoted market value were listed separately for each of the
above six groups of common stock. All were reported as current assets under the balance sheet
caption "listed securities" with the exception of the Owens-Corning Fiberglas shares reserved
for exchange of preferred stock. The latter was reported in the other security investments
section of the balance sheet.

EXHIBIT 2

OWENS-ILLINOIS GLASS COMPANY
Highlights

	1962	1961	1960	1959	1958
Net Sales	$627,766,400	$596,424,600	$561,042,300	$552,676,900	$508,459,900
Earnings before U.S. and Foreign Taxes on Income	59,060,200	61,858,900	61,287,100	80,031,400	69,249,100
Net Earnings	33,160,200	34,358,900	33,187,100	40,831,400	37,772,000[a]
Taxes Excluding Social Benefits Taxes	33,511,100	34,746,700	34,904,700	46,002,800	36,671,900
Working Capital	155,363,200	159,793,100	168,154,600	164,535,300	159,794,200
Land, Buildings, Equipment, and Timberlands, net	255,634,700	250,135,700	211,196,900	209,073,500	197,485,100
Long-term Debt	96,452,000	98,302,400	97,200,000	98,200,000	100,000,000
A Common Share:					
Earnings	4.09	4.26	4.10	5.20	4.82[a]
Annual Cash Dividend Rate	2.50	2.50	2.50	2.50	2.50
Taxes Excluding Social Benefits Taxes	4.58	4.76	4.79	6.37	5.13
Cash Flow	8.60	8.12	7.23	8.11	(not shown)
Equity	$350,429,400	$229,225,800	$324,619,600	$310,057,700	$284,156,200
Equity a Common Share	36.81	35.19	33.25	31.56	28.24
Annual Preferred Dividend requirement	3,278,200	3,291,700	3,291,900	3,292,000	3,292,000
Shares Outstanding:					
Common	7,310,310	7,301,110	7,287,710	7,216,692	7,148,287
Preferred	813,721	822,921	822,941	822,991	822,991

[a]Includes nonrecurring gain of 70 cents a share realized from the sale of certain assets of the Kaylo Division and the sale of 98,386 common shares of Continental Can Company, Inc.

EXHIBIT 3

		1959	1960	1961	1962	% of Stock Owned by O-I in 1966
Monsanto	EPS	2.18	2.40	2.40	2.70	
	DPS	1.00	1.00	1.00	1.05	~1 1/2
Continental	EPS	3.20	2.21	2.87	3.26	
Can	DPS	1.80	1.80	1.80	1.80	~3
Container Corp.	EPS	1.83	1.57	1.92	1.72	
	DPS	1.00	1.00	.90	.825	~1-2
OCF	EPS	2.43	2.19	2.13	2.14	
	DPS	.80	1.00	1.00	1.00	~30
Pa. Glass Sand	EPS	1.67	1.65	1.76	2.01	
	DPS	.90	1.00	1.00	1.00	~4

non-current assets under the heading "investments, at cost, deposits, etc."

The company's balance sheets always indicated that supplementary information concerning the listed securities could be found elsewhere in the annual report. Sometimes this information was presented in a footnote to the financial statements, sometimes in a section of the annual report entitled "financial review," and sometimes in both places. Some of the supplementary information about listed securities supplied in the annual reports issued for years 1958 through 1962 is summarized in Exhibit 1.

Owens-Illinois "highlights," which appeared prominently just inside the cover of each of the annual reports, are also reproduced as Exhibit 2.

QUESTIONS

1. Compute investment earnings for 1959-1962 (pretax) under cost, equity, and market value methods. You may ignore capital gains on the sale of Container Corp. shares because such gains are not material.

2. Which securities are current assets and which are long-term investments?

3. State and defend an accounting policy for investments for O-I. Consider both balance sheet presentation and income statement presentation.

APPENDIX A
OWENS-ILLINOIS GLASS COMPANY

History of Acquisition of Listed Security Investments

1. Owens-Corning Fiberglas Corporation—acquired 1938

The company's 1935 annual report stated that " . . . a 25-year license agreement has been entered into with Corning Glass Works of Corning, New York under which your company and Corning will cooperate in research and development work in connection with glass fibers."

Owens-Corning Fiberglas Corporation was formed in 1938 to acquire from Owens-Illinois Glass Company and Corning Glass Works the assets these companies used in the development and production of glass fiber products, including plants at Newark, Ohio, and Corning, New York. Since its inception an equal percentage of its common stock has been owned by Owens-Illinois Glass and Corning Glass, each of these companies owning 49.77 per cent at first and about 31 per cent each in 1962. The remainder of the common stock is publicly held. By the end of 1939 Owens-Illinois owned 15,501 preferred shares and 60,423 common shares of Owens-Corning. These shares were carried on the books as an investment (non-current asset) until 1951. In 1951, in order to comply with New York Stock Exchange listing requirements for Owens-Corning Fiberglas, Owens-Illinois sold enough of the Owens-Corning common stock to reduce their ownership to 33 per cent. Corning Glass Works did likewise. (Market price at the time was $34.75.) At the end of 1951, Owens-Illinois had over 1,000,000 shares of Owens-Corning (the increase in the number of shares resulted from conversion of preferred shares into common and common stock splits) and in 1952, after the stock was listed and a public market was created, Owens-Illinois began carrying this stock on their balance sheet as a current asset. No reason was given in the 1952 annual report for this change.

2. Monsanto Chemical Corporation—acquired 1957

In 1953, Owens-Illinois invested $8,000,000 in the purchase of 250,000 shares of the Plax Company (50 per cent interest). It exchanged this interest, in 1957, with the Monsanto Chemical Company for 325,000 shares of Monsanto common stock. Stock dividends and small additional purchases of this stock apparently have increased this to 366,003 shares in 1963, carried at a cost of the original market value of the Monsanto stock exchanged. The Monsanto common shares have been reported as a current asset since 1957. Prior to 1957, the Plax stock had been carried under other investments, not as a current asset.

3. Continental Can Co., Inc.—acquired 1956

In 1956 when Continental Can Co., Inc. acquired the Robert Gair Corp., Owens-Illinois received 417,886 shares of Continental Can common stock in exchange for its ownership in Robert Gair Corporation. Owens had obtained its Robert Gair shares in 1952 in exchange for one of its operating divisions and had carried it as a current asset until 1956. From 1956 to 1962 the company carried the Continental Can stock as a current asset. In 1963 it disposed of its last shares of Continental Can stock in accordance with an agreement entered into when the stock was acquired.

4. Container Corporation of America—acquired 1933

In 1933, Owens-Illinois acquired 16,000 shares of 7% cumulative preferred stock of Container Corporation of America, which it subsequently sold or converted into common stock (50,000 shares). Small amounts of additional common stock were apparently bought and sold periodically. In 1955, Owens-Illinois held 70,000 shares of Container Corporation common. The stock was split four for one in 1956 and by the end of that year Owens-Illinois held 270,000 shares. Recently it has been disposing of shares in this company at the rate of exactly 20,000 shares per year.

No reason for this apparent systematic divestiture is given in the annual reports. The Container Corporation of America stock was carried as an investment until 1951. Since 1952 the Container Corporation stock has been reported as a current asset.

5. Pennsylvania Glass Sand—acquired 1936

In 1936 Owens-Illinois sold one of its subsidiary companies to Pennsylvania Glass Sand in exchange for 15,309 trust certificates for voting shares. This was reported as an investment until 1951 and carried as a current asset thereafter with no change in amount since 1952.

Case 11 - 3

Xenia Industries, Inc.

As was his custom, Mr. Robert Bowen often discussed the financial statements he received on his stockholdings with an accounting friend, Mr. Andrew Franklin. Mr. Bowen had recently been appointed a director of Xenia Industries after purchasing the holdings of one of the original stockholders, and he had been making a detailed examination of the financial statements in preparation for taking an active part in the affairs of the company. Xenia's balance sheet contained among the assets, an account called "investments in subsidiaries." Mr. Franklin suggested that Mr. Bowen probably should seek additional information about the nature of the items included in this account.

Further investigation revealed that Xenia had two subsidiary companies in which it owned 100 per cent of the outstanding capital stock and one other company in which it had a 90 per cent ownership interest. The records revealed the following investment information:

	Balance 12/31/74
1. The Oates Manufacturing Company (owned 100 per cent) (Acquired January 1, 1969, at a cost of $175,000)	$240,000
2. Jackson Valve Company (owned 100 per cent) (Acquired January 1, 1969, at a cost of $270,000)	270,000
3. Santos Mining Company (owned 90 per cent)- a Nigerian company (Acquired June 30, 1974, at a cost of $70,000)	70,000
Total Balance of Investment in Subsidiaries as shown on December 31, 1974, Balance Sheet	$580,000

[1] This case was prepared by Associate Professor John K. Shank as the basis for class discussion rather than to illustrate effective or ineffective handling of an administrative situation.

EXHIBIT 1

XENIA INDUSTRIES, INC.

Comparative Balance Sheets
December 31

ASSETS		1973		1974
Current Assets:				
Cash	$129,000		$ 42,000	
Marketable Securities	55,000		25,000	
Accounts Receivable (net)	110,000		160,000	
Inventory	152,000		222,000	
		$446,000		$449,000
Long-term Assets:				
Plant and Equipment	$370,000		$460,000	
Less: Accumulated Depreciatio	108,000	262,000	90,000	370,000
Goodwill		90,0C0		90,000
Patents		50,000		50,000
Other Intangibles		20,000		40,000
Investment in Subsidiary Companies		500,000		580,000
Other Assets		14,000		66,000
Total Assets		$1,382,000		$1,645,000

LIABILITIES AND STOCKHOLDERS' EQUITY

Current Liabilities:				
Accounts Payable	$210,000		$115,000	
Accrued Expenses	60,000		80,000	
Accrued Taxes	62,000	$332,000	97,000	$292,000
Mortgages Payable		125,000		100,000
Reserve for Deferred Taxes		30,000		50,000
Capital Stock ($100 par)	$500,000		$540,000	
Additional Paid-in Capital	100,000		180,000	
Retained Earnings	295,000	895,000	483,000	1,203,000
Total Liabilities and Stockholders' Equity		$1,382,000		$1,645,000

EXHIBIT 2

XENIA INDUSTRIES, INC.

Income Statement for Year Ended
December 31, 1974

Sales		$3,500,000
Less Cost of sales		2,600,000
Gross Margin		$ 900,000
Less: Selling Expenses	$400,000	
Administrative expenses	135,000	535,000

Income from Operations		$ 365,000
Other Income and Expense:		
Deduct: Other Expenses	$ 40,000	
Add: Equity in Earnings of Subsidiary	10,000	30,000
Profit before Taxes		$ 335,000
Income Taxes		102,000
Profit after Taxes before Extraordinary Charges		$ 233,000
Extraordinary Items (net of taxes)[a]		30,000
Net Income		$ 203,000

Analysis of Changes in Capital

Additional Paid in Capital	
Balance, December 31, 1973	$ 100,000
Add: Premium on Sale of Capital Stock	80,000
Balance, December 31, 1974	$ 180,000
Retained Earnings	
Balance, December 31, 1973	$ 295,000
Add: Net Income	203,000
	$ 498,000
Deduct: Cash Dividends	15,000
Balance, December 31, 1974	$ 483,000

[a]Because of a modernization program undertaken by your company, some excess facilities were disposed of by sale. Book value at time of sale was $110,000; originally the facilities cost $200,000. Sales price was $50,000.

EXHIBIT 3

.XENIA INDUSTRIES, INC.

Condensed Subsidiary Balance Sheets
December 31, 1974
(000 omitted)

	Oates Manufacturing Company	Jackson Valve Company	Santos Mining Company	Totals
Current Assets	$300	$200	$ 45	$545
Property Assets (net)	50	150	35	235
Other Assets	10	140	60	210
Total	$360	$490	$140	$990
Current Liabilities	$ 20	$ 70	$ 5	$ 95
Long-term Debt	100	100	80	280
Owners' Equity				
Capital Stock	175	200	50	425

Additional Paid- in Capital	—	50	—	50
Retained Earnings	65	70	5	140
Total	$360	$490	$140	$990
Dividends Received by Xenia Company since Acquisition through December 31, 1974	$ 25	$100	—	$125

Total Owners' Equity of Each Company at Date of Acquisition of Stock was as Follows:

Capital Stock	$175	$200	$ 50
Additional Paid-in Capital		50	
Retained Earnings (deficit)		(100)	15
Total	$175	$150	$ 65
1974 Earnings	$ 10	$ 50	$(10)[a]
1974 Depreciation Expense	$ 8	$ 15	$ 4

[a]Since acquisition, June 30, 1974.

Discussions with the company accountant revealed that Xenia has been recording in its investment account the undistributed earnings of the Oates Manufacturing Company. Xenia did not consolidate Oates because it was a much different business from Xenia's. The other investments were maintained at the original cost, recording revenue on Xenia's books only to the extent dividends were received. Jackson Valve was carried at cost because the management of Xenia was actively trying to divest a major part of Jackson's operations. No buyer had yet been found but negotiations were in process with several interested parties. Santos Mining was carried at cost because of management's general reluctance to count undistributed profits of a foreign sub. There was, however, no particular reason to question the political or economic stability of Nigeria. Earnings of Santos were reinvested in the business as a matter of policy. It was unlikely that any of Santos' earnings would ever be repatriated.

Mr. Bowen had been concerned about the working capital position of Xenia Industries. He knew that the company would have to seek additional short-term borrowing from the banks and he was concerned about the effects of preparing consolidated statements on the various parts of the Xenia financial statements, as well as the effects on a statement of sources and application of funds. Among other things it was his impression that bankers put a great deal of emphasis on such factors as working capital, debt/equity ratios, earnings, return on investment, and other more or less standard ratios.

Further questioning revealed that one of the important factors leading to the purchase of the Jackson Valve Company was several important patents that Jackson had developed. Jackson had charged the patent development costs to expense as they were incurred, but Xenia's management was certain these patents would contribute materially to future growth and sales for at least 10 years beyond the acquisition date. The excess of purchase price over book value on this acquisition was attributable to the patents.

QUESTIONS

1. Which subsidiaries, if any, should be consolidated?

2. Prepare consolidated statements for 1974 under your assumptions from Question 1.

3. Prepare a memo for Mr. Bowen analyzing the differences between the consolidated statement ratios and those of the individual firms.

Case 11-4

International Telephone
& Telegraph Corporation (A)[1]

"The difficulty with consolidated financial statements," said Mr. Herbert C. Knortz, senior vice president and comptroller of International Telephone and Telegraph Corporation (ITT), "is that we've obviously got to have them in order to report responsibily to the shareholding public. But there's almost no way to prepare them without running the risk of either confusing or misleading someone. Morever, in ITT we've really got the problem in spades—not just because we have so many legal business entities within the ITT complex, but also because our businesses are so diverse as to product and market. I think our consolidations policy is in full accord with the best requirements of the accounting profession but I'm still not happy with it."

BACKGROUND

In 1969, ITT was one of the largest industrial corporations in the world. Based on 1968 performance, it ranked eleventh in sales volume in *Fortune* magazine's listing of "The 500 Largest Industrial Corporations," up from a ranking of twenty-first the preceding year. Financial statements for 1968 are presented in exhibits 1 and 2. The company's 10-year growth record is summarized in Exhibit 3. "That record," Mr. Knortz said, "is really a monument to Hal Geneen (ITT's chairman and president]. When he came here in 1959 he said he'd double our sales and profits within 5 years, and he did. Then, in 1964 he made the same statement, and he's done it again. There may be a lot of talk about the difficulty of managing so-called conglomerates, but Mr. Geneen has shown that it can be done."

For the year 1968, more than half of ITT's revenues and profits were produced by its manufacturing operations. (See Exhibit 4 for financial data by major product

[1] This case was made possible by the cooperation of International Telephone and Telegraph Corporation. It was prepared by Professor Richard F. Vancil as the basis for class discussion rather than to illustrate either effective or ineffective handling of an administrative situation.

groups.) During the preceding few years, however, the company had pursued its announced policy of increasing its activities in the field of consumer and business services. Acquisitions during this period included Continental Baking Company ("Wonder" bread and "Hostess" cakes), Levitt and Sons, Incorporated (residential home construction), Sheraton Corporation of America ("world's largest hotel chain"), Avis, Inc. ("Number Two" in rental cars), Aetna Finance Company (consumer installment loans), and many others. ITT continued to operate telephone utilities, the original business on which the company was founded in 1920, in Puerto Rico, the Virgin Islands, Chile, and Peru as well as producing about 20 per cent of the telephone equipment sold outside of the United States.

Most of ITT's acquisitions were effected through an exchange of shares with the shareholders of the company being acquired. Typically, ITT would create a new series of its cumulative convertible preferred stock and exchange it for the common stock of its merger partner. Such an exchange was usually a nontaxable transaction for the individual shareholder, and was treated as a pooling of interests in ITT's accounting records. The effect of such transactions during 1968, for example, may be observed by comparing the sales and revenues for 1967 as originally reported (Exhibit 3) with the same figure as restated for 1967 (Exhibit 2).

CONSOLIDATIONS POLICY

"Our consolidations policy is the clearest one possible under the circumstances, I think," said Mr. Knortz. "The first sentence in the footnotes to our annual report tells it all: 'The consolidated financial statements include the accounts of all significant majority-owned subsidiaries except the finance subsidiaries. Even for the finance subs we used the equity method, which means we reflect the full effect of their current operations as a single entry in our income statement. And our annual report includes supplementary financial statements for those subs [see Exhibit 5].

"The principal reason for not consolidating the finance subs," Mr. Knortz went on, "is that it isn't usually done by industrial companies. Many manufacturing companies have captive finance companies to handle the receivables generated by their sales, but these subs are so different from the primary operations of their parent that they've not consolidated on the grounds that it would be confusing. We want our financial statements to be as clear as possible—and as comparable as possible to those of other companies—so we follow the traditional practice.

"Frankly, I'm quite happy that we don't consolidate them, for another reason. One of the keystones in our growth has been to increase the effectiveness with which our stockholders' equity is employed. This means not only making good investments, but also making appropriate use of debt capital to leverage the stockholders' return. Although we had nearly a billion dollars of long-term debt at the end of 1968, our return on equity set a record. Unfortunately, the bond-rating bureaus don't always view us as the blue-chip we really are. They look at our financial ratios on a consolidated basis and say that we've got a little more debt than a manufacturing company ought to have to earn the best bond rating. Obviously if our finance subs were consolidated, our capitalization ratios would look even worse.

"Actually, as we've pointed out to the bond fellows time and again," Mr. Knortz concluded, "our corporation is so diverse that the only way to evaluate our debt securities is in terms of the businesses we're in. Many of our businesses only make sense as an investment if they're highly leveraged. Utilities are perhaps the best example, but the same thing is true of a hotel chain [see Exhibit 6] or the car rental business. In each of those businesses, our operations are conservatively financed; we meet the highest financial standards for those particular industries. Yet, all of the activities are consolidated in our regular statements, and the bond analysts then apply the standards that would be applicable to a manufacturing company. I don't think that our consolidations policy needs to be changed, but I do know that it's costing our stockholders money in terms of a higher interest rate on our bonds. I suppose that we are faced with a continuing program of education and disclosure."

QUESTIONS

1. Using the available data, evaluate the capital structure of ITT and such of its components as you think necessary to illustrate Mr. Knortz's comments in the last paragraph of the case.

2. What, if anything, should ITT do to deal with the problem raised by Mr. Knortz?

EXHIBIT 1

Consolidated Balance Sheets
as of December 31, 1968 and 1967
Thousands of Dollars

	1968	1967
Assets		
Current Assets		
Cash	$ 296,839	$ 168,176
Accounts and notes receivable	638,172	607,344
Inventories	705,851	637,352
Other current assets	120,269	99,815
	1,761,131	1,512,687
Investments, Deferred Receivables and Other Assets		
Finance subsidiaries (Page 35)	125,270	107,437
Other investments, at cost	166,817	121,675
Accounts receivable due subsequent to one year	59,564	56,232
Other assets	73,825	72,258
	425,476	357,602
Plant, Property and Equipment, at cost	2,882,438	2,599,558
Less—Reserves for depreciation	1,046,645	963,475
	1,835,793	1,636,083
	$4,022,400	$3,506,372

Liabilities and Stockholders' Equity

Current Liabilities

Loans and current maturities of long-term debt	$ 376,169	$ 355,690
Accounts payable and accrued charges	563,215	418,238
Accrued taxes	149,180	108,053
	1,088,564	881,981
Reserves and Deferred Liabilities	202,641	164,240
Deferred Income Taxes	69,340	54,905
Long-Term Debt (Page 31)	931,772	848,991
Minority Equity in Subsidiaries Consolidated	77,991	61,973
	2,370,308	2,012,090
Stockholders' Equity		
Cumulative Preferred Stock (Page 31)	372,637	375,483
Common Stock		
Authorized 100,000,000 shares, $1 per value		
Outstanding 59,059,251 and 57,579,387 shares	59,059	57,579
Capital Surplus	388,613	343,478
Retained Earnings	831,783	717,742
	1,652,092	1,494,282
	$4,022,400	$3,506,372

The accompanying notes to financial statements are an integral part of the above statements.

EXHIBIT 2

Consolidated Income
for the years ended December 31, 1968 and 1967
Thousands of Dollars

	1968	1967
Sales and Revenues		
Manufacturing	$2,351,456	$2,066,555
Consumer and business services	1,513,566	1,336,953
Telecommunication utilities	201,480	174,293
	4,066,502	3,577,801

Costs and Expenses (including depreciation of $158,333 and
$142,982)

Costs of sales and operating expenses—		
Manufacturing	1,825,844	1,633,846
Consumer and business services	1,103,289	973,222

Telecommunication utilities	117,579	94,401
Selling and general expenses	663,235	572,904
	3,709,947	3,274,373
	356,555	303,428
Equity in net earnings of finance subsidiaries	10,773	11,288
Income from Operations	367,328	314,716
Dividends, interest and other income	32,172	28,003
Interest and other finfncial charges	(86,775)	(85,851)
	312,725	256,868
Income Taxes and Minority Equity		
U.S. and foreign income taxes	(125,548)	(98,161)
Minority common stockholders' equity in net income	(7,015)	(4,940)
Income before Extraordinary Items	180,162	153,767
Gain on sale of Comsat shares—$16,842 and $6,939 for the respective years (net of applicable income taxes of $10,104 and $4,036), less provision for obsolescence of radio communications facilities—$4,600 and $3,400 for the respective years (net of applicable income taxes of $1,600 in each year)	12,242	3,439
Recovery in 1967 on war damage award of $17,400 applied to reserve for foreign operations	—	—
Net Income	$ 192,404	$ 157,306
Per Share of Common Stock, after recognition of residual securitie:		
Income before extraordinary items	$2.58	$2.29
Extraordinary items	.19	.06
Net income	$2.77	$2.35
Pro Forma net income (after extraordinary items) per share of Common Stock giving effect to conversion as of the beginning of the year of all dilutive convertible securities although such full conversion is unlikely for some time	$2.66	$2.26

The accompanying notes to financial statements are an integral part of the above statements.

EXHIBIT 3

Ten-Year Summary*

(Dollar amounts in thousands except per share figures)

	1968	1967	1966	1965	1964	1963	1962	1961	1960	1959
Results for Year										
Sales and revenues	$4,066,502	2,760,572	2,121,272	1,782,939	1,542,079	1,414,146	1,090,198	930,500	811,449	765,640
U.S. and foreign taxes	$ 290,436	204,069	162,179	135,615	120,034	87,345	65,812	54,133	50,266	45,343
Income before extraordinary items	$ 180,162†	119,221†	89,910	76,110	63,164	52,375	40,694	36,059†	30,570†	29,036
Per common share	2.58	2.27	2.04	1.79	1.55	1.35	1.21	1.09	.98	.95
Return on stockholders' equity	12.2%	11.7%	11.5%	10.8%	9.9%	9.1%	8.6%	8.0%	7.4%	7.2%
Dividends per common share	$ .87-1/2	.77-1/2	69-3/8	.61-7/8	.55	.50	.50	.50	.50	.50
Gross plant additions	$ 362,069	238,141	168,049	145,629	119,336	123,241	114,584	105,311	66,809	84,219
Provision for depreciation	$ 158,333	116,120	73,875	63,737	50,713	39,378	31,763	31,341	25,606	27,433
R & D expenditures	$ 210,000	210,000	220,000	182,000	174,000	170,000	150,000	131,000	126,000	117,000

Year-End Position										
Net current assets	$ 672,567	528,713	318,957	367,012	308,055	333,849	296,155	268,422	269,324	222,269
Plant, property and equipment (net)	$1,835,793	1,305,829	895,438	789,849	668,240	572,469	462,323	391,347	288,461	355,115
Total assets	$4,022,400	2,961,172	2,360,435	2,021,795	1,668,853	1,469,168	1,235,781	1,088,310	923,944	932,269
Long-term debt	$ 931,772	744,675	433,834	428,134	309,795	293,408	266,815	182,509	148,478	165,500
Stockholders' equity	$1,652,092	1,143,568	820,007	739,620	659,925	592,429	483,531	465,061	415,814	415,088
Stockholders' equity per common share	$ 16.83	17.39	16.78	15.69	15.06	14.29	14.11	13.76	13.26	13.36
Year-End Statistics										
Orders on hand (Manufacturing)	$1,529,000	1,257,000	1,233,000	1,140,000	1,004,000	917,000	778,000	731,000	623,000	551,000
Shares of common stock outstanding (thousands)	59,059	49,940	42,168	40,530	38,720	36,924	33,258	32,750	31,362	31,060
Stockholders	185,184	130,671	109,203	106,298	104,413	100,269	92,362	94,719	87,818	88,230
Employees	293,000	236,000	204,000	199,000	185,000	73,000	157,000	149,000	132,000	136,000

*The above data are as reported in the ITT Annual Reports for the respective years, except that number of shares and per share amounts have adjusted for 2-for-1 stock split effective January 26, 1968.

†Extraordinary credits in 1968, 1967, 1961 and 1960 amounted to $12,242, $3,539, $7,620 and $7,902, respectively.

EXHIBIT 4

Principal Product Groups	Sales & Revenues		Income*	
	1968	1967	1968	1967
Manufacturing—				
Telecommunications Equipment . . .	21%	21%	24%	22%
Industrial and Consumer Products . .	24	24	18	19
Defense and Space Programs	7	8	1	3
Natural Resources	6	5	12	11
	58	58	55	55
Consumer and Business Services—				
Food Processing and Services	17	17	8	9
Consumer Services	16	16	11	9
Business and Financial Services . ·. .	4	4	10	9
	37	37	29	27
Utility Operations	5	5	16	18
Total	100%	100%	100%	100%

*Before extraordinary items

General Grouping of Net Assets *as of December 31, 1968*
Thousands of Dollars

	Consolidated	Manufacturing	Consumer and Business Services	Telecommunication Utilities
ASSETS				
Current Assets	$ 1,761,131	$ 1,332,999	$ 369,842	$ 58,290
Investments, Deferred Receivables and Other Assets .	425,476	125,149	266,138	34,189
Plant, Property and Equipment	2,882,438	1,497,085	740,455	644,898
Reserves for Depreciation	(1,046,645)	(640,080)	(277,952)	(128,613)
	4,022,400	2,315,153	1,098,483	608,764
LIABILITIES				
Current Liabilities	1,088,564	695,763	254,823	137,978
Reserves and Deferred Liabilities	271,981	210,434	28,524	33,023
Long-Term Debt	931,772	442,797	277,999	210,976
Minority Equity in Subsidiaries Consolidated	77,991	44,035	9,336	24,620
	2,370,308	1,393,029	570,682	406,597
NET ASSETS	$ 1,652,092	$ 922,124	$ 527,801	$ 202,167
NET ASSETS EMPLOYED				
United States and Canada	$ 1,082,661	$ 527,029	$ 483,112	$ 72,520
Foreign	569,431	395,095	44,689	129,647
	$ 1,652,092	$ 922,124	$ 527,801	$ 202,167

The accompanying notes to financial statements are an integral part of the above statement.

EXHIBIT 5

ITT Finance Subsidiaries

Combined Balance Sheets *as of December 31, 1968 and 1967*
Thousands of Dollars

	1968	1967*
ASSETS		
Cash	$ 43,003	$ 42,059
Notes and installment obligations receivable, ($58,738 and $63,936 pledged to secure short-term obligations) net of unearned income and reserves—		
Affiliated companies	59,227	62,952
Other customers	449,613	406,445
Investments in life insurance companies, at underlying equity	24,448	19,283
Investments in property, leased to affiliated companies	13,462	13,990
Other assets	16,991	15,209
	$606,744	$559,938
LIABILITIES		
Bank loans and other short-term obligations	$284,943	$243,742
Accounts payable and accrued charges	21,309	19,878
Long-term debt, due 1969-87—average interest rate 5.5%	175,222	188,881
	481,474	452,501
ITT EQUITY		
Subordinated debt and advances	32,153	22,708
Capital stock and capital surplus—increased in 1968 by capital contribution	55,897	53,613
Retained earnings—$18,271 restricted as to payment of dividends	37,220	31,116
	125,270	107,437
	$606,744	$559,938

Combined Income and Retained Earnings *for the years ended December 31, 1968 and 1967*
Thousands of Dollars

	1968	1967*
INCOME (including $7,744 and $7,994 from affiliated companies)		
Interest	$ 63,700	$ 61,862
Commissions	4,785	4,530
Rentals and other income	5,563	3,355
	74,048	69,747
EXPENSES		
Interest	25,891	24,038
Administrative expenses, etc.	37,048	33,874
U. S. and foreign income taxes	5,102	4,770
	68,041	62,682
	6,007	7,065
Equity in net earnings of life insurance companies	4,766	4,223
NET INCOME	10,773	11,288
Add—Retained earnings at beginning of year	31,116	23,516
(Deduct)—Dividends	(4,669)	(3,688)
RETAINED EARNINGS at end of year	$ 37,220	$ 31,116

1967 restated to include the accounts of Thorp Finance Corporation added through a pooling of interests.

EXHIBIT 6

INTERNATIONAL TELEPHONE AND TELEGRAPH CORPORATION A(A)

Condensed Financial Statement for
Sheraton Corporation of America and Subsidiaries Consolidated (See Note)
(000 omitted)

Consolidated balance Sheets: Dec. 31, 1968

ASSETS

Current Assets	$ 60,505
Investments, Deferred Receivables, and Other Assets	20,661
Plant, Property, and Equipment	336,533
Reserves for Depreciation	(134,748)
Total Assets	$282,951

LIABILITIES

Current Liabilities	$ 47,884
Reserves and Deferred Liabilities	3,499
Long-term Debt	150,265
Minority Equity in Subsidiaries Consolidated	1,541
Total Liabilities	$203,189
NET ASSETS (including $10,204,000 due to ITT)	$ 79,762

Statement of Consolidated Income: Year Ended Dec. 31, 1968

Sales and Revenues: Hotels, Buildings, and Other	$242,732	
Manufacturing	65,164	$307,896
Operating Costs and Expenses: Hotels, Buildings, and Other	$227,493	
Manufacturing	59,495	286,988
Income from Operations		$ 20,908
Other Deductions		
Debt Expense, Net of Other Income	$10,497	
Minority Interest in Net Income	303	
U. S. and Foreign Income Taxes	3,872	14,672
Income before Extraordinary Items		$ 6,236
Net Gains from Disposition of Properties, Less Taxes Thereon		3,947
Net Income		$ 10,183

Note: Includes Thompson Industries, Inc., a Manufacturing Subsidiary.

Source: Offering circular dated July 1969 (recast and condensed by casewriter).

Case 11 - 5

Harte-Hanks Newspapers, Inc.[1]

"Newspapers have traditionally been run in a manner to keep people informed via good journalism and perhaps to persuade to a particular political or economic philosophy through editorials. Recently there has emerged a trend within the industry toward newspaper groups where management, while continuing to stress the production of high-quality newspapers, is more concerned with maximizing return on investment rather than persuading the newspaper audience to any political philosophy. Utilizing central office staffs of highly qualified and motivated managers, group newspapers, possibly best typified by Gannett or Knight, have led the way and have turned in impressive records of growth. Market recognition has followed, and the two companies currently sell at 25-33 times earnings. We believe Harte-Hanks is developing along comparable lines and has the potential for similar or superior earning performance. The new management team which joined the company in September of 1970 has an excellent reputation within the industry."

So begins a Wall Street report written in 1973 by White, Weld, who, it should be noted, also has underwritten Harte-Hanks' various stock offerings.

Less than 3 years before, Harte-Hanks did not exist as a legal entity. There were 20 or so small corporations in Texas, each of which was controlled by the Harte and Hanks families and trusts established by them and each of which managed a small to medium size newspaper. Although the various companies had generally been profitable and were growing at reasonable rates, the owners recognized the need to restructure their corporate and financial affairs in order to meet the challenges and take advantages of the opportunities that the rapid changes of the early 1970's foreshadowed. Late in 1970, in events which for our purposes can be considered as simultaneous, these various corporations were brought within the rubric of one holding company, Harte-Hanks Newspapers, Inc., and a new management team was brought in.

[1] This case was prepared by Laird H. Simons, III, under the supervision of Associate Professor John K. Shank, as the basis for class discussion, rather than to illustrate either the effective or ineffective handling of an administrative situation.

EXHIBIT 1

HARTE-HANKS NEWSPAPERS, INC. AND SUBSIDIARIES
Consolidated Balance Sheet
June 30, 1972

ASSETS		*LIABILITIES AND SHAREHOLDERS' EQUITY*	
Cash	$ 5,027,447	Accounts Payable	$ 2,039,158
Trade Receivables	6,007,985	Accrued Expenses and	2,001,604
Other Current Assets	2,071,960	Other Liabilities	
Investments and		Other Current Liabilities	6,738,778
Other Assets	1,871,135	Long-term Debt	11,845,276
Property, Plant, and		Other Liabilities	186,558
Equipment (net)	18,272,824	Common Stock	3,478,407
Intangible Assets and		Additional Paid-in Capital	6,955,330
Deferred Charges	26,143,267	Retained Earnings	26,149,507
	$59,394,618		$59,394,618

Consolidated Income Statement
Year Ending June 30

	1972	1971
Revenues		
Newspaper Advertising	$39,962,983	$28,584,704
Newspaper Circulation	10,655,149	7,523,219
Television Revenues	3,243,794	2,903,906
Other	1,003,434	976,843
	54,865,360	39,988,672
Cost and Expenses		
Editorial, Production, and Distribution	30,818,868	25,109,940
Advertising, Selling, General, and Administrative	14,680,059	8,780,924
Goodwill Amortization—Note L	367,490	15,694
Other	2,182,956	1,153,206
	48,049,373	35,059,864
Income before Income Taxes and Extraordinary Items	6,815,987	4,928,808
Income Taxes	3,201,458	2,185,982
Income before Extraordinary Items	$ 3,614,529	$ 2,742,826
Extraordinary Items, Net of Applicable Tax—Note K	---	1,063,576
Net Income	$3,614,529	$ 3,806,402
Average Number of Shares of Common Stock Outstanding after Giving Retroactive Effect to the Shares Issued in the Reorganization and Poolings of Interests—Note A	3,268,989	3,119,247
Earnings per Average Share of Common Stock—		

Note 1:

Income before Extraordinary Items	$1.11	$ .88
Extraordinary Items	——	.34
Net Income	$1.11	$1.22

Since that time the company had experienced rapid growth, both internally and by acquisitions. (See Exhibit 1 for 1972 financial statements.) By the time of the *Yakima Herald* acquisition, Harte-Hanks had gone public and had already expanded through acquisition into half a dozen states. (For a summary of its 1971-1972 acquisitions, see Exhibit 2.)

To foster management's aim of becoming a major publicly held company in the information business, a number of rather explicit goals were established. Those directly applicable to their acquisitions policies are as follows:

1. Maintain at least 80 per cent of corporate revenues from newspapers.

2. Maximize the long-term value of the common shareholder equity in the company.

3. Double 1971 earnings per share by 7/1/76.

4. Enjoy a price-earnings ratio that is in the upper 25 per cent of the industry by 7/1/76.

5. Generate over 50 per cent of total revenues from outside Texas by 7/1/75.

To this point, although non-Texas operations have accounted for 28 per cent of the revenues, they have accounted for only 10 of the profits. This would imply that the potential earnings improvement through better productivity and market penetration are still to be realized from the recently acquired newspapers. Harte-Hanks is not buying earning gains through acquisitions; rather it is buying the potential for earning growth. Initially an acquisition may be slightly dilutive, but the new properties provide the basis on which the company can effect the technological, administrative, and marketing changes that it hopes will result in significant incremental profit contribution in succeeding years.

In this regard, the company's own set of acquisition criteria are quite instructive. First, the company looks at the overall economic health of the acquiree's local market. It must be currently viable and growing in size and must show promise of continuing improvements, both qualitatively and quantitatively. Second, the newspaper to be acquired must satisfy unique informational needs better than anyone else in the market. Every market must have its own identity regarding local news and advertising, especially, as is often the case, if the community is in the shadow of a major city. Identifying such needs requires considerable market research. Satisfying them requires intense product development. Third, the acquisition candidate must be, or have the potential for becoming in 1 year, the most effective means in the market for disseminating the information and filling the local advertising and news needs that have been identified. Finally, there must be qualified management available, either within the acquisition candidate or within Harte-Hanks, that can deal creatively with the unique characteristics, opportunities, and problems of that particular market.

Once these criteria are met, the potential acquiree must also meet several quantitative objectives before an offer will be made. The investment must be small enough in relation to the projected financial returns of the acquiree so that the discounted present value rate of return is attractive. There must be no appreciable initial dilution of earnings per share. The price paid must be less than twenty times the expected annualized earnings at the end of 12 months.

This was the framework within which the Yakima acquisition was evaluated. It had come to the attention of Harte-Hanks that the family that owned the *Yakima Herald-Republic* was considering the sale of their entire interest. The family patriarch, W. H. Robertson, whose father had begun the paper in 1890, was 73. His sister, Helen Crum, who held most of the remaining shares, was somewhat older. Having seen what had happened to other newspapers that had passed into estates and been sold to the highest bidder, they chose to find an appropriate buyer for their life's work before retiring.

The *Yakima Herald-Republic* was attractive to a group newspaper for a variety of reasons. It serviced a natural geographic area that was partially bounded by mountains and inhabited by about 175,000 residents (46,000 households). It was the only newspaper in the area, having a circulation of about 38,000 in both its daily and Sunday editions. Papers from Spokane and Seattle with subscribers numbering several thousand provided little competition. Yakima was a potential growth area. A fertile region of agriculture and livestock, it was not susceptible to the vagaries of the aerospace industry. It also had recently been traversed by a new superhighway. Although the population had not yet grown, the growth of businesses and shopping centers was marked. These facts, when combined with the presence of the founder's grandnephew, James Tonkin, as a capable publisher who would stay on, the willingness to the patriarch to give advice as needed, and the existence of generally sound management at all levels satisfied the qualitative criteria Harte-Hanks imposed.

The stumbling block appeared to be the price. Other groups such as Gannett and Lee had expressed interest in the paper. It would be necessary to go high, higher than the quantitative criteria would permit, to be successful in the acquisition. This would be the first exception to their rules. Harte-Hanks had stressed rapid turnaround situations in which a large multiple could be paid on the assumption that substantial profit improvement was possible the first year. This was not the case with this well-run and technologically advanced paper. The asking price was in the $12 to $15 million range, or about forty times 1971 earnings. For the 20X earnings criteria to be met, after-tax profits, now 8 per cent of sales, would have to increase to 16 per cent of sales (see Exhibit 3). It was clear and fully acknowledged by the company that such a large percentage improvement, perhaps ultimately possible, would not take place in just a few years. Management's explanation for paying so much stressed the location of the newspaper. They had a strong desire to have their company geographically diversified and to this point had been unable to locate a newspaper in the dynamic growth area of the Pacific Northwest. They felt it important to have this beachhead, not to mention a satisified publisher in an acquired company who could attend regional journalism conferences and describe the benefits of being in the Harte-Hanks group.

Having determined that the *Yakima Herald-Republic* was desirable, Harte-Hanks made an initial offer of its common stock in exchange for all the capital stock of

EXHIBIT 2

HARTE-HANKS PROPERTIES ACQUIRED AFTER JANUARY 1971

	Masthead	Date Acquired	Method	Price (000)	Goodwill	Per Share Effect[a]
1. Journal Publishing Co., Hamilton, Ohio	Journal News	May 1971	Cash	$ 7,634	$ 5,905	3.4¢
2. News Publishing Co., Framingham, Mass.	South Middlesex Daily News	June 1971	Cash	4,309	3,250	1.9¢
3. Ypsilanti Press, Ypsilanti, Mich.	The Press	Sept. 1971	Cash	1,952	1,820	1.1¢
4. Independent Publishing Co., Anderson, S.C.	Anderson Independent and Daily Mail	Feb. 1972	Notes	7,363	7,483	4.3¢
5. Woodbury Daily Times, Woodbury, N.J.	Daily Times	Feb. 1972	Notes	3,039	2,638	1.5¢
6. Budde Publications, San Francisco, Cal.	San Francisco Progress	June 1972	Stock 64,908(shs)	2,220	–0–	N.A.
7. Republic Publishing Co., Yakima, Washington	Yakima-Herald Republic	Sept. 1972	Stock 482,200(shs)	12,778	–0–	N.A.
8. Van/De Publishing Co., California	Pennysaver (Orange and Santa Clara Counties)	Sept. 1972	Cash & Notes	6,950	6,337	3.7¢
9. San Diego Group McKinnon Newspaper Group Star News Publishing Co. Publishers Offset Inc.	11 weekly and bi-weekly newspapers in San Diego County	Oct. 1972	Common Stock 82,811 (shs.) Cash & Notes	7,033	7,026	4.1¢
			TOTAL	$53,278	$34,461	20.0¢

a Assumes 4,320,758 shares outstanding and a 40-year amortization period.

EXHIBIT 3

REPUBLIC PUBLISHING COMPANY

Balance Sheet
June 30, 1972

ASSETS

Current Assets

Cash	$ 541,839
Trade Receivables, Less Allowance for Doubtful Accounts of $15,000	301,398
Current Maturities of Municipal Bonds Including Accrued Interest	34,635
Inventory of Newsprint—at lower of cost (first-in, first-out method) or Market	60,112
Prepaid Expenses	9,876
Total Current Assets	947,860

Investments and Other Assets

Long-term Portion of Municipal Bonds	86,754
Other Investments Less Allowance for Losses of $1,080,000	170,000
Other	44,713
	301,467

Property, Plant, and Equipment—on the Basis of Cost

Land	198,337
Building and Improvements	1,595,036
Equipment and Furniture	1,420,114
	3,213,487
Less Allowance for Depreciation	1,806,433
	1,407,054
Construction and Equipment Installations in Progress (estimated additional cost to complete of $240,000)	221,869
	1,628,923
	$2,878,250

LIABILITES AND STOCKHOLDERS' EQUITY

Current Liabilities

Accounts Payable	$ 317,358
Accrued Expenses and Other Liabilities	302,880
Prepaid Subscriptions	68,954
Federal Income Taxes, Including Deferred	40,436
Total Current Liabilities	729,628

Stockholders' Equity
Preferred Stock 5% Cumulative, Par Value $100
a share: Authorized—20,000 Shares; Issued
and Outstanding—16,319 shares — 1,631,900

Common Stock:
Class A-(Voting) Par Value $10 a share;
Authorized—3,500 shares; Issued and
Outstanding—2,600 shares — 26,000
Class B—(nonvoting) Par Value $10 a Share;
Authorized—31,500 Shares; Issued and
Outstanding—23,400 shares — 234,000

Additional Paid-in Capital	5,543
Retained Earnings	251,179
	2,148,622

$2,878,250

REPUBLIC PUBLISHING COMPANY
Statement of Operations

	Year Ended December 31				Year Ended	
	1967 (unaudited)	1968 (unaudited)	1969	1970	1971	June 30, 1972
Revenues						
Newspaper Advertising	$2,265,996	$2,419,732	$2,593,342	$2,693,969	$3,089,159	$3,339,339
Newspaper Circulation	669,307	739,219	800,785	875,124	914,515	918,241
Other	62,921	48,978	64,946	81,983	54,123	62,378
	3,028,224	3,207,929	3,459,073	3,651,076	4,057,797	4,319,958
Costs and Expenses						
Editorial, Production, and Distribution	1,757,396	1,770,653	1,856,732	2,054,863	2,284,120	2,392,124
Advertising, Selling, General, and Administrative	700,146	793,239	871,034	890,496	987,008	1,067,819
Depreciation and Amortization	221,933	224,913	195,601	194,537	165,434	156,386
	2,679,475	2,788,805	2,923,367	3,139,896	3,436,562	3,616,329
Income before Federal Income Taxes and Extraordinary Items	348,749	419,124	535,706	511,180	621,235	703,629
Federal Income Taxes—Note F						
Current	151,455	191,724	281,967	267,993	291,954	361,954
Deferred (credit)	323	22,144	(11,839)	(27,154)	(13,779)	(41,084)
	151,778	213,868	270,128	240,839	278,175	320,552
Income before Extraordinary Items	196,971	205,256	265,578	270,341	343,060	383,077
Extraordinary Items—Note B	305,122	—	—	(42,097)	(1,130,000)	—
Net Income (Loss)	$ 502,093	$ 205,256	$ 265,578	$ 228,244	($ 786,940)	$ 383,077

Republic Corporation (the Herald). The Republic owners, however, had no interest in the stock of a budding newspaper group; they wanted cash. This presented a problem to Harte-Hanks whose earnings were already suffering from the goodwill amortization of half a dozen previous acquisitions (see Exhibit 4). Republic Corporation's acquisition would result in the largest amount of goodwill yet purchased, and Harte-Hanks was not willing to take on this additional eps impact.

Sometime toward the end of fiscal 1972 a plan was developed that seemed to offer all parties concerned what they wanted. An agreement was worked out whereby Harte-Hanks would offer 485,200 shares of its common stock for all the

EXHIBIT 4

From Harte-Hanks 1972 Annual Report

Harte-Hanks has more amortizable goodwill on its books than any company in the industry. Isn't this a great handicap?

"It is true that our earnings per share would have been $1.22 instead of $1.11 this past year—an increase of 30 per cent instead of 26 per cent—had our new affiliates joined us prior to October 1970, when the new goodwill accounting rule became effective. In our opinion, this rule should not apply to our industry. Newspapers that have secure franchises in good markets do not decline in value and, therefore, should not be subjected to an accounting rule which presupposes that a newspaper franchise is amortizable."

"A case in point is our purchase of the Anderson newspapers, where we incurred $7.6 million in goodwill. Today we feel that the value of the Anderson newspapers is considerably higher than it was seven months ago when we made the purchase; yet; we must write off nearly $200,000 annually in non-tax deductible goodwill for the next 40 years simply because we purchased Anderson after October 1970. I believe that most industry observers realize that the application of the goodwill to newspaper acquisitions generally produces unrealistic results, and that they will, therefore, focus their attention on earnings per share before goodwill amortization."

White Weld Report—February 12, 1973

Appendix II

The 1970 ruling of the Accounting Principle Board on purchase acquisitions presents an anomalous situation for newspapers. The ruling required the writing off of goodwill created in the "purchase" acquisition, as distinguished from a "pooling of interest" acquisition made solely for common stock, and required the writing off of such goodwill created 1971 or thereafter over a period of no more than 40 years. However, newspapers unlike most businesses, have few fixed assets relative to real worth or earning power and consequently generate considerable goodwill in a purchase acquisition. As a consequence, newspaper goodwill is essentially a capitalization of a paper, "franchise" worth and reflects the difficulty of market entry. A large capital commitment is required to carry the losses incurred while a newspaper is starting up. In most cases, it is so large that it constitutes a virtual prohibition to entry. In effect most newspapers are a "legal monopoly." Thus writing off "goodwill" has less validity for the newspaper business than for other businesses. Some companies have avoided the write off by making acquisitions with common stock on pooling of interest basis.

EXHIBIT 5
Selling Stockholders

The names of the selling stockholders, the number of shares to be sold by each of them, and their respective holdings after such sales are as follows:

Name	Number of Shares Presently Owned	Number of Shares To Be sold	Number of Shares To Be Owned after Sale
James B. Barker	100	100	—
Georgia Mayse Bassano	4,876	2,500	2,376
Walter Bassano	4,177	2,500	1,677
Anita L. Budde	18,109	9,000	9,109
Henry Budde	45,109	15,000	30,109
Conway C. Craig	70,514	1,600	68,914
Ethel M. Foster	200	100	100
Matthew Craig Gannaway	200	100	100
Houston H. Harte	673,328	4,500	668,828
Mabel Hurt	200	200	—
Robert M. Jackson	17,796	1,800	15,996
Bertie K. Mayse	12,682	1,000	11,682
Mary Jo Stone	4,876	2,000	2,876

Former Republic Stockholders

Helen Crum	106,742	106,742	—
David R. Millen	1,540	1,540	—
Lorna R. Miller	9,122	9,122	—
Steven G. Millen	1,680	1,680	—
Ruth B. Robertson	20,353	20,353	—
W.H. Robertson	306,395	306,395	—
Iva Simmons	240	240	—
James E. Tonkin	22,499	22,499	—
Nancy Tonkin	5,022	5,022	—
Robert Wright	1,447	1,447	—

Pacific National Bank, Trustee for:

Anne Llewelyn Millen	720	720	—
Kemberly Elaine Millen	720	720	—
Sally Tonkin	240	240	—
Susan Tonkin	240	240	—
Hiram Robertson Wright	240	240	—
Jennifer Jean Wright	80	80	—
William Carlton Wright	240	240	—

Pacific National Bank, Custodian for:

Anne Llewelyn Millen	960	960	—
Kimberly Elaine Millen	960	960	—
Sally Tonkin	960	960	—
Stacy Tonkin	960	960	—
Susan Tonkin	960	960	—

Hiram Robertson Wright	960	960	—
Jennifer Jean Wright	960	960	—
William Carlton Wright	960	960	—

EXHIBIT 6
Accounting Interpretations

The Institute staff has been authorized to issue interpretations of accounting questions having general interest to the profession. The purpose of the interpretations is to provide guidance on a timely basis without the formal procedures required for an APB Opinion and to clarify points on which past practice may have varied and been considered generally accepted. These interpretations, which are reviewed with informed members of the profession, are not pronouncements of the Board. However, members should be aware that they may be called upon to justify departures from the interpretations. Unless otherwise stated, the interpretations are not intended to be retroactive.

From the *Journal of Accountancy*, September 1971:

POOLING WITH "BAILOUT"

Question—Paragraph 48-a of APB Opinion Number 16 specifies that a combined corporation may not agree to directly or indirectly retire or require all or part of the common stock issued to effect a business combination and paragraph 48-b specifies that a combined corporation may not enter into financial arrangements for the benefit of the former stockholders of a combining company if a business combination is to be accounted for by the pooling of interests method. Would an arrangement whereby a third party buys all or part of the voting common stock issued to stockholders of a combining company immediately after consummation of a business combination cause the combination to not meet these conditions?

Interpretation—The fact that stockholders of a combining company sell voting common stock received in a business combination to a third party would not indicate failure to meet the conditions of paragraphs 48-a and 48-b. "Continuity of ownership interests," a criterion for a pooling of interests under ARB No. 48, is *not* a condition to account for a business combination by the pooling of interests method under APB Opinion Number 16. The critical factor in meeting conditions of paragraphs 48-a and 48-b is that the voting common stock issued to effect a business combination remains outside the combined corporation without arrangements on the part of any of the corporations involving the use of their financial resources to "bailout" former stockholders of a combining company or to induce others to do so.

Either the combined corporation or one of the combining companies may assist the former stockholders in locating an unrelated buyer for their shares (such as by introductions to underwriters) so long as compensation or other financial inducements from the corporation are not in some way involved in the arrangement. If unregistered stock is issued, the combined corporation may also agree to pay the costs of initial registration.

From the *Journal of Accountancy*, November, 1972:

COMBINATION CONTINGENT ON "BAILOUT"

Question—An accounting interpretation of APB Number 16—"Pooling With 'Bailout' "—issued in September 1971 indicates that former shareholders of a combining company may sell voting common stock received in a business combination accounting for as a pooling of interests. Would the accounting for a combination be affected by the fact that its consummation is contingent upon the purchase by a third party or parties of all or part of the voting common stock to be issued in the combination?

Interpretation—Yes. A business combination should be accounted for as a purchase if its consummation is contingent upon the purchase by a third party or parties of *any* of the voting common stock to be issued. This would be the case, for example, if the parties to the combination have agreed that consummation of the combination will not occur until there is a commitment by a third party for a private purchase, a firm public offering, or some other form of a guaranteed market for all or part of the shares to be issued. Including such a contingency in the arrangements of the combination, either explicitly or by intent, would be considered a financial arrangement which is precluded in a pooling by paragraph 48-b of APB Opinion Number 16.

It should be noted that this accounting interpretation does not modify the previous interpretation on "Pooling Without 'Bailout,' " which states that shareholders may sell stock received in a pooling and that the corporation may assist them in locating an unrelated buyer for their shares. Although shareholders may sell stock received in a pooling, consummation of the business combination must first occur without regard to such a sale and cannot be contingent upon a firm commitment by the potential purchaser of the shares to be issued.

outstanding capital stock of Republic. The 16,319 shares of Republic preferred stock were valued at $100 per share (par value, liquidation value, and price at which the company had redeemed shares in the past) and a price was fixed for the Harte-Hanks common (about $25) so that a ratio of approximately four shares for one was established. Class A (voting) and Class B (nonvoting) were held in excactly the same percentages by the Republic shareholders, so that those shares of Harte-Hanks common not given in exchange to the preferred stockholders, were distributed according to the percentage ownership of the Republic common. Immediately on the consummation of the deal, Harte-Hanks was to make a public offering of its own shares and to include with this offering (as a secondary offering) all the shares given to the Republic holders and some of the shares held by Harte-Hanks insiders (see Exhibit 5 for the selling shareholders). Harte-Hanks would receive the proceeds from only 274,400 of the 800,000 shares sold and merely act as a vehicle whereby the selling shareholders could receive cash for their holdings.

This arrangement was felt by the company to be fully within the letter of Accounting Principles Board (APB) Opinion No. 16 (see interpretation in Exhibit 6). When filed with the SEC, however, the Commission raised objections. It insisted that the Republic shareholders, recipients of Harte-Hanks stock, bear the risk of the market for a reasonable period before selling their Harte-Hanks shares. The period for this particular acquisition was determined by refusing to permit filing of the registration statement before the deal was signed. Thus, the length of time necessary to review the registration statement before permitting it to become effective serves to define "reasonable." Although the company felt that this "interpretation" of APB No. 16 was in fact a change from the opinion itself, which had no holding period requirement, it was compelled to renegotiate that portion of the deal that dealt with the timing for the secondary offering. Although the agreement was signed on September 19, 1972, the secondary offering did not take place until October 25. During that period, the market price of Harte-Hanks common stock declined from $26.50 to $22.50, resulting in a significant reduction in the amount of cash received by the Republic shareholders.

QUESTIONS

1. Recast the June 30, 1972, Harte-Hanks financial statements as they would have looked if the *Yakima Herald* acquisition had been made as of 6/30/72 under:

   (a) Pooling of interest accounting.
   (b) Purchase accounting.

2. Does the acquisition qualify for pooling of interest treatment under generally accepted accounting principles?

3. Should the regulations regarding amortization of goodwill be suspended for newspaper companies?

Case 12-1

Allegheny Ludlum Industries, Incorporated [1]

The financial summary section of the 1969 annual report of Allegheny Ludlum Industries, Incorporated, contained the following statement:

Effects of LIFO Accounting

For a number of years, the Corporation has used the Last-In First-Out (LIFO) method of accounting for its steel inventories. In periods of extended inflation, coupled with uncertain supplies of raw materials from foreign sources, and rapid increased and fluctuations in prices of raw materials such as nickel and chrome-nickel scrap, earnings can be affected unrealistically for any given year.

Because of these factors, Allegheny Ludlum will apply to the Internal Revenue Service for permission to discontinue using the LIFO method of accounting for valuing those inventories for which this method has been used. If such application is granted, the LIFO reserve at December 31, 1969, of $12,300,000 would be eliminated which would require a provision for income taxes of approximately $6,150,000. The Corporation will also seek permission to pay the increased taxes over a ten-year period. If Allegheny Ludlum had not used the LIFO method of accounting during 1969, net earnings for the year would have been increased by approximately $1,500,000.

The full financial statements and related notes for 1969 are shown as Exhibit 1. Allegheny Ludlum had switched from average cost to LIFO in 1950, soon after LIFO was first recognized as an acceptable inventory valuation method by the Internal Revenue Service. Like 1969, that was also a period of rising prices for the corporation. As a result, it saved $1,475,000 in income taxes by using LIFO in 1950. No specific explanation was given in that annual report, or in any subsequent one, for the change in accounting methods. Perhaps the best clue is the bold-faced heading, "LIFO Again Reduces Tax Payments," in the 1951 annual report in connection with a paragraph which disclosed that LIFO reduced income taxes by $1,530,000 that year.

[1] This case was prepared by Assistant Professor John K. Shank as a basis for class discussion rather than to illustrate either effective or ineffective handling of an administrative situation.

Copyright © 1970 by the President and Fellows of Harvard College. Revised July 1971.

Most other steel companies also adopted LIFO during the early 1950s. It still continues to be the most commonly used method in that industry.

The following stories relating to the proposed change back to the average cost method appeared in the Wall Street Journal during the Spring of 1970.

MARCH 4

ALLEGHENY LUDLUM ASKS IRS APPROVAL
TO SWITCH SYSTEM OF ACCOUNTING

Company Says Change in Method of
Valuing Inventories Could Add
$6 Million to Net for '70

Allegheny Ludlum Steel Corp. is seeking permission to change its accounting system in a move that could add more than $6 million to its net income this year.

The big specialty steelmaker said that it asked the Interal Revenue Service for permission to discontinue using the last-in first-out, or LIFO, method of valuing its inventories, a widely-used accounting system.

Allegheny Ludlum said the move was made necessary "because of the effect of continuing inflationary increases in cost of raw materials." It said the income gain from the elimination of LIFO would be treated as extraordinary income for this year since it would result from elimination of LIFO reserves established in prior years.

It wasn't immediately clear whether other steel companies would follow suit, but it would be attractive for them, having the effect, if granted, of boosting earnings during a period when operations are turning slack for most steelmakers.

In addition, by boosting Allegheny Ludlum's net income by $6,150,000 the change would increase its tax load by a similar amount. It said it is seeking permission to pay those higher taxes over a 10-year period.

Under the LIFO system, a company charges against its current operations the latest cost it paid for raw materials. So, if it has materials in its stockpiles for which it paid, say, 50 cents a pound, $1 a pound and $2 a pound at varying times, current operations would be charged by the latest price.

Theoretically at least, raw material prices rise and fall, so that at some point the company could be using $2 a pound materials and charging current operations only 50 cents a pound. Due to recent inflation, though, raw material prices rarely have swung down after a series of increases.

For specialty steelmakers, the squeeze in the cost of nickel last year was especially painful. Nickel-bearing scrap about doubled in price and the LIFO accounting method was then penalizing current operations.

(Reprinted by permission of the Wall Street Journal)

APRIL 15

ALLEGHENY LUDLUM PLAN TO CHANGE
ACCOUNTING DRAWS HOLDER'S FIRE

United Corp. Says Its Will Seek
Backing of Other Shareholders
in Attack at Annual Meeting

United Corp., the largest stockholder of Allegheny Ludlum Steel Corp., said it will oppose a proposed change in Allegheny Ludlum's accounting methods at the steel company's annual meeting in Pittsburgh next week.

William M. Hickey, president of the closed-end investment company, disclosed United's plan in New York. He said he is asking other holders of Allegheny Ludlum preferred to join in opposing a management proposal to discontinue using the last-in, first-out, or LIFO, inventory accounting system. United Corp. owns 33% of Allegheny Ludlum's preferred stock outstanding and 5.8% of the company's total voting stock.

An Allegheny Ludlum spokesman in Pittsburgh said the plan to change its inventory accounting method was "a management decision approved by the board" that isn't subject to shareholder approval. The subject isn't on the agenda for the April 24 annual meeting, he said, and indicated management would have sufficient proxies to defeat any move to bar the change.

LIFO, a widely used accounting system, involves a company charging against its current operations the latest cost it paid for raw materials. Thus, it could have materials in its stockpiles for which it paid $1 a pound and $2 a pound at different times with current operations being charged by the latest price. Theoretically, it could be using $2 a pound materials and charging current operations only $1 a pound, which would serve to improve reported earnings.

Owing to recent inflation, however, raw material prices have rarely swung down after a series of increases.

Mr. Hickey, in a letter to other preferred stockholders, said dropping LIFO would cost Allegheny Ludlum $6 million in increased Federal income taxes. He added that a projected earnings improvement would be "artificial" and "illusory and transitory."

When Allegheny Ludlum announced March 3 that it would ask Internal Revenue Service for permission to discontinue the LIFO accounting method, it said that the change would result in an extraordinary increase of $6.2 million in both earnings after taxes and income taxes in 1970. The increase in income would stem from elimination of LIFO reserves established in prior years.

Allegheny Ludlum has said it is seeking to pay the higher taxes over a 10-year period.

(Reprinted by permission of the Wall Street Journal)

APRIL 17

The *Journal* reported that the corporation had scheduled a special shareholders' meeting to follow the regular one. The proposed change would be the subject of discussion at the special meeting.

APRIL 27

THREE BIG STEEL FIRMS'
PROFIT FELL IN 1st QUARTER

Wheeling-Pittsburgh Net Off 92.5%
Allegheny Ludlum, Interlake Earnings Down

Strike May Hurt 2nd Period

. . .

Acrimonious Debate

Much of the Allegheny Ludlum meeting was taken up by an acrimonious debate between E. J. Hanley, chairman, and Richard Smith, who identified himself as counsel of United Corp., New York, a closed-end investment company. United is the largest stockholder in Allegheny Ludlum, owning 33% of the outstanding preferred shares and 5.8% of the total voting stock.

The debate was over management's proposal to change inventory accounting by dropping the "last-in, first-out" accounting system. Mr. Hanely reiterated management's belief that the LIFO method penalizes profit in an inflationary period, such as now, by charging the latest price paid for a raw material against current operations as the materials are used. In a period of steadily rising prices, the latest price will be above the price actually paid for the material used.

United had solicited proxies from preferred shareholders to oppose the accounting change. Mr. Smith called the move "an unnecessary dissipation of corporate cash." If the change is made, 1970 earnings would be increased about $6.2 million, but corporate Federal income taxes would rise by a like amount, reflecting liquidation of LIFO reserves. "Money spent for taxes is money lost forever," Mr. Smith said, quoting a stockholder.

A resolution by Mr. Smith calling on directors not to approve the change was soundly defeated. Allegheny Ludlum originally announced the move as a management decision subject only to approval by the Internal Revenue Service. However, after United Corp. raised objections, Allegheny said it would submit the proposal to a vote at a special shareholders meeting later this year, assuming the IRS first approves. (Reprinted by permission of the Wall Street Journal)

QUESTIONS

1. Why do you think the management of Allegheny Ludlum decided to discontinue the use of the LIFO method?

2. Why do you think the management of United Corp. objected to this decision?

3. If you were a shareholder in Allegheny Ludlum, would you vote with management or with United Corp. on this matter?

4. Assuming the change is made, how should it be reflected in the 1970 annual report?

EXHIBIT 1

ALLEGHENY LUDLUM INDUSTRIES, INCORPORATED

Statement of Consolidated Earnings and Earned Surplus
Year ended December 31, 1969 with comparative figures for 1968 (Note 1)

Sales and revenues:	*1969*	*1968*
Sales	$536,467,782	$487,886,449
Interest, dividends, royalties and other—net	2,142,791	2,800,520
	538,610,573	490,686,969
Costs:		
Employee costs (Note 10):		
Wages and salaries	167,186,276	150,426,045
Social security taxes	7,798,203	6,927,109
Pensions and other (Note 9)	25,997,519	23,254,394
	200,981,998	180,607,548
Materials, services and other costs (Note 10)	269,078,614	245,225,136
Depreciation and amortization (Note 5)	13,513,230	12,857,955
Interest and amortization of debenture expense	6,194,703	4,083,720
State, local and miscellaneous taxes	6,308,901	5,561,142
Federal taxes on income, including $6,226,000 deferred taxes (1968—$2,948,000) (Notes 5 and 9)	20,183,000	19,474,400
Total costs and income taxes	516,260,446	467,809,901
Net earnings	22,350,127	22,877,068
Balance in earned surplus at beginning (1968 adjusted by $8,538,454 representing earned surplus of pooled subsidiaries) (Note 1)	154,450,304	147,615,312
	176,800,431	170,492,380
Deduct—Dividends declared:		
On $3.00 Convertible Preferred Stock—$3.00 per share	4,998,505	3,938,031
On $2.70 Cumulative Preferred Stock (Note 6)	120,536	108,546
On Common Stock—$2.40 per share	11,363,923	11,228,563
By pooled subsidiaries to former shareowners	431,347	766,936
	16,914,311	16,042,076
Balance in earned surplus at end (Note 6)	$159,886,120	$154,450,304
Earnings per common share (Note 10):		
Primary	$3.44	$3.58
Fully diluted	$3.27	$3.35

See accompanying notes to financial statements.
Reproduced from *Allegheny Ludlum 1969 Annual Report*

ASSETS	*1969*	*1968*
Current Assets:		
Cash	$10,981,416	$ 9,912,103

Marketable securities—at cost (approximately market) and accrued interest	409,416	409,416
Notes and accounts receivable—trade, less estimated allowances of $910,333 (1968—$960,109)	66,187,027	51,519,456
Miscellaneous accounts receivable	1,805,991	1,817,497
Inventories (Note 2):		
Raw material	20,898,597	22,258,978
Semi-finished	82,953,011	70,734,562
Finished	33,165,618	32,993,793
Supplies	3,203,763	3,022,748
	140,220,989	129,010,081
Prepaid expenses (Note 9)	9,836,111	4,749,156
Total current assets	229,440,950	197,417,709
Investments (Note 3)	8,182,559	8,169,702
Fixed Assets—at Cost:		
Land	4,142,978	4,027,115
Buildings, machinery and equipment	408,076,470	377,692,025
	412,219,448	381,719,140
Less Accumulated depreciation and amortization ..	210,929,712	199,414,778
	201,289,736	182,304,362
Unamortized Expenses	702,024	750,035
Excess of Cost of Investments in Subsidiaries over Equities in Net Assets at Date of Acquisition	1,311,896	156,295
	$440,927,165	$388,798,103

See accompanying notes to financial statements.

LIABILITIES	1969	1968
Current Liabilities:		
Notes payable and current portion of long-term debt	$ 17,743,772	$ 13,496,480
Accounts payable—trade	24,372,904	18,499,118
Accrued liabilities:		
Payrolls, royalties and other expenses (Note 9) ..	14,638,259	10,515,441
Vacation allowances	8,530,942	7,929,589
Taxes, other than Federal taxes on income	5,321,336	3,619,974
	28,490,537	22,065,004
Dividends payable—preferred	1,510,429	1,170,021
Provision for Federal income taxes (Note 9)	4,445,309	903,645
Total current liabilities	76,562,951	56,134,268
Long-Term Debt (Note 4)	99,408,277	78,168,947
Reserves (Note 9)	10,322,963	11,261,297
Deferred Federal Income Taxes (Note 5)	5,241,535	—

Capital Stock and Surplus:
Capital stock (Notes 1, 6 and 7):
$3.00 Convertible Preferred Stock—$1.00 par value—
authorized 2,200,000 shares; outstanding 2,013,905

shares (1968—2,012,468)	2,013,905	2,012,468
Cumulative Preferred Stock, issuable in series—no par value—authorized 1,000,000 shares—none outstanding	—	—
Common Stock—$1.00 par value—Authorized 20,000,000 Shares; outstanding 4,748,978 shares (1968—4,731,641)	4,748,978	4,731,641
Surplus:		
Capital surplus (Note 8)	82,973,354	82,270,096
Earned surplus (Note 6)	159,886,120	154,450,304
	249,622,357	243,464,509
Less Cost of 4,500 common shares in treasury	230,918	230,918
	249,391,439	243,233,591
	$440,927,165	$388,798,103

See accompanying notes to financial statements.

Notes to Financial Statements

December 31, 1969

(1) Principles of consolidation:

The consolidated financial statements include the accounts of the Corporation and all wholly-owned domestic and Canadian subsidiaries. In both the current and prior year are the accounts (on a calendar year basis) of companies (Jacobsen Manufacturing Company, National Material Corporation and Good Steel Service Inc.) acquired in 1969 in transactions, recorded as poolings of interests, involving the issue or delivery of 610,210 shares of $3.00 Convertible Preferred Stock and 60,900 shares (including 38,500 held in treasury) of Common Stock.

(2) Inventories:

Inventories are stated at cost, which is not in excess of market. Cost was determined under the "last-in, first-out" method as to steel inventories. Other inventories are stated at standard (which approximates actual) or average cost. The amount applied to reflect inventories under the "last-in, first-out" method was increased by $3,085,325 during 1969 to $12,302,942 at year end.

(3)

Included herein are:

Investments in unconsolidated affiliated companies, at cost, less reserves of $1,400,000	$6,464,679
Miscellaneous investments, at cost	1,717,880
	$8,182,559

The Corporation's equity in unconsolidated affiliated companies exceeded the carrying values by approximately $15,719,000 at December 31, 1969 and the Corporation's share of the net earnings for the year then ended amounted to approximately $526,000. During the year dividends $68,200 were received from these companies.

(4) Long-term debt:

Amounts due beyond one year:
Notes payable:

3% Notes due January 1, 1972	$ 3,400,000
3.75% Notes due September 15, 1977	4,200,000
4 5/8% Notes due May 1, 1990	25,000,000
5 1/4% Note due May 1, 1979	1,700,000
6% Note due September 1, 1976	600,000
Prime rate notes and other obligations due	
January 15, 1971 and September 16, 1972	787,500
Bank Notes due November 15, 1971	39,000,000
Other notes	297,352
	74,984,852
4% Convertible Subordinated Debentures due	
October 1, 1981	5,703,200
4 3/4% Sinking Fund Debentures due June 1, 1986	11,375,000
3.6% to 6% Rental obligations due to 1989	7,345,225
	$99,408,277

Annual prepayments are required: on the 3% Notes, $100,000; on the 3.75% Notes, $600,000; on the 4 5/8% Notes, $1,250,000 beginning in 1971; on the 5 1/4% Note, $200,000; on the 6% Note, $100,000; on the Prime rate notes and other obligations, $562,500; on the other notes, $60,400; on the 4% Convertible Subordinated Debentures, $810,000; on the 4 3/4% Sinking Fund Debentures, $725,000; and on the Rental obligations, approximately $385,000.

The Bank Notes represent borrowings under a bank credit agreement whereby the Corporation may borrow up to $45,000,000 during the period ending November 15, 1971, such borrowings bearing interest at the prime rate. On November 15, 1971, the Corporation may convert the then outstanding borrowings and the remaining unborrowed portion under the credit agreement into a term borrowing bearing interest at the rate of ¼ of 1% in excess of the prime rate and repayable quarterly over a five-year period.

The 4% Convertible Subordinated Debentures are convertible into shares of Common Stock. At December 31, 1969, the conversion price, which is subject to adjustment, was $52.00 per share, and 109,677 shares of Common Stock were reserved for conversion.

The various Notes and the Indentures under which the Debentures were issued contain provisions restricting the payment of dividends on Common Stock (otherwise than in capital stock). However, no portion of the consolidated earned surplus was thereby restricted at December 31, 1969. The Notes and Indentures also contain various other restrictions relating to additional indebtedness, mortgages and liens and the purchase or redemption of capital stock or subordinated indebtedness.

The Rental obligations consist of indebtedness under certain lease-purchase agreements; the leased properties have been treated as assets and related lease obligations have been treated as the long-term indebtedness.

(5) Depreciation and deferred Federal income taxes:

The Corporation and its subsidiaries provide depreciation for financial reporting purposes based on straight-line rates whereas accelerated rates are utilized primarily for tax purposes. Deferred Federal income taxes applicable to the excess of depreciation used for tax purposes over that provided for financial reporting purposes amounted to $3,563,000 in 1969.

(6) Capital stock:

Shares of $3.00 Convertible Preferred Stock may be converted at any time into Common Stock. At December 31, 1969, the conversion rate, which is subject to adjustment, was on a share for share basis. At the option of the Corporation, the $3.00 Convertible Preferred Stock may be redeemed in whole or in part after June 30, 1972, at prices commencing at $65.00 per share and reducing by $1.00 per share each year to $60.00 per share, plus accrued dividends. In the event of voluntary liquidation, the holders of $3.00 Convertible Preferred Stock are entitled to receive the lesser of $65.00 per share, plus accrued dividends, or an amount equal to the redemption price then in effect. As a result of such preference, at December 31, 1969, $41,398,506 of the consolidated earned surplus of the Corporation was not available for payment of dividends on the Common Stock.

At December 31, 1969, 2,435,270 shares of Common Stock were reserved for conversions of $3.00 Convertible Preferred Stock and 4% Convertible Subordinated Debentures and for outstanding options and the granting of options under the Employees' Stock Option Plans.

In connection with the merger of Jacobsen Manufacturing Company, each outstanding share of $2.70 Cumulative Preferred Stock of the Corporation (aggregating 80,414 shares) was converted into one share of $3.00 Convertible Preferred Stock.

(7) Stock options:

The Employees' Stock Option Plan, adopted by shareowners in 1955, authorized the granting of options to purchase shares of Common Stock, exercisable during a period of ten years from the granting dates at prices not less than 95% of the fair market value at such dates. In 1967, in connection with the acquisition of a company, options of that company were converted into options for $3.00 Convertible Preferred Stock. Options were exercised in 1969 for $4,643 shares of Common Stock at option prices ranging from $31.08 to $41.43 per share (aggregating $175,354), and for 8,212 shares of $3.00 Convertible Preferred Stock at option prices ranging from $15.05 to $36.00 per share (aggregating $245,082). Options terminated in 1969 as to 724 shares of $3.00 Convertible Preferred Stock. At December 31, 1969, 6,003 common shares were subject to outstanding options at prices ranging from $32.38 to $41.43 per share (aggregating $239,202) and 5,685 shares of $3.00 Convertible Preferred Stock were subject to outstanding options at prices ranging from $15.05 to $36.00 per share (aggregating $184,349).

Shareowners approved a new qualified employees' stock option plan in April 1969 under which options may be granted for common shares at prices not less than the fair market value at the dates granted, exercisable during a five-year period from such dates. At December 31, 1969, no options had been granted and 300,000 shares of Common Stock were reserved for the granting of options under the 1969 plan.

(8) Capital surplus:

The changes in capital surplus for the year ended December 31, 1969 are as follows:

Balance at December 31, 1968, as previously reported	$78,933,784
Adjustments relating to acquisitions of pooled subsidiaries	3,336,312
Balance at December 31, 1968, as adjusted	82,270,096
Excess of principal amount of 4% Convertible Subordinated Debentures over par value of 6,154 shares of Common Stock issued upon conversion, less adjustments for cash paid in lieu of fractional shares and unamortized debenture expense	295,677
Excess of option price over par value of 4,643 shares of Common Stock and 8,212 shares of $3.00 Convertible Preferred Stock issued pursuant to stock options	407,581
Balance at December 31, 1969	$82,973,354

(9) Retirement plans:

Substantially all of the employees of the Corporation and its subsidiaries are covered by non-contributory, and on plans. The total pension expense for the year was $10,738,000 which includes amortization of prior service cost over periods ranging from 15 to 40 years. In 1969, the Corporation and certain subsidiaries recorded prepaid and accrued pension costs of $3,807,000 in addition to the normal pension contribution for 1969. Applicable current deferred Federal income taxes have been provided. Except for $4,290,000 accrued in prior years by a subsidiary and included in "Reserves," it is the policy to fund pension costs accrued.

(10) Other matters:

In 1969, the Corporation and its subsidiaries reflected an investment credit of $1,450,000 in income.

Primary earnings per share have been determined on the basis of the number (monthly weighted average) of shares outstanding and after deduction for dividend requirements on preferred stock. Exercise of outstanding stock options would have no material effect on primary earnings per share.

Fully diluted earnings per share have been determined on the assumption that all $3.00 Convertible Preferred Stock and 4% Convertible Subordinated Debentures outstanding at the beginning of each year had been converted into Common Stock at the beginning of each such year, appropriate adjustments having been made for actual conversions, related annual dividends and interest cost net of applicable income taxes. It is further assumed that the stock options outstanding at the end of each year had been exercised at the beginning of each such year and that the proceeds therefrom were utilized to reacquire Common Stock at a price equal to the higher of the market price at each year-end or the average for such year.

Included in the 1969 employee costs and in materials, services and other costs are costs of goods sold aggregating $420,041,845 and general, selling and administrative expenses aggregating $50,018,767.

The Corporation has agreed with the insurance companies from which Titanium Metals Corporation of America ("Timet"), a 50%-owned company, has borrowed $30,000,000 under loan agreements that if at any time the net working capital of Timet falls below $12,500,000 it will make an investment in Timet in an amount equal to 50% of such deficiency. At December 31, 1969, the net working capital of Timet as defined in the loan agreements was $17,134,581.

(11) Subsequent event:

On March 3, 1970, the Corporation announced its intention to apply to the Internal Revenue Service for permission to discontinue the "last-in, first-out" (LIFO) method of accounting as to steel inventories commencing with the year 1970. The amount of the LIFO reserve at December 31, 1969 was $12,302,942 and the elimination thereof would require a provision for income taxes of approximately $6,150,000. The Corporation will ask permission to pay the additional income taxes over a ten-year period.

Accountants' Report　　　　Peat, Marwick, Mitchell & Co.
Certified Public Accountants
Henry W. Oliver Building
Pittsburgh, Pa. 15222

The Shareowners and the Board of Directors Allegheny Ludlum Steel Corporation:

We have examined the consolidated balance sheet of Allegheny Ludlum Steel Corporation and subsidiaries as of December 31, 1969 and the related statement of earnings and earned surplus for the year then ended. Our examination was made in accordance with generally accepted auditing standards, and accordingly included such tests of the accounting records and such other auditing procedures as we considered necessary in the circumstances.

In our opinion, the accompanying consolidated balance sheet and statement of consolidated earnings and earned surplus present fairly the financial position of Allegheny Ludlum Steel Corporation and subsidiaries at December 31, 1969 and the results of their operations for the year then ended, in conformity with generally accepted accounting principles applied on a basis consistent with that of the preceding year.

Peat, Marwick, Mitchell & Co.
January 27, 1970 (except for Note 11
as to which the date is March 3, 1970)

Case 12-2

Control Data Corporation (E)[1]

"The possible revision of our depreciation policies for leased equipment is an important matter, but perhaps less important than the related question of what, if anything, we should do about research, development, and marketing costs." The speaker, Mr. B. R. Eng, Controller of Control Data Corporation, was talking about the review of accounting policies that the company had undertaken in the Spring of 1965. Background information about the company and its depreciation policy on leased equipment is given in the (D) case in this series.

"You see," Mr. Eng continued, "it takes just as much development expense, marketing expense, programming costs, etc. to handle a lease order as it does an outright sale. But the revenue to be derived from the lease orders is spread over several years. To charge off all of these costs and expenses at the time they are incurred is not consistent with the accounting principle of matching costs against related revenues. Nor, as I suggested before, can such charge-off be justified on the basis of conservatism. In short, to charge off all costs and expenses related to lease orders at the time such costs are incurred is not a proper determination of income, because it understates current income and overstates future income.

"For example, I know of three companies—companies that are well known and somewhat larger than Control Data—that follow the practice of deferring their development and programming costs, and I believe they all do it by capitalizing those costs as a part of the cost of their leased equipment, thereby deferring such costs to future periods as a part of their depreciation expense.

"Now the problem," Mr. Eng went on, "is much harder to deal with for those types of expenses than it is for the cost of equipment. When we build a piece of equipment, we have an order for it and can identify the costs of producing the equipment to fulfill the order. Research, development, and even marketing

---

[1] This case was made possible by the cooperation of Control Data Corporation. It was prepared by Professor Richard F. Vancil as the basis for class discussion rather than to illustrate either effective or ineffective handling of an administrative situation.

expenses are much more speculative. We're really trying to put ourselves in a position to win an order, but a lot of the money we spend turns out to be wasted. The research doesn't yield anything, or the customer listens to our pitch and then buys from someone else. On balance, of course, the total amount is well spent, at least we're still making a profit in a tough business, but the old saw about 'half our advertising money is wasted, we just don't know which half' is true. As a result of all this uncertainty, we've been very conservative and have expensed all such costs in the year they were incurred.

"That policy has finally caught up with us this year. Fiscal year 1965 is the best year we've ever had, at least if you measure it in terms of the success of our products in the market place. The total domestic orders booked for our standard computer systems in fiscal '65 increased more than 65% over the prior year. Worldwide, the percentage increase in orders booked was nearly 50%. All that sounds great, and our profits should skyrocket too, until we start doing our accounting.

"Now, in the normal course of events, a new order goes into our backlog and it may be several months before the system is installed and accepted by the customer. Even on an outright sale, therefore, we don't have a perfect matching of costs and revenues because all of the costs are incurred before the sale is finally recognized. On lease orders, and that was 63% of computer system orders in 1965 [see Exhibit 1], the problem is compounded because when the system is installed, we only recognize the rental income not the sales value.

"So," Mr. Eng continued, "what happens? Here [Exhibit 2] is a tentative operating statement for 1965 on a consolidated basis. Our standard computer systems account for the bulk of the revenue and expense. We've had such a good year that our profits went down. Now I don't really believe that, nor do I think that it would be fair to our stockholders to tell them that. Therefore, we began really rethinking our accounting policies several months ago. It's easy to identify the major cost elements that are causing the problem. One is the cost of equipment depreciation to be charged against rental income, and we've already talked about that. The other two big ones are marketing expenses and research and development expenses."

Marketing Expenses

"I'm not sure that we're taking the right approach," Mr. Eng said, "but what we're doing is asking ourselves a series of four questions. Our total marketing expense for the year is just over $15 million, broken down approximately like this [see Exhibit 3]. The first question is, which types of marketing expenses should be considered for deferral? Second, within an expense category, is the entire amount related to the order-producing activity, or only part of it? We're pretty sure that any deferral of marketing expenses ought to be related to orders booked, not systems installed. Third, should those expenses be related to all orders booked or only to lease orders? And fourth, if we do defer a portion of those costs, how should they then be amortized against subsequent revenue? Each one of those questions is very difficult to answer.

"The six main categories of domestic marketing expenses run the gamut from those that are matched against revenue pretty well to those where matching is almost impossible. Sales commissions are an example of the first type. Our salesmen are salaried, but they also get a commission based on revenue received. A lease order thus produces a stream of commissions for the salesman. Corporate marketing administration is an example of the second type. We can't live without it, but it's hard to identify any revenue that it produces, much less the period in which the revenue is received.

"The second question," Mr. Eng continued, "is even tougher. More than half our total marketing expenses is incurred in the field offices, and that's where the orders are produced. Now, one of the strengths of this company is that we have a very effective marketing management information system. Each salesman and each analyst in every office keeps track of how he spends his time every day, and those data are then summarized using computers produced by a well-known manufacturer. The cobbler's children don't always go barefoot. As a result, we know fairly precisely how our field marketing effort was allocated for each week in each field office. For fiscal '65, an over-all summary looks approximately like this [see Exhibit 4]. It's pretty easy to exclude the 22% of the time spent on other products, but what about administrative time? That really takes us back to first question, except that there are several levels of administrative costs to deal with. The salesmen and analysts have some nonproductive time. Then there's the costs for managers, secretaries and clerks in the field offices, which are allocated between the field sales and applications activities. Then there's more of the same at the regional offices, only it's set out separately in this summary. And then, of course, there's corporate administration.

"The third question is perhaps a little easier, because we can differentiate clearly between lease orders and purchase orders. The final question is judgment again."

Research and Development Costs

"For R & D," Mr. Eng went on, "the questions are similar, but the answers are different, or at least a lot more difficult. We spent $16.5 million in this category in fiscal '65 [see Exhibit 5], and all of it in one sense or another, was intended to produce future revenue. Our R & D activities are decentralized. The Corporate Research Center is true research. They work on very theoretical stuff like information theory, microcircuitry, advanced memory techniques, and so forth. They have a very small staff actually, considering how productive they have been.

"Most of R & D money is spent in the divisional research labs and is really aimed at developing new, marketable products or improving existing ones. The Computer Division has the biggest budget, of course, and more than half their efforts are on products already being marketed. On the other hand, they spent over $3 million on projects that were not identifiable with any existing or proposed product line. Our philosophy is that having such projects in a development lab produces a better, more interesting working environment than would be possible if all such projects were done at the corporate lab—as some companies do.

"The only other major R & D budget," Mr. Eng concluded, "is in the Peripheral Equipment Division. They produce equipment that is incorporated into all our standard computer systems, and more than half their effort is to improve those products."

Assignment

1. What portion, if any, of CDC's expenses for marketing, research and development should be deferred in fiscal year 1965 and amortized against revenues in subsequent years? Develop an explicit policy for determining the amount of such costs to be capitalized, and quantify the effects of your policy for 1965.

2. What policy should be adopted to govern the amortization of deferred expenses?

EXHIBIT 1

CONTROL DATA CORPORATION (E)
COMPUTER SYSTEM ORDERS BOOKED, FY 1965

| | Domestic Orders* | | Worldwide Orders | |
| | Per Cent of Total | Lease | Per Cent of Total | Lease |
Product Line	Domestic Orders	Ratio**	Worldwide Orders	Ratio**
Old product lines	10.8%	46%	9.3%	43%
Lower 3000 series	23.0	75	26.0	62
Upper 3000 series	30.4	86	34.7	80
6600	32.2	55	26.7	53
8090	3.6	40	3.3	38
Totals	100.0%	68%	100.0%	63%

*Domestic orders amounted to 80% of worldwide orders booked during the year.
**Orders booked for leased systems for each product line, as a percentage of the total orders booked for that product line.

EXHIBIT 2

CONTROL DATA CORPORATION (E)
CONDENSED CONSOLIDATED OPERATING STATEMENTS
FISCAL YEARS ENDED JUNE 30, 1964 (ACTUAL) AND 1965 (TENTATIVE)
(in thousands)

| | Actual FY 1964* | | Tentative FY 1965 | |
	Amount	%	Amount	%
Net sales	$105,453		$127,800	
Rentals and service income	25,619		32,700	
Total Revenue	$131,072	100.0	$160,500	100.0
Cost of sales, rentals and service	78,857	60.2	97,400	60.7
Gross profit	$ 52,215	39.8	$ 63,100	39.3
Operating expenses:				
Marketing	$ 10,378	7.9	$ 15,300	9.5
Other sales & service engineering	4,386	3.3	6,900	4.3
Product management	1,474	1.1	2,100	1.3
General and administrative	6,911	5.3	9,800	6.1

Total Operating Expenses	$ 23,149	17.6	$ 34,100	21.2
Research and development	12,323	9.4	16,500	10.3
Interest and other deductions	1,715	1.3	3,300	2.1
Other income	(187)	(.1)	(300)	(.2)
Total Expenses	$ 37,000	28.2	$ 53,600	33.4
Net earnings before income taxes	$ 15,215	11.6	$ 9,500	5.9
Provision for income taxes	9,197	7.0	4,900	3.0
Net Earnings	$ 6,018	4.6	$ 4,600	2.9

*Restated from amounts reported in FY 1964 to reflect three acquisitions during FY 1965 that were recorded as poolings of interests.

EXHIBIT 3

CONTROL DATA CORPORATION (E)
MARKETING EXPENSE, FY 1965 (APPROXIMATE)
(in thousands)

Regional marketing administration (five regional offices in U.S.)	$ 3,300
Field office expenses:	
Sales expense (salesmen's salaries, travel expenses and related costs)	4,700
Sales commissions	1,000
Applications expenses (analysts' salaries and related costs)	2,400
Corporate marketing administration (marketing adm., sales adm., contract adm., and corp. applications engineering)	2,100
Advertising and graphic arts expenses	1,200
International sales and marketing expenses	600
Total Marketing Expenses	$15,300

EXHIBIT 4

CONTROL DATA CORPORATION (E)
APPROXIMATE DISTRIBUTION OF TOTAL MARKETING EFFORT
BY FIELD SALESMEN AND ANALYSTS

Type of Activity	Per Cent of Total Hours
1. Marketing standard computer systems (sales calls and demonstrations, applications engineering, etc.)	61%
2. Marketing other products	22
3. Administrative time (general office work, reports, conferences, meetings, training, etc.)	17
Total	100%

EXHIBIT 5

CONTROL DATA CORPORATION (E)
RESEARCH AND DEVELOPMENT EXPENSES, FY 1965 (APPROXIMATE)
(in thousands)

Corporate Research Center			$ 900
Computer Division			
Continuing development work on existing products:			
Old products	$ 300		
Lower 3000 series	1,800		
Upper 3000 series	1,900		
6600	1,300		
8090	100	$5,400	
Development work on products about to be introduced:			
1700 series	$ 100		
3500 series	200	300	
Development work not identifiable with specific products:			
Applicable to all product lines	$ 800		
Applicable to no product line	3,100	3,900	
Total Computer Division			9,600
Peripheral Equipment Division			
Development work on equipment used in existing systems (printers, readers, etc.)	$1,800		
Development work on equipment for new systems	1,200		
Total Peripheral Equipment Division			$ 3,000
Research and development expenses in 13 other divisions and international (no division spending more than $600,000 in FY 1965)			$ 3,000
Total Research and Development Expenses			$16,500

Case 12-3

Bethlehem Steel Pension Plan [1]

BACKGROUND [2]

The economic impact of pension funds has increased dramatically over the past decade. The book value of the assets of all private non-insured pension funds increased from $33 billion in 1960 to $106 billion in 1971. During this same period, the total assets of the 100 retirement plans with the largest values of reported assets increased from $18 billion to $48 billion. These plans accounted for nearly half the assets of all private non-insured pension plans. In 1971, these 100 largest pension plans covered 5.9 million active and vested employees and provided $2.7 billion in benefits to 935,000 retired employees.

During the period 1960 to 1971, there was also a substantial shift in the way pension funds invest their assets. Investments in stock for the 100 largest plans rose from 38 per cent of total pension assets in 1960 to 59 per cent in 1971. For the same period, investments in bonds and debentures dropped from 52 per cent of total assets to 25 per cent. This compares with 61 per cent in stocks and 30 per cent in bonds for all retirement plans in 1971. The remainder of investment assets were in cash, real estate, and other miscellaneous investments.

DISCLOSURE

ABP Opinion No. 8 (Accounting for the Cost of Pension Plans) states that pension plans are of sufficient importance to an understanding of financial statements that the following disclosures should be made in the footnotes:

[1] This case was written by William J. Rauwerdink, Research Assistant, under the supervision of Associate Professor John K. Shank, as the basis for class discussion rather than to illustrate either the effective or ineffective handling of an administrative situation.

Copyright © 1974 by the President and Fellows of Harvard College. Distributed by the Intercollegiate Case Clearing House, Soldiers Field, Boston, Mass. 02163. All rights reserved to the contributors. Printed in the U.S.A.

[2] U.S. Department of Labor, Labor-Management Services Administration, *The 100 Largest Retirement Plans 1960-1971*, January 1973.

1. A statement that the plan exists and an identification of the employee group covered.

2. A statement of the company's accounting and funding policy.

3. The provision for pension costs in the current period.

4. The excess, if any, of actuarially computed "vested" benefits over the total of pension fund assets.

5. The nature and effect of matters affecting comparability of periods presented (e.g., changes in actuarial assumptions, plan amendments, and amortization policy for "past" and "prior" service cost).

In calculating the annual pension charge, APB No. 8 defines minimum and maximum allowable amounts. The annual cost "should not be less than the total of (1) normal cost, (2) an amount equivalent to interest on any unfunded prior service cost, and (3) . . . [in the case of Bethlehem Steel] the amount, if any, by which 5% of such excess (i.e., the unfunded "vested" benefits) at the beginning of the year is more than the amount of reduction, if any, in such excess (i.e., the unfunded "vested" benefits) during the year. . . ."[3]

The maximum provision is roughly defined as the total of (1) "normal" cost, (2) 1/10 of the "past service" liability, (3) interest on the unfunded "prior service" cost.

In addition, the Welfare and Pension Plans Disclosure Act of 1959 requires administrators of employee benefit plans that provide retirement benefits and cover twenty-six or more employees to file reports with the Secretary of Labor. Included among these reports are Form D-1 (initial plan description) and Form D-2 (annual financial reports).

Portions of the 1972 Form D-2 disclosing the pension "normal" costs for Bethlehem Steel are shown in Exhibit 1.

BETHLEHEM STEEL

Due to delays in actuarially determining the liabilities for a given fiscal year, the preceding year's prior and past service liabilities closely approximate the amounts used in determining the following year's allowable range for pension expense. Bethlehem's 1971 Form D-2 indicated a year-end accrued past service liability of $1,267,893,000. The unfunded prior service liability was $749,270,000 at that date.

Also, footnotes to Bethlehem's 1971 annual report disclosed vested benefits of $145,000,000 in excess of pension trust assets.

In August of 1972, a revision in pension plan terms took effect that caused a substantial change in vested benefits and the "past service" liability.

Exhibit 2 contains portions of the Bethlehem Steel and Pension Trust Fund audited reports for 1972. The notes to these statements indicate the pension accounting policies used and the amount of the unfunded "vested" liability as required by APB Opinion 8. Supplemental data is given below.[4]

---

[3] APB Opinion 8, American Institute of Certified Public Accountants, New York, New York.
[4] From annual reports and Form D-2.

	1970	1971	1972
Income before Taxes and Pension Charge (millions)	$180.75	$277.8	$282.5
Pension Charge (millions)	46.6	56.6	80.9
Employees Covered			
Retired	29,000	31,000	34,000
Employed	129,000	123,000	117,000
EPS	2.05	3.14	3.02
Outstanding Common Shares (millions)	44.0	44.4	44.4

QUESTIONS

1. Using the guidelines of APB Opinion 8, calculate the minimum and maximum for pension expense for Bethlehem Steel for 1972.
   (a) Using asset and liability data from the 1971 Form D-2.
   (b) Using asset and liability data from the 1972 Form D-2.

   Note: for both parts (a) and (b), use 1972 normal cost of $17.3 million.

2. Does the Bethlehem annual report adequately meet APB disclosure requirements? Is the disclosure adequate to evaluate the economic significance of the pension plan? What additional disclosures, if any, would you recommend?

3. What is the nature of a balance sheet liability reflecting pension costs?

4. What is the nature of an unfunded prior service liability?

EXHIBIT 1

THE BETHLEHEM STEEL PENSION PLAN

Part IV

Part IV data for trust or other separately maintained fund are to be completed for a plan involving a trust or other separately maintained fund. It also is to be completed for a plan which: (1) Has incurred expenses other than: (a) Payments for unfunded benefits or (b) Insurance or annuity premiums or subscription charges paid to an insurance carrier or service or other organization; or (2) Has assets other than: (a) Insurance or annuity contracts or (b) Contributions in the process of payment or collection.

Part IV—Section A
Statement of Assets and Liabilities

Name of Plan: Pension Plan of Bethlehem Steel Corporation and Subsidiary Companies

File No. WP–17205

For Year Beginning January 1 1972 and Ending December 31 1972

Item	ASSETS¹	End of Prior Year	End of Reporting Year
1. Cash		$ 272,070	$ 1,552,028
2. Receivables:			
a. Contributions: (See Item 18)			
(1) Employer		56,438,111	40,713,278
(2) Other (Specify)			
b. Dividends or experience rating refunds			
c. Other (Specify) Accrued interest		1,876,051	1,645,369

3. Investments: (Other than real estate)		
a. Bank deposits at interest and deposits or shares in savings and loan associations	15,500,000	47,000,000
b. Stocks:		
(1) Preferred	17,356,280	15,003,286
(2) Common	364,598,306	386,239,137
c. Bonds and debentures:		
(1) Government obligations:		
(a) Federal	17,816,587	22,231,985
(b) State and municipal		
(2) Foreign government obligations	1,516,875	924,375
(3) Nongovernment obligations	104,845,575	82,918,910
d. Common Trusts:		
(1) (Identify)		
(2) (Identify)		
e. Subsidiary organizations (See Instructions)		
(Identify and indicate percentage of ownership by this Plan in the subsidiary)		
(1) _____ % _____		
(2) _____ % _____		
4. Real estate loans and mortgages		
5. Loans and Notes Receivable: (Other than real estate)		
a. Secured		
b. Unsecured (Commercial Paper)	975,562	7,000,000
6. Real Estate:		
a. Operated		
b. Other real estate		
7. Other Assets:		
a. Accrued income		
b. Prepaid expenses		
c. Other (Specify)		
8. **Total Assets**	$581,195,417	$605,228,368
LIABILITIES		
9. Insurance and annuity premiums payable	$	$
10. Unpaid claims (Not covered by insurance)		
11. Accounts payable		
12. Accrued expenses		
13. Other liabilities (Specify)		
14. Reserve for future benefits	581,195,417	605,228,368
15. **Total Liabilities and Reserves**	$581,195,417	$605,228,368

¹ The assets listed in this statement must be valued on the basis regularly used in valuing investments held in the fund and reported to the U.S. Treasury Department, or shall be valued at their aggregate cost or present value, whichever is lower, if such a statement is not so required to be filed with the U.S. Treasury Department.

9

Part IV—Section B
Statement of Receipts and Disbursements

–5–

Name of Plan: Pension Plan of Bethlehem Steel Corporation and Subsidiary Companies

File No.	WP– 17205

For Year Beginning January 1, 1972 and Ending December 31, 1972
(Month) (Day) (Year) (Month) (Day) (Year)

CASH RECEIPTS

Item
1. Contributions: (Exclude amounts entered in Item 2)
   a. Employer (Schedule 1) ... $ 96,478,273
   b. Employee
   c. Other (Specify)
   d. Total Contributions ... $ 96,478,273
2. Dividends and Experience Rating Refunds From Insurance Companies
3. Receipts From Investments:
   a. Interest ... $ 6,474,396
   b. Dividends ... 13,989,552
   c. Rents
   d. Other (Specify) Collateral for securities loaned ... 35,410,600
   e. Total Receipts From Investments ... 55,874,548
4. Receipts From Sale of Assets:
   a. Sales to parties-in-interest ... $
   b. Sales to others and maturities (including accrued interest) ... 296,737,412
   c. Total Receipts From Sale of Assets (Schedule 2) ... 296,737,412
5. Other Receipts:
   a. Loans (Money borrowed) ... $
   b. Other (Specify) Miscellaneous income, etc. ... 34,703
   c. Total Other Receipts ... 34,703
6. **Total Receipts** ... $ 449,124,936

CASH DISBURSEMENTS

7. Insurance and Annuity Premiums Paid to Insurance Carriers and Payments to Service Organizations (Including Prepaid Medical Plans) ... $
8. Benefits Provided Directly by the Trust or Separately Maintained Fund ... 80,686,929

9. Payments to an Organization Maintained by the Plan for the Purpose of Providing Benefits to Participants (Attach latest operating statement of the Organization showing detail of administrative expenses, supplies, fees, etc.) . . . .

10. Payments or Contract Fees Paid to Independent Organizations or Individuals Providing Plan Benefits (Clinics, hospitals, doctors, etc.) . . . .

11. Administrative Expenses:
    a. Salaries (Schedule 3) . . . . $. . . . .
    b. Allowances, expenses, etc. (Schedule 3) . . . .
    c. Taxes . . . .
    d. Fees and commissions (Schedule 4) . . . .
    e. Rent . . . .
    f. Insurance premiums . . . .
    g. Fidelity bond premiums . . . .
    h. Other administrative expenses (Specify) . . . . _____
    i.   Total Administrative Expenses . . . .

12. Purchase of Assets:
    a. Investments: (Other than real estate)
       (1) Purchased from parties-in-interest . .(including accrued interest)$. . . .331,737,276. . . .
       (2) Purchased from others . . . .
    b. Real Estate:
       (1) Purchased from parties-in-interest . . . .
       (2) Purchased from others . . . . _____
    c.   Total Purchase of Assets . . . . 331,747,276. . . . . .

13. Loans (Money loaned) . . . .

14. Other Disbursements (Specify)
    a. Collateral repaid upon return of securities loaned . . . $. . . . . .35,410,600. . . .
    b. Miscellaneous expense, etc.   173
    c.   Total Other Disbursements 35,410,773
15.   Total Disbursements . . . . $ 447,844,978

11

Part IV—Section E   −6−
Trust Fund Pension Plan Data

            Pension Plan of Bethlehem
Name of Plan Steel Corporation and Subsidiary Companies | File No. | WP− 17205

This section is to be completed to the extent applicable for those pension plan benefits funded through the medium of a trust.

1. Number of Participants:

       a. Retired 31,500

       b. Active (exclude those in 1c.) 117,000

       c. Separated from employment with vested
          benefits 2,500

2. **Type and Basis of Funding.**—The methods of funding and determination of costs currently being used for the Plan are to be stated here. (See instructions.)

                              See Exhibit I

3. **Actuarial Assumptions and Methods**
       Attach a statement of the actuarial assumptions and methods currently being used in determining the contributions.   A copy of the latest actuarial report which includes such a statement in respect of contributions may be submitted in lieu of the foregoing.   Any such statements or reports submitted as attachments should be appropriately identified.   Where under the type and basis of funding, figures are entered in Item 4, below, a further statement is required showing the actuarial assumptions and methods used in deriving the liabilities of the pension plan, including a description of the precise meaning **assigned** to each of the terms of Item 4 below with respect to the amounts shown.   (See instructions.)

a. Statement of actuarial assumptions attached . . . . [X] Yes   [ ] No

b. Actuarial report attached . . . . [ ] Yes   [x] No

4. Amount of current and past service liabilities as determined by the last actuarial valuation:

   a. (1) Total accrued actuarial liability including any past service or supplemental cost (Before any offset for as- $ 1,754,000.00
   sets entered in b.) ....

   (2) Current service or normal cost (Use the annual amount from the last valuation) .... $ 17,325.00

   b. Enter the amount of the applicable reserves [1] .... $ 581,195.00

5. Date of last valuation ....December 31, 1971.........

   State the name and business address of the actuary or other person who made the valuation.

   Name ....Alexander & Alexander, Inc...

   Address ....1185 Avenue of the Americas, New York, N. Y. 10036

   [1] This is the amount of assets appropriate actuarially to represent an offset against the total liability of 4 a (1).   Assets should be valued on the basis regularly used for the fund in reports to the United States Treasury Department or on the basis of aggregate cost or present value, whichever is lower, if not reported to the United States Treasury Department.

                                          15

BETHLEHEM STEEL CORPORATION AND SUBSIDIARY COMPANIES PARTICIPATING IN THE PENSION PLAN OF BETHLEHEM STEEL CORPORATION AND SUBSIDIARY COMPANIES SUMMARY OF ACTUARIAL BASIS OF COST CALCULATIONS

Interest (including Fund Earnings and Capital Appreciation):	It is contemplated that the earnings of the fund, inclusive of capital growth, will amount to 6% per annum, compounded annually. Prior to August, 1972, a 7% per annum rate had been assumed.
Mortality and Termination Rates:	*Pre-Retirement*: A discount has been taken in respect of anticipated mortality and terminations of employment. Separate sets of rates of decrements, including allowances for mortality and turnover have been prepared for each entry age, based on the past experience of the companies participating in the Plan. Sample rates of decrement per 100 are as follows:

| Year | Entry Age | | |
	20	30	40
1	30.17	30.25	30.43
10	5.32	5.55	6.09
20	2.57	3.12	1.69

Post-Retirement: Group Annuity Table for 1951, adjusted separately for salaried and hourly employees to reflect current pensioner mortality experience.

Future Earnings: Salaried Employees: It is anticipated that relative average earnings levels will proceed as shown by the following specimen ratios:

Age	Ratio of Final 10 year Average Earnings At retirement to Present Earnings
30	1.606
40	1.256
50	1.101

Hourly-Paid Employees: It has been assumed for calculation purposes that future earnings levels will remain unchanged.

Retirement Age: It is assumed for actuarial purposes that employees will retire at the close of the fiscal year ending June 30 in which they attain age 63 (beginning August 1, 1972, age 62 in the case of salaried employees.) If on the calculation date they are older than such age, it is assumed that they will retire on the following June 30.

EXHIBIT 2

The Bethlehem Steel Pension Plan

Notes to Consolidated Financial Statements

A. Accounting Policies

Principles of Consolidation—All majority owned subsidiaries of Bethlehem, except two ocean transportation subsidiaries with vessels under construction for long-term charter to unaffiliated interests, are consolidated. In December, 1972, it was decided that a subsidiary engaged in activities in the shelter market, which had been accounted for by the equity method since acquisition, would be consolidated because of its increased significance. The 1971 statements have been restated for comparability, which did not have a significant effect on any account and did not change net income.

Investments in unconsolidated majority owned subsidiaries are accounted for by the equity method. Investments representing 50% or less of the voting stock are accounted for by the equity method or carried at cost, as appropriate. Investments accounted for by the equity method are carried at cost plus advances, adjusted for Bethlehem's equity in their net income since organization or acquisition less dividends received.

Inventories—Inventories (other than contract work in progress, which is valued at cost less billings, adjusted for estimated partial profits or losses) are valued at the lower of cost or market using the last-in, first-out (LIFO) method, adopted in 1947, in costing the principal portion thereof and the first-in, first-out or average cost method in costing in costing the remainder.

Property, Plant and Equipment—Property, plant and equipment is valued at cost. Gains or losses on disposition of property, plant and equipment are normally credited or charged to accumulated depreciation. Maintenance and repairs are charged to expense as incurred.

Depreciation—For financial accounting purposes depreciation is computed under the straight line method and for Federal income tax purposes substantially all depreciation is computed under accelerated methods. The depreciation rates used for both purposes are based on lives established by the U.S. Treasury Department in connection with guideline and asset depreciation range procedures.

Research and Development Costs—Research and development costs are charged to expense as incurred.

Pensions—Pension costs under Bethlehem's Pension Plan for its employees include current service costs, which are accrued and funded on a current basis, and prior service costs, which are amortized and funded over periods of not more than 40 years. The various actuarial assumptions which enter into the determination of pension costs are reviewed periodically and revised as appropriate.

Income Taxes—The provision for Federal income taxes for any year is reduced by the full estimated investment tax credits for the year. Provision is made to reflect the tax effects of reporting income and expense at different times for financial accounting purposes and for Federal income tax purposes.

Foreign Exchange—Accounts in foreign currencies are translated into U.S. dollars on the basis of appropriate official or free rates of exchange.

Net Income Per Share—Net income per share is calculated by dividing the average number of shares outstanding during a year into the net income for the year.

B. Inventories

	December 31,	
	1972	*1971*
	(dollars in thousands)	
Ore, fluxes, fuel and coal chemicals	$121,231	$138,478
Pig iron, alloys, scrap and manufacturing supplies	75,238	76,503
Finished and semi-finished Products	218,709	182,698
Contract work in progress	66,527	76,303
	$481,705	$473,982

The amounts included above for inventories valued by the LIFO method are less than replacement or current cost by $220,000,000 at December 31, 1972.

C. Property, Plant and Equipment

	December 31,	
	1972	*1971*
Class of Properties	*(dollars in thousands)*	
Steel producing and fabricating, and miscellaneous	$4,398,011	$4,313,410
Raw material (net of depletion)	416,073	412,686
Transportation	172,615	183,973
Shipbuilding and ship repair	159,696	150,913
Total (at cost)	$5,146,395	$5,060,982
Less accumulated depreciation ...	3,015,881	2,900,006
	$2,130,514	$2,160,976

D. Investments

Investments in companies accounted for by the equity method include advances of $10,164,000 at December 31, 1972, and $2,034,000 at December 31, 1971.

Bethlehem's share in the net income of companies accounted for by the equity method amounted to $220,000 and $6,231,000 in 1972 and 1971, respectively, which amounts are included in interest, dividends and other income.

E. Long-Term Debt

	December 31,	
	1972	*1971*
	(dollars in thousands)	
Consolidated Mortgage Bonds		
2¾%, Series J. Due 1976	$ 17,565	$ 17,929
3%, Series K. Due 1979	25,149	25,149
3¼% Debentures. Due 1980	3,218	3,268
5.40% Debentures. Due 1992	137,817	143,892
6 7/8% Debentures. Due 1999	100,000	100,000
9% Debentures. Due 2000	150,000	150,000
4¾%–8¼% Notes. Due 1973 through 1976	17,217	16,938
4½% Subordinated Debentures. Due 1990	109,919	113,454
5¼%–5 5/8% Obligations related to pollution control revenue bonds: Due 1997 and 2002	58,000	—
4¾%–9¼% Notes and Lease Subsidiaries. Due 1973 through 1997	41,503	23,476
	$660,388	$594,106
Less unamortized debt discount	3,819	3,660
	$656,569	$590,446
Less amounts due within one year	14,421	11,486
	$642,148	$578,960

The effective interest rate of any individual debt issue is not materially increased above the stated rate by any applicable debt discount.

The amounts shown above are net of securities owned and available for sinking fund requirements. The aggregate of (a) the excess of sinking fund requirements over such securities owned and (b) maturities is as follows in the next five years: 1973 $14,421,000; 1974 $13,610,000; 1975 $18,166,000; 1976 $41,330,000 and 1977 $21,998,000.

F. Commitments and Contingent Liabilities

Based on its proportionate stock interest in certain associated raw material enterprises, Bethlehem is entitled to receive its share of the raw materials produced by such enterprises and is committed to pay its share of their costs, including amortization of their long-term indebtedness. Bethlehem's share of such amortization averages approximately $7,400,000 annually through 1983. In addition, Bethlehem has guaranteed indebtedness of various enterprises, including that of certain associated enterprises, with maturities averaging approximately $2,500,000 annually through 1991. Bethlehem has also entered into lease agreements which provide for rental payments averaging approximately $5,000,000 annually through 1997.

At December 31, 1972, Bethlehem had placed purchase orders in respect of a substantial portion of the estimated cost of completion, $520,000,000, of the then authorized additions and improvements to its properties.

G. Capital Stock

During 1972 and 1971 Bethlehem reacquired 94,397 and 233 shares, respectively, of its Common Stock and used 79,872 and 471,090 shares, respectively, in the acquisitions mentioned in Note L.

The authorized capital stock includes 20,000,000 shares of Preferred Stock, par value $1 per share, none of which has been issued.

H. Special Incentive Compensation Plan

Under the Special Incentive Compensation Plan in effect under Article Tenth of Bethlehem's Amended Certificate of Incorporation, certain executives receive special incentive compensation in the form of dividend units. The aggregate number of dividend units credited for any year is determined by dividing an amount equal to 2% of the consolidated net income for the year by the market value per share of Bethlehem Common Stock at the beginning of the year. Each dividend unit entitles the holder to receive cash payments equal to cash dividends paid on a share of Common Stock after the crediting of the unit and during his life, but in any event until the 15th anniversary of the termination, by death or otherwise, of his service with Bethlehem, subject to earlier termiantion in certain circumstances. The charges to expense for the Plan in 1972 and 1971 were $613,000 and $523,000, respectively.

I. Pensions

Effective August 1, 1972, the amounts charged to income for pensions include the increased costs resulting from increased benefits arising out of the union agreement of August 1, 1971, and from revisions in actuarial assumptions. Such revisions in actuarial assumptions did not have a material effect on consolidated net income for 1972. The excess of the actuarially computed value of vested benefits over the market value of the Pension Trust Fund amounted to $591,000,000 at December 31, 1972.

Exhibit 2 (continued) Pension Trust Fund

	December 31 (dollars in thousands)	
Statements of Assets	*1972*	*1971*
Cash and accrued interest receivable	$ 3,198	$ 2,148
Contributions receivable from employing companies	40,713	56,438
Investments, at cost:		
Short-term obligations	76,232	34,292
Long-term bonds, notes and other obligations	83,843	106,363
Preferred stocks	15,003	17,356
Common stocks	386,239	364,598
Total	$605,228	$581,195

The Pension Trust Fund is not the property of Bethlehem and therefore is not included in the consolidated financial statements. The aggregate market value of the assets of the Fund was more than the cost thereof at December 31, 1972 and 1971.

	Year (dollars in thousands)	
Statements of Changes in Fund	*1972*	*1971*
Balance in Fund, January 1	$581,195	$562,472
Add:		
Contributions from employing companies	80,754	56,449
Income from investments	21,002	21,858
Net gain on disposition of investments	2,964	7,919
	$685,915	$648,698
Deduct: Pension payments	80,687	67,503
Balance in Fund, December 31	$605,228	$581,195
Pensioners at year end	31,444	28,804

Report of Independent Accountants

To the Trustees of the Pension Trust of
Bethlehem Steel Corporation and Subsidiary Companies:

In our opinion, the accompanying statements of assets and statements of changes in the Fund present fairly the assets of the Pension Fund under the Pension Trust of Bethlehem Steel Corporation and Subsidiary Companies at December 31, 1972 and 1971 and the changes in the Fund during the years, in conformity with generally accepted accounting principles applied on a consistent basis. Our examinations of these statements were made in accordance with generally accepted auditing standards and accordingly included such tests of the accounting records and such other auditing procedures as we considered necessary in the circumstances, including confirmation by the custodian of investments owned at December 31, 1972 and 1971.

Price Waterhouse & Co.
60 Broad Street
New York, N. Y. 10004
January 31, 1973

Case 12-4

Verona Products, Inc.[1]

.

John Cook, financial vice president of Verona Products, had a problem. Because management had decided to lease an additional factory building, he was faced with deciding the appropriate accounting treatment for the lease transaction.

The lease began on January 1, 1974, and was to extend through the 20 years ending December 31, 1993. The yearly rental rate was $115,200, exclusive of taxes, maintenance, and insurance which were to be provided by Verona. (Payment was to be made each December 31.) The building's original construction cost had been $479,000 but market value was now somewhere in excess of $1,000,000. From conversations with the lessor, Mr. Cook determined that the lease was to include interest charged at an 8 per cent rate. The building was assumed to have a 25-year remaining life as of 1974. At the end of the initial 20-year lease period, Verona would have the option of renewing for another 10 years at a rate equal to 1/2 the annual payment during the first 20 years.

QUESTIONS

1. If Verona wanted to capitalize the lease they would do so at "present market value." Given the lease payment terms and the interest rate charged, calculate the market value placed on the buildings by the lessor.

2. What is the difference in earnings impact for Verona for 1974 and 1975 between:
   (a) treatment as a lease, or
   (b) capitalizing the lease and charging compound interest and depreciation as expenses?

[1] This case was written by Geoffrey J. Mansfield, under the supervision of Associate Professor John K. Shank, as the basis for class discussion rather than to illustrate effective or ineffective handling of an administrative situation.

3. What would the balance sheets look like in 1974 and 1975 with capitalization?

4. What accounting treatment should Mr. Cook adopt for the "lease" described?

EXHIBIT 1

VERONA PRODUCTS, INC.

Income Statements
For Years Ending December 31
(000's omitted)

	Actual	Pro Forma	
	1973	1974	1975
Net Revenues	$2,700	2,980	$3,450
Expenses:			
Cost of Sales[a]	1,750	1,960	2,200
Marketing and Administration	325	370	425
Income before Taxes	625	650	825
Provision for Taxes	310	325	410
Net Income	$ 315	$ 325	$ 415
Earnings Per Share	3.15	3.25	4.15
[100,000 shares]			

[a]Includes $115,200 lease payment in 1974 and 1975.

EXHIBIT 2

VERONA PRODUCTS, INC.

Balance Sheets
As of December 31
(000's omitted)

	Actual	Pro Forma	
	1973	1974	1975
ASSETS			
Current Assets			
Cash	$ 275	$ 370	$ 425
Marketable Securities	75	75	400
Accounts Receivable	425	500	602
Inventories	600	700	854
Other	50	50	50
	1,425	1,695	2,325

Property Assets			
Buildings and Equipment	1,270	1,270	1,270
Office Furniture and Equipment	125	325	350
Autos and Trucks	40	50	60
Leasehold Improvements	35	135	190
Accumulated Depreciation	(270	(410)	(470)
	1,200	1,370	1,400
Total Assets	$2,625	$3,065	$3,725

LIABILITIES AND OWNERS' EQUITY

Current Liabilities			
Accounts Payable	$ 185	$ 210	$ 235
Accrued Expenses	260	290	330
Income Taxes	165	255	370
	610	755	935
Deferred Income Taxes	560	785	1,085
Long-Term Mortgage Note	565	510	455
Shareholders' Equity			
Common Stock	100	100	100
Retained Earnings	790	915	1,150
	890	1,015	1,250
	$2,625	$3,065	$3,725

(Dividends in 1974 are $200,000; in 1975, $180,000.)

Case 13-1

Innovations, Inc.[1]

"I'd like your views on some discussions I've been having with my accountants, David." David Rosenkrantz, a recent graduate of a prestigious business school and newly appointed executive assistant to the president of Innovations, Inc., listened expectantly as his boss, Rachel Guildenstern, continued. "As you know, in the ten short years since my sister and I started Innovations, we have pioneered some exciting new concepts in household notions. By intensively substituting capital for labor in our manufacturing operations while retaining an old-world flavor in our marketing and promotion programs, we have succeeded in providing our customers with the quality and panache they desire at very competitive prices. Also, our aggressive utilization of debt has allowed us to maintain a good return even on relatively modest margins. (See exhibits 1 and 2 for current financial statements.)

"Now I am wondering whether or not we should extend our innovative philosophy to our financial statements, as well. It seems to me that, due to our highly leveraged financial position, we have been benefiting from recent inflationary trends and that there should be some way to make our shareholders aware of it. When I asked Arthur (Arthur Block, senior partner of DeFunis, Block and Kahlmann, Innovation's accountants) about it, he said that, although we could include what he called general price-level adjusted statements in our annual reports as supplementary information, he would advise against it. He said that there were great differences of opinion in the accounting profession regarding the marginal utility of the supplementary data due to problems associated with index selection, income recognition, and the like. He also told me that price level information would only confuse most investors—'obfuscate, not illuminate' were his words, I believe—and that they would be unable to analyze it. What do you think?"

[1] This case was written by David Clark, MBA student, under the supervision of Associate Professor John K. Shank, as the basis for class discussion rather than to illustrate effective or ineffective handling of an administrative situation.

"Well," Rosenkrantz began, "I think that Mr. Block has raised some interesting points, but there are other considerations here, as well. For instance, our balance sheet is pretty heavy with fixed assets, some of which, like the San Francisco warehouse, have been on our books for 10 years. Since general prices have risen considerably in that period, price level adjustments would probably result in significantly higher depreciation charges for us.

"On the other hand," he continued, "I don't think that we should decide against including the information just because our average shareholder doesn't understand it. There are a lot of things that they don't understand. Anyway, we may be *required* to present this sort of data in the near future, especially if the current rate of inflation holds up. If we do it this year, though, we will surely call attention to ourselves in the financial press; I don't know whether that will hurt us or help us until I do the numbers."

Rachel Guildenstern glanced at her watch. "All right." she replied. "I have to go up to Portland to look at a possible acquisition tomorrow; you can work up the figures[2] while I'm gone. We'll talk about it again when I get back and come to some sort of decision so that we can get the '73 annual report off to the printers on time. I really do think we should go ahead on this, but I would hate to fall on my face."

EXHIBIT 1

INNOVATIONS, INC.

Comparative Balance Sheets
As of December 31, 1973 and 1972
($000,000)

ASSETS	1973	1972
Cash	$ 6.3	$ 6.1
Accounts Receivable	8.0	7.6
Inventories	3.2	3.0
Total current assets	$ 17.5	$ 16.7
Plant and Equipment	$124.8	$115.6
Less Accumulated Depreciation	43.5	37.2
	$ 81.3	$ 78.4
Other Assets	$ 4.9	$ 4.9
	$103.7	$100.0
LIABILITIES		
Accounts Payable	$ 12.8	$ 12.2
Accruals	0.2	0.2
Other Current Liabilities	3.7	3.5

[2] Exhibit 3 contains general price level data (the Gross National Product Implicit Price Deflator). Exhibit 4 presents aging information for plant and equipment, common stock and surplus, other assets, and other liabilities.

Total Current Liabilities	$ 16.7	$ 15.9
Long-term Debt	$ 63.5	$ 61.6
Other Liabilities	$ 1.0	$ 1.0
Common Stock and Surplus	$ 17.5	$ 17.5
Retained Earnings	5.0	4.0
	$ 22.5	$ 21.5
	$103.7	$100.0

EXHIBIT 2

INNOVATIONS, INC.

Statement of Income and Retained Earnings
For the year ended December 31, 1973

Sales		$100.0
Opening Inventory	$ 3.0	
Purchases	80.2	
Closing Inventory	3.2	
Cost of Goods Sold		80.0
Gross Margin		$ 20.0
Depreciation		6.3
Other Expenses		5.0
Operating Profit		$ 8.7
Interest (@ 7.5 per cent)		4.7
Profit before Tax		4.0
Profit after Tax		2.0
Retained Earnings, 12/31/72		$ 4.0
		$ 6.0
Less Dividends Paid, 1973		1.0
Retained Earnings, 12/31/73		$ 5.0

EXHIBIT 3

INNOVATIONS, INC.

Implicit Price Deflators for Gross National Product
For years 1963-1973
(1958 = 100)

Year	GNPI	GNPI as % of Index (12/31/73)
1963	107.2	1.478
1964	108.8	1.456
1965	110.9	1.428

1966	113.94	1.390
1967	117.59	1.347
1968	122.30	1.294
1969	128.20	1.235
1970	135.24	1.171
1971	141.60	1.118
1972	146.10	1.084
1973	153.94	1.029

Quarterly Averages

	1972			*1973*
I	144.85	1.093	149.81	1.057
II	145.42	1.089	152.46	1.039
III	146.42	1.082	155.06	1.021
IV	147.63	1.073	158.36	1.000

Source: U.S. Department of Commerce Bureau of Economic Analysis: *Survey of Current Business*, February 1974, for 1973 data; 1972 *Business Statistics* for all other data.

EXHIBIT 4

INNOVATIONS, INC.

Analysis of Selected Accounts
($000,000)

A. *Plant and Equipment, 1972 balance sheet:*
   Investments in

	Gross Amount	Accumulated Depreciation	Net Amount
1971	$ 10.9	$ 1.1	$ 9.8
1970	23.1	3.5	19.6
1968	26.1	6.5	19.6
1965	16.3	6.5	9.8
1963	39.2	19.6	19.6
12/31/72 Totals:	$115.6	$37.2	$78.4
1973 Balance Sheet			
Prior Investments	$115.6	$37.2	$78.4
1973 Depreciation on Prior Investments		5.8	(5.8)
1973 Investment (1st qtr.)	9.2	0.5	8.7
12/31/73 Totals	$124.8	$43.5	$81.3

B. *Common Stock and Surplus*

Year of Addition Amount

1970	$ 4.375
1966	4.375
1963	8.75
Balance, 12/31/72 and	$17.5
12/31/73	

C. *Other Assets, Other Liabilities*

(For simplicity, assume that these accounts first appeared during 1968 and have remained constant.)

Case 13- 2

Forever Stores, Inc. [1]

Karl Stone, president and principal stockholder of Forever Stores, Inc., sat at his desk reflecting on the condition of his business in general, and on the 1973 results (see Exhibits 1 and 2) in particular. It hadn't been a great year, he mused, but it hadn't been a disaster either. At lease he didn't have to worry about the energy crisis; his 94 jewelry stores were all located in high pedestrian-traffic areas of major metropolitan areas, and he had recently been assured by his regional managers that there had been no noticable slump in sales. Still, Stone felt mildly uncomfortable about another problem in the U.S. economy that didn't seem to want to go away: inflation. He felt that if he could only get some feel for the parameters of the situation as it affected Forever, he would be better able to deal with it. With this in mind he called his assistant, a recent graduate of a well-known eastern business school, into his office.

"Carole," he began, "I have the feeling that we're getting clobbered by rising prices, but these statements look as healthy as ever. Since it looks as though inflation is here to stay, at least for a while, I think that this might be a good time to review some of our financial policies: capital structure, dividend policy, credit policies, things of that sort. But I have to be able to *see* what I'm fighting first; I need *information*. Do you see what I'm driving at?"

Carole Schultz shifted in her chair. "Yes, I believe I do," she replied. "What you're referring to are price-level adjusted financial statements; the techniques involved here have been part of GAAP for years, but have been largely ignored in practice. They relate a company's reported results to general price-level changes in the economy."

Stone leaned back, looking slightly relieved. "Excellent. What do you need to construct these statements?"

[1] This case was prepared by David Clark, MBA student, under the supervision of Associate Professor John K. Shank as the basis for class discussion rather than to illustrate either effective or ineffective handling of an administrative situation.

"First, I'll need a table of the Gross National Product Implicit Price Deflator (GNPI) going back to 1963, the year the company was formed," she responded, "but I can get that at the library (see Exhibit 3). Then, in addition to the basic financial statements, I'll need schedules that show the age of individual items in our 'non-monetary' accounts: Plant and Equipment, Other Current Assets, Other Assets, Other Liabilities, and Common Stock and Surplus (Exhibit 4). I'll get on it right away."

"Fine," replied Stone. "While you're at it, I'd like you to think about the implications of the figures you come up with. I'd like to know what kinds of decisions the price-level adjusted data will help us make, and I'd also like to get your ideas on some of the weaknesses or pitfalls that we should watch out for. I have a meeting with another director later today, so I'd like to go over your results with you before then. I'll see you at three."

Carole got up and turned to leave. Before she reached the door Stone called out, "Oh, and don't worry about lunch; I'll send one of the boys out for sandwiches."

EXHIBIT 1
FOREVER STORES, INC.

Comparative Balance Sheets
at 12/31/73 and 12/31/72
($000,000)

	December 31	
	1973	1972
ASSETS		
Cash	$ 2.4	$ 2.3
Accounts Receivable	56.3	53.7
Inventories	34.3	32.7
Other Current Assets	0.6	0.6
Total Current Assets	93.6	89.3
Plant and Equipment	10.6	10.6
Less Accumulated Depreciation	3.9	3.4
	6.7	7.2
Other Assets	3.4	3.5
	$103.7	$100.0
LIABILITIES		
Accounts Payable	$ 31.5	$ 29.9
Accruals	4.4	4.2
Other Current Liabilities	1.4	1.3
Total Current Liabilities	37.3	35.4
Long-term Debt	15.3	14.9
Other liabilities	10.5	10.1

Common Stock and Surplus	33.6	33.6
Retained Earnings	7.0	6.0
	40.6	39.6
	$103.7	$100.0

EXHIBIT 2
FOREVER STORES, INC.

*Statement of Income
and Retained Earnings
for year ended December 31, 1973
($000,000)*

Sales		$100.0
Cost of Goods Sold		
Opening Inventory	$32.7	
Purchases	81.6	
Closing Inventory	34.3	80.0
Gross Margin		20.0
Depreciation		0.5
Other Expenses		13.8
Operating Profit		5.7
Interest (@ 7.5%)		1.7
Profit Before Tax		4.0
Profit After Tax		2.0
Retained Earnings, 12/31/72		$ 6.0
		8.0
Less: Dividends paid, 1973		1.0
Retained Earnings, 12/31/73		$ 7.0

EXHIBIT 3
FOREVER STORES, INC.

*Implicit Price Deflators for Gross National Product
for years 1963-1973*
(1958 = 100)*

Year	GNPI	GNPI as % of index (12/31/73)
1963	107.2	1.478
1964	108.8	1.456
1965	110.9	1.428
1966	113.94	1.390
1967	117.59	1.347
1968	112.30	1.294
1969	128.20	1.235
1970	135.24	1.171
1971	141.60	1.118
1972	146.10	1.084
1973	153.94	1.029

Quarterly Averages

	1972		1973	
I	144.85	1.093	149.81	1.057
II	125.42	1.089	152.46	1.039
III	146.42	1.082	155.06	1.021
IV	147.63	1.073	158.36	1.000

*Source: U.S. Department of Commerce Bureau of Economic Analysis: *Survey of Current Business,* February 1974, for 1973 data; 1972 *Business Statistics* for all other data.

EXHIBIT 4
FOREVER STORES, INC.

Chronological Analysis of
Selected Accounts
($000,000)

Plant and Equipment

Year Acquired	Gross Investment	Accumulated Depreciation* 12/31/72	Net Amount 12/31/72	12/31/73
1963	$ 3.6	$1.8	$1.8	$1.6
1965	1.5	0.6	0.9	0.8
1968	2.4	0.6	1.8	1.7
1970	2.1	0.3	1.8	1.7
1971	1.0	0.1	0.9	0.8
	$10.6	$3.4	$7.2	$6.7

*All Plant and Equipment depreciated straight-line over 20 years.

Common Stock and Surplus

Year Acquired	Year Acquired
1963	$16.8
1966	8.4
1970	8.4
	$33.6

Other Current Assets,
Other Assets and
Other Liabilities

(For simplicity, assume that entire amounts appearing on
1972 statements were acquired in 1968.)

Case 13-3

Ohio Valley Industries[1]

As the stock market slid to record lows during mid-1974, Ohio Valley's president, Lynn Griffin, had become particularly anxious to investigate possible acquisition candidates. Griffin was aware of reports which indicated that price/earnings ratios had reached their lowest level in 25 years with over 80% of the stocks listed on the major exchanges selling at 10 times earnings or less. Another report claimed that 40% of publicly traded stocks were selling below reported book value.

Ohio Valley was primarily a manufacturer of industrial grinding wheels. Thus, although Ohio Valley had fairly large cash flows and stable profitability, very little growth could reasonably be anticipated. The prospect of combining forces with a firm in a more growth-oriented situation was very attractive (especially considering the current "bargain basement" prices).

Discussions with several firms proved fruitless, but on December 31, 1974, Ohio Valley did successfully acquire 97% of the stock of Badger Bionics. Badger was solidly established in the technology-based medical equipment industry. The purchase price was $2 million in cash. The company was to be operated as a consolidated subsidiary.

Griffin was quite sure this acquisition would require use of the "purchase" accounting method which had been reaffirmed by the Accounting Principles Board in Opinion No. 16. However, she felt uncertain about the correct application of the "fair value" provisions of that Opinion (see Exhibit 1).

Exhibit 2 presents the December 31, 1974 balance sheets of Ohio Valley and Badger Bionics. Griffin had asked the Ohio Valley accounting department to bring to her attention any situations that could affect the valuation of the Badger

---

[1] This case was prepared by William J. Rauwerdink, Research Assistant, under the supervision of Associate Professor John K. Shank as the basis for class discussion rather than to illustrate either effective or ineffective handling of an administrative situation.

Copyright © 1974 by the President and Fellows of Harvard College.

investment. The following list of items was presented to her in early February, 1975, as the financial statements for the 1974 Annual Report were being finalized:

1. The Accounts Receivable and Payable "agings" are representative of industry expectations.

2. Of the marketable securities, $100,000 are considered to be temporary investments of currently excess corporate resources. These have a current market value of $108,000. The balance in this account is a long-term commitment carried at cost ($30,000). It represents 5% of the stock of Sherman Corp., a privately held firm. Ohio Valley's share of Sherman's book value is $48,000. However, a reputable independent investment banker felt the shares would be worth $65,000 on the open market. Mr. Hayes, Senior Controller, has calculated that if Sherman's estimated future cash flow were capitalized, Ohio Valley's pro rata indicated share would be $114,000.

3. Land similar to that held by Badger was recently sold for approximately $300,000. However, Badger's president maintains that the property he purchased is irreplaceable and that applying "similar" property values to it would be arbitrary and inaccurate. This land is not related to Badger's business. It is being held as an investment. Also Ohio Valley has no readily apparent use for this land. A real estate consultant hired by Ohio Valley felt confident that with time to develop its full potential, the land value will be substantially in excess of that achieved by other sellers. The consultant has estimated that investing an additional $150,000 will yield a developed value of $650,000.

4. Book inventories are valued using the LIFO technique. Substantially all of Badger's materials inventory consists of precious metals which fluctuate wildly in price, but currently can be sold on the spot commodity market at 275% of book value. The finished inventory has an estimated selling value of about $4.7 million. Only minimal incremental sales costs will be required to sell it. The Badger production manager has estimated that completing the unfinished inventory will cost, on average, $2,100 per unit. Historically, Badger has earned income of about 20% (before income tax which averages around 50%) on its products.

5. Badger's physical plant, while relatively old, is in excellent operating condition. There are no plans to replace this capacity. An independent appraiser has estimated that the current replacement cost of a comparably equipped new plant would be $10.2 million. The plant is about 50% depreciated. The real estate consultant estimated that the plant could probably be sold now, as is, for about $3 million assuming a buyer could be found.

6. The plant sits on land owned by Iroquois County. Badger negotiated a 30 year land lease from the County Industrial Development Agency in 1964. The annual rental cost is $20,000. The lease Badger currently holds would have cost $40,000 per year if negotiated today.

7. The long-term debt owed is due as follows: $900,000 at the end of 4 years, $1,700,000 at the end of 6 years. Both loans are at 12% annual interest.

8. The Badger finaancial statements do not mention the ownership of a key patent. Badger's president reported that since successfully filing for the patent, the company has received no offers to purchase the patent nor have they solicited any Badger has always planned to use the patent, he said, not sell it. Badger has spent

about $100,000 to develop the patent. The president has estimated its market value to be around $400,000. Mr. Hayes has calculated that the estimated discounted cash flow from products directly related to the patent is $260,000. This calculation is based on the remaining 12 years of patent protection.

A few days after Griffin reviewed this list, she received two additional pieces of information regarding the Badger acquisition. The holder of the other 95% of the stock of Sherman Corp. reportedly sold his holdings for $2.47 million. Also, an unfortunate fire had just destroyed one building in the Badger complex. The damage was total. Book value of the building, net of accumulated depreciation was $380,000. However, a recent insurance appraisal had valued the building at $415,000. The building was insured for $332,000, but settlement of the claim would probably take 6 to 8 months.

The 1974 financial statements had to go to the printer by February 20, 1975 and the independent auditors wanted to know as soon as possible how Ohio Valley would record the Badger investment.

QUESTIONS

1. Prepare a consolidated balance sheet as of the date of purchase.

2. Prepare a consolidated income statement for 1975. Individual income statements for the two firms are found in Exhibit 3.

EXHIBIT 1

Opinion #16*

Recording Assets Acquired and Liabilities Assumed

87. An acquiring corporation should allocate the cost of an acquired company to the assets acquired and liabilities assumed. Allocation should follow the principles described in paragraph 68.

First, all identifiable assets acquired, either individually or by type, and liabilities assumed in a business combination, whether or not shown in the financial statements of the acquired company, should be assigned a portion of the cost of the acquired company, normally equal to their fair values at date of acquisition.

Second, the excess of the cost of the acquired company over the sum of the amounts assigned to identifiable assets acquired less liabilities assumed should be recorded as goodwill. The sum of the market or appraisal values of identifiable assets acquired less liabilities assumed may sometimes exceed the cost of the acquired company. If so, the values otherwise assignable to noncurrent assets acquired (except long-term investments in marketable securities) should be reduced by a proportionate part of the excess to determine the assigned values. A deferred credit for an excess of assigned value of identifiable assets over cost of an acquired company (sometimes called "negative goodwill") should not be recorded unless those assets are reduced to zero value.

Independent appraisals may be used as an aid in determining the fair values of some assets and liabilities. Subsequent sales of assets may also provide evidence of values. The effect of taxes may be a factor in assigning amounts to identifiable assets and liabilities (paragraph 89).

88. General guides for assigning amounts to the individual assets acquired and liabilities assumed, except goodwill, are:

a. Marketable securities at current net realizable values.

b. Receivables at present values of amounts to be received determined at appropriate current interest rates, less allowances for uncollectibility and collection costs, if necessary.

c. Inventories:

(1) Finished goods and merchandise at estimated selling prices less the sum of (a) costs of disposal and (b) a reasonable profit allowance for the selling effort of the acquiring corporation.

(2) Work in process at estimated selling prices of finished goods less the sum of (a) costs to complete, (b) costs of disposal, and (c) a reasonable profit allowance for the completing and selling effort of the acquiring corporation based on profit for similar finished goods.

(3) Raw materials at current replacement costs.

d. Plant and equipment: (1) to be used, at current replacement costs for similar capacity[1] unless the expected future use of the assets indicates a lower value to the acquirer, (2) to be sold or held for later sale rather than used, at current net realizable value, and (3) to be used temporarily, at current net realizable value recognizing future depreciation for the expected period of use.

e. Intangible assets which can be identified and named, including contracts, patents, franchises, customer and supplier lists, and favorable leases, at appraised values.[2]

f. Other assets, including land, natural resources, and nonmarketable securities, at appraised values.

g. Accounts and notes payable, long-term debt, and other claims payable at present values of amounts to be paid determined at appropriate current interest rates.

h. Liabilities and accruals—for example, accruals for pension cost,[3] warranties, vacation pay, deferred compensation—at present values of amounts to be paid determined at appropriate current interest rates.

[1] Replacement cost may be determined directly if a used asset market exists for the assets acquired. Otherwise, the replacement cost should be approximated from replacement cost new less estimated accumulated depreciation.

[2] Fair values should be ascribed to specific assets; identifiable assets should not be included in goodwill.

[3] An accrual for pension cost should be the greater of (1) accrued pension cost computed in conformity with the accounting policies of the acquiring corporation for one or more of its pension plans or (2) the excess, if any, of the actuarially computed value of vested benefits over the amount of the pension fund.

i. Other liabilities and commitments, including unfavorable leases, contracts, and commitments and plant closing expense incident to the acquisition, at present values of amounts to be paid determined at appropriate current interest rates.

An acquiring corporation should record periodically as a part of income the accrual of interest on assets and liabilities recorded at acquisition date at the discounted values of amounts to be received or paid. An acquiring corporation should not record as a separate asset the goodwill previously recorded by an acquired company and should not record deferred income taxes recorded by an acquired company before its acquisition. An acquiring corporation should reduce the acquired goodwill retroactively for the realized tax benefits of loss carry-forwards of an acquired company not previously recorded by the acquiring corporation.

89. The market or appraisal values of specific assets and liabilities determined in paragraph 88 may differ from the income tax bases of those items. Estimated future tax effects of differences between the tax bases and amounts otherwise appropriate to assign to an asset or a liability are one of the variables in estimating fair value. Amounts assigned to identifiable assets and liabilities should, for example, recognize that the fair value of an asset to an acquirer is less than its market or appraisal value if all or a portion of the market or appraisal value is not deductible for income taxes. The impact of tax effects on amounts assigned to individual assets and liabilities depends on numerous factors, including imminence or delay of realization of the asset value and the possible timing of tax consequences. Since differences between amounts assigned and tax bases are not timing differences (APB Opinion No. 11, *Accounting for Income Taxes*, paragraph 13), the acquiring corporation should not record deferred tax accounts at the date of acquisition.

Amortization of Goodwill

90. Goodwill recorded in a business combination accounted for by the purchase method should be amortized in accordance with the provisions in paragraphs 27 to 31 of APB Opinion No. 17, *Intangible Assets*.

Excess of Acquired Net Assets Over Cost

91. The value assigned to net assets acquired should not exceed the cost of an acquired company because the general presumption in historical-cost based accounting is that net assets acquired should be recorded at not more than cost. The total market or appraisal values of identifiable assets acquired less liabilities assumed in a few business combinations may exceed the cost of the acquired company. An excess over cost should be allocated to reduce proportionately the values assigned to noncurrent assets (except long-term investments in marketable securities) in determining their fair values (paragraph 87). If the allocation reduces

the noncurrent assets to zero value, the remainder of the excess over cost should be classified as a deferred credit and should be amortized systematically to income over the period estimated to be benefited but not in excess of forty years. The method and period of amortization should be disclosed.

92. No part of the excess of acquired net assets over cost should be added directly to stockholders' equity at the date of acquisition.

EXHIBIT 2

Balance Sheet Data
12/31/74
(000 omitted)

Assets		Ohio Valley		Badger
Cash		$ 7,400		$ 110
Marketable Securities (at cost)		10,800		130
Accounts Receivable (net)		11,200		1,890
Days Outstanding	0-30=$7,500		$790	
	31-60= 2,500		680	
	61-90= 1,200		420	
Inventory		12,700		2,120
Finished Goods	=8,000		500 units 1,420	
Work in Progress	=3,000		500 units 550	
Raw Materials	=1,700		150	
Land		1,400		175
PP&E (net)		53,900		2,455
		$97,400		$6,880

Equities		Ohio Valley		Badger
Accounts Payable		$ 7,200		$1,560
Days Outstanding	0-30=$6,000		$770	
	31-60= 1,200		430	
	61-90= zero		360	
Notes Payable		1,200		440
Deferred Taxes		2,000		
Long-term Debt				
(due after 6 years)		12,500	(after 4 years)	900
(due after 10 years)		*20,000	(after 8 years)	1,700
Common Stock (1,800,000 shares @ $10)		18,000		
Common Stock (100,000 shares @ $1)				100
Retained Earnings		36,500		2,180
		$97,400		$6,880

*This debt was issued late in 1974 to yield 9% to maturity.

EXHIBIT 3

INCOME STATEMENTS

Year Ending 12/31/75

(000 omitted)

	Ohio Valley	*Badger*
Sales (net)	$98,600*	$7,940
Cost of Goods Sold	61,750	3,170
Selling, General & Administrative	20,500	2,112
Depreciation	3,800	320
Lease Expense	—	60
Other (net)	1,710**	318
Income before taxes	10,840	1,960
Provision for taxes	5,420	980
Net Income	$ 5,420	$ 980

*Including $1,000,000 of sales to Badger. The gross margin on these sales was $300,000. All of these items were fully consumed by Badger during 1975.
**Including $485,000 of dividends received from Badger. On the books of Ohio Valley, the investment in Badger was carried using the cost method.

Case 14-1

Data Consultants, Inc.[1]

In the summer of 1973, John Wilson, an investor in a variety of small companies, had an option to purchase a controlling interest in Data Consultants, Inc. (DCI).

Data Consultants, Inc., was a small, closely held company engaged actively in several related fields. The company conducted business and industry surveys, developed special computer programs, and offered various management services such as information planning, guidance in mathematical techniques, and marketing research. The customers of the company included both government agencies and commercial firms. The results of the operations of the company for the fiscal year ended July 31, 1973, are shown in Exhibit 1. The balance sheet appears in Exhibit 2.

Beginning in the fall of 1972 DCI had implemented a new strategy, designed to reduce the fluctuations in its level of activity and provide a better basis for long-term, profitable growth. Although the company had been profitable in each of the last several years, profits had been somewhat erratic because most of the company's projects were of relatively short duration (2 to 3 months) with the result that sales volume was erratic and unpredictable. The new strategy was to seek longer-term projects that might run for 18 to 30 months, thus permitting a more stable work flow, better work force planning, and, management hoped, eventually higher profits. By July 31, 1973, a major shift in the nature of the company's projects had been achieved; nearly three-quarters of the activity in the month of July had been on long-term projects.

Mr. Wilson did not contemplate any further basic changes in the company's way of doing business. However, he was not satisfied with the financial data provided to the board of directors. Also, he felt the company's reports to the shareholders were inadequate; first, the accounts of the company were maintained on a modified cash basis rather than an accrual basis, which sought to match revenues and related costs;

[1] This case was prepared by Associate Professor John K. Shank as the basis for class discussion rather than to illustrate either the effective or ineffective handling of an administrative situation.

EXHIBIT 1

DATA CONSULTANTS, INC.

Statement of Earnings
For the Year Ended July 31, 1973[a]

Revenues		$12,100,000
Costs and Expenses		
Research and Development	$3,200,000	
Sales and Marketing	2,900,000	
Contract Installation Expenses	8,250,000	
Service Costs	1,300,000	
Administrative Expenses	950,000	
Depreciation	700,000	17,300,000
Operating Loss		(5,200,000)
Gain on Sale of Marketable Securities		1,300,000
Net Loss before Taxes		$(3,900,000)

[a]Statement prepared on a modified cash basis:
  1. Revenue recognized only when actually received in cash.
  2. All expenses (except depreciation) recognized when paid in cash.

and second, the company had used its independent public accountant primarily to prepare tax returns, rather than to assist in the preparation of financial reports for stockholders.

Mr. Wilson wanted to review the company's general accounting policies before he exercised his option to purchase the stock. Accordingly, he arranged a meeting to discuss this matter with the company's auditors, his personal auditors, and an executive from another business in which he had an interest.

EXHIBIT 2

DATA CONSULTANTS, INC.

Comparative Balance Sheet
July 31

ASSETS		1973[a]	1972
Cash		$ 1,800,000	$ 3,100,000
Marketable securities		3,600,000	6,800,000
Property and Equipment			
Land, Buildings, and Equipment	$8,000,000		
Less Accumulated Depreciation	2,000,000	6,000,000	5,700,000
		$11,400,000	$15,600,000

LIABILITIES AND EQUITY

Equipment Notes Payable	$ 1,700,000	$ 2,000,000
Common Stock and Paid-in Capital	3,200,000	3,200,000
Retained Earnings	6,500,000	10,400,000
	$11,400,000	$15,600,000

ᵃBefore consideration of tax loss carryback.

AUGUST 24 MEETING

The meeting to discuss the accounting policies of DCI was held on Friday, August 24, 1973. Prior to the meeting, Mr. Wilson had received the statements shown in exhibits 1 and 2 from Fred Kneads, the controller of DCI. Three other men were at the meeting in addition to Wilson and Kneads: Jeff Davis of the Fraser Construction Company, Price Anderson of the CPA firm of Anderson, Mitchell and Company (the firm frequently used by Mr. Wilson), and Peter Bird present auditor of DCI. John Wilson was the controlling shareholder of Fraser Construction.

Wilson: This morning I'd like to discuss the accounting policies of DCI. Of course, if necessary, I hope you will make suggestions as to possible changes in the company's accounting policies. Has Fred (Kneads) provided you with copies of the company's latest financial statements? (All nod in agreement.) Naturally, I am quite disturbed with the net operating loss of over $5 million for the year ended July 31, 1973, for two reasons: First, the contracts obtained by the company during fiscal 1973 are up 30 per cent over last year and management seems to think they were profitable, but the statements indicate a large loss; second, although I can't put my finger on it, I don't think the present set of statements are adequate for my needs. . . .

I'd like to pass around an agenda that I think will help us focus this discussion.

Wilson: Price, you have been very patient, but I can see that you are itching to make some comments, so the podium is yours.

Anderson: Thanks, John. I have some ideas and I'd like to express them in the form of a revised statement for the company for 1973. As you know, I've had the company's 1973 statement for a day or so now and with Fred's help I revised the statements. Now, I'd like to distribute copies of them to you. (Mr. Anderson distributes a statement that has been recast and is shown as the first column of Exhibit 3.) . . . . Of course, John, these are rough drafts subject to refinement, but I think they'll help to express my ideas.

Wilson: Fantastic, Price. The loss of $3.9 million is now a profit of $1.6 million. That's better! (All laugh). Perhaps you could tell me where you buy your pencils.

Anderson: Let me assure you, John, it isn't just a sharp pencil (smiling). Fortunately, Fred maintained records of his accumulated costs by contracts, portion of contracts completed, including information on payments received and estimates of the percentage completion on each contract. With this information, Fred and I were able to revise the financial statements using the following underlying assumptions:

EXHIBIT 3

DATA CONSULTANTS, INC.

Alternative Earnings Statements
For the year ended July 31, 1973

	Completed Contract Basis	*Percentage of Cost Completion Basis*	*Economic Earnings Basis*
Contract Income			
Billings on Completed Contracts	$16,400,000	$16,400,000	$16,400,000
Related Installation Costs	7,050,000	7,050,000	7,050,000
	9,350,000	9,350,000	9,350,000
Plus Earnings Recognized on Open Contracts	—	1,500,000	1,000,000
	9,350,000	10,850,000	10,350,000
Other Operating Expenses			
Research and Development	3,200,000	3,200,000	
Sales and Marking	2,900,000	2,900,000	5,000,000
Service Costs	1,300,000	1,300,000	1,300,000
Administrative Expenses	950,000	950,000	950,000
Depreciation Expense	700,000	700,000	700,000
	9,050,000	9,050,000	7,950,000
Operating Earnings	300,000	1,800,000	2,400,000
Gain on Temporary Investments	1,300,000	1,300,000	2,100,000
Net Earnings before Taxes	$ 1,600,000	$ 3,100,000	$ 4,500,000

[a]See exhibits 4 and 5 for an explanation of the three alternative methods and for additional information related to the calculations.

1. accrual—that is, matching costs and revenues—instead of merely showing the net cash flow from operations.

2. revenue recorded when billed to customer.

3. costs deferred—that is, shown as assets rather than expenses—for contracts not completed.

John, these assumptions can be taken as replies to the first three questions on your agenda. I'd like to comment on each assumption.

First, I used the accrual method to estimate the results of operations rather than the modified cash basis. Let me explain it this way. If all contracts had been completed during the accounting period, all bills paid, and all invoices collected, there'd be no difference between the cash profit and the accounting accrual profit. But, if on the other hand, you spend money on a contract one period and collect the fee in the second period, you show a cash loss in the first, a cash profit in the second, and have no reasonable estimate of the

EXHIBIT 4

DATA CONSULTANTS, INC.

Explanation of the alternative accounting methods:

Completed Contract Method

1. Expense all development and marketing costs as incurred.
2. Expense all service and administrative costs as incurred.
3. Defer contract installation costs until contracts are completed and billings are rendered.
4. Recognize revenues when billings are rendered.
5. Recognize securities gains or losses only when realized.

Percentage of Costs Completion Method

1. Expense all development and marketing costs as incurred.
2. Expense all service and administrative costs as incurred.
3. Recognize expected contract income (contract billings less contract installation costs) on the basis of percenage of installation costs incurred to total expected installation costs.
4. Recognize security profits or losses when realized.

Economic Earnings Method

1. Expense all Service and administration costs as incurred.
2. Defer development and marketing costs for the year. Charge to contracts on the basis of: (contract amount/total value of contracts awarded). In subsequent years, development and marketing expense for the year will equal beginning of the year deferral plus actual costs for the year less ending deferral.
3. Recognize expected contract income on the basis of percentage of value added on the contracts (determined from independent estimates).
4. Recognize security gains or losses at year's end whether or not the securities are actually sold.

results of operations for either period. Therefore, in general, the new statements reflect the accrual basis of accounting rather than the modified cash basis. I might add that during the fiscal year ended July 31, 1972, the year before last, the cash profit was approximately equal to the accounting profit. This occurred because most of the projects were of short duration. They were started, completed, and customers' payments were received, all during fiscal 1972.

At the beginning of this last accounting period (fiscal 1973), according to our calculations, there were neither accounts receivable nor uncompleted contracts of any significant amount. Note that at the end of fiscal 1973 accounts receivable on contracts completed or partially completed and deferred costs totaled over $5 million. This reflects the company's new policy of seeking larger and longer-term contracts.

I understand that the company is attempting to work out a new form of contract that would make some provision for advance and progress payments on longer-term contracts. Of course, the adoption of the "accrual basis" does not mean we don't have to prepare cash budgets. Also, to complete the picture, a statement summarizing the sources and uses of funds for the year should be prepared.

Second, revenue has been recorded at the time the customer was billed, rather than when his payments are received. Previously, only a memorandum file of accounts receivable was maintained. It seemed to me that you "make your profit" when you completed the contract and bill the customer.

Third, costs incurred on the uncompleted unbilled portion of contracts was deferred to the time period when the revenue will be recognized. Development costs not clearly associated directly with specific uncompleted contracts are included in cost of service. That is, they are written off during this accounting period.

Let me sum up by telling you what my intentions were. I tried to accumulate costs and revenues as they were incurred and earned, respectively; i.e., I tried to match together costs and related revenues.

Wilson: Jeff, would you like to comment on Price's remarks.

Davis: Well, let me describe the accounting policy we follow at Fraser Construction for revenue recognition and the matching of costs and revenues. We have a similar problem. Perhaps our experience may suggest a better way to deal with the questions raised in your agenda. Somewhere in my briefcase here . . . I have a Fraser annual report with me and . . . if I can find it, I'd like to read directly from the *Notes to the Financial Statements* . . . ah, here it is.

> "Note C—Unbilled Costs and Profits Included in Sales: The company follows the procedure reflecting, on a percentage-of-completion basis, the costs incurred and related profits on fixed-price contracts with progress payment provisions as sales in the month in which such costs are incurred. Included herein are unbilled costs and related profits of $1,000,000 in excess of progress billing of $1,900,000 at November 30, 1972, and unbilled costs and related profits of $500,000 in excess of progress billings of $700,000 at November 30, 1971. In addition, costs on cost-plus fixed-fee government contracts amounting to $100,000 in 1972 and $150,000 in 1971 are included."

In other words, Price, we take into account not only progress billings, which are "legally enforceable" claims as you refer to them, but also the value of work completed but not billed. It seems to me our accounting policy provides a pretty good matching of costs and revenues.

I guess you can argue that our policy is not so "conservative," but the policy is based on competent business judgment that has been substantiated over the years; *and* the amounts involved are material. Also, our annual report is signed by the auditors.

The auditors agreed to that accounting policy years ago and I guess it's really up to them to decide such things as a company's accounting policy anyway.

Wilson: I couldn't disagree more. This matter of setting accounting policy is very important to me and I think it demands the involvement of all our managers and the auditors in the discussion . . . but, management has the final word on accounting policy.

Now, from my understanding thus far, it seems to me that all three proposals have some shortcomings in terms of really reflecting the economics of business. Without going into a criticism of your proposals, let me just suggest another. First, although it's true that we probably earn a part of the ultimate profit each day as work on a project progresses, it seems to me that we earn because of the work that our people do, not just because costs are incurred. In the early stages of many projects there are substantial costs for computer time that we purchase from service bureaus. I don't think we make a profit on buying that service; our profit is more related to the idea of value added by the work of our staff. Second, we incur major costs for product development and marketing, the sole purpose of which is to ultimately produce contract revenue and profit. I don't see how any of your proposals match these costs with revenue. Finally, although no one has mentioned it yet, the company had a quite successful year in the management of its temporary investments—more successful than it first appears. Wouldn't our statements be more informative if we recognized the *fact* that, as of the end of the year, we've got a gain of $800,000 in the securities that we're holding? After all, if we didn't make that money this year, when did we make it?

My problem, of course, is that I'm not an accountant, so I don't know whether my ideas conform to the generally accepted principles. But that's why we've got two CPA's at this meeting. I may be wrong in my suggestions, in the sense that they're not the best way to measure what happened. I'm anxious to hear such arguments. I may also be wrong in the sense that my suggestions are not permissible. If so, I'd like to know about it, but I'd also like to know *why* the traditional principles are set up the way they are, so I can re-think my ideas. What do you say?

Mr. Wilson's Agenda

1. How does Data Consultants, Inc., make a profit?

   by developing a product?
   by finding customers and signing a contract?
   by performing work on a contract?
   by completing a contract?
   by billing a customer?
   by being paid by a customer?

2. When should the company recognize sales revenue?

3. When should the company recognize expenses?

4. What accounting policies best reflect our conclusions on these questions?

Fred, could you describe briefly the results of the operations of the company during fiscal 1973 (see Exhibit 1) and give us your thoughts on the first item on the agenda.

Kneads: Gladly, John. First, the company statements of profit and loss have always been drawn up on a modified cash basis. That is, all our expenses are recorded when they are paid out and all our revenue arises when our customers pay us for the services we provide. An exception is expenditures for fixed assets. The depreciation expense on our statements is the same as we are allowed for tax purposes. That way, you see, we do not anticipate revenue that we may not be able to collect, and the statement reflects very closely the change in our flow of cash during the year. Also, it is essentially the same as the statement we submit to the tax authorities.

Wilson: Fred, I've always believed a company's financial statements should reflect the basic economics of the business. Why don't you start by telling us how DCI makes a profit?

Kneads: Surely, let me show how by describing a typical series of events from start to finish. Since many of our new contracts are linked with new computer software packages developed in our research department, I will start there. Furthermore, to give you a sense of the time element let me break the year into four equal periods. During period 1, we pay the wages of our research staff and the expenses for the computer time and supplies they use in their work. They may complete a project in one quarter or it may take several quarters. Upon completion, the new development or technique is turned over to our sales engineers who attempt to match the capabilities of our new program with the needs of a customers. Sometimes, of course, the customer describes his needs to us first and the program or technique is developed specifically for that customer. Let's assume that the customer is found in period 4 and a contract is completed by period 6. At this point we have either integrated the program to run on the customer's equipment or trained the customer's staff in the use of the technique. For the first six periods then (or about a year and a half) we, out of our own pocket, paid for developing, selling, and delivery.

Normally, after the customer is satisfied that our service or program is functioning satisfactorily, we bill him some time during the initial period of use. Usually, customers pay the amount of the contract over the next two quarters in accordance with our terms of payment. If we mail the invoice in the sixth period, we frequently receive half of the amount in the seventh period and half in the eighth. Also, our service department handles inquiries from the customer for four periods after installation for which we do not charge any fee. Thus, most of our contracts last for about ten periods, or 2 1/2 years from initial development to final services. Some contracts are only a few months long, but we're now 10 months into another contract that we expect will run for 2 more years.

To sum up, gentlemen, our cash outflow is spread fairly evenly over the life of our contracts, and our cash inflow usually is received in two parts at the end of the contract.

To answer your question directly, Mr. Wilson, I guess we make a profit when we receive more money during a month then we pay out.

QUESTIONS

1. For this question, please confine your discussion to the determination of pre-tax net income. Exhibits 3, 4, and 5 present and explain income statements reflecting the accounting policies suggested, respectively, by Messrs. Anderson, Davis, and Wilson. The company also has the alternative of continuing to use the modified cash basis, as shown in Exhibit 1.

   (a) Of these four alternatives, which one would you recommend to Mr. Wilson as the most appropriate for DCI? Why?

(b) If you think that some other combination of accounting policies would be better than any of the four, describe your proposal and support it.

2. Please revise the balance sheet in Exhibit 2 to make it consistent with the method of income determination that you selected in Question 1(a). The revised balance sheet should also reflect the effects of federal income taxes. You may assume that:

(a) The appropriate tax rate is 50 per cent on operating income and 30 per cent on capital gains.

(b) The company will continue to use the modified cash basis for determining taxable income.

(c) The company's tax-basis loss for fiscal 1973 can be used to claim a refund of taxes paid in prior years. The amount of the refund to be received is $1,950,000 (50 per cent of the net loss of $3,900,000).

3. (a) Using the revised balance sheet from Question 2 and your income statement from Question 1, prepare a funds flow statement (all financial resources) for DCI for the year ended July 31, 1973.

(b) How and why would this statement differ from one prepared directly from exhibits 1 and 2?

EXHIBIT 5
DATA CONSULTANTS, INC.

Additional Information

A. *For Percentage Completion Calculations*

Open Contracts at 7-31-73

Contract Amount	Billings to Date	Costs Incurred to Date	Anticipated Costs to Complete	Total Expected Profit
$3,600,000	—	$1,200,000	$400,000	$2,000,000

1. Percentage of expected total costs incurred to date.	75%
2. Value added percentage (independent estimate)	50%

B. *Deferred Marketing and Development Costs*

$$\left(\frac{\text{Value of Open Contracts at Year's End}}{\text{Total Value of Contracts for the Year}}\right) \times \begin{array}{l}\text{Total Development} \\ \text{and Marketing Expense} \\ \text{for the Year}\end{array} = \begin{array}{l}\text{Deferred} \\ \text{Development} \\ \text{and} \\ \text{Marketing} \\ \text{Expense at} \\ \text{Year's End}\end{array}$$

$$\left(\frac{\$3,600,000}{\$16,400,000 + \$3,600,000}\right) \quad \times \quad \$6,100,000 \quad = \quad \$1,100,000$$

C. *Security Trading Profits*

	Cost	Market Price	Gain[a]
1. Securities sold during the year	$3,200,000	$4,500,000	$1,300,000
2. Securities still held at year's end	3,600,000	4,400,000	800,000

[a]These securities have been held by DCI for 18 months; thus, any gains are taxable at the capital gains rate.

Case 14-2

Measurex Corporation[1]

Measurex Corporation designs, manufactures, and markets digital computer process control systems for producers of sheet products, primarily paper manufacturers. Measurex's equipment is designed to increase the efficiency of the production process by monitoring the physical characteristics of the material flow using a combination of radiation, infrared and optical sensors linked to a digital computer, and appropriate output devices. Although Measurex's systems are most widely used in papermaking, they have applications in the tile, rubber, plastics, and metal industries.

Measurex markets its system on short or long-term leases as well as on a sale basis. Each Measurex system sells for between $200,000 and $500,000, with an average of $275,000 to $300,000. The firm also offers short-term (12 to 42 months) and long-term (66 to 102 months) leases. Long-term leases allow the lessee to renew at the expiration of the lease term with an accompanying reduction in the monthly rental to 25 per cent of the original charge; a separate charge is made for service. Lessees also retain the right to evaluate the system for the initial 6 months of the lease and to return the device for a refund within that period.

Incorporated in California in early 1968, Measurex has shown significant growth in revenues, profits, and assets during its corporate history (Exhibit 1). Customers have shown a clear preference for long-term leases; as of January 1972 only one user had chosen to purchase the equipment. At the same time, orders for new systems have grown from twenty-seven in fiscal year 1971 to forty-six orders in 1972 and fifty in the first half of 1973. A significant number of users have been repeat customers. Measurex has financed the growth in outstanding leases by maintaining lines of credit with domestic banks and through Eurocurrency

[1] This case was prepared by Steven E. Levy, Research Assistant, under the supervision of Associate Professor John K. Shank, as the basis for class discussion rather than to illustrate either the effective or ineffective handling of an administrative situation.

borrowings. In addition, the firm has spent large sums on research and development throughout its history; in January 1972 it held four domestic patents and had applied for nine domestic and thirty-four foreign patents.

Measurex made a public offering of common stock in March 1972. Issued at $20, the shares quickly rose to $40 and were quoted, in November 1973, in the mid-$20s. Measurex's stock attracted a substantial following among institutional investors and brokerage houses, having been selected "No. 1 Baby Blue Chip" in a poll of western security analysts. Analysts predicted earnings per share of $0.85 to $0.90 in fiscal year 1973 and $1.20 in 1974. At the same time, a number of individuals and publications called attention to alleged flaws in several aspects of Measurex's accounting practices. Yet, as 1973 drew to a close, corporate officials strongly defended the firm's policies and institutional analysts continued to recommend the purchase of Measurex's shares.

QUESTIONS

1. What rate of discount is Measurex using to compute the present value of its lease contracts receivable? (Hint: What is the present value of the payment streams discounted at 4 per cent? at 6 per cent?)

2. What figure would Measurex report for sales revenue in 1972 if the lease payments were discounted at 10 per cent?

3. What is the impact of the discount rate on the reported earnings of Measurex? How do you think that discount rate should be determined?

4. Evaluate Measurex's inventory, tax, depreciation, and R&D accounting policies in terms of the firm's general reporting strategy.

5. What is the relationship between Measurex's accounting practices and its overall corporate strategy?

Note: In considering Question 1, you may assume that the timing of receipt of the aggregate cash flows from the long-term lease contracts receivable is as follows:

	1972	*1971*
1972	$ —	$1,109,000
1973	3,162,000	1,300,000
1974	3,680,000	1,324,000
1975	3,864,000	1,301,000
1976	4,037,000	1,314,000
1977	3,953,000	914,000
1978	2,415,000	908,000
1979	2,415,000	909,000
1980	2,413,000	—
Total	$25,939,000	$9,079,000

EXHIBIT 1.

MEASUREX CORPORATION
Highlights
For the Current Year

	1972	Percent Increase from 1971
Operating revenues	$16,336,000	90%
Income before extraordinary credit:		
Amount	1,727,000	67%
Per share	.71	37%
Average number of common shares	2,429,000	22%

Measurex Corporation and Subsidiary Companies
Notes to Consolidated Financial Statements

1. Summary of Significant Accounting Policies

Basis of Consolidation:

The accompanying consolidated financial statements include the accounts of the Company and its subsidiaries all of which are wholly owned excepting directors' qualifying shares. All significant intercompany items have been eliminated.

Lease Accounting:

Measurex offers its customers both short-term and long-term leases. Generally, short-term leases have terms from 12 to 42 months and long-term leases have terms from 66 to 102 months.

Substantially all the amounts shown as "Sales" are represented by long-term leases accounted for on the financing method. Such method recognizes as revenue at the time of shipment of a system an amount equal to the lesser of (a) the discounted amount of future committed lease payments discounted at a rate which the Company believes approximates the customer's borrowing rate or (b) the cash purchase price of the system. The excess of the aggregate committed lease payments over the discounted amount of such payments is recognized as interest income on the sum-of-the-digits method over the term of the lease.

In years prior to 1972 it was the Company's practice to record residual value on financing leases; had this practice been continued in 1972 net income would have been increased by approximately $336,000, or $.15 per share. (In fiscal year 1972 the American Institute of Certified Public Accountants published an Accounting Interpretation recommending that in accounting for financing leases residual value not be recorded; the Company has conformed to this recommendation.)

Short-term leases are accounted for on the operating method whereby the aggregate rentals are reported as revenue on a straight-line basis over the term of the leases. Under the operating method the statement of income reflects, as expenses, depreciation of the leased property and amortization of the installation costs.

Since its inception it has been the Company's practice to grant its customers an initial period, generally six months following installation, in which to evaluate the system. During the initial period the customer may return the system and require the refund of all rentals theretofore paid. Although no systems have been returned through November 30, 1972, provisions have been made which management believes to be sufficient to provide for losses which may result from returns.

MEASUREX CORPORATION AND SUBSIDIARY COMPANIES

Operating Summary for all Years

(Dollar amounts in thousands except per-share income)

	1972	1971	1970	1969	1968[1]
Operating revenues	$16,336	$ 8,613	$3,527	$ 302	$ (334)
Income (loss) before taxes and extraordinary credit[2]	2,887	1,974	(25)	(781)	(334)
Income (loss) before extraordinary credit[2]	1,727	1,034	(25)	(781)	(334)
Extraordinary credit[2]		545			
Net income (loss)	$ 1,727	$ 1,579	$ (25)	$ (781)	$ (334)
Net income (loss) per common and common equivalent share:					
Income before extraordinary credit[2]	$ .71	$ .52	$ (.02)	$ (.72)	$ (1.16)
Extraordinary credit[2]		.27			
Net income (loss)	$ .71	$ .79	(.02)	$ (.72)	$ (1.16)

Financial Position at Year-End
(November 30)

	1972	1971	1970	1969	1968[1]
Working capital	$ 8,021	$ 5,219	$ 764	$ 665	$ 362
Total assets	34,657	18,296	8,222	2,765	750
Capitalization:					
Long-term debt	10,386	9,033	1,649	835	62
Shareholders' equity	20,099	7,155	5,464	1,496	530

[1] From inception on January 18, 1968, to November 30, 1968.
[2] Extraordinary credit arises from reduction to provision for federal income taxes utilization of net operating loss carry-forward.

592

MEASUREX CORPORATION AND SUBSIDIARY COMPANIES

Consolidated Statements of Income

For the years ended November 30, 1972 and 1971

	1972	1971
Operating Revenues		
Sales	$15,201,000	$8,041,000
Rental and service income	1,135,000	572,000
	16,336,000	8,613,000
Cost of sales, rentals and services	7,058,000	3,073,000
Gross profit	9,278,000	5,540,000
Selling, general and administrative expenses	6,414,000	3,458,000
	2,864,000	2,082,000
Interest income	607,000	275,000
Interest expense	(584,000)	(383,000)
	23,000	(108,000)
Income before taxes on income and extraordinary credit	2,887,000	1,974,000
Taxes on income	1,160,000	940,000
Income before extraordinary credit	1,727,000	1,034,000
Extraordinary credit—reduction of provision for federal income taxes through utilization of net operating loss carry-forward	—	545,000
Net income	$ 1,727,000	$1,579,000
Net income per common and common equivalent share:		
Income before extraordinary credit	$ .71	$ .52
Extraordinary credit	—	.27
Net income	$ .71	$ .79

See accompanying notes.

MEASUREX CORPORATION AND SUBSIDIARY COMPANIES

Consolidated Statements of Changes in Financial Position

For the years ended November 30, 1972 and 1971

	1972	1971
Resources Provided		
Issuances of common stock for cash	$11,210,000	$ 42,000
Issuance (cancellation) of warrants	(42,000)	70,000
Additions to long-term debt	13,160,000	10,329,000
Reduction in non-current portion of lease contracts receivable	2,417,000	4,178,000
	$26,745,000	$14,619,000
Resources Applied		
To operations:		
Net income	$(1,727,000)	$(1,579,000)
Non-working capital items entering into the determination of net income:		
Depreciation and amortization	(707,000)	(524,000)
Non-current portion of deferred taxes on income	(874,000)	(355,000)
Net book amount of systems (including installation costs) on leases converted from short-term to long-term	(741,000)	(573,000)
Additions to non-current portion of lease contracts receivable related to sales which did not create working capital	13,649,000	7,109,000
Working capital applied to operations	9,600,000	4,078,000
Payments and current portion of long-term debt	11,807,000	2,944,000
Additions to systems leased to others under short-term leases (including installation costs)	317,000	845,000
Additions to fixed assets	1,373,000	651,000
Additions to investment in new product development	915,000	631,000
Additions to residual value of systems leased to others	—	551,000
Other	(69,000)	464,000
Increase in working capital	2,802,000	4,455,000
	$26,745,000	$14,619,000

Changes in Components of Working Capital:

Current assets—increase (decrease) in:

Cash	$ 721,000	$ 843,000
Current portion of lease contracts receivable	1,726,000	683,000
Accounts receivable	(606,000)	1,959,000
Inventories	2,256,000	1,537,000
Prepaid expenses	(105,000)	77,000
Increase in current assets	3,992,000	5,099,000
Current liabilities—increase (decrease) in:		
Long-term debt due within one year	63,000	(66,000)
Trade accounts payable	262,000	243,000
Accrued expenses	755,000	427,000
Deferred taxes on income	110,000	40,000
Increase in current liabilities	1,190,000	644,000
Increase in working capital	$ 2,802,000	$ 4,455,000

See accompanying notes.

MEASUREX CORPORATION AND SUBSIDIARY COMPANIES

Consolidated Balance Sheet
November 30, 1972 and 1971

ASSETS	1972	1971
Current assets:		
Cash	$ 1,871,000	$ 1,150,000
Current portion of lease contracts receivable	2,619,000	893,000
Accounts receivable	1,457,000	2,063,000
Inventories	4,991,000	2,735,000
Prepaid expenses	26,000	131,000
Total current assets	10,964,000	6,972,000
Lease contracts receivable less current portion and valuation provision .	17,222,000	5,989,000
Systems leased to others under short-term leases (including installation costs), at cost less accumulated depreciation and amortization of $261,000 (1972) and $174,000 (1971)	1,066,000	1,691,000
Residual value of systems leased to others under long-term leases ...	691,000	691,000
Fixed assets, at cost less allowance for depreciation	2,631,000	1,466,000
Investment in new product development less accumulated amortization of $814,000 (1972) and $451,000. (1971)	1,491,000	962,000
Other	592,000	525,000
	$34,657,000	$18,296,000

See accompanying notes.

	1972	1971
LIABILITIES		
Current liabilities:		
Long-term debt due within one year	210,000	$ 147,000
Trade accounts payable	955,000	693,000
Accrued expenses:		
Payroll and payroll related items	989,000	466,000
Initial and continuing services	421,000	212,000
Other	218,000	195,000
Deferred taxes on income	150,000	40,000
Total current liabilities	2,943,000	1,753,000
Long-term debt less amount due within one year ...	10,386,000	9,033,000
Deferred taxes on income	1,229,000	355,000
	14,558,000	11,141,000
Contingent liabilities		
SHAREHOLDERS' EQUITY		
Preferred stock, $1 par value:		
Authorized: 1,000,000 shares; issued and outstanding: none		
Common stock, without par value:		
Authorized: 5,000,000 shares; issued and outstanding:		
2,597,284 shares (1972) and 1,927,406 (1971)	68,000	34,000
Additional paid-in capital	17,865,000	6,682,000
Retained earnings	2,166,000	439,000
	20,099,000	7,155,000
	$34,657,000	$18,296,000

MEASUREX CORPORATION AND SUBSIDIARY COMPANIES

Consolidated Statements of Shareholders' Equity
For the years ended November 30, 1972 and 1971

| | Common Stock | | | Additional Retained | |
	Shares	Amount	Paid-In Capital	Earnings	Total
Balance, December 1, 1970	1,901,011	$33,000	$ 6,571,000	$(1,140,000)	$ 5,464,000
Issuance of warrants to purchase 72,000 shares of common stock			70,000		70,000
Other issuances (including 24,245 shares upon exercise of employee stock options)	26,395	1,000	41,000		42,000
Net income for the year ended November 30, 1971 ...				1,579,000	1,579,000
Balance, November 30, 1971	1,927,406	34,000	6,682,000	439,000	7,155,000
Public offering of common stock less related expenses of $1,114,000	600,000	30,000	10,829,000		10,859,000
Cancellation of warrant to purchase 42,000 shares of common stock			(42,000)		(42,000)
Other issuances (including 65,878 shares upon exercise of employee stock options)	69,878	4,000	396,000		400,000
Net income for the year ended November 30, 1972				1,727,000	1,727,000
Balance, November 30, 1972	2,597,284	$68,000	$17,865,000	$ 2,166,000	$20,099,000

See accompanying notes.

See Note 2.

Inventory Valuation:

Purchased parts and components are stated at the lower of average cost or market. Finished sub-assemblies and systems and work in process are stated at the lower of standard cost (which approximates actual cost) or market.

See Note 3.

Properties:

The Company provides for depreciation and amortization by charges to expense which are sufficient to write off the costs of the assets over their estimated useful lives, on a straight-line basis.

The basis for computing depreciation and amortization is as follows:

Class of Property	*Estimated Useful Lives*
Systems leased to others under short-term leases	9 Years
Installation costs on systems leased to others under short-term leases	4 years
Buildings	25-40 Years
Machinery and equipment	2-10 Years

Investment in New Product Development:

The Company is capitalizing new product development costs which are identifiable to significant new systems or products having a potential commercial value; those costs not meeting these criteria are charged to selling, general and administrative expense currently. The capitalized costs are being amortized to expense over the anticipated useful life of the system or product, or three years from the beginning of routine production, whichever is shorter. Costs applicable to projects abandoned are written off in the year of abandonment.

See Note 5.

Taxes on Income:

Deferred taxes are provided on all significant differences between taxable income and pre-tax income as shown in the accompanying consolidated statements of income except taxes are not provided on the income of the Company's Domestic International Sales Corporation subsidiary inasmuch as management believes that the payment of taxes on such income can be deferred indefinitely by investing and distributing such income as the DISC regulations allow.

Investment tax credit on fixed assets is recognized on the flow-through method. Generally, it is the Company's policy to allow the end-user of the leased Measurex system to claim the related investment tax credit; unclaimed investment tax credit is recognized by the Company either as additional sales or as financing income over the term of the lease.

Deferred taxes arise principally as a result of the following differences between taxable income and pre-tax income as shown in the accompanying consolidated statements of income:

(a) new product development costs which have been deferred in the accompanying financial statements are expensed for tax purposes.

(b) long-term leases, which are reported under the financing method for financial statement purposes, are reported under either the installment method or the operating method for tax purposes, and

(c) losses upon non-collection and system return are deducted for tax purposes as the losses are incurred.

See Note 8.

Net Income per Common and Common Equivalent Share:

Net income per common and common equivalent share has been computed based upon the average number of common shares outstanding during the year assuming the exercise of employee stock options and stock warrants to the extent that such options and warrants were dilutive. In this computation, the proceeds from the assumed exercise of the options and warrants are assumed to have been used to purchase shares of common stock at the average market price for the period such options and warrants were outstanding. The number of shares used in the computation was 2,429,000 in 1972 and 1,994,000 in 1971.

2. Lease Contracts Receivable

Lease contracts receivable are summarized below:

	1972	*1971*
Aggregate lease payments to be received under long-term leases accounted for under the financing method	$25,939,000	$9,079,000
Less unearned financing income	4,449,000	1,774,000
	21,490,000	7,305,000
Less amount due within one year	2,619,000	893,000
	18,871,000	6,412,000
Less reserve for non-collection and system returns	1,649,000	423,000
	$17,222,000	$5,989,000

For a more complete description of lease transactions, see Note 1—"Lease Accounting."

The aggregate amount of principal payments due in years subsequent to 1972 are set forth below:

1973	$ 2,619,000
1974	3,048,000
1975	3,201,000
1976	3,343,000
1977	3,277,000
Thereafter	6,002,000
	$21,490,000

With respect to certain leases which have been or will be accounted for under the financing method, the Company has arranged financing with Manufacturers Hanover Trust Company ("Manufacturers") in amounts not to exceed $7,456,000 through November 30, 1973. Pursuant to such arrangement, the Company sells to Manufacturers such lease contracts receivable and related equipment on a full recourse basis and participates with Manufacturers in revenues received from the customers pursuant to purchase or lease renewal options. The effective interest rate of this arrangement varies between 8¾% and 10%. As of November 30, 1972 the Company had received $3,456,000 from Manufacturers pursuant to this agreement and was contingently liable to Manufacturers for approximately $2,990,000 of such amount.

3. Inventories

Inventories are as follows:

	1972	1971
Purchased parts and components	$3,077,000	$1,232,000
Finished sub-assemblies and systems	1,064,000	1,085,000
Work in process	850,000	418,000
	$4,991,000	$2,735,000

See Note 1—"Inventory Valuation."

4. Fixed Assets

Details of fixed assets less allowance for depreciation are set forth below:

	1972	1971
Buildings (under construction in 1971)	$1,127,000	$ 350,000
Machinery and equipment	1,025,000	537,000
Leasehold improvements	—	9,000
	2,152,000	896,000
Less allowance for depreciation		
(see Note 1—"Properties")	293,000	164,000
	1,859,000	732,000
Land	772,000	734,000
	$2,631,000	$1,466,000

5. New Product Development

Total new product development expenditures:

	1972	1971
Capitalized (before amortization)	$ 915,000	$ 631,000
Charged to operating expenses currently	953,000	634,000
	$1,868,000	$1,265,000
Amortization of capitalized costs	$ 363,000	$ 273,000

See Note 1—"Investment in New Product Development."

6. Long-Term Debt

Details of long-term debt are presented below:

	1972	1971
Credit agreement with banks	$ 8,935,000	$7,110,000
4% mortgage payable in annual installments of $83,000	249,000	332,000
8¾% mortgage payable in monthly installments from 1973 to 1998	1,050,000	380,000

Capitalized lease obligations on equipment used by Measurex (8¾% interest rate)	362,000	158,000
2% above prime subordinated note	—	1,200,000
	10,596,000	9,180,000
Less amount due within one year	210,000	147,000
	$10,386,000	$9,033,000

The credit agreement with Bank of America and Manufacturers Hanover Trust Company allows the Company to borrow up to $20,000,000 through November 30, 1973. The funds borrowed as of November 30, 1973 are repayable in 66 monthly installments are determined by a formula related to the Company's rental receipts, but in no case will the installments be less than 1/66th of the November 30, 1973 borrowed funds.

Borrowings under the credit agreement bear interest at ½% above the prime interest rate to November 30, 1973 and thereafter at 1% above prime. In addition, the Company is required to maintain compensating balances with the bank equal to the greater of 20% of the borrowed funds or $1,000,000; such compensating balance requirements at November 30, 1972 raise the Company's cost of borrowed funds under this agreement to approximately 7½% per annum.

The credit agreement prohibits payment of cash dividends and requires the Company to keep working capital and indebtedness within specified levels. As collateral for the credit agreement, the banks may require the Company to assign its rights to future rentals on certain systems leased to end users. As of January 23, 1973, the banks had not requested any collateral.

As of January 23, 1973, borrowings under the credit agreement have increased to $11,565,000.

The aggregate amount of principal payments of long-term debt required to be paid for each of the five years following fiscal year 1972 is set forth below:

1973	$ 210,000
1974	1,817,000
1975	1,802,000
1976	1,693,000
1977	1,661,000
Thereafter	3,413,000
	$10,596,000

Subsequent to November 30, 1972, the Company arranged for a $7 million Eurocurrency borrowing.

7. Profit-Sharing Plans

The Company presently has an employee cash profit-sharing plan whereby up to 10% of the consolidated pre-tax income may be contributed to the plan. The plan is subject to annual renewal and has been renewed for 1973. The Company's contributions under the plan are set forth below:

	Percent of Pre-Tax Income	Amount
Year ended November 30, 1972	7.9%	$248,000
Year ended November 30, 1971	8.2%	178,000

The Company also has an annually renewable bonus plan whereby the Company's president is paid 1% of pre-tax (and pre-profit-sharing) income.

8. Taxes on Income

The components of taxes on income are as follows:

	1972	1971
Provision for federal income taxes which would be required in the absence of the availability of the net operating loss carry-forward		$545,000
Deferred taxes	$1,283,000	457,000
Investment tax credit (recognized under the flow-through method)	(123,000)	(80,000)
	$1,160,000	$940,000

As of November 30, 1972 the Company had a net operating loss carry-forward for federal income tax purposes of approximately $9,000,000 of which amount approximately $500,000 will expire in 1973, $700,000 in 1974, $1,500,000 in 1975, $400,000 in 1976 and $5,900,000 in 1977, if not theretofore used to reduce taxable income. If the net operating loss carry-forward is utilized, it will not affect financial statement income in the year of utilization but will reduce federal income taxes otherwise payable.

In 1972 the Company formed a Domestic International Sales Corporation ("DISC"). Through the proper utilization of a DISC, federal income taxes on transactions with foreign customers may be indefinitely deferred. The 1972 statement of income includes $430,000 of DISC-related income for which no federal income tax provision has been made inasmuch as management believes they will be able to defer the payment of such tax indefinitely.

See Note 1—"Taxes on Income."

9. Qualified Stock Option Plans

Under the Company's qualified stock option plans, 405,000 shares of common stock have been reserved for granting of options to officers and key employees of which 150,000 shares are subject to shareholder approval. Options may be granted at prices not less than 100% of the fair market value of the stock at the date of grant and become exercisable either 1/3 each year commencing one year from the date of grant. Options expire if not exercised within five years from the date of grant. Information concerning options granted under the plans is set forth below:

	Shares Available for Grant	Options Outstanding Shares	Options Outstanding Price per Share	Options Outstanding Total
Balance, December 1, 1971	30,802	179,124	$ 33-$15	$1,670,000
Additional shares reserved for grant	150,000			
Options granted	(58,750)	58,750	$17-$32	1,424,000
Options terminated	9,852	(9,852)	(9,852)	(147,000)
Options exercised		(65,878)	$33-$15	(331,000)
Balance, November 30, 1972	131,904	162,144	$33-$32	$2,616,000
Options exercisable at November 30, 1972		30,286	$33-$15	$ 280,000

10. Warrants

At November 30, 1972, the Company has the following warrants to purchase common stock outstanding:

Shares	Price per Share	Expiration Date
12,000	$15.00	December 29, 1975
18,000	$13.33	May 30, 1977

Auditors' Report

To the Board of Directors
Measurex Corporation

We have examined the consolidated balance sheet of Measurex Corporation and Subsidiary Companies sheet of Measurex Corporation and Subsidiary Companies as of November 30, 1972, and the related consolidated statements of income, shareholders' equity and changes in financial position for the year then ended. Our examination was made in accordance with generally accepted auditing standards and accordingly included such tests of the accounting records and such other auditing procedures as we considered necessary in the circumstances. We previously examined and reported upon the consolidated financial statements of Measurex Corporation and Subsidiary Companies for the year ended November 30, 1971.

In our opinion, the above-mentioned financial statements present fairly the consolidated financial position of Measurex Corporation and Subsidiary Companies at November 30, 1972 and 1971, and the consolidated results of their operations and changes in financial position for the years then ended, in conformity with generally accepted accounting principles applied on a consistent basis, except for the change, with which we concur, in accounting for residual value on finance leases as described in Note 1 of Notes to Consolidated Financial Statements.

Lybrand, Ross Bros. & Montgomery
Palo Alto, California

January 23, 1973

Case 14 - 3

The Patterson Company[1]

Andrew Patterson, the founder and president of the Patterson Company, was muttering under his breath about meddling accountants making up new rules and regulations to increase their fees at the expense of hard working businessmen when his new executive assistant, Tom Rogers, recent graduate of a well-known eastern business school, came into the office and sat down.

"Tom," Patterson began, "I've just been on the phone with our auditors about the 1971 annual report to the stockholders. It seems a group of learned gentlemen called the Accounting Principles Board has come up with another change in the way we present our financial statements to the public. Starting this year we're going to have to include in the annual report a 'statement of changes in financial position.' As far as I'm concerned that's just a fancy way of saying, 'where did we get the money and where did it go.' We've never put this kind of statement in our annual report before although we've used 'where got-where gone' statements internally for years."

"What do you mean by a 'where got-where gone statement,' " Rogers asked.

"Oh, that's just a recap of changes in balance sheet items from year to year," Patterson replied. (See Exhibit 1 for the preceding year's statement.)

"Yes I see." Rogers said. "I've always called that a funds flow statement."

"Anyway," Patterson continued, "I told the auditors we'd put our internal 'where got-where gone' statement in the annual report but they seemed to think that there would be some question of its compliance with the Accounting Principles Board Opinion."

"Now, Tom, you must have studied some of this in business school. I want you to do a funds flow statement that will satisfy the auditors. I don't want them taking exception to our financial statements over a little thing like that. The earnings per share is all anyone ever looks at anyway. You might be able to do this statement so

[1] This case was prepared by Jonathan Brown, Research Assistant, under the supervision of Assistant Professor John K. Shank, as the basis for class discussion rather than to illustrate either effective or ineffective handling of an administrative situation.

that I have a better idea of the flow of funds through the company, but I doubt it. I've been making a profit for too long not to be able to *feel* where the money comes from and where it goes."

The Patterson Company is a medium-sized manufacturer of appliances and engineering equipment with operations wholly within the United States and Canada. The company has permanent non-controlling investments in several of its suppliers and there are minority investors in several of the company's consolidated subsidiaries. A portion of the engineering equipment is sold under long-term installment contracts to companies with generally high credit ratings.

The following supplementary information is taken from the books and records of the company.

Principles of Consolidation:

The Patterson Company consolidated financial statements include all significant subsidiaries that are more than 50 per cent owned. All significant intercompany transactions are eliminated in consolidation. Dividends of $950,000 ($850,000 in 1970) were paid out in 1971 to minority shareholders of consolidated subsidiaries. Investment in affiliated companies (those 20 per cent to 50 per cent owned) is recorded on the equity method; $1,000,000 in dividends was received ($900,000 in 1970) from these affiliated companies in 1971.

Income Taxes:

The company recognizes the deferred income tax liabilities and benefits resulting from timing differences between financial and tax accounting. The major differences relate to allowances for depreciation. Investment tax credits are amortized over 5 years for financial reporting purposes. Deferred investment tax credit amortized in 1971 amounted to $850,000 ($875,000 in 1970). Credits taken in 1971 were $1,200,000 ($1,100,000 in 1970).

Depreciation:

Provision for depreciation is based on annual rates calculated to amortize the cost of depreciable assets over their estimated economic lives. Such provisions are computed mainly on the straight-line method. During 1971 the amounts provided for depreciation totaled $16,710,000. Depreciation expense included in the beginning inventory was $2,430,000 and $3,422,000 was included in the ending inventory.

Intangibles Arising from Previously Acquired Businesses:

The excess of purchase price over net assets at date of acquisition for companies acquired after October 30, 1970, is being amortized over 40 years using the straight-line method. Such excess arising from businesses acquired before that date is not being amortized since, in the opinion of management, there has been no decrease in value.

Pension Costs:

The company accrues pension expense at amounts equal to normal costs plus interest on unfunded prior service costs and, for certain plans, a portion of prior service costs. Total pension expense was $8,500,000 in 1971 and $7,500,000 in 1970. The company funds pension costs as it is deemed necessary to maintain the financial integrity of the pension trust. None of the

1971 expense was funded. During 1971, the benefits provided under certain plans were increased and at December 31, 1971, the actuarially computed value of vested benefits for all plans exceeded the total of the pension fund and balance sheet accruals by approximately $10,000,000.

Warranty Reserves:

The company maintains warranty reserves for several of its product lines. In 1971, a total of $7,430,000 of expense was charged against operations. Actual charges against the reserve in 197i amounted to $6,512,000.

Long-term Financing:

The company repaid $27,000,000 of its long-term debt to one bank and borrowed $20,000,000 as part of a long-term line of credit of $25,000,000 negotiated with a group of insurance companies. The company also retired a term loan in the amount of $8,090,000 during the year.

Changes in Property Assets:

Property assets with a total cost of $13,277,000 and accumulated depreciation of $8,130,000 were sold for a gain of $1,300,000, which is included in other income. The company purchased property, plant, and equipment amounting to $23,153,000 in 1971.

Long-term Receivables: (in thousands of dollars)

	Gross Receivables	Unearned Interest	Net Receivables
December 31, 1970	59,212	11,072	48,140
Sales in 1971	17,240	3,965	13,275
Collections in 1971	14,865	3,500	11,365
December 31, 1971	61,587	11,537	50,050

Research and Development and Marketing Expenditures.

These expenses are charged to operations in the period in which they are incurred.

Allowance for Doubtful Accounts:

Included in selling, general, and administrative expenses are allowances for doubtful accounts totaling $9,874,000. Charges against the reserve for doubtful accounts were $10,451,000 in 1971.

QUESTIONS

1. On the basis of the information provided, prepare a consolidated statement of changes in financial position for 1971 for the Patterson Company.

2. What are the significant differences in the quality of disclosure for a shareholder and for the company between your statement of changes in financial position and that used by the company for internal control purposes, as shown in Exhibit 1.

EXHIBIT 1

THE PATTERSON COMPANY
"Where Got—Where Gone" Statement
(000 omitted)

	1970
Sources	
Decrease in Short-term Investments	$ 878
Decrease in Property, Plant, and Equipment	7,825
Decrease in Goodwill	520
Increase in Accounts Payable	2,017
Increase in Interest and Other Accruals	212
Increase in Accrued Taxes	1,148
Increase in Warranty Reserves	584
Increase in Deferred Taxes	949
Increase in Accrued Pension	317
Increase in Minority Interest	1,363
Increase in Retained Earnings	21,129
	$36,942
Total	
Uses	
Increase in Cash	$ 6,789
Increase in Accounts Receivable	4,728
Increase in Inventories	15,202
Increase in Pre-paid Expenses	393
Increase in Long-term Receivables	910
Increase in Net Investment in Uncon- solidated Affiliates	2,670
Decrease in Notes Payable	250
Decrease in Long-term Debt	6,000
Total	$36,942

EXHIBIT 2

THE PATTERSON COMPANY
Statement of Income
(000 omitted)

	1971	1970
Net Sales	$658,285	$598,365
Other Income (net)	1,763	1,873
	660,048	600,238
Costs and Expenses		
Cost of Goods Sold	390,837	345,737
Selling, General, and Administrative Expenses	203,142	187,274
Interest	6,138	6,513
Depreciatio	15,718	14,320
Amortization of Goodwill	526	520
	616,361	554,364
	43,687	45,874

Equity in Net Earnings of Affiliated Companies	4,230	3,570
Minority Interest in Earnings of Consolidated Subsidiaries	2,981	2,213
Income before Taxes and Extraordinary Charge	44,936	47,231
Income Taxes	16,467	17,532
Income before Extraordinary Charge	28,469	29,699
Extraordinary Charge for Discontinuation of Certain Operations, Net of Income Tax credit of 2,260.		

Costs Incurred to Date	1,260		
Estimated Future Costs	1,000	2,260	
Net Income		26,209	29,699
Dividends Paid in Cash during the Year		9,300	8,570

EXHIBIT 3

THE PATTERSON COMPANY
Statement of Financial Position

	Year Ended December 31,		
	1971	*1970*	*1969*
ASSETS			
Current Assets			
Cash	16,682	13,267	6,478
Short-term Investments—at Cost (approximate market value)	7,076	4,309	5,187
Accounts Receivable (less allowances for doubtful accounts, 1971, 1,267; 1970, 1,844.)	83,192	71,928	67,200
Inventories—at Lower fo Cost (first-in, first-out method) or Market			
Finished Products	113,768	108,963	98,315
Work in Process, Raw Materials, supplies	47,147	48,815	44,261
Prepaid Expenses	5,148	6,213	5,820
Total	273,013	253,495	227,261
Property, Plant, and Equipment			
Land	5,037	4,912	4,730
Buildings	77,147	73,341	71,803
Machinery and Equipment	164,051	158,106	155,476
	246,235	236,359	232,009
Less Allowance for Depreciation	119,449	110,869	98,694
	126,786	125,490	133,315
Long-term Receivables	50,050	48,140	47,230
Investments in Unconsolidated Affiliates	19,470	16,240	13,570
Goodwill	40,514	41,040	41,560
	509,833	484,405	462,936

	Year Ended December 31,		
	1971	*1970*	*1969*

LIABILITIES AND SHAREHOLDERS' EQUITY

Current Liabilities:			
Notes Payable	3,000	3,500	3,750
Accounts Payable	13,835	10,634	8,617
Interest and Other Accruals	3,481	4,023	3,811
Accrued Taxes	7,018	6,377	5,229
Current Portion of Long-term Debt	6,000	6,000	6,000
Reserve for Warranties	4,718	3,800	3,216
Total	41,162	34,334	30,623
Long-term Debt	44,910	60,000	66,000
Deferred Income Taxes and Investment Credit	12,660	12,010	11,061
Accrued Pension Benefits	14,730	6,230	5,913
Minority Interest	8,767	6,736	5,373
Reserve for Loss on Discontinued Operations	1,000		
Shareholders' Equity:			
Common Stock	6,300	6,200	6,200
Additional Paid-in Capital	77,529	73,029	73,029
Retained Earnings	302,775	285,866	264,737
	386,604	365,095	343,966
	509,833	484,405	462,936

Case 14-4

NVF Company [1]

In late 1968, NVF Company, a manufacturing firm, made an exchange offer to the shareholders of Sharon Steel Corporation. For each share of Sharon common, the holder was to receive $70 of 5% subordinated debentures and 1.5 common stock purchase warrants. By March 1, 1969, approximately 86% of the Sharon common shares had been tendered and, as a result, the 1969 NVF annual report recorded the effects of the transaction. Because of the sizable difference between the coupon rate on these debentures and the rate required by the market, a significant bond discount asset (deferred debt expense) appeared among NVF's assets. It is interesting to note that the New York Stock Exchange originally refused to list these debentures because of the uncertainty that the interest payments would be covered.

QUESTIONS

1. What was the cash equivalent value of the Sharon stock acquired? What was the book value of the stock acquired?

2. What disclosures should be included, either on the balance sheet or in the footnotes, to fairly represent this financial situation to the shareholder?

3. NVF is amortizing this discount on the straight-line method. What are the advantages of this method? What are the disadvantages?

[1] This case was prepared by Laird H. Simons, III, Research Assistant, under the supervision of Associate Professor John K. Shank, as the basis for class discussion rather than to illustrate either effective or ineffective handling of an administrative situation.

EXHIBIT 1

NVF COMPANY AND SUBSIDIARIES
Consolidated Balance Sheet
December 31

	1969	1968 pro forma- unaudited (note 2)
ASSETS		
Current assets:		
Cash and short-term securities	$ 4,635,000	$ 3,910,000
Receivables, less allowance for doubtful accounts of $274,000 and $245,000	34,019,000	26,484,000
Inventories (note 3)	47,258,000	46,393,000
Other current assets	112,000	358,000
Total current assets	86,024,000	77,145,000
Properties at cost, less accumulated depreciation, depletion and amortization (note 4)	130,088,000	136,437,000
Deferred debt expense (note 1)	51,881,000	56,609,000
Prepaid expenses and other assets	4,831,000	1,530,000
	$272,824,000	$271,721,000
LIABILITIES AND STOCKHOLDERS' EQUITY		
Current liabilities:		
Notes payable	$ —	$ 2,000,000
Long-term debt payable within one year	10,811,000	6,321,000
Accounts payable	15,500,000	10,999,000
Wages, salaries and other employee costs	10,944,000	12,618,000
Federal and state taxes on income (note 6)	1,751,000	315,000
Other current liabilities	3,079,000	4,820,000
Total current liabilities	42,085,000	37,073,000

Long-term debt (note 7)	39,209,000	49,089,000
Accrued employee benefits	802,000	2,652,000
Noncurrent and deferred income taxes (note 6)	12,560,000	9,954,000
Minority interest	15,490,000	14,720,000
	112,146,000	113,488,000
5% subordinated debentures, due 1994 (note 8)	93,886,000	99,066,000
Excess of equity over cost of investment (note 2)	18,182,000	19,685,000
Stockholders' equity (note 9):		
Preferred stock, $1 par value; 5,000,000 shares authorized in 1969, none issued	—	—
Common stock, $1 par value; authorized, 10,000,000 shares (1,000,000 in 1968); issued 967,408 shares (731,787 in 1968)	967,000	732,000
Capital in excess of par value	29,981,000	27,966,000
Retained earnings	17,662,000	10,784,000
	48,610,000	39,482,000
Total stockholders' equity	$272,824,000	$271,721,000

See accompanying notes to consolidated financial statements.

Notes to Consolidated Financial Statements
(Information relating to 1968 is unaudited)

(1) Acquisition of Sharon Steel Corporation:

Under an exchange offer, the company acquired, as of March 1, 1969, 1,415,235 common shares of Sharon Steel Corporation (approximately 86%) in exchange for $99,066,000 principal amount of 5% subordinated debentures due 1994 and 2,122,852 common stock purchase warrants. Deferred debt expense of $56,609,000 attributable to the 5% subordinated debentures was recorded and is being amortized on the "bonds outstanding" method. The value of $22,129,000 assigned to the warrants issued with respect to the exchange has been reflected as part of the cost of investment in Sharon.

(2) Principles of Consolidation:

The consolidated statements include the accounts of NVF Company and all of its subsidiaries. Sharon Steel Corporation and subsidiaries have been included for the year, with appropriate adjustment made for pre-acquisition income. At the date of acquisition, Sharon's net worth exceeded the cost of investment by $19,835,000. This amount is being amortized into income over a ten-year period.

For the purpose of providing a comparison, 1968 financial statements have been presented on a pro forma basis, consolidating the financial statements of NVF and Sharon for that year on the assumption that the acquisition of Sharon by NVF had been effected as of January 1, 1968.

(8) Subordinated Debentures:

The 5% subordinated debentures due 1994 are redeemable in whole or in part at any time at the option of the company at prices reducing ¼ of 1% each year from 105% on December 31, 1969. Additionally the company is required to make cash sinking fund payments on January 1 of each year for five years commencing 1989 to retire by redemption 10% of the outstanding debentures on the November 15 immediately preceding each such January 1 less any debentures previously retired.

The warrants issued in connection with the acquisition of Sharon Steel Corporation entitled the holders thereof to purchase one share of common stock of NVF at $22 per share. The principal amount of any of the 5% subordidated debentures due 1994 held by a warrant holder may be applied by him toward payment of the purchase price upon exercise of the warrant. The warrants expire on January 31, 1979. The purchase price is subject to adjustment in certain events.

4. A growing minority (of purists?) feel that this netting process should be combined with discount amortization using the compound interest method. Why does this come closer to representing the economic realities of the situation? Why might a company desire to avoid this method as long as it is optional?

5. What was the yield rate at date of issue on the 5% debentures? Compute interest expense on the debentures for 1969 as NVF would calculate it and under a market yield calculation approach.

Case 14-5

Vitreometals Inc.[1]

In May 1959, C. R. Newton, president of Vitreometals, Inc., was discussing with W. P. Mason, vice president and treasurer, some problems encountered in their efforts to secure funds for working capital and other purposes. A tentative loan agreement had been worked out a short time previously with financial institutions by which $720,000 in mortgage money and $480,000 from sale of prior preferred stock was to have been secured. When the agreements were submitted to counsel for the lending institutions to work out the details, several questions arose over terms and conditions to be written into the loan and stock purchase agreements.

Originally, Vitreometals and the lending institutions had tentatively agreed that net assets were to be maintained at a minimum of $2 million. For this purpose net assets were defined as being equal to total net worth, less appraisal surplus and goodwill. However, when counsel for the lending institutions worked out the customary loan and purchase convenants, it was stipulated that in addition to appraisal surplus and goodwill, certain assets such as deferred research and development costs, plant-move and start-up expense, and blueprints and drawings related to a package building plan were also to be deleted in arriving at "net tangible assets" to be maintained. As a result of these deletions, it was apparent that Vitreometals might find it difficult to maintain the net tangible assets at the minimum level specified.

Newton said to Mason: "Bill, I don't think these lawyers, or the professional accountants, understand some of the problems a small growing company like ours is up against. Those drawings of the package building plan are just as hard assets as the machinery in our plant and ought to be included in determining the minimum net tangible assets requirement. As a matter of fact, you know that those plans and

[1] Name of the company and persons have been disguised. This case was prepared by Henry Key, Professor of Accounting, Texas Christian University, as a basis for class discussion. Cases are not designed to present illustrations of either correct or incorrect handling of administrative situations.

engineering drawings are the main assets we acquired from the Builtwell Company. The other assets were insignificant, yet those boys want to throw out the best assets we acquired as if they have no value at all. Sometimes I think public accountants and lawyers hinder a growing business more than they help."

Mason replied: "Yes, I know what you say is largely true, Bob. The accountants and the lawyers have developed a lot of so-called generally accepted principles and conventions that are applied to financial statements in a rather indiscriminate manner. It grows out of practices of the past that have largely disappeared from the business scene, but the attitude of accountants toward these soft assets is still prevalent. The bulletins of the American Institute of Certified Public Accountants have a great deal of weight and influence in such matters; in fact, perhaps too much."

"I think it is time some of these concepts that have no real validity in fact ought to be changed," stated Newton. "If someone would bring these matters out into the open and get them thoroughly examined and discussed, maybe some helpful changes could be brought about.

"And while we are on the subject," continued Newton, "I have often wondered why the accounting profession has never developed some way to show on the balance sheet the value of such intangibles as our licensing agreements with Foreco, Ltd., of Canada, Sollingen-Stahlblechbau of Germany, Emailleries-Girondaux of Belgium, Ceramic Enamel Corp. of South Africa, Lesperes Reunies of France, Smalterie Lombardi, S. A. of Italy, and the others. These licensing and royalty agreements represent tremendous asset values in terms of future income to the company, yet they are hidden away in an obscure footnote to the balance sheet if they are mentioned at all. They ought to be quantified in monetary terms on the balance sheet. That would give a truer picture of the sound going concern value of a company like ours than present accounting and legal practices permit."

Vitreometals, Inc., was organized in the early 1920s to produce porcelain enamel products for one principal customer. It had not been singularly successful but had managed to remain on the business scene until after World War II. In 1946, Newton, a recent business school graduate, stumbled onto the company while looking about for a good postwar business in which he could try out some of his ideas on management and product development. He was impressed with the favorable qualities of procelain enamel on metal as a durable product with strength, beauty, and general flexibility in use. Many areas, he felt, had not been tapped in the market for such a product and, in general, companies manufacturing and marketing such products were unimaginative and lacking in managerial know-how.

Newton acquired a 50 per cent interest in Vitreometals, Inc., and became vice president in 1946. The first year showed a small profit, but, more important, Newton was convinced that vast possibilities existed that were not being exploited for the products line. In 1947 he was able to arrange a plan by which the company acquired the remaining outstanding stock, thus removing outside ownership and giving him a free hand to carry out his long-range plans.

THE BASIC BLUEPRINT

As Newton envisioned the future of Vitreometals, four groups of problems needed to be isolated and dealt with. The first task, it seemed to him, was (1) to strengthen top management, (2) to set goals, and (3) to build a flexible organization. Seasoned and skilled men, who shared Newton's philosophy of how a small company ought to be managed, joined the organization. These top executives set about selecting and training younger men to provide the organizational strength needed. Once the management group was formed, brainstorming for ideas was carried on continually.

A timetable was set for achieving selected goals. From 1947 to 1952, all possible effort was to be devoted to product development. From 1952 to 1957, emphasis was to shift to the kind of plant or plants that would eventually be needed for the growing company. By 1958 it was expected that a modern plant would be ready to turn out a wide range of products for a rapidly expanding domestic and world market.

The stereotyped chart concept of organization was tossed out the window. ("It just gets in the way when you need your employee talents most," said Newton. "Whenever abilities are needed on a problem, we work crossways, not up and down, to get the maximum value out of the talents we have in the company.")

FINANCING METHODS

The second group of problems revolved around financing methods. "In a small growing company engaged simultaneously in product research and development and standard production, there is always an acute problem of working capital shortage. Research and development costs overbalance the nominal income from limited product sales, hence reinvestment is inadequate as a source of funds" Newton noted. "Such a situation places a strain on the credit position of a company." It was as much a part of the 10-year plan originating in 1947 to develop the company financially as in other respects—to build a solid foundation that would serve as a base for carrying out growth financing programs in the future.

Vitreometals might have followed the conventional method of meeting its pressing financial needs with heavy mortgage debt. Instead, it chose to follow the somewhat unorthodox route of equity financing through public sale of stock. Several factors mitigate against the typical small firm using this method. But Vitreometals wanted to establish a public market for its shares to be in a better position for meeting future needs. A modest offering of common stock in 1949 was absorbed by the public with good distribution. A second offering of common stock with warrants for purchase of additional common was successfully distributed in 1952. Almost all of the warrants had been exercised before expiration date in 1955.

PRODUCT DEVELOPMENT

A third major set of problems centered around the product line. Initially, one main product with one principal customer characterized the company. Newton and his associates realized that a growing, dynamic company would require a product line offering diversification, flexibility, and market depth. Every conceivable use for ceramic coated metals was examined, without limitation concerning the engineering and production problems involved. Research and development costs mounted to more than $3,000,000 by the end of the 10-year period, and in 1957 more than 90 per cent of sales were accounted for by products that were not in the line in 1947. Newton remarked: "It is really surprising what a handful of brilliant technicians can do when they are working together on a well-conceived, specifically identified goal."

EXPANSION PLAN

The fourth set of problems involved (1) acquiring key plants related to Vitreometals and gaining well-qualified people for the growing organization, (2) expanding into world wide markets, and (3) exploiting the profit potential. From 1952 to 1958, two companies were acquired as subsidiaries and a third was brought under voting control in a foreign country to round out the structure for realizing the profit potential. Connections with some minor companies were also made during this period. Penetration of foreign markets had been effected principally through licensing agreements under which Vitreometals furnished technical and production know-how.

FUTURE OUTLOOK: THE PAYOFF

During 1958 the company incurred heavy moving and start-up costs as operations were transferred to a modern new leased building on a long-term contract. Working capital was again reduced to an unsatisfactory level, so additional common stock was publicly distributed. Outstanding convertible debentures in the amount of $420,000 were also converted into common stock.

These moves furnished the base for the next major financing mentioned at the beginning of the case. This was undertaken early in 1959, to provide $720,000 through a mortgage note and $480,000 through sale of prior cumulative preferred (callable) stock. Common stock warrants were attached to each convenant giving holders the right to purchase common stock during the next 15 years.

The tentative loan commitment had provided that appraisal surplus and goodwill should be subtracted from total equity to arrive at the $2 million of net assets to be maintained. However, counsel for the lending institutions proposed to delete not only appraisal surplus and goodwill, but also the package building plan asset, plant-move and start-up expense, and deferred research and development costs from total equity to arrive at net tangible assets to be maintained. Newton and Mason both felt that the tentative commitment definition should be honored, proposing that these values be established: the package building plan, $48,000; plant-move and start-up expense, $144,000; and deferred research and development costs, $564,180. They further proposed that if these amounts were accepted, no further additions would be made to these accounts. Also, these accounts were to be reduced by applicable amortizations and write offs in the future.

SALES GROWTH

The following table shows consolidated sales and net income (or loss), after income taxes, for the period 1945-1956, inclusive.

Table 1

Year	Sales	Net Income after Tax
1945	$ 131,600	$(30,160) loss
1946	325,610	18,120
1947	465,440	11,760
1948	689,520	15,490
1949	726,850	(25,790) loss
1950	891,320	5,400
1951	1,267,140	23,330
1952	1,458,440	24,240
1953	2,382,220	50,290
1954	2,409,020	51,470
1955	2,435,700	(140,230) loss (strike)
1956	3,473,590	104,490

EXHIBIT 1

VITREOMETALS, INC.
Consolidated Balance Sheets,
December 31, 1958, and 1957

ASSETS	1958	1957
Current Assets		
Cash	$ 201,480	$ 201,240
Accounts and Notes Receivable (Note 1)	796,980	769,620
Inventories at Lower of Cost or Market	685,130	749,750
Claim for Refund of Prior Years' Federal Income Taxes	14,350	1,870
Prepaid Expenses (Note 1)	41,520	50,760
Total Current Assets	$1,739,460	$1,773,240
Investment in Affiliated Companies, at Cost (market December 31, 1958, $84,000) (Notes 1-2)	27,420	27,420
Plant and Equipment (Notes 3-4)		
Land, Buildings, Machinery, and Equipment	$2,107,920	$1,648,080
Less: Accumulated Depreciation	443,880	533,760
Net Plant and Equipment	$1,664,040	$1,114,320
Goodwill from Acquisition of Subsidiary	152,640	152,640
Package Building Plan Acquisition	48,000	48,000
Other Assets		
Cash Surrender Value of Life Insurance (Note 4)	$ 25,980	$ 22,620
New Plant Start-up Expense	144,000	—
Deferred Charges—Research and Development Expense	564,180	413,280

Total Other Assets	$ 734,160	$ 435,900
Total Assets	$4,365,720	$3,551,520
Liabilities and Stockholders' Equity		
Current Liabilities		
Notes and Mortgages Payable, Current		
Portion (Notes 1-4)	$ 694,920	$ 368,640
Accounts Payable and Accrued Liabilities	933,120	710,940
Total Current Liabilities	$1,628,040	$1,079,580
Long-term Notes and Mortgages Payable,		
Less Current Portion above (Notes 1-4)	408,960	338,050
Convertible Suborindated Debentures,		
5 3/4% due 1971		420,000
Minority Interest		
5% Cumulative Preferred Stock (Note 5)	33,600	33,600
Stockholders' Equity		
Capital Stock, Par Value $1.00 Per Share;		
Authorized 600,000; Issued and Outstand-		
ing, 476,470 (1958); 306,360 (1957) (Note 6)	$ 476,470	$ 306,360
Capital in Excess of Par Value of		
Common Shares—Exhibit B	1,316,480	736,880
Appraisal Surplus—Exhibit B	364,820	457,650
Retained Earnings—Exhibit B	137,350	179,400
Total Stockholders' Equity	$2,295,120	$1,680,290
Total Liabilities and Stockholders' Equity	$4,365,720	$3,551,520

EXHIBIT 2

VITREOMETALS, INC.

Statement of Changes in Stockholders' Equity
for the Year Ended December 31, 1958

	Common Stock, Par $1	Capital in Excess of Par Value	Appraisal Surplus	Retained Earnings
Balance, January 1, 1958	$306,360	$736,880	$457,650	$179,400
Consolidated Net Income for Year Ended December 31, 1958, per Exhibit C				8,600
Amortization and Write Off of Appraisal (Note 3)			(92,830)	(8,120)
Dividends Paid on Subsidiary Preferred Stock				(1,680)
Amortization of Bond Discount on Conversion to Stock				(40,850)
Proceeds of Issue of 170,110 Shares of Common Stock	170,110	579,600		
Balance, December 31, 1958—Exhibit A	$476,470	$1,316,480	$364,820	$137,350

EXHIBIT 3

VITREOMETALS, INC.
Statement of Consolidated Income
for the Years Ended December 31, 1958 and 1957

	1958	1957
Total Revenues	2,886,580	$3,387,110
Cost of Goods Sold	2,412,710	2,810,270
Gross Profit	$ 473,870	$ 576,840
Selling and Administrative Expenses	440,740	396,350
Income from Operations	$ 33,130	$ 180,490
Other Income (charges) (net)	(37,010)	(66,480)
Net Income (loss before Federal Income Taxes)	$ (3,880)	$ 114,010
Federal Income Taxes		7,800
Net Income (loss) after Provision for Federal Income Taxes	$ (3,880)	$ 106,210
Refund of Federal Income Taxes due to Net Operating Loss Carrybacks	12,480	1,870
Consolidated Net Income—Exhibit B	$ 8,600	$ 108,080

Notes Accompanying Financial Statements, December 31, 1958

Notes Accompanying Financial Statements, December 31, 1958

Note 1: Accounts receivable of $401,040 are assigned as security for notes payable-bank in the amount of $328,740. A total of 24,000 shares of Foreco, Ltd., common stock are assigned as security for notes payable in the amount of $60,000. Unexpired insurance premiums of $11,600 are pledged against notes payable of $60,000. Unexpired insurance premiums of $11,600 are pledged against notes payable of $11,900.

Note 2: Investment in affiliated companies of $27,420 is as follows:

Company	Investment	% Owned
Foreco, Ltd.	$24,300	23
A	3,000	33
B	120	49
C	—	10
	$27,420	

Note 3: As a result of independent appraisals, the fixed assets are shown at cost plus an appraisal increment of $416,300 (net of amortization). Depreciation on the amount of appreciation has been charged in the amount of $8,120 to consolidated retained earnings and in the amount of $25,990 to consolidated appraisal surplus. In addition, the balance of the appraisal increment on the A-Plant, which was disposed of in 1958, was written off in the amount of $66,840.

Note 4: Plant and equipment having a book value of $1,664,040, together with cash surrender value of life insurance amounting to $25,980, are pledged to secure notes and mortgages of $471,220.

Note 5: Dividends on the 5% cumulative preferred stock of Subsidiary E have been paid up to and including December 1, 1958.

Note 6. Of the 123,530 shares of Vitreometals, Inc., common stock unissued at December 31, 1958, 17,140 shares are held for the redemption of warrants that expire September 1, 1962.

Auditor's Opinion

To the Board of Directors
Vitreometals, Inc.
Alton, Connecticut

We have examined the balance sheet of Viteometals, Inc., and its subsidiaries, Company D and Company E, as of December 31, 1958, and the related statements of income and changes in stockholders' equity for the year then ended. Our examination was made in accordance with generally accepted auditing standards and accordingly included such tests of the accounting records and such other auditing procedures as we considered necessary in the circumstances, except for inventories of Company D.
Inventories of Company D, which amounted to $173,090, were taken by responsible employees of the company and priced at the lower of cost or market. We did not verify the condition or quantities of merchandies at December 31, 1958, of Company D, such quantities and values being stated at company figures. However, a responsible officer of the company did certify to the quantities, condition, and valuation of the inventory.
Subject to the foregoing, in our opinion, the accompanying consolidated balance sheet and statements of consolidated income and statement of changes in stockholders' equity present fairly the consolidated financial position of Vitreometals, Inc., and its subsidiaries, Company D and Company E at December 31, 1958, and the results of consolidated operations for the year then ended, in conformity with generally accepted accounting principles, applied on a basis consistent with that of the preceding year.

Alfred D. Sessions
Certified Public Accountant

QUESTIONS

1. If all the dates in the case were changed so that the financial statements covered the years 1973 and 1974 instead of 1957 and 1958, what changes in accounting and reporting practices would be required in order to conform to GAAP?

2. If you accept the Vitreometals statements as being typical for the late 1950's, do you think the changes in accounting and reporting practices since then represent significant improvement, some improvement, or no improvement at all?

3. What changes would be required regarding the actions of the independent CPA?

4. What further changes in accounting and reporting practices would you predict for the next 15 years?

Index